The Making of Song Dynasty History

In this ambitious work of political and intellectual history, Charles Hartman surveys the major sources that survive as vestiges of the official dynastic historiography of the Chinese Song dynasty (960–1279). Analyzing the narratives that emerge from these sources as products of Song political discourse, Hartman offers a thorough introduction to the texts and the political circumstances surrounding their compilation. Distilling from these sources a "grand allegory of Song history," he argues that the embedded narratives in these sources reflect tension between a Confucian model of political institutionalism and the Song court's preference for a non-sectarian, technocratic model. Fundamentally rethinking the corpus of texts that have formed the basis of our understanding of the Song and of imperial China more broadly, this far-reaching account of historiographical process and knowledge production illuminates the relationship between official history writing and political struggle in China.

CHARLES HARTMAN is Professor of Chinese Studies in the Department of East Asian Studies at the University at Albany, State University of New York.

T0382163

The Making of Song Dynasty History

Sources and Narratives, 960–1279 CE

Charles Hartman

University at Albany, State University of New York

CAMBRIDGE
UNIVERSITY PRESS

University Printing House, Cambridge CB2 8BS, United Kingdom

One Liberty Plaza, 20th Floor, New York, NY 10006, USA

477 Williamstown Road, Port Melbourne, VIC 3207, Australia

314-321, 3rd Floor, Plot 3, Splendor Forum, Jasola District Centre, New Delhi - 110025, India

103 Penang Road, #05-06/07, Visioncrest Commercial, Singapore 238467

Cambridge University Press is part of the University of Cambridge.

It furthers the University's mission by disseminating knowledge in the pursuit of education, learning and research at the highest international levels of excellence.

www.cambridge.org
Information on this title: www.cambridge.org/9781108819992
DOI: 10.1017/9781108877176

First published 2021
First paperback edition 2022

A catalogue record for this publication is available from the British Library

ISBN 978-1-108-83483-4 Hardback
ISBN 978-1-108-81999-2 Paperback

To the memory
of
Friedrich A. Bischoff (1928–2009),
Professor of East Asian Languages and Literatures,
Indiana University
1964–1982

Contents

Contents

Figures

Tables

Preface

This book is the first volume in a projected two-volume study of the Chinese Song dynasty (960–1279). *The Making of Song Dynasty History: Sources and Narratives* surveys the major sources that survive as vestiges of official dynastic historiography. It then constructs the master narratives that emerge from these sources and frames these narratives as products of Song political discourse. A subsequent volume on the structures of governance in Song will study the political and social realities behind that discourse.

This book has been a long time in the making, and many people have helped along the way. Paul Smith has been for over two decades a faithful scholarly companion, an erudite sounding board, a friend, and an endless source of stimulating encouragement. Valerie Hansen regularly invited me to address her class in Song documents at Yale, and I have learned much from her and her students. Ari Daniel Levine, a consummate scholar and editor, gave the manuscript a close read, and the finished book is much better for his meticulous attention to all issues, large and small. Friends among the American community of Song scholars – Maggie Bickford, Beverly Bossler, John Chaffee, Hugh Clark, Pat Ebrey, Bob Hymes, Anna Shields, Hoyt Tillman, and Hilde De Weerdt – have all helped to solve research problems and to bring this volume to completion.

As indistinct visions of this book first began to take shape in the early 2000s, I was able to invite three graduate students from Harvard to come to Albany. Over a four-year period, I read with Sung Chia-fu, Li Cho-ying, and Liu Guanglin many of the primary texts that form the backbone of this book. They will recognize our conversations on every page, and their scholarship, erudition, and friendship are among the lasting memories of my research on Song history.

I am grateful to Dr. Tseng Shu-Hsien and the staff of the Center for Chinese Studies at the National Central Library, Taipei for research support during autumn 2012. Writing of this book began in 2013 during a term at the Institute for Advanced Study in Princeton, and I am grateful to Nicola di Cosmo and the IAS staff for providing the optimal environment for academic work. Christian Lamouroux's kind invitation enabled me in the spring of 2016 to present the essential arguments of this book in four lectures at the École des hautes études en sciences sociales in Paris.

My thanks also to Deng Xiaonan of Peking University and Bao Weimin of Renmin University for their sustained interest and support for my research among the community of Song scholars in China. In Taiwan, I am grateful to Huang K'uan-ch'ung at Academia Sincia, Fang Cheng-Hua at National Taiwan University, and Li Cho-ying at National Tsing Hua University for invitations to present research from this book. Lectures on Song issues given at Cornell, Harvard, Princeton, the University of Pennsylvania, the University of Michigan, Rutgers, and Yale enabled me to garner helpful suggestions from scholars at these institutions and their students.

I am especially grateful to Luo Yinan and Chang Wei-ling for many years of sustained, fruitful conversations on problems of Song history. Likewise, my interaction with Ho Koon-wan and a generation of younger scholars in Hong Kong – Lincoln Tsui, Chu Mingkin, and Jack Cheung – has strengthened the arguments in this book. Thanks also go to Chen Yunru, Hans van Ess, Lee Tsong-han, Victor Mair, Freda Murck, Julia Murray, Joanna Handlin Smith, and Xu Yongming for many years and many forms of advice and support.

To my longest-standing friend in sinology, Bill Nienhauser of the University of Wisconsin, may the dedication to this volume bring back memories of a time and place, gone but not forgotten, that continues to inspire.

My colleagues at the University at Albany, James Hargett, Anthony DeBlasi, Susanna Fessler, Fan Pen Chen, and Andrew Byon have quietly assumed more than their share of the chores of local university life in order to afford me more time for "Charles's book." I could not have written this book in Albany without their support and that of Chen Yu-hui, bibliographer for East Asian studies, and the interlibrary loan office of the UAlbany Library. My colleague John Person helped with issues of Japanese romanization.

Finally, my wife Li-yun and my daughter Katy have lived with this book as long as I have. Neither could I have written this book without them. My gratitude to them is as great as their patience and love.

A Note on the Text

Chinese characters are given for proper names, places, book titles, and technical terms upon their first mention in the text. Dates for persons follow Chang Bide, Wang Deyi, et al., *Songren zhuanji ziliao suoyin* (Taipei, 1976) and Li Yumin, *Songren shengzu xingnian kao* (Beijing, 2010). Dates follow the traditional Chinese lunar calendar converted into Western notation. Thus, for example, 1144/3/18 corresponds to the eighteenth day of the third month of the fourteenth year of the Shaoxing 紹興 reign period. Equivalencies between Chinese and Western years follow P. Hoang, *Concordance des chronologies néoméniques chinoise et européenne* (Shanghai, 1910). The beginning of the bibliography contains a list of abbreviations for primary sources that are cited frequently in the notes.

Introduction

Toward a Dynamic Historiography of the Song Dynasty

> The Qing period is renowned as a pinnacle of Classical scholarship,
> but they could never match the Song scholars in historiography.
>
> Chen Yinke (1890–1969)

Over the past two decades scholars in China have made remarkable progress toward a "living" history of Song political institutions. At a Hangzhou conference in 2001 to review the past century of scholarship on Song and to chart a path forward, Deng Xiaonan critiqued prevalent research that treated these institutions as autonomous units, boxes with labels on organization charts, frozen in time and place. She proposed to study institutions as dynamic, living organisms shaped by ever-changing historical "processes" and linked to each other and larger society through complex networks of "relationships."[1] Twenty years later, the continuing fruits of this new scholarship have transformed our understanding of the dynasty and its place in the larger history of China. This volume attempts to build upon this research and to apply similar concepts to the study of the Song historical sources themselves. This attempt at "living historiography" treats historical works as ever-changing, dynamic creations continually shaped by social and political processes and intersecting relationships among compilers, editors, copyists, printers, and readers. In this process, I hope to demonstrate the depth of Chen Yinke's insight that the Song era marked a pinnacle in the development of Chinese historiography, or, as I have written elsewhere, a "maturity" whose achievements the scholarly world has yet fully to recognize.[2]

The Making of Song Dynasty History: Sources and Narratives has grown from a series of individual studies I began in the late 1990s to describe each of the principal primary sources for Song history. However, I had written only two articles when I began to doubt that the single-work-per-article format would enable me systematically to address larger issues that I had come to realize

---

[1] Deng Xiaonan, "Zouxiang 'huo' de zhidushi."

[2] Hartman, "Chinese Historiography in the Age of Maturity." For the quotation from Chen Yinke see his "Preface to the Reprinting of *Westerners and Central Asians in China under the Mongols*," *Chen Yinke xiansheng lunwenji*, 1:683, cited in Chia-fu Sung, "Between Tortoise and Mirror," 1.

affected all the works I proposed to study.[3] For example, neither book I had written about had survived in its original format. A combination of forces related to the intellectual and political movement known as the Learning of the Way (*daoxue* 道學) and the proliferation of commercial printing had drastically transformed both works. Modern readers were not reading what the reputed Song authors of these works had originally written. A static historiography of titles, authors, dates, and editions would hardly suffice to describe these supposedly primary sources, much less enable modern scholars to access their contents with confidence.

A vital task for the historian of Song is to see through and work around the coloration that these forces, especially the *daoxue* movement, have painted upon the primary source collections. This book will describe these colors in detail and attempt to account for the painters and their motives. Although this *daoxue* influence arose in the late twelfth and peaked in the mid-thirteenth century, this process of historical coloring is closely related to another, older phenomenon – the inseparable nature of history (what happened) and historiography (writing about what happened) in Song. The Song period experienced an especially close identity between the makers of political history and the shapers of its historiographical record. Ouyang Xiu 歐陽修 (1007–1072), Sima Guang 司馬光 (1019–1086), and Zhao Ruyu 趙汝愚 (1140–1196), for example, were senior statesmen and historians. The great historians Li Tao 李燾 (1115–1184), Li Xinchuan 李心傳 (1167–1244), and Lü Zhong 呂中 (*jinshi* 1247) labored privately, but also worked as officials in the dynasty's formal historiographical operation to interface their own private and the state's official historiography. This book attempts to unravel this complex nexus of processes and relationships that intertwined politics, history, and both private and official historiography in Song.

Because Song history and Song historiography are so closely linked in these ways, they must be studied together to be delinked. The dynasty's history cannot be understood without first understanding the nature and origin of the surviving historical texts; yet these texts cannot be understood without first understanding Song political and intellectual history. My solution to this chicken-and-egg conundrum is to focus on the rhetoric of the texts as evidence of the political processes from which they grew. In my view, Song history emerged from a historiographical process in which successive politicians/historians used rhetoric to reorganize facts they culled, often for contemporaneous political purposes, from an already existing and ever-growing corpus of political and historical records. Thus, I read historical documents not to

---

[3] Hartman, "Bibliographic Notes on Sung Historical Works: *Topical Narratives from the Long Draft Continuation of the Comprehensive Mirror That Aids Administration* by Yang Chungliang" and "Bibliographic Notes on Sung Historical Works: The Original *Record of the Way and Its Destiny* by Li Hsin-ch'uan."

determine reliable facts but to detect traces of the initial rhetorical construction and subsequent reconstruction of the stories they present. Often, the visible traces of this linguistic manipulation enable us to observe a story that is very different from and usually truer than the "facts" that that history purports to contain.[4]

Of course, the idea of history as a rhetorical construct is basic to Western postmodern theories of historiography. Two ideas are fundamental. First, most of what many scholars accept as historical "fact" is actually a subsequently created image or projection of earlier events. Second, because these post hoc images were created with and transmitted by language, they are literary artifacts; and these artifacts can be changed as time moves on. Although my earlier studies were undertaken independently of these theoretical considerations, this book is the first major study to reference contemporary deconstructionist theories to analyze the dominant rhetorical features of Song historiography. However, readers will quickly realize that this book does not systematically impose these postmodern perspectives on the sources; rather, the sources, when read as literary artifacts, readily confirm their own history of rhetorical manipulation. And my reading of Song sources relies upon methodology derived largely from traditional sinology, not postmodern theory.

Sources

Since the four works of Song history writing I will examine in this book are all products of official Song historiography – and chosen for that reason – we may begin with a brief description of that operation. Song historians, like their counterparts in the modern West, conceived history as a sequence of "events" (*shi* 事). Unlike the Western historian, however, whose task was first to define and mark off his primary events from the undifferentiated flow of time, the Song historian found his events already predefined by a bureaucratic process in which he himself was not the initiating agent.[5] Government interagency communications in Song required the authoring official to define at the beginning of his document the "event" about which he was corresponding, something like the topic line of a modern interoffice memo. If the event did not originate with him, he was to restate the "event" as he found it already defined in prior documentation on the issue.[6] The official Song historiographical process

---

[4] For a more extended discussion and application of these principles see Hartman, "The Making of a Villain: Ch'in Kuei and *Tao-hsüeh*"; also Cai Hanmo [Charles Hartman], *Lishi de yanzhuang*, 2–97.

[5] Veyne, *Writing History*, 34–36, views reality as an infinitely dividable series of sub-events from which the historian selects and then orders into meaningful plots. See also White, "Historical Text as Literary Artifact," in *Tropics of Discourse*, 90–93.

[6] Sima Guang, *Shuyi*, 1.1b–2b; Xie Shenfu, *Qingyuan tiaofa shilei*, 16.234–35.

began when records of these "events" were transmitted to the court history office. When this system was inaugurated in 983/8, the monthly submissions from the Secretariat and from the Bureau of Military Affairs were simply called "events sent to the history office."[7] Thus, in Song, the bureaucratic process of government defined the constituent elements of history – yet another twist on Étienne Balazs's famous axiom that in China, "history was written by officials for officials."[8]

The Song founders inherited the institutions and procedures of an earlier court-based historiographical operation that had evolved in Tang, had survived the tenth century, and, although slow to be revived in early Song, had evolved by the mid-eleventh century into a mature and politically important institution of Song government.[9] As is well known, the basic operation processed routine administrative documents through multiple and lengthy stages of manipulation and compression. Modern scholars, based on a passage from the Southern Song encyclopedist Zhang Ruyu 章如愚 (jinshi 1196), describe a three-stage process of transcription, transmission, and transformation.[10] Figure 0.1, organized time-wise from left to right, depicts the entire production process of official historiography from the initial collection of documents (listed on the far left) through to compilation of the official dynasty history (the final column on the right), in this case the Song History of 1345.

The process centered on the person of the emperor and his function as chief presiding officer at his "court," a series of regular audiences and meetings between him and his senior administrators. The initial transcription phase (jizai 記載) began with the "Diary of Activity and Repose" (Qiju zhu 起居注), a record of the emperor's actions, as recorded by two official court diarists who accompanied him at audiences and elsewhere; the "records of current administration" (shizheng ji 時政記) were monthly summaries, compiled by one of the chief councilors, of their discussions with the emperor. In addition, some government agencies were required to send copies of their actions to the history office; and, finally, families of deceased officials above a certain rank submitted biographical records of their kinsmen for inclusion in the historical

[7] SHY, zhiguan, 6.30a–b.
[8] Balazs, "L'histoire comme guide de la pratique bureaucratique," 82.
[9] For the Tang see Twitchett, The Writing of Official History under the T'ang. There is no monograph on official Song historiography in English. See, however, Kurz, "The Consolidation of Official Historiography during the Early Northern Song Dynasty"; Hartman, "Chinese Historiography in the Age of Maturity"; and Sung Chia-fu, "The Official Historiographical Operation of the Song Dynasty." There are three book-length studies in Chinese. Most comprehensive is Wang Sheng'en, Songdai guanfang shixue yanjiu. Song Limin, Songdai shiguan zhidu yanjiu, focuses on development of the court historiographical agencies. Cai Chongbang, Songdai xiushi zhidu yanjiu offers authoritative accounts of the major works produced.
[10] Song Limin, Songdai shiguan zhidu yanjiu, 5–6; Sung, "Official Historiographical Operation," 191.

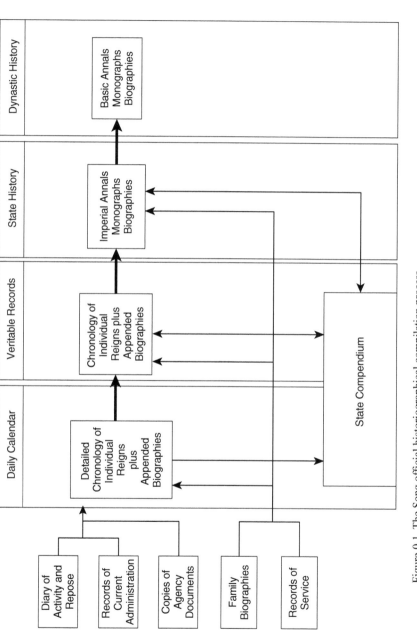

Figure 0.1 The Song official historiographical compilation process

Sources: Hirata Shigeki, "Sōdai no nikki shiryō kara mita seiji kōzō," 30; Cai Chongbang, *Songdai xiushi zhidu yanjiu*, 1–8; Hartman and DeBlasi, "The Growth of Historical Method in Tang China," 24.

record. The transmission phase (*bianji* 編集) ensued when the history office processed the assembled documents into a "daily calendar" (*rili* 日歷), a day-by-day chronicle, completed monthly.[11] Upon the death of an emperor, which concluded one imperial reign, or one "court," the transformation phase (*zuan-xiu* 纂修) began, and the "daily calendar" was reworked and edited into "veritable records" (*shilu* 實錄), a compressed chronicle of one imperial reign. Periodically, an emperor would order that existing veritable records of several past reigns be combined into a "state history" (*guoshi* 國史). This process involved transforming the veritable records, which followed a day-by-day chronological format, into the tripartite annals–monographs–biographies format that the state histories and the eventual final, dynastic history would assume.

Figure 0.1 and the above paragraph present a theoretical and highly idealized description of official court historiography. Surviving Song writings teem with complaints about non-adherence to established protocols, political interference, favoritism, negligence, lassitude, and corruption at all stages of the operation. Typical are the observations of Xu Du 徐度 (1106–1166), who worked in the court history office during the 1130s. He lamented deficiencies in many of the principal sources of primary documentation. For example, since the court diarists were stationed too far away at audiences to hear discussion of the memorials, officials submitted their own summaries of those discussions; and to save time and evade complications they usually reported that the emperor had said nothing. Beyond the chief councilors' monthly summaries, agency reports were often the only record of administrative actions, and agencies often neglected to submit copies of their actions as required. Family-submitted biographies were usually nothing more than puffery of dubious historical value. Finally, Xu observed, once composed from these sources, the daily calendar became set and no additions were permitted.[12]

As Xu Du implied, the daily calendar formed the basis of all subsequent stages of compression. But its timely compilation was the exception rather than the norm. Compilation did not resume in early Song until 988, and was suspended from 1007 through 1043 and again from 1054 through 1067. Seldom compiled contemporaneously thereafter, the daily calendar was often not completed until many years later, often in co-ordination with the veritable records. For example, a definitive *Shenzong Daily Calendar* (*Shenzong rili* 神宗日歷), covering the years 1067 through 1085, was not established until 1116, at which point the *Shenzong Veritable Records* (*Shenzong shilu* 神宗實錄) had

---

[11] For an 1162 list of items to be included in the daily calendar see Chen Kui, *Nan Song guan'ge lu*, 4.39–40, translated in Sung, "The Official Historiographical Operation," 194–95.
[12] Wang Mingqing, *Huizhu lu, houlu*, 1.68–69. *Wenxian tongkao*, 191.5556–57, quotes this passage in the introduction to its section on dynastic histories.

already been through three revisions.[13] As a result, officials responsible for compiling the veritable records were often forced to reconstruct the calendar decades after the events had transpired. Edicts to compile veritable records, especially in Southern Song, often lamented gaps in needed information and therefore asked the public to submit relevant documentation.[14] The long delays between an event and its final presentation in the state history offered many opportunities for political and personal intrusions into the process. The veritable records were a crucial phase of the operation, essentially the last chance to control the historical record before its final codification into the state history. The veritable records of the Taizu, Taizong, Shenzong, and Zhezong reigns were rewritten multiple times in response to ongoing political change.[15] We will explore in detail in the chapters to follow how these features of "living historiography" have affected the surviving record of Song history.

Contributing to these problems of co-ordination was the somewhat hapha-zard administration of court historiography, especially in Northern Song. The dynasty inherited a physical building in Kaifeng called the Institute of Historiography (*shiguan* 史館), which Taizong rebuilt; but the location was used as a library and archival storage rather than as working space for court historians. The usual procedure was to appoint ad hoc committees of scholars and officials, usually seconded from other assignments, to work on specific compilation projects. The project was then assigned an allocation of tempor-ary work space somewhere in the imperial city, with an accompanying budget and support staff. To maintain secrecy and security, space was often assigned within the inner court, the private imperial residence where eunuchs provided security, services, and supervision. Thus, before the government reorganiza-tion of 1082, temporary staff working in temporary quarters performed most of the court's historiography. However, after 1082, historiographical opera-tions were concentrated in the new Imperial Library (*Bishu sheng* 秘書省), where they remained until the end of the dynasty. Although the Southern Song Imperial Library was located far outside the imperial city, eunuchs still provided support and were routinely rewarded when the projects were completed.[16]

---

[13] Cai Chongbang, *Songdai xiushi zhidu yanjiu*, 40–42.

[14] See, for example, Hartman, "The Reluctant Historian," 101–12, for difficulties compiling the *Qinzong Veritable Records* in 1166.

[15] Cai Chongbang, *Songdai xiushi zhidu yanjiu*, 64–101; Wang Deyi, "Bei Song jiuchao shilu zuanxiu kao."

[16] Gong Yanming, *Songdai guanzhi cidian*, 148, 256–62; Sung, "Official Historiographical Operation," 179–90. For the Southern Song Imperial Library see the still unmatched study by Winkelman, *The Imperial Library in Southern Sung China*, based largely on Chen Kui, *Nan Song guan'ge lu*. To avoid needless detail, I sometimes write in this book "history office" to refer generically to officials and projects connected to court historiography, regardless of the time period.

This oversight reflects the fact that the Song founders sanctioned the re-establishment of court historiography only on the condition that they control its contents and productions. In 994 Taizong implemented a system of imperial preapproval for monthly submissions of the court diary. In a procedure known as "submitting to the throne" (*jinyu* 進御), drafts were first submitted for imperial review, and after approval were then forwarded to the history office. This preapproval requirement was eventually applied to the records of current administration, the veritable records, and the state histories. Ouyang Xiu and others objected to the practice, which violated older Tang precedents that precluded the emperor from monitoring the historiographical record, but made little headway in removing the surveillance.[17] As we shall see in the chapters that follow, this tension between the monarchy and Confucian literati over the proper role of history in governance profoundly shaped the contours of the surviving historical record. In essence, history for the monarchy was a vehicle to exert its legitimacy and strengthen political control. For the literati, history was a source of rhetorical precedent for use in political dialogue, and much of that dialogue was directed against imperial expressions of absolute authority.

The result of this tension can be seen in Figure 0.2, a timeline of historio-graphical production plotted against major political developments over the course of the entire dynasty. Despite the difficulties enumerated above, the Northern Song managed tolerably well to sustain its official historiographical operations. The initial *Three Courts State History* (*Sanchao guoshi* 三朝國史), covering the period from 960 through 1022, was completed in 1030. The early 1080s saw the second installment of the *State Compendium* (*Guochao huiyao* 國朝會要), completed in 1081, followed in 1082 by the *Two Courts State History* (*Liangchao guoshi* 兩朝國史), covering the period 1022 through 1067. Since Emperor Shenzong was still alive, dynastic history was now up to date. However, partisan struggles over the New Policies intensified after his death in 1085 and slowed this progress. Rival political factions produced competing versions of the *Shenzong Veritable Records* in 1091 and in 1096; a failed attempt at a compromise version followed in 1101, another wholesale revision came in 1136, and yet another attempted revision in 1138.[18] The timeline shows only the three completed versions of 1091, 1096, and 1136.

The Jurchen invasions and the relocation to the south in 1127 further derailed the pace of historiographical work. The dynasty lost access to its historical archives in Kaifeng; and, in any case, the daily calendars for the Huizong and Qinzong reigns, covering 1100 through 1127, had not been maintained. Although the 1136 revisions to the *Shenzong Veritable Records* settled to

---

[17] Wang Sheng'en, *Songdai guanfang shixue yanjiu*, 76–82; on eunuch supervision see 87–89.
[18] Cai Chongbang, *Songdai xiushi zhidu yanjiu*, 82–98.

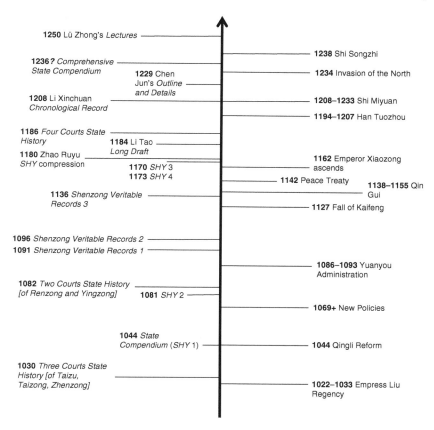

Figure 0.2 Timeline of major historiographical works

some degree the historical stance on the New Policies, the advent of Qin Gui 秦
檜 (1090–1155), as sole councilor in 1138 brought yet another setback to the
resumption of routine court historiography. To camouflage opposition to his
policy of a negotiated peace with the Jurchen, Qin Gui put his son, Qin Xi 秦熺
(d. 1166), in charge of the Imperial Library in 1142; and he remained there until
Qin Gui's death in 1155. Qin Xi used the office to compile a highly partisan
daily calendar for the period from 1127 through 1142 that provided historical
justification and a sympathetic account of Qin Gui's policies; that done, after
1142 he suspended the daily calendar as well as efforts to fill the lacunae for
Northern Song history between 1100 and 1127.[19]

---

[19] See Hartman, "The Making of a Villain" 69–74.

Political changes in the wake of another Jurchen invasion, the abdication of Emperor Gaozong 高宗 (r. 1127–1162), and the ascension of Xiaozong 孝宗 (r. 1162–1189) altered the political climate for court historiography in 1162. Xiaozong had no good opinion of Qin Gui, whose political support came largely from the Jiangnan region in the southeast. Therefore, after concluding another peace with the Jurchen in 1165, he turned to a coalition of Sichuan and Fujian literati to form a new administration. As a result, Li Tao, a Sichuan native with a national reputation for his private work as a historian, was called to the capital and appointed to the Imperial Library with a mandate to rebuild and resume its historiographical operations. The sudden cluster of activity on the timeline between the completion of the third *State Compendium* in 1170 and the *Four Courts State History* (*Sichao guoshi* 四朝國史) in 1186 reflects the influence of Li Tao and the political support he received from the literati coalition. As Chapter 2 on Li Tao will explain, the view of Northern Song history he embedded into his monumental *Long Draft Continuation of the Comprehensive Mirror That Aids Administration* (*Xu zizhi tongjian changbian* 續資治通鑑長編) was intended to support the policies his coalition advocated to Emperor Xiaozong. The same political forces also supported efforts, begun by Zhao Ruyu in 1180, to rework the successive state compendia into a single *Comprehensive State Compendium* (*Zonglei guochao huiyao* 總類國朝會要) that would better serve the research and rhetorical needs of his literati allies for political reform.

In fact, the half-century that began with Li Tao's arrival at the Imperial Library in 1167 and extended through the publication by Chen Jun 陳均 (1174–1244) of his *Chronologically Arranged Complete Essentials in Outline and Details of the August Courts* (*Huangchao biannian gangmu beiyao* 皇朝編年綱目備要) in 1229 is the seminal period in the evolution of what I will describe in Part II of this book as the grand allegory, the master narrative of Song history. Although Li Tao was not himself a *daoxue* practitioner, many of his coalition partners were active supporters of the movement, or allied socially and politically to those who were. Chen Junqing 陳俊卿 (1113–1186), the coalition leader from Fujian, was close to Zhu Xi 朱熹 (1130–1200) and was Chen Jun's grand uncle. As a political leader, Chen Junqing advocated and attempted to practice a form of literati governance that positioned itself against the unilateral exercise of power by the emperor; by his designated proxies such as Qin Gui; or through non-literati actors within the monarchy such as eunuchs, imperial favorites (often referred to throughout this book as "the close," a direct translation of the Song Chinese term), and affinal kinsmen. Events between 1190 and 1210 – the rise to power of the autocratic affine Han Tuozhou 韓侂冑 (1152–1207), his purge of Zhao Ruyu and his coalition in 1194, the imposition of the Qingyuan-era proscription against *daoxue* in 1196, the disaster of the

Kaixi war in 1206, and the gradual return to autocracy under Shi Miyuan 史彌
遠 (1164–1233) after 1208 – all combined to form the political and social
backdrop for the final consolidation of the grand narrative of Song history. This
narrative would explain how literati such as the *daoxue* adherents had struggled
to preserve the legacy of the Song founders as exemplars of a benevolent
governance that had brought back to life the Confucian models of antiquity.

The first part of this book offers in-depth studies of the four largest collections of primary sources that initially arose as productions of official Song state
historiography and that have survived, after a fashion, to this day. These works
are the *Recovered Draft of the Song State Compendium* (*Song huiyao jigao* 宋
會要輯稿), Li Tao's *Long Draft*, Li Xinchuan's *Chronological Record of
Important Events since 1127* (*Jianyan yilai xinian yaolu* 建炎以來繫年要
錄), and the *Song History* (*Songshi* 宋史). A glance at the footnotes to this
book, or almost any monograph on Song history, will attest that these works are
the sources most widely used by Song historians today. However, unlike
existing studies, my research draws explicit parallels between the contents of
these works (such as their organizing principles and basic themes, as well as
variations in chronological coverage) and the political convictions, associations, and careers of their compilers. This "living historiography" presents each
work as the product of the political forces that shaped its creation, subsequent
reception, and transmission to the present.

In addition to being vital sources for the modern historian of Song, these four
works contain material from each stage of official historiography and thus
provide the opportunity to obtain an archaeological perspective on the formation of Song historical narratives. One may envision four tiers or stages of this
process. The base level of "primary texts" comprises self-authored documents
written contemporaneously with the event in question. The unique function of
the *State Compendium* in the Song historiographical operation – no other
dynasty had a similar process – as an ongoing catch basin of material from
all stages of historiographical production – means that the *Recovered Draft*, as
Figure 0.1 indicates, preserves material from the earliest "transcription" stage
of production. Scholars who regularly consult the work are soon able to
recognize these documents, which most likely are copies of primary documents
generated by state agencies, then forwarded for inclusion in the daily calendar,
and deposited from there directly into the *State Compendium*. However, as
Chapter 1 on the *State Compendium* demonstrates, the present *Recovered Draft*
is a specialized subset of the theoretical entirety of the Song *State
Compendium*. In addition, the work's tortured transmission to the present
requires that its documents be archaeologically examined to determine from
which stage of the compilation process they derive. In short, the book contains
many documents that are indeed primary transcriptions, but also many that
derive from later stages of the compression process.

Taken together, Li Tao's *Long Draft* and Li Xinchuan's *Chronological Record* once contained a day-by-day chronological history of China that extended for over 200 years, from 960 through 1162.[20] One goal of this book is to present the magnitude of this achievement in the context of the overall history of Chinese historical writing. More importantly for Song, the chapter on the *State Compendium* will show the extensive involvement of both Li Tao and Li Xinchuan in the formation of the present text of the *Recovered Draft*. In short, three of the four works under review in this book derive from the hands of two historians who lived only forty miles from each other in Sichuan. Since both the *Long Draft* and the *Chronological Record* are based on daily calendars and veritable records, they are best conceived as a secondary level of surviving documentation. Both share a similar methodology and goal: to offer the private historian's corrections to the omissions, errors, and distortions of official history. To this end, the relationship between the main text of these works and their self-authored commentary is crucial. Following a tradition that extended from Ouyang Xiu and Sima Guang in Northern Song, both Sichuan historians introduced private sources to critique the official narratives. Those passages in both the *Long Draft* and the *Chronological Record* without commentary represent daily-calendar or veritable-records text that the two Sichuan historians accept as unproblematic. Passages with commentary employ a process they call "discussion" (*taolun* 討論). This process cites outside sources to correct the veritable records in order to generate a revised main text that the historians believe presents a more credible narrative. As such, both works directly challenged imperial authority to control the dynasty's history. Li Tao repeatedly asked Emperor Xiaozong to confer an official imprimatur on the *Long Draft*, but he received little more than a pro forma note of appreciation and imperial calligraphy to grace the title page of his work.

Chapter 3 on Li Xinchuan discusses the entirety of Li Xinchuan's career and his surviving works as the mature development of the Sichuan tradition of dialogue historiography. Chapter 4, "The *Daoxue* Historians," studies a series of historians from Fujian who appropriated the works of the Sichuan historians and used them to develop a distinctive *daoxue* historiography. I have elsewhere characterized this development as a move from a documentary toward a pedagogic perspective on the function of history.[21] Li Xinchuan was certainly familiar with *daoxue* philosophy and exegesis and also sympathetic to the movement's political goals. But the overtly didactic and moralistic voices of the *daoxue* historians ran counter to the Sichuan tradition of historiographical

---

[20] As is well known, the present, reconstituted version of the *Long Draft* has lost original coverage for a total of thirty-four years, from 1067/4 through 1070/3, from 1093/7 through 1097/3, and from 1100 through the end of the Northern Song in 1127.

[21] Hartman, "Chen Jun's *Outline and Details*"; Cai Hanmo, *Lishi de yanzhuang*, 293–343.

dialogue. Therefore, the works of Zhu Xi, Chen Jun, and Lü Zhong stand at yet a third level of remove from the primary sources: they are pedagogic abridgments of the longer documentary histories of Li Tao and Li Xinchuan. Unfortunately, the popularity of *daoxue* historiography and its spread throughout the academic world of late Song, plus the Mongol invasions of Sichuan that destroyed the province's libraries and printing establishment, consigned both the *Long Draft* and the *Chronological Record* to textual degradation, commentarial intrusions, and a general oblivion that the Qing academicians in the eighteenth century were only able partially to redress.

Finally, the *Song History*, the official dynastic history of Song completed by Yuan court historians in 1345, is the end of the line for the historiographical processes that are the subject of this book. Recently, the question has emerged whether the *Song History* is a primary source. The older generation of scholars tends to think it is, and uses the work accordingly; younger scholars express reservations, and are more cautious. In truth, the question admits no single answer. The Qing academicians labeled the *Song History* the worst of the twenty-four dynastic histories. They noted that the Yuan historians had merely cut and pasted from the Song veritable records and state histories. As a result, the work was verbose, contradictory, poorly researched, and sloppily edited – all valid criticisms. Yet the Qing scholars also observed that the Yuan historians were fervent *daoxue* advocates, and they owed their political careers to that adherence.

Chapter 5 on the *Song History* reveals the legacy of late Song *daoxue* historiography on the Yuan historians and how they used its principles and themes to create an overarching structure and narratives for the *Song History*. Since, in this sense, the *Song History* depends on the perspective of writers like Chen Jun and Lü Zhong, the work represents a fourth and final stage of remove from the theoretical purity of the primary sources at the very beginning of the historiographical operation. Yet this *daoxue* structure is indeed but an outer shell, inside which reigns the textual chaos the Qing scholars so lamented. As one of the greatest contemporary scholars of the work has observed, many passages, especially in the technical monographs, are so corrupt they cannot be understood unless collated against parallel passages in other Song texts, and therefore they should not be considered primary sources.[22] In short, the *Song History*, like the *Recovered Draft of the State Compendium*, is a vast kaleidoscope of textual passages that derive from many points within the Song historiographical operation. The archaeology of any given passage must first be understood before that passage can be confidently used for historical research.[23]

---

[22] Gong Yanming, *Songshi zhiguanzhi buzheng*, preface, 1–6.

[23] For more on the notion of textual archaeology in relation to the text of the *Song History* see Hartman, "A Textual History of Cai Jing's Biography in the *Songshi*"; Cai Hanmo, *Lishi de yanzhuang*, 162–216.

Narratives

The second half of this book describes the controlling narratives that the Yuan historians imposed on their sources and explains how these narratives grew from political change within the Song dynasty itself.[24] Chapter 6 describes how the first elements of this metanarrative, which I call the "grand allegory of Song history," began to form within the Confucian political discourse of the mid-eleventh century, and how this process of narrative formation continued to develop over the course of the dynasty. A distinctive Song genre of history writing known as "precious instructions" (*baoxun* 寶訓) or "sagacious administration" (*shengzheng* 聖政) facilitated the beginning of this process and supported its growth. This genre selected stories from the larger flow of official historiography in order to foreground certain actions of the founding emperors as exemplars for contemporaneous action. The first work in this genre, the *Precious Instructions from Three Courts* (*Sanchao baoxun* 三朝寶訓) was completed in 1032. Entries were arranged chronologically within thematic classifications, a format that made these works especially suitable for use at the imperial Classics Mat sessions. First read there in 1039, *Precious Instructions from Three Courts* remained a staple of imperial study until the end of the dynasty.[25]

This new genre, essentially a kind of exemplar historiography, focused upon a small set of uplifting themes and illustrative actions from the past and so brought an organizing vision to the disparate events of the more orthodox, yet also more diffuse, historiographical genres such as the daily calendars and veritable records. In short, the "precious instructions" imposed political values on otherwise random historical events. They were also probably the only Song history that most Song emperors read. Emperor Gaozong, for example, studied *Precious Instructions from Three Courts* continuously for twenty-two years. Emperor Xiaozong began immediately after his ascension in 1162 and spent eighteen years with the book.[26] Imperial tutors in the Classics Mat sessions would often focus on entries from specific thematic groups that they deemed especially relevant to contemporaneous issues. Li Tao was careful to keep the influence of this genre at bay in the *Long Draft*, but the *daoxue* historians were only too happy to embrace their utility and cherry-pick their contents with abandon. Entries from the genre also formed a staple of thirteenth-century encyclopedias.[27]

---

[24] For a more detailed synopsis see Hartman, "*Song History* Narratives as Grand Allegory."

[25] For studies of the genre see Wang Deyi, "Songdai de shengzheng he baoxun zhi yanjiu"; Deng Xiaonan, *Zuzong zhi fa*, 370–98; Sung, "Official Historiographical Operation," 202–4, and the sources there cited; also Cai Hanmo, "Lu You *Zhongxing shengzheng cao* kao."

[26] *SHY, chongru*, 7.3a–b, 7a, 9a, 12a–b.

[27] Xu Zhenxing, "*Gujin yuanliu zhilun* zhong de Songdai *baoxun* yiwen."

Closely related to the rise of this new semipopular genre of historiography was the increasing use of "precedents" (*gushi* 故事) as a rhetorical strategy in policy discussions. An individual precedent – the citation of a relevant historical event in the context of policy discussion – could be included in a memorial; or precedents could be submitted, often at audience or Classics Mat sessions, individually or in groups as a distinct genre of remonstrance. A precedent created a mode of analogical thinking that invoked past actions (both real and supposed) as justification for contemporaneous policy proposals. Many precedents came not from the veritable records but from the *Precious Instructions of the Three Courts*.[28] Over time, the most rhetorically successful of these precedents coalesced into a group of Confucian political preferences known as the "policies of the ancestors" (*zuzong zhi fa* 祖宗之法).[29]

I demonstrate that the grand allegory of Song history can be analyzed into three controlling themes or organizing principles. All three components of the metanarrative grew from active, ongoing political discourse, beginning in the Qingli 慶曆 period (1041–1048) and culminating in the Jiading 嘉定 period (1208–1224), when the third and final component assumed definitive form. Chapter 8, "An Empire of Benevolence," studies how the Confucian concept of "benevolence" (*ren* 仁) came to define the character of the Song state. Although present during the mid-eleventh-century Confucian revival, this association grew during the subsequent Yuanyou 元祐 period (1086–1093), when officials who opposed a return of the New Policies charged that harsh economic aspects of those policies had deformed the benevolent character of earlier Song rule. In making this argument, these officials enhanced the allegedly benevolent nature of the reign of Emperor Renzong 仁宗 (r. 1022–1063) and then retroactively postulated this quality back to the founder himself. The result was a historical narrative that plotted an axis of positive political value from Taizu, through the Qingli period, to Yuanyou. After 1125, the political purge of Cai Jing 蔡京 (1047–1126) and other followers of the New Policies created political space for this distinctive Yuanyou narrative to emerge as a central pillar of a new Restoration (*zhongxing* 中興) historiography.

Chapter 9, "From Soldier to Sage," explores how Emperor Taizu 太祖 (r. 960–976), the Song founder and a typical exemplar of tenth-century militarism, came eventually to acquire the qualities of the Confucian sage-emperor Yao 堯. Always honored as the dynastic founder, the process of elevating Taizu above all his successors and ascribing to him the origin of Song greatness began in earnest in 1131 when Emperor Gaozong proclaimed his intention to restore the Song throne to the line of Taizu descendants, a process he completed when, invoking the precedent of Yao's abdication in favor of Shun 舜, he abdicated in

---

[28] See for example Cheng Ju, *Beishan ji*, 28.9b–13a.
[29] For an overview see Lamouroux and Deng, "The 'Ancestors' Family Instructions'."

favor of Emperor Xiaozong in 1162. Chapter 9 also contains detailed analyses of two major narratives of the Song founding by Taizu – "Fighting over Chen Bridge," and "A Banquet for the Generals." I demonstrate that although the sources of these narratives date to the mid-Northern Song, their final textual codification took place during the 1130s and reflects that period's need to recast the history of the Song founding in ways that would support the dynasty's attempt at Restoration after 1127.

Lastly, Chapter 10, "The Lineage of Evil," explains the origin and growth of the premise that a series of "autocratic councilors," beginning with Cai Jing and extending through Qin Gui, Han Tuozhou, Shi Miyuan, and Jia Sidao 賈似道 (1213–1275) dominated Song governance for long periods of time and perpetrated policies antithetical to the "policies of the ancestors." This historical conception arose with the political rise of *daoxue* and its intensification of the Confucian moral dichotomy between gentlemen (*junzi* 君子) and petty men (*xiaoren* 小人) and the application of this dichotomy to Song history. This process began in the 1160s with Zhu Xi's campaign to frame Qin Gui as a "petty man" and culminated in the political protests against Shi Miyuan in the 1220s.[30]

Chapters 8 through 10 concentrate on the origin and historical usage in Song political discourse of each of these three thematic clusters. Although, for want of a better word, I call these narrative elements "themes" or sometimes "motifs," they are perhaps best understood as rhetorical force fields. Each came to stand for a guiding political ideal that then drew random historical events into larger thematic clusters. Just as the electromagnetic force of a magnet will pull scattered iron filings into distinctive shapes, so the force of these ideals pulled disparate events into patterns of meaning that came to define the Song historical field.

These rhetorical magnets functioned in three ways. First, they filtered events to determine which could best serve as building blocks for larger narrative structures. Second, they organized these events into meaningful patterns. Third, they assigned political value to the events. The timing of these three functions with respect to any given event tracks, and perhaps even constitutes, the development of Song political and intellectual history. To take a well-known, concrete example, the first state history of 1030 contained an event whereby Taizu in 968 ordered the newly aligned gates of his renovated palace opened wide to permit an unobstructed view into the audience chamber, likening the spacious prospects to the openness of his own mind.[31] In 1038

---

[30] For an extended discussion of these three themes see Hartman, "*Song History* Narratives as Grand Allegory," 50–56.

[31] The inclusion of this event without commentary in the *Long Draft* (*Changbian*, 9.199–200) and in the annals of the *Eastern Capital Miscellany* (*Dongdu shilüe*, 2.3a) strongly suggests that the story was part of the *Taizu Veritable Records* and the state history of 1030.

Shi Jie 石介 (1005–1045) included this story in his *Records of Sagacious Administration from the Three Courts* (*Sanchao shengzheng lu* 三朝聖政錄), thus selecting out and foregrounding the event above others in the existing historiographical record.[32]

By mid-century, the process of affixing a rhetorical meaning to the passage was already under way. In 1068 the adviser Qian Yi 錢顗 (*jinshi* 1046) equated Taizu's mind with the "rectified mind" (*zhengxin* 正心) of the *Great Learning*, thus highlighting the event's potential as a rhetorical component of Confucian political discourse. The straightened (rectified) alignment of the gates became now a metaphor for the moral rectification of Taizu's mind, itself a Confucian precondition for the good governance that supposedly flowed from that mind; and so the young Emperor Shenzong was advised to emulate the rectified mind of Taizu.[33] By the end of Northern Song, the passage had become a rhetorical touchstone for imperial openness to remonstrance and was grouped with other Taizu anecdotes that had come to stand for various principles of Confucian literati governance. In 1126, for example, Luo Congyan 羅從彥 (1072–1135) provided the event with an explicit Confucian commentary that linked Taizu and the sage-emperors of antiquity via a metaphor in the *Book of Documents* whereby the sage-emperor Shun "threw open the doors [of communication between the court and the empire]."[34] In the twelfth century, aided by the political elevation of Taizu and the *daoxue* push for greater participation in governance, the anecdote became a staple of political discourse. Chen Junqing in 1162, for example, used the story to admonish the new Emperor Xiaozong that he should inaugurate a period of "open/fair" (*gong* 公) governance as opposed to the "closed/private" (*si* 私) policies that then prevailed.[35] By the end of Song, Chen Jun and Lü Zhong cited the story as evidence that Taizu had been a *daoxue* sage who had acquired the mind of Yao and Shun. And the Yuan historians included the story among a group of fifteen anecdotes, strategically placed at the conclusion of the Taizu annals in the *Song History*, to portray the dynastic founder as the fountainhead and exemplar of Song Confucian governance.[36]

Western historians since Hegel have acknowledged that "narrativity" cannot exist without an underlying system of moral order: if every story

is a kind of allegory, points to a moral, or endows events ... with significance that they do not possess as a mere sequence, then it seems possible to conclude that every

---

[32] The work does not survive, but this passage is quoted in the early Southern Song encyclopedia, Zeng Zao, *Leishuo*, 19.17b.

[33] Zhao Ruyu, *Songchao zhuchen zouyi*, 2.11.

[34] Luo Congyan, *Zun Yao lu*, 1.116–117; Legge, *The Shoo King*, 41. See also Sima Guang, *Sushui jiwen*, 1.14.

[35] *Zhu Xi ji*, 96.4912.   [36] *Huangchao gangmu*, 2.28; *Huangchao dashiji*, 3.67–68; *SS*, 3.49.

historical narrative has as its latent or manifest purpose the desire to moralize the events of which it treats.[37]

The above paragraphs propose that the moral order behind the narratives that formed the grand allegory of Song history was Confucian. I use "Confucian" in this book to refer to a distinctive group of government officials – "literati" because most had earned *jinshi* (進士) status – that generated in the 1030s and 1040s both a theory and an attempted practice of governance that were self-consciously based on moral principles found largely in the *Great Learning*, the *Analects*, the *Mencius*, and the *Book of Documents*. Often termed in English "Neo-Confucians" and viewed in Chinese as the initiators of a distinctive "Song learning" (*Song xue* 宋學), there is no doubt that literati committed to these principles constituted a powerful intellectual and political force in Song.[38] Sima Guang's monumental *Comprehensive Mirror That Aids Administration* systematically applied these principles to pre-Song Chinese history; and every historian studied in this book was in this sense Confucian and applied the same principles to create a history of their own dynasty.

Yet, despite the fact that Confucian moral principles undergird all three of the narrative clusters identified above, we cannot conclude that the only moral imperative in Song historiography was Confucian. The dynamic in Song, always latent and sometimes overt, between official and private historiography reflects tension about precisely what moral order should underlie "narrativity." The monarchy, as the driver of official historiography, did not necessarily share the same moral commitments as the Confucian literati who used that historiography to generate the historical narratives we read today. The rise of a committed Confucian reform movement in the Renzong era challenged the monarchy on many fronts, including historiography.[39] This reform was directed against the mainstays of imperial power – its monopoly of financial resources, its control over the military, and the authority accorded its legions of non-literati governmental actors. Although Song monarchs proffered lip service to the moral and practical imperatives of these reforms, no monarch ever embraced the totality of the Confucian challenge. The intensity of twelfth-century *daoxue* opposition reflects the reality that the post-1127 monarchy that Emperor Gaozong and Qin Gui re-created exceeded the grasp of its Northern Song prototype in all these areas. In essence, the grand allegory is an exemplar historiography that crafted an imaginative vision of the monarchy's past in order to critique the monarchy's present and pending actions. The

---

[37] White, "The Value of Narrativity in the Representation of Reality," in *The Content of the Form*, 14.
[38] For the standard treatment in English see Bol, *"This Culture of Ours"*; of the many works in Chinese see Chen Zhi'e, *Bei Song wenhuashi shulun*.
[39] Lamouroux, "Song Renzong's Court Landscape."

argumentative rhetoric of Qian Yi's 1068 memorial to Emperor Shenzong – emulate Taizu and so improve yourself and dynastic governance – lies at the heart of Song Confucian remonstrance and the historiography that grew from it.

As we will explore later in Chapter 11, the reality at the core of the grand allegory was an ongoing political conflict between the practitioners of two contrasting visions of governance. On the one hand, the Song monarchy inherited from the military regimes of the Five Dynasties a technocratic organization. The leader delegated power through ad hoc appointments to various technical specialists – in military administration, finance, accounting, and technology – in return for their personal loyalty to him. If he performed well, the appointee could retain his post for extended periods. Accordingly, the rulers devoted minimum attention to horizontal integration among units and maximum attention to vertical control. Eager for support from all quarters, the Song monarchs were nonsectarian and eclectic. As a result, little beyond adulation of the royal house drove whatever narrativity existed in the veritable records.

On the other hand, the Qingli reformers sought to revamp existing agencies and create new ones that would transform Confucian political principles into a Confucian institutionalism. This new vision of shared governance was encapsulated in a sentence the chief councilor Wen Yanbo 文彥博 (1006–1097) addressed to Emperor Shenzong in 1071: "Your Majesty governs together with us who are your officials."[40] In contrast to the inherited model, this vision gave preference to ordered hierarchies of units, each with a defined relationship to the others. A primary concern thus became horizontal co-ordination among these units. The moral attainments of Confucian education replaced technical expertise as a qualification for office. Officials rotated through these offices in fixed sequences on limited tours of duty with only token imperial oversight. Thus, a broader concept of loyalty to these principles and institutions, often described as the "essential body of the state" (*guoti* 國體) and supported by "public, or fair, opinion" (*gonglun* 共論), replaced the earlier notion of personal loyalty to the ruler. Finally, in contrast to technocratic governance, where literary ability was merely another technical skill, as committed Confucians ascended into higher office, their scholarship and literary skills, honed through examination culture, became vital tools for contributing to shared governance. It is this vision of Confucian literati governance that drove the narratives that transformed the unstructured events of official historiography into the grand allegory we read today.

---

[40] *Changbian*, 221.5370. For commentary see Yu Yingshi, *Zhu Xi de lishi shijie*, 1:287–312; Deng Xiaonan, *Zuzong zhi fa*, 408–21.

Part I

Sources

L'histoire se fait avec des texts.
Fustel de Coulanges (1830–1889)

1 *The Song State Compendium*

Introduction

The *Song huiyao* 宋會要, rendered here generically as the *Song State Compendium*, presents a unique and vital resource for students of Song history. Unfortunately, the tortuous and convoluted transmission of the received text has rendered this work the most problematic, yet perhaps also the richest, of the four major sources for Song history. The first *huiyao* 會要 (collected essential documents), a state-sponsored collection of official documents, was issued in 1044, and the court subsequently updated these compilations throughout the dynasty. A selection from these original collections was first printed in late Song. No copies of this Song edition survive. But large portions of the work were copied into the early Ming *Yongle Encyclopedia* (*Yongle dadian* 永樂大典). Efforts began only in the nineteenth century to retrieve from the encyclopedia and reassemble these Song documents. This chapter will later review the epic 200-year struggle of scholars to reconstruct the collection and resolve its many puzzles. However, despite its status as a milestone of modern Song scholarship, the 2014 edition of the *Recovered Draft of the Collected Essential Documents of the Song Dynasty* (*Song huiyao jigao* 宋會要輯稿) provides only a fragmentary reflection of the original Song collections. Major questions remain about the compilation history of the original collections and about the relationship of the present *Recovered Draft* to these earlier *huiyao* collections. These questions must first be addressed in order to understand how best to unlock the riches of the *Recovered Draft*.[1]

---

[1] The phrase *huiyao* originated in the *Rituals of Zhou* (*Zhouli*), where military officers submitted monthly "essential details" (*yao*) of their unit rosters and weaponry to two sub-ministers at the Zhou dynasty court. At the end of the year, the ministers then "collected" (*hui*) the monthly submissions into an annual report. See Sun Yirang, *Zhouli zhengyi*, 5.205, 226–27; trans. Biot, *Le Tcheou-li*, 1:53, 56; cf. *Yuhai*, 185.4a–b. There is a large secondary scholarship on the *Song huiyao*. Essential are Wang Yunhai, *Song huiyao jigao kaoxiao*, revised and incorporated into *Wang Yunhai wenji*; also Chen Zhichao, *Jiekai* Song huiyao *zhi mi*. In addition to these specialized works, most surveys of Song historiography include a section on the *huiyao*. Particularly helpful is Cai Chongbang, *Songdai xiushi zhidu yanjiu*, 149–72; also Song Limin, *Songdai shiguan zhidu yanjiu*, 197–213. Liu Lin's introduction (*xuyan*, 1–21) to the 2014 edition

This chapter contains two interrelated parts. The first part describes the role of the *huiyao* in Song historiography and politics. Modern scholarship on Song historiography largely views the original *huiyao* collections as uniform, bureaucratic productions of the court history office, routinely compiled under the formal aegis of a current chief councilor. Against this view, I argue that the present text of the *Recovered Draft* reflects a partial subset of the original collections. The history of the original *huiyao* and of this subset reveals that its intellectual shapers were not faceless bureaucrats – although many of these certainly worked on the *huiyao* – but rather some of the most influential of Song historians: Wang Zhu 王洙 (997–1057), Li Tao, and Li Xinchuan. In all cases, these historians were allied to known, and occasionally dominant, political networks. The leaders of these networks, and their historians, viewed these compilations as historical justification for the policy preferences that the networks advocated.

Given these links between politics and history, the second part analyzes the present text of the *Recovered Draft* in order to determine if traces remain of the political history of its compilation and the historical views of its compilers. Using the digital, Web-based edition of the *Recovered Draft* maintained by the Research Center for Digital Humanities (RCDH) at National Taiwan University, this second part plots the distribution of all the datable entries in the database. Preliminary conclusions suggest that the distribution of entries reveals both editorial choices and overall patterns of Song history that transcend these editorial choices.

The Origins and Distinctiveness of the Song Dynasty *Huiyao*

The *huiyao* were originally a series of working reference collections – intended for government use – of dynastic actions and precedents. Since neither earlier nor later dynasties maintained such collections, the *huiyao* constitute a unique Song institution and a distinctive feature of Song government and historiography. The first *huiyao* compilation appeared as a private work in the mid-Tang period. Production of the first Song *huiyao* between 1030 and 1044 coincided precisely with the emergence of a distinctive literati governance during the reign of Emperor Renzong. Because convenient access to historical precedent enhanced the ability of literati officials to influence court decision making, the *huiyao* developed as a useful resource that aided these officials in their political

---

of the *Song huiyao jigao* offers a summary of prevailing opinion on a range of issues that influenced the editing of the work. The editors of this printed edition had access to a punctuated, digital version produced at Academia Sinica in Taiwan and available through their online database Scripta Sinica. Tu Hsieh-chang 杜協昌 at the Research Center for Digital Humanities (RCDH), National Taiwan University, has in turn designed and maintains a highly flexible full-text search interface for the Scripta Sinica edition.

struggles with other sectors of governance. What follows shows that the compilation and maintenance of the *huiyao* collections over the course of the dynasty correlate strongly with the historical fortunes of literati governance in Song.

Descriptions of the original *huiyao* collections, as well as perusal of the modern *Recovered Draft*, suggest the affinity of the *huiyao* genre to the encyclopedias of the time. In 1013, well before the first *huiyao* initiative in 1030, the court completed work on *The Imperial Book Treasury as Grand Tortoise* (*Cefu yuangui* 冊府元龜), an enormous "encyclopedic vision of history" whose purpose was to provide an imperial reference collection for "events from successive ages that pertain to rulers and their servitors."[2] The *Grand Tortoise* combined organizational features from both traditional ency- clopedias and the standard histories. The work, whose coverage terminated in 959, employed a two-tiered classification system of thirty-one sections (*bu* 部) and 1,104 subsections (*men* 門) to classify and group a wide range of pre-Song texts. This two-tier system descended from early Tang encyclopedias such as the *Classified Collection of Literary Texts* (*Yiwen leiju* 藝文類聚), and the early Song *Great Peace Imperial Reader* (*Taiping yulan* 太平御覽) continued this structure. These traditional encyclopedias arranged individual entries in loose chronological order within each subsection.

In the *Grand Tortoise*, however, after a brief preface, each subsection used the same precise system of calendric notation as the annals sections of the standard histories to arrange individual entries in strict chronological sequence. The earlier *Tang Compendium* (*Tang huiyao* 唐會要) and the *Five Dynasties Compendium* (*Wudai huiyao* 五代會要), completed in 961 and 963 respec- tively, had used the same calendric notation but did not adopt the two-tiered classification system of the encyclopedias. The *Grand Tortoise* thus constituted a new genre of historiography. Its purpose was to project the moral legitimacy of the Song monarch and to assert his sole authority to interpret the past and to apply its lessons for contemporary action and future precedent. Departing from the format of the earlier Tang *huiyao*, the Song *huiyao* adopted both the dating and the classification regimens from the *Grand Tortoise*.[3] However, the chan- ged political circumstances between 1013 and the early 1040s enabled the compilers of the first Song *huiyao* to put their own stamp on the genre as a tool for literati officials to garner their own set of precedents. If the *Grand Tortoise* was a repository of pre-dynastic precedents through which the emperor could profess his moral authority, the *huiyao* quickly became a repository of dynastic

---

[2] Sung Chia-fu, "Between Tortoise and Mirror," 24–36, 82–143; the same author's "Cong *Cefu yuangui* lun Beisong chuqi leishushi lishi shuxie caozuo de dianfan yiyi." For a brief précis see Hartman, "Chinese Historiography in the Age of Maturity," 42–44.

[3] Yamauchi Masahiro, "*Sappu genki* to *Sō kaiyō*." For the Tang *huiyao* see Twitchett, *The Writing of Official History under the T'ang*, 109–18.

precedents by which literati officials could lay claim to an authority of their own.

For example, the second *huiyao* collection, completed under the chief councilor Wang Gui 王珪 (1019–1085) in 1081, was divided into twenty-one sections (*lei* 類). Individual entries were first separated into categories, then arranged chronologically within each of 854 subsections (*men*).[4] In his request to update the original 1044 collection, Wang noted that court officials found the *huiyao* format, in which events were ordered into categorized, chronological sequences, the most convenient way to search for dynastic precedents.[5] Cheng Ju 程俱 (1078–1144) later seconded this opinion:

> During policy discussions at court, one would never send down requests [for information] to the State History Office but always to the State Compendium Office. Because events [in the *Compendium*] are arranged into categories, one can trace for any issue its development, pros and cons, and origins from 960 to the present. It is more convenient than the state history where events are scattered and abbreviated and whose proper sequence is therefore difficult to discern.[6]

Later historians would revise the contents of the 1081 *huiyao*, but they retained as optimal its essential framework of twenty-one sections, and these form the basic divisions of the present *Recovered Draft*. Table 1.1 shows the seventeen categories of the present *Recovered Draft*, the number of "unique datable entries" (a concept to be explained later in this chapter), and the percentage of entries in each category. These categories are identical to those in Wang Hui's *huiyao* of 1081.[7]

Thus, the *huiyao* were not intended as histories but rather as reference repositories of possible precedents. Since the modern *huiyao* is a direct descendent of these collections, the modern text, despite all its problems, usually presents, compared to other available sources, the closest direct connection to the primary documents that once formed the base of the original *huiyao*. At the same time, as Figure 0.1 demonstrates, although the Song scholars did not view the *huiyao* collections primarily as "historical archives" in the modern sense, the collections nevertheless became closely intertwined over the course of the dynasty with the official historiographical process. For example, work on the first *huiyao* began in 1030/7 only one month after submission of the first definitive state history of the dynasty, the *Three Courts State History*. Clearly, the first *huiyao* was not a source for the first state history. Like its predecessor,

---

[4] *Yuhai*, 51.35b–37a.   [5] *Huayang ji*, 8.16a–b; *QSW*, 53:1151.143.

[6] *Lintai gushi jiaozheng*, 2.95. Documents concerning subsequent *huiyao* often repeat these principles; see, for example, Shi Shidian's request in 1179 to compile a *huiyao* for the first decade of Xiaozong's reign; anonymous, *Nan Song guan'ge xulu*, 4.197–98.

[7] The 1081 *huiyao* had five subdivisions within the "ritual" category, thus twenty-one categories versus the seventeen for the *Recovered Draft*, which does not subdivide this category.

Table 1.1 *State Compendium* categories

Category		Number of unique datable entries	Percentage of total unique dated entries
Emperors	帝系	1,219	2
Empresses	后妃	605	1
Ritual	禮	7,477	13
Music	樂	410	1
Regalia	輿服	373	1
Ceremonies	儀制	1,963	3
Learning	崇儒	1,408	2
Calendar	運曆	183	1
Omens	瑞異	560	1
Official positions	職官	17,869	31
Official selection	選舉	4,882	9
Daoism and Buddhism	道釋	213	1
Financial administration	食貨	8,851	15
Penal law	刑法	2,659	4
Army	兵	4,356	8
Regional administration	方域	2,250	4
Border peoples	蕃夷	1,805	3
Total		57,083	100

the *Tang Compendium*, the first Song *huiyao* was rather a work that reorganized an already completed state history into preset categories of reference.[8]

Ample citations in the surviving *Recovered Draft* from the various state histories compiled in Northern Song indicate that this pattern (categorization of existing dynastic histories and incorporation into the *huiyao*) persisted for some time. For example, the second *huiyao* was compiled between 1070 and 1081, whereas the *Two Courts State History*, which covered the reigns of Emperors Renzong (r. 1022–1063) and Yingzong (r. 1063–1067), was compiled between 1077 and 1082, more or less simultaneously with the *huiyao*. However, as the dynasty progressed, political factionalism dramatically slowed the court's ability to complete the state histories. This slowdown in turn affected the timely compilation of the *huiyao* and ultimately changed their original character as a categorized rewrite of an already completed state history. Under Emperor Xiaozong in Southern Song, the compilation of the *huiyao* became regularized and its character began to merge with that of the daily calendar (*rili*). As the second part of this chapter will show, these changes are readily apparent in the distribution and character of material in the *Recovered Draft*.

---

[8] Twitchett, *The Writing of Official History under the T'ang*, 116.

In general, over the course of the dynasty the Song court history office produced three varieties of *huiyao* compilations. First were the primary *huiyao*, the initial documentation for the designated period of coverage. Second, beginning in Southern Song, the primary *huiyao*, now compiled roughly at ten-year intervals, were then combined after the death of a given emperor to form a consolidated *huiyao* of his reign. Last were collected and categorized, or comprehensive, *huiyao*, which edited and recategorized multiple existing *huiyao* into a single source reference for the entire dynasty.[9] In all cases, however, the *huiyao* never lost their initial character as an indexing and reference source for prior dynastic precedents.

The First and Second Collections

The edict for the first *huiyao* ordered that the work "edit and chronologically order dynastic precedents and changes to regulations."[10] Scholars who had worked on the *Three Courts State History* began the project in 1030, but in 1037 control passed to the younger Wang Zhu. Wang was a career scholar who, beginning in 1032, held a long series of appointments in court libraries and academic agencies. In addition to his work as a historian, he was also a bibliographer, a ritual expert, and a literary editor, being, for example, in 1039 the first person to define the corpus of the Tang poet Du Fu. He was a member of the political network centered on Fu Bi 富弼 (1004–1083) and Fan Zhongyan 范仲淹 (989–1052), the renowned advocates of the Qingli "minor reform" in the late 1030s and early 1040s. Wang was neither a political operative nor a policy expert, but the group's historian and archivist. In addition to his work on the first *huiyao*, he was also the lead researcher in 1043–1044 on the *Precedents from the Era of Great Peace* (*Taiping gushi* 太平故事), a reference work that culled early Song precedents for use as justification and guidance for implementation of the reformers' central agenda, the "ten-point memorial" of 1043/9.[11] Wang Zhu submitted the first *huiyao*, entitled the *State Compendium* (*Guochao huiyao* 國朝會要), in 150 *juan* in 1044/4; the *Precedents from the Era of Great Peace* in twenty *juan* followed five months later in 1044/9. The *Precedents*, to be studied in more detailed in Chapter 6, was a more focused subset of the former, and Fu Bi ordered that copies be made available to officials in the Secretariat and the Bureau of Military Affairs for use in policy formulation and implementation.[12]

---

[9] Chen Zhichao, *Jiekai* Song huiyao *zhi mi*, 89–92.
[10] Chao Gongwu, *Junzhai dushuzhi jiaozheng*, 14.659; *Changbian*, 109.2541.
[11] For Wang's work on Du Fu see Hartman, "The Tang Poet Du Fu and the Song Dynasty Literati," 46–47. For Fu Bi's request to compile the *Taiping gushi*, see *Changbian*, 143.3455–56.
[12] *Yuhai*, 49.6b–7a.

These facts suggest close co-ordination between the first *huiyao* collection and the political objectives of the Qingli reform. While the original *huiyao* project may have been conceived in 1030 as a simple "indexing" of the state history, by 1044 the political necessity of a comprehensive collection of selected dynastic precedents for reform was compelling. In this connection, one should note that Wang Zhu and his superiors decided to extend *huiyao* coverage for the twenty-one-year period beginning with Emperor Zhenzong's death in 1022, the last year of state history coverage, down to the "present" of 1043. By so doing, they not only foregrounded their preferred sources for the history of the period 960–1022, but also began the process of culling material for the history of the ten-year regency of Empress Liu, 1023–1033, against whose policies and personnel the reformers had first defined themselves politically. Since no daily calendar had been maintained for the first twenty years of Renzong's rule, Wang Zhu's *huiyao* became, in essence, the earliest formal record for the entire period between 1022 and 1043.[13]

Just as the *State Compendium* arose from the need of the Qingli reformers for precedents to justify their call for political change, so the request for a continuation of their work came soon after the advent of the New Policies in 1069. In 1070/9 the Hanlin scholar Wang Gui requested permission to extend *huiyao* coverage from 1044 through 1069. After noting the utility of the format and the necessity of preserving documents before they became lost, his memorial, in addition to proposing to extend coverage past 1044, stated two justifications for making revisions to the 960–1043 material as well. First, the original compilation had been hastily executed, and many items were omitted. Second, many documents were merely "clerical verbiage" and should not be transmitted to posterity.[14] Work commenced according to these guidelines and was completed in 1081/9, when Wang, then chief councilor, submitted the finished work, aptly entitled *Enlarged and Revised State Compendium* (*Zengxiu guochao huiyao* 增修國朝會要) in 300 *juan*. His submission memorial notes that the new *huiyao* contained "extensive additions and deletions to the old text" and that the documents had been edited for brevity with the goal of retaining as many "events" as possible. Clearly, the work was intended not only to continue but to replace the earlier *State Compendium* of 1044. The *Enlarged and Revised State Compendium* of 1081 thus covered the period 960–1077 and included all the New Policies as "precedents."[15]

---

[13] Cai Chongbang, *Songdai xiushi zhidu yanjiu*, 41. The daily calendar had, in fact, not been maintained since 1007. As soon as Zhenzong died in 1022, Empress Liu ordered the daily calendar for his entire reign summarily compiled, but did not order that the calendar be subsequently maintained during the new Emperor Renzong's reign; see *SHY, zhiguan*, 18.79a.

[14] Wang Gui, *Huayang ji*, 8.16a–b.

[15] *Changbian*, 316.7642. Unlike for the other major *huiyao*, surviving sources identify no leading historian behind the compilation of the 1081 work. Song Minqiu and Zeng Gong were involved but only marginally. The two scholars rewarded upon the work's completion were both minor

A Hundred-Year Hiatus

Wang Gui's *Enlarged and Revised State Compendium* remained the standard, and essentially the only, *huiyao* collection for almost one hundred years. No evidence suggests that the antireform, Yuanyou administration from 1086 through 1093 attempted to revise the work. Upon his ascension in 1100, Emperor Huizong ordered the work updated. A subsequent order in 1106 authorized revisions to all of the post-1067 material. Given that Cai Jing had placed his son, Cai You 蔡攸 (1077–1126), in charge of *huiyao* revisions, the order suggests an attempt by the Cai family to rewrite the early history of the New Policies. Considerable work was accomplished on the project, but by 1118 only 110 *juan* of revisions to the first three sections (on emperors, empresses, and rites) had been submitted. Wang Yinglin 王應麟 (1223–1296) describes these as mostly changes to existing material with only sporadic entries for events after 1077.[16] According to Hong Mai 洪邁 (1123–1202), another 400 *juan* of material had been prepared; but, because submission on a major holiday would increase their stipends, the office personnel were waiting for such a day to submit the finished work. The Cai family controlled the billets in the *huiyao* office, together with most other court academic and literary agencies, and used these positions to augment the salaries of members of their political faction.[17] Therefore, when Wang Fu 王黼 (1079–1126) took control of the government in 1120, he immediately terminated fifty-eight book compilation projects, including the *huiyao*, dismissing the Cai appointees and reassigning the clerks to other offices. The *huiyao* manuscript languished unsubmitted in the empty office and was eventually lost.[18]

In the chaos of the relocation to the south after 1127, there was little time for the *huiyao*. In 1139/12 Liu Caishao 劉才邵 (1086–1158) noted the lack of any *huiyao* records subsequent to 1077 and requested that work on updating the collection begin. Emperor Gaozong approved, but neither funds nor office space were allocated.[19] Liu renewed his request in 1143, noting that a proper *huiyao* was essential to preserving Gaozong's legacy.[20] A similar conversation occurred again on 1161/1 between the emperor and the chief councilor Chen Kangbo 陳康伯 (1097–1165). Gaozong acknowledged that the *huiyao* were depositories of "the precedents of the founders" and added that the former councilor Tang Situi 湯思退 (d. 1164) had thwarted previous attempts to resume compilation. He again ordered work to begin, but the transition to

minions of Wang Gui; see *SHY, zhiguan*, 67.1a. Most probably, Wang Gui himself, who first proposed the work in 1070, was its guiding intellectual force.

[16] *Yuhai*, 51.36b–37a.
[17] For this system see Wang Yunhai, *Wang Yunhai wenji*, 499–500, and Lamouroux, *Fiscalité*, 196–97.
[18] Hong Mai, *Rongzhai suibi*, 13.173–74; Chen Zhensun, *Zhizhai shulu jieti*, 5.162.
[19] *Yaolu*, 133.2490.   [20] Huang Huai, *Lidai mingchen zouyi*, 277.1b–2a.

Emperor Xiaozong in 1162 and the return of Tang Situi as councilor in 1163–1164 further delayed the work.[21] Not until 1168/11, under the administration of Chief Councilor Chen Junqing, was the *huiyao* office formally reconstituted. The clear implication from this record of delay is that the administrations of Qin Gui and Tang Situi had little interest in updating the *huiyao*.

Resumption under Emperor Xiaozong

On the contrary, Chen Junqing and his allies favored a more open and participatory system of government, where the reference function of the *huiyao* could prove useful to policy formation, as it had initially in 1044. Chen Junqing, who became chief councilor on 1168/10/13, was the first councilor to carry the concurrent title of "director of compilation for the *State Compendium*" (*tiju bianxiu guochao huiyao* 提舉編修國朝會要).[22] On 1169/4/12, library vice director Wang Dayou 汪大猷 (1120–1200), a key associate of Chen Junqing, submitted plans for the long-delayed revision. He proposed rejecting all of the material submitted in 1118 by Cai You as politically motivated by "the needs of the moment." He requested, therefore, that the veritable records and other works be consulted in order to "return to what is most proper." In order not to divide the Shenzong reign into two bodies of material (the existing Wang Gui compilation with coverage from 1067 through 1077 and the new compilation that would cover events from 1078 through 1085), he requested permission to redo all the Shenzong-period material, beginning from 1067.[23] Wang soon left the Library, but the renowned historian Li Tao assumed his position, supervised the compilation, and wrote the preface for the finished work, which he submitted in 1170/5, a mere year and a half after the office had been created.

Li Tao's preface to this work, known as the *Continued Four Courts Compendium* [*of Shenzong, Zhezong, Huizong, and Qinzong*] (*Xu sichao huiyao* 續四朝會要) reviews the hundred-year hiatus in *huiyao* compilation and offers an important statement of the basic conception of Northern Song history that Li used to organize the new *huiyao* continuation. He viewed the advent of the New Policies in 1067 as a fundamental dividing line in the history

---

[21] *Yaolu*, 188.3642.

[22] The title was added to his portfolio on 1168/11/28; see *SHY, zhiguan*, 18.32a; *SS*, 164.3878; and Gong Yanming, *Songshi zhiguanzhi buzheng*, 233. Dedicated space for compilation of the *huiyao* at the Imperial Library probably dates from this time. In the Southern Song, the *huiyao* office was located in the rear of the Imperial Library compound directly opposite the office of the daily calendar. The physical proximity of these two offices within the Library doubtless reflects their close working relationship after 1168. See Winkelman, *The Imperial Library in Southern Sung China*, 16 and end map. Winkelman's account draws heavily upon the *Nan Song guan'ge lu* by Chen Kui, who was posted to the library in the 1160s and 1170s and played a central role in reviving the *huiyao* genre during these years.

[23] *SHY, zhiguan*, 18.33a–b.

of the dynasty. In his opinion, the existing *huiyao* compilation well represented the policies of the founders and the continuation of these policies through 1067. On the contrary, because the period from 1067 through 1127 witnessed both repeated deviations from those principles and attempts to return to them, "the way was different between the two periods." The many "turns" during this latter period, Li maintained, had produced a plethora of documentation, only about two-thirds of which the history office had been able to reclaim. Li Tao thus made three important claims for his *huiyao* continuation: (1) it presented a full account of the principles of the founders, (2) the New Policies constituted a deviation from those principles, and (3) the documentation for the subsequent periods of alternation between these two political viewpoints was not complete.[24]

In addition to articulating Li Tao's stance on the New Policies, the preface also presents evidence to understand the relationship between the *huiyao* that Li Tao compiled in 1170 and the *Long Draft*, which, as we shall explore in Chapter 2, he was then in the process of writing. On the one hand, Li Tao delivered to the court his second submission of *Long Draft* material, covering the years 960 through 1067, in 1168/4, one year *before* he began work on editing the *huiyao* material. On the other hand, he delivered his fourth *Long Draft* submission, covering the years 1067–1127, in 1177, seven years *after* completing work on the *huiyao* which also covered this period. This difference appears manifest in the roughly 630 citations to various *huiyao* in the commentary to the present text of the *Long Draft*.

Figure 1.1 shows the number of these citations per year in the *Long Draft*. The dotted vertical line marks 1078, the first year of the Yuanfeng reign period and the end of coverage in Wang Gui's *State Compendium* of 1081. The vast

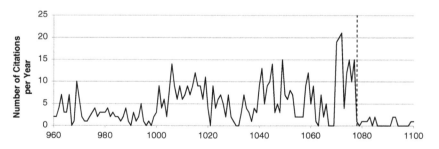

Figure 1.1 Frequency of *State Compendium* citations in the *Long Draft*
Source: *Wenyuange Siku quanshu, dianziban*. Search on the term *"huiyao"* (會要) in commentary to *Siku quanshu* edition of the *Long Draft*.

---

[24] *Wenxian tongkao*, 201.5773.

majority of these citations occur throughout the material from 960 through 1077. Only fourteen citations occur in material dated after 1078. We may thus conclude that Li Tao consulted and cited the earlier 1044 and 1081 *huiyao* of Wang Zhu and Wang Gui when he compiled the *Long Draft* for the period 960–1067; but he did not cite his own 1170 *huiyao* continuation in the *Long Draft* segments he submitted in 1177. We may surmise from this pattern that Li Tao felt it unnecessary to cite his own *huiyao* of 1170 because he had probably already incorporated its most important entries from the various veritable records into the *Long Draft*. We see here evidence for the close relationship between Li Tao's activities as a private and as an official historian. A more crucial point, however, is that because Li Tao edited the *huiyao* for the period 1067–1127, it is most probable that this *huiyao* material conformed to his presentation of the history of this same period in the *Long Draft*.

Surviving evidence concerning the size and division of the 1170 *huiyao* in relation to its 1081 predecessor also provides a hint about Li Tao's treatment of the New Policies. Although Li Tao retained Wang Gui's twenty-one major divisions of the 1081 *huiyao*, he reduced the number of subsections from 854 to 666, while expanding the overall size from 150 to 300 *juan*. As is well known, the New Policies spawned a proliferation of government initiatives and new agencies to administer them, and this growth continued unabated until the end of Northern Song. The existing *Recovered Draft* treats these agencies in the sections on "officials" (*zhiguan* 職官) and on the "economy" (*shihuo* 食貨), which are among the lengthiest sections in the work. It is possible that Li Tao's reduction in the number of these subsections reflects an attempt to contain the historical image of this proliferation and to constrain the history of the New Policies within the boundaries of pre-1067 government. As we shall see in the discussion of Li Tao in the next chapter, although the *Recovered Draft* provides generous coverage of the New Policies years, the *Long Draft* allots greater proportional coverage to this period, and especially to the revocation of the New Policies in 1086, than does the present *Recovered Draft*.

The administration of Chen Junqing acted quickly to continue the momentum of the recently completed *huiyao* project. A month after its submission in 1170/5, work began to compile a *huiyao* collection for the reign of Emperor Gaozong (r. 1127–1162). Although Li Tao left the Library a month later, his assistant, Chen Kui 陳騤 (1128–1203), continued work on the new project. Because Gaozong was still alive, compilation of his veritable records had not yet begun, and the existing daily calendar was sporadic and incomplete. The Library therefore issued a widespread call for the submission of Gaozong-era documents, which were incorporated directly into the *huiyao* project. By 1173, the work was complete, and Chen Kui submitted the *Restoration Compendium* (*Zhongxing huiyao* 中興會要) in 200 *juan*. In this case, the *huiyao* proved to be among the earliest of the official histories of the Gaozong reign; the history office, again under Li Tao, did not complete the *Gaozong Daily Calendar* (*Gaozong rili* 高宗日歷) until 1177. As we shall discuss below, this compilation history is also readily apparent in the distribution of entries in the present *Recovered Draft*.

This brief survey reveals that the entire *huiyao* collection for the period 1067 through 1162 – over 100 years of Song history, including the New Policies, the fall of Northern Song, and the restoration under Gaozong – was compiled, largely by Li Tao and Chen Kui, in the five-year period between 1168 and 1173. We will explore below the implications of this fact for the proper interpretation and use of the *Recovered Draft*.

New Paradigms

The political forces early in Emperor Xiaozong's reign that gave rise to the resurgence of the *huiyao* initiated two divergent tendencies in the continuing evolution of the genre. First was a desire to avoid the hiatuses of the past and keep the *huiyao* collection, now up to date through 1162, as current as possible. Second was an inclination to combine the now multiple collections into one comprehensive work. These two currents were both, to some degree, responses to the expanding involvement of the *daoxue* movement in politics. However, the two tendencies often worked at cross-purposes. This tension remains apparent in the present structure of the *Recovered Draft* and provides important clues to its origins.

With the first concern in mind, in 1173/9 Chen Kui began work on yet another *huiyao* that would cover the first decade of Xiaozong's reign, the Qiandao period from 1162 through 1173. Six years later, in 1179/7, the Imperial Library submitted the work, the *Qiandao [period] Compendium* (*Qiandao huiyao* 乾道會要). Chen Kui's work set the precedent for a series of *huiyao* that would be assembled in regular and relatively quick succession, and this practice continued until the end of the dynasty. Adopting a concrete plan eventually suggested by Zhen Dexiu 真德秀 (1178–1235) in 1209, an edict of 1214 stipulated that the Imperial Library would assemble appropriate documents every two years, classify them into categories, and submit a single, free-standing collection every decade.[25] The result was a succession of individual *huiyao* volumes that would cover the entire reign of an emperor and would be complete and available shortly after his reign ended. Ultimately, three individual *huiyao* were compiled for the reign of Xiaozong (in 1179, 1186, and 1192), three for Ningzong (in 1203, 1213, and 1221), and perhaps as many as five for Lizong.[26]

This regular production schedule kept the collection up to date and minimized lost documentation. However, the proliferation of individual titles

---

[25] Anonymous, *Nan Song guan'ge xulu*, 4.204.
[26] For details see Cai Chongbang, *Songdai xiushi zhidu yanjiu*, 159–67.

Table 1.2 Primary *huiyao* compilations

Title		Period of compilation	Number of *juan*	Years covered	Primary compiler
State Compendium	國朝會要	1030–1044	150	960–1043	Wang Zhu
Enlarged and Revised State Compendium	增修國朝會要	1070–1081	300	960–1077	Wang Gui
Revised State Compendium	重修國朝會要	1100–1118	110 [+400]	1067–1106 (?)	Cai You
Continued Four Courts Compendium	續四朝會要	1168–1170	300	1067–1127	Li Tao
Restoration Compendium	中興會要	1170–1173	200	1127–1162	Chen Kui
Chunxi Compendiums	淳熙會要	1173–1179	158	1162–1173	Chen Kui
		1179–1186	130	1174–1183	Wang Huai
		1186–1192	80 [=368]	1183–1189	
Jiatai Period Xiaozong Compendium	嘉泰孝宗會要	1200–1201	200	1162–1189	
Qingyuan Period Guangzong Compendium	慶元光宗會要	1196–1200	100	1189–1194	
Ningzong Compendiums	寧宗會要	1202–1203	150	1194–1201	[1194–1201 period revised in 1221]
		1213	110	1202–1211	
		1221	110 [=360]	1212–1220	
Ningzong Compendium	寧宗會要	1242	150	1194–1224	Shi Songzhi

Source: Wang Yunhai, "Songdai guanxiu benchao huiyao," *Wang Yunhai wenji*, 28–31; Cai Chongbang, *Songdai xiushi zhidu yanjiu*, 150–65.

removed the convenience of the *huiyao* as a "one-stop" reference for dynastic precedents, a feature of the original design that persisted well into the Southern Song. For example, the *Enlarged and Revised State Compendium* of 1081 remained the single-source, authoritative reference for over ninety years. But the new *huiyao* collections produced by the Library under Li Tao and Chen Kui in the 1160s and 1170s, beneficial as these were as historical repositories, now forced busy officials to consult multiple *huiyao* compilations. Therefore, in 1200, the imperial librarian Shao Wenbing 邵文炳 (*jinshi* 1163), in an effort to halt the increasing fragmentation of the genre, proposed to consolidate the three individual *huiyao* from Xiaozong's reign, a total of 368 *juan*, into a single *Xiaozong Compendium* (*Xiaozong huiyao* 孝宗會要). He emphasized that the consolidated work would eliminate duplication and be easier to consult than the three existing separate volumes. The resulting consolidation, in a much-reduced 200 *juan*, both reorganized and standardized the subsections of the individual volumes and re-edited all the entries for consistency.[27] In a similar process, the three *huiyao* volumes for the Ningzong reign were eventually condensed from a combined total of 360 *juan* to a 150-*juan* consolidation during the administration of Chief Councilor Shi Songzhi in 1242.[28]

The second Xiaozong-era innovation in the *huiyao* genre began with Zhao Ruyu's push in 1180/10 for a comprehensive and unified *huiyao* collection whose coverage would extend from the beginning of the dynasty to the present. A *jinshi* of 1166, Zhao came into his position as vice director of the Imperial Library following the ascent of Zhou Bida 周必大 (1126–1204) into the assistant councilorship in 1180/6. Both shared strong political and personal ties to *daoxue* adherents. Both would become chief councilors, Zhou in 1187 and Zhao in 1194, when Zhao's failed confrontation with Han Tuozhou ignited the Qingyuan-period proscription of *daoxue*. Zhao Ruyu's biographer counts Wang Yingchen 汪應辰 (1118–1176) and Li Tao as among Zhao's most influential mentors.[29] We will have occasion in Chapter 6 to explore Zhao's politics and its relationship to his influential anthology, *The Ministers Memorials from the August Courts* (*Huangchao mingchen zouyi* 皇朝名臣奏議), completed in 1186. His 1180 proposal for a comprehensive *huiyao* both inherits the historical vision of his mentors and foreshadows the political stance of his subsequent anthology.

Although Zhao Ruyu remained only several months at the Library, he left explicit instructions that the comprehensive *huiyao* was to be assembled using four works: (1) Wang Gui's *State Compendium* of 1081, (2) Li Tao's *Continued*

---

[27] Anonymous, *Nan Song guan'ge xulu*, 4.204; *Yuhai*, 51.38b–39a.

[28] Cai Chongbang, *Songdai xiushi zhidu yanjiu*, 162–65.

[29] See the long funeral inscription for Zhao by Liu Guangzu, *QSW*, 279:6318.81–100, and the detailed reconstruction of Zhao's political and intellectual life in Yu Yingshi, *Zhu Xi de lishi shijie*, 2:198–204.

Four Courts Compendium of 1170, (3) Chen Kui's *Restoration Compendium* of 1173, and (4) the *Qiandao Compendium*, the just-completed first installment for Xiaozong's reign covering the years 1162 through 1173. The compression was to create a unified set of sections and subsections, standardize the level of detail in the individual entries, "and combine everything into one work such that there is maximum coverage with minimal verbiage, the historical dynamic flows smoothly, and the text is clear."[30] Zhao's proposal was approved. And so began the first in a long series of actions that would culminate in the present *Recovered Draft*.

Song sources are opaque on the connection between Zhao's 1180 proposal and the *Comprehensive State Compendium* (*Zonglei guochao huiyao* 總類國朝會要) that the Imperial Library submitted in 1210.[31] But the best sources attribute the book to Zhang Congzu 張從祖 (d. 1208), who worked in the Imperial Library from 1204 until his death in 1208.[32] Zhang was a Chengdu native with close ties to his fellow Sichuan scholars Xu Yi 許奕 (1170–1219) and Wei Liaoweng 魏了翁 (1178–1237), both of whom worked together with Zhang in the Library during this period and praised his work as a historian.[33] After the assassination of Han Tuozhou in 1207, the new administration under Shi Miyuan utilized *daoxue* scholars to help establish its political and historical legitimacy. Among the many new initiatives at the Library during this period were (1) a call in 1208 to complete the long-stalled comprehensive *huiyao* that Zhao Ruyu had begun in 1180, (2) Zhen Dexiu's proposal in 1209 to rewrite the entire history of Emperor Ningzong's early reign, and (3) Xu Yi's suggestion in 1210 that the Library obtain a copy of Li Xinchuan's *Chronological Record* from Sichuan.

The *Comprehensive State Compendium* comprised 588 *juan* and contained entries that dated from 960 through 1173. The *Recovered Draft* preserves 579 brief annotations, or sourcing tags, that have permitted scholars to reconstruct the constituent sources of the *Comprehensive State Compendium*.[34] This research confirms that the work submitted in 1210 adhered closely to the guidelines that Zhao Ruyu had set down thirty years earlier in 1180. The work utilized only the four sources that Zhao had stipulated and coverage terminated at 1173. Its 588 *juan* represented a 40 percent compression of the

---

[30] *Yuhai*, 51.39b–40a.
[31] For the most comprehensive study see Wang Yunhai, "Songchao *Zonglei guochao huiyao* kao," in *Wang Yunhai wenji*, 134–51.
[32] Anonymous, *Nan Song guan'ge xulu*, 4.203; *Yuhai*, 39b–40a.
[33] Anonymous, *Nan Song guan'ge xulu*, 8.295, 314, 328, 9.370. See Wei's grave inscription for Xu Yi and his funeral prayer for Zhang Congzu; *QSW*, 311:7110.61–62, 7131.399–400; also *SHY, xuanju*, 22.22a, where Zhang and Xu both served as examiners for the *jinshi* examination of 1205.
[34] For example, "the above material is from the *Restoration Compendium*" (以上中興會要). See Wang Yunhai, "Songchao *Zonglei guochao huiyao* kao," 142–44; Chen Zhichao, *Jiekai* Song huiyao zhi mi, 75–80; Liu Lin, "xuyan," 7–9; Aoyama Sadao, *Sōkaiyō kenkyū biyō: mokuroku*, contains a full listing of these annotations. They can also be easily accessed and tabulated via the search engine in the digital SHY database.

four earlier *huiyao* from which it had drawn. Post-1173 material, although readily available in the *Guangzong Compendium* and the *Xiaozong Compendium*, completed in 1200 and 1201 respectively, was not used. Modern scholars have therefore concluded that much of the work was completed in the early 1180s and put aside for many years, only to be taken up again by Zhang Congzu at the Library toward the end of the Han Tuozhou years and hastily completed after 1208.[35]

An important confirmation that the 1210 work not only followed Zhao Ruyu's guidelines but also adhered to his political views on Northern Song history may be found in what the sourcing tags reveal about coverage for the period 1067–1077, the crucial years of the New Policies. As we have seen above, Wang Gui's *Enlarged and Revised State Compendium* of 1081 and Li Tao's *Continued Four Courts Compendium* of 1170 overlapped in their coverage of this period. Modern historians would consider Wang Gui's work the clearly preferable source. But an analysis of the sourcing tags for the years 1067–1077 in the *Recovered Draft* reveals that the vast bulk of this material derives not from Wang Gui's *huiyao* but from Li Tao's reworking of 1170.[36] The choice by Zhao Ruyu and Zhang Congzu to follow Li Tao's coverage of the New Policies reflects their own view of Northern Song history, a view that placed positive historical value on the Song founders Taizu and Taizong, on the Qingli and Yuanyou periods, and contrasted these periods with the New Policies and their aftermath.

When Li Xinchuan arrived in the capital to assume his duties as a court historian in 1226, he found Zhang Congzu's manuscript of the 1210 *Comprehensive State Compendium* in the Imperial Library. Li Xinchuan's initial mandate at the Library was to supplement gaps and deficiencies in the formal state history for the period from 1127 through 1224. Although there is no evidence that he worked directly on the *Comprehensive State Compendium* in the 1220s, he would certainly have had access to the manuscript at the Library.[37] Most probably, increasingly autocratic tendencies in the Shi Miyuan administration had once again forestalled work on the comprehensive *huiyao*. Li Xinchuan eventually continued what Zhao Ruyu and Zhang Congzu had begun, and his continuation forms the base of the *Recovered Draft*. But many details remain unclear.

Chen Zhensun 陳振孫 (1179–1262), a contemporary bibliographer, records a *Comprehensive State Compendium*, also in 588 *juan*, and makes four statements about the book: (1) Li Xinchuan compiled it, (2) he combined "three books into one," (3) it was printed in Sichuan, and (4) the blocks are now in the

---

[35] Chen Zhichao, *Jiekai* Song huiyao *zhi mi*, 86.
[36] Chen Zhichao, *Jiekai* Song huiyao *zhi mi*, 75, 79.
[37] For Li's career at the Library see Hartman, "Li Hsin-ch'uan and the Historical Image," 320–28, and the sources there cited.

Directorate of Education.[38] Modern scholars have questioned and debated each of these points, and there is no consensus.[39] Court politics forced Li Xinchuan to return to Sichuan in 1233/2. But after Shi Miyuan died in 1233/11, a new Duanping administration once again embraced a *daoxue* banner, recalled its advocates such as Wei Liaoweng and Zhen Dexiu to court, and proposed administrative changes modeled on Northern Song Yuanyou-period policies. An up-to-date comprehensive *huiyao* that would mirror those historical values was on the agenda of the new administration, as it had been earlier in 1180 and in 1208. Therefore, in 1234/3, Li Xinchuan was ordered to "continue the *State Compendium*," using the resources of the Sichuan provincial government in Chengdu.[40] He recruited two Sichuan protégés, Gao Side 高斯得 (1201–1279) and Mou Zicai 牟子才 (*jinshi* 1253), and, according to his *Song History* biography, "completed the work in 1236."[41] If Chen Zhensun's entry is taken literally, then we must conclude that Li Xinchuan, working in Sichuan, in a little over two years, used the *Xiaozong Compendium*, the *Guangzong Compendium*, and the various segments of the *Ningzong Compendium* to supplement the pre-1174 material already assembled by Zhang Congzu. The work was then printed and the blocks transported to Hangzhou.

The major difficulty with this scenario is that the Mongols invaded Sichuan in 1235. Gao Side's own father was killed in 1235/9, and by 1236/10 the Mongol armies had destroyed Chengdu. It seems difficult to conceive that Li Xinchuan could complete such a large project under these difficult circumstances. Yet if we concede that perhaps not all of the blocks were carved in Sichuan, but later in Hangzhou when Li Xinchuan returned in 1238 as vice director of the Library, it is possible to accept all of Chen Zhensun's assertions. The identical number of *juan* – 588 – in the earlier and later collections suggests that Li Xinchuan quickly appended post-1174 entries onto the existing structure and format of the earlier work.[42] At least two important sections in the *Recovered Draft* preserve labels that identify the material in these sections as deriving from these two collections. One of these labels reads "The *Comprehensive State Compendium* as previously submitted [to court]"

---

[38] *Zhizhai shulu jieti*, 5.163.

[39] Most skeptical is Chen Zhichao, *Jiekai* Song huiyao *zhi mi*, 82–85. Less so are Wang Yunhai, "Songchao *Zonglei guochao huiyao* kao," 144–48; and Cai Chongbang, *Songdai xiushi zhidu yanjiu*, 167–68. Liu Lin, "xuyan," 5–12, largely follows Wang Yunhai.

[40] *Songshi quanwen*, 32.2685.

[41] *SS*, 438.12984. The biographies of Gao and Mou also record their participation in the project; *SS*, 409.12322, 411.12355.

[42] Liu Lin, "xuyan," 11, discounts Chen Zhensun's testimony that the work contained 588 *juan* and "combined three works into one." However, he accepts Chen's statement that the work was printed in Sichuan and that the blocks were stored in the Directorate of Education, where Chen himself served in 1245–1246. Although Liu Lin ignores the problem of the Mongol invasion, his scenario seems more probable if Chen Zhensun's entry refers only to the Zhang Congzu's portion of the work, submitted in 1210.

(*Jingjin zonglei guochao huiyao* 經進總類國朝會要); the second reads "The *Continued Comprehensive State Compendium* as previously submitted [to court]" (*Jingjin xu zonglei guochao huiyao* 經進續總類國朝會要).[43]

This scenario supports the conclusion that the modern *Recovered Draft* reconstructs a specialized subset of the primary Song *huiyao* collections: today's *Song huiyao* is a comprehensive yet condensed distillation begun by Zhao Ruyu in 1180, as continued under Zhang Congzu between 1204 and 1210, and as supplemented by Li Xinchuan in the mid-1230s. The process can be better understood and illustrated in Figure 1.3 below after a consideration of the history and nature of the *Recovered Draft*.

The *Recovered Draft*

If Chen Zhensun is to be believed, the state printed the Zhang Congzu/Li Xinchuan *Comprehensive State Compendium* in the mid-thirteenth century. The catalogue of the early Ming imperial library records one, probably incomplete, exemplar of this "*Song huiyao*."[44] Between 1403 and 1408, a team of over 2,000 scholars and scribes copied its contents, along with many other works, into the *Yongle Encyclopedia*, the largest reference collection ever compiled in China. Because the encyclopedia was organized not by topics but by rhyming categories, its editors divided up and parceled out the contents of the *Song huiyao* into almost 400 different locations throughout the encyclopedia, thus destroying the original work's structure and organization. The original Song imprint did not survive the Ming; and only a single manuscript copy of perhaps 80–90 percent of the *Yongle Encyclopedia* survived into the Qing. Only 3–4 percent survives today.

In the eighteenth century, the scholars of Emperor Qianlong's imperial academy recovered from the *Yongle Encyclopedia* two major works on Song history – Li Tao's *Long Draft* and Li Xinchuan's *Chronological Record*. Since the Ming editors had copied both works intact into the encyclopedia under the character *song* 宋, the recovery process was relatively straightforward,. The *Song huiyao*, however, presented a much more formidable problem, and Qianlong's scholars apparently never formulated a plan to reconstruct the work. However, early in the nineteenth century, Xu Song 徐松 (1781–1848), a young scholar whom the Qing academy had tasked to recover Tang prose texts from the *Yongle Encyclopedia*, realized the value of the *Song huiyao*

---

[43] For the first of these sections see *SHY, dixi*, 5.1a, 6.1a, 7.1a, 16a. The second section, a series of important data on commercial tax collections, begins its post-1174 entries with the label *Jingjin xu zonglei huiyao* (*SHY, shihuo*, 18.8a). Entries within this section are sub-labeled as being from the *Xiaozong huiyao*, *Guangzong huiyao*, and *Ningzong huiyao* (*SHY, shihuo*, 18.18b, 20a, 31a–b).

[44] Yang Shiqi, *Wenyuange mulu*, 2.13b; Liu Lin, "xuyan," 10.

quotations in the encyclopedia. A historian by nature, by 1810 he had utilized the resources of the Tang project surreptitiously to locate and copy between 500 and 600 *juan* of *Song huiyao* material from throughout the encyclopedia. He and two other scholars worked intermittently to organize this material, but after Xu's death in 1848, his library and the manuscript passed into the hands of the Liulichang booksellers in Beijing. In 1860, the Anglo-French invasion of Beijing destroyed the sole copy of the *Yongle Encyclopedia*, making Xu Song's manuscript the only surviving copy of the *Song huiyao* quotations from the encyclopedia.

At some point, the scholar Miu Quansun 繆荃孫 (1844–1919) purchased the manuscript. He presented it in 1887 to the newly formed Guangya shuju in Canton, where he and Tu Ji 屠寄 (1856–1921) formed a plan to refashion the material into their own work on Song institutions rather than try to reconstruct the work the Yongle editors had copied. With this goal in mind, they extensively reorganized and reworked Xu's manuscript. The project was never completed, and in 1915 the former Guangya shuju manager sold both Xu's manuscript and the unpublished Guangya manuscript to the book collector and erstwhile publisher Liu Chenggan 劉承幹 (1881–1963). Liu tasked two additional scholars with completing Miu's plan. They continued to work on the two manuscripts, adding and integrating material from other Song sources. With the project still incomplete, in 1931 the Beiping Library finally bought what remained of Xu's original manuscript. Asked to evaluate its condition, Ye Weiqing 葉渭清 (1886–1966), a scholar of Song history, advised "best no one do any more editing on this!" In 1936, with a subvention of $2,500 from the Harvard-Yenching Institute, the library published 200 photostatic copies of Xu's manuscript, now aptly entitled *Recovered Draft(s) from the Collected Essential Documents of the Song Dynasty*.[45]

Understanding the *Recovered Draft*

The *Recovered Draft* thus represents the remnants of an unsuccessful attempt by Xu Song to reconstruct an already incomplete work that had been copied into an already fragmenting *Yongle Encyclopedia*. His efforts then suffered mightily at the hands of subsequent scholars and printers who wanted to use his manuscript to make another book. This complex history of the *Recovered Draft* – plus the fact that the work copied into the *Yongle Encyclopedia* was itself a consolidation of separate *huiyao* collections, plus the fact that two of these collections (covering the period from 1067 through 1162) were compiled between 1168 and 1173 – therefore raises the question: to what degree do the

---

[45] For brief accounts of the history of the *Recovered Draft* see Liu Lin, "xuyan," 2–5; Chen Zhichao, *Jiekai* Song huiyao *zhi mi*, 5–7; and, in more detail, *Wang Yunhai wenji*, 38–61.

entries in the *Recovered Draft* reflect actual patterns of Song governance and how has the complex history of the *Recovered Draft* affected that reflection.[46]

The versatility of the Web-based version of the *Recovered Draft* maintained by the Research Center for Digital Humanities (RCDH) at National Taiwan University makes it possible to answer this question. The database contains over 80,000 separate entries from the 1936 edition of the *Recovered Draft*. Computerized textual analysis can date over 70,000 of these entries.[47] However, duplicate and multiple entries that derive from or describe the same event comprise a significant percentage of these dated entries. Unfortunately, these duplications do not occur in predictable patterns but cluster in certain sections of the *Recovered Draft*. Some duplicates were introduced during the Ming copying, others during the Qing; some may have already been present in the *Comprehensive State Compendium*.[48] Although these duplicates help us to understand the genesis of the *Recovered Draft*, they must be eliminated in order to obtain a more accurate picture of the work's coverage of Song history. Once these duplicates have been eliminated, the database returns over 57,000 unique, datable entries. This data set forms the basis of the following analysis.

The solid line in Figure 1.2 indicates the total number of entries for each year of Song from 960 through 1224. The dotted line calculates a ten-year moving average. The yearly average across all years is 218 entries; the median is 192. The vertical lines demarcate the reign spans of the thirteen Song emperors who ruled during this period. The chart shows wide variation in the number of entries per year. These range from a low of only thirty-three entries in 967 to a high of 688 entries in 1133. However, the history of these two eras presents roughly similar circumstances: in the late 960s, Taizu launched campaigns against the Northern and Southern Han to expand the incipient Song state; in the mid-1130s, Gaozong fought against the Jurchen and pseudo-Qi states to solidify the Restoration. Yet, even accounting for the greater size and complexity of government under Gaozong, this enormous disparity in the number of

---

[46] It is unlikely that the editors of the *Yongle Encyclopedia* influenced these patterns in a significant way. Unlike the later *Siku quanshu* project under the Qing emperor Qianlong, there is no evidence that the Ming court imposed any ideological filters on the content of the *Yongle Encyclopedia*, let alone any that would have influenced the work's depiction of Song history. In addition, as explained above, the Ming editors parceled out the contents of the *Song huiyao* over almost 400 rhyme categories. Given this methodology, it is difficult to conceive how systematic censorship could have been imposed.

[47] Umehara Kaoru, *Sōkaiyō shūkō hennen sakuin*, tabulated over 63,000 datable entries. The distribution of Umehara's entries across each of the imperial reigns correlates well with the RCDH data.

[48] The problem is complex and highly technical; see Wang Yunhai, "*Song huiyao jigao* chongchu bianfu chengyin kao," in *Wang Yunhai wenji*, 242–57. Wang does not consider the possibility that the late Song *Comprehensive State Compendium* may already have contained duplicate entries.

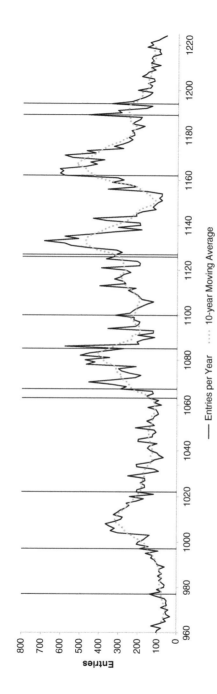

Figure 1.2 Unique datable entries, per year, in the *Recovered Draft Compendium*

entries suggests that the *Recovered Draft* does not present – and that the compilers of its sources probably were never able to present, nor ever intended to present – a consistent, chronologically balanced coverage of Song history.

The data reveal four chronological peaks: (1) an initial peak in the middle of Zhenzong's reign, about 1008; (2) virtually all of Shenzong's reign, with a peak at 1082 and a subsequent spike in 1086, a year after his death; (3) the early reign of Gaozong, with a peak, the high point in the data set, in 1133; and (4) the early Xiaozong reign with twin peaks in 1163 and 1165 and another in 1171. Alternatively, there are four conspicuous low points. First, the two initial reigns of Taizu and Taizong are well below the average. Virtually the entire reign of Renzong also falls below the average. Significantly, there is a unique and dramatic drop during the administration of Qin Gui, beginning in 1144 and lasting until his death in 1155. Finally, discounting the spikes in 1189 and 1194 (caused by intense ritual activity surrounding respectively the ascension of Emperor Guangzong and the death of Xiaozong), there is a gradual but significant decline in the number of entries per year after 1173.

Clearly, no single factor can account for all this variation. One can in fact detect at least three interacting dynamics that have influenced this diffuse chronological pattern. First – and most basic – are gaps in the primary, contemporary record. Two periods stand out. We have seen in the Introduction that essential features of the mature system of court historiography did not function until the early 990s. Therefore, the primary historical record for the first two Song reigns was much shallower than that for subsequent reigns. Likewise, as will be detailed in Chapter 3, after 1143 Qin Gui curtailed the routine function of the court history office as a collection point for primary documentation, and subsequent Song historians were never able to fill this lacuna.[49] Accordingly, these two pronounced dips below the average represent periods for which primary documentation had not been collected and was therefore not available to the compilers when the initial *huiyao* for these periods were first assembled in 1044 and 1173 respectively.

Second, one could argue that the four peaks represent periods of increased government activity. At least two of the four peaks can certainly be understood in this way. Following the treaty of Chanyuan in 1005, Emperor Zhenzong began a period of state building that lasted well into the middle portion of his reign. Likewise, Emperor Shenzong's launch of the New Policies early in his reign began an intense period of state activism that lasted throughout his reign. The smoothed data sharpen both trends. However, it is harder to argue that the two later peaks in the early Gaozong and early Xiaozong years represent a proportional increase in actual state activity when compared to the earlier Zhenzong or Shenzong periods.

---

[49] For details see Hartman, "The Making of a Villain," 68–74.

It is more probable that these spikes come from editorial choices to highlight these periods in relation to the other periods of Song history.

In addition to the spikes in the early Gaozong and early Xiaozong periods, editorial selection probably also explains the decline in entries after 1173 and during the Renzong era. We have seen above that Zhang Congzu's *Comprehensive State Compendium* ended in 1173 and that Li Xinchuan added entries after that date in great haste and under difficult circumstances. The Renzong-era dip is more difficult to explain, but perhaps reflects the contours of the 1081 *huiyao* submitted under Wang Gui, which by Southern Song had become the definitive and only *huiyao* for the Renzong period. Despite the similarities – from the modern perspective – between the Qingli reforms and the New Policies, the Shenzong-era reformers saw the Renzong reign, especially its latter years, as a period of financial and institutional decay that the New Policies were devised to address. Renzong-era figures such as Ouyang Xiu, Han Qi 韓琦 (1008–1075), Fu Bi, and Sima Guang had opposed the New Policies, and the 1081 *huiyao* most likely downplayed their earlier precedents and opinions from the Qingli era. Although Li Tao's *Long Draft* made a valiant attempt, Southern Song historians, no matter how sympathetic to the Qingli reformers, were never able to bypass or augment the fundamental documentary stance that Wang Gui's 1081 *huiyao* had imposed on the Renzong era.

If the Renzong-era dip results from the 1081 *huiyao*'s negative historical stance against this period, the Gaozong- and Xiaozong-era peaks, in contrast, result from positive historical emphasis put on these periods, initially by Li Tao and Chen Kui as compilers of the *Continued Four Courts Compendium* and the *Restoration Compendium* and subsequently by Zhang Congzu and Li Xinchuan as compilers of the *Comprehensive State Compendium*. As we have seen above, the *huiyao* for the Gaozong reign (1127–1162) were compiled between 1170 and 1173 amidst a concerted drive to backfill, augment, and revise the incomplete and politically unsatisfactory *Gaozong Daily Calendar*.[50] The *Restoration Compendium* (1173) was actually completed four years before the *Gaozong Daily Calendar* (1177). Chen Kui thus enjoyed a surfeit of documentation for the *Restoration Compendium* and he made the most of this opportunity. Likewise, Chen's efforts on the first Xiaozong-period *huiyao*, the *Qiandao Compendium*, benefited from the collection of contemporary documentation for the Xiaozong daily calendar which had been maintained consistently since his ascension in 1162.

The twin peaks in the data set for Southern Song thus both derive from two original compilations, both completed in the 1170s when a surfeit of documentation was accessible to their compilers. But politics also played a large role. In

[50] Cai Chongbang, *Songdai xiushi zhidu yanjiu*, 45–47.

1180, Zhao Ruyu designated both these works for inclusion in the first comprehensive *huiyao*. We will explore the politics of this period in Chapter 6. Anticipating that discussion, two trends appear prominent in the historiographical focus of the Xiaozong period. As soon as Gaozong abdicated and Emperor Xiaozong ascended the throne in 1162, the official historians set about to ratify official propaganda that framed the transition as a parallel to that from Yao, the legendary founder of the primal Chinese polity who had abdicated in favor of his chosen successor, Shun. The *Gaozong Sagacious Administration* (*Gaozong shengzheng* 高宗聖政), completed in 1166, mirrored this figural pairing and cast Gaozong and his actions during the late 1120s and early 1130s as the origin and basis of the Restoration.[51] Onto this early base, the ensuing politics of the 1160s and 1170s pitted literati officials, such as Chen Junqing, Zhou Bida, and Zhao Ruyu, against palace insiders, such as Long Dayuan 龍大淵 (d. 1168), Zeng Di 曾覿 (1109–1180), Zhang Yue 張說 (d. 1180), and their allies. Li Tao and Chen Kui were closely allied to the former group and so embraced a historiographical perspective that highlighted how both Gaozong and Xiaozong had acted to constrain the latter group. In addition, each period witnessed large military operations, which always increased the documented volume of state activity.

Conclusion

The *Recovered Draft* entries for Southern Song are different – both from Northern Song and from each other. Chen Kui's compilations from the 1170s relied upon material from a more fundamental layer of the historiographical process, either a copy of the primary document itself or an entry in the daily calendar. As shown above, the *Restoration Compendium* of 1173 was compiled amidst a reconstruction and revision to the basic historical record of Gaozong's reign; and the *Qiandao Compendium* for the 1162–1173 period utilized virtually contemporary documents. Thus, the closer the date of an entry between 1127 and 1173 to 1179, the deeper was Chen Kui's available source base. This fact accounts for the peaks during the early Xiaozong years and probably also for the peak during the early Gaozong reign, since Xiaozong-era politicians, seeking to align the histories of the two periods, sought Gaozong-era precedents for their contemporary policies. The Qin Gui trough results both from the suppression of document collection during his rule and from the desire of Xiaozong-era historians to minimize his historical role by foregrounding

---

[51] For details see Hartman [Cai Hanmo], "Lu You *Zhongxing shengzheng cao* kao." In 1189, the ascension of the third Southern Song emperor Guangzong extended these analogies by pairing Guangzong with Yu, the third legendary emperor of antiquity. This analogical framework remained central to official and private historiography until the end of Song; see the commentary by Lü Zhong in *Huangchao zhongxing dashiji*, 22.771–72 and 24.797–98.

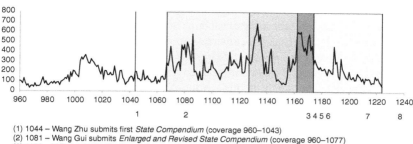

(1) 1044 – Wang Zhu submits first *State Compendium* (coverage 960–1043)
(2) 1081 – Wang Gui submits *Enlarged and Revised State Compendium* (coverage 960–1077)
(3) 1170 – Li Tao submits *Continued Compendium of the Four Courts* (coverage 1067–1127)
(4) 1173 – Chen Kui submits *Restoration Compendium* (coverage 1127–1162)
(5) 1179 – Chen Kui submits *Qiandao Compendium* (coverage 1162–1173)
(6) 1180 – Zhao Ruyu orders compilation of the *Comprehensive State Compendium* (coverage 960–1173)
(7) 1210 – Imperial Library submits Zhang Congzu's *Comprehensive State Compendium* (coverage 960–1173)
(8) 1236 – Li Xinchuan submits *Continued Comprehensive State Compendium* (coverage 960–1224)

Figure 1.3 Evolution of the *Recovered Draft Compendium*

material from before and after the period of his rule. Finally, the post-1174 entries revert partially to the earlier model. They derive from the consolidated *Xiaozong Compendium*, the primary *huiyao* for Guangzong, and the consolidated and primary *huiyao* for Ningzong. In other words, although Li Xinchuan compiled the post-1174 entries, circumstances forced him to use, once again, second-order sources that had already been edited to alter the historical footprint of Han Tuozhou, a project to which, as we shall see in Chapter 3, Li Xinchuan was himself hardly adverse. Thus, the organizational contours of the present *Recovered Draft* were fixed in the 1170s and reflect the needs and vision of its compilers and their political sponsors. The post-1174 material is essentially an "appendix," but one that continues Zhang Congzu's realization of Zhao Ruyu's initial conception for the work.

The modern *Recovered Draft* thus presents a complex mosaic of intertwining influences that descend from the primary *huiyao* compilations, from the *Comprehensive State Compendium*, and from the latter work's convoluted transmission to the present. However, once these influences are identified and differentiated, the strengths and weaknesses of the data become apparent, and modern students of Song history can better utilize the unique riches of the collection. Clearly, the varying depth of the textual base presents pitfalls for those who rely on the work for diachronic studies. The danger is acute for the early Song and for the post-1174 years; yet the problems in each case are different. The lack of documentation for the early Song provided space for Qingli historians to backdate precedents they favored, and subsequent generations largely accepted this early "history" without question. Therefore, uncritical acceptance of *huiyao* sources for early Song risks accepting the teleological constructions of later ages. The danger of the post-1174 entries is the opposite: they present a condensed, sketchy, and partisan sample of the period's once ample original documentation.

On the other hand, the *Recovered Draft* favors synchronic studies of institutions and issues during the years of peak coverage. The modern study of Song history, drawn to the depth of these resources, has indeed demonstrated an outsize interest in the New Policies, the early Restoration, and the reign of Emperor Xiaozong. Because the documentation is richer, diachronic studies also tend to dwell upon these periods. The result is an illusion that the history of these periods is somehow of greater overall import than that of other periods – that more happened during the peaks than in the troughs. And such indeed seems to have been the intention of the compilers of the *Comprehensive State Compendium*. But, at the same time, the riches of the peaks also afford more detailed insight into the deeper structures of Song political life. Later chapters of this book will utilize these resources to delve deeply into the politics of the historiography of the 1130s and the 1160s – not because what happened during these periods was normative for what happened in the troughs but to understand how and why the peaks themselves were created.

2   Li Tao and the *Long Draft*

Introduction

His pivotal role in shaping the surviving corpus of primary sources for Song history makes Li Tao the most influential of the Song historians who worked on the history of their own dynasty. Together with the *huiyao* collections, in whose compilation, as we have seen in the previous chapter, he was centrally involved, his monumental *Long Draft* has become the principal modern resource for Northern Song history. There are two aspects to the centrality of the *Long Draft* for modern students of Song; the first concerns its methodology, the second its content. This section argues that these two aspects are intimately related and that one cannot be understood in isolation from the other. In addition, sufficient details of Li Tao's biography survive to enable an appraisal of the relationship between his political career and his work on the *Long Draft*. This chapter seeks, therefore, to understand the mechanics and the message of his masterpiece within the political context of the times in which he lived.

Li Tao worked on the *Long Draft* from the early 1140s through 1183, first during his long career in Sichuan local administration and later as an official historian at the Imperial Library in the capital. This forty-year period, which extended from the Qin Gui years well into the reign of Emperor Xiaozong, witnessed political conflict and contentious debates about how a proper Song governance should be "restored" (*zhongxing*) after the loss of the North in 1127. This question in turn compelled a definition of the principles upon which the Song state had initially been founded. History, and in particular Li Tao the historian, played an active role in these debates. Evidence indicates that Li Tao compiled the *Long Draft* as a "resource guide" for policy formulation and that contemporary readers understood the work in this way. Exactly what had been the foundations of Northern Song rule? Exactly what should be restored and how? Completed fifty years after the fall of Kaifeng, the *Long Draft* was, and remains, the earliest account of Northern Song history that is both comprehensive and cohesive. And Li Tao's answers to the fundamental questions of his own day remain the cornerstones of our understanding of that history today.

The dissolution of Li Tao's original *Long Draft*, together with the disappearance of his collected works, limits our ability to research his work and its relation to his official career. As is well known, major portions of the *Long Draft*'s main text and commentary, principally the Huizong and Qinzong years (1100–1127), have been lost. Furthermore, the transmitted text contains both later accretions to Li Tao's original commentary and entries where, research suggests, his original commentary has probably disappeared from the text. The modern edition of the *Long Draft*, completed in 1995 and reprinted in 2004, is a milestone achievement and represents the culmination of 200 years of scholarly efforts to salvage and rebuild the work. But the precise relationship between this modern reconstruction and Li Tao's lost original will always remain to some degree speculative.

Likewise, only fragments of Li Tao's collected works, originally 120 *juan*, survive. These were collected by Fu Zengxiang 傅增湘 (1872–1949) and printed in 1943. Although not extensive, they provide important clues about his intellectual and political orientation.[1] In addition to these fragments from his collected works, only two titles from his once large body of freestanding scholarship on the classics and history survive. These are a commentary on the *Shuowen* dictionary and the *Extensive Discussions on the Six Dynasties Comprehensive Mirror* (*Liuchao tongjian boyi* 六朝通鑑博議). Little studied until recently, this latter work affords a unique, albeit narrow and difficult, perspective on his political thinking.[2]

The major primary source for Li Tao's biography is the "spirit path stele" (*shendaobei* 神道碑) composed by Zhou Bida in 1201. Zhou, a former chief councilor and outstanding scholar, had been a close colleague of Li Tao, and a supporter of the historian and his family. His inscription is an admirable example of the genre – a detailed and laudatory account of Li's life intended for public display at the beginning of the path that led to his tomb. Zhou composed this biography at the family's request seventeen years after Li's death. At that time, Zhou Bida was still a target of the Qingyuan persecution, which was not relaxed until the following year. It is tempting to read Zhou's strident defense of Li Tao's career as a historian and imperial adviser as a challenge to the policies of the Han Tuozhou administration. The same political battlefronts on which Zhou and Li had fought together during the earlier reign of Emperor Xiaozong continued unabated under the young Emperor Ningzong, and the persecution

---

[1] Fu Zengxiang, *Songdai Shuwen jicun*, 52.1a–54.8b, collected eighty-one pieces. A more recent edition, Fu Zengxiang, *Songdai Shuwen jichun jiaobu*, 4:52.1714–54.1788, edited by Wu Hongze, adds an additional thirty-four works. For other collections of Li Tao's surviving writings see Wang Chenglüe and Yang Jinxian, *Li Tao xuexing shiwen jikao*, 76–188; and *QSW*, 210:4661.176–4667.283.

[2] For a detailed study and edition see Choi Sung-hei, "Li Tao (1115–1184) *Liuchao tongjian boyi* yanjiu." For helpful bibliographic notes on Li Tao's lost and surviving works see Wang Chenglüe and Yang Jinxian, *Li Tao xuexing shiwen jikao*, 55–75.

grew from and exacerbated these political fault lines. The details of Zhou's biography largely accord with what can be gleaned from the surviving fragments of Li's collected works, with a careful reading of his Six Dynasties history, and with the political orientation of the reconstructed *Long Draft*. In this sense, the heightened rhetoric of Zhou's inscription foregrounds for us the intertwining politics of Li's government service and his work as a historian.[3]

The other primary source for Li's biography is the tomb inscription (*muke* 墓刻) composed by his son Li Bi 李壁 (1159–1222) for internment with the body in 1185. In contrast to the more usual and fuller "tomb record and inscription" (*muzhiming* 墓誌銘), Li Bi's text is little more than a list of his father's official positions followed by a short assessment of his life and personality. Li's text is more somber and less strident than Zhou's detailed account. According to his son, Li Tao devoted his life to Emperor Xiaozong, to recovery of the North and reintegration of the Song state. His prodigious learning earned him respect from both emperor and colleagues. He relied upon his learning to formulate policy recommendations that took changing strategic circumstances into account but disregarded the momentary partisan politics of the issues. These forthright and learned opinions rendered him a difficult ally, and his career thus suffered a number of political reversals. Li Bi implies that the emperor intended to appoint his father to the chief councilorship, but that Li Tao died before the appointment was made. He does not mention the *Long Draft*.[4]

The Historian from Sichuan

Li Tao was born in Danleng 丹稜, Meizhou 眉州, south of the Sichuan metropolis of Chengdu in 1115. His father, Li Zhong 李中, had earned the *jinshi* degree in 1109, served as a mid-level official in Sichuan, and "had full knowledge of dynastic precedents."[5] Li Tao himself passed the *jinshi* in 1138 at age twenty-three, but he declined a routine entry-level position in the civil service in order to continue his studies at a mountain retreat outside Danleng. His purpose there was to prepare a portfolio of fifty essays on the historical background of contemporary policy questions. The essays were the initial

---

[3] For the text see Zhou Bida, *Wenzhong ji*, 66.7b–23b; *QSW*, 232.5183.396–406; and Wang Chenglüe and Yang Jinxian, *Li Tao xuexing shiwen jikao*, 40–50. Unless otherwise referenced, statements in the following biography of Li Tao are based on Zhou Bida's inscription.

[4] For Li Bi's inscription see *QSW*, 274:6687.2–3; Wang Chenglüe and Yang Jinxian, *Li Tao xuexing shiwen jikao*, 38–40. A surviving portion of the *Yongle dadian* (10,421.1a–12a) gathers five biographical texts on Li Tao: (1) his *Songshi* biography (*SS*, 388.11914–20); (2) a short but vital passage from *Yaolu*, 183.3520; (3) Li Bi's *muke*; (4) Zhou Bida's *shendaobei*; and (5) Zhu Xi's criticism of the *Long Draft* from *Zhuzi yulei*, 130.3132–33. The last item manifests the *Yongle dadian* editors' acceptance of *daoxue* unhappiness with the *Long Draft*. See Hartman, "The Reluctant Historian"; also Cai Hanmo [Charles Hartman], *Lishi de yanzhuang*, 217–67.

[5] *Yaolu*, 183.3520.

requirement for participation in a multi-staged "decree examination" (*zhike* 制科). Li Tao and his essays failed to obtain the required endorsement of the Sichuan circuit supervisor, and in 1142 he assumed his first administrative position as assistant magistrate of Huayang 華陽, a county of Chengdu.

Aside from two periods of mourning for his parents, Li Tao spent the next twenty-five years in Sichuan provincial administration, eventually advancing into the supervisory ranks at the circuit level. His historical research probably evolved from his preparations for the decree examination. By the late 1150s, his work had attracted the attention of the Imperial Library in the capital. The renewal of hostilities with the Jin in the early 1160s and the ascension of Emperor Xiaozong in 1162 created a new political landscape favorable to Li Tao and to his historical project. In 1163 he submitted to the court the first installment of what would eventually become the *Long Draft*. This generated a recommendation that he be called to the capital, but shifting politics and a mourning period for his mother delayed the appointment.

Li Tao was already fifty-two years old when he arrived for the first time in Lin'an in 1167. He was appointed to the Imperial Library and served there three times over the next sixteen years. Shifting political alliances ended his first term in 1170. After two tours in the provinces as prefect, he returned as library director in 1176, but a scandal involving his sons and the decree examination forced him the next year into provincial office once again. In the decade after 1167, both at the library and in his provincial posts, he continued to work on the *Long Draft*, submitting additional installments in 1168, 1175, and 1177. Li Tao was clearly the guiding intellectual force at the library during the decade from 1167 through 1177, during which time he oversaw a formidable array of official compilations. The historians at the Imperial Library during this decade largely closed the books, at least officially, on the history of Northern Song. In 1183, Li Tao submitted a revised version of the *Long Draft* and was appointed once again to the Library with a concurrent appointment as imperial tutor. He took ill in the winter of 1183 and died the following year.[6]

Li Tao's roots in Sichuan are central to understanding his careers as historian, local administrator, and imperial adviser. Meizhou had an intense tradition of local scholarship and government service in the Song. Based on local gazetteers, the prefecture produced 898 *jinshi* recipients over the course of the dynasty, as compared to 659 for the much larger Chengdu and 658 for Lin'an.[7] Li Tao and his sons were often compared to the famous Su Xun 蘇洵 (1009–1066) and sons Su Shi 蘇軾 (1036–1101) and Su Zhe 蘇轍 (1039–1112), the Northern Song Meizhou clan that had done so much to define

---

[6] For modern biographical studies of Li Tao see Xu Gui, "Li Tao nianbiao," Wang Deyi, *Li Tao fuzi nianpu*; and Wang Chenglüe and Yang Jinxian, *Li Tao xuexing shiwen jikao*, 1–38.

[7] Chaffee, *Thorny Gates of Learning in Sung China*, 196–202.

the eleventh-century tradition of literati scholarship and government service. In addition to its scholarship, Meizhou was also an important center of early printing. The so-called "seven histories of Meishan," a precursor to the later series of official dynastic histories, were printed there in 1144.[8] Most of Sichuan escaped the turmoil of the Jin invasions, and the province's libraries had grown undisturbed for over a century and a half. In 1148, the emperor ordered a systematic search in Sichuan for books to restock the newly built Imperial Library in Lin'an.[9]

The prosperity of Sichuan derived not only from the combined agricultural fertility and mineral wealth of the land but also from its large population. Chengdu circuit had a higher population density that any other area of Song, almost twice that of the capital, Kaifeng, in the late Northern Song.[10] Historically, its geographical isolation and its strategic location as a trading entrepôt to Central Asia enabled the area to maintain an economic and often political independence from the nuclear centers of Chinese civilization on the North China plain. Economically, for example, Sichuan's large iron deposits enabled it to mint its own iron coinage in the mid-tenth century. In early Song, the area's merchants developed the world's first paper currency, which the provincial government at Chengdu appropriated in 1024.[11] Known as "Heaven's Storehouse," control over Sichuan was central to the economic and military viability of the Song state.

This importance increased dramatically after the dynasty lost control of the North in the mid-1120s. Upon the conclusion of the peace treaty with the Jin in 1142, three armies totaling 100,000 troops were stationed across the two Lizhou circuits in northern Sichuan. These troops, comprising one-third of all Song military forces, defended the now heavily militarized border against a Jin invasion through the Sichuan passes.[12] During Li Tao's entire lifetime, three generations of the Wu family, beginning with Wu Jie 吳玠 (1093–1139), dominated these armies. Well characterized as a "military entrepreneur," Wu and his descendants repeatedly challenged the Song court for control and disposition of the resources necessary to support his forces.[13]

And those resources were considerable. A contemporary observer estimated the annual cost of Wu Jie's army in the 1130s at "upwards of 40 million strings."[14] Li Xinchuan reckoned the cost in cash alone at 22 million

---

[8] Chao Gongwu, *Junzhai dushuzhi jiaozheng*, 184.   [9] *Yaolu*, 157.2990.

[10] Chen Zhichao, "Songdai renkou de zengzhang yu renkou fenbu de bianhua," 228–33.

[11] Von Glahn, "The Origins of Paper Money in China," 66–72.

[12] Xu Gui, "Nan Song Shaoxing shinian qianhou 'neiwai dajun' renshu kao."

[13] Smith, *Taxing Heaven's Storehouse*, 215. For a succinct review of the distinctive political and economic conditions in Sichuan during the Southern Song see Lin Tianwei, *Songdai shishi zhiyi*, 178–219. In English see Lo, *Szechwan in Sung China*.

[14] Zhuang Chuo, *Jile bian*, 93.

strings.[15] In order to raise these sums, the provincial administration increased the extractions from monopoly sales; it also retained funds that had previously gone to the court, which, in turn, sanctioned the sale of offices, promotions, and tax exemptions. Additionally, the province began to issue excess quantities of "cash-pulls" (*qianyin* 錢引), the twelfth-century version of Sichuan paper currency.[16] The resulting inflation caused widespread economic hardship. As a result of these measures, Sichuan tax levies more than doubled from 16 million strings in 1128 to 37 million strings in 1137.[17] As a point of contrast, the annual expenses of the "traveling court" in 1134 were between 16 and 20 million strings. This amount covered the emperor's expenses and the salaries of all court officials. This cash came directly from monopoly sales in those areas over which the court maintained direct military control.[18] In other words, in the mid-1130s, the Sichuan military cost twice as much as did the entire operation of the central court.

After the peace of 1142, the Song court brought the "house armies" (*jiajun* 家軍) of central China under its control, but the older model lived on in Sichuan. Li Dai 李迨 (d. 1148), an auditor sent out to Sichuan in 1137, reported that Wu Jie's army had 50,749 soldiers and 17,700 "officials" (*guanyuan* 官員), for a ratio of more than one officer to every three soldiers.[19] In addition to their outsize representation, the "officers" accounted for over 90 per cent of salary costs. Compounding the expense was the practice of denominating a portion of officers' salaries in commodities such as rice and silk but paying in cash based on the local market value of the commodity. The army commanders manipulated these markets to ensure that they received the highest possible remuneration.[20]

Sichuan remained a "house army" in the sense that its officer corps turned their positions into vehicles to enrich their families. Reporting in 1168, Yu Yunwen 虞允文 (1110–1174), a Sichuan native and political associate of Li Tao, described the commanders as "having placed their relatives throughout the army; their salaries are paid by the court, but they work entirely for their own interests."[21] The officers used the labor of the soldiers to staff their own business enterprises, padded the official rosters to inflate army expenses, and swindled the troops of pay and rations. In short, Yu Yunwen describes a force

[15] *Chaoye zaji, jia*, 15.323–24; Wang Shengduo, *Liang Song caizheng shi*, 124. *Yaolu*, 83.1583, puts the revenue of the Sichuan General Command Office (*Zongling suo*) in 1134 at 33.42 million strings, expenditures at 33.93 million strings, for a deficit of 510,000 strings. Cash payments, probably to Wu Jie's army alone, totaled 19.55 million strings.

[16] He Yuhong, "Nan Song chuanshan zhanqu junfei de xiaohao yu chouji," 33–36.

[17] Guo Zhengzhong, "Nan Song zhongyang caizheng huobi suishou kaobian," 175–76.

[18] Guo Zhengzhong, "Nan Song zhongyang caizheng huobi suishou kaobian," 176.

[19] *Yaolu*, 111.2076–80; *QSW*, 190:4195.294–97. Despite his own statistics, Li Dai pegs the ratio of soldiers to officers at six to one.

[20] *Yaolu*, 110.2068.   [21] *QSW*, 240:4586.56–57.

whose leadership was so corrupt and whose soldiers were so demoralized that the army would be useless in combat. As a result, he worked, unsuccessfully, to develop local militia forces independent of the regular army.[22] Despite such court attempts to regain control of Sichuan, in 1182 Zhao Ruyu wrote in frustration that the Wu family "views the Sichuan army as an old family possession."[23] Several years later, Liu Zheng 留正 (1129–1206) warned that the Wus had exercised military control in Sichuan for so long that the soldiers "call themselves the 'Wu family army' and know nothing of the court."[24]

In the late 1150s, Li Tao, then magistrate of Shuangliu 雙流 county near Chengdu, submitted to the court a chart that compared Sichuan military costs in 1126 versus 1156 in relation to the budget of Chengdu circuit. He put 1156 cash outlays for the army at 23 million strings. Chengdu's revenues that year were only 9.8 million strings, and the circuit ran a 10 percent deficit of 949,600 strings. In 1127, by contrast, there had been a surplus of 574,300 strings. Li Tao placed these stark figures, which document the undiminished and continuing military costs in Sichuan after the 1142 peace, against Emperor Renzong's financing of the Tangut wars in the 1030s and 1040s. Those wars called for a similar expansion of local revenue, but after the war Renzong had acted quickly to downsize military ranks, rescind special tax levies, and return military farmland to the peasants. In this way, he followed policies of the dynastic founders and thus returned the area to economic prosperity. With both rhetorical indirection and hyperbole, Li Tao concludes that although Emperor Gaozong has followed the "precedents of Renzong" and ordered similar measures, his policies have yet to be fully implemented in Sichuan. But once in effect, the "age of Renzong will return in less than a year."[25]

As a historian from Sichuan, the political and economic circumstances of the province following the loss of North in 1127 were central to the formation of Li Tao's historical vision. As his studies of the province's finances attest, he believed that Sichuan contributed more to the dynasty than it received in return. Despite its strategic location on the Jin border and its population's loyalty to the center, the province continued to suffer from the chronic militarism that reassertion of central military control after the peace of 1142 had to some degree relieved in other provinces. This failure of Sichuan to enjoy the full benefits of the Restoration contibuted to Li Tao's historical emphasis that the early Northern Song emperors had done better by the province than their Southern Song heirs.

---

[22] *Chaoye zaji, jia*, 18.408; Gong, "The Reign of Hsiao-tsung," 732–33.
[23] *QSW*, 273:6187.426.   [24] *SS*, 391.11974.
[25] Li Tao's preface to the chart survives: *QSW*, 210:4663.217–19. For dating of the preface to about 1160, see *Wenxian tongkao*, 24.710.

The Origins of the *Long Draft*

It was under these circumstances that Li Tao conceived and began work on what would eventually become the *Long Draft*. Zhou Bida wrote that in 1135, at age twenty, Li Tao composed fourteen policy essays on "Restoring Orthodoxy" (*Fanzheng yi* 反正議). The phrase *fanzheng* alludes to the conclusion of the *Spring and Autumn Annals* where Confucius reveals that the purpose of the book has been "to bring order to our disordered times and restore us to orthodoxy." The phrase was common in early Southern Song as a metaphor for restoration.[26] Li Xinchuan mentions Li Tao's essays in his account of Emperor Xiaozong's early life and places the ideas of these essays in the context of the policy to restore the dignity and authority of the Taizu branch of the imperial clan, from which Xiaozong came. Their major proposal was that the court should ennoble selected imperial clan members as "princes" and deploy them in highly visible defensive and offensive capacities in order to bolster the image of the dynasty and counter any popular inclination toward an alternative.[27] Li Tao's proposal is perhaps best understood against the background of the tense military conflict in 1134 and 1135 between the Song state and the Qi dynasty under the puppet emperor Liu Yu 劉豫 (1073–1143), a buffer state created by the Jin to administer North China in 1130/7.

If such was indeed an implication in Li Tao's essays, his timing could not have been worse. The Jin dissolved the Qi in 1137, and in 1138/7 Emperor Gaozong made Qin Gui chief councilor. The two embarked on a policy of concentrating political and military power around the person of Gaozong. The peace negotiated with the Jin in 1142 sealed Gaozong's position as emperor and Qin Gui's position as sole chief councilor. All of Li Tao's biographers emphasize his hostility to Qin Gui and his policies. They relate that when Qin Gui first heard of Li Tao's reputation, the councilor contacted him, but that Li Tao, angered by the peace policy, spurned his advances and so, writes Li Bi, "made himself a recluse in distant places for thirty years."[28]

It is possible that Qin Gui's return as chief councilor prompted Li Tao to continue his studies rather than to accept an introductory-level post in 1138. When Li Tao finally emerged from his studies and assumed his post in 1142, he had produced the fifty policy essays necessary to secure a recommendation to take the decree examination to identify "those virtuous and honest, able to speak directly and remonstrate fully," an old characterization of the decree examination. Modern students of the sociology of the Song examination system have largely ignored the decree examinations because the number of participants was minuscule. Known simply as the "great examination" (*dake* 大

---

[26] Li and Hartman, "A Newly Discovered Inscription," 416–17, 436; for another example in a 1129 memorial by Hu Yin see *SS*, 435.12919.
[27] *Chaoye zaji, yi*, 1.500.   [28] *QSW*, 274.6687.3. See also *Yaolu*, 183.3520.

科), these were, however, the most prestigious – and difficult – of all Song examinations.[29] Only thirty-four individuals successfully completed this examination between 964 and 1205; only one, Li Tao's son Li Hou 李垕 (d. 1180) in 1171, completed the process in Southern Song.

In 1130, Emperor Gaozong, as part of his program for dynastic renewal, announced a decree examination, which had not been held since 1094. Additional decrees followed in 1134 and 1137, but there were no successful candidates. The examination entailed a three-stage process. The candidate first composed fifty essays on policy issues. Candidates and their essays that obtained the endorsement of a senior court official were then graded into three ranks by a small group of senior officials. Those in the upper two ranks then proceeded to the Imperial Library, where, under the direction of the Censorate, court scholars posed "six topics" (*liu ti* 六題). Each topic, on which the candidate was required to write at least 500 characters, was a citation of five or six characters in length that could come either from the main text or from the commentaries to the nine classics, the seventeen histories, or other pre-Qin works. Routinely, three of the questions were to be formulated as "clear topics" (*ming ti* 明題), citations taken more or less verbatim from their source texts, and thus easy to recognize; but three were to be "opaque topics" (*an ti* 暗題), citations whose wording the examiners could alter in varying degrees, thus disguising the text and increasing the difficulty of recognizing the source text.[30] Those who passed four topics moved to the final stage, during which the emperor personally administered a single policy question drafted by the chief councilors. These procedural details, and their manipulation, later played a critical role in Li Tao's career. Although Li Tao himself never faced the "six topics," two of his sons, Li Shu 李塾 (d. 1180) and Li Hou, did. A controversy over the 1177 decree examination engulfed both sons and forced Li Tao from the capital just as he was completing the *Long Draft* and at the peak of his influence at court.

Li Tao's "Preface to *Decree Examination Topics*" (*Zhike timu bian xu* 制科 題目編序), probably written between 1138 and 1140, explains his attitude toward the examination and his preparations. He acknowledged the structure of the examination process as a combination of remonstrance, which requires conceptual understanding of policy issues in their historical contexts, and the rote memorization necessary for passing the "topics." He affirms his

---

[29] Cai Tao, *Tiewei shan congtan*, 2.29. Li Xinchuan, for example, begins his section on examinations with decree examinations, from which these details are largely taken, *Chaoye zaji, jia,* 13.254–55. Because the entire *State Compendium* section on these examinations has survived (*SHY, xuanju*, 10.1a–11.41a), there are excellent secondary studies; see Nie Chongqi, "Songdai zhiju kaolüe," and Wang Deyi and Nie Chongqi, *Songdai xianliang fangzheng ke ji cike kao*, 1–55.

[30] Nie Chongqi, "Songdai zhiju kaolüe," 180–82.

commitment to the larger "benefits the ancients derived from speaking directly and remonstrating fully," but admits he has difficulty maintaining a similar commitment to memorization. Therefore, he has taken about 100 passages each from over fifty books, and disguised them as "opaque topics." He and his friends divert themselves guessing these citations as they would riddles – a pastime, he maintains, more productive than playing chess.

The preface combines lighthearted jocularity with a serious historical analysis of the flaws in the decree examination process and its manipulation by senior officials. The preface contains the earliest example in Li Tao's surviving writings of the kind of remonstrance by historical analogy that would subsequently inform so much of the *Long Draft*. Li recalls that at the decree examination in 1070 the palace essay of Kong Pingzhong 孔平仲 (1046?– 1104) offended Wang Anshi 王安石 (1021–1086), so Wang maneuvered to disparage Kong and deny him any benefit from his success. Three years later, Wang used the failure of another hapless candidate to recognize any of the six topics as a pretext to characterize the entire process as a useless memory exercise, and no more decree examinations were called during Shenzong's reign.[31] Noting that Gaozong's three decrees had yet to produce a successful candidate, Li Tao implied that court officials have, like Wang Anshi, increased the difficulty of the "topics" as a way to eliminate the public presentation of "full remonstrance" at the final palace essay stage of the examination.[32]

Gaozong's decree calling the next examination in 1140 survives and is the actual edict to which Li Tao responded. The edict notes that the extraordinarily difficult times require candidates whose scholarship embraces ancient and modern issues and whose direct criticisms will improve government operations.[33] As Li Tao understood, the examination demanded extensive intellectual and scholarly preparation; but it was also high-level, and potentially high-stakes, political theater. For example, the palace question put to Li Hou in 1171 asked him to comment on civil and military corruption, financial mismanagement, deficiencies in military leadership, agricultural shortages, rural poverty, ineffective famine relief, currency problems, and a "clerical" mentality among provincial officials.[34] Clearly, any answer that "spoke directly" on even one of these issues would wade into highly political matters and offend powerful constituencies.

Ye Shi 葉適 (1150–1223), who was a great admirer of the *Long Draft*, also composed a collection of fifty essays, probably also written in the 1170s for the decree examination. These survive and provide a concrete example of the genre and its role in the politics of policy formation.[35] The essays are divided into

---

[31] *Changbian*, 215.5245–47, 246.6002.
[32] For the text see *Wenxian tongkao*, 33.978–79; *QSW*, 210:4663.219–20; also Ye Shaoweng, *Sichao wenjian lu*, 120–21.
[33] *SHY, xuanju*, 11.24b.   [34] *SHY, xuanju*, 11.30a–b.
[35] For an analysis see De Weerdt, *Competition over Content*, 90–128.

broad administrative categories (administrative structure, finance, military, etc.) and focus on contemporary problems such as those posed to Li Hou in 1171. The investigation and formulation of the "solutions" rely heavily on historical examples and parallels, often to earlier Song, specifically Northern Song, history. Although Ye Shi's essays were written before he could have seen the completed *Long Draft*, he doubtless saw the relationship between the remonstrance function of the essays and the *Long Draft*.

However, Zhang Tao 張燾 (1092–1166), the pacification commissioner for Chengdu circuit at the time, declined to recommend Li Tao and his essays. Most probably, given the political climate in Lin'an following the peace treaty of 1142, Zhang saw little chance that Li Tao would succeed and considerable risk that, if he passed the preliminary qualifications, his final policy essay would offend the now entrenched administration of Qin Gui, just as Kong Pingzhong had offended Wang Anshi. As a result, Li Tao turned to local administration, but he did not abandon his studies. When he submitted the *Long Draft* in 1183, he wrote that he had been working on the book for forty years. The inference is strong that Li Tao transferred the energy he had previously devoted to preparation for the decree examination into administration – and into historical scholarship.

As is well known, the *Long Draft* was conceived, presented, and accepted as a continuation of work that Sima Guang had begun on Song history. Among Sima's projects had been a book of tables that illustrated institutional changes in Song court offices as well as a listing of officials who had occupied those offices. Sima had ordered the work composed in 1069 for future use at his Classics Mat sessions with Emperor Shenzong. In doing so, he followed the model of his own earlier *Chronological Charts* (*Linian tu* 歷年圖), which served as a framework for the emerging *Comprehensive Mirror*. These tables of Song institutions were eventually completed and submitted to the court in 1081. However, the original had disappeared, and Li Tao could find only a fragmentary manuscript whose integrity he doubted. But he set out to complete and expand the scope of the work according to the guidelines that Sima had set in his original preface. In 1159, he eventually submitted a *A Continuation of the Tables of [Changes to] the Hundred Offices and [Appointments of] Senior Court Officials* (*Xu baiguan gongqing biao* 續百官公卿表), in 142 *juan*, to the court history office.[36]

Li's surviving preface, as well as his prefaces to the subsections on censors and remonstrators, provides ample information to understand the work's close relationship to the *Long Draft*. First, Li Tao, preserving Sima Guang's

---

[36] *SHY, chongru*, 5.35b–36a; *Yuhai*, 47.39a, 119.32a–b; Wang Chenglüe and Yang Jinxian, *Li Tao xuexing shiwen jikao*, 72. For Li Tao's preface see *Wenxian tongkao*, 202.5800–3; and *QSW*, 210:4663.211–12. For Sima Guang's original preface see *Sima Guang ji*, 65.1361–63.

definition of who was a "senior official," included all civil, military, and eunuch officials at or above grade six in the personal rank system (*cong liu pin* 從六品). The tables thus presented a full spectrum of senior and mid-level court officials and were not limited, as are the tables in the present *Song History*, to the top strata of civil officials. In other words, the tables presented all the players and the full political complexity of court government. Second, the tables were chronologically arranged – Li Tao calls them year-tables (*nianbiao* 年表) – and he provided a precise date for each appointment, a feature that he insists ensures their reliability. The work covered the period from 960 through 1125. Dates were taken from official sources – the veritable records and state histories – which existed for the pre-1100 period. He was forced, however, to rely on private sources for the Huizong period and admits that the coverage for this latter period is accordingly spotty and uncertain.

Third, the top register on every page contained a "record of major events" (*dashiji* 大事記), a feature copied from the twenty-third chapter of Sima Qian's *Grand Scribe's Records*.[37] Thus, the tables were more than a simple record of who had held what position; they also contained an evaluation of what had been "major events." A version of Sima Guang's "record of major events" for the Song through 1067 survives in the last four chapters of his *Record of Surveying the Past* (*Jigu lu* 稽古錄).[38] Although sparse and terse in the manner of the *Spring and Autumn Annals*, these assembled events already provide the theoretical skeleton on which Li Tao would construct the major themes of the *Long Draft*. The three portions of the tables – offices, appointments, and events – interacted to provide an interpretive overview of the relationship between personnel appointments, policy decisions, and political change. And the *Long Draft* would provide the details, just as Sima Guang's *Comprehensive Mirror* had provided the details for the earlier *Chronological Charts*.

Li Tao intended his tables to be understood not only as interpretive history, but also ultimately as remonstrance. For example, the preface to the table of remonstrators concluded that the data demonstrates two theories about how remonstrators should be appointed: (1) solely by the emperor, or (2) by the emperor after consulting with his chief councilors. The implication, which would have been immediately apparent to any reader in the 1150s, is that they should not be appointed solely by the chief councilor.[39] Another remonstrative aspect of the tables was their emphasis on recording the earliest occurrence of measures or institutions of which Sima Guang or Li Tao approved. Despite their brevity, Sima's tables provide generous coverage for

[37] For a translation see Chavannes, *Les mémoires historiques de Se-ma Ts'ien*, 3:186–200.
[38] Sima Guang, *Jigu lu dianjiao ben*, 17.659–20.760.
[39] *Wenxian tongkao*, 203.5814–15; *QSW*, 210:4663.215; Wang Chenglüe and Yang Jinxian, *Li Tao xuexing shiwen jikao*, 72.

these events.[40] Among Li Tao's works was a *First Occurrence of Dynastic Events* (*Benchao shishi* 本朝事始), which was probably a list of such events scheduled for inclusion in the *Long Draft*.[41]

The strongest evidence that the tables were not only remonstrance but also prelude to the *Long Draft* is the concluding line from the preface: "the precedents will appear separately in a continued account." Both Zhou Bida and Li Xinchuan agree that "the *Long Draft* began here."[42] They probably based this conclusion on the common language between the general preface to the tables and the memorial that accompanied Li Tao's submission of the first seventeen-*juan* installment of the "precedents" in 1163.[43] In both documents, Li Tao emphasized his concern as a historian for "the precedents of our dynasty." He writes in the preface that "continuing the work of Sima Guang, I will bring into accord the many opinions about the virtuous achievements of our glorious founders." In other words, the tables completed Sima Guang's goal of providing a textually secure and chronologically accurate scaffolding on which precedents, because they occupied key locations in the scaffold, could thus be showcased. The 1163 memorial advances the project by moving from datable facts to the discussion of their interpretation. Because "learned literati" have differing opinions about major dynastic events, Li maintained, there is no consensus about what happened and thus no agreement about what the precedents should be. And therefore, "moved by my sense of what is just, I offer these discussions in order to bring these many opinions into accord" (臣輒發憤 討論, 使眾說咸會於一). We will explore below exactly what Li Tao means by "discussion." "Accord," I will argue, means that he hoped the book would provide a basis for agreement on which Northern Song "precedents" should serve to underpin the Song restoration.

The Reign of Emperor Xiaozong and the Politics of the *Long Draft*

Between his *jinshi* degree in 1138 and his arrival in Lin'an in 1167, Li Tao held a series of seven appointments at the local and provincial levels of Sichuan government. Most of these were "close to the people" (*qinmin* 親民), a category of office that placed him in direct administrative contact with the populace. At least once, in 1146, he refused an academic position in order to continue in local government. This career made the historian an on-the-ground administrator of government policies in Sichuan and gave him sustained experience of the effect of those policies on the population.

---

[40] *Jigu lu dianjiao ben*, 17.661, 662, 663, 671, 681, etc.
[41] Wang Chenglüe and Yang Jinxian, *Li Tao xuexing shiwen jikao*, 65.   [42] *Yaolu*, 183.3520.
[43] *Wenxian tongkao*, 193.5611; *QSW*, 210:4661.181; Wang Chenglüe and Yang Jinxian, *Li Tao xuexing shiwen jikao*, 158–59.

Zhou Bida relates several incidents that show Li Tao both protesting those policies and working to ameliorate their implementation. In 1151, Fu Xingzhong 符行中 (d. 1159), the head of the Sichuan General Command Office, ordered Li Tao to increase the salt tax quota for Jianzhou 簡州, the prefecture adjoining his native Meizhou. Li Tao protested the increase and insisted in putting his objections on the record. The incident caused Zhang Jun 張浚 (1097–1164), the former chief councilor then retired in Sichuan, to remark that Li Tao "had the spirit of a remonstrator."[44] This dispute between Li and Fu was a minor struggle in the growing tension between the Sichuan General Command Office and officials in the local administration over control of resources during the administration of Qin Gui. From 1148 through 1155 Fu Xingzhong, acting as Qin Gui's representative in Sichuan, increased tax extractions despite orders from the court that they be reduced and that the arrears be forgiven. After Qin Gui's death in 1155, Fu was indicted for not following these orders and for using some of the funds he thus extracted to bribe the sole councilor.[45]

In 1164, working in the office of the fiscal commissioner for Tongchuan 潼川 circuit, Li Tao devised a system of "tax covenants" (keyue 科約) that protected residents by making it more difficult for local officials to levy and collect illegal taxes. After assuming this office, he indicted four prefects and magistrates within the circuit for such extractions. He then drew up a list of all legitimate taxes owed in each jurisdiction along with an estimate of the tax amounts due in each category based on an average of the past three years. He publicized these lists in each jurisdiction and encouraged the reporting of infractions. These "covenants" between local officials and residents remained in place long after Li Tao moved on.[46]

Finally, when Li Tao was first promoted into the higher circuit-level admin-istration in 1159, he supported his superior's efforts to reorganize the Sichuan military and reduce its expenses. That superior was Wang Gangzhong 王剛中 (1103–1165), appointed pacification commissioner for Sichuan in 1158/9. A jinshi of 1135, Wang soon ran afoul of Qin Gui, but resumed his court career in 1156 as a historian in the Imperial Library, where he worked on the "precious instructions" for the Zhezong and Huizong reigns.[47] He was also appointed tutor to the heir apparent, the future Xiaozong. He prepared a book of pre-cedents from Han and Tang history that argued for a robust military stance against the Jin, at the same time as he advocated for military reform by imposing civil oversight over army officers, reducing pay supplements, retiring older soldiers, and opening military farms. He was, in short, the ideal patron, both intellectually and politically, for Li Tao. After arriving in Sichuan, Wang

---

[44] *Yaolu*, 162.3076.
[45] *SHY, zhiguan*, 70.45b, 76.72a. *Yaolu*, 167.3166, relates a story that Fu once sent birthday congratulations to Qin Gui along with two golden statues of lions to support the letter.
[46] Zhou Bida, *shendaobei, QSW*, 232:5183.398.   [47] *Yuhai*, 49.11a–b.

added the experienced local administrator and historian to his staff and, most probably, arranged for the submission of Li Tao's chronological tables to the Imperial Library.[48]

In 1161, the Jin launched a military foray into Sichuan as part of their more extensive invasions to the east. Wang Gangzhong personally rode overnight to spur the Wu family general, then Wu Lin 吳璘 (1102–1167), to action, resulting in a decisive victory. When Wang declined to claim credit, Li Tao pointed out that the victory had resulted from steps Wang had taken to better integrate the Sichuan military into the civil administration by intervening in the selection of officers, by selecting capable military officers for civil posts, and by reforming the system for veteran soldiers.[49] In his epitaph, Sun Di 孫覿 (1081–1169) writes that before his death in 1165 Wang summarized for his former pupil and now emperor a four-point plan for military and economic restoration. The first point called for military farms along the model that Emperor Taizong had created in the early Song: "the details are all in the state history, from which they can be retrieved and implemented."[50]

The death of Qin Gui in 1155 created an opening for new political leadership to emerge in the capital.[51] Following the Jin invasion of 1161, the emperor called an eleven-member deliberative conference to consider the logistics of a military response.[52] Eight of its members had risen to national prominence through opposition to the remnants of Qin Gui's administration and its policies. Two members, Yu Yunwen from Sichuan and Chen Junqing from Fujian, would later go on to become chief councilors. A third, Wang Yingchen 汪應辰 (1118–1176), would soon be posted to Sichuan, where he would arrange for Li Tao's move to Lin'an. In short, Li Tao's emergence on the national scene and – very probably – his commitment to what would become the *Long Draft* were directly related to the support he received from this post-Qin Gui political alliance and to its interest in the contemporary political relevance of his historiographical project.

This group represented a geographical alliance between Sichuan and Fujian scholars against officials from the Jiangnan area that had formed the base of Qin Gui's support. Like Li Tao, many of its members were serious scholars who often took an academic approach to administrative problems. Chen Junqing, for example, was a close friend of Zhu Xi and an advocate of Fujian *daoxue*. They cast their opponents as "capable clerks" whose only goal was to advance their careers by increasing revenue extraction.[53] Teraji Jun cites a series of

[48] *SS*, 386.11862–64; see also Wang's funeral inscription (*muzhiming*) by Sun Di in *QSW*, 161:3493.88–96.
[49] *SS*, 386.11863.   [50] *QSW*, 161:3493.93.
[51] The analysis in these two paragraphs follows Teraji Jun, *Nan-Sō shoki seijishi kenkyū*, 432–45.
[52] *Yaolu*, 190.3681.
[53] See Chen Junqing's 1167 characterization of his political opposition as "capable clerks," quoted in his biography by Zhu Xi, *Zhu Xi ji*, 96.4918.

memorials between 1155 and 1160 that call for stricter oversight of provincial tax collection, fiscal reform, and a national audit.[54] Finally, all members of the new alliance were irredentist to some degree and advocated a more robust military stance against the Jin. In short, this group echoed at the national level many of the same concerns that Li Tao had voiced as a local administrator in Sichuan. Therefore, in matters of geography, scholarship, and internal and external dynastic policy, Li Tao found natural allies in the developing Sichuan–Fujian axis at court.

Yu Yunwen's victory over the Jin invaders at Caishi in 1161/11, followed by Emperor Gaozong's abdication and Xiaozong's ascension in 1162/6, encouraged the new alliance to press for the recall of Zhang Jun, Qin Gui's old nemesis from Sichuan, advocate for war against the Jin, and admirer of Li Tao's remonstrative spirit. In 1163, the year that Li Tao submitted the first installment of his history to court, Zhang pressed his invasion, and the Song forces suffered a disastrous defeat at Fuli on 1163/5/24. Xiaozong decided reluctantly to negotiate an end to the war and recalled Tang Situi, a leader of the Jiangnan officials and protégé of Qin Gui, to manage the task as chief councilor. These developments dealt the new alliance a temporary setback. A recommendation to bring Li Tao to the capital in 1164 went nowhere when Tang Situi forced the recommender from office.[55]

A key member of the group, however, Wang Yingchen, arrived in Sichuan in 1164/5 as pacification commissioner and prefect of Chengdu. Li Tao was in mourning for his mother, but as soon as the mourning period was over, Wang recommended to the senior councilors that Li be brought to court. Wang's letter noted Li Tao's dual accomplishments as a historian and local administrator. In language that echoed Li Tao's own descriptions of his work, Wang wrote that the historian had resolved discrepancies in the details of dynastic precedents to derive what are "most appropriate" versions that can be transmitted with confidence to posterity. He also noted his expertise at all levels of local administrative regulations and procedures.[56]

When Wang Yingchen recommended Li Tao, his letter went to four officials: the two chief councilors Ye Yong 葉顒 (1100–1167) and Wei Qi 魏杞 (*jinshi* 1142) and the two assisting councilors Jiang Fu 蔣芾 (*jinshi* 1151) and Chen Junqing. These four councilors shared common political goals, and their appointments in 1167/1 marked the first time in Xiaozong's reign that all four senior civil positions in government had been filled. Although this coalition would dissolve within a year, it was the dominant political alliance at the moment, and it summoned Li Tao to court. Good evidence suggests that its

---

[54] Teraji Jun, *Nan-Sō shoki seijishi kenkyū*, 443–44; for the memorials see *Yaolu*, 170.3249, 171.3265–67, 174.3325, 175.3355–56, and 187.3635.
[55] See the biography of Hong Zun, *SS*, 373.11568.
[56] Wang Yingchen, *Wending ji*, 13.18a–b; *QSW*, 215:4768.35.

leaders thought that Li Tao's talents as a historian might prove useful to their political goals.

As was customary in such cases, before he was assigned his new position at court, Li Tao had an interview with the emperor. At his audience on 1167/8/14, he wasted little time making his points. He addressed three issues. First, in order to formulate a fundamental long-term plan to recover the north, Xiaozong should follow the precedents of the dynastic founder Taizu. Second, he suggested that the number of remonstrators be increased and that the investigating censors overseeing the Six Ministries be permitted to bypass their regular chain of command and memorialize directly to the emperor. Third, he advocated extensive military reforms, including a freeze on increases in troop size, reductions in the officer's corps, verification of military rosters, and an end to "private donations" by military commanders to the court.[57]

Thus, in his first meeting with the emperor, Li Tao presented proposals for reforming fundamental civil and military institutions together with historical justification for their implementation. He was appointed junior compiler in the Office of the State History, adjacent to the Imperial Library. Upon the recommendation of Wang Yingchen, still in Sichuan, Li Tao was ordered to submit the continuation of his Taizu-era material, which, Wang noted, was essentially complete through 1100, and the Library was to edit and deposit a clean copy in the "imperial archives" (*bige* 秘閣), a select section of the Library that was intended for imperial use.[58] The following month, the Hanlin scholar Liu Gong 劉珙 (1122–1178), an important member of the governing coalition, engaged the emperor on the subject of what makes a good historian. They concluded that he should possess a combination of discrimination, scholarship, and administrative ability. The conversation suggests that Li Tao's appointment was perhaps part of the coalition's effort to strengthen and control the history office.[59]

When Li Tao arrived in the capital, the great issue of the moment was the dismissal of the general Qi Fang 戚方, supreme commander of the imperial army at Zhenjiang. With 47,000 troops under his command, Qi Fang's rank and stature were comparable to Wu Lin's in Sichuan. A primary goal of the Ye–Wei–Jiang–Chen government was to regain control over military costs that had escalated during the wars of the early 1160s. But military corruption and collusion between military leaders and the eunuchs who supervised most court accounting procedures posed major challenges. Jiang Fu targeted Qi Fang's army for a 4,000-troop reduction, but insisted to the emperor that

---

[57] None of these memorials survive. This paragraph is based on the synopses in Li Tao's biography by Zhou Bida, *QSW*, 232:5183.398; and in his *Song History* biography, *SS*, 388.11914–15.

[58] *SHY, chongru*, 4.14b, 5.37a–b.

[59] *Songshi quanwen*, 24B.2050. Their consensus repeated the great Tang historian Liu Zhiji's opinion on the three necessary qualities of a good historian; see Ouyang Xiu, *Xin Tang shu*, 132.4522.

reductions in personnel without simultaneous imposition of financial controls would be useless. To this end, the emperor agreed in 1166/12 to establish, under the chief councilors, a State Finance Office (*Guoyong si* 國用司), with authority to conduct monthly audits of all government units, both inner and outer court, civil and military, court and province.[60]

The administration launched a major investigation of Qi Fang. Comparing him to a common bandit, censors determined that he had oppressed and financially exploited his troops by diverting 40 percent of their compensation and then bribed two eunuchs to camouflage the court accounting. Two-thirds of his wealth was ordered confiscated and distributed among the troops. He and the two eunuchs were severely punished and placed in southern confinement.[61] As the affair was concluding, the emperor and Ye Yong agreed that similar practices were pervasive throughout the other armies, and they hoped that the example of Qi Fang would encourage reforms elsewhere. Ye Yong pointed out, however, that the court could not punish every general as it had Qi Fang. The long-term solution was for Xiaozong to emulate the personnel management policies of the founding emperor Taizu. History showed that superior emperorship, in consort with the "policies of the ancestors," had transformed the rough soldiers of the Five Dynasties into the illustrious civil and military leaders of the Renzong period. Xiaozong could do likewise and thus ensure the longevity of the dynasty.[62]

In short, all three points on which Li Tao addressed Xiaozong at his initial audience reinforced the actions that the current administration had undertaken several weeks earlier against Qi Fang. Furthermore, both his rhetoric and his historical framing of contemporary issues mirrored the policies of his superiors who had brought him to the capital.

Eight months elapsed between the initial order for Li Tao to submit his compilation and its formal delivery on 1168/4/25. On the one hand, there were distractions. Research on the calendar and on ritual matters took time from his historical work. He was also drawn into a nasty and highly visible dispute with Hong Mai over a protocol issue. On the other hand, the order to submit all his material through 1100 forced Li Tao to rethink the format of his project. The 1167 edict refers to his work as the *Continuation of the Comprehensive Mirror That Aids Administration* (*Xu zizhi tongjian*); but Li Tao's 1168 memorial explains that he has recast his material as a "long draft" and that his submission includes material only through 1067, not 1100. Most scholars argue that the vastly greater quantity of primary sources for the reigns after 1067 forced Li

---

[60] *SHY, zhiguan*, 6.20a–21a; *QSW*, 234.5225.285; *Chaoye zaji, jia*, 17.387–88; *Songshi quanwen*, 24B.2042–43.

[61] *SHY, zhiguan*, 71.18b–19b; *Songshi quanwen*, 24B.2049–50.

[62] See Yang Wanli's biography of Ye Yong, *QSW*, 240:5360.75–76. Zhu Xi's biography of Chen Junqing gives much of this narrative to Chen; see *Zhu Xi ji*, 96.4921–22.

Tao to change the format of his compilation, and Li Tao's own memorial indeed mentions this problem.[63]

But the issue was greater than the simple problem of time versus the amplitude of the sources. We have seen in Chapter 1 that Li Tao's preface to the 1170 *Continued Four Courts Compendium* perceived the year 1067 as marking a fundamental shift in the nature of the Song state. His decision to confine his 1168 submission to the pre-1067 material also reflects this per-ceived division. The year 1067 marked not only a political but also a historiographical divide whose dimensions Li Tao probably only fully under-stood after his arrival at the library. As of 1167, the existing historiographical record for the pre-1067 period, the veritable records and state histories, had long been written. Although he would attempt to annotate and correct this record, the basic source materials were settled and in place. On the contrary, sources for the post-1067 period presented a host of intertwined historiogra-phical and political problems. There were at least three, often conflicting, versions of the *Shenzong Veritable Records* and two versions of the *Zhezong Veritable Records*. Those for the Huizong and Qinzong reigns were still, in Li Tao's view, incomplete. Draft state histories for the Shenzong and Zhezong reigns had been completed in 1104 and 1122 respectively, but Li Tao viewed both works as imbued with the troubled politics of the late Northern Song.

In short, before Li Tao could apply the "long-draft" method to comment on the primary sources, those sources needed to be present in complete and official, thus sanctioned, versions. Therefore, Li Tao's work as a historian henceforth proceeded along two closely related fronts. First, he worked in his official capacity as a compiler in the State History Office to complete the veritable records and state histories through 1127. Second, he proceeded simultaneously to continue his "long-draft" project on this same material for the 1067–1127 period. In theory, the dividing line between the two projects was clear. The first was official history; the second was not. But, in truth, the line was often fluid and opaque. Li Tao exploited this ambiguity to develop his own brand of quasi-official historiography, seeking to obtain for the *Long Draft* an imperial sanction similar to those that the formal, official sources enjoyed.

Li Tao thus attempted to co-ordinate the official historical sources for the 1067–1127 period (the veritable records, the state history, and the *Compendium*) with the political interpretations that he would present in the *Long Draft* about what had happened during this period. If the first *Long Draft*

---

[63] Pei Rucheng and Xu Peizao, *Xu zizhi tongjian changbian kaolüe*, 21–23; Sudō Yoshiyuki, "Nan-Sō no Ri Tou to *Zoku shiji tsugan chōhen* no seiritsu," 485–86. There are several versions of Li Tao's 1168 submission memorial. For condensations see *Wenxian tongkao*, 193.5611–12; and *Yuhai*, 47.43a–44b. The longer version, reprinted in *QSW*, 210:4661.178–79, derives from the front matter in the thirteenth-century imprint, *Songben Xu zizhi tongjian changbian*. For both texts, see Wang Chenglüe and Yang Jinxian, *Li Tao xuexing shiwen jikao*, 159–60.

submission of 1168 presented Li Tao's views on Taizu and the policies of the founders, then the post-1067 material would illustrate how the politics of the Shenzong era had deformed those same policies and led to the debacle of 1125–1127. Politically, these were still unsettled issues in 1168, and many of the goals of Li Tao's coalition were directed against what they perceived as continuations of the misguided policies from these earlier eras.

It is highly likely Li Tao realized that the main text and interlinear commentary of the "long-draft" format could provide a better medium than the finished *Comprehensive Mirror* model for articulating the historical background of the political choices that confronted those who were tasked with continuing the "restoration." He would present these choices as contemporary versions of the same choices that had faced the emperors and political leaders of pre-1127 Song, with the implicit warning that the wrong choices could lead to similar disasters.

The "long-draft" format offered a more flexible tableau for presenting arguments that the state should "restore" appropriate precedents of the founders and unmake the deviations from these policies that the Shenzong era had inaugurated. In short, it provided a more nuanced format for presenting a historical image of Northern Song that the Ye–Wei–Jiang–Chen alliance could use in policy formulation with the emperor and in political struggles with their opponents. As we shall also see below, when Li Tao eventually presented his 1067–1100 material in 1175, he asked Xiaozong to convene a formal deliberative conference to review the major issues and apply an official imprimatur on his historical take on the period. The contemporary political implications of such an imprimatur would have been substantial, and Emperor Xiaozong wisely sidestepped the request.

Proceeding thus on two fronts, the day before Li Tao submitted his first installment of the *Long Draft*, the chief councilor Jiang Fu submitted the completed *Qinzong Veritable Records* as well as the Qinzong annals for the state history. Since Li Tao had edited the former and compiled the latter, he was accorded a promotion. However, he deftly declined the promotion, citing a precedent that conferred promotion only upon completion of the full state history. Noting that during the Northern Song the state history projects had been completed in four to five years but that work on the *Four Courts State History* (Shenzong through Qinzong, 1167–1127) had been now under way for over ten years, he pressed for permission to accelerate its compilation, thus also gaining control over the process.[64]

But the *Huizong Veritable Records* presented far larger problems. Fortunately, the *Recovered Draft* preserves two long memorials that Li Tao wrote in 1169/12 that detail his proposed solution. These memorials make clear

---

[64] *SHY, zhiguan*, 18.69a–b; *QSW*, 210:4661.182.

the extensive correlation between the *Long Draft* and the official compilations on which he worked. The chief councilor Tang Situi had submitted a draft of the *Huizong Veritable Records* in 1158. But Tang had been a protégé of Qin Gui, had continued many policies of the Huizong era, and, as we have seen in Chapter 1, was no supporter of a robust state historiography. Not surprisingly, Li Tao found the *Huizong Veritable Records* even more inferior than those that covered the Shenzong and Zhezong eras.

Li Tao began his memorials by citing the many precedents for revisions to existing veritable records. He maintained that in all cases these revisions had been undertaken to supply information that was lacking, for whatever reason, in the earlier version. This process necessitated recourse to nonofficial sources. He relates that his research for the *Long Draft* has restored 10–20 percent of the omissions in the Zhezong veritable records. But the Huizong-era records were unique: even basic information, such as, for example, the appointment dates for major officials, was often manifestly wrong. He emphasized that the state history could not be compiled on such a weak foundation.

He therefore proposed to classify the entries in the existing *Huizong Veritable Records* into four categories and to revise accordingly: "retain what is fact, omit what is false, insert what is lacking, and correct what is mistaken." He asked permission to prepare in this way and submit the initial year (1100) as a sample for approval, thus establishing guidelines to revise the whole work. Li Tao framed his request to undertake this recompilation as an extension of the authorization he had earlier received to complete and submit the *Long Draft*. He requested directly that "I be given special permission to devote my full attention to a critique of the events of the Huizong era and to compile them into the *Long Draft*, which, when complete, can then assist in the compilation of the state history."[65] On 1170/2/24 he submitted three months of the initial year, which contained twenty-one revised entries. However, Li Tao lost his Library position in the summer of 1170, and all work on the revision stopped. It resumed only in 1176 when he returned to the Library and recruited Lü Zuqian 呂祖謙 (1137–1181) to help with the work, which was finished on 1177/3/9.[66] Since, as we shall see below, the Huizong-era portion of the *Long Draft* was completed on 1177/7/5, it is clear not only that the two projects mirrored each other but also that Li Tao compiled both works, probably during his absence from the capital between 1170 and 1176.

Li Tao's request to revise the *Huizong Veritable Records* must also be understood in the context of his participation in ongoing political developments at court. The governing Ye–Wei–Jiang–Chen coalition began to weaken in 1167/12 when Emperor Xiaozong removed Ye and Wei as chief councilors and did not replace them. When Li Tao saw the emperor again at a revolving

---

[65] *SHY, zhiguan*,18.58a–b, 69b–70a; *QSW*, 201:4661.185–88.   [66] *SHY, zhiguan*, 18.70a–b.

audience on 1168/9/14, the emperor's decision to govern without his top civil advisers was the first item on the historian's agenda. He noted that emperors in earlier dynasties had utilized one of two options: either they relied upon a single councilor, or they relied upon a collaborative group. Rejecting both models, as Xiaozong had done, forced the emperor to rely upon "close favorites" and to govern from the "center" (i.e. the inner palace). Accordingly, he did not have the benefit of consultation with his civil advisers. Zhou Bida remarks obliquely in his biography that Li Tao's memorial "had perhaps some target in mind." Modern Chinese scholars, no doubt correctly, understand this target to be Zeng Di.[67]

We noted briefly in the Introduction, and will explore in detail in another book, the role of "the close," or "favorites," in the Song political system, especially during the reign of Xiaozong. By juxtaposing Zeng Di against the civil councilors, Li Tao criticized the emperor's reluctance to fill the vacant councilor positions and his preferred recourse to Zeng Di, a leader of the technocratic, inner-court bureaucracy. Because this preference fostered a mode of governance that issued exclusively from the "center," Li Tao warned that the entire onus of administration thus fell personally on the emperor rather than being diffused among the standard, line organs of governance. At the same audience, Li Tao also spoke against the large number of "facilitated degrees" (*tezouming* 特奏名) in proportion to the number of regular "advanced degrees" (*jinshi*) conferred through the triennial examination process. For him, "facilitated degrees" were simply another form of imperial patronage that unleashed large numbers of aging, underqualified, and corrupt officials upon the populace. At the examinations in 1169, the emperor conferred 391 *jinshi* and 291 *tezouming*. Li Tao raised the issue again in 1177, but to no effect. At the 1181 examinations, the proportions reversed: there were now 470 *tezouming* versus only 380 *jinshi*; in 1184, the proportions increased again: 699 *tezouming* were conferred against only 394 *jinshi*. In other words, between Li Tao's arrival at court and his death, the number of *jinshi* remained constant, but the number of "facilitated degrees" increased by 140 per cent.[68] Clearly, Li Tao was arguing against a prevailing trend to confer more "facilitated degrees."

Li Tao probably viewed these two issues on which he addressed Xiaozong in 1168 as related. Both addressed the proper role of civil officials, especially *jinshi* accredited literati, in governance. At the top of the official hierarchy, the imperial sidestep around the chief councilors and reliance upon Zeng Di undermined civil authority and undercut the councilors' role as leaders of the civil bureaucracy. At the bottom of the hierarchy, the proliferation of "facilitated-

---

[67] Xu Gui, "Li Tao nianbiao," 60.
[68] For "facilitated degrees" see Chaffee, *Thorny Gates of Learning in Sung China*, 24–28; for the statistics see Fu Xuancong, *Song dengkeji kao*, 949, 964, 1043, 1057, 1063, 1078. For other unsuccessful efforts during Xiaozong's reign to halt the increase see *Chaoye zaji, yi*, 15.777–78.

degree" holders, who often obtained and usually never left entry-level "close-to -the-people" positions, corrupted the most fundamental layer of local admin- istration. In both cases, Li Tao implied that the emperor's practice was debasing the fundamentals of good governance. Zhou Bida writes that following the audience, the emperor ordered that a committee be assembled to investigate the examination quotas and imperial patronage, but that his "close attendants" blocked the proceedings.

Although Li Tao's memorial was certainly not the only source of pressure, late in 1168/8 Xiaozong indeed appointed Chen Junqing and Yu Yunwen as dual chief councilors. This partnership embodied the political alliance between Fujian and Sichuan, and lasted for almost two years, until 1170/6. Yu was a fellow Sichuanese and advocate of Li Tao.[69] The historian was promoted and, with the backing of the councilors during these two years, accelerated work on a series of historical projects, including revisions to the *Huizong Veritable Records* and the compilation of the *huiyao*, as described above. In 1170/3, the court ordered the *Long Draft* submission of 1168, the five-court history from 960 through 1067, copied in a style and formatting identical to Sima Guang's original *Comprehensive Mirror*, with Li Tao's offices and titles placed in the same position as those of Sima Guang.[70] The order officially confirmed Li Tao's aspirations for the *Long Draft* and his own status as a historian successor to Sima Guang. It also acknowledged the current administration's receptivity to a historical work that manifested Sima Guang's political ideals.

The Chen–Yu councilorship began to diverge over the feasibility of a military invasion to recover the North. Yu Yunwen had been lauded as a "Confucian general" for his decisive victory at Caishi that reversed the Jin invasion in 1161/11. He had since served in the Bureau of Military Affairs and, just prior to his appointment as councilor in 1169, had completed a two-year term as pacification commissioner for Sichuan, where he had attempted to regain court control over the military following the death of Wu Lin in 1167. Reportedly, he and Xiaozong had formulated plans for a two-pronged attack on the North, with Yu leading from Sichuan and the emperor along the Huai valley.[71]

These plans put Li Tao in some difficulty. At their audience in 1168/9, Li had remarked that no one was qualified to lead an invasion of the North. When the emperor replied that he himself would do so, Li reminded him that Emperor Zhenzong, at the head of Song forces in 1004, had negotiated the peace of Chanyuan. But Xiaozong countered that he hoped to recover the North, citing precedents from the Taizu and Taizong era where those emperors had

[69] *SS*, 383.11797.   [70] *SHY, chongru*, 5.37b–38a.
[71] Gong, "The Reign of Hsiao-tsung," 736–37; Yang Wanli's *shendaobei* for Yu Yunwen at *QSW*, 240:5361.101, 104–5.

personally commanded victorious military campaigns. Li Tao advised that Song should "govern itself well and wait for an opportune moment." The implication was that the state should develop a secure economic foundation based on agricultural prosperity before attempting military action to recover the North. Because Yu Yunwen advocated increased taxes to finance an immediate invasion, Chen Junqing and Li Tao opposed the emperor's plan.[72]

It was at this juncture that Li Tao compiled his only other surviving work, his treatise on Six Dynasties history. Modern students of this work place its composition in the 1168–1170 period and read the work as a detailed alternative to contemporary plans for a northern invasion.[73] In this work, Li Tao uses the issues and personalities of Six Dynasties history to put forth his own comprehensive plan for eventual recovery of the North. In the paraphrase of the *Siku* editors, the work advocates reunification through a return to the founding principles of the Song state rather than through ill-conceived and hasty stratagems for military conquest.[74]

In the final weeks before his departure from the capital on 1170/6/27, Li Tao also advocated for changes to the dynasty's program of major state rituals. Although too complex a subject to examine in detail here, his ideas for ritual reform accord both with his interpretation of Northern Song history and with his contemporary political orientation in favor of civil and against "close" governance. The Song had two major venues at which regular sacrifices were offered to a wide range of deities and dynastic ancestors. These were the triennial suburban sacrifices and the so-called Hall of Light (*mingtang* 明堂). Song opinion had long been divided over the proper relationship between the two venues. In addition to the purely ritual issues, the suburban sacrifices were the main vehicle for the conferral of imperial patronage – cash payments, promotions, and "protection" appointments – that constituted the lifeblood of Song officialdom. Simply put, Li Tao favored confining the suburban sacrifices as a vehicle for offerings to "Heaven," while transferring sacrifices to the lesser deities and to the dynastic ancestors to the Hall of Light. Such adjustments would have lowered overall government expenses by reducing the amount of imperial patronage dispensed at the suburban sacrifices.[75]

The historian couched his proposals as a return to the "policies of the ancestors" and as a continuation of Sima Guang's position on these issues. Emperor Shenzong had removed the deities and ancestors from the Hall of

---

[72] Zhou Bida at *QSW*, 232:5183.399.
[73] Pei Rucheng and Xu Peizao, *Xu zizhi tongjian changbian kaolüe*, 2; Choi, "Li Tao *Liuchao tongjian boyi* yanjiu," 51–53; Xiong Bin and Huang Bo, "Yi shi lun zheng: Songdai Sichuan shijia de qianchaoshi yanjiu," 62.
[74] Ji Yun et al., *Qinding Siku quanshu zongmu*, 88.1167.
[75] *SS*, 388.11917; for Li Tao's memorials see *QSW*, 210: 4662.191–94; for a useful overview see Liu, "The Sung Emperors and the *Ming-t'ang* or Hall of Enlightenment."

Light, reserving the rites as an exclusive sacrifice to his own father. His change thus emphasized their "filial" aspect. Sima Guang advocated unsuccessfully for the traditional position that these rites should honor a wide range of deities and ancestors. In the early Southern Song, Gaozong readmitted some deities, but after his abdication in 1162, the Shenzong-era interpretation of the rites again emphasized the "father," now, in this case, Gaozong. Although Xiaozong generally supported Li Tao's ideas on ritual, because these reforms would have downgraded Gaozong's status as "father," Gaozong's retainers resisted. A key sub-contingent among "the close," they joked at a deliberative conference that Li Tao seemed to have read every book except the *Classic of Filial Piety*.[76] Although Li Tao memorialized three times on the issue, his reforms were not implemented until 1188, when Zhou Bida, then chief councilor, inaugurated them a year after Gaozong's death.[77] Although it is perhaps an oversimplification to align the controversy in this way, Li Tao's stance on the Hall of Light attempted to align Xiaozong, the policies of the ancestors, and the civil literati against Gaozong, the New Policies of the Shenzong era, and "the close."

The widening policy differences between Chen Junqing and Yu Yunwen, followed by Chen's departure from the councilorship in 1170/5, as well as Li Tao's confrontations with "the close," all combined to render his continuation at the Library problematic. Accordingly, he requested an outside assignment and was transferred to the provincial government of Hubei. According to Zhou Bida, Li was recalled to the Library in 1172. But Yu Yunwen, then in Sichuan, feared Li Tao's influence over the emperor on the northern issue and had him reassigned, as prefect of Luzhou, back to Sichuan. Li Tao continued to work on the *Long Draft* and in early 1175 offered his "third submission," which covered the years 1067–1100.[78] By 1176/1, he was back in the capital as director of the Imperial Library with a personal mandate from the emperor to devote his full time to historical work. Xiaozong was again ruling without benefit of chief councilors. Gong Maoliang 龔茂良 (d. 1178), a Fujian native and ally of Chen Junqing, served as assisting councilor and remained the highest appointed civil official at court during most of Li Tao's second period in the capital.

It appears that little had been accomplished on the dynasty's various historiographical projects during Li Tao's five-and-a-half-year absence from the capital. Within the next year and a half, however, under his direction, the Library submitted the *Gaozong Daily Calendar* (on 1176/3/3) and the *Huizong Veritable Records*, which Gong Maoliang

---

[76] Zhou Bida, *Yutang zaji* (*Shuofu* ed.), 79.1b.   [77] *Songshi quanwen*, 27B.2351.

[78] The primary sources do not agree on the date of the third submission. Xu Gui, "Li Tao nianbiao," 69; and Pei Rucheng and Xu Peizao, *Xu zizhi tongjian changbian kaolüe*, 23–25, accept late 1174. However, Tang Jianghao, "Li Tao zhuanjin *Xu zizhi tongjian changbian* zhi shi, ci, juan, ce xutan," 157–63 argues convincingly for 1175/2/22.

submitted on 1177/3/9.[79] Several months later, on 1177/7/5, Li Tao sub-mitted the final portion of the *Long Draft*, covering the reigns of Huizong and Qinzong. The almost simultaneous completion of the two projects underscores their close connection and the indeterminate line between Li Tao's work as an official and as a private historian. Upon seeing the completed draft, Emperor Xiaozong is reported to have remarked, "It enables me to read and consult the policies of our dynastic house and thus to bring about more effective administration."[80]

Despite Xiaozong's mandate that he focus on historical projects, Li Tao continued to advise on a wide range of cultural and political issues. Zhou Bida writes that during this period Li Tao was especially outspoken in deliberative councils. Almost immediately upon his return, he renewed his call for reform of the suburban sacrifices. When an earthquake slightly damaged one of the columns in the ancestral shrine to Taizu, Li Tao pushed for a "substantial" response and advocated for enhancements to Taizu's ritual status within the ancestral ritual complex. In the autumn of 1176, Li Tao and Zhou Bida were appointed imperial tutors, which carried the right to address remonstrance directly to the emperor. Li Tao raised again the issue of facilitated degrees, upping the ante by calling for a complete return to the Yuanyou system of four-part *jinshi* examinations (in classics, poetry, *fu*, and discourse) as advocated by Su Shi. Finally, he called for removing Wang Anshi and his son from their status as acolytes in the Confucian temple and replacing them with Fan Zhongyan, Sima Guang, Ouyang Xiu, and Su Shi.[81] Such a change to the dynasty's ritual recognition of political and intellectual achievement would have sanctioned the values that the *Long Draft* had identified in Northern Song history, and was highly controversial, even among Li Tao's political allies. Xiaozong consented only to removing the portrait of Wang Anshi's son from the temple. The father remained until 1241.

In winter 1176, Li Tao requested that Lü Zuqian assist him in revising the *Huizong Veritable Records*. When the work was finished, Lü was scheduled to present a "revolving memorial," probably in connection with the completion of the project. Although Lü himself does not make the link explicit, his two 1177 memorials on governance clarify what he and Li Tao no doubt hoped Xiaozong would take as their interpretation of the historical lessons that the Huizong period offered

---

[79] *SHY, zhiguan*, 18.102b; *Yuhai*, 48.17b–18a.   [80] Zhou Bida, *Wenzhong ji*, 107. 20b.

[81] Li Xinchuan, *Chaoye zaji, yi*, 4.569; *Daoming lu*, 8.96. Zhou Bida is silent on this controversy, probably because so many of the coalition members like Chen Junqing and Gong Maoliang resisted these changes, fearing they would cause too much political backlash. In 1168, Wei Shanzhi had called for the Ch'eng brothers to be named acolytes. Li Tao's preference for Sima and Su confirms his lack of enthusiasm for radical *daoxue* agendas. For a full review of this issue see Neskar, "The Cult of Worthies," 271–301.

to the present.[82] The first memorial is a long discourse on how Xiaozong should rely upon the formal structure of government and not exercise unilaterally his own decision-making authority. He should rely upon the duly appointed chief councilors and their subordinates, not upon informal personnel such as "the close." Such irregular delegation ultimately weakens both imperial authority and the underlying "administrative structure" (*zhiti* 治體).

In essence, Lü charges that Xiaozong's arrogation of his councilors' authority has enabled downstream agencies throughout government to usurp authority from subordinate units and led to a general breakdown of regular administrative order. Into this vacuum Xiaozong had invited "the close," whom the emperor has permitted to act as his surrogates for properly appointed functionaries. The latter have been "blocked" in the performance of their duties and in their careers. Such conditions, if allowed to continue, will lead to administrative dysfunction, just as blockages of circulation in the body lead to illness and death. The second memorial urges Xiaozong to strengthen the principle of "magnanimity and reward for devotion" (*kuanda zhonghou* 寬大忠厚), which he attributes to the Song founders and posits as the foundation of the Song "administrative structure." Failure to fully implement this vision impedes effective government and makes recovery of the North impossible.[83]

Although neither the *Huizong Veritable Records* nor the Huizong portion of the *Long Draft* survive, it is not difficult to read Lü Zuqian's memorials against the imprint that Li Tao's works have left upon the surviving image of the Huizong age. Irregular, ad hoc administrative units, often run by individuals with close personal connections to the emperor, destroyed the "administrative structure" of the founders, "blocked" and demoralized the regular bureaucracy, and eventually destroyed the country's capacity to resist the Jin invasions. The message to Xiaozong was clear: reinstitute the policies of the founders and distance yourself from the failed legacy of Huizong, or a fate similar to his awaits you.

Although the Huizong section of the *Long Draft* may or may not have inspired Xiaozong to "effective administration," its message was not lost on "the close." On 1177/6/9 Zeng Di succeeded in ousting Gong Maoliang as assisting councilor. Li Tao submitted the last portion of the *Long Draft* a month later. In the following month, a coalition led by Zeng Di, the eunuchs, and their

---

[82] Lü Zuqian, *Donglai ji*, 3.11a–16b; *QSW*, 261:5869.37–40. The memorials are cited in Lü's *Songshi* biography (*SS*, 434.12873–74), which explicitly links the completion of the *Huizong Veritable Records* and these memorials.

[83] Two years later, in 1179, Shi Hao, during the controversy over the 1179 examinations and the ensuing political struggle between the chief councilor Zhao Xiong and Zeng Di, also attributed the principle of *kuanda zhonghou* to the founders. See Shi Hao, *Maofeng zhenyin manlu*, 10.10b.

literati allies engineered a scandal that implicated Li Tao and forced him from the capital.

In 1171, Li Hou, Li Tao's second son, had fulfilled his father's earlier ambition and passed the decree examination for those who could "speak directly and remonstrate fully," the only person in Southern Song ever to do so. During 1176–1177, he was posted to the history office, where he worked together with his father. In 1177, Zhou Bida recommended Li Shu, Li Tao's fourth son, for the same decree examination, which Li Shu took with three other candidates. Zeng Di engineered an order drastically increasing the difficulty of the examination by requiring that all six "citations" be "opaque"; that all six derive from commentary, not main text; and that candidates must answer five correctly. In addition, he arranged for Qian Liangchen 錢良臣 (d. 1189), a political ally hostile to Zhou Bida, Gong Maoliang, and Li Tao, to conduct the examinations. As a result of these measures, all four candidates failed. In anger, Li Hou drafted a question for the Imperial University examinations in which he asked students to review the history of the decree examination and noted that even under the laxer standards of Northern Song, Su Xun 蘇洵 (1009–1066) had failed, and Fu Bi and Zhang Fangping 張方平 (1007–1091) had barely passed. Given the circumstances, the impertinence of the question played into Zeng Di's hands. A censorial inquest ensued, and Li Hou and Li Tao were dismissed from their positions. Li Tao was posted to serve as prefect of Changde in modern Hunan.[84] The affair was but one skirmish in Zeng Di's ultimately successful campaign against Gong Maoliang and his allies.[85]

In Hunan, Li Tao lifted restrictions against merchant participation in the tea trade. Such actions were in keeping with his general philosophy against fully regulated government monopolies and in favor of the use of merchants as middlemen between the government and consumers of monopoly products. Such thinking was a continuation of the economic policies that Zhao Kai 趙開 (1066–1141) had implemented in Sichuan in the 1130s. After his return to Sichuan in 1180, Li Tao composed a major epitaph for Zhao Kai, forty years after the latter's death. The text is Li's sole surviving example of this genre and this biography provides a rare window into his thinking on the history of Southern Song economic policy.

Both Li Hou and Li Shu died in 1180, perhaps the result of an accident or an epidemic. According to Zhou Bida, the emperor appointed Li Tao prefect of

---

[84] *Chaoye zaji, jia*, 13. 255–59; *SHY, xuanju*, 11.33a–34b; *SS*, 156.3650–51; Fu Xuancong, *Song dengkeji kao*, 1017–19.

[85] For a study of the larger political confrontation between Gong Maoliang and Zeng Di see Chang Wei-ling, "Cong Nan Song zhongqi fan jinxi zhengzheng kan daoxue xing shidafu dui 'huifu' taidu de zhuanbian," 93–104. Chang states that Li Tao and his sons were victims of this purge, as were also Lin Guangchao, Lou Yue, Chen Fuliang, and others. She understands Li Xinchuan's account to allude to Zeng Di, Wang Bian, and Gan Bian as the coalition that engineered the failure of Li Shu; see ibid., 102 n. 107.

Suining 遂寧, a major Sichuan post, to distract him from his grief. Among the measures he undertook in this office was a resumption of his earlier efforts to reform the Sichuan military. He personally inspected troops, opened training facilities, and retrieved soldiers who had decamped to the marketplaces. He also worked to moderate an ordered increase in the wine sales tax for the prefecture and advocated a return to the system of subcontracting out wine sales to individual households. All his recorded economic measures as prefect in Hunan and at Suining reveal him opposing measures that derived from Wang Anshi's New Policies and advocating a return to pre-1067 practice.

During these years, Li Tao followed Lü Zuqian's advice and continued to revise the *Long Draft*. Sometime in 1182, probably before Zhou Bida left the state council in the ninth month, Li Tao was ordered to submit his final revisions to the court. On 1183/3/3 he submitted a clean copy of the revised manuscript, involving changes to 4,450 entries. The emperor insisted he return to Lin'an, and in the summer of 1183 he was again appointed imperial tutor and assigned to work on the state history in the Library. Large portions of the *Four Court History*, the final version of the official history of the dynasty from 1067 through 1127 – much of it based on material in the *Long Draft* – had been submitted in 1180, but the entire work remained unfinished. On 1183/7/17, Li Tao requested ten additional postings to the Library, including You Mou 尤袤 (1127–1194) and Liu Qingzhi 劉清之 (d. 1190), in order rapidly to complete the work.[86]

As usual, the historian continued to speak out in ever more direct ways on political and administrative issues. In contrast to his two earlier periods at court, he was now unaffiliated politically to higher administration, which was now under the increasing sway of Wang Huai 王淮 (1126–1189). This independence, combined with his seniority and strong relationship with Xiaozong, emboldened him to speak with new directness. He advocated for a truly consultative decision-making process, one that would resemble the "struggles" between the Tang Emperor Taizong (r. 626–249) and his contentious adviser Wei Zheng 魏徵 (580–643) in contrast to the servile deference that Song councilors like Wang Gui had rendered imperial authority. This observation was possibly aimed at Wang Huai, whom Li Tao also suggested should follow the precedents of the founders and attend the emperor's tutorial sessions.[87] Lastly, in a remark aimed directly at the heart of the Xiaozong court, Li Tao suggested that those funds which the emperor and his "close" had diverted since the beginning of his reign from the Ministry of Revenue into his personal Inner Treasury should be returned to the control of the properly appointed finance officials.

[86] *SHY, zhiguan*, 18.59; *SS*, 388.11918.   [87] *SS*, 388.11919.

Li Tao was taken ill in the winter of 1183 and resigned in 1184/2. His "last will" is both a distillation of his lifelong advice to Xiaozong and an epitome for the *Long Draft:* "Take Taizu as your master when planning for the future; take Renzong as your model when managing officials." He died in Lin'an, and Xiaozong ordered government transport to take his body back to Sichuan for burial.

As was customary, Zhou Bida composed a series of ten dirges to mourn his passing and laud his accomplishments.[88] Many of the poems are routine examples of the genre. Most telling, however, are the figures that Zhou chose to serve as historical metaphors for the values he saw as paramount in Li Tao's life. He compared his outspokenness to Ji An 汲黯 (d. 108 BCE?), and his loyalty to Liu Xiang 劉向 (79–8 BCE). Ji An was an official under the Han emperor Wudi who spoke out at great risk to his own life against modifications to dynastic institutions proposed by Zhang Tang 張湯, a technocratic functionary.[89] In his arguments against the New Policies of Wang Anshi, Sima Guang had already invoked the dichotomy between Ji An and Zhang Tang as a prototype for his own preference for proper staffing of existing dynastic institutions rather than for the institutional modifications of the New Policies. As Sima stressed to Emperor Shenzong, "the old policies of the founders cannot be discarded." When the emperor replied that the men and policies must go together, Sima replied, "If you have the right men, there is no need to worry about bad policy; but without the right men, even good policies are useless."[90] Ji An therefore became a touchstone metaphor in Southern Song for opposition to the New Policies; and Sima's advice to Shenzong is later reflected in Li Tao's advice to Xiaozong to "take Taizu as your teacher; Renzong as your model."

By pairing Ji An with Liu Xiang, the legendary Eastern Han scholar and bibliographer, Zhou Bida emphasized that Li Tao expressed his loyalty to Xiaozong and the dynasty through his learning and scholarship. Much of Liu Xiang's scholarship attempted to ground Han administrative policy in precedents drawn from the Zhou classics.[91] The same poem explains that Li Tao was unique in his ability to apply his encyclopedic knowledge of history to "make connections to the present." This formulation, in conjunction with the parallels to Ji An, stresses the connection between Li Tao's historical scholarship and the contemporary political world of Emperor Xiaozong's reign in which Li Tao lived and worked.

---

[88]   *Wenzhong ji*, 7.14b–15b.
[89]   See Loewe, *A Biographical Dictionary*, 179–81 and 692–94, for Ji An and Zhang Tang.
[90]   Li Yumin, *Sima Guang Riji jiaozhu*, 98–100. Shenzong himself compared Sima Guang to Ji An; see Ji, *Politics and Conservatism in Northern Song China*, 150.
[91]   Loewe, *A Biographical Dictionary*, 372–75.

Method and Message in the *Long Draft*

The *Long Draft* marks the apogee in China of a historiographical method known as "investigation of differences" (*kaoyi* 考異). Pioneered a century earlier by Sima Guang, a "long draft" is an annalistic history whose format comprises both a main text and a commentary. The main text features a series of discrete, chronologically ordered events. The compiler constructs his presentation of these events using language quoted from those sources he has evaluated as most credible. The commentary both cites these sources at greater length and also records conflicting sources that the compiler has declined to incorporate through citation in the main text. Sima Guang had prepared a "long draft" of the *Comprehensive Mirror*, but he viewed the format as an intermediate stage between source collection and the finished work. Sima's final format presented a compressed main text but relegated the commentary to a separate appendix. Modern scholarship agrees that Li Tao, by expanding the scope of his commentary and by placing the commentary on the same page together with the main text, developed "investigation of differences" far beyond Sima Guang and created a new genre of Chinese historiography.[92]

Under Li Tao's learned and skillful brush, "investigation of differences" became a powerful vehicle to negotiate the political tensions in his conflicting sources and to apply the lessons he discovered in those sources to the issues of his own day. Many scholars have followed Li Tao's own lead and understand the *Long Draft* as an attempt to use private sources, as recorded in the work's interlinear commentary, to correct the deficiencies of the official historical record. Yet there is more to Li Tao's method. Close reading of the commentary reveals that the main text of many entries presents an often difficult compromise between multiple versions of the same event. Accordingly, the alternative narratives in the commentary sometimes work at cross-purposes to the main text. This subtle interplay between main text and commentary often generates an ambiguity that delighted some readers such as Ye Shi but angered others such as Zhu Xi. And their discomfort with Li Tao's method was a partial cause of the decline into which the work eventually fell.

The manuscript of the *Long Draft* that Li Tao submitted to the court in 1183 contained four parts. The main narrative, with its interlinear commentary, extended from 960 through 1127 and comprised 980 *juan* in 604 fascicles (*ce*). There was also a ten *juan* list of corrections made to over 4,450 entries since the original submissions in 1168, 1175, and 1177. Li Tao also prepared an abridgment entitled *Selected Essentials* (*juyao* 舉要) in sixty-eight *juan* and an index in five *juan*. The four parts totaled 1,063 *juan* in 687 fascicles and were

---

[92] Pei Rucheng and Xu Peizao, *Xu zizhi tongjian changbian kaolüe*, 76–78; Yan Yongcheng, *Nan Song shixue yanjiu*, 131.

deposited in the Imperial Library.[93] The modern text that the eighteenth-century academicians retrieved from the *Yongle Encyclopedia* and reconstituted in 520 *juan* therefore differs significantly from Li Tao's final submission. The following section, while considering the historical forces that deformed Li Tao's original work into its modern guise, seeks to describe the relationship between methodology and message in the modern *Long Draft* – the only text available to modern scholars.

As described above, the *Long Draft* contains both main-text narrative and a commentary comprising 12,660 interlinear notes.[94] The interplay between main text and commentary is key to understanding the work's method and its message. Li Tao's commentary serves at least four separate, but related, functions. First, it provides supplemental information: it identifies sources for the main text, provides biographical and other informational details, and inserts cross-references to other related passages. Second, within the broad category of "investigation of differences," it explores differing accounts of the same event, amounting to a kind of source criticism. Third, it flags unresolved issues for later investigation. And lastly, Li Tao sometimes uses the commentary directly to offer his own opinions and evaluations.[95]

Reactions to the work, even among Li Tao's allies, were mixed. In 1188, Zhou Bida, now councilor, penned a colophon on a fragmentary draft of the *Comprehensive Mirror* upon which Li Tao had once previously appended his own colophon. The fragment demonstrated how Sima Guang and Fan Zuyu 范祖禹 (1041–1098) had condensed the Tang portion of the *Comprehensive Mirror* down from 600 or 700 to a final eighty-one *juan*. In his comment, Li Tao admired the ability of his forebears to bring about this degree of compression despite the profusion of sources for Tang history. Zhou seconded this opinion, and lamented that Li Tao had been unable to complete a similar compression of the *Long Draft*. In his view, the *Long Draft* was an unfinished work and too long.[96]

Ye Shi penned the fullest contemporary assessment of the *Long Draft* that survives. He made the extraordinary claim that the *Long Draft* was the greatest work of history since the *Spring and Autumn Annals*, surpassing the achievements even of Sima Qian and Sima Guang. Ye argued that, given the antiquity of the periods on which he worked, Sima Guang, despite all his efforts, had been unable to surmount the fragmentary, haphazard state of his sources and

[93] *Wenxian tongkao*, 193.5612; *Chaoye zaji, jia*, 4.113.
[94] For this count see Yan Yongcheng, *Nan Song shixue yanjiu*, 131. The longest note, at *Changbian*, 265.6498–513, runs to 10,655 Chinese characters.
[95] For this classification see Pei Rucheng and Xu Peizao, *Xu zizhi tongjian changbian kaolüe*, 79–82. This fourfold classification refers only to Li Tao's genuine commentary, not to the subsequent accretions of pseudocommentary, on which see ibid., 83–95.
[96] For Li Tao's colophon see *Wenxian tongkao*, 193.5603–4; and *QSW*, 210:4664.236–37; for Zhou Bida's colophon see *QSW*, 230:5127.327.

organize them into a unified, trustworthy history. But Li Tao, like Confucius, worked on periods much closer to his own time, and both were thus able to establish solid chronologies upon which to ground their sources. Ye explained that Li Tao first resolved inconsistencies in the chronologies of the veritable records, the state histories, and other bureaucratic documents and brought them into "a single [chronological] alignment." Into this structure he then brought private histories, crosschecking official and unofficial accounts, "such that the perverse and correct frames of mind [of the historical actors] become clearer chapter after chapter." He concluded that Li Tao "did not dare complete the work himself, but made its broad outlines emerge from its profusion of detail, its utter prolixity become utter simplicity."[97] Ye Shi thus construes Li Tao's methodology as a three-stage process: (1) he used the chronological precision of official sources to establish a consistent, unified chronology; (2) he used unofficial sources to verify and adjust the content of official sources; and (3) he did so in such a way that the "broad outlines" and "utter simplicity" that he perceived in his sources emerged as self-evident from their "utter prolixity."

Ye Shi's observations offer a solid foundation upon which to analyze the methodology of the *Long Draft*. The following discussion will focus on the veritable records as the work's chronological base, its comingling of official and private sources, and the use of commentarial "discussion" to elicit a unified message from its "utter prolixity." In general, the veritable records served as Li Tao's textual base for the *Long Draft*. In addition to his own 1169 statement to this effect, there is also Zhou Bida's testimony from the 1190s. Zhou explained that when he was compiling his own edition of Ouyang Xiu's works he had not collated quotations from Ouyang's memorials in the veritable records or in the *Long Draft* because both texts had been abbreviated and were thus identical to each other. Zhou attributed this abbreviation to court historians who had excerpted the original memorials for inclusion in the veritable records, and he concluded that "the *Long Draft* is based on those veritable records."[98]

Modern scholars have compared the *Long Draft* text against the surviving *Taizong Veritable Records* and quotations of other veritable records in late Song encyclopedias and have confirmed Zhou's opinion.[99] Li Tao's decision to ground the *Long Draft* on the veritable records arose naturally from the nature of the veritable records and their relation to other official sources, as these existed in the mid-twelfth century. As can be seen above in Figure 0.2, when Li

---

[97] *Wenxian tongkao*, 193.5613; *Ye Shi ji*, 12.210; *QSW*, 285:6472.156–57. For an additional Ye Shi explanation of his appraisal of the *Long Draft* see his *Xixue jiyan*, 25.7b.

[98] For Li Tao's statement see *SHY, zhiguan*, 18.58b. Zhou Bida noted that the veritable records and the *Long Draft* cited eighty-eight of the 168 memorials that Zhou included in Ouyang Xiu's collected works; see *Ouyang wenzhong gong wenji*, 114.17a.

[99] Pei Rucheng and Xu Peizao, *Xu zizhi tongjian changbian kaolüe*, 39–56; Yan Yongcheng, "*Xu zizhi tongjian changbian* Shenzong chao qucai kao," 61–63; see also Yan Yongcheng's edition of Qian Ruoshui, *Taizong shilu*, introduction, 15–17.

Tao began work on the *Long Draft* completed veritable records existed for the years from the dynastic founding in 960 through to 1100, whereas the two existing state histories covered only through 1067, and the first two *huiyao* collections only through 1077. Since the daily calendars were nonexistent or fragmentary for many periods, the veritable records furnished the most consistent chronological coverage across the longest time span. However, only for the reigns of Zhenzong, Renzong, and Yingzong (998–1067) did veritable records exist in a single, uncontested version. The veritable records for the reigns of Taizu and Taizong (960–997), and for those of Shenzong and Zhezong (1067–1100), existed in multiple, conflicting versions; and those for the Huizong and Qinzong reigns (1100–1127) were still works in progress when Li Tao arrived in Lin'an.

These conflicting official sources presented Li Tao with his greatest challenge and also his greatest opportunity as a historian. In order to resolve discrepancies in this official record, Li Tao made recourse to nonofficial sources. As we have seen in the Introduction, Song official historiography was organized to process official documents into official history; therefore, many viewed the comingling of official and nonofficial sources as a dilution, if not an outright violation, of this established process.[100] As justification for mixing the two streams, Li Tao invoked Sima Guang. Commenting on a surviving fragment of Sima Guang's diary, Li noted that Sima Guang had compiled his diary and what subsequently became known as the *Su River Records* (*Sushui jiwen* 涑水記聞) as phases of a process to collect private accounts that contradicted Song official history. Sima hoped that his notes might serve one day as source material for a continuation of the *Comprehensive Mirror*. Li, who made extensive use of the *Su River Records*, observed that Sima's plan provided the basis for his own *Long Draft*.[101]

As Li Tao's invocation of the Sima Guang precedent implies, this historiographical method challenged the monarchy's claim to exclusive control over official history. As in so many other aspect of Song political culture, this challenge began in the Qingli period, when Ouyang Xiu undertook to rewrite the existing official history of the Tang and Five Dynasties. Comingling of official and unofficial sources was but one modification that the Qingli scholars introduced into official historiography by which they sought to transform that process from one directed solely toward the needs of emperor and court to one that addressed the larger needs of the emerging literati class.[102]

---

[100] For examples see Pei Rucheng and Xu Peizao, *Xu zizhi tongjian changbian kaolüe*, 66; also Sung, "The Official Historiographical Operation of the Song Dynasty," 195–96.

[101] *Wenxian tongkao*, 197.5683; *QSW*, 210:4665.238–39.

[102] For this aspect of Ouyang Xiu see Hartman, "Chinese Historiography in the Age of Maturity," 44–46; and Sung, "Between Tortoise and Mirror," 144–214.

By Li Tao's time, long-running disputes over the historical depiction of the New Policies had made comingling a grudgingly accepted practice. In his 1163 submission memorial to the court, Li Tao stated that his aim was "to take the various accounts [of the imperial ancestors' achievements] and assemble them all into one" (*xian hui yu yi* 咸會於一).[103] Some scholars argue that this ambiguous phrase means simply that Li aimed to bring the disparate accounts physically together into one book. Others, however, see a grander intention and understand the phrase to mean that he aimed to resolve the conflicting accounts into a unified historiographical narrative.[104]

Li Tao's decision in 1168 to change his format from a "comprehensive mirror" – a direct continuation of Sima Guang's finished work – to a "long draft" is crucial to understanding his goals for the *Long Draft* and the relationship between methodology and message in the work. As we have explored above, the prodigious quantity and conflicting quality of the post-1067 sources certainly influenced his decision. Equally important, however, was his realization, upon arriving in Lin'an in 1167, that the "long-draft" format afforded better potential for aligning the historiographical and political goals of his work.

The switch to "long-draft" format signaled his ultimate intention toward a unified history, not simply a collection of conflicting opinions on that history. As we have seen, Li called the process by which this unification was to be achieved "discussion" (*taolun* 討論), and his contemporaries agreed that Li Tao was the leading master of this genre.[105] "Discussion" is essentially the process of textual and historical analysis through which the optimal "unified" interpretation of an event is achieved. Scholars generally concur that entries in the *Long Draft* main text that have no commentary are veritable-record entries that Li Tao accepts as unproblematic. Those with commentary, however, are veritable-record text that Li Tao has deemed it necessary, after "discussion," to alter in some way.[106] In such cases, the main text consists of snippets of various

---

[103] *Wenxian tongkao*, 193:5611.

[104] For the simpler interpretation see Sudō Yoshiyuki, "Nan-Sō no Ri Tou to *Zoku shiji tsugan chōhen* no seiritsu," 483–84. Sudō points out, correctly, that the phrase also occurs in Li Tao's 1159 preface to his chronological tables of senior government officials, where a non-metaphorical interpretation seems more appropriate. Pei Rucheng and Xu Peizao, *Xu zizhi tongjian changbian kaolüe*, introduction, 5–8, along with most other Chinese scholars, prefer the more expansive understanding.

[105] For Li Tao's uses of the term in reference to his own historiographical practice see *Wenxian tongkao*, 193.4611; and *QSW*, 210: 4661.187; for contemporary praise of Li Tao's "discussion" see Han Biao, *Jianquan riji*, 2.11b.

[106] Pei Rucheng and Xu Peizao, *Xu zizhi tongjian changbian kaolüe*, 89. These conclusions, however, rarely consider the possibility that portions of Li Tao's original commentary may not survive in the transmitted text. When utilizing the *Long Draft*, scholars should remember that although the main text indeed represents what Li considers the most reliable narrative, it may not reproduce verbatim the corresponding veritable record.

sources that Li Tao has stitched together to arrive at what he considers the most credible telling of the event. Li Tao's commentary usually quotes the longer passages from which these snippets derive and explains the reasons for his choices. Often, in order to justify these choices, the commentary will adduce sources that are not eventually cited in the main text. The main text of the *Long Draft*, therefore, consists largely of previously formulated text that Li Tao has "cut and pasted" to assemble his version of credible history.

Almost any commentated "event" in the *Long Draft* may illustrate this methodology. For example, on 1126/2/1 the military officer Yao Pingzhong 姚平仲 (1099–1180) led a raid out from besieged Kaifeng in order to rescue several high-level hostages held by the encircling Jurchen invaders. The raid failed and undermined ongoing diplomatic negotiations with the Jurchen. Since the future Emperor Gaozong was one of the hostages and Li Gang 李綱 (1083–1140), a future chief councilor, had supported the raid, its historical treatment remained politically sensitive. To further complicate the historian's task, a major primary source was Li Gang's own self-serving memoir in which he naturally absolved himself of responsibility for the debacle. Li Tao's main-text entry on the raid contains 1,028 characters. Of these, an initial forty-five characters constitute a "headline," which delineates the event, and probably derives from existing official sources, probably the *Qinzong Veritable Records*. To explicate this headline Li uses three extracts, totaling 245 characters from Li Gang's memoir. He balances this account, however, with two long quotations from a much lesser known memoir by one of the hostages, totaling 699 characters. Finally, he writes thirty-seven characters from his own brush that splice together these quotations into what he believes to be a balanced historical narrative of the raid and its aftermath. Thus although Li Tao personally composed only 3 percent of the *Long Draft* main text of this event, his commentary cites other sources to defend his textual choices and to explain which parts of both memoirs he has chosen to accept and which to reject.[107]

Li Tao's methodology and format thus place the historian in open dialogue with his sources. Modern Chinese scholars quite rightly insist that this dialogue constitutes an innovative development in Chinese historiography. Although Li Tao acknowledged Sima Guang's "investigation of differences" (*kaoyi*) as his inspiration, Li Tao in truth advanced the technique far beyond its original scope. Central to this advance was Li's decision to insert his commentary into the main text, thus enabling the reader to participate immediately and directly in the historian's dialogue with his sources. The first editions of the *Comprehensive Mirror* had not included the "investigation of differences," and

---

[107] For this passage see Huang Yizhou et al., *Xu zizhi tongjian changbian shibu*, 53.1645–48; for an extended analysis see Hartman, "The Reluctant Historian," 118–130; and Cai Hanmo [Charles Hartman], *Lishi de yanzhuang*, 233–48.

the two texts were not combined in the unified format in which they are read today until the Yuan period. Superficially, the *Long Draft* commentary resembles the interlinear format of earlier commentary on the classical canon, but unlike this model, where the author comments upon a largely fixed text, Li Tao is both devising his main text and simultaneously commenting upon his own work.

In essence, Li Tao often writes two stories at the same time. His main text presents his own best judgment on the many events he has chosen to include in his larger narrative. At the same time, the commentary functions simultaneously in two ways. Although Li Tao uses the commentary to defend his main text, the inclusion of "discarded" passages also permits the reader to construct his own alternative narrative. In this way, the *Long Draft* straddles the line between public and private historiography. The main text presents a series of suggested corrections to the official veritable records, but the commentary illustrates that only recourse to private sources can enable those corrections. The commentary both defends and challenges the main-text narrative. In this way, Li Tao both enters into "discussion" with his readers and continues the literati tradition of using writings from the "notebook" (*biji* 筆記) genre to challenge the imperial monopoly on official history.

Precisely because its original goal of "merging all [accounts] into one" was never realized, the *Long Draft* presents less a history than a sourcebook for history. Like its inspiration, the *Comprehensive Mirror*, it had a twofold official and private audience. Officially, Li Tao presented the *Long Draft* to the emperor, the ultimate arbiter of official history, as a sourcebook that would enable the official, political unification of Northern Song history as a guide for the policies of the Restoration. Yet simultaneously and privately, the same book could also serve Li Tao's political allies as a source for relevant political precedents in their struggle to shape that Restoration.

Given this characterization of the *Long Draft* as a "sourcebook for history," it may seem counterintuitive to attempt to delineate its "message." Yet there can be no doubt that Li Tao believed that the unified political message he perceived in the sources would be self-evident to those who persevered through his "discussions." At its simplest, that message is identical to Li Tao's final advice to Emperor Xiaozong that he should take Taizu as his mentor when planning for the future and Renzong as his model when managing officials. We have briefly explored above the political circumstances in which Li Tao composed the *Long Draft*, how resurgent literati political forces in Xiaozong's reign urged a "restart" of early Song policies supposedly once advocated by Taizu and in this way opposed the continuation of Qin Gui-style governance.

Li Tao's rhetorical emphasis on Taizu set in motion a chain of historiographical consequences. Chapters 6 and 7 will explore how literati scholars in the Qingli period, in order to create an alternative to the politics of Empress Liu's regency, had been the first to codify an image of Taizu as a proponent of literati governance. Therefore, among the reasons Li Tao and his allies embraced Qingli was because Qingli had embraced Taizu. In both cases, literati officials invoked Taizu in support of their own governance and against the alternative models practiced by Empress Liu, by Qin Gui, and, in the Xiaozong years, by no less than the political network of the retired Emperor Gaozong and Empress Wu. Likewise, when Wang Anshi framed the New Policies as alternatives to the "old policies of the ancestors," he had unknowingly put himself on the wrong side of a rising political and rhetorical tide that would, in Southern Song, slowly elevate Taizu to the status of Sage. The result was an axis of positive, literati political value that progressed from Taizu through Qingli to Yuanyou and beyond. Li Tao brought precisely this message to his first audience with the emperor, when, upon his arrival in Lin'an in 1167, he presented Xiaozong a set of "Taizu precedents and the request that they be adopted as political standards."[108]

Li Tao's allocation of space in the *Long Draft* reflects his support for this axis of political value. A comparison of the number of entries per year in the *Long Draft* versus those in the *Recovered Draft Compendium* reveals how Li Tao's political focus shaped the *Long Draft*'s coverage across different periods of Northern Song history. We have seen in Chapter 1 that, despite its complex compilation history, the *Recovered Draft* can still provide a sense of the depth and distribution of primary documentation on Northern Song history that existed during Li Tao's lifetime in the official historical record. Figure 2.1 shows how Li Tao's emphasis in the *Long Draft* varies from the allocation of space in the *Recovered Draft*.[109] The relative coverage of the two works departs significantly during four periods. As would be expected, the *Long Draft* contains more extensive coverage of the Qingli period (1041–1048), the Xining period (1068–1077), and the Yuanyou period (1086–1093). Alternatively, the *Long Draft* significantly underweights the later reign of Taizong (983–997), the entire Zhenzong reign (998–1022), and the regency of Empress Liu (1023–1033). The alignment of coverage for the reigns of Taizu and early Taizong

---

[108] See Zhou Bida's biography of Li Tao at *QSW*, 232:5183.398. Wang Deyi suggests, probably correctly, that "standards" here alludes to strategies to recover the North; see *Li Tao fuzi nianpu*, 26.

[109] As in Figure 1.2, *SHY* data counts the number of entries per year normalized by dividing the yearly totals by the total of all entries between 960 and 1099, multiplied by 100. *Long Draft* data was derived by counting the number of pages devoted to each year in the Zhonghua shuju edition. There is no text for the years 1067–1070 and 1093–1097. These *Long Draft* lacunae certainly distort the overall contours of the present *Long Draft* data. Hypothetically, a similar exercise conducted on the original *Long Draft*, complete from 960 through 1127, would reduce to some degree the extreme peaks that the present, truncated text produces. However, the clear patterns of divergence between the present *SHY* and *Long Draft* data suggest that such hypothetically reduced *Long Draft* peaks would not affect my conclusions concerning the general allocation of space between the two works.

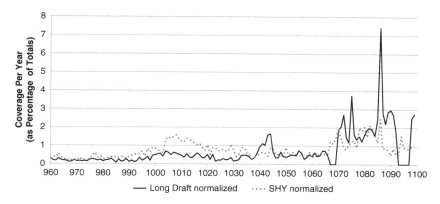

Figure 2.1 Coverage per year: *Long Draft* versus *Recovered Draft Compendium*

reflects the paucity of sources from this period, a deficiency neither work could surmount. Also noteworthy is the close alignment of coverage for the latter reign of Emperor Renzong and for the reign of Yingzong (1046–1067). In brief, this comparison shows that Li Tao underutilized material for the period 983–1033, but augmented the official record for the Qingli, Xining, and, drastically so, the Yuanyou periods.

An analysis of material within each of these periods reveals that, although the character of his sources for the early, middle, and late Northern Song periods differed dramatically, Li Tao consistently shaped those sources to express his preference for the Taizu–Qingli–Yuanyou axis of positive political value. In other words, the allocation of space within the main text of the *Long Draft* expresses this historiographical perspective and its attendant political values. As is well known, the bulk of the *Long Draft* consists of memorials submitted in the course of court decision making. In this respect, Li Tao also followed Sima Guang, who devoted over two-thirds of the *Comprehensive Mirror* to quoted memorials. As Robert LaFleur has well observed, Sima did not intend these lengthy quotations as documentation of the actual events themselves but rather as samples of reflection and opinion on those events. In short, the historians do not focus on the events but on how the sovereign and his advisers reacted to those events.[110] This emphasis generates a profusion of detail on the workings of the deliberative process, on interactions among official personnel and government agencies, on administrative mechanics,

---

[110] See LaFleur, "Beyond Commentary: Memorials, Remonstrance, and the *Zizhi Tongjian*'s Moral World," Chapter 5 of "A Rhetoric of Remonstrance," especially 165–74.

and on political ramifications – all of which the historians intend as didactic lessons in governance. Therefore, the number of memorials included on any specific event or issue does not necessarily reflect a modern sense of its actual historical importance as much as the importance the historian has perceived in the didactic benefit of the resulting discourse that the event generated. This focus explains why Li Tao dwelt upon the Qingli, Xining, and Yuanyou periods: these periods offered maximum potential for foregrounding, positively and negatively, lessons in governance that Li Tao held to be important for his audience. With the exception of the early period, where he was constrained by the paucity of sources, the other periods (983–1033, 1046–1067) offered diminished potential in this regard, and Li Tao trimmed the coverage accordingly.

Given this focus, Li Tao's perception of how well the memorials on a given event may illustrate the principles of literati governance, as these are reflected in his preferred Taizu–Qingli–Yuanyou continuum of political value, determined which memorials he included. Although a systematic analysis of the entire *Long Draft* from this perspective remains to be undertaken, research on selected portions reveals that Li Tao employed consistent editing techniques to shape his discourse. The relative paucity of records from the reigns of the first emperors, as well as revisions under Emperors Taizong and Zhenzong to reframe the Taizu reign to their own advantage, created unique problems for the historiography of the founding. Pei Rucheng and Xu Peizao count 830 citations to official sources in the Taizu and Taizong sections of the *Long Draft* (*juan* 1–42), the majority being of the state histories, the veritable records, and the *huiyao* collections. There are also 280 citations to private sources, and Li Tao maintains roughly this three-to-one ratio for the remainder of the work.[111] Among the "official" sources was the "old Taizu veritable records," the first history of the Taizu reign, completed in 980. Because the revised version of 999 superseded the earlier work, the "old records" were suppressed and had become by Li Tao's time an exceedingly rare book. Nevertheless Li Tao, in order to rebalance the historical depiction of Taizu, sought out the text and cited it a total of forty-two times in the seventeen *juan* of the *Long Draft* devoted to Taizu's reign.

Despite these difficulties, Li Tao found opportunities to fashion his early Song material into discourse that portrayed the founders as supporters of literati governance and in ways that address contemporary Southern Song issues. *Juan* 27–29, which cover the period from 986/1 through 988/12, presents a case in point.[112] The Song defeat at Qigou Pass in 986/4 marked a turning point in Taizong's failed campaign to recover the sixteen prefectures from the Khitan.

[111] Pei Rucheng and Xu Peizao, *Xu zizhi tongjian changbian kaolüe*, 39–49. These figures do not include an additional 280 citations to the *Comprehensive Mirror* that occur in the *Long Draft* chapters on very early Song history.

[112] I am indebted to Zhang Yuan, "Tan Song shi jiaoxue zhong de shiliao fenxi," 145, for this example.

The emperor had relied exclusively on the Bureau of Military Affairs for advice, and the chief councilors took advantage of the disaster to press for their greater involvement in military decision making. Against this scenario, Li Tao took pains to insert into the bare-bones veritable-record chronology a series of memorials that analyzed Song military options and argued for expansion of the chief councilors' portfolio. These begin with a 986/6 memorial from Chief Councilor Li Fang 李昉 (925–996), who pointed out that, because warfare costs are imposed upon the entire country, his office should be involved in military decisions.[113] Concluding the series is a memorial from Luo Chuyue 羅 處約 (958–990), a young recipient of the 983 *jinshi* degree, in which Luo argued for abolishing the separate Finance Commission and incorporating its functions into a recentralized Tang administrative structure headed by the chief councilors. Luo argues that such a move would enable the chief councilors to co-ordinate accounting functions across state agencies.[114]

Immediately following Luo's memorial, and concluding *juan* 29, Li appends a conversation between Taizong and Chief Councilor Zhao Pu 趙普 (922–992) on the status of their efforts at state building. Taizong remarks to his councilor that Taizu restored the power of the monarchy and ended the excessive militarism of the Five Dynasties. He affirms his intention to work with his councilors to develop his brother's vision into an institutional system (*gangji* 綱紀) that will be "utterly impartial ... without faction and without prejudice." This juxtaposition of Luo's memorial and the Taizong–Zhao Pu dialogue is entirely Li Tao's device; neither document was included in the original veritable records. Li's explained in his commentary that he retrieved the undated memorial from Luo's state history biography and inserted the text at the end of 988.[115] Likewise, he retrieved the imperial dialogue from the *Precious Instructions from Three Courts* of 1032.[116]

Li Tao's joining of these two documents as a conclusion to his dialogue on Qigou Pass implies that the founders ultimately would support a civil-based governance in which the chief councilors, within a balanced political system, exercised authority over the state's civil, military, and financial affairs. Li Tao, the historian, certainly knew that no early Song emperor had ever actively supported such a scenario; but Li Tao the politician also knew that no contemporary reader could fail to relate this "discourse" to the struggles in their

---

[113] *Changbian*, 27.617.   [114] *Changbian*, 29.660–62.

[115] The memorial remains in Luo's *Song History* biography; see *SS*, 440.13033–35. By virtue of its inclusion in the *Long Draft*, the text became a staple of *daoxue* historiography; see Chen Jun, *Huangchao gangmu*, 3.65; and Lü Zhong, *Huangchao dashiji*, 4.89.

[116] The received edition of the *Long Draft* contains no commentary after this dialogue, but the passage clearly derives from the *Sanchao baoxun*; see the quotation in Zhang Gang (1083–1166), *Huayang ji*, 22.10b. Since Li Tao often acknowledged quotations from the *Sanchao baoxun* (there are sixteen in *juan* 18–42, the Taizong years), this entry probably reflects an instance where original commentary has dropped from the received *Long Draft* text.

own time over expansion of the authority of the councilors' office. Although the councilors' routine concurrent appointment as commissioners of military affairs had begun in 1162, the relationship between the bureau and the councilors remained fraught, as the struggle between civil and military officials over the tenure in the bureau of the imperial affine Zhang Yue between 1165 and 1171 attests. Likewise, in 1166, the year before Li Tao arrived in Lin'an, chief councilors Jiang Fu and Chen Junqing convinced Emperor Xiaozong to create a State Finance Office under the jurisdiction of their office. The move generated persistent opposition from inner-court interests, and the brief period in which the chief councilors exercised, on paper, control over civil, military, and financial affairs ended with Chen Junqing's departure from court in 1170.

As the *Long Draft* moves into the Renzong reign, its sources present easier opportunities to apply the lessons of the past to the political necessities of the present. Han Qi, a major proponent of the Qingli reforms, had supervised the compilation of the *Renzong Veritable Records* in the 1060s.[117] Thus, Li Tao's base source for the period was probably already predisposed toward his message. For example, *juan* 140–152 cover the months from 1043/3 through 1044/10, a period that witnessed the rise and fall of the Qingli reform movement under Fan Zhongyan, Han Qi, Fu Bi, and Ouyang Xiu. Given a profusion of material, Li expresses his opinion through the allocation of more main-text space to the advocates and less to the opponents of this reform. The thirteen *juan* in question contain quotations from 117 memorials, 106 of which derive from the pro-reform group. They manifest three basic compositional techniques. First, memorials that Li cites without comment indicate that he agrees with their opinion. These constitute the backbone of the main-text narrative and frame his "discourse" on the reforms. Although significant political opposition doomed the reforms, Li does not cite a single memorial that opposed reform. Second, if he generally supports one perspective on an issue but deems other opposing arguments also credible, he then devises for his main text a composite narrative that relies primarily upon his preferred position but also incorporates the accepted opposing arguments. The commentary then explains his rationale. Third, if he judges opposing sides on an issue to present equally valid arguments but deems neither position fully adequate, he cites both in equal proportions, but inserts elements from a third party and thus offers a compromise solution.[118] In this way, Li's own political perspective and judgment frame the presentation of every discourse.

Detailed studies of Li Tao's treatment of sources for the Shenzong period, 1067–1085, also confirm a similar methodology, but one now vastly

---

[117] Cai Chongbang, *Songdai xiushi zhidu yanjiu*, 78–80.

[118] See Lee, "Different Mirrors of the Past," 29–73, with examples of each formulation. Lee actually perceives four categories, but his first two – verbatim quotation from memorials Li approves and exclusion of those he opposes – reflect the same principle of exclusivity, and I have condensed them into one category.

complicated by contending versions of the veritable records.[119] The political aftermath of the New Policies generated three different and conflicting *Shenzong Veritable Records*. An initial version, guided by Fan Zuyu, was completed under the antireform administration in 1091/3. Fan had worked with Sima Guang on the *Comprehensive Mirror*, and this first version of Shenzong's veritable records was highly critical of the New Policies. When reform advocates returned to power under Emperor Zhezong in 1094, they prosecuted the historians who had worked on the earlier records for defaming Emperor Shenzong, and they used Wang Anshi's diary to compile another version that portrayed his policies in a positive light. Largely under the direction of Cai Bian 蔡卞 (1058–1117) and Cai Jing, this version was finished in 1096/11. As a working draft, they had copied out the 1091 text in black ink, then added corrections and additions in red ink and erasures in yellow. They disseminated a final copy in black ink, but secluded the working draft within the palace and burned the 1091 original. But twenty years later the hidden draft was subsequently leaked to the public and so survived into Southern Song. This draft then served as the source for another set of "new" revisions completed under Fan Chong 范沖 (1067–1141), Fan Zuyu's son, in 1136/1. This new version was once again favorable to the antireformers, but Fan Chong condensed or omitted many historically useful details that the pro-reform 1096 edition had added.[120]

In addition to 201 generic references to "veritable records" between *juan* 210 and 363 (1070–1085), Li Tao's commentary refers 640 times to either the "black," the "red," or the "new" edition, by which he designates the editions of 1091, 1096, and 1136. Table 2.1 illustrates how Li Tao utilized these three versions as well as the "private" accounts of Wang Anshi and Sima Guang.

At first sight, it may appear that Li prefers the reformist over the antireformist versions, since he cites the red edition 370 times and Wang's diary 224 times. However, his preferred version is the first black edition of 1091, the earliest and most stridently antireformist account. Since the original text of this edition had been burned, Li used the red and new editions to reconstruct the lost black text, and then used this reconstruction as the base for his main-text narrative. But, since the black text often omitted or distorted details of the New Policies, Li supplemented the black text with material from the reformist red edition. Such supplements find their way into the main text a total of 125 times; and material from the red edition is used 245 times in the commentarial

---

[119] The following relies heavily upon Yan Yongcheng, "*Xu zizhi tongjian changbian* Shenzong chao qucai kao"; and Li Huarui, *Wang Anshi bianfa yanjiushi*, 114–65. For a detailed English-language study of Li Tao's utilization of sources for the Shenzong period see Levine, "A Performance of Transparency."

[120] For detailed studies of the *Shenzong shilu* see Wang Deyi, "Bei Song jiuchao shilu zuanxiu kao," 87–98 and Cai Chongbang, *Songdai xiushi zhidu yanjiu*, 82–98.

Table 2.1 *Long Draft* major source utilization for the period 1070–1085 (*juan* 210–363): number of citations

Work	Main text		Commentary	Totals
	As base	As supplement		
Shenzong Veritable Records 神宗實錄				
Black edition 黑本	107	–	21	128
Red edition 朱本	–	125	245	370
New edition 新本	75	–	67	142
Private accounts				
Wang Anshi's *Diary*日錄	69	71	84	224
Sima Guang's *Diary*日記	15	12	33	60
Sima Guang's *Su River Records*	20	13	30	63

Source: This table combines and adapts the separate tables in Yan Yongcheng, "*Xu zizhi tongjian changbian* Shenzong chao qucai kao," 64; and Yan Yongcheng, *Nan Song shixue yanjiu*, 130. Li Huarui, *Wang Anshi bianfa yanjiushi*, 117, counts 170 citations to any one of the three *Shenzong shilu* between *juan* 210 and 277 (1070/4 and 1076/7).

"discussion." The major purpose of these supplements is to document the extent and excesses of the New Policies. In essence, Li uses the reformist triumphalism that Cai Bian and Cai Jing had built into the red edition of 1096 to present a historical argument that the New Policies had deformed the policies of the ancestors.

The reign of Shenzong doubtless presented Li Tao with his greatest challenge as a historian. Although he worked through the different biases in the three versions of the veritable records to distill a detailed and factually accurate narrative of the New Policies, his deep-seated distaste for those policies and their aftermath pervades and colors the *Long Draft*. His selection of private sources to evaluate and augment the veritable records performs much of this coloring. Despite ample quotations from Wang's diary, the vast majority of his private sources are anti-New Policies. These include memoirs written by the Yuanyou administrators and their descendants, such as Sima Guang, Fan Zhen 范鎮 (1008–1088), Wei Tai 魏泰, Su Zhe, and Shao Bowen 邵伯溫 (1057– 1134). Most often cited are the *Collection to Venerate Yao* (*Zun Yao ji* 遵堯集) (forty citations) by Chen Guan 陳瓘 (1057–1122) and the *Unofficial History* (*Ye shi* 野史) (forty-five citations) by Lin Xi 林希 (1035–1101).[121] Li Tao cites almost all of Chen Guan's collection, which Chen wrote specifically to counter the use of Wang's diary in the red veritable records and for which Chen was prosecuted in 1111.[122] Lin Xi's work was composed in the midst of the New

[121] For a detailed discussion, see Li Huarui, *Wang Anshi bianfa yanjiushi*, 135–49.
[122] Huang Yizhou, *Xu zizhi tongjian changbian shibu*, 30.1006–7.

Policies era when he opposed reform; but, unhappy over his treatment during the Yuanyou period, he sided with the reformers under Zhang Dun 章惇 (1035–1105) and abandoned his earlier antireform memoirs. When the political tide turned again in the early Southern Song, his grandson rewrote and disseminated his history.[123] In his commentary, Li Tao cites the work, which is filled with virulent, personal attacks against the reformers, to color Wang's underlings as profit-grubbing "petty men."

Li Huarui, summarizing the *Long Draft*'s narrative on the New Policies, makes five points: (1) Li Tao restored and preserved the black, Yuanyou history of the period; (2) he reconstructed a factual account of the New Policies to demonstrate in detail how Wang Anshi changed the policies of the ancestors; (3) he absolved Emperor Shenzong and placed responsibility for these changes on Wang; (4) he maintained that Wang employed morally corrupt, unscrupulous "petty men" to implement the policies; and (5) he took pains to document how the New Policies harmed the population.[124] Each of Li Huarui's five points can be further related to advice about government that Li Tao proffered throughout his career to Emperor Xiaozong. As we have seen, Li advocated that the emperor should ground his policies on those of the Yuanyou period; he should restore and implement the policies of the ancestors (and the *Long Draft* provided a sourcebook on how to do so); he should not be misled by his advisers as Shenzong had been; he should not employ non-literati officials in key positions; and he should not pursue policies that harm the people (such as excessive taxation).

Any attempt to reduce a work as complex and nuanced as the *Long Draft* to a single message would be overly simplistic. As explained above, Li Tao directed his efforts toward at least three discernible audiences: as with Sima Guang's *Comprehensive Mirror*, the primary audience was an audience of one – the *Long Draft* was a handbook of governance for Emperor Xiaozong. Another audience was the official historiographical office that Li Tao hoped, in conjunction with the emperor, would use the resources collected in the *Long Draft* formally to resolve major issues of Song history. A final audience was the broader coalition of literati officials to whom Li Tao was politically allied and whom he hoped would use his work as a resource guide for policy formation.

Tsong-han Lee's analysis of the *Long Draft* narrative for the Qingli years discerns two overriding concerns. Although both are directed primarily at the emperor, they also pertain to the work's wider literati audience. First is a focus on the administrative skills necessary for the effective management of officials – their recruitment, placement, and supervision. For example, the *Long Draft*'s meticulous recording of position transfers, promotions, and demotions –

---

[123] Chen Zhensun, *Zhizhai shulu jieti*, 5.151.
[124] Li Huarui, *Wang Anshi bianfa yanjiushi*, 148.

especially as seen in relation to evolving historical "events" – provides a vast casebook for Song personnel management.[125] Second, and related, is Li Tao's emphasis on the need to govern in ways that strengthen the dynasty's proper institutional structures. Like Sima Guang, Li Tao advocated a literati conception of government: "the system" (*jigang*) was an interlocking structure of hierarchically related offices, each with prescribed functions and relationships to other offices. Government worked best, and maximized the effectiveness of each official in the system, when the highest authorities governed in ways that enforced and strengthened the hierarchical definitions and boundaries of each office. In this sense, the *Long Draft* presents a vast historical argument for the superiority of literati governance.[126]

The Fate of a Masterpiece

The emperor promised to write a preface for the *Long Draft*, just as Emperor Shenzong had done for the *Comprehensive Mirror*. But he never did. Likewise, he never convened the deliberative conferences that Li Tao had requested in 1174 and again in 1183. In both requests, Li had drawn parallels to the famous Han dynasty conferences in 51 BCE at Stone Canal Pavilion and in 79 AD at White Tiger Hall. Han emperors had convened these meetings to resolve competing interpretations in advance of an imperial imprimatur for a unified interpretation of the canon.[127] Li's 1183 memorial emphasized that, given the dueling histories of the New Policies, the *Long Draft* still contained many conflicting and thus unresolved accounts. Thus, despite forty years of effort, he could not guarantee that no contradictions remained. Only a deliberative conference, acting on the ultimate authority of the emperor, could resolve the remaining conflicts and enable the final completion of the work. Without such sanction, he feared that criticism from parties unhappy over his choices could endanger the survival of the work. In conclusion, he requested an imperial preface specifically to protect the work from future destruction, just as Shenzong's preface had saved the *Comprehensive Mirror* in the late 1090s.[128]

Li's memorial reveals how he hoped to complete the *Long Draft*. In fact, the problems were more political than historical, and he was asking Xiaozong for a lot. Because the state history for the 1067–1127 period was still incomplete in 1183, the official historiographical position on the New Policies had yet to be finalized. Thus, Li Tao was not asking for a conference simply to resolve minor historical quibbles; he was asking the emperor to use the *Long Draft* as a vehicle to endorse a Taizu–Renzong–Yuanyou model of governance before

[125] For an example where Li Tao directly declares this intention see *Changbian*, 151.3685.
[126] Lee, "Different Mirrors of the Past," 54–62.
[127] Twitchett and Loewe, *The Cambridge History of China, Volume 1*, 757, 763.
[128] *Wenxian tongkao*, 193.5612–13; *QSW*, 210:4661.180–81.

the completion of the official history. If the emperor and the conference accepted this gambit, the state history office, with or without Li Tao, would be required to align the state history with the newly established historical and political line. The request continued Li Tao's strategy of using the *Long Draft* to influence the direction and content of the state history. In addition, by soliciting an imperial preface, he was asking Xiaozong to sanction in perpetuity the *Long Draft*'s historical perspective.

These were all politically charged issues, but the politics had already shifted against Li Tao. In 1182/9, Zhou Bida left the State Council, and Wang Huai advanced as the senior chief councilor. Wang, a native of Jinhua in Zhejiang, headed a different political network than the Sichuan–Fujian coalition that had sponsored Li Tao and his history. Wang lacked the drive for reform that animated his opponents, and he doubtless saw little political advantage in a conference that would ratify the historiographical orientation of the *Long Draft* and enable Li Tao to surround the work, along with its historical and policy perspectives, with an imperial imprimatur. There is no record that Emperor Xiaozong or any top official for the remainder of his reign took an interest in the *Long Draft*. After Li Tao's death, the emperor ordered Hong Mai in 1185/6 to complete the *Four Courts State History* for the 1067–1127 period. Li Tao had worked for many years to co-ordinate the state history and the *Long Draft*. He had achieved this goal in the annals and monographic sections, and only the biographies remained unfinished. But Hong had had a difficult relationship with Li. When the emperor pressed Hong to finish the work, he hastily combined Li Tao's drafts with inferior biographies from Wang Cheng's *Eastern Capital Miscellany* (*Dongdu shilüe* 東都史略), and Wang Huai submitted the finished work in 1186. The result was hardly the state history that Li had envisioned, and was roundly criticized by later historians.[129]

Song sources are vague on the disposition of the various installments and revisions to the *Long Draft* that Li Tao submitted between 1163 and 1183.[130] In 1191/10 Emperor Guangzong asked the Directorate of Education for a copy of the work. Vice Director Peng Guinian 彭龜年 (1142–1206) replied that the Directorate possessed only the sections submitted by Li Tao in 1175 from Luzhou. He added that the Imperial Library, however, possessed both the initial five-court installment copied in the same format as Sima Guang's

---

[129] *Chaoye zaji, jia*, 4.110–11, 9.187; see Hartman, "The Reluctant Historian," 109–10.

[130] Pei Rucheng and Xu Peizao, *Xu zizhi tongjian changbian kaolüe*, 1–2; followed by Yan Yongcheng, "Jin qichaoben *Xu zizhi tongjian changbian* tanyuan," 8, argue that the court held three copies of the complete *Long Draft*: (1) the original installment drafts, (2) a clean copy of those installments executed in the format of the *Comprehensive Mirror*, and (3) Li Tao's final submission of 1183. However, the order to execute a copy in the format of the *Comprehensive Mirror* came in 1170, when only the initial, five-court installment (covering 960–1067) had been submitted (*SHY, chongru*, 5.37b–38a). There seems no evidence that the order was subsequently extended to apply to the later installments.

Comprehensive Mirror in 1170 and the final manuscript that Li had submitted in 1183. Peng advised the emperor to access the *Long Draft*, as Li Tao had intended, through the *Selected Essentials*. The emperor ordered an abridgment, but the work was apparently never completed. Later, in 1194 Peng submitted a work entitled *The Sage's Mirror for Inner Cultivation* (*Neizhi shengjian* 內治聖鑑), a collection of dynastic precedents for regulating the inner court, for which he drew upon the resources of the *Compendium* and the *Long Draft*, presumably using the Directorate's Luzhou edition. The emperor inquired whether Peng's work was an abridgment of the *Long Draft*, and Peng informed him that no, even an abridged version of the *Long Draft* would be much longer than the twenty-*juan* work he had just submitted.[131] This exchange reveals that the *Long Draft* was indeed being used, in the decade after its submission, as Li Tao had envisioned – as a collection of precedents to illustrate the principles of literati governance.

There is evidence that manuscript copies, both complete and partial, circulated among the literati coalition's top leaders. Zhou Bida possessed a copy, as did Chen Junqing, who retired around 1182 to Fujian and whose copy eventually served as the major source for Chen Jun's *Outline and Details*.[132] Zhou Mi 周密 (1232–1291), in his notebook, the *Random Recollections from the Guixin Quarter* (*Guixin zashi* 癸辛雜識), tells an intriguing tale of how Han Yangu 韓彥古 (d. 1192) obtained a copy of the 1183 manuscript even before the clean copy could be submitted. The court had ordered the Lin'an city government to furnish the scribal manpower for the enormous transcription project. Han Yangu, whose brother Han Yanzhi 韓彥質 was Lin'an mayor at the time, bribed the scribes to prepare a secret copy, which they delivered to him before they completed the official copy. Han's interest in the *Long Draft* seems unusual, since the Han brothers were sons of the famous general Han Shizhong 韓世忠 (1190–1151), and Han Yangu was related by marriage to Xiaozong's "favorite" Zeng Di. He was thus closely allied to powerful anti-literati forces, not known for their interest in history. Nevertheless, in 1193, their third brother Han Yanzhi 韓彥直 submitted to court the *Water-Heart Mirror* (*Shuixin jing* 水心鏡), a 167-*juan* work on Song history. The Han brothers were strong advocates for the rehabilitation of the disgraced general Yue Fei 岳飛 (1103–1141). Although no direct evidence links the two works, it is probable Han Yanzhi's history drew upon his brother's copy of the *Long Draft* to present a view of Song history more favorable to military and affinal interests.[133] Li Tao was furious at Han Yangu when he discovered the theft. The

---

[131] *QSW*, 278:6295.118, 6297.145–47.   [132] Hartman, "Chen Jun's *Outline and Details*," 282.
[133] Zhou Mi, *Guixin zashi*, 38–39; for Han Yanzhi's tenure as Lin'an mayor, see Qian Yueyou, *Xianchun Lin'an zhi*, 48.5a–b; for the *Shuixin jing*, see *SS*, 364.11371.

story reveals that political persuasions other than its intended literati audience might find useful affirmation in the work's profusion of detail.

Scholarship on the transmission of the *Long Draft* divides the work's bibliography into three related, but separate, topics: (1) the original, complete "nine-court" edition (covering 960–1127) as submitted by Li Tao in 1183; (2) a truncated "seven-court" edition (covering 960–1066, 1070–1092, and 1098–1099) as reconstituted in 520 *juan* by the Four Treasuries academicians from the *Yongle Encyclopedia*; and (3) surviving Song imprints of an abridged "five-court" edition in 108 *juan* (covering 960–1067).[134] However, the relationship among these three versions of the text (the first being hypothetical since no copy survives; the second and third both extant) is unclear. Scholars generally concur that the full *Long Draft*, as submitted in 1183, was never printed.[135] Commercial bookstores, however, soon began printing abridgments, and three exemplars of an abridged five-court version survive. These editions omit about 30 percent of the text (as recovered from the *Yongle Encyclopedia*), mainly by eliminating shorter entries.[136] Also unclear is how mentions in Song sources of various early editions relate either to Li Tao's original work or to these surviving Song imprints.

For example, a letter from Zhu Xi to Li Tao's son, Li Bi, written in 1197 or 1198, mentions no less than four editions of the *Long Draft*, one of which he specifies as "the edition printed by Wang [Yingchen]." Zhu also mentions a "Fuzhou edition," a "Chengdu edition," and a "Nanjian edition," which seems to have been in the planning stages when Zhu wrote.[137] Unfortunately, lack of context makes it impossible to determine whether Zhu refers here to printed or to manuscript editions, or whether these editions were complete, nine-court versions. Certainly, Wang Yingchen's edition was a five-court version. Wang Yingchen was stationed in Sichuan through 1168, had recommended Li Tao's five-court manuscript to court, and died in 1176; therefore, Zhu Xi probably refers to an early printing of the five-court version that could well be the ancestor of the three Song exemplars that survive.

In addition, the catalogue of the great mid-thirteenth-century bibliophile Zhao Xibian 趙希弁 (d. 1250+) describes a 946-*juan* Sichuan edition that

---

[134] Pei Rucheng and Xu Peizao, *Xu zizhi tongjian changbian kaolüe*, 1–18.

[135] Pei Rucheng and Xu Peizao, *Xu zizhi tongjian changbian kaolüe*, 1–4.

[136] Pei Rucheng and Xu Peizao, *Xu zizhi tongjian changbian kaolüe*, 9–16. The exemplar in the Liaoning Provincial Library was reproduced in 1995 as *Songben Xu zizhi tongjian changbian*, with a preface by Chen Zhichao. Another exemplar in the National Library of China, entitled *Xu zizhi tongjian changbian cuoyao*, was reproduced in 2004 in the series *Zhongguo zaicao shanben*. A second exemplar of the *cuoyao* edition is in the Seikado Library. To my knowledge, no specialist of Song printing has examined any of these exemplars, and their points of origin remain unknown. They are generally believed to date from the early thirteenth century.

[137] *Zhu Xi ji*, 38.1740–42. Wang Deyi, *Li Tao fuzi nianpu*, 123–25, dates the letter to 1197; Chen Lai, *Zhuzi shuxin biannian kaozheng*, 468, prefers 1198.

some scholars of Song printing accept as a reference to a printed edition.[138] This could well be the Chengdu edition to which Zhu Xi refers. Thus, if the full *Long Draft* was ever printed, it was probably in Sichuan, Li Tao's home base, where manuscripts of the full work certainly circulated and served as the base for abridgments that proliferated in the early thirteenth century. Two such works survive largely intact: the *Topical Narratives from the Long Draft Continuation of the Comprehensive Mirror That Aids Administration* (*Xu zizhi tongjian changbian jishi benmo* 續資治通鑑長編紀事本末) by Yang Zhongliang 楊仲良 and the *Administrative Records from the Period of Great Tranquility, Fully Classified* (*Taiping zhiji tonglei*) by Peng Baichuan 彭百川. Yang and Peng were both fellow natives of Meishan in the generation after Li Tao, and Yang Zhongliang was probably related to him by marriage.[139] Certainly, the immediate legacy of the *Long Draft*, in both manuscript and print, was strongest in Sichuan. The Mongol destruction of Sichuan in the 1230s, however, destroyed the printing blocks for Yang's work and would certainly also have destroyed any Sichuan printing blocks of the *Long Draft*, if they existed.

Also in the 1230s, the great Lin'an fire of 1231 burned almost the entire Imperial Library compound, including the emperor's personal library (*bige*), where Li Tao's final 1183 submission had been deposited.[140] Probably, all of Li Tao's original manuscript submissions to the court perished at this time. Since the Mongol army recovered large portions of the *Long Draft* from the Imperial Library in 1276, these were probably copies that had been moved into the library from other locations, such as the Directorate copy of the Luzhou submission that Peng Guinian had used, or copies that the library acquired after its reopening in 1232.

Thus, the combination of the Lin'an fire and the Mongol invasions of Sichuan probably destroyed those few printed or manuscript copies of the full, nine-court *Long Draft* that existed in the early thirteenth century. By the late Song, even native Sichuan historians working at court could no longer access the complete work, but consulted the *Long Draft* in separate sections, and some of these sections were no longer available. For example, Li Xinchuan's disciple, Gao Side, worked intermittently in the Imperial Library

---

[138] Chao Gongwu, *Junzhai dushuzhi jiaozheng*, 1110–11; Poon, "Books and Printing in Sung China," 290.

[139] On the first work see Hartman, "Bibliographic Notes on Sung Historical Works: *Topical Narratives from the Long Draft Continuation of the Comprehensive Mirror That Aids Administration*"; and Cai Hanmo, *Lishi de yanzhuang*, 270–92; on the second see Deng Guangming, "Dui youguan *Taiping zhiji tonglei* zhu wenti de xin kaosuo." For similar compressions of the *Long Draft* that do not survive see the list in Yan Yongcheng, *Nan Song shixue yanjiu*, 342–44.

[140] The garden and the compilation hall at the rear of the compound were the only structures that survived; see *Nan Song guan'ge xulu*, 2.170.

from the mid-1240s through the mid-1260s. His biography records among his projects a *Huizong-era Long Draft* (*Huizong changbian* 徽宗長編). If Gao could still consult Li Tao's original, it is difficult to see the rationale for this undertaking. The *Huizong-era Long Draft* apparently formed part of Gao's project to combine Li Tao's *Long Draft* and Li Xinchuan's *Chronological Record* into a unified "long draft" for the entire Song, from 960 through 1162.[141]

This reception history suggests that because many scholars and historians perceived the *Long Draft* as an unfinished work, they viewed its text as a base for improvements and continuations rather than as a masterpiece to be preserved intact. One may detect at least three developments in the post-Li Tao, thirteenth-century history of the *Long Draft*. First were efforts by Sichuan historians who were Li Tao's direct intellectual heirs to continue his work. Zhu Xi's letter, for example, alludes to Li Bi's ongoing efforts both to revise and to augment his father's original draft and to extend its coverage into Southern Song.[142] Li Xinchuan's entire career and surviving *oeuvre* can be viewed as a continuation of Li Tao's work; and Gao Side's unrealized project to combine the *Long Draft* and the *Chronological Record* continued a goal that perhaps originated with Li Tao himself and so persisted through three generations of Sichuan historians. Second were works that drew upon the *Long Draft* to compile shorter compilations in more accessible formats such as the "topical narratives" of Yang Zhongliang and Peng Baichuan. Although these works are not totally free of *daoxue* influence, they represent in this respect a middle ground between the *Long Draft* and the last category, the "outline and details" (*gangmu* 綱目) histories of Chen Jun and his successors. As we shall explore in Chapter 4, these short, selective works, although based upon the *Long Draft* and *Chronological Record*, manifest an overt *daoxue* agenda both in the selection of main entries (*gang*) and in their commentarial details (*mu*).

The boundaries between these categories were fluid. As the popularity of *daoxue* grew over the course of the thirteenth century, even Li Tao's direct Sichuan disciples such as Gao Side succumbed to its influence. Gao's biography, for example, records a *Chronological Record of the Gaozong Reign in Outline and Details* (*Gaozong xinian yaolu gangmu* 高宗繫年要錄綱目), clearly an adaptation of his teacher's *Chronological Record* in the *daoxue*

---

[141] *SS*, 409.12328; Gao Side, *Chitang cungao*, 7.23a; Yan Yongcheng, "Jin qichaoben *Xu zizhi tongjian changbian* tanyuan," 9. Late in his life, Gao wrote a poem entitled "Reading the *Zhezong-era Long Draft*" (*Du Zhezong changbian* 讀哲宗長編), also suggesting that he conceived, and probably accessed, the post-1067 *Long Draft* in the individual, reign-specific installments in which Li Tao had originally written them; see *Chitang cungao*, 6.14b–15a.

[142] Yan Yongcheng, "Jin qichaoben *Xu zizhi tongjian changbian* tanyuan," 10, suggests that Li Tao himself had drafted such a continuation and that surviving citations of a "*Shaoxing*-era long draft" in the *Song huiyao* and in Zhang Ruyu's *(Shantang) Qunshu kaosuo* derive from his manuscript.

"outline-and-details" format.[143] Such adaptation of material originally in "long-draft" format into the more accessible but doctrinally focused "outline-and-details" format reduced the appeal and need for the original works. The survival of the 108-*juan* five-court edition should be understood in this context. Focused on the founders and the Renzong era, before the controversial New Policies had arisen, the work served as a convenient repository of useful precedents and contained little that could contest the *daoxue* narrative on Northern Song history. Despite Li Tao's obvious anti-New Policies perspective, the latter sections, bulky and complex, offered little appeal for politicians, printers, or educators in late Song.

Finally, one can detect important variations in how different geographical regions received and reworked the *Long Draft*. Significantly, all the editions mentioned in Zhu Xi's letter derive from either Sichuan or Fujian. Certainly, this pattern relates to the robust printing industries in both regions; but, more importantly, it reflects the original Sichuan–Fujian political coalition of the early Xiaozong era during which and for which Li Tao had composed the work. In short, the literati of these areas continued to perceive value in the *Long Draft*, but their different uses reflect the different ways they perceived this value. Respect for the integrity of the *Long Draft* was naturally greatest in Sichuan, where the work was perhaps printed in full and where doctrinally neutral abridgments such as those by Yang Zhongliang and Peng Baichuan maintained its strong Sichuan character. In Fujian, the strong *daoxue* movement prompted drastic reworkings of the *Long Draft* but did not ultimately contradict its advocacy of literati governance. By contrast, Zhejiang scholars helped themselves to the work's copious sources but combined these indiscriminately with other sources to compile their encyclopedias and "statecraft" handbooks; but surviving sources do not reveal any editions or freestanding adaptations of the *Long Draft* from Zhejiang.[144]

Conclusion

When the reconstructed *Long Draft* was first printed in 1819, the scholar Sun Yuanxiang 孫原湘 (1760–1829), drawing upon Li Tao's first submission memorial of 1163, wrote that the work presented "discussions" on the most contentious and sensitive issues of Song history – the founding at Chen Bridge, the death of Taizu and his immediate heirs, the peace treaties of 1005 and 1044,

---

[143] *SS*, 409.12327.
[144] At least two early thirteenth-century Zhejiang works utilized the full, nine-court version of the *Long Draft*. Xu Ziming, author of the *Chronological Record of the Song State Council* (*Song zaifu biannian lu*), was a native of Yongjia; Zhang Ruyu, who compiled the *Qunshu kaosuo*, was a native of Jinhua. On the latter's use of the *Long Draft* see Tang Kaijian and Chen Wenyuan, "*Shantang kaosuo* zhong baoliu de *Changbian* yiwen."

the Tangut wars, and the struggles over the New Policies. On all these issues Li
Tao had used private sources to fill in the lacunae or amend the distortions of the
official record. When his contemporaries could not or dared not speak on such
sensitive issues, he spoke "as a Song official on Song matters" with an integrity
found only in the legendary historians of antiquity, "resolving all opinions into
one."[145]

In their biographies of Li Tao, both Zhou Bida and Li Bi stress the historian's
loyalty to the Emperor Xiaozong. They understand this loyalty as Li Tao's
strong and persistent advocacy to the emperor for a total restoration (*zhongxing*) of Northern Song greatness. Politically, this restoration requires rebuilding the institutions of Qingli/Yuanyou literati governance as essential
preparation for the military recovery of the North. Li Tao's position was not
merely academic but grew from his lived experience as an official in Sichuan
provincial administration and later at court.

Scholars have long recognized the affinity between the concrete program for
dynastic renewal that Li Tao outlined in his *Extensive Discussions on the Six
Dynasties Comprehensive Mirror* and his *Long Draft* narrative.[146] Li drew
upon Six Dynasties history to insist that the leadership of Sun Quan 孫權
(181–252), the first emperor of the Wu dynasty who forged an alliance with the
Sichuan Han kingdom, had enabled the military defeat of the Northern forces
under Cao Cao 曹操 (155–220) at the Red Cliff in 208. Li Tao held that Sun
Quan's skills in personnel management enabled his elevation to the emperorship of Wu in 229. But after he became emperor, Sun abandoned his ambition to
recover the North and permitted his government to dissolve into internal
disorder.[147] In Li Tao's work, Sun Quan is an obvious type for Emperor
Xiaozong. Li thus advocates for a more effective alliance between "Wu" (the
Song center at Lin'an) and Sichuan.[148] Li's early concern with excessive costs
in the Sichuan military, his support of Wang Gangzhong's actions in 1161, and
his own measures at Suining in 1180 to reform the Sichuan military all display
his personal commitment to strong oversight of imperial forces in the province
and against the disposition of the Sichuan military as a "house army." In Li
Tao's opinion, corruption in the Sichuan military both undermined dynastic
legitimacy and weakened the Wu–Shu alliance, without which a viable defensive posture, let along recovery of the North, was impossible.

---

[145] Sun Yuanxiang, *Tianzhenge ji*, 43.7b–8b, also cited in Pei Rucheng and Xu Peizao, *Xu zizhi
tongjian changbian kaolüe*, Introduction, 5–6. To remove any ambiguity from Li Tao's 咸會於
一 Sun Yuanxiang altered the phrase to read 咸歸於一.

[146] Ji Yun et al., *Qinding Siku quanshu zongmu*, 88.1167; Pei Rucheng and Xu Peizao, *Xu zizhi
tongjian changbian kaolüe*, Introduction, 2–3, cite a similar opinion by Peng Yuanrui 彭元瑞
(1731–1803).

[147] For Li Tao's assessment of Sun Quan see Choi, "Li Tao *Liuchao tongjian boyi* yanjiu," 127–34.

[148] Choi, "Li Tao *Liuchao tongjian boyi* yanjiu," 178–81.

The *Long Draft* links the origins of literati governance back to Taizu's policy that imposed civilian control over the military governors of the Five Dynasties. Li Tao's historical stance on Taizu supports his concept of total restoration as a realization of literati efforts to control the military establishment of their own time. As Chief Councilor Ye Yong explained to Xiaozong in the wake of the dismissal of Qi Fang in 1167, if His Majesty could only emulate the management style of Taizu, then the perfection of the Renzong era could be achieved. In other words, recovery of the North could only be achieved through return to the founding principles of Song. Those principles eschew the deviations of the New Policies and their covert continuation under Qin Gui and other practitioners of technocratic governance. Throughout his career in local government, Li Tao worked wherever possible to ameliorate the impact of actions he linked historically to the New Policies. From his youthful refusal to co-operate with Qin Gui to his career resistance against Zeng Di's network of "the close," Li Tao consistently sided with advocates of literati against technocratic governance. The profuse documentation in the *Long Draft* to establish the perfidy of the New Policies also presents a historical argument against what Li Tao experienced as the evils wrought by the technocrats of his own age.

A proper administrative balance between sovereign and councilor in the context of a robust remonstrance function was central to the concept of literati governance. The *Long Draft* originated in extensive charts that correlated the appointment tenures of officials against the historical outcomes of their actions in those offices. This focus underscored Li Tao's view that optimal governance arose when sovereign and councilor co-operate to identify and place the best officials in the most suitable positions. But unilateral exercise, either by the monarch or by his designate, of this primary function of personnel administration undermines the "public" nature of government and consigns administration to the "private" – to "the close" against which Li Tao and his allies contended. Li Tao's warning against too many facilitated degrees and Lü Zuqian's warning upon submission of the *Huizong Veritable Records* against the dangers of unilateral imperial decision making both address fundamental tenets of literati governance whose history the *Long Draft* so carefully re-created.

Introduction

Students of the Song dynasty dread the question whether Li Tao or Li Xinchuan was the greater historian. Even the Qing academicians could not decide. In 1773 they noted in their initial evaluation of Li Xinchuan's masterpiece, *The Chronological Record of Important Events since 1127*, that Li Xinchuan had followed Li Tao's methodology but that he had been "more precise and thorough," thus suggesting that Li Xinchuan had surpassed his forerunner. Writing a decade later, however, after completion of the *Siku* project, the editors seemed to temper this earlier judgment: "Li Tao followed Sima Guang, but, in some areas did not equal him; Li Xinchuan followed Li Tao and equaled him in every way." This later formulation suggests that although neither of the Sichuan historians equaled Sima Guang, their individual achievements were similar to each other.[1] Then again, the Qing scholar Sun Yuanxiang, a great admirer of Li Tao, ultimately declared Li Xinchuan the better historian.[2]

Indeed, both Li Tao and Li Xinchuan followed in Sima Guang's historiographical footsteps. But Li Xinchuan, who lived a generation after Li Tao, had his predecessor's example before him, and learned from the *Long Draft* how Li Tao had adapted Sima's methodological principles for use on Song dynasty sources. Furthermore, although Li Tao labored privately for many years as a historian in Sichuan, he revised the entire *Long Draft* after he gained access in 1167, as an official historian at age fifty-two, to the Imperial Library in the capital. And yet, as we have seen, although Li Tao enjoyed political support at court, his active involvement in court politics also complicated his task as a historian. Li Xinchuan, however, labored in provincial isolation as a private scholar in Sichuan and completed the works that established his reputation as a historian well before his arrival in Lin'an in 1226.

---

[1] For the 1773 *tiyao* see Li Xinchuan, *Jianyan yilai xinian yaolu* (*SKQS* edition), *mulu*, 27b; for the later notice, see Ji Yun et al., *Qinding Siku quanshu zongmu*, 47.657–58.

[2] *Yaolu*, appendix, 3977.

As historians, Li Tao and Li Xinchuan share many similarities. As the Qing academicians recognized, both worked consciously in a historiographical tradition that both perceived as emanating from Sima Guang. Both viewed their work as a corrective to the deficiencies of official history. Both worked as private scholars and also as official historians at the Imperial Library, thus blurring the line between their private and official historiography. Both received support from important Sichuan officials. Yet there were also significant differences in their careers. As we have seen, Li Tao had a long and active career in local Sichuan administration before his arrival in Lin'an. He had practical experience in government that Li Xinchuan lacked. This experience, plus Li Tao's much higher personal rank upon arrival at court, made him a much more active figure in court politics during the 1160s and 1170s than Li Xinchuan could hope to become during the 1220s and 1230s. Additionally, the Sichuan faction at court was more powerful during Emperor Xiaozong's reign than during Emperor Lizong's. In short, if Li Tao was the consummate scholar-official who successfully blended his scholarly and his official careers, Li Xinchuan, despite his time in Lin'an, remained more purely a scholar, who, in the words of one observer, "stayed far from the center of power and trusted too much to his historical texts and documents."[3]

Like Li Tao, Li Xinchuan was a scholar of broad interests whose writings spanned classical exegesis, history, and belles lettres. Most of this larger corpus, including 100 *juan* of his collected works, is now lost.[4] Only four works, all on history, have survived. *The Chronological Record of Important Events since 1127* is a day-by-day history from the beginning of the Southern Song in 1127 through to Emperor Gaozong's abdication in 1162. The *Chronological Record* remains for modern historians the indispensible, if perhaps not entirely definitive, account of this period.[5] While working on the *Chronological Record*, Li also compiled the *Diverse Notes on Court and Province since 1127*, which he completed in two installments in 1202 and 1216. Bibliographers often classify the *Diverse Notes* as a "notebook" (*biji*), but the work constitutes in fact a topical index and vade mecum to the *Chronological Record*.[6] Both the *Chronological Record* and the *Diverse Notes* are relatively early works, completed at least a decade before Li arrived in Lin'an. The *Record of the Way and Its Fate*, a history of the *daoxue* movement with a preface dated 1239, near the end of his Lin'an career and only five years before his death, provides the only example of Li's later historiographical

---

[3] Zhou Mi charged that Li's isolation in Sichuan and overreliance upon mere documents rendered him ill-informed about many court events; see *Qidong yeyu*, 3.59–60.

[4] Fu Zengxiang, *Songdai Shuwen jicun*, 77.1a–15a, collects thirty-five randomly preserved texts from Li Xinchuan's corpus.

[5] The standard edition is now *Jianyan yilai xinian yaolu*, edited by Hu Kun (2013).

[6] *Jianyan yilai chaoye zaji*, edited by Xu Gui (2000).

work. Finally, fragments of a minor work, the *Corrections of Errors in Old Accounts* (*Jiuwen zhengwu* 舊聞證誤), also survive, and provide a window into Li's working methodology as a historian.[7] All four works will be discussed in this chapter.

The Life of Li Xinchuan

Li Xinchuan was a native of Jingyan 井研 county in Longzhou 隆州, a major salt-producing area about sixty miles south of Chengdu in Sichuan.[8] His grandfather had been the first in his family to hold office, and the family became known locally in the next generation for its scholarship. His father, Li Shunchen 李舜臣 (d. 1182), was a prodigy who could reputedly read at age three, then acquired broad learning in pursuit of his wider ambitions. He attained the *jinshi* degree in 1166. But his strident irredentist tracts alienated court leaders who had just the year before negotiated peace with the Jin, and he remained for over a decade in local Sichuan civil and educational posts. In 1179, probably due to the influence of his fellow Sichuanese then chief councilor Zhao Xiong 趙雄 (1129–1193), he was appointed to the Court of the Imperial Clan in Lin'an where he worked on Emperor Shenzong's genealogy.[9] His three sons, Li Xinchuan and his two younger brothers, Li Daochuan 李道傳 (1170–1217) and Li Xingchuan 李性傳 (1174–1254), accompanied their father to the capital. Li Shunchen's scholarly reputation was formidable enough to earn him a slot, in 1180, on the committee to conduct the Directorate School qualifications for the *jinshi* examination.[10] The father apparently held similar aspirations for his sons. In the same year, Li Daochuan, aged ten, sat for the entrance examination at the Directorate School.[11] When Li Shunchen died in Lin'an in 1182, his three sons returned to Sichuan.[12]

The Li brothers spent the next fifteen years preparing for the *jinshi* examination. Li Xinchuan and Li Daochuan finally sat together for the exam in 1196. Daochuan passed and began his official career; but Xinchuan, aged twenty-

---

[7] Li Xinchuan, *Jiuwen zhengwu*, edited by Cui Wenyin (1981). For a useful survey of Li's surviving as well as his lost works see Wang Deyi, "Li Xinchuan zhushu kao"; also Chaffee, "Li Hsin-ch'üan," 212–14.

[8] For Li Xinchuan's biography see the still unsurpassed *nianpu* by Wang Deyi, "Li Xiuyan xiansheng nianpu"; also Chaffee, "Li Hsin-ch'üan." Lai Kehong, *Li Xinchuan shiji zhuzuo biannian*, should be consulted along with the corrections in Liang Taiji's review, reprinted in the latter's *Tang Song lishi wenxian yanjiu conggao*, 447–68.

[9] *SS*, 404.12223–24.   [10] *SHY, xuanju*, 21.2b.

[11] Wang Deyi, "Li Xiuyan xiansheng nianpu," 6708.

[12] For a posthumous memoir of Li Shunchen's years in Lin'an, an accolade to his scholarship, and a tribute to the accomplishments of his three sons see the "Inscription for Mr. Li's Pavilion of Perpetual Devotion," composed by Lou Yue at the request of Li Daochuan in 1213; Lou Yue, *Gongkui ji*, 60.9a–11b; *QSW*, 265:5971.59–60.

nine, failed.[13] Rather than continue to prepare for subsequent attempts, he abandoned pursuit of the degree and devoted his full time to his scholarly interests. Some scholars attribute his *jinshi* failure to Han Tuozhou's blacklisting of *daoxue* scholars, but Li Daochuan, whose understanding and advocacy of *daoxue* was much stronger than his brother's, passed the same examinations in the same year.[14] Whatever the case may be, Li Xinchuan remained for the next thirty years in Sichuan and worked at home in Longzhou as a private scholar. His biographers mark 1197 as the beginning of his efforts as a historian. Over the next two decades, he completed the *Chronological Record* and the *Diverse Notes*. After completing the second installment of the *Diverse Notes* in 1216, he compiled several works of classical commentary, perhaps for instructional use in the Chengdu academies, where he apparently taught from time to time.[15]

During this period, he also compiled an enormous work on the contemporaneous history of Sichuan. Entitled *An Account of the Western Frontier from 1201 through 1221* (*Xichui taiding lu* 西陲泰定錄), a thirteenth-century bibliography described the work in ninety *juan* as divided between an initial section in thirty-seven *juan* that chronicled, from 1201 through 1211, the origins and aftermath of the Wu Xi 吳曦 (d. 1206) rebellion, followed by a continuation that brought the narrative up to 1221. Li used a tabular format similar to Sima Qian's tables in the *Grand Scribe's Records* that enabled him to align local events in Sichuan with policy pronouncements from the court in Lin'an. The work was probably never printed, since not even fragments survive. One purpose seems to have been to establish a historical record of the conduct of local officials during the rebellion, to distinguish between those who had remained loyal to the Song and those who had not. At any rate, Li Xinchuan's *Account of the Western Frontier* demonstrates his concern for the history of Sichuan and for his homeland's larger role in the Song empire.[16]

In 1225, Cui Yuzhi 崔與之 (1158–1239), Cao Yanyue 曹彥約 (1157–1228), Xu Yi, Wei Liaoweng, and eventually a total of twenty-three officials supported his appointment to court as part of a recruitment drive for new talent following the ascension of Emperor Lizong in 1224.[17] This strong support derived from Li Xinchuan's already established reputation as a historian both in Sichuan and empire-wide.[18] He arrived in Lin'an in 1226, aged sixty, and was appointed

---

[13] Li Xingchuan passed the *jinshi* in 1211; Li Xinchuan was eventually awarded the degree by imperial decree in 1226; see Fu Xuancong, *Song dengkeji kao*, 1169, 1290, 1448.

[14] Lai Kehong, *Li Xinchuan shiji zhuzuo biannian*, 50–51.

[15] Wang Deyi, "Li Xiuyan xiansheng nianpu," 6732; "Li Xinchuan zhushu kao," 6771–74.

[16] Chen Zhensun, *Zhizhai shulu jieti*, 5.158; *Chaoye zaji, yi*, 9.653; Wang Deyi, "Li Xinchuan zhushu kao," 6785.

[17] Wei Liaoweng, *Heshan xiansheng daquan wenji*, 77.4a; *SS*, 410.12344, 438.12984.

[18] For Li's empire-wide reputation at this time see Li Xiaolong, *Cui Qingxian gong yanxing lu*, 2.12.

proofreader in the Imperial Library, where he began work on the state histories for the post-1127 era, precisely the same period he had treated in the *Chronological Record* and the *Diverse Notes*. He would remain at the Imperial Library for the next seven years. Still a commoner at the time of his appointment, the following year he was granted official status. He was promoted again in 1229 and was conferred the *jinshi* degree in 1231 as part of patronage dispensed in connection with the seventy-fifth birthday of the emperor's mother. The records of the Imperial Library state that his *jinshi* degree resulted from the emperor's appreciation of a memorial he presented at the revolving audience whose "opinions were detailed, clear, and concealed nothing."[19]

He also submitted with Du Zheng 度正 (1190–1231) a memorial in late 1231 advocating changes to the dynastic ancestral temple.[20] However, a censorial indictment forced his return to Sichuan in 1233. The grounds for the indictment are unclear, but may be related to Li's political advocacy for *daoxue*. As early as 1211, his younger brother, Li Daochuan, who died in 1217, had proposed including the Northern Song *daoxue* masters for worship as acolytes in the imperial temple.[21] Li Xinchuan returned to the issue in 1233, and requested that Sima Guang, Zhou Dunyi, Shao Yong, Zhang Zai, the Cheng brothers, and Zhu Xi be added as acolytes, but his request was denied.[22] The previous year Li had recommended that the emperor recruit his friend Li Fan 李燔 (1164–1233), whom Li praised as the pre-eminent surviving disciple of Zhu Xi, to serve as imperial tutor. The emperor approved the idea, but the appointment was not forthcoming.[23] The recommendation had a possibly subversive context. After a successful career in provincial administration, Li Fan had gone into reclusion in the 1220s to protest Chief Councilor Shi Miyuan's manipulation of the imperial succession in 1224. Since Shi Miyuan was still in power in 1233, Li's recommendation could possibly be construed as an attack on the chief councilor. Li Xinchuan's negative opinion of Shi Miyuan appears in the 1239 *Record of the Way and Its Fate*, and his conflicts with Shi's nephew, Shi Songzhi, would complicate the historian's last years in Lin'an.

In 1233, however, the court, apparently anxious it should not waste Li's talents as a historian, ordered that he report to the Sichuan provincial administration in Chengdu and work on updating the *State Compendium*. As we have discussed above in Chapter 1, he remained in Sichuan until 1237 when the Mongol incursions forced his permanent relocation to the east. He returned to court as assistant director of the Imperial Library in 1238/3 and resumed work on the *Four Restoration Courts State History (Zhongxing Sichao guoshi* 中興

---

[19] *SS*, 41.794; anonymous, *Nan Song guan'ge xulu*, 6.227.   [20] *SS*, 41.795.
[21] For the text see Li Xinchuan, *Daoming lu*, 8.94–96; for a synopsis see Chaffee, "The Historian as Critic," 317–18.
[22] *SS*, 429.12769.   [23] *SS*, 430.12784–85.

四朝國史) and the corresponding veritable records. Later in the year, he was promoted to full director of the Library.[24] He brought with him to Lin'an two younger scholars, Gao Side and Mou Zicai, whom he had recruited in Sichuan to assist on the *State Compendium*. In an apparent push to complete the state history, Li also recruited an additional four scholars to the Imperial Library, Qian Shi 錢時 (1175–1244), Zhao Ruteng 趙汝騰 (d. 1266), Liu Hanbi 劉漢弼 (*jinshi* 1216), and Xu Yuanjie 徐元杰 (1194–1245), to work on the project. All were younger scholars with *daoxue* inclinations and antagonistic to Shi Songzhi.[25]

As in the time of Li Tao, Li Xinchuan and the other historians at the Imperial Library became embroiled in political struggles at the highest levels of government. The impetus to bring Li Xinchuan back to the history office probably came from Cui Yuzhi, who had been among Li's early supporters and who assumed duties as nominal chief councilor following the dissolution of the pro-*daoxue* Duanping administration in 1236. In 1238/10, in an effort to forestall Shi Songzhi from following in his uncle's footsteps, Gao Side memorialized the emperor and advocated a dual councilorship with divided duties.[26] The effort achieved little except the enmity of Shi, who in 1239/1 became chief councilor. Cui Yuzhi left office in 1239/6 and was dead by the end of the year. Within another year, Shi Songzhi indeed became sole chief councilor, a post he held until the end of 1244.

Li Xinchuan's only surviving memorial dates from 1240/7 and is preserved in his *Song History* biography. In the summer of 1240 a famine, exacerbated by a decade of warfare against the Jurchen and the Mongols on the northern border, had reduced the population of Lin'an to cannibalism. Li's memorial attributed the famine to the government's failure to plan for the aftermath of these military operations. Government hoarding of grain, an influx of refugees, and failure to remit taxes have caused resentment among the population to rise to dangerous levels. Corrupt local officials do nothing to prohibit the spread of war profiteering and banditry. The failure of the monarch and his councilors to develop consistent strategies, to curtail opulence and luxury at court, and to accept forthright criticism have further increased popular resentment. Li urged the monarch to rid himself of self-serving advisers and so open the way for honest suggestions to stem the famine.[27] Shortly after submitting this memorial

---

[24] *SS*, 42.816; anonymous, *Nan Song guan'ge xulu*, 7.248, 254, 9.359.

[25] Anonymous, *Nan Song guan'ge xulu*, 7.286, 8.303, 320, 332, 9.350, 355; *SS*, 407.12293, 409.12322, 411.12355, 424.12653, 12660; Wang Deyi, "Li Xiuyan xiansheng nianpu," 6757–60.

[26] *SS*, 409.12322–23. For Shi Songzhi see Richard L. Davis, *Court and Family in Sung China*, 142–57.

[27] *SS*, 438.12984–85. Fu Zengxiang, *Songdai Shuwen jicun*, 77.1a–b, cites this memorial from Huang Huai and Yang Shiqi, *Lidai mingchen zouyi*, 310.6a–7a. The Ming editors follow the confusing text of Li's *Song History* biography and misdate the text to 1236. This error has been

and before work on the state history project was complete, the Censorate again indicted Li, and he was permitted to return to his new home in Huzhou 湖州 with a sinecure.[28]

Shi Songzhi became sole councilor in the last month of 1240 and took immediate steps to defuse the historical and cultural issues that fueled his political opposition. A month later, in 1241/1, the court issued an edict that confirmed the *daoxue* claim of direct inheritance from Mencius; enshrined Zhou Dunyi, Zhang Zai, the Cheng brothers, and Zhu Xi as acolytes in the Confucian temple; and removed Wang Anshi from that status.[29] Shi Songzhi also moved quickly to complete, and put his own stamp upon, the official version of recent history. With Li Xinchuan now gone, he ordered Gao Dingzi 高定子 (*jinshi* 1202), an uncle of Gao Side, to submit the basic annals of the *Four Restoration Courts State History* and the *Ningzong Veritable Records*, and the elder Gao immediate complied.[30] Shi Songzhi's choice of Gao Dingzi was politically astute. In 1238, Li Xinchuan had tasked Gao's nephew, his top assistant Gao Side, to finalize the veritable records of the Guangzong and Ningzong reigns (the period 1190–1224), the most recent and therefore most politically sensitive part of the project.

Gao Side's biography in the *Song History* writes that after his uncle submitted the manuscript Shi Songzhi rewrote the conclusion of the Ningzong portion to hide the complicity of his uncle Shi Miyuan in deposing the Crown Prince and installing an obscure kinsman as the future Emperor Lizong.[31] Gao Side, Du Fan 杜範 (1182–1245), and others protested the revision, but the work had already been formally submitted. The biography writes that Li Xinchuan retained a copy of Gao's original manuscript and added the sparse annotation "drafted by Mr. Gao, formerly of the court history office," in order to register his opposition to the changes.[32] Despite these tensions, Gao Dingzi, who seems to have retained good relations with both sides, requested that Li Xinchuan be returned to his position to work on the remaining monographic and biographic sections of the state history, but nothing seems to have come of the request. On the contrary, Li Xinchuan's sinecure was removed, and he went into official retirement the following year. He died in Huzhou in 1244, aged seventy-seven.[33]

---

corrected in Lai Kehong, *Li Xinchuan shiji zhuzuo biannian,* 210–11. For a detailed synopsis of the memorial see Chaffee, "The Historian as Critic," 328–29. Li's criticism is restrained compared to other memorials on the issue but shares many of the same themes. See the memorial of Du Fan at *SS*, 407.12283–85, translated in Davis, *Court and Family in Sung China*, 131–32.

[28] *SS*, 438.12985.
[29] For a fuller discussion see Li and Hartman, "A Newly Discovered Inscription," 447–48.
[30] *Songshi quanwen*, 33.2745; *Yuhai*, 46.51a.   [31] Chaffee, *Branches of Heaven*, 203–5.
[32] *SS*, 40912322–23; Cai Chongbang, *Songdai xiushi zhidu yanjiu*, 138–39.
[33] For a fuller account of Li's later career see Hartman, "Li Hsin-ch'uan and the Historical Image," 320–28.

Corrections of Errors in Old Accounts

In the preface to the *Diverse Notes* of 1202 Li Xinchuan remembered visiting the court at Lin'an with his father twenty years earlier, where he saw the genealogical archives and overheard the policy discussions of senior councilors. Returning to Sichuan, he grew to lament that the post-1127 history of the dynasty remained fragmented and inchoate. He resolved to remedy this deficiency and began to gather the source materials that would eventually comprise the *Chronological Record* and the *Diverse Notes*.[34] The preface to the second collection of the *Diverse Notes* from 1216 constitutes Li Xinchuan's fullest articulation of his goals as a historian. First, he wished to bring order to the varied and dispersed historical accounts of the Restoration. Second, he wished to complete the lacunae in the official history of the period. And finally, he wished to make the results of his researches accessible as a statecraft resource for policy makers.[35] Li's preface to the *Record of the Way and Its Fate* from 1239 summarizes along similar lines, albeit in more modest and bureaucratic terms, his tasks as an official historian: "It has fallen to me in my lack of talent to assemble old and lost documents since the Restoration, to record and copy them in chronological order, and to present them successively to the proper authorities."[36]

Each of these three goals may be conceived as one stage or process in Li's overall historiographical operation. The first stage entails verifying matters of fact in the historical record and correcting both inadvertent errors and intentional distortions. The second stage consists of organizing the now established facts into small, but definitive, narratives. In the final stage, these narratives are organized into larger patterns of meaning; in short, a discourse that Li hoped would assist statecraft thinkers and political leaders. Each of Li's surviving works can be assigned a relative position and function in this threefold schema. The *Corrections of Errors* corresponds to the first stage, as does much of the genuine commentary in the *Chronological Record*. The main text of the *Chronological Record* and the *Diverse Notes* reflect the second stage of narrative building. And lastly, both the *Chronological Record* and the *Diverse Notes*, but especially the *Record of the Way and Its Fate*, also display the final stage, in which Li organized his narratives into a higher-order discourse that projected his own political values.

As John Chaffee astutely observed, Li Xinchuan "is ever concerned with particulars."[37] At first glance, the *Corrections of Errors in Old Accounts* seems the slightest of Li's surviving works. Its entries appear to display none of the

---

[34] *Chaoye zaji, jia*, 3.
[35] *Chaoye zaji, yi*, 481; Nie Lehe, "*Jianyan yilai xinian yaolu* yanjiu," 10.
[36] *Daoming lu*, preface, 1; Hartman, "Li Hsin-ch'uan and the Historical Image," 328.
[37] Chaffee, "The Historian as Critic," 317.

higher-order and second- and third-stage historiographical processes of his other works. Yet the work provides an important window onto the most fundamental of Li's historiographical operations – the verification of fact and the elimination of errors in source texts. Wang Deyi framed the work as a harbinger of Qing dynasty evidential scholarship (*kaozheng* 考證), the proximate origin of the modern Chinese textually based criticism of historical sources.[38] *Corrections of Errors*, originally in fifteen *juan*, was printed in Sichuan around 1210. By the early Ming, no complete copy had survived, and the Qing academicians recovered only 140 entries from the *Yongle Encyclopedia*. They then organized these surviving entries into the four *juan* of the present *Siku quanshu* edition.[39]

Most extracts concern Northern Song, but some entries in the fourth *juan* concern early Southern Song. Each entry begins with a passage quoted from a named source, followed by Li's justification for his corrections. The following passage illustrates the format and flavor of the entries.

"In 974, one ordered the Secretariat and the Bureau of Military Affairs to compile records of current administration and forward them to the court historian." (This is from *Shilin's Table Talk* by Ye Mengde.)

I comment: According to the *Veritable Records*, on 1006/5/5, at the request of Wang Qinruo and Chen Yaosou, the Bureau of Military Affairs first established its records of current administration, which were sent monthly to the Secretariat. During the Dazhong xiangfu period [in 1012/6], it was further ordered that these *Records* be sent directly to the history office. The practice did not begin in 974. Ye is wrong.[40]

The quoted sentence occurs in a long account by Ye Mengde 葉夢得 (1077–1148) of the development of court historiography from the early Tang to his own day.[41] The issue concerns precisely when the Bureau of Military Affairs began to send a monthly record of its activities to the court history office. In Ye Mengde's day, both the Secretariat and the BMA sent their own records independently, and Li Xinchuan apparently believes Ye has mistakenly projected this practice back to 974.[42] Li's conclusion that the practice began only in 1006 has two implications. First, the *Long Draft* records an earlier proposal from the Secretariat in 989/10 that the BMA forward its records to the Secretariat for incorporation into the Secretariat's account of its own actions, thus producing a unified record that could then be sent to the history office. Li Tao states that this request was so ordered and comments that "the BMA

---

[38] Wang Deyi, "Li Xinchuan zhushu kao," 6782–85.
[39] See Ji Yun et al., *Qinding Siku quanshu zongmu*, 88.1168; and Balazs and Hervouet, *A Sung Bibliography*, 107–8, which states erroneously that the work is not in the *Siku quanshu*.
[40] Li Xinchuan, *Jiuwen zhengwu*, 1.6.   [41] Ye Mengde, *Shilin yanyu*, 2.24–25.
[42] At this time, the historian Hu Meng suggested a similar procedure, but implementation was not successful. See *SHY, zhiguan*, 6.30a; and Kurz, "The Consolidation of Official Historiography during the Early Northern Song Dynasty," 14–17.

records of current administration probably starts here."[43] Li Xinchuan has reasoned, however, that if Wang Qinruo 王欽若 (962–1025) and Chen Yaosou 陳堯叟 (961–1017), who headed the BMA in 1006, requested permission to submit their own records, then BMA records were probably not, despite the 989 edict, submitted regularly before 1006. In short, Li distinguishes between when an edict ordered an action and when that action actually began. Second, Wang and Chen assumed control of the BMA on 1006/2/26, only two months before their request, and ran the agency together until 1017.[44] They were thus also responsible for the second action whereby the BMA bypassed the Secretariat and forwarded its records directly to the history office. Clearly, the pair, who built the BMA into an administrative center on par with the Secretariat, seized an opportunity to control the historical narrative of their activity at the BMA. Both actions in 1006 and in 1012 therefore document the rising importance of the BMA and Wang Qinruo in the political structure of early Song.

This entry is typical of many in the *Corrections of Errors*. Li Xinchuan uses the precise dating of official historiography, in this case the *Veritable Records*, to correct dating errors in private accounts. This focus on careful dating, however, is not gratuitous, but rather is a prelude to the Sichuan school of historiography's preoccupation, as in this entry, with the historical "origins" of a given institution or administrative operation. And this preoccupation, in turn, reflects the importance of precedent in Song political culture, a topic we will discuss in detail below. In short, Li rarely corrects a date for its own sake, but to highlight a larger historical implication that the corrected date then brings into sharper focus. For example, a *Long Draft* entry under 1054/8/13 records the conferral of academic office upon the former chief councilor Liang Shi 梁適 (1000–1069), whom a censorial indictment had forced from office the previous month. In his commentary, Li Tao quotes the accusation of Mei Yaochen 梅堯臣 (1002–1060) in his notebook, *The Blue Cloud Stallion* (*Biyun xia* 碧雲騢), that Liang, whom Mei's narrative maintains had close ties to court eunuchs, had obtained this appointment via an inner-court directive, namely a shortcut around the regular appointment process. Li Tao found this assessment too harsh and so excluded this detail from his main-text narrative in the *Long Draft*. In his correction, however, Li Xinchuan notes that Liang's academic reappointment came only thirty-nine days after his dismissal. This short period of time violated the precedent that chief councilors dismissed from office via censorial indictments could not retain or soon regain academic office. He cites three Renzong-era cases of former chief councilors who waited an average of ten years before reappointment, and therefore concludes that there must be

---

[43] *Changbian*, 30.691; also *SHY, zhiguan*, 6.30b.
[44] Liang Tianxi, *Song Shumi yuan zhidu*, 956–59.

some substance to Mei Yaochen's charge.[45] In this entry, Li invoked the historical force of precedent to argue that, despite Li Tao's reservations, Liang's appointment must have been irregular and therefore proof of his ties to court eunuchs.

In a letter he wrote to Li Xinchuan in the mid-1220s, Liu Zai 劉宰 (1166–1239) recalled his reaction upon first reading a copy of the *Corrections of Errors* that Li Daochuan had given him a decade earlier. Unlike a modern reader, who may likely find many of Li's corrections mere nitpicking, Liu Zai marveled at how Li's erudition enabled him not only to punch holes in commonly accepted truisms about the dynasty's past but also to uncover its more deeply guarded secrets.[46] For example, as we shall see in our examination of the *Song History* in Chapter 5, the motif that Emperor Zhenzong was given to opulence had already by Southern Song become such a truism. An early touchstone passage occurred in Sima Guang's *Su River Records* where Wang Dan 王旦 (957–1016) asked Li Hang 李沆 (947–1004) his opinion of the just-concluded peace treaty with the Khitan. Li replied, "It's fine, but I now fear the emperor's inclination toward opulence will grow." Wang disagreed, but later in Zhenzong's reign remarked, "I must admit that Li Hang was prescient." Li Xinchuan's correction to this passage remarked tersely, "According to the *State History*, peace with the Khitan was achieved in 1005/12. At this time, Li Hang had been dead for some time." Li Hang died in 1004/7, almost a year and a half before the treaty was concluded.[47]

In addition to this entry on the *Su River Records*, the existing *Corrections of Errors* contains sixteen entries that correct or develop passages from Li Tao's commentary to the *Long Draft*. Most other entries comment on privately compiled works in the notebook (*biji*) genre; the largest number, sixteen entries, correct *Waving the Duster* by Wang Mingqing 王明清 (1127–?), a work that also served as a major source for the *Chronological Record*. In short, although fragments from an originally minor work, the present text of the *Corrections of Errors* demonstrates that Li Xinchuan, ever concerned with particulars, cast a wide and nonpartisan net in his efforts to bring order to the Song past.

The *Chronological Record*

Shortly after the first copy of the *Chronological Record* arrived about 1212 in the capital, Lou Yue 樓鑰 (1137–1213) acquired a copy from the Imperial

---

[45] Li Xinchuan, *Jiuwen zhengwu*, 2.24; *Changbian*, 176.4272; Mei Yaochen, *Biyun xia*, 4.
[46] Liu Zai, *Mantang ji*, 10.19a–20b; *QSW*, 299:6827.270–71.
[47] Li Xinchuan, *Jiuwen zhengwu*, 1.12; Sima Guang, *Sushui jiwen*, 6.120. Li Hang and Wang Dan served together on the Council of State from 1001 until Li's death in 1004. Other versions of the story do not mention the peace treaty and thus avoid the chronological inconsistency. See Wang Pizhi, *Shengshui yantan lu*, 2.13.

Library, read it to the end, and remarked, "now I understand that the requitals from Heaven make no error."[48] This cryptic phrase was not only elegant flattery but also a critical assessment that placed the *Record* in a historiographical mainstream that prioritized a core function of the Chinese historian – to assist Heaven as the ultimate source of moral authority in rendering judgments on human actions. The phrase "the requitals of Heaven" comes from a pivotal chapter in *The Grand Scribe's Records* where Sima Qian questioned the impartiality of the "Way of Heaven," or "divine justice" (*tiandao* 天道): why do the virtuous suffer in privation, while the evil prosper and rule the world? Sima did not question the reality of this injustice. But he did claim for history, and for himself, the ability, by accurately describing this reality, to bring clarity to what the vagaries of Heaven often leave murky.[49] Thus, Lou Yue, one of the *Record*'s earliest and most informed readers, both compared Li Xinchuan to Sima Qian and saw his work as a realization of the highest ideals of Chinese historiography.

Before examining why the *Record* elicited such high praise, it may be useful to consider how the politics of the decade prior to 1212 affected its composition. Li began work on the *Record* during the Qingyuan proscription of "false learning," which began in 1196/8 and lasted through 1202/2. As soon as the proscription ended, Han Tuozhou imposed tighter restrictions on the private writing and dissemination of historical works. These restrictions were imposed because reports came from the border that works on Song history were being smuggled to the Jurchen. At issue were privately printed versions of historical works completed over the past twenty years: the *Long Draft*, Wang Cheng's *Eastern Capital Miscellany*, and the histories by Xiong Ke 熊克 (1118–1190). The court banned the printing of these works and ordered that copies already in circulation be submitted to the court history office for review. In 1202/7, any work deemed to contain "matters offensive to the state body" (*shi gan guoti* 事干國體) was ordered destroyed.[50] Li's own preface to the second installment of the *Diverse Notes*, dated 1216, states that because of the 1202 ban he feared retribution from the Han Tuozhou administration. He therefore discontinued work on the *Diverse Notes* and resumed work, which he had begun in 1197, on the supposedly less interpretive *Chronological Record*.[51]

---

[48] *Gongkui ji*, 60.9a; *QSW*, 265:5971.59.

[49] Sima Qian, *Shiji*, 62.2124–26, the biography of Bo Yi and Shu Qi; see Nienhauser, *The Grand Scribe's Records*, 7:1–8, and especially the "translators note" at 7. For *tiandao* as "divine justice," see Qian Zhongshu, *Guanzhui bian*, 1:306.

[50] *SHY, xingfa*, 2.132a–b, 132b–133a. Li Xinchuan compares the 1202 ban to Qin Gui's ban on private histories; see *Chaoye zaji, jia*, 6.149–50; cf. Poon, "Books and Printing in Sung China," 60–61.

[51] *Chaoye zaji, yi*, 481. This preface also compares the 1202 ban on private histories to the Qin Gui-era inquisitions and notes the fate of Li Guang and his family, who were punished for compiling a private history; see Hartman, "The Making of a Villain," 76–77, 99–102.

Scholars concur that Li had completed an initial draft of the *Record* by late 1205.[52] The murder of Han Tuozhou in 1207/11 and the advent of a new administration under Shi Miyuan, in which Li's younger brother, Li Daochuan, actively participated, created the political opening for submission of the work to court. Yang Fu 楊輔 (*jinshi* 1166), then Sichuan defense commissioner, ordered Li Xinchuan to prepare the work for submission; and Yang himself took a copy of the revised *Record* with him when he departed for Lin'an in 1208/7. Li Daochuan took another copy with him when he left for Lin'an in 1209. In 1210/9, following a suggestion from Xu Yi, ten court historians jointly requested that Li Daochuan submit his copy "so that it may serve as an aid to the composition of the state history."[53] As we have seen in Chapter 1, Xu Yi was a Sichuan native and a close associate of Wei Liaoweng, with whom Xu had worked in the court history office several years earlier when their Sichuan colleague Zhang Congzu had completed the *Comprehensive State Compendium*.

Thus, both the *Record* and the first installment of the *Diverse Notes* were composed during periods when the Han Tuozhou court monitored intellectual orientation and especially the writing of history. Li Xinchuan's treatment of Qin Gui in the *Record* may serve as a prime example to illustrate the interaction between contemporaneous politics and the work's composition. Writing in 1198, only one year after completion of the first installment of the *Gaozong Veritable Records* (*Gaozong shilu* 高宗實錄), Wang Mingqing lamented the pro-Qin Gui tenor of the court's official history of the Gaozong years. He noted that after Qin's death in 1155, although Gaozong had dismissed his most extreme partisans, the ensuing spirit of political reconciliation had prevented an accurate account of Qin Gui's administration in the first official history of the period, the *Gaozong Sagacious Administration* (*Gaozong shengzheng*) of 1166. According to Wang Mingqing, Qin's adherents still controlled the court history office three decades later; and the ongoing *Gaozong Veritable Records* continued to conceal the nefarious aspects of his rule.[54]

Li Xinchuan thus faced a dilemma: an accurate portrayal of Qin Gui in the *Record* presented the danger that readers would take his depiction of Qin as a historical type for Han Tuozhou and thus read the *Record* as an attack on the Han administration. Thus, if he corrected the biased official historical record by inserting details of Qin's partisanship, he risked drawing Han Tuozhou's scrutiny over private history writing upon himself and the *Record*. However,

[52] Kong Xue, "*Jianyan yilai xinian yaolu* zhushu shijian kao," 53–56.
[53] *Yaolu*, appendix, 3979, reprints this memorial; *SS*, 397.12096, 436.12945. This paragraph is based on the detailed analysis in Liang Taiji, "*Xinian yaolu, Chaoye zaji* de qiyi jishu ji qi chengyin," 200–5.
[54] Wang Mingqing, *Yuzhao xinzhi*, 4.65. For excellent details on Li Xinchuan's revisionist take on Qin Gui see Yan Yongcheng, *Nan Song shixue yanjiu*, 240–47.

Han's decision to invade the North altered this dynamic. As lead-up to the invasion, in 1206/4 Han revoked Qin Gui's patent of nobility and changed his posthumous name to "erroneous and vile" (*miuchou* 謬醜).[55] Of course, this move was intended to buttress Han's impending reversal of Qin's non-aggression pact with the Jin, but the downgrade also opened the door for a more nuanced historical assessment of Qin Gui's rule.

Although largely complete by 1205, the *Record* was hastily revised between Han's death in 1207/11 and 1208/7 when the first clear copy left Sichuan for Lin'an. Recent scholarship reveals that Li Xinchuan undertook these revisions to insulate the work against charges that it might "contain matters offensive to the state body," the same standard that Han had applied in his 1202 injunction against private histories.[56] A close reading of the *Record*'s commentary demonstrates that during this revision period Li made changes to passages that touched upon three sensitive areas. The first two involved offenses to the imperial dignity (demeaning references to the imperial person and diplomatic language that reflected negatively on Song).

But the third and largest number of changes concerned Qin Gui. Li made careful revisions and inserted new material to document the nefarious qualities of the Qin administration.[57] We will examine one of these passages in detail below. For example, he added to the *Record* at this time his narrative of Qin Gui's last great inquisition against Zhang Jun and fifty-three other officials, a tale that became a major feature of Qin's subsequent biography.[58] The 1207–1208 transition from Han Tuozhou's autocracy to the reform administration under Shi Miyuan both provided the political backdrop for these revisions and enabled Li to refashion the historical significance of the Qin Gui years. Before 1207, a full account of the Qin Gui years would have been read as an attack on the Han Tuozhou regime. After 1208, the same account remained a strong indictment of autocracy but could also be read as a caution to the new administration to adhere to its professed program of political reform. Yet, as I have explained elsewhere, Li's treatment of Qin Gui in the *Chronological Record* constitutes a balanced presentation of his historical role when compared to the *daoxue* histories of the mid-thirteenth century.[59]

---

[55] *SS*, 473.13765.

[56] Since the Northern Song, this phrase encompassed negative references to imperial affines (*Changbian*, 169.4069). Han Tuozhou was himself an imperial affine, his mother being the younger sister of Emperor Gaozong's Empress Wu, who lived until 1197. Han's uncle, Wu Yi, was also married to Qin Gui's granddaughter.

[57] Kong Xue, "*Jianyan yilai xinian yaolu* zhushu shijian kao," 55–56.

[58] Liang Taiji, "*Xinian yaolu, Chaoye zaji* de qiyi jishu ji qi chengyin," 195–96. For other passages relating to Qin Gui, see *Yaolu*, 124.2334, 149.2816–17, 150.2841, 154.2907, 155.2505, 164.2933, and 165.3141–42.

[59] Hartman, "The Making of a Villain," 86.

After the murder of Han Tuozhou in 1207, a swift transition to the new administration under Shi Miyuan prompted extensive revisions to the historical record. These revisions affected not only those records for the immediate 1195–1207 period, but also entailed a new focus for the existing and already compiled history of the earlier 1127–1194 period. The compilation of a "state history" for the Gaozong reign had been ordered in 1202/2, only days prior to the ban on private histories.[60] Given other priorities, the project gained little immediate traction. But Li Xinchuan's frenzied 1208 revisions to the draft *Record*, as well as the urgency of the new regime's historians to acquire his work "as an aid to compiling the state history," suggest that these historians saw in the revised *Record* a potential handbook to refashion the existing historical compilations – the *Daily Calendar* and the *Veritable Records* of Gaozong's reign – into a more suitable post-Han Tuozhou version of Southern Song's foundational period. During his years in Lin'an in the 1220s and 1230s, Li Xinchuan would personally continue these efforts, but under very different political circumstances.[61]

That the surviving *Chronological Record* covers only the reign of Gaozong, whereas the surviving *Diverse Notes* encompass material that spans the three reigns of Emperors Gaozong, Xiaozong, and Guangzong, gives rise to the question whether Li Xinchuan ever completed his chronological history through 1194. The publisher's advertisement preceding the Song edition of the *Diverse Notes* reprints two documents from the court history office, dated 1223, that order the provincial government at Longzhou to copy the Xiaozong and Guangzong portions of Li's *Chronological Record* as part of the court's ongoing revisions to the veritable records for these two reigns.[62] The bibliographer Chen Zhensun notes that Li completed the Xiaozong and Guangzong portions of the *Record* but that the Mongol invasions of Sichuan had rendered the work inaccessible.[63] Given that the court ordered Li himself to work on the history of these reigns after his 1226 arrival in Lin'an, one may plausibly conclude that he had at least completed draft chronologies for these periods, but that they were never printed in Sichuan or elsewhere.[64]

[60] *SS*, 38.731.   [61] Hartman, "Li Hsin-ch'uan and the Historical Image," 320–28.

[62] *Yaolu*, appendix, 3982–84; Cai Chongbang, *Songdai xiushi zhidu yanjiu*, 107–9. The documents are signed by nine history office officials whose titles match those recorded for 1223 in anonymous, *Nan Song guan'ge xulu*, 9.374, 380, 386; one of these was Wei Liaoweng.

[63] *Zhizhai shulu jieti*, 4.120.

[64] Li's student Gao Side probably completed his draft history of the Xiaozong reign; see Lai Kehong, *Li Xinchuan shiji zhuzuo biannian*, 159–160. The contentious debate in China over Li's original title for the *Chronological Record* – was it the *Gaozong Chronological Record* (*Gaozong xinian yaolu*) or the *Chronological Record since 1127* (*Jianyan yilai xinian yaolu*)? – addresses the question of Li's initial plan for the scope of his work. Did he initially intend to write a history only of Gaozong's reign or a history that would extend from 1127 to his own day? A recent summary of this debate leans toward the latter hypothesis; see Hu Kun, editorial comment, *Yaolu*, 2–7.

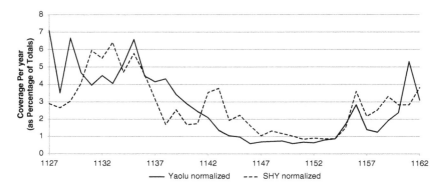

Figure 3.1 Coverage per year: *Chronological Record* versus *Recovered Draft Compendium*

Figure 3.1 plots the relative coverage of the *Chronological Record* against that of the *Recovered Draft of the State Compendium*.[65] As might be expected, the overall contours of the coverage are similar in both works. The variations, however, show how Li Xinchuan both adjusted to his own purpose and worked around Qin Gui's manipulation of the primary source base. Li devotes outsize coverage to four periods: (1) the early formative years of the Restoration (1127–1130), (2) the years of successful Song consolidation (1133–1136), (3) the immediate post-Qin Gui years (1156–1157), and (4) the advent of the Jin war and the imperial transition (1161–1162). Coverage of the second and third periods tracks the primary base, but Li has inserted added emphasis on the first and the last periods. This coverage of the early period lays down an in-depth account of the founding principles of the Restoration as a departure from the corruption of late Northern Song. Coverage of the latter period details not only the political convulsions caused by the Jin invasion of 1161 but also literati efforts to build a post-Qin Gui administration. Alternatively, the inversion in coverage midway through the Qin Gui years from 1137 through 1155 shows Li Xinchuan's commitment to the administration of Zhao Ding 趙鼎 (1085–1147) and the arguments against Qin Gui's peace policy. The decline in coverage after

---

[65] Data for the *Recovered Draft* is based on the number of entries per year, as explained in Chapter 1 above. Data for the *Chronological Record* use the same methodology as that for the *Long Draft* in Chapter 2 above and are based on the number of pages devoted to each year in the Zhonghua edition of 2013. The first five *juan* of the *Chronological Record* contain entries prior to 1127, and these have been omitted in order to maintain chronological consistency with the *Recovered Draft*. On the other hand, Gaozong's rule ended on 1162/6/11. The *Yongle Encyclopedia* completes the year 1162 by adding material from the *Zhongxing shengzheng*, and the *Siku* editors have retained this material. This graph also includes this material in order to maintain chronological consistency for 1162 with the *Recovered Draft*.

the 1142 peace indicates Li's disinclination to chronicle in detail the cultural achievements of Qin's regime.

Facts and Sources

We may recall that the *Chronological Record* is the only one of Li Xinchuan' surviving works that simultaneously manifests all three of the historiographical functions from fact-finding, through the creation of narrative, and finally to the formation of a singular historical discourse. The following treatment of the *Chronological Record* follows this tripartite conception of the work. We begin with an examination of the work's sources in an effort to understand how the *Chronological Record*'s methodology to establish the reliability of facts and events contained in earlier historical accounts resembles the *Corrections of Errors*. As Xu Yi described the book to the court, Li

adopted the *Gaozong Daily Calendar* and the *State Compendium* as his base, then cast a wide net for old lost and scattered documentation. He accepted what he found trustworthy, explicated what he trimmed, and left open what he found doubtful. He then assembled the best accounts, searching for a considered middle between prolixity and terseness, and so composed this book.[66]

Modern scholars have extrapolated from this passage the following principles: (1) unannotated text in the *Record* represents *Daily Calendar* entries that Li has judged unproblematic; (2) annotations explain and justify any changes he has made to the *Daily Calendar*; (3) annotations also record any unresolved doubts about an issue, in which case Li would not include the matter in the main *Record* text; and (4) his narratives of contested events derive from a comparison of all extent sources to arrive at the "best version."[67]

Scholars agree that Li Xinchuan's primary source was the *Gaozong Daily Calendar* (*Gaozong rili*), completed in 1176. Understanding the origin and nature of this primary official source is key to understanding Li Xinchuan's historiographical challenges, his solutions, and the magnitude of his achievement. As we have seen in the Introduction, maintaining the daily calendar was a primary responsibility of the court history office. A list, codified in the 1160s, of items to be included confirms the calendar's character as a chronicle of daily court activities, understood as the activities of the emperor and his senior officials. The focus was on two general categories of events: those relating to policy formation and implementation, and personnel actions for senior and mid-level officials. To be included were all major ritual actions; all documents resulting from court audiences either presented in person or submitted in writing along with any imperial responses, formal edicts and inner directives,

---

[66] *Yaolu*, appendix, 3980; *QSW* 304: 6937.27–28.
[67] Kong Xue, "*Jianyan yilai xinian yaolu* qucai kao," 46–47.

amnesties, and all requests from agencies to deviate from their established protocols; functional appointments and personnel actions for officials above stipulated grades; special appointments for meritorious conduct; and finally, biographical information on senior officials entered under the date of their deaths.[68] Since all of these were routine, continuing court functions, one might expect a relatively even chronological coverage across the *Gaozong Daily Calendar*.

However, the discussion of the *Recovered Draft of the State Compendium* in Chapter 1 revealed the uneven depth of historical coverage over the course of the Gaozong reign, from 1127 through 1162, as portrayed in Figure 1.1. This unevenness derives from the politics behind the compilation of the *Gaozong Daily Calendar*.[69] Despite the rapid political turnover and military chaos of the early Gaozong years, his advisers appear to have kept up the court's historiographical operation; and Xu Du, who worked in the history office during the late 1130s, claimed that the primary sources for the first decade of Gaozong's rule, especially after the court's return from the sea in 1130/4, were complete.[70] He goes on to explain, however, that after Qin Gui attained power as sole councilor in 1138, he purged and rewrote these archives to remove any negative reference to himself or his supporters. In 1140/2, Qin Gui consolidated all historiographical operations in the Imperial Library and placed his son Qin Xi 秦熺 in charge. Under Qin Xi's direction, an updated *Daily Calendar since 1127 (Jianyan yilai rili* 建炎以來日歷), in 590 *juan*, was prepared and submitted in 1143/2.[71] In addition, Qin Gui suspended compilation of the contemporaneous daily calendar, a hiatus that lasted until his death in 1155. A diarist newly appointed in 1156/3 reported that the office had not been staffed since 1143, and that no diary had been maintained after that date.[72]

Two imperatives guided Qin Xi's monopoly of court historiography: to massage the historical record of Qin Gui and his administration, and to justify his major policy incentive to achieve a negotiated peace with the Jin. The *Daily Calendar since 1127*, for example, contained an appendix that lauded the return of Gaozong's mother from Jin captivity as a result of the peace treaty of 1142. The historical record after 1138, therefore, was not empty, but consisted, in Xu Du's opinion, "of nothing but flattery from his partisans that does not deserve to be transmitted as truth to later generations."[73] Efforts began immediately after Qin Gui's death, therefore, on three fronts: to restore some political balance to

---

[68] Chen Kui, *Nan Song guan'ge lu*, 4.39–41.
[69] For a more extended discussion see Hartman, "The Making of a Villain," 68–75.
[70] Wang Mingqing, *Huizhu lu, houlu*, 1.69. For some contradictory evidence see Hartman, "The Making of a Villain," 75 n. 27.
[71] *Yaolu*, 148.2798. Li Xinchuan quotes Xu Du's account in his main text entry on the submission of the *Jianyan yilai rili*, thus signaling his support for Xu's opinion.
[72] *Yaolu*, 172.3287; *SHY, zhiguan*, 2.18b.   [73] Wang Mingqing, *Huizhu lu, houlu*, 1.69.

the existing *Daily Calendar since 1127*, to backfill the 1143–1155 period, and to resume normal court historiographical operations after 1155. The full record of these efforts is too complex to present here.[74] In brief, given the lingering influence of Qin Gui's partisans and the delicate problem of how to present the emperor's own shifting political stances, the results were fragmentary, ambiguous, and unsatisfactory. As late at 1175/7 an official at the Imperial Library reported that the daily calendar was still incomplete and requested additional funds and another call for submission of relevant documents.[75] A year later, and only two months after returning to Lin'an as director of the Imperial Library, Li Tao submitted the finished work in 1,000 *juan*. With a note more of frustration than of humility, the great historian wrote in his memorial of submission,

Seeing that for over three score of years many more than one historian has gathered and joined together this great multiplicity of documents, how could I myself dare to insure they are free from omissions, contradictions, and departures from truth?[76]

Li Tao's reservations were apparently well founded and Li Xinchuan's challenge was formidable. An edict of 1195/1/11 ordering completion of the *Gaozong Veritable Records* noted that the existing history of the post-1142 period, presumably the *Daily Calendar*, was satisfactory and should not be changed.[77]

From the *Chronological Record*'s initial audience until modern times, readers have marveled at the multitude of sources that Li Xinchuan invoked to correct the daily calendar's "departures from truth." At least four scholars have separately tabulated citations in the *Record*'s commentary to determine the total number of these sources.

Table 3.1 summarizes these results, dividing the sources into eight generic categories and listing the number of titles cited in each category. The most frequently cited titles within each of the first three categories are also listed. The first six categories present few problems, since these titles are roughly equivalent to "books" in the modern sense. The categories of "individual literary texts" and "individual documents," however, attempt to account for the many discrete literary compositions and bureaucratic documents that Li cites as individual texts, without attribution to any other source. Many of these documents were perhaps already included in the daily calendar.

---

[74] For an excellent synopsis see Cai Chongbang, *Songdai xiushi zhidu yanjiu*, 45–47. See also Hartman, "The Making of a Villain," 70 n. 15, 73–74, and *Yuhai*, 47.40a–41b.

[75] *SHY, zhiguan*, 2.23b.   [76] *Wenxian tongkao*, 194.5640; *QSW* 210:4663.210.

[77] *SHY, zhiguan*, 18.73a–b. The *Gaozong Veritable Records* was submitted in two installments. The 1197 submission covered the years 1127 through 1136; the 1202 submission covered 1137 through 1162. Li Xinchuan's commentary to the *Chronological Record* cites the veritable records only through 1135/4, strongly suggesting he did not yet have access to the second installment. Thus, since Qin Gui assumed power only in 1138, Li's "base text" for the Qin Gui years remained the daily calendar, whose pro-Qin Gui take on post-1142 history the edict of 1195 stipulated was not to be changed.

Table 3.1 Sources cited in Li Xinchuan's autocommentary to the *Chronological Record*[a]

Category and title of work	Number of titles cited	Number of citations
Official histories 官方史書	35	
Gaozong Daily Calendar 高宗日歷		959
Undifferentiated [*State*] *History* 史		114
State Compendium 會要		85
Various *Veritable Records* 實錄		82
Private accounts 私史, 雜史, 筆記	170	
Minor Calendar of the Restoration 中興小歷		526
Remnant History of the Restoration 中興遺史		312
Diary of Zhu Shengfei 秀水閒居錄		109
Waving the Duster 揮麈錄		100
Compendium of Treaties 三朝北夢會編		66
The Recluse's Rustic Records 林泉野記		54
Biographies 傳記, 行狀, 碑銘	150	
Zhao Ding 趙鼎事實		36
Zhang Jun 張浚行狀 (朱熹)		36
Han Shizhong 韓世忠神道碑 (趙雄)		22
Hong Hao 洪浩行述 (洪适)		14
Li Gang 李綱行狀		10
Yue Fei 岳候傳		10
Local histories 地方志	16	
Collected works 文集, 別集	30	
Records of inscribed names 題名	50	
Individual literary texts 單篇詩文	40	
Individual documents 單篇奏狀	285	
Total	776	

[a] This table combines data from Yamauchi Masahiro, "Ken'en irai keinen yōroku chūkoin hemmoku sakuin hika," Nie Lehe, "*Jianyan yilai xinian yaolu* yanjiu," 39–53; Sun Jianmin, "Qushe zhi ji jian jingshen – lüelun *Jianyan yilai xinian yaolu* de qucai," and the list of cited titles in the appended index volume to Li Xinchuan, *Jianyan yilai xinian yaolu* (Shanghai: Shanghai guji chubanshe, 1992), 4: 509–614. The classifications and the number of titles cited follow Sun Jianmin's synopsis of the 1992 index. The number of citations follows the 1992 index or Yamauchi. The number of "individual documents" follows Nie Lehe. As its title indicates, this chart excludes citations in the pseudo-commentary.

Rather than viewing the *Chronological Record* as a commentary upon the *Gaozong Daily Calendar*, it is better to view the *Calendar* as the major sourcebook for the *Record*. On the one hand, Liang Taiji estimates that 90 percent of unannotated main text in the *Record* reproduces *Calendar* entries. On the other hand, annotated main text either corrects entries in the *Calendar* or inserts material from other sources that the *Calendar* did not contain.[78] A simple

[78] "*Jianyan yilai xinian yaolu* qucai kao," 163–66.

comparison of the size of the two works – 1,000 *juan* for the *Calendar* and 200 *juan* for the *Record* – demonstrates that Li Xinchuan has bypassed upwards of 80 percent of the *Calendar*'s contents. While the *Calendar* thus provided the basic structure for the *Record*, Li's attitude toward his official source is highly critical. Nie Lehe has analyzed the 347 citations to the *Calendar* in the first forty-five *juan* of the *Record*. In only seventy-one cases does Li endorse the *Calendar* version of events against contradictions in other sources. One hundred and twenty-three citations criticize the *Calendar* either for its total omissions or for overly brief treatments. Eighty-seven cases dismiss the *Calendar* version as too erroneous to admit into the main text. In the remaining sixty-six cases, Li Xinchuan declines to decide the issue and preserves in the commentary both the *Calendar* and its contradicting source.[79]

To counter the overwhelming court-centered nature of the *Daily Calendar*, Li relied heavily upon primary sources that provided a variety of alternative perspectives. Yamauchi, for example, counted twenty-eight histories of the Jin and pseudo-Qi dynasties or memoirs of officials who served these regimes. Three of the most frequently quoted private histories – the *Remnant History of the Restoration* (*Zhongxing yishi* 中興遺事), the *Compendium of Northern Treaties*, and the *Recluse's Rustic Record* – contained eyewitness accounts of happenings in the provinces, with often sympathetic treatment of military figures that were often at odds with the court. Half of the most-cited biographies (those of Han Shizhong, Hong Hao, and Yue Fei) likewise detail military issues.

By far, the most frequently cited nonofficial source is Xiong Ke's *Minor Calendar of the Restoration* (*Zhongxing xiaoli* 中興小歷). Modern scholars routinely discount the *Minor Calendar* in favor of the *Chronological Record* as an authoritative history of the Gaozong era. But understanding Li's use of the work is key to understanding his goals for the *Record*. Xiong Ke was a literary prodigy, a *jinshi* of 1157, and an eventual partisan of Wang Huai, chief councilor during most of the 1180s. Xiong worked in the Imperial Library from 1180 through 1183, shortly after completion of the *Gaozong Daily Calendar* in 1176.[80] His *Minor Calendar*, essentially a first pass at compressing the official *Daily Calendar*, was completed shortly before the end of Wang Huai's tenure as councilor in 1188. Li Xinchuan criticized the work as "evasive, and neither insightful nor learned," adding that it had never been submitted to court.[81] As we have seen, because Emperor Gaozong lived until 1187, the *Daily*

---

[79] "*Jianyan yilai xinian yaolu* yanjiu," 65; see also Kong Xue, "*Jianyan yilai xinian yaolu* qucai kao," 46.

[80] Anonymous, *Nan Song guan'ge xulu*, 8.291, 325, 9.366; *SS*, 445.13143–44; J. Kurata in Franke, *Sung Biographies*, 417–19.

[81] *Chaoye zaji, jia*, 6.150; the autocommentary at *Yaolu*, 177.3390, accuses Xiong Ke of distorting the *Daily Calendar* to reflect favorably on Wang Huai's father.

Calendar and *Minor Calendar* still reflected a positive appraisal of Qin Gui and of Gaozong's foreign policy, a view widely shared by mainstream, non-*daoxue* officials like Wang Huai. Although he was a Fujian native, Xiong Ke's history represented a non-Sichuan, non-Fujian historiography that reflected the viewpoint of Jiangnan officials, like Qin Gui and Wang Huai, who had prospered from Gaozong's policies. The vast majority of Li Xinchuan's citations to the *Minor Calendar* in his autocommentary therefore not only correct the details of Xiong Ke's botched compression of the *Daily Calendar*, but more importantly build a solid historical foundation for altering the still prevailing positive image of Qin Gui and accordingly the character of the early Restoration period.[82]

The English word "commentary" usually connotes an explanatory appendage to an otherwise theoretically self-contained and intrinsically coherent text. As detailed in the previous chapter, however, Li Tao's methodology of the *Long Draft* created an interactive and symbiotic dialogue between his main-text narratives and his interlinear commentary. Li Xinchuan refined this symbiosis in the *Chronological Record*, and his commentarial text is integral to all three of the work's historiographical operations. Unfortunately, in the course of its transmission, the *Record* acquired successive layers of later commentary that Li Xinchuan did not write. Since no copy of the work survived after the Ming, the Qing academicians reconstructed the present text of the *Chronological Record*, as they did the *Long Draft*, from quotations in the early Ming *Yongle Encyclopedia* into which these Song works had been copied. The Qing scholars noted the discrepancy between Li Xinchuan's original commentary and the subsequent layer, but their reconstruction made no attempt to distinguish between the two. Rather, they themselves added yet an additional layer of commentary.[83]

In the late 1990s three scholars independently established this hybrid nature of the interlinear commentary in the reconstructed text of the *Record* and realized the importance of distinguishing between the various layers in order to better understand the mechanics of Li Xinchuan's methodology and the meaning of the work.[84] These scholars recognized three layers: (1) Li Xinchuan's own commentary, which I call the autocommentary; (2) an additional layer, or layers, acquired sometime during the 200 years between the *Record*'s submission to the court in 1212 and its incorporation into the *Yongle Encyclopedia* in 1407, which I will call the pseudocommentary; and (3) the

---

[82] For an excellent comparison of the *Chronological Record* and the *Minor Calendar* see Yan Yongcheng, *Nan Song shixue yanjiu*, 240–47; also Liang Taiji, "*Jianyan yilai xinian yaolu* qucai kao," 166–70; Hartman, "The Making of a Villain," 75–76; and Balazs and Hervouet, *A Sung Bibliography*, 79–80.

[83] Ji Yun et al., *Qinding Siku quanshu zongmu*, 1:657; reprinted in *Yaolu*, appendix, 3975–76.

[84] Kong Xue, "*Jianyan yilai xinian yaolu* zhuwen bianxi"; Hartman, "The Making of a Villain," 79–86; and Liang Taiji, "*Yaolu* zizhu de neirong fanwei ji qi suo jieshi de xiuzuan tili."

Qing academicians' own comments, which are immaterial to this discussion. These scholars also recognized the distinctive mid-thirteenth-century *daoxue* perspective in the pseudocommentary. We must discount this pseudocommentary when evaluating the *Record* as an example of Li Xinchuan's historiography; but that same material will help to understand the changing intellectual atmosphere in which the *Record* was later received and that led to its eventual demise as a freestanding work. We will therefore reserve discussion of the pseudocommentary until the next chapter, where it more properly belongs.

Li Xinchuan's autocommentary in the *Record* expands upon the methodology established by Sima Guang and Li Tao. As he does in *Corrections of Errors*, Li employs basic "investigation of differences" (*kaoyi*) to refine the factual accuracy of details concerning time, place, person, title, and event. As he explained this procedure in a passage to be examined below, "I remove uncertainty by evaluating incidents together and establish evidence by verifying the times [of the incidents]."[85] Another function of the autocommentary is to provide additional information not written into the main text. For example, Li often provides biographical details of native place and heritage upon an official's first appearance. These notes often identify lesser known scions of powerful Northern Song officials. This information is not gratuitous, but provided readers a sense of the individual's regional and family affiliations, both major factors in Song politics. Another function is to provide a technical breakdown of details summarized in the main text, for example financial statistics or more precise geographical particulars.

Constructing Narratives

Liang Taiji counts sixteen separate functions of the autocommentary.[86] Half of these serve in different ways to make connections between events that are separated in time; in other words, to construct narratives. Like the *Daily Calendar*, the *Record* is a day-by-day chronicle and whenever possible records events under a precise daily date. The autocommentary to many entries, however, makes reference to other related events that have occurred either before or after the primary recorded event. A particular concern is to identify the "ancestor," or original precipitating event, in a sequence of events to which Li has determined the primary event is historically related. The phrase "for the ancestor of this event see [an earlier date]" (*shizu jian* 事祖見 ...) refers backwards in time to a past event. An opposite function, where the autocommentary links the primary event to something in the future, is termed "an anticipative origin," or "foreshadowing" (*zhangben* 張本). Early in the

---

[85] *Yaolu*, 165.3141.   [86] "*Yaolu* zizhu de neirong," 207–27.

Record, when recapping the movements in late 1126 of Prince Kang, the future Emperor Gaozong, Li Xinchuan explained,

the annalistic format should not recollect events that have already been recorded. But in this case, the battles with the Jin and the establishment of Prince Kang's headquarters are all anticipative origins to events after the [1127] Restoration. Therefore, I describe them in detail to complete the beginning and the end [of the story].[87]

Such narrative building techniques seldom occur in Sima Guang or Li Tao, and constitute a major innovation of Li Xinchuan. They are, by contrast, totally absent in Xiong Ke's *Minor Calendar*.

Other autocommentarial functions create narrative links by providing outcomes and dates for requested or suggested administrative actions, by indicating that two events are somehow related (other than as an ancestor or anticipative origin), and by indicating either the known or the suspected cause or impetus for an action. Another autocommentarial function is to earmark unsolved problems for future attention. Often these comments suggest that additional documentation or future research will be necessary to resolve the issue. These comments seem sometimes intended for Li Xinchuan himself, as if he contemplated a future revision, and sometimes intended for his successors, in the hope that future historians would be able to resolve the remaining "contradictions and departures from truth."

At this point, it may be helpful to examine a typical entry and its commentary to illustrate the interaction between the main text and autocommentary in the *Record*. The following entry records as the primary event the death of one Deng Shaomi 鄧紹密 on 1129/2/5:

Fan Qiong, brigadier general for imperial defense and bandit suppression, led his troops from Dongping and arrived at Shouchun. His soldiers seized the prefect, the Senior Compiler in the Hall for Promoting Literature Deng Shaomi, and killed him. Previously, when Fan Qiong reached Shouchun, he marched southward past the city walls. The soldiers manning the ramparts saw his flags and laughed: "This general's never going to kill the foreigners; all he does is march around." When Qiong heard this, he became angry and notified the prefecture to search for those who had taunted him. Shaomi found one soldier, sent him out, and Qiong ordered the man beheaded. When Qiong's troops entered the city to obtain supplies, Shaomi's troops, resentful that their colleague had been beheaded, took up their weapons and drove off Qiong's soldiers. His troops then put on their armor and entered the city, looting and burning. Shaomi was killed by marauding soldiers. Zhao Xuzhi, magistrate of Xiacai county, was also killed, and everything in the city was burned to the ground. Later, Shaomi was [posthumously] conferred personnel rank at grade 4B.[88]

Li's autocommentary to this entry makes four points. First, he identifies his source as the *Remnant History of the Restoration*, thereby indicating that the

---

[87] *Yaolu*, 1.22.   [88] *Yaolu*, 20.458–59.

Daily Calendar did not contain this event.[89] Second, he corrects the *Minor Calendar*, which implausibly placed the army of Fan Qiong 范瓊 (d. 1129) in Huaixi two months earlier. Third, he corrects a statement in the *Records of the Restoration Loyal and Righteous* (*Zhongxing zhongyi lu* 中興忠義錄) by Gong Yizheng 龔頤正 (1140–1201) that Deng Shaomi was killed by Jin soldiers defending Shouchun, adding that he suspects that Gong has mistakenly followed an error in the *State Compendium*. And lastly, from the *Daily Calendar* for 1132/4/22, he quotes a petition from Deng's wife for posthumous preferment based on the nature of Deng's death. She reported that her husband had gone to a location about 100 kilometers south of Shouchun to subdue a bandit horde, but the bandits took him captive instead. When he refused to renounce the Song and cursed them, they killed him. Li Xinchuan notes that the wife's petition contradicts the account of Deng's death in the *Remnant History*, but he includes the wife's testimony in his autocommentary, awaiting further documentation.

The death of Deng Shaomi on 1129/2/5 is the primary chronological event. The word "previously" in the main text signals events that occurred prior to the primary event. The information that Deng was "later" posthumously promoted leads into the autocommentary where Li details three sources and three different accounts of Deng's death. Foregrounding the *Remnant History* in the main text indicates his preference as a historian for this version over the other two sources, both of which he concludes had ulterior motives to varnish Deng's demise. The petition from his wife, who stood to benefit from the preferment, probably did secure Deng's promotion and the official documentation that confirmed his status as a Song martyr. Gong Yizheng then found and uncritically took this document from the *State Compendium*. Yet, Li admits that there could be common ground between the version he has foregrounded and the wife's petition, and so signals his reservation. Although it is not mentioned in the autocommentary, this entry plays an important role in the larger narrative of 1129. Fan Qiong was implicated in the Miao–Liu mutiny the following month, then subsequently indicted and executed in 1129/7.[90] The story of his impulsive and destructive behavior at Shouchun is an undeclared "anticipative origin" for his own demise and a vivid example of how the disintegration of military discipline brought misery to the population during the early Restoration – a motif the *Daily Calendar* hardly emphasized.[91]

---

[89] The *Remnant History* does not survive as a freestanding text. The work was, however, a major source for Xu Mengxin's *Compendium of Treaties with the North*. The present text of this work contains an anonymous account of the Shouchun debacle that was either Li Xinchuan's immediate or a parallel source; see *Huibian*, 121.7b–8a. Li follows the details of this account closely but rewrites its author's more colloquial language.

[90] *Yaolu*, 25.591–92, 594.

[91] Li Xinchuan's larger narrative on Fan Qiong at *Chaoye zaji, jia*, 7.153–54, identifies his demise as a turning point in Emperor Gaozong's initial efforts to rein in recalcitrant military commanders.

Another example of the interdependent relationship between autocommentary and main text will illustrate Li Xinchuan's skill as a historian in sifting through the slimmest of evidence to ferret out a long-suppressed narrative. The primary event, dated 1153/10/22, records the dispatch of an official from the Ministry of Revenue, one Zhong Shiming 鍾世明, to assess flood damage along the Yangzi river upstream of Jiankang. The following translation uses the time markers in the passage to divide the text into five segments.

[1] 1153/10/22. The Vice Minister of Revenue Xu Zongyue reported: "Floods have destroyed the polder fields in Xuanzhou and Taipingzhou. Our ministry requests that you depute the Assistant for National Granaries and acting concurrent Ministry of Revenue officer Zhong Shiming to proceed to the area and make arrangements." Approved.

[2] *After this*, Zhong Shiming reported that damage to thirteen larger polders in Wuhu and Dangtu counties in Taipingzhou and two in Xuanzhou would require several million work units to repair. He requested use of grain normalization funds to support the populace and rebuild the polders. Also approved.[92]

[3] *Before this*, floods engulfed Xuanzhou and Taipingzhou. At that time, Gong Wu, magistrate of Liyang county, submitted to Qin Gui a plan to repair the polders, and Qin then appointed the prefectural administrator Ding Si as assistant supervisor for Jiangnan East circuit to travel there and co-ordinate the work.

[4] *At this point*, the order to send out Zhong Shiming replaced Ding Si. One also attached Gong Wu to the Jiangnan East circuit grain normalization office in order to oversee corvée labor. Zhang Jin, magistrate of Dangtu county, reported that the floods had displaced over half the population, and there was not sufficient manpower to undertake repairs. Accordingly, one followed Zhang's advice and constructed a long embankment 180 *li* around to protect the small polders. This was quickly completed, but most of Gong Wu's ten thousand corvée laborers died.

[5] *Before this*, Cao Yong, the mayor of Lin'an, recommended the wine storehouse manager Gong Fu to Qin Gui to serve as overseer for Qin's estates in Pingjiang prefecture and Xiuzhou. Gong Fu was now promoted, appointed provisional censor for the Six Ministries with a mandate to serve as inspector for post stations, and he proceeded to the two affected counties. Whenever Gong Fu encountered a depleted polder he forced the owner to sell it to him at a low price, and the people suffered greatly.[93]

Li Xinchuan's autocommentary reveals that he used six documents from the *Daily Calendar* to reconstruct this narrative. Two documents were routine appointment notices for Zhong Shiming and Ding Si 丁襈.[94] A third

[92] The translation abridges some details; for the full report see *SHY, shihuo*, 7.49a–50a.
[93] *Yaolu*, 165.3141–42.
[94] Zhong Shiming's notice is also preserved verbatim at *SHY, shihuo*, 7.49a.

document, dated two months earlier at 1153/8/22, conferred production from the Eternal Harvest polder in Jiankang to Qin Gui, with the polder to be jointly administered by Jiankang prefecture and the Jiangnan East circuit fiscal commissioner.[95] The other three documents, however, were indictments from 1156 and 1158, after Qin Gui's death in 1155, against Zhong Shiming and the Gong brothers.[96] Li confides that no other source mentions wrong-doing by Zhong and the Gongs; he adds that censorial indictments, which are often based on rumor, can be untrustworthy as history. But in this case, he can verify the charges in the indictments by cross-checking the events in question against the timeline of the appointments. He concludes, therefore, that the indictments reflect "public opinion" (*tianxia gonglun* 天下公論) and are credible. Returning to the primary event, Li observes that it was highly irregular to dispatch a capital-based, mid-level Ministry of Revenue official to oversee matters in the provinces. He concludes, therefore, that the motive of Xu Zongyue 徐宗說 (d. 1162) for dispatching Zhong was to focus resources on restoring production on Qin Gui's Eternal Harvest polder after the floods.

The entry thus serves as a good example of how Li used the *Daily Calendar* as a sourcebook rather than as a guidebook for Song history. The first three segments in the main-text narrative derive from official appointment notices and from Zhong Shiming's report on the flood damage. But segments 4 and 5 rely upon wording from the subsequent indictments of Zhong and the Gong brothers. In short, although this information was present in the *Daily Calendar*, Li Xinchuan constructed from these facts the following narrative. In the autumn of 1153 floods along the Yangzi destroyed polders in Jiangnan East circuit south of Jiankang, including the Eternal Harvest polder whose production the state had recently awarded to Qin Gui. Gong Wu 龔鍪, the brother of Qin Gui's private estate manager Gong Fu 龔釜, proposed a plan of repairs, and Ding Si, a provincial administrator, was assigned to oversee the project. But Vice Minister of Revenue Xu Zongyue, either on his own initiative or at Qin Gui's request, delegated an official from the ministry to work with Gong Wu to speed up the work. Conducted in the dead of winter, these measures cost the lives of almost 10,000 corvée laborers. At the same time, Gong Fu, perhaps at Qin Gui's direction, took advantage of conditions to buy up polder land in the area.

As mentioned above, this was an entry Li Xinchuan constructed during final revisions to the *Chronological Record* in 1208 in order to provide additional

---

[95] *Yaolu*, 165.3136, also records this action, as do the annals at *SS*, 31.578.

[96] *SHY, zhiguan*, 70.44b, preserves a brief summary of Zhong's dismissal on 1156/3/22; also *Yaolu*, 171.3283.

details on the Qin Gui era. He appended a final note to the autocommentary that explains his rationale:

During Qin Gui's autocratic administration, anything touching on his private affairs was omitted from the records of current administration and *Daily Calendar*, and furthermore he banned private histories. As a result, later generations have been totally unaware of his many actions that brought suffering to the people for his own benefit. I have therefore now written of these events to demonstrate this truth.[97]

Creating a Political Discourse

The *Chronological Record*, therefore, is not a mechanical reworking of the *Daily Calendar* but a complex and textured layering of intersecting narratives that combine to articulate larger themes and ultimately, as in the *Long Draft*, to advance certain political perspectives. We will concentrate here on several recurrent clusters of themes from the *Record* and reserve for the conclusion of this chapter a summary of those perspectives as gleaned from the totality of Li's surviving works. Two major, interrelated clusters are irredentism and fiscal stability. As we have seen, Li Xinchuan's father was an ardent irredentist, and his son inherited his conviction that the Restoration could never be complete until the dynasty recovered its former territory in the North. This irredentism assumes many forms in the *Record*, including admiration for military leaders who fought the Jin and for others who resisted the Jin occupation. A typical example of this theme is Li's account of the death of Zong Ze 宗澤 (1059–1128) in 1128/7. Zong, then regent of Kaifeng, rallied local troops and resistance fighters to beat back the final Jin assault on the capital. But the new court under Gaozong, intent on moving south, rejected his plans for a counterattack and his pleas for reinforcements. On his deathbed, he averred he would die without regret if his subordinates continued the fight. When they agreed, his last words were to shout three times "Cross the Yellow River!" Despite local support for Zong's son to assume his post, the court appointed the inept Du Chong 杜充 (d. 1140), whose subsequent defection to the Jin removed all hope of northern recovery.[98] Li fashioned this account of Zong's death from nonofficial sources to foreground his irredentist message; the *Minor Calendar*, by contrast, records only the appointment of Du Chong, and omits any mention of Zong Ze's death.[99]

The dozens of detailed descriptions of battles that Li has included in the *Record* also contribute to this irredentist cluster. Li has painstakingly reconstructed these accounts from private, often firsthand, witnesses to the encounters. These battle narratives not only eulogize the resistance but also describe

[97] *Yaolu*, 165.3142.   [98] *Yaolu*, 16.394–95; Kaplan, "Yueh Fei," 85–87.
[99] *Zhongxing xiaoli*, 4.40; *Huibian*, 112.6b–11a.

Song military weaknesses and those responsible for its defeats. For example, the *Record* is largely positive on Han Shizhong, perhaps the most capable Song commander of the 1130s. Yet Li has cobbled together from five different sources (two biographies of Han, one government document, and two private histories) a narrative of Han's defeat at a naval battle near Zhenjiang on the Yangzi river in 1134/4.[100] The most often cited example of Li's concern for military history is his reconstruction of the battle at Caishi in 1161/11. The 6,000-character autocommentary analyzes over ten sources to conclude that credit for the Song victory belongs to Yu Yunwen. Li details the biased nature of many of these accounts and concludes, "Generally, a critical evaluation in the narrative genre must exhaust all factual evidence. Even the slightest slide into personal emotion renders the narrative untrustworthy for later generations."[101]

Yet another contributor to this irredentist cluster is the generous coverage devoted to the anti-peace perspective in policy discussions during 1138 (*juan* 118–124), the crucial year in which Gaozong tasked Qin Gui with negotiating peace with the Jin. As does Li Tao in the *Long Draft*, Li Xinchuan expresses his own opinions through generous quotation of memorials whose perspective he endorses and through more niggardly treatment of those he does not. Although it remains unclear how many of these anti-peace tracts were included in the reconstructed *Daily Calendar* of 1176, Li has certainly drawn on outside sources to expand the calendar's anti-peace coverage.[102] This preponderance of anti-peace memorials in the *Record* has created the widespread view that those opposed to the peace process outnumbered its supporters.[103] Yet coverage for 1138 in Xiong Ke's *Minor Calendar*, although much shorter than in the *Chronological Record*, presents a more balanced account of the debates on war and peace and probably represents a more representative distillation of the *Daily Calendar*'s coverage on this issue.[104]

Li Xinchuan's opinions on fiscal stability are closely related to his stance on war and peace. A constant theme throughout his writings, including his sole surviving memorial, is the cost of warfare and how to manage the dynasty's fiscal policies in order to foster a prosperous rural economy and simultaneously

---

[100] *Yaolu*, 32.747–748.

[101] *Yaolu*, 194.3787–99. For discussions of this passage see Sun Jianmin, "Qushe zhi ji jian jingshen," 87; and Nie Lehe, "*Jianyan yilai xinian yaolu* yanjiu," 81–83. Li's outsize efforts to confirm Yu Yunwen's credit for the Caishi victory may indeed have had ulterior motives. Yu Yunwen, a major Sichuan official and chief councilor during the 1160s and 1170s, was a patron of Li Shunchen, and Li Xinchuan maintained good relations with Yu's descendants. The Caishi autocommentary may be seen as evidence to support the charge in Li Xinchuan's biography that his works favored his Sichuan compatriots; see *SS*, 438.12985.

[102] See, for example, *Yaolu*, 119.2226 and 120.2244.

[103] See, for example, Tao Jing-shen, "The Move to the South and the Reign of Kao-tsung," 677–79.

[104] *Zhongxing xiaoli*, 25.295–304.

support a military strong enough to prevail against the Jin and complete the Restoration. Essentially, Li agrees with the twelfth-century *daoxue* consensus that a strong dynastic economy must be a precondition for successful military action. In turn, the prosperity of local agricultural communities constitutes the foundation for dynastic economic and military strength. We have cited in Chapter 2 Li Dai's report from 1137 on the finances of Sichuan and his conclusion that excessive military costs impose an unsustainable tax burden on the population. Li Xinchuan's autocommentary explains that he has included Li Dai's full text because the memorial presents a comprehensive analysis of the province's financial problems.[105]

Li also cites in full another memorial written in 1135/2 by the censor Zhang Zhiyuan 張致遠 (1090–1147), a political ally of Zhao Ding, that argued for a full-scale reordering of dynastic financial administration. In Zhang's view, a balkanization of fiscal administration, a legacy of the New Policies, fostered a cadre of self-proclaimed financial experts whose profiteering had corrupted the state agencies for the wine and salt monopolies, currency, and grain supply. At court, the Ministry of Revenue had degenerated into little more than a sales outlet for monk certificates and patents of nobility. Zhang admits the pressing need for military funding but argues that the real problem is the plethora of extractions that sap "the strength of the people." Proper financial management would restore this "base of the state." Zhang proposed a centralization of financial controls under a reorganized Ministry of Revenue, increased authority for its top officials, regular audits to balance income and expenditures, and elimination of the independent monopoly and grain stabilization agencies. He opposed an increase in the wine tax, the return of New Policies market trade, and extension of the salt monopoly into Fujian. As we shall see below, Zhao Ding was one of Li Xinchuan's political heroes, and this memorial, whose proposals were never to be realized, encapsulated an institutionalist vision of financial administration that twelfth- and thirteenth-century political reformers, including Li Xinchuan, would continue to endorse. The autocommentary therefore observes that because this memorial contains "an overall plan for state finance," Li has included its full text in the *Record*.[106]

The *Diverse Notes*

Apart from the four major compilations studied in this book – the *State Compendium*, the *Long Draft*, the *Chronological Record*, and the *Song History* – Li Xinchuan's *Diverse Notes on Court and Province since 1127* may arguably be the single most useful book for the study of Song governance. In his pioneering study, John Chaffee has rightly termed the *Diverse Notes* "a

---

[105] *Yaolu*, 111.2076–80.   [106] *Yaolu*, 85.1611–13.

handbook of government."[107] The work presents a systematic survey of political institutions and agencies, policies, protocols, personalities, personnel management, finance, and foreign policy. Despite the title, the coverage is often comprehensive, from the beginning of the dynasty to Li Xinchuan's own day. His approach combines historical analysis and political comment. The essay or "note" (*ji* 記) genre afforded Li greater freedom than did the chronological format of the *Record* to construct his historical narratives and integrate them into a coherent political message. Li expresses his own viewpoint both directly and indirectly over the almost 800 topics of the *Diverse Notes*. His contemporaries immediately recognized the work's comprehensive nature and historical value. The bibliographer Chen Zhensun wrote that the *Diverse Notes* was "the most detailed private history compiled since our move south."[108]

As we have seen above, Li composed the two twenty-*juan* installments of the *Diverse Notes* – with prefaces dated 1202 and 1216 – intermittently as he worked on the *Chronological Record*. And scholars have long speculated on the relationship between the two works. The *Siku* editors noted astutely that the *Notes* were hardly "diverse" (*za* 雜) but related to the *Record* "as warp does to woof," thus implying a conceptual connection between the two works.[109] They further observed that the thirteen thematic categories into which Li divided the *Diverse Notes* rendered its organizational mechanism similar to that of the *huiyao* collections. Since the first installment of the *Notes* was completed six years before the *Record*, the contemporaneous bibliographer Zhao Xibian wrote tellingly that the "*Chronological Record* most probably took its standards from [these notes]."[110] A printer's blurb on the first Song printing of the *Notes* at Chengdu advertised that they had been compiled as a "preparatory outline" (*zhangben* 張本) for the *Record*. Although the truth was certainly more complex, the advertisement assured that since the "*Records* for the three courts [of Gaozong, Xiaozong, and Guangzong]" have already been submitted to court, "the contents of this book are all verified events; you need no longer harbor doubts about them."[111]

The *Siku* editors quote the opinion of the early Qing scholar Wang Shizhen 王士禎 (1634–1711) that the utility of the *Notes* derives from their unique

---

[107] Chaffee, "The Historian as Critic," 323. [108] *Zhizhai shulu jieti*, 5.158.

[109] Ji Yun et al., *Qinding Siku quanshu zongmu*, 81.1079–80.

[110] Chao Gongwu, *Junzhai dushuzhi jiaozheng*, 1116. Zhao Xibian knew Li Xinchuan's works well and compiled a volume of supplemental annotations to the *Chronological Record*; see *Junzhai dushuzhi jiaozheng*, 1113.

[111] *Yaolu*, appendix, 3984. Liang Taiji, "*Xinian yaolu*, *Chaoye zaji* de qiyi jishu ji qi chengyin," 194–200, argues convincingly that this passage is a printer's advertisement. Liang accounts for factual differences between the existing texts of the *Record* and the *Notes* by suggesting that both texts were in accord prior to Li's 1208 revisions to the *Record*. He concludes that differences between the two works arose because Li did not make subsequent revisions to the *Notes* and his original 1202 version was then printed in Chengdu without his consent.

juxtaposition of larger focus and minute detail – Li Xinchuan lasers in on the dynasty's major unsolved problems with a profusion of illuminating detail.[112] In this connection, the resemblance between the *Diverse Notes* and the *huiyao* is only superficial. Li's thirteen thematic categories combine *huiyao* categories (monarchs, sacrifices, rites, examinations, official positions, finance, the military, and border defense) with categories more often encountered in bibliography (court events, cultural works, specific incidents, and precedents). Furthermore, unlike the *huiyao* genre, which did not evaluate or distinguish between major and minor events, the details of each individual entry in the *Notes*, when read in the context of their surrounding entries, combine to create a comprehensive yet critical analysis of the Song government's performance in each of his thirteen subject categories.

Table 3.2 lists the thirteen subject categories into which Li organized the *Diverse Notes*, the number of entries within each category in the installments of 1202 and 1216, the combined number of entries per category in both installments, the percentage of each category based on these combined totals, and a brief description of the category's contents. One notices immediately that the two largest categories are, as in the *Recovered Draft of the State Compendium*, the bureaucratic system and state finance. In other words, Li's portrayal of governance in the *Diverse Notes* relies upon a documentary base similar in scope to that of official historiography. However, the two other largest categories, the imperial house and precedents, highlight areas important to Li's personal, more critical view of Song governance. The 1216 installment begins with two expansive biographies of Emperors Gaozong and Xiaozong that, although they focus on the imperial transitions in 1162 and 1189, offer an in-depth political history of the monarchy from 1127 through 1189.[113] The other entries on the imperial house provide biographies of emperors, empresses, consorts, princes, and princesses that focus on their official titles and ranks, and, by implication, their salaries. Although careful not to include "matters offensive to the state body," Li was highly critical of powerful elements within the monarchy, and one must often read between the lines of his entries – always alert for hints of irony. For example, a seemingly prosaic list of imperial affinal kin who attained the topmost grade in the military personal rank system (*jiedushi* 節度使) notes a drastic increase in their number after the move south, recording twenty-two such appointments in Southern Song. The list reveals that most empresses' kin managed only one or two such appointments, but five of Empress Wu's relatives attained the top grade.[114]

The category of precedents contains two types of entries. First are entries clearly labeled in the text as "precedents" (*gushi*). For example, the entry on

[112] Ji Yun et al., *Qinding Siku quanshu zongmu*, 81.1079.   [113] *Chaoye zaji, yi*, 1.495–2.535.
[114] *Chaoye zaji, jia*, 12.239.

Table 3.2 The thirteen subject categories in Li Xinchuan's *Diverse Notes on Court and Province since 1127*

Subject category		1202	1216	Total	Percentage	Content
The imperial house	上德	52	28	80	10	Biographies of emperors, empresses, princes, and princesses
Imperial sacrifices	郊廟	37	0	37	5	Imperial rituals; ritual and religious institutions
State ritual functions	典禮	19	15	34	4	Court ritual and ceremonial functions
Cultural works	制作	23	4	27	3	Production of seals, regalia; court historiography
Court events	朝事	39	10	49	6	Major policy initiatives, chronologically arranged
Specific incidents	時事	2	28	30	4	Narratives of person- and time-specific events and issues
Diverse events	雜事	19	24	43	5	Notes on matters of lesser interest
Precedents	故事	52	22	74	9	Precedent-setting events and protocols
The bureaucratic system	官制	89	78	167	21	Court and provincial government agencies, personnel management of officials
Selecting officials	取士	44	10	54	7	Examination system, schools
Finance and taxation	財賦	90	19	109	14	Taxation, budgets, state monopolies, grain management, transportation, state agriculture, currency, treasuries
The military	兵馬	39	11	50	6	Army units, military administration, militias, weapons manufacture, horse administration
Border defense	邊防	16	15	42	5	Defense policy, major battles, insurrections
Totals		521	264	796	99	

"revolving audiences" (*zhuandui* 轉對) begins by citing the "precedent" that every fifth day one official from the court's officer corps was to be allocated time to address the emperor on a nonroutine matter of the official's choice. But the bulk of the entry describes how chief councilors in Southern Song manipulated this institution to deflect potential criticism from reaching the emperor.[115] Second, many entries in this category are lists of officials who have attained some unusual distinction, for either good or ill. There is, for example, a list of officials who served as imperial drafters before the age of thirty and those who served as chief councilors before forty.[116] Then there is the impressive record of one Mo Zichun 莫子純 (1159–1215), an otherwise undistinguished official who managed to be promoted in personal rank faster than any other official in dynastic history.[117] From a modern perspective, it is difficult to establish a relationship between these two types of "precedent" entries, but the intent is certainly, as Wang Shizhen observed, to create a textured picture of the many facets of Song political culture. Li Xinchuan will often, in fact, spell out the intended implication for even the most prosaic of his lists. An enumeration of the number of assisting chief councilors that served under each emperor finds that the greatest number served under Gaozong (forty-eight over thirty-six years). Li attributes the high turnover to Qin Gui's reluctance to permit potential rivals long enough tenures in the office to challenge his authority.[118]

The three chapters on the bureaucratic system form the core of the first *Diverse Notes* of 1202. The first two of these chapters treat respectively the capital-based offices, then circuit-level provincial units. This coverage is not comprehensive, but highlights those offices and positions that exercised real power, important moments in their history, changes to their administrative structure, and relationships to other units. For example, the twenty-eight entries on central court positions focus exclusively on the chief councilor and the Bureau of Military Affairs, concluding with one entry each on eunuch agencies and the Postern Office, totally excluding second-tier offices such as the Six Ministries.[119] A uniquely conceived third chapter collects data on patents of nobility, supplemental academic appointments, merit appointments, and clerical rosters. The common focus is on the relentless growth of officialdom, both in total numbers and in cost, especially for non-literati officials such as the imperial clan, imperial affines, and clerks.

For example, one entry details the annual cost in 1125 of salaries at the highest military rank (*jiedushi*) for twenty-six imperial princes, eleven other imperial clan members, two former chief councilors, four generals, ten imperial affines, and seven eunuchs at 700,000 strings.[120] As a point of comparison, these sixty officials comprised only 0.15 percent of the roughly 40,000 officials in service during this period. Since annual state revenue was between 70 and 80 million strings, the salaries for these sixty individuals, most of who

---

[115] *Chaoye zaji, jia*, 9.170; Hartman, "Sung Government and Politics," 117–18.
[116] *Chaoye zaji, jia*, 9.177.   [117] *Chaoye zaji, yi*, 11.680.   [118] *Chaoye zaji, jia*, 9.174–75.
[119] *Chaoye zaji, jia*, 10.196–211.   [120] *Chaoye zaji, jia*, 12.239.

performed only token, if any, functional duties, consumed almost 1 percent of total state revenue.[121] This chapter also contains vital statistics on the fluctuations in numbers of officials from early Song through 1201, emphasizing their fourfold growth over this period.[122]

The entries on taxation and state revenue are likewise fundamental to Li Xinchuan's political message. As Chaffee has noted, Li was "remarkably fond of statistics," and, one might add, most fond of financial statistics.[123] The four chapters on finance in the 1202 installment begin with a statistical survey of the relentless growth of state revenue from the beginning of the dynasty, emphasizing that the continuation of extra levies imposed early in the Southern Song have "exhausted the resources of the people."[124] The ensuing entries offer an in-depth and systematic account of how the state extracted these resources: monopolies on salt, tea, and alcohol; special levies for military support; corvée exemption fees; land taxes; import duties; and currency fees. The fourth chapter reviews the agencies responsible for raising and managing this income. These entries are not simple rehashes of bureaucratic protocols, but often feature incidents and statistics that bolster Li's view that much of this revenue was squandered in corruption and needless extravagance.

For example, Li's brief history of the Left Reserve Treasury (*Zuozang fengzhuang ku* 左藏封樁庫) chronicles the unsuccessful attempts of civil officials at the end of the twelfth century to audit and prevent transfers from this supposedly public, "court" treasury into the monarchy's Inner Treasury. The entry ends with commentary that tabulates an unprecedented 2.5 million strings dispersed from the Left Reserve in autumn of 1200 for construction and maintenance of Empress Wu's mausoleum.[125] This sum represented more than twice the total monthly cash salaries for the entire roster of capital-based officials.[126] Li penned this entry no later than 1202, probably shortly after he received news in Sichuan of the disbursements. Han Tuozhou was the nephew of Empress Wu, and the expenditures on her tomb were a form of state patronage. Given this contemporary, critical nature of the *Notes*, one may well understand why Li felt compelled to suspend his work in the face of the

---

[121] Wang Shengduo, *Liang Song caizheng shi*, 692.

[122] *Chaoye zaji, jia*, 12.249–50; Hartman, "Sung Government and Politics," 53. Also included in the second installment is a precise enumeration of the different classes of officials and their methods of entry into service for the year 1213, a unique data set fundamental for understanding the composition of the Song civil service; see *Chaoye zaji, yi*, 14.757–58; Chaffee, *Thorny Gates of Learning in Sung China*, 24–27.

[123] Chaffee, "The Historian as Critic," 324. The same penchant is also apparent in the *Chronological Record*, in which the entries for most years conclude with provincial statistics on population, taxation, and revenue; see Nie, "*Jianyan yilai xinian yaolu* yanjiu," 88–87.

[124] *Chaoye zaji, jia*, 14.289.   [125] *Chaoye zaji, jia*, 17.383–84.

[126] *Chaoye zaji, jia*, 17.379, puts this figure at 1.2 million strings in 1189; see also Wang Shengduo, *Liang Song caizheng shi*, 133, which is based on the numbers in *SHY, shihuo*, 56.65a–66b.

Han administration's injunction against private compilations that touched on "matters offensive to the state body," a formulation that, as we have seen above, specifically included the monarch and his affinal kin.

If the section on state finance is largely about revenue collection, the concluding sections on the military and on border defense describe the expenditure of that revenue. The 1202 installment details the major Song armies, including regional militias, their numbers and costs, horse administration, and weapons manufacture. The sections on border defense begin with a brief résumé of policy makers' views on war and peace, then describe major battles from 1127 through 1164, and conclude with a detailed history of negotiations that led to the peace of 1164.[127] The 1216 installment contains much briefer sections on the military and the border, since Li set forth the basic facts and his views in 1202. The 1216 finance section is largely devoted to Sichuan province, as is the border section, which describes local insurrections in the southwest. Of particular interest are three entries that survey developments among the Jurchen, the Tanguts, and the Mongols. These long entries combine official historiography's ethnological focus on steppe customs along with a day-by-day record of recent Mongol military activity. The account of Genghis Khan's incursions into Shandong references events that had occurred only two and half years prior to the 1216 dating of the preface. Clearly, Li Xinchuan received up-to-date information, probably via his connections to Chengdu regional administration, on the impact of Mongol expansion in North China.[128]

The second installment of the *Diverse Notes* also contains a history of Han Tuozhou's invasion of the North in 1206 and the resulting rebellion in Sichuan.[129] These many examples of recent, even ongoing events in the *Diverse Notes* testify to Li Xinchuan's conception of the close relationship between history and political commentary. Evidence suggests that Li continued to compose installments of the *Diverse Notes* throughout his life.[130] He worked, for example, simultaneously on the second installment of the *Notes* and on *An Account of the Western Frontier from 1201 through 1221*, his monumental history of contemporary Sichuan. His portrayal of Mongol military prowess in the context of Song historical experience with the Tanguts and the Jurchen is prescient. He writes both with an eye toward the past and with

[127] *Chaoye zaji, jia*, 19.448–20.471.   [128] *Chaoye zaji, yi*, 19.847–54, on the Mongols.
[129] *Chaoye zaji, yi*, 18.825–38.
[130] Writing in 1241, Zhang Duanyi 張端義 recorded a conversation with Li Xinchuan, in which the historian stated that he had compiled six installments of the *Diverse Notes*; see *Gui'er ji*, 1.1. The *Siku* editors speculate that these later installments were never printed, but Wang Deyi suggests that the implied third and fourth installments, probably compiled between 1216 and 1226, were most likely printed in Sichuan; see Wang Deyi, "Li Xinchuan zhushu kao," 6781. Late Song sources and the *Yongle Encyclopedia* indeed quote a number of passages from the *Diverse Notes* that are not in the received edition of the first two installments; see *Chaoye zaji*, appendix, 909–29.

a historian's sense of the importance of an accurate record of present events for the future. This fusion of history and reportage is central to Li Xinchuan's historiographical outlook and to his distinctive voice as a historian.

The Record of the Way and Its Fate

The *Record of the Way and Its Fate*, with a preface dated 1239, over three decades after the *Chronological Record*, may initially appear as a slight and easily overlooked afterthought compared to his earlier magna opera. The small work, however, is key to understanding Li Xinchuan's later career, to comprehending the thirteenth-century fate of the Sichuan tradition of analytical historiography, and to placing the *daoxue* movement within the larger framework of Song history. Since I have published extensively on the *Record of the Way*, I will summarize those findings here.[131]

The received ten-*juan* edition of the *Record of the Way* is not Li Xinchuan's original work but rather a drastic expansion and revision undertaken by the Yuan scholar Cheng Rongxiu 程榮秀 (1263–1333) and printed in 1333. Cheng was a descendant of Cheng Yi, and he reworked Li's original text to foreground the history of the Cheng Yi–Zhu Xi school of *daoxue* over other strains of the movement. In this process, Cheng not only distorted Li's conception of *daoxue* but also mangled his historiographical method. However, two surviving *juan* from the *Yongle Encyclopedia*, the great Ming encyclopedia of 1407, contain the first half of Li's original text; in addition, guidelines drawn from this text then make possible a confident reconstruction of the second half of the original work.[132]

The original *Record of the Way* contained fifty-six entries. A typical entry has three parts: (1) a primary source document; (2) Li Xinchuan's reconstruction of the historical background of the source document, which he constructs by quoting other related documents; and (3) his own critical notes on uncertainties, problems, and questions for future research. On the one hand, this tripartite structure is similar to the relationship between text and commentary in the *Chronological Record*, and derives ultimately from Li Tao's *Long Draft*.[133] On the other hand, the format of the *Record of the Way* resembles that of the *Diverse Notes*, since Li's freedom to choose the documents for inclusion permits him wide latitude to shape the sources into his preferred historical

---

[131] Hartman, "Bibliographic Notes on Sung Historical Works: The Original *Record of the Way*" and "Li Hsin-ch'uan and the Historical Image," combined and revised as "*Daoming lu* fuyuan yu Li Xinchuan de daoxue guan" in Cai Hanmo, *Lishi de yanzhuang*, 344–448.

[132] For details see Hartman, "Bibliographic Notes on Sung Historical Works: The Original *Record of the Way*," 39–61; *Lishi de yanzhuang*, 420–48.

[133] Hartman, "Bibliographic Notes on Sung Historical Works: The Original *Record of the Way*," 14–15.

narrative. Li worked on the *Record of the Way* from 1224 through 1239. Thus, this continuity of methodology reveals the *Record of the Way* as an extension of his earlier work. As mentioned above, his efforts to continue the chronological record for the post-Gaozong reigns extended well into his later career. And, as we have seen, evidence suggests that additional collections of *Diverse Notes* were compiled after the second installment of 1216. Li's work on the *Record of the Way* thus proceeded apace with his larger, ongoing works on Southern Song history, and the view of *daoxue* that emerges from the reconstructed, original text must be understood in the context of his other writings.

The structure of the original *Record of the Way*, as well as Li's preface, presents Song *daoxue* as a political movement that developed in three phases. The first *juan* of the original work, presenting phase one, began with Sima Guang's recommendation of Cheng Yi as Classics Mat tutor in 1085, then progressed through Zhang Dun's persecution of the Yuanyou administrators in the 1090s, the inquisitions against Cheng learning under Cai Jing in the early twelfth century, and the re-emergence of Cheng learning in the 1130s under Zhao Ding, and ended with the reinstatement of the ban in 1136. The second phase, in *juan* two, coincided with the autocracy of Qin Gui from 1136 through the lifting of the ban in 1156. *Juan* three and four covered the period from the request of Chen Jia 陳賈 for an official condemnation of *daoxue* in 1183 and concluded with a censorial request from 1202 to end the proscription against *daoxue* adherents that had begun in 1196. A fifth *juan*, with no commentary, contained documents between 1208 and 1224 that recommended honors be granted to various *daoxue* figures.

Li's preface portrays each of the periods as a political and moral struggle between leaders who supported *daoxue* – Sima Guang, Zhao Ding, and Zhao Ruyu – against leaders who suppressed the movement – Zhang Dun and Cai Jing, Qin Gui, and Han Tuozhou. This dichotomy coincides closely with the "lineage of evil" motif that arose as an explanatory framework for Song history after 1208. The *Record of the Way* thus encapsulates a master narrative for Song history as a political and moral struggle between proponents of the Confucian "Way" (*dao* 道) and "its learning" (*xue* 學) and their opponents, a subject that will be examined in Chapter 7 below. Li's preface explains that the Way is the political manifestation of Confucian principles as articulated in the *Analects* and *Mencius*; learning is the private scholarship and moral cultivation necessary to understand and internalize those principles. The true *daoxue* adherent practices the former when in office and cultivates the latter when out of office.[134]

---

[134] For a translation and analysis of the preface see Hartman, "Li Hsin-ch'uan and the Historical Image," 328–36.

In the preface, however, Li Xinchuan is decidedly pessimistic about the future prospects, the "fate," of *daoxue*. And this pessimism accords with the intense criticism of Song political institutions so pervasive in the *Diverse Notes*, especially the installment of 1216. In addition to overt political suppression from the lineage of autocratic councilors, Li labels apostasy from within as an equally strong threat to the *daoxue* teachings. He describes false adherents who have no true understanding of *daoxue* "learning" and superficially embrace its "Way" out of political expediency and opportunism. Li's preface names no names. However, Shi Miyuan, sole councilor from 1208 through 1233, employed officials who had studied with *daoxue* teachers, and he professed outward allegiance to the movement's principles in a political move to demarcate his administration from that of Han Tuozhou.

After Shi's death, these officials formed the Duanping administration (1234–1236); but their superficial embrace of the Way could not surmount international and domestic challenges. This failure then facilitated the return of autocracy under Shi's nephew, Shi Songzhi. The nephew, following his uncle's policy, also outwardly espoused *daoxue*, and engineered the state's formal embrace of the Cheng Yi–Zhu Xi teachings in 1241.[135] As we have seen above, Li contended, in his later years, against Shi Songzhi's revisionist historiography and his politics. The irony was that the same politician Li Xinchuan had framed as the historical continuation of the Cai Jing, Qin Gui, and Han Tuozhou autocracy had himself confirmed the validity of the politics that Li had framed as the historical opposition to that autocracy. It must have seemed to Li Xinchuan that, despite the praise he had received from Lou Yue, he had failed in his mission as a historian to render the Way of Heaven – divine justice – immune from the vagaries of fate. If Sima Qian wondered in the *Grand Scribe's Records* why the virtuous suffer and the evil rule the world, Li Xinchuan mused in the *Record of the Way and Its Fate* why the *daoxue* teachings had failed to produce the political order its proponents had promised.

Conclusion

Li Xinchuan's exclusive focus on Song history and the loss of his collected works, which prevents a full reconstruction of his intellectual development, have hitherto denied him recognition as one of the greatest of Chinese historians. His colleagues soon recognized that his fusion of Sichuan "dialogue" historiography and contemporaneous reportage created a powerful platform to refashion a dynastic history relevant to their ongoing political struggles. Li Xinchuan conceived the *Chronological Record* and the *Diverse Notes* as

---

[135] For these developments see Li and Hartman, "A Newly Discovered Inscription," 447–48.

complementary works that would, in their totality, present his views on contemporary history. The *Chronological Record*'s analytical source criticism established a base narrative that Li deemed credible. In turn, the *Notes* function as a guide or index to the *Record*. Their topical arrangement enabled Li to group together "events" into meaningful sequences whose significance might otherwise have been missed. The *Record* and the *Notes* may thus be understood as Li Xinchuan's solution to the problem of the prolixity of the *Long Draft* and the need for a new genre of historical writing that would analytically compress the growing enormity of the Song historical record.

As distilled in the *Record of the Way and Its Fate*, Li viewed Restoration history as a moral and political struggle between two approaches to governance. His preferred vector, emanating from Sima Guang, through Zhao Ding and Zhao Ruyu, advocated an institutional approach to governance that emphasized control by civil officials with *jinshi* backgrounds, administering agencies according to fixed principles, if not actual protocols, whose origins Li traced ultimately to the Song founders. By contrast, the opposing vector, personified by Cai Jing, Qin Gui, and Han Tuozhou, governed through associations of the influential and ad hoc combinations of decentralized agencies, largely administered by military-grade and other non-literati officials, plus the ever-present coterie of literati apostates. Only during his formative years under Emperor Xiaozong did Li Xinchuan experience this first model of governance, and Xiaozong emerges in the *Diverse Notes* as the most successful of the Southern Song emperors. But after the advent of Han Tuozhou in 1194, when Li was twenty-seven, he experienced, in his view, an almost unbroken series of autocratic regimes and unsuccessful attempts to return to the literati model. This pessimism, perhaps more apparent in the *Record of the Way*, was nonetheless the underlying voice of Li's historiography from the beginning.

If *daoxue* failed to provide a political solution to the crisis of thirteenth-century governance, the movement came to dominate the century's historiography. Although sympathetic to the intellectual and political claims of *daoxue*, Li Xinchuan recoiled at the univocal and simplistic focus of its historiography. In spite of all his efforts at contemporary reportage, Li Xinchuan's basic methodology looked backwards toward Li Tao and the hallmark Sichuan tradition of dialogue historiography. For this reason, Li Xinchuan, for all his genius and industry, was a retrograde figure – the consummate practitioner of twelfth-century historiography in its waning thirteenth-century days. The following chapter will demonstrate the critical role of *daoxue* historiography in the finalization of the grand allegory and its influence on the Yuan compilers of the *Song History*.

4   The *Daoxue* Historians

The period between the completion of Li Tao's *Long Draft* in 1183 and the *Chronologically Arranged Complete Essentials in Outline and Details of the August Courts*, completed by Chen Jun in 1229, marks a seminal half-century in the development of Song historiography. The crucial element during this period was the evolution of the *daoxue* teachings from a localized, intellectual movement into an empire-wide political force. As Chapter 2 has shown, although Li Tao was sympathetic to the *daoxue* political agenda, he did not permit the movement's still-incipient historiography to impact the *Long Draft*. Only several decades later, Li Xinchuan faced a radically altered landscape for the historian. The political rise of *daoxue* after 1208 required new, focused narratives that historicized and legitimated the movement's political goals. Building upon what Zhu Xi had begun, this new *daoxue* historiography grew rapidly in Fujian. But the Fujian historiography had little patience for the painstaking historical precision and transparent, dialogue historiography of the Sichuan school. These opposing trends were already well under way during Li Xinchuan's lifetime and doubtless contributed to his overall pessimistic outlook for the future of Song historiography, if not for the dynasty itself.

We have also seen in Chapter 2 how shifts in the political, intellectual, and military landscape in the thirteenth century condemned Li Tao's *Long Draft* to abridgment, repurposing, and eventual dissolution. These same forces affected Li Xinchuan's corpus as well. Both the *Chronological Record* and the *Diverse Notes* were printed in Sichuan before Li's departure for Lin'an in 1225. The Mongol attacks on Sichuan in the 1230s, however, destroyed the printing blocks, and no imprint of either work survives.[1]

Jia Sidao, during a tour as Yangzhou prefect and district administrator, reprinted the *Chronological Record* in 1253. No imprint of this edition survives. His colophon praised the work as the only comprehensive history of the Gaozong reign. He also noted the importance of Gaozong's residence in Yangzhou during 1127–1129: it was here that, in the face of great difficulties,

---

[1] Manuscript tracing copies of Song editions of the *Diverse Notes* do survive and form the textual basis of the modern edition; see *Chaoye zaji*, Xu Gui's editorial comment, 5–6.

Gaozong restored the Classics Mat sessions, named Cheng Yi's disciple Yang Shi 楊時 (1053–1135) as his tutor, welcomed remonstrance, and "supported our succession of the Way" (*fuchi daotong* 扶持道統). Jia proclaims that these actions were the founding principles of the successful Restoration.[2] Thus, less than ten years after Li Xinchuan's death and twelve years after the court's recognition of *daoxue* in 1241, Jia promoted the *Chronological Record* as a window into the *daoxue* history of the dynasty.

As is well-known, the eighteenth-century Qing academicians recovered the current texts of both the *Long Draft* and the *Chronological Record* from the *Yongle Encyclopedia*. But both works were extracted from that source already encrusted with layers of pseudocommentary by thirteenth-century *daoxue* authors that had not originally been part of these works. The purpose of this pseudocommentary is identical to Jia Sidao's postface to his edition of the *Chronological Record*: to overlay the events in the *Long Draft* and the *Record* with a *daoxue* historical narrative that valorizes the movement's political priorities, makes those priorities fundamental dynastic principles, and extends those principles back to the dynastic foundings in 960 and 1127.[3] The vast majority of this pseudocommentary derives from three sources. First, the work known today as the *Sagacious Administration from the Two Restoration Courts of the August Song Augmented with Lectures by Famous Confucians* (*Zengru mingru jiangyi huang Song zhongxing liangchao shengzheng* 增入名儒講議皇宋中興兩朝聖政) is a combination and drastic commercial reworking of the official *Gaozong Sagacious Administration* (*Gaozong shengzheng*) of 1166 and the *Xiaozong Sagacious Administration* (*Xiaozong shengzheng* 孝宗聖政) of 1192. These works of official historiography were intended as didactic guide-books of imperial governance for use by the next emperor. The genre featured comments on important entries written in the name of the sitting chief councilor. In 1192, one of the first committed *daoxue* councilors was Liu Zheng, and the commentary written in his name is an early, official reflection of the movement's political views. This convergence of the official *shengzheng* format and an incipient *daoxue* historiography marks a critical juncture in the evolution of Song historiography. As the *daoxue* teachings spread through the intellectual world of the thirteenth century, commercial publishers repackaged these works, added other commentary, and advertised the book as "augmented with lectures by famous Confucians."[4] The writings of Lü Zhong, to be studied

---

[2] Reprinted in *Yaolu*, appendix, 3976–77.

[3] For the *Record* see the discussion in Hartman, "The Making of a Villain," 68–86; Liang Taiji, "*Yaolu* zizhu de neirong fanwei ji qi suo jieshi de xiuzuan tili"; Kong Xue, "*Jianyan yilai xinian yaolu* zhuwen bianxi." For the *Long Draft* see Pei Rucheng and Xu Peizao, *Xu zizhi tongjian changbian kaolüe*, 83–95.

[4] Liang Taiji, "*Shengzheng* jinben fei yuanben zhi jiu xiangbian," demonstrates convincingly that the present text constitutes a drastic commercial modification and revision of the work's original

later in this chapter, constitute the second major component in the pseudocommentary to the *Chronological Record*; and the third is an unknown work entitled *The Tortoise and Mirror of the Restoration* (*Zhongxing guijian* 中興龜鑑) by one He Fu 何俌.[5]

Since the source edition of the *Chronological Record* employed by the *Yongle Encyclopedia* compilers for their transcription has long since disappeared, scholars are uncertain on precisely when this *daoxue* commentary was inserted into the work. The Qing academicians suggested that the Ming compilers had done the deed, and subsequent scholarship has largely adopted this view. However, recent research points toward a much earlier date. The modern editor of the *Chronological Record* suggests that this pseudocommentary was already present in an edition privately printed sometime in the late thirteenth century, a copy of which then served as the base text for the *Yongle* compilers.[6]

This timing coincides perfectly with the culmination of a distinctive *daoxue*-inspired narrative of Song history that began with Zhu Xi in the 1160s, accelerated during the post-1208 period with the works of the Fujian historian Chen Jun, and culminated in the works of another Fujian historian, Lü Zhong, about 1250. As is well known, this century witnessed the growth of *daoxue* from a loose association of local scholars with avant-garde intellectual and political stances into a broad-based social and political movement that reached into the highest levels of government.[7] As it struggled during this period against its political foes, the movement developed a corresponding historiography to support its intellectual and political goals. This chapter will survey the surviving writings of these historians, then conclude by distinguishing between their activities as historians, the *daoxue* historiography they practiced, and the *daoxue* history they produced.

Zhu Xi

Zhu Xi's historiography can be traced back to Cheng Yi's insistence that history must remain auxiliary to the pursuit and cultivation of moral understanding.[8] This understanding reposed in the Confucian classics, the primary object of

---

  shengzheng format; see also Hartman, "The Making of a Villain," 83–84; and Hartman [Cai Hanmo], "Lu You *Zhongxing shengzheng cao* kao."

[5] Hartman, "The Making of a Villain," 85–86. See also the careful study of the *Zhongxing guijian* in Wang Shengduo and Chen Chaoyang, "*Songshi quanwen* chayin shilun wenxian yanjiu," 475–78, in which the authors are likewise unable to identify the work with confidence.

[6] *Yaolu*, Hu Kun editorial comment, 15–16, 22–23. I concur with this view.

[7] For a recent survey see Tillman, "The Rise of the *Tao-Hsüeh* Confucian Fellowship in Southern Sung."

[8] Zhu Xi's anthology of the Cheng brothers' thought, the *Reflections on Things at Hand*, groups Cheng Yi's pronouncements on the theory of history after the preface to his commentary on the *Spring and Autumn Annals*. See Zhu Xi and Lü Zuqian, *Jinsi lu*, 3.20b–26a; trans. Wing-tsit Chan, *Reflections on Things at Hand*, 114–19. For a useful summary of Zhu Xi's ideas on history

study that must always precede the study of secondary disciplines, such as history. As is well known, Cheng Yi held that the world contained patterns of moral order (*li, yili* 理, 義理): the perception and internalization of these patterns and the moral values they contained constituted true knowledge; and this knowledge then became an epistemology that undergirded all other modes of inquiry. Thus, sage-authors had embedded in well-written history – and two of the Confucian classics, the *Documents* and the *Spring and Autumn Annals*, were histories – discoverable traces of these moral patterns. Of course, the writers of later histories, especially official histories, were not sages; and so the moral patterns in their histories were more difficult to discern. According to Zhu Xi, Cheng Yi's favorite work of modern history was Fan Zuyu's *Tang Mirror* (*Tangjian* 唐鑑), a work that selected 332 events from the Tang period and provided a commentary that generated an explicit "discourse" that drew forth the moral messages of the Tang past for contemporary policy.

Thus, a major goal of *daoxue* historiography was to rewrite existing historical works, and to write new ones, in ways that would render more visible, and thus more easily internalized by the student, the moral patterns (*yili*) of past human actions. Or, in other words, the purpose of history was to extract (or create) from historical facts narratives that both embodied the values and taught the lessons of the Confucian classics. Zhu Xi's efforts as a *daoxue* historian developed along three parallel lines, each of which focused on a specific period of history. First, his lasting legacy as a historian remains the *Outline and Details of the Comprehensive Mirror That Aids Governance* (*Zizhi tongjian gangmu* 資治通鑑綱目), which reworked Sima Guang's *Comprehensive Mirror* and covered the period from mid-Zhou through 959. We will discuss this work in detail below.

Second, a lesser work, the *Records of the Words and Deeds of Illustrious Ministers at Five [Song] Courts* (*Wuchao mingchen yanxing lu* 五朝名臣言行錄), collected biographical material on ninety-seven Northern Song officials, and was first printed at the Jianyang commercial printing center in Fujian in 1172. Zhu supplemented the official biographies of these officials with additional material from private histories, collected works, and notebooks. Although modern scholars view the work as an unbiased collection of pristine primary sources, as we shall see below, Zhu Xi's disciples held that he had infused the work with subtle insights into the deeper rhythms of Northern Song history.[9] Lastly, Zhu's views on early Southern Song history merged with his views on contemporaneous politics. Seven long chapters in the *Conversations*

see Huang, "Chu Hsi as a Teacher of History"; for greater detail see Qian Mu, *Zhuzi xin xue'an*, 5:1–150.

[9] Many Song imprints of the work survive, including the copy reprinted in the *Sibu congkan*. For a modern appraisal see Wang Deyi, "Zhu Xi *Wuchao* ji *Sanchao mingchen yanxing lu* de shiliao jiazhi."

of *Zhu Xi* (*Zhuzi yulei* 朱子語類) record Zhu Xi's discussions with his students on Song dynasty history, and two of these chapters focus on Southern Song personalities.[10] Many of these discussions revolve around his efforts to cast the historical image of Qin Gui as a nefarious minister who had oppressed the *daoxue* movement.[11]

Already in the 1160s, Zhu Xi conceived a plan to rework Sima Guang's *Comprehensive Mirror* into a more user-friendly guide to the moral lessons of history. He often expressed dissatisfaction with the *Comprehensive Mirror*, as well as with Li Tao's *Long Draft*. In his view, the moral lessons of history were too difficult to retrieve from the strict chronological format and overwhelming detail of these expansive works. Since both Sima Guang and Li Tao had composed their works as correctives to state history and to furnish a historical "discourse" for use at the highest levels of court policy formation, Zhu Xi's criticism was in this sense warranted.[12] As early as 1167, therefore, he devised a new format, the "outline and details," to render the moral lessons of history accessible to a wider audience of students and scholars. The result, the *Outline and Details of the Comprehensive Mirror That Aids Governance*, was completed by his students and first printed in 1219.[13]

Each typical entry in this work is divided into two parts. The "outline" (*gang*) is a brief, headline-like text that, using a coded language similar to the *Spring and Autumn Annals*, telegraphs or "outlines" the moral value of a specific historical event. These *gang* were printed in large type and arranged in chronological order. Underneath each *gang*, its supporting "details" (*mu*) discoursed on the moral value of the event in the *gang* in two ways. First, quotations of other historical texts in the *mu* placed the *gang*'s event in relation to other events both before and after the event under discussion. The resulting structure linked separate events across time and created a narrative that drew forth the moral values telegraphed in the *gang*. Second, quotations from the writings of *daoxue* scholars were appended to highlight the moral significance of the events in question, in essence to link the lessons now revealed from history and the moral values of the classics.

We may contrast the historiography of Sima Guang and his Sichuan heirs with that of Zhu Xi and his *daoxue* disciples as follows. For the former, history is a primary value; and its lessons emerge as self-evident from a balanced and transparent presentation of texts. Thus, Sima Guang delegated to others the assembly of primary texts, but reserved to himself the choice of which texts to weave into his primary narrative and which to consign to commentary. For the latter, history is a secondary enterprise, a repository of examples to illustrate

[10] *Zhuzi yulei*, 127.3042–133.3201; for Southern Song see 131.3138–132.3184.
[11] Hartman, "The Making of a Villain," 117–43.
[12] See *Zhuzi yulei*, 130.3132–33, 134.3204–7; and Hartman, "The Reluctant Historian."
[13] Lee, "Making Moral Decisions."

a priori moral and ethical values. The primary task of the historian is to select which events will serve as *gang* – to decide how history will illustrate these values. Thus, Zhu Xi, after drawing up the guidelines for the *Outline and Details*, left the selection of texts to his students.[14]

This shift can be described as a move away from an archival or documentary approach that viewed historical works as guides to bureaucratic practice, and toward a pedagogic approach that viewed them as guides to moral behavior.[15] This shift, as argued above, closely tracked the rise of *daoxue* over the last century of Song rule. The divide also manifested a strong regional difference. Beginning in the 1140s, Li Tao in Sichuan rekindled Sima Guang's legacy as a historian, and this tradition continued under Li Xinchuan and his assistants. Local literati and administrators supported the work of both historians, who benefited from the province's tradition of independent historiography and its well-developed printing industry. These traditions began and flourished independently of the *daoxue* movement, which influenced Sichuan scholars only in the early thirteenth century. Beginning in the 1230s, however, Mongol attacks on Sichuan ended the area's tradition of historical research; its archives and printing establishments were destroyed, and scholars were forced to flee eastward as refugees. As we have seen, no copy of any Sichuan imprint of a work by Li Tao or Li Xinchuan has survived.

On the contrary, the economic growth of Fujian as a manufacturing and trading center on the southeast coast continued undisturbed over the course of the Southern Song. Zhu Xi skillfully exploited the area's economic and political resources as he worked to build his empire-wide reputation as a synthesizer and promoter of the *daoxue* teachings. Zhu Xi's family had connections to the Fujian printing industry that enabled him to print his works quickly and to distribute them widely through his students and through the network of private *daoxue* academies in Fujian and beyond. Thus, while the historiographical traditions of Sichuan waned, the *daoxue* historiography that originated with Zhu Xi in Fujian continued to flourish locally and spread until the end of the dynasty.[16]

Chen Jun

If Zhu Xi's *Outline and Details of the Comprehensive Mirror* abridged and reworked Sima Guang's magnum opus and so began the shift from documentary to pedagogic history, Chen Jun's *Outline and Details* in the same way

---

[14] Hartman, "The Making of a Villain," 143–46.
[15] Hartman, "Chen Jun's *Outline and Details*," 275–281; Ge Zhaoguang, "Cong *Tongjian* dao *Gangmu*."
[16] For connections between *daoxue* and the Fujian printing industry see Chia, *Printing for Profit*, 79–99; for *daoxue* academies in Fujian see Walton, *Academies and Society*, 41–49.

reworked Li Tao's *Long Draft* and Li Xinchuan's *Chronological Record* and so completed this transition. In so doing, Chen Jun not only applied *daoxue* historiography to the dynasty's own history, but also, in the process, compiled the first single-authored, uniform history of Song from the dynasty's inception down to the author's own time. Chen Jun's two works, his history of Northern Song – the *Chronologically Arranged Complete Essentials in Outline and Details of the August Courts* – and his history of Southern Song through 1189 – the *Chronologically Arranged Outline and Details of the Two Restoration Courts* – are seminal milestones in the development of the grand allegory of Song history and vital to understanding the narratives that would influence the compilers of the *Song History* in 1345.[17]

Chen Jun 陳均 (1174–1244) was an only slightly younger contemporary of Li Xinchuan, and both shared youthful ambitions to bring order to the still vacillating history of their dynasty. And just as his Sichuan origins guided the goals and ultimate fate of Li Xinchuan's ambitions, so did Chen Jun's Fujian origins determine the course, content, and disposition of his historiographical labors. Chen Jun was born into one of the great literati lineages of Putian 莆田, Xinghua 興化 prefecture, on the Fujian coast. His granduncle was Chen Junqing, chief councilor from 1168 through 1170, leader of the literati coalition that had embraced Li Tao, and a political supporter of Zhu Xi, whom Chen recommended three times for office. When the elder Chen retired and returned to Putian in 1182, he brought back to Fujian copies of the Song dynastic histories and Li Tao's *Long Draft*. Intellectual leadership of the lineage, as well as Chen's library, passed to his fourth son, Chen Mi 陳宓 (1171–1230), who was a direct disciple of Zhu Xi. At some point, Chen Jun moved in with Chen Mi, who was his uncle, despite the latter being only three years older. Chen Jun acted both as study companion and amanuensis to his uncle, and their intellectual and political fortunes developed in tandem.[18]

Chen Mi was the most politically active of Chen Junqing's sons; and, when he obtained a court position in 1214, Chen Jun moved with him to the capital. In 1216, however, Chen Mi submitted a memorial that attacked the chief councilor, Shi Miyuan. This attack extended into the second generation a political feud that had begun in the Xiaozong era when Chen Junqing clashed over court policy with Shi Miyuan's father, Shi Hao 史浩 (1106–1194). Evidence indicates that Chen Jun and Chen Mi worked together to condense the *Long Draft* and produce a *daoxue*-inspired history of Song that would validate the principles of literati governance as well as the administration of Chen Junqing. After submitting his memorial, Chen Mi lost his post and left the capital; Chen Jun entered the Imperial University, where he remained for the next decade and

---

[17] The following section is based on Hartman, "Chen Jun's *Outline and Details*."
[18] For biographical sources on Chen, see Hartman, "Chen Jun's *Outline and Details*," 281 n.14.

continued to work on the history project. In 1226, just as Li Xinchuan was arriving in Lin'an, Chen, now aged fifty-two, resigned his university position and returned to Putian. By 1229, he had completed at least the Northern Song portion of his *Outline and Details* and had solicited prefaces from three influential Fujian officials – Zhen Dexiu, Zheng Xingzhi 鄭性之 (1172–1255), and Lin Jie 林岊 (*jinshi* 1187). Zhen Dexiu was just emerging at this time as an empire-wide advocate for *daoxue*; Zheng Xingzhi, a first-place *jinshi* in 1208, would go on to serve from 1235 through 1237 as assisting chief councilor in the Duanping administration.

In contrast to the loss of Song Sichuan imprints for the works of Li Tao and Li Xinchuan, two early imprints of Chen Jun's Northern Song history survive, and these testify to the immediate popularity of his work.[19] The complex relationship between these two imprints, together with the work's prefaces, as well as information gleaned from contemporaneous bibliographies, enables us to understand in detail how political forces shaped both the content and the reception of Chen Jun's work. Remarkably, the four prefaces reveal the author and his supporters in a tense dialogue over the nature of the book, its proper audience, and how best to proceed toward dissemination. Chen's own preface, written while his work was still in manuscript, argues defensively against three criticisms he anticipates the book will receive: that it usurps the authority of the official historians, that it abridges the fullness of the official record, and that it cannot hope to resolve the many contradictions in that record. He defends his book against these charges, but envisions his work primarily as a private study aid for students.[20]

The prefaces of Zhen Dexiu and Zheng Xingzhi, on the other hand, urge Chen Jun to submit his work to the court for use in the emperor's Classics Mat sessions. Zhen's preface is divided into three sections and is the longest of the group. An opening segment of direct discourse reveals Chen again distancing his work from official history and from Zhu Xi. While acknowledging Zhu Xi's *gangmu* as his inspiration, he avers that because his subject is Song history and not the history of earlier periods, he has not dared to inject moral verdicts on specific events into his *gang*, as Zhu Xi had done. Thus, he has not titled his work an "outline and details" but simply "complete essentials" (*beiyao* 備要). He requests from Zhen a synopsis of the work, which he doubtless hoped would serve as an imprimatur from the senior scholar and an additional bulwark against potential criticism. Zhen's synopsis, a key document in Song dynasty historiography that we will examine in Chapter 7, constitutes the earliest summary of Song history to contain all major elements of the grand allegory.

---

[19] On these imprints see Hartman, "Chen Jun's *Outline and Details*," 288–99.
[20] For these prefaces see *Huangchao gangmu*, frontmatter, 1–6; also Hartman, "Chen Jun's *Outline and Details*," 284–87.

Zhen's preface places Chen Jun's work squarely in the tradition of *daoxue* historiography. He agrees that Chen has not, like Zhu Xi, followed a strict *Spring and Autumn Annals* program and "lodged praise and blame" into the diction of his *gang*. Nevertheless, Zhen perceives in the work a carefully crafted and coherent stance on Northern Song history that he feels should serve as an agenda for present political reform – a reform that would move the administration of Shi Miyuan away from the policies of Wang Anshi toward those of the "founders." He holds that Chen's book articulates this message not in *Chunqiu* verbal codes but in the "judgments on selection and rejection" that are manifested in the topics that the work treats. He maintains that such judgments require moral authority and that Chen Jun has acquired that authority from his family ties to the former chief councilor Chen Junqing and from his association with "virtuous *shidafu*" (*xian shidafu* 賢士大夫). In sum, Zhen's preface makes the implied claim that the profusion of the original primary sources – the state histories and Li Tao – renders them morally diffuse and neutral, whereas the focused and targeted selections of Chen Jun provide a narrative of Northern Song history that is both morally and politically compelling.

Zheng Xingzhi's preface, dated fall 1229, relates that Zheng and several friends, attracted to the enormous utility of Chen Jun's work, have already taken steps to print the book. Despite Chen's initial objections, the preface ends with his permission to print. The earlier of the two surviving imprints inserted the phrase *gangmu* into the title, which accordingly read *Huangchao biannian gangmu beiyao*, the title by which the work is known today. The typographical format of this first edition followed the first edition of Zhu Xi's *Outline and Details of the Comprehensive Mirror*. As prefect of Quanzhou 泉州 in 1219, Zhen Dexiu had sponsored the initial printing of Zhu Xi's *Outline and Details*, and the same typographical layout was then used to print Chen Jun's work. In addition to this visual confirmation, Zheng's preface makes the specific claim that he viewed Chen Jun's work as a continuation of the spirit of Zhu Xi. Both Zhen Dexiu and Zheng Xingzhi went to Lin'an in 1234 as key members of the Duanping reform administration. In early 1235, Zheng requested that the court order Chen Jun to submit his work, which Zheng specifically calls "the *Long Draft Outline and Details*." Although Chen submitted a manuscript, the second of the two surviving imprints shows his efforts to bring both printings into accord with his revised manuscript. These efforts included moves to omit the phrase *gangmu* from the title and to excise passages from his original text that were now deemed "offensive to the state body."[21]

These efforts reveal that Chen Jun was sensitive to the increased scrutiny his work would receive as court-sanctioned history. The Southern Song portions of

---

[21] For an analysis of these passages see Hartman, "Chen Jun's *Outline and Details*," 303–6.

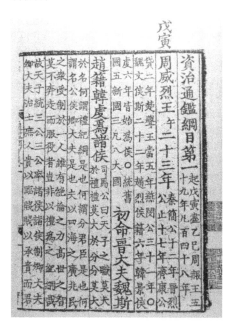

Figure 4.1 Zhu Xi, *Outline and Details for the Comprehensive Mirror*, first
1219 edition, Wenling.
After Chen Jian and Ma Wenda, *Song Yuan banke tushi*, 4 vols. (Beijing:
Xueyuan chubanshe, 2000), I. 131.

his work treat in profuse detail the achievements of Chen Junqing as chief
councilor, while virtually ignoring Shi Hao; and, as we have seen, Chen Jun's
own unsuccessful political career was closely linked to that of his uncle, Chen
Mi, and the latter's opposition to Shi Miyuan. When Chen's work was completed in 1229, Shi Miyuan was still firmly in power, and Chen, as a reclusive
and vulnerable provincial scholar, appears to have been reluctant to subject
himself and his work to the vicissitudes of court politics and the scrutiny that
would certainly follow submission. Even in 1235, Chen remained cautious. He
insisted on personally supervising the preparation of his manuscript for court
submission, refused the official position offered as reward, and insisted on
retaining his title as "University student" until his death at age seventy. Chen
Jun's caution proved prophetic. Inherently weak, the Duanping administration
dissolved in 1237, and Shi Songzhi, Shi Miyuan's nephew, assumed power in
1238. Under these circumstances, despite the state's recognition of the *daoxue*
teachings in 1241, Chen Jun's work was consigned to official oblivion at court.
In Fujian, however, the work proliferated in the province's *daoxue* academies.

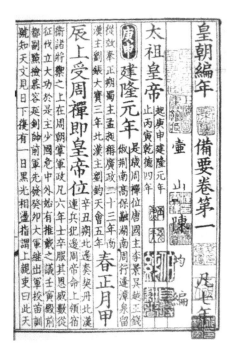

Figure 4.2 Chen Jun, *Chronologically Arranged Complete Essentials in Outline and Details of the August Courts*, first 1229 edition
Reproduced from *Huangchao biannian beiyao*, in the series *Zhonghua zai zao shan ben* (Beijing: Beijing tushuguan chubanshe, 2004).

Probably by 1250, the second segment covering Southern Song history from 1127 through 1189 was in print; and by 1260 a third installment that extended coverage through 1224 – possibly the work of a Zhen Dexiu disciple – was added to the series.

Summarizing, then, the evolution of the *Outline and Details*, Chen Jun (and probably also Chen Mi) conceived and composed the nucleus of the work as a private challenge to the policies of Shi Miyuan. Zheng Xingzhi and Chen Dexiu, Fujian statesmen with empire-wide ambitions, recast the work as a continuation of Zhu Xi's *Outline and Details of the Comprehensive Mirror* and propagated this revision as a historical justification for their program of political reform during the Duanping administration. Reacting against the autocracy of Shi Miyuan, these reformers cast their policies as a return to the supposed principles of the dynastic founder, Taizu, as these principles had supposedly been developed and implemented during the Qingli and Yuanyou administrations of Northern Song. This narrative, already present in Li Tao, cast Wang Anshi as an opponent of these dynastic principles. Extending this counternarrative to the Southern Song, the completed *daoxue* trilogy created a lineage of Wang Anshi extenders – Qin Gui, Han Tuozhou, and Shi Miyuan – that, like Wang, had all acted to thwart attempted returns to the policies of the dynastic founder.

Despite Chen Jun's personal reluctance, his supporters and those who continued his work made two claims for his achievement: (1) that he had extended the principles of Zhu Xi's outline and details to the subject matter of Song history, and (2) that he had abridged Li Tao's *Long Draft* as his major source for that subject matter. Figure 4.3, a comparison of the relative coverage of the *Long Draft* and the Northern Song portion of the *Outline and Details*, confirms these claims and reveals the nature of Chen Jun's debt to his source.[22] Focus on the Qingli and Yuanyou periods remains in both works. Coverage in the two works through 1067 is relatively consistent, although Chen increased space for the Song foundation while decreasing that for the Zhenzong years. Also, in keeping with the smaller scale and didactic aim of his work, he drastically reduced Li Tao's coverage of the New Policies and Yuanyou years to bring these years into proportion with the scale of his treatment of the Qingli period. The spikes around 1100 and again during 1125–1127 are to some degree deceiving. Both periods witnessed political reversals of the New Policies, and Chen Jun's "details" contain long denunciations, especially of Cai Jing and his allies. Likewise, much of the 1125–1127

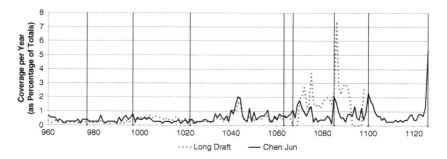

Figure 4.3 Coverage per year: Chen Jun versus *Long Draft*

[22] This chart reflects page counts for each year's coverage in the Zhonghua shuju editions of *Changbian* and *Huangchao gangmu*, normalized as a percentage of the total number of pages in each work. As with the earlier comparison between *SHY* and *Changbian*, the *Changbian* lacunae for the years 1067–1069, 1093–1097, and 1100–1126 certainly distort the *Changbian* data to some degree.

coverage, while chronicling the fall of Kaifeng, frames this defeat as a failure of the New Policies, and includes long extracts from memorials that denounce its advocates and their allies, while extolling and quoting at length Li Gang, a subsequent *daoxue* hero of the Restoration.[23] These spikes thus reinforce the content of the earlier spikes during the Qingli and New Policies eras.

Lü Zhong's *Lectures on Song History*

If Chen Jun composed the first organic history of the dynasty, and the first to articulate a coherent *daoxue* vision of that history, Lü Zhong then interpreted and refined that vision, and his *Lectures* quickly became the prism through which Song history would come to be viewed. Despite his pivotal role, little was known until recently of Lü or his works. I first pointed out his importance in 1998, and Zhang Qifan published a preliminary article in 1999.[24] Although his lectures on Northern Song history were taken into the *Siku quanshu*, those on Southern Song history were long presumed lost. A Ming manuscript of the latter, however, survives in Taiwan and eventually enabled Zhang Qifan and Bai Xiaoxia to publish a modern edition of both works in 2014.[25]

Ironically, one reason for the delayed awareness of Lü's importance was the contemporaneous popularity of his work. His *Lectures*, written for students preparing for *jinshi* examinations, were so often reprinted and reworked in late Song, and appeared under such a variety of titles and permutations, that later scholars had difficulty recognizing the essential coherence of his corpus. Even such basics as the original title of the works and their attribution to Lü became lost in an ensuing and enduring bibliographic muddle.[26] It is now possible, however, to recognize *Lectures on Major Events of the August Courts* (*Huangchao dashiji jiangyi* 皇朝大事記講義) and *Lectures on Major Events of the August Courts of the Restoration* (*Huangchao zhongxing dashiji jiangyi* 皇朝中興大事記講義) as the final and most sophisticated articulation of the *daoxue* interpretation of Song history before the demise of Song.

Despite the popularity of Lü Zhong's works, the diminished quantity of surviving documentation from late Song has forced scholars to rely largely

---

[23] On Zhu Xi's promotion of Li Gang see Hartman, "The Reluctant Historian," 138–39.

[24] Hartman, "The Making of a Villain," 80–82; Zhang Qifan, "*Dashiji jiangyi* chutan."

[25] Lü Zhong, *Leibian Huangchao dashiji jiangyi. Leibian Huangchao zhongxing dashiji jiangyi* (Shanghai: Shanghai renmin chubanshe, 2014). This work reprints Zhang's 1999 article (874–84), Zhang and Bai's report on the Ming manuscript of the Southern Song material (885–97), and Huang Huixian's in-depth article on Lü Zhong and his works (898–924). For a summary of current research on Lü Zhong see Wang Shengduo and Chen Chaoyang, "*Songshi quanwen* chayin shilun wenxian yanjiu," 457–74. This section has also benefited from two unpublished papers on Lü Zhong, one by Jaeyoon Song and another by Ari Levine. I am grateful to both scholars for sharing their research with me.

[26] Huang Huixian, "Lü Zhong yu *Huangchao dashiji xintan*," 909–15.

upon Ming and Qing gazetters to reconstruct his career. He was a native of Jinjiang 晉江, a city adjacent to Quanzhou on the Fujian coast, where his grandfather in 1172 and his father and uncle together in 1199 had passed the *jinshi* exams. Lack of further information suggests that their careers were local and that Lü Zhong was born into an established Fujian literati family, albeit one lacking the national stature of Chen Jun's. He received his own *jinshi* in 1247, ranking sixth among 527 candidates who passed.[27] He was initially posted as instructor in the prefectural school at Zhaoqing 肇慶, about fifty miles west of modern Guangzhou. While in Zhaoqing, he reportedly added shrines at the school to Zhou Dunyi and to Bao Zheng 包拯 (999–1062). His capital career began in the early 1250s when he obtained an entry-level position in the Imperial Library's history office, followed by a stint as tutor to the imperial clan. He was then promoted to an administrative position in the Imperial University and to the staff of the emperor's Classics Mat. He returned to Fujian to attend to the burial of his older brother, but returned to the capital in 1258 as administrative assistant in the Imperial Library. He was removed, however, probably by Chief Councilor Ding Daquan 丁大全 (d. 1263), and posted out as prefect of Tingzhou 汀州, in Fujian. After serving a full tour in 1260–1261, he returned to the Imperial Library, but seems to have died shortly thereafter.[28]

The gazetteer biographies include several sentences from Lü Zhong memorials that critique various government policies. However, Fang Hui's 方回 (1227–1286) biography of Lü Wu 呂午 (1179–1255) contains an account that brings Lü Zhong's political views into clearer focus. Fang relates that Lü Zhong was close to his townsman Hong Tianxi 洪天錫 (d. 1272) when they were together in the capital. In 1254 Hong was appointed censor with the secret support of the eunuch Dong Songchen 董宋臣, and Hong consulted Lü upon which topics he might remonstrate. Lü, frustrated that his own position afforded him no opportunity to proffer criticism, and unaware of the secret alliance between Hong and Dong, replied with a long list of grievances against the eunuchs and their allies among Empress Xie's kinsmen.[29] In another example of Lü's political inclinations, Lü Zhong probably supported the protests of the "six gentlemen," Imperial University students who protested Ding Daquan's removal of Chief Counciler Dong Hui 董槐 (*jinshi* 1213) in 1256. The University administration, of which Lü was then a member, supported the students, and Ding imposed sanctions on the University.[30] Ding's subsequent

---

[27] Fu Xuancong, *Song dengkeji kao*, 1590.
[28] The above relies upon Huang Huixian, "Lü Zhong yu *Huangchao dashiji* xintan," 898–904, and the sources there cited.
[29] Fang Hui, "Zuoshi Lü gong jiazhuan," 12b–13a, appended to Lü Wu, *Zuoshi jiancao*.
[30] *SS*, 418.12529; anonymous, *Songji sanchao zhengyao jianzheng*, 2.217–18; Huang Huixian, "Lü Zhong yu *Huangchao dashiji* xintan," 903–4, also links Lü with this event.

dismissal of Lü from his Imperial Library post several years later may derive from this earlier encounter.

The date of a surviving preface to the *Lectures* on Northern Song, written by one Liu Shifu 劉實甫 (*jinshi* 1244) in 1247, the same year that Lü Zhong received his *jinshi* degree, implies that Lü had probably begun work on his project well before that year, perhaps as part of his own exam preparation.[31] The latest datable reference in the *Lectures* is to a 1234 memorial by Wei Liaoweng. The work was thus composed sometime between 1234 and 1247, more probably toward the earlier end of that range, a period that witnessed the downfall of the Duanping administration and the rise of Shi Songzhi.[32] Liu's preface states that he first saw a version of the work in his days at the Imperial University, thus sometime before his *jinshi* in 1244. However, his preface neither names the work's author nor cites its title. An author strip often copied into Ming and Qing manuscripts gives Lü Zhong's title as instructor in the Zhaoqing provincial school and names as copyeditor one Miao Lie 繆烈 (*jinshi* 1238), a Fujian native and instructor in the provincial school at Fuzhou.[33] These facts suggest that Lü completed the Northern Song segment of the *Lectures*, probably in Fujian in the late 1230s or early 1240s; that manuscript copies circulated widely and perhaps anonymously among students preparing for the exams; and that a commercial Fujian printer, perhaps to take advantage of Lü's own exam success in 1247, published at least the Northern Song portion shortly thereafter.

Other evidence helps to further date and politically place Lü Zhong's work as a historian. A late Song bibliography mentions him as the joint author of a collection of evaluative comments on selected passages from Zhu Xi's *Outline and Details of the Comprehensive Mirror* that "extracted examples of positive and negative historical change and rendered judgments upon them." The work, entitled *Discussions and Judgments on the Outline and Details* (*Gangmu lunduan* 綱目論斷), contained a colophon by Xu Qingsou 徐清叟 (*jinshi* 1214) and was compiled in conjunction with the submission of Zhu Xi's history for Classics Mat use at the start of the Duanping administration in 1234.[34] If this entry is correct, then Lü Zhong's *Lectures* on Song history should perhaps be viewed as a continuation of earlier work to render more accessible Zhu Xi's history of pre-Song China, and futhermore as evidence of his familiarity with Zhu Xi's *daoxue* historiography. Xu Qingsou was a senior Fujian literatus who had opposed Shi Miyuan and formed close ties to the Duanping administration under Zhen Dexiu and Wei Liaoweng. He would go

[31] For Liu's preface see *Huangchao dashiji*, 31–2.
[32] Huang Huixian, "Lü Zhong yu *Huangchao dashiji* xintan," 907–9.
[33] Wang Shengduo and Chen Chaoyang, "*Songshi quanwen* chayin," 465–66.
[34] Chao Gongwu, *Junzhai dushuzhi jiaozheng*, 1114.

on to serve as assiting chief councilor from 1252 through 1255 when he and Lü Zhong were known as "renowned literati" in Lin'an.

The description of the *Discussions and Judgments on the Outline and Details* as interpretive judgments on selected historical events could also well describe the *Lectures*. Liu Shifu described the work he prefaced as "classifying into groups the major events of each reign, with groups for each successive reign and explanations for each successive event, searching out their origins and their ends, illuminating the subtle and the hidden, speaking of short-term [events] yet pointing toward their long-term [connections and implications]." The modern text of the *Lectures* contains 339 entries on Northern Song and 408 on Southern Song. Each entry contains three parts: a title that states the topic of the entry, one or more events arranged in chronological sequence within the topical entry, and Lü Zhong's comments or "lectures." These latter sometimes occur after individual events, but usually follow the last event in the entry and summarize Lü's thoughts on all the historical events included in the topical entry.

Scholars have noted that Lü Zhong's *Lectures* combine the formats of Zhu Xi's *gangmu* and the "topical narrative" (*jishi benmo* 紀事本末) of Yuan Shu 袁樞 (1131–1205).[35] Although Lü Zhong's debt to his predecessors is clear, he has in fact created a new format. His *Lectures* maximize the power of the "topical narrative" to categorize and group events under topical headings; at the same time, by softening the rigid division between *gang* and *mu*, Lü Zhong is able both to maintain chronological continuity and to insert his own comments into each entry. This power to define the topical categories and to select which events to include in each topic enables him to define his fields of historical inquiry and to decide which events would be included and which excluded; in other words, to create his own narratives from the existing chronologies of Song history available to him. As will be shown below, Chen Jun's *Outline and Details* was the proximate source for these details; thus, Lü's "events" came to him to some extent preselected. At the same time, six introductory essays (three each at the beginning of the portions on Northern and Southern Song) furnish an over-arching interpretive structure for the work. Lü has crafted the diction and rhetoric of the topic titles to reinforce the themes of these introductory essays. Thus, as one reads the work, the introductory essays prefigure the topics to come; and the topical entries, once encountered, refer back to and reinforce the message of the essays.

The semantic content and rhetorical structure of the topic titles differ in the Northern and Southern Song portions of the *Lectures*, and this difference reinforces one of Lü Zhong's major themes: that the character of the Song state changed forever with the advent of the New Policies. The titles in the Northern Song portion can be divided into general, and generally value-neutral,

---

[35] Wang Deyi, "Songdai Fujian de shixue," 171.

topics that occur across most reigns ("ascending the throne," "imperial succession," "seeking remonstrance") as opposed to groups of events that occurred
only once ("pacifying Sichuan," "the Heavenly letters descend"). Among the
former category are topics that treat the major civil institutions of governance:
the chief councilors, the Censorate, the Secretariat drafters, the academic
agencies, and the Classics Mat. Employing a value-neutral diction, these
sequences of topics occur for the reigns of Taizong through Yingzong, but
cease for the reigns of Shenzong and after.[36] In contrast, the diction of the titles
for topics that treat the New Policies characterizes them as groups of events that
disrupted the pre-Shenzong order and destroyed the unity of early Song
governance. Thus the divisive rhetoric of gentlemen and petty men dominates
many topics for the Zhezong and Huizong reigns.[37] The titles in the *Lectures* on
Southern Song focus more on specific policies, actions, and personalities than
on institutions, and follow chronological order more closely than do their
Northern Song counterparts.

The diction of a special set of topic titles also transmits a distinct *daoxue*
perspective. There are two subcategories within this group. The first treats the
actions and careers of *daoxue* paragons from Zhou Dunyi through Zhu Xi as
well as the various inquisitions against the *daoxue* movement.[38] The second
and much more numerous category imposes a value-laden *daoxue* rhetoric
upon otherwise neutral events. The first entry in this category, entitled
"Rectifying the Mind and Cultivating the Body" (*zhengxin xiushen* 正心修
身) includes two apocryphal anecdotes that enable Lü Zhong to quote in his
comments Zhu Xi's equation of Taizu with the sage-emperors Yao and Shun.[39]
All of the titles that employ the *junzi/xiaoren* distinction also contribute to the
daoxue narrative of Song history as a struggle between positive and negative
moral forces. Taken in their totality, these entries project the ideals and politics
associated with Southern Song *daoxue* back to the beginning of the dynasty and

[36] For Taizong see *Huangchao dashiji*, 4.88–97; for Zhenzong, 6.132–49; for Renzong,
8.175–9.199; and for Yingzong, 13.256–60. These sections also include entries on financial,
legal, and provincial institutions, but Lü Zhong's focus is clearly on the civil organs of the court
and control by civil-side literati. For example, his entry on the Renzong-era Financial
Commission selects four events between 1034 and 1059 that emphasize (1) literati control
over the commission through a unique system of in-house promotion through its sub-agencies
and (2), as theoretically desirable, commission oversight of all budgeting functions, including
those of the Inner Treasury. He then cites a passage from Wang Anshi's 10,000-word memorial
of 1059 to argue that the New Policies and the government reorganization of 1082 destroyed this
pre-Shenzong-era system of financial control. See *Huangchao dashiji*, 9.197–99.

[37] For example, of the forty-seven Zhezong-era entries, sixteen employ the *junzi/xiaoren* dichotomy; of the eighteen Huizong entries, ten employ this diction. See *Huangchao dashiji*, 20.-
347–57 and 21.362–74.

[38] *Huangchao dashiji*, 14.272–74, 18.334–35, 22.380; *Zhongxing dashiji*, 4.491–92, 22.775, 23.-
784–85, 788–89, 25.812–13, 814–15, 817–18, 27.843–44.

[39] *Huangchao dashiji*, 3.67–68.

create the illusion that these ideas formed a consistent thread that ran through Song history.

Lü Zhong's format is ideally suited to categorizing and shaping essentially disparate events into the larger organic patterns of *daoxue* historiography. For example, a topic entitled "benevolent governance" (*renzheng* 仁政) groups together five incidents between 983 and 994. In the first incident, Taizong remarks to Zhao Pu that he has removed oppressive Five Dynasties tax levies and declares his intention to abolish land taxes entirely. The remaining four events all concern tax remissions and emergency measures enacted in famine-stricken areas.[40] In other words, by grouping these five events together, Lü frames the last four tax remissions as examples of Taizong's general desire to reduce tax levies, and labels all five as examples of his "benevolent governance." In reality, tax remisions for famine areas were routine policy since the taxes could not anyway be collected; futhermore, Taizong never followed through on his intention to abolish land taxes.

The second component of a typical *Lectures* entry is a text (or texts) that details a specific, dated historical event or set of events. Lü Zhong relied heavily upon Chen Jun's *Outline and Details* for this component of his entries. Comparing the two works, the diction for the same event is often identical, or parallel in ways that make clear Lü's debt to Chen.[41] Yet Lü has not slavishly copied his predecessor. Chen Jun's format carefully distinguished between *gang* and *mu*, but Lü copied and combined text indiscriminately from both. A typical entry from the *Lectures* begins with a Chen *gang*, then selects and reworks text from the ensuing *mu*. Since these passages now become the "primary" texts upon which Lü delivers his "lecture," the resulting narrative elevates material that was secondary, supportive, or evaluative in Chen Jun into the higher category of "primary source" in the *Lectures*. This process allows Lü Zhong, while adhering closely to his predecessor's text, to bend the shape of the ensuing narrative to his own ends. For some entries, it can be shown that Lü went back to the *Long Draft* to retrieve language more suited to his purposes.[42]

Lü's comments or "lectures" upon his preselected and assembled historical events comprise the third component of the topical entries. These lectures

---

[40] *Huangchao dashiji*, 5.109–10. All five events are taken from Chen Jun; see *Huangchao gangmu*, 3.67–68, 72, 76, 80, 5.96.

[41] I am indebted to Jaeyoon Song for this observation on the Northern Song *Lectures*. My own research has confirmed his opinion and also established the same relationship between Lü's Southern Song *Lectures* and Chen Jun's *Liangchao zhongxing biannian gangmu*. The origin of Lü Zhong's material for the reigns of Guangzong and Ningzong (the period 1190–1224) remains uncertain. There seems no relationship between Lü's text and the anonymous *Xubian liangchao gangmu beiyao*, which also covers this period. The latter work derives from the Sichuan historiography of Li Xinchuan; see Hartman, "Chen Jun's *Outline and Details*," 310–11.

[42] See, for example, *Huangchao dashiji*, 3.61, and the source texts at *Huangchao gangmu*, 1.19; and *Changbian*, 3.62.

reinforce themes already outlined in the three introductory essays in each portion. The three essays in the Southern Song *Lectures*, for example, are described as "general discussions" (*tonglun* 統論).[43] Taken in their entirety, these essays present an extended, multifaceted, and sophisticated appraisal of Song history. They also manifest a distinctive and consistent rhetorical structure. The essays are sequential; the second and third in each series build upon and circle out from the initial essay.[44] The essays on Southern Song are much longer than those on Northern Song. They summaraize and enlarge upon ideas from the first series and were clearly written for a subsequent, and conceptually independent, volume on Southern Song.[45]

The opening essay on Northern Song is entitled "On the Essence of Governance" (*Guoti lun* 國體論) and outlines Lü's ideas on the theoretical principles of Song governance. As always, the character *ti* 體 carries overtones of "body," and the essay thus treats the basic principles by which the body of state should be organized and how it should function. The title's full implication is thus "on good goverance and the body of the state." The second essay, "On Institutions" (*Zhidu lun* 制度論) describes the regulatory mechanisms that translate these principles into practice. The third essay, "On the State Dynamic" (*Guoshi lun* 國勢論) analyzes the military and diplomatic position of the Song state relative to its neighbors and to its historical predecessors. The second and third essays in the Southern Song sequence repeat these titles (*Zhongxing zhidu lun, Zhongxing guoshi lun*), but the first essay is different. "On the Restoration Model" (*Zhongxing guimo lun* 中興規模論) posits three evolutionary paradigms for dynastic governance: founding, maintaining, and restoring. The latter can succeed only if the polity can generate "worthies and gentlemen" capable of restoring the "benevolence and rightness" of the founders. In Lü's view, neither the Song nor any earlier dynasty had achieved a true restoration. Lü chastizes Southern Song literati for repeated moral failures and details a long string of bad choices, opportunistic politicians, and autocratic councilors that destroyed the Song restoration.[46]

An analysis of all six essays and a depiction of their themes as these are dispersed throughout Lü's individual lectures would require a specialized study. We concentrate, therefore, on the first essay, "On the Essence of Governance," which contains Lü's theory of Song governance along with his basic narrative of its historical fate. The tract also presents a prime example of *daoxue* historiography in its final phase. All three essays that precede the Northern Song *Lectures* employ an identical rhetorical structure: two sets of complementary bipolarities, much like the x and y axes on a graph, define the

[43] *Zhongxing dashiji*, 1.429.   [44] My thanks to Ari Levine for this observation.
[45] See Lü Zhong's own comment at *Zhongxing dashiji*, 1.436.
[46] *Zhongxing dashiji*, 1.429–36.

theoretical and historical fields of inquiry.[47] In this first essay, one axis comprises the two poles of "latitude" (*kuan* 寬) and "rigor" (*yan* 嚴). Latitude (or forbearance, leniency) and rigor (or strictness, exactitude) are two modalities of governance that the ruler can apply at his discretion.[48] On the second axis are "benevolent intent" (*renyi* 仁意) and "the political system" (*jigang* 紀綱). Lü insists that, in contrast to earlier dynasties, an intent or inclination toward benevolent rule was the fundamental mind-set of Taizu and his successors. The political system, by which Lü means the physical organs and practical mechanics of governance, is the vehicle that transforms this imperial intent into policy and concrete government. Lü assumes that if the ruler can properly balance latitude and rigor then the political system will effectively transmute his benevolent intentions into successful administration.

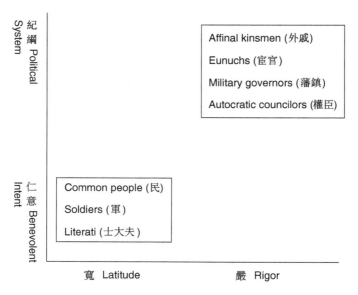

Figure 4.4 Theoretical and historical fields of inquiry in Lü Zhong, "On the Essence of Governance"

---

[47] I am grateful to Ari Levine for the graph analogy; the concrete realization of that analogy is mine.

[48] The political contrast between *kuan* and *yan* dates to the Western Han, if not before. *Yan* describes an urgent, serious command, and one that therefore carries severe punishment with no possibility of latitude or amnesty (*kuan*) for noncompliance. *Yan* can also mean "grave, awesome," and often describes the imperial demeanor or bearing. *Kuan* originally described a large, spacious room, and therefore large-hearted, magnanimous. See Wang Fengyang, *Gu ci bian*, 647, 861–62.

However, the ruler's task is not merely to choose between latitude and rigor but also to adjust these modalities as necessary to regulate the various components of the body politic. For this model, Lü divides the Song polity into two constituencies. The first includes the common people, common soldiers, and literati officials (*shidafu*). Their support and unity enable the emperor to obtain and hold the empire. The second, however, which frustrates governance, includes the emperor's affinal kin, eunuchs, "military governors" (*fanzhen* 藩鎮 – by which Lü means the contemporaneous senior military leadership) – and autocratic ministers.

The first group should be encouraged with latitude, the second restrained with strictness. Both axes must function in consort to achieve this goal, "for latitude means the fulfillment of benevolent intent; and rigor means rectification of the political system. Benevolent intent and the political system must be promulgated together for good governance to be realized." Thus, good governance – a healthy political system that effectuates benevolent rule and mainains a political balance between all elements of the polity – ensues from application of the proper modality to the proper group at the proper time. Lü maintains that this governance model derives from antiquity as expressed in two ideas of Mencius: (1) only the king who does not insist on killing can unify the realm; but (2) his virtue alone is not sufficient, absent effective institutions, to bring about benevolent rule.[49] Lü insists that the Song founders' embrace of the first principle manifested their benevolent intent, and that the political system they created demonstrated the second.

Having laid down this theroretical base, Lü proceeds to a historical analysis that makes the claim for Song exceptionalism. He provides four examples to demonstrate how the founders applied these principles and so surpassed the Han and Tang. Building upon his bipartite analysis of the Song polity, he provides one example each of how the Song founders restrained the four dangerous elements in the second constituency. They gave generous emoluments to affinal kin but did not permit them to interfer at court or to serve in provincial positions, thus avoiding the disasters of Eastern Han when affinal kin controlled the state.[50] They did not slaughter eunuchs but restrained their power by assigning them carefully prescribed duties, and thus avoided disasters as when the Zhou dynasty cook Yiya and eunuchs conspired to manipulate the succession.[51] They took back power from the military governors, and thus avoided the provincial separatism of late Tang. Finally, Taizong established the position of assisting chief councilor and created the remonstrance organs to investigate "nefarious" officials, and thus prevented the emergence of strongmen, or in Song terms, "autocratic ministers," such as Wang Mang 王莽 (33 BCE–23 CE) and Cao Cao 曹操 (155–220) in Han, or Zhu Wen 朱溫

---

[49] Legge, *Mencius*, 136–37, 289.
[50] Twitchett and Loewe, *The Cambridge History of China, Volume 1*, 174.
[51] *Zuo Tradition*, 1:337.

(852–912) in late Tang. "Thus they used the political system to exert rigor in those places where rigor was necessary."

The political system was also the mechanism through which the founders expressed their benevolence and so brought about the unity of the people, soldiers, and literati. However, balance between latitude and rigor also played an important role in how the system regulated these groups. In accordance with the rulers' intent, the people were not excessively taxed, corvéed, or punished; yet strictures prevented excess such as theft and treachery. Solders were well treated, yet military regulations ensured order. Officials were given ample opportunities for advancement, yet quotas and strict rules at the Ministry of Personnel regulated their careers. In each case, although latitute defined the ruler's primary policy, corresponding rigor prevented abuse and disorder.

The actualization of benevolent rule thus depends on this balance between latitude and rigor. For example, if bandits are not supressed, then benevolence flows to the bandits, and people resent the state. If monoply laws are not stricly enforced, then the benefits of the rulers' benevolence accrue to profiteers. Thus, brave soldiers suffer when cowards are rewarded; good officials suffer when the rules of promotion are violated. "For without benevolent intent there is no foundation upon which to ground the political system, and without the system there is no way to exercise benevolent intent." Lü argues that the political system became subsequently too weak to execute the founders' original intent, and thus few people benefited from their benevolence. Wang Anshi and his followers then maintained that the founders' benevolence had been insufficient and their original foundations flawed.

Lü then atttacks the historical justification of the New Policies. Failing to appreciate this balance of the founders, Wang argued that while Taizu and Taizong had been rigorous (*yan*), Zhenzong and Renzong had been too lax (*kuan*), and this latitude led to the political and economic difficulties of the 1060s. The New Policies would thus correct the empire's ills by re-exerting the rigor of the founders. Lü admits that the political structure had indeed deteriorated by the Renzong era, but compares the problems to those of an aging house with cracking walls and a leaking roof. Such minor, non-structural defects are easily repaired; and Fan Zhongyan already outlined the work to be done, but Wang elected rather to demolish the entire structure and build another house. "In the process, not only did he destroy the political system of the founders but also the concept of loyalty and tolerance upon which they had founded our state."

Zhang Dun and Cai Jing continued and exacerbated these policies, applying excessive rigor to the people (through increased taxes) and to the literati (through political repression), all the while showering excess latitude on eunuchs such as Gao Qiu 高俅 (d. 1126) and Tong Guan 童貫 (1054–1126). So rigor became repression and latitude became license. Lü concludes his essay with one of the many counterfactuals to which he is devoted: suppose Fan Zhongyan's minor reforms, which dealt with many of the same problems as the New Policies, had succeeded? The New Policies would never have happened, the balanced policies of the founders would have continued, and the political structure they created would have endured.[52]

This intial essay sets up a series of premises that the subsequent essays and lectures develop and confirm. First, a sense of Confucian benevolence motivated the Song founders Taizu and Taizong. Second, these ideals prompted them to create policies and political structures that promoted the prosperity of the populace under the leadership of the literati. Third, these policies included actions to restrain the power of other state actors who are presumed to be antithetical to these values – the affinal kin, eunuchs, military leaders, and bureaucratic strongmen. Fourth, employing latitude and rigor where appropriate, Zhenzong and Renzong continued the founders' governance model. Fifth, the advent of Wang Anshi and the New Policies destroyed the founders' intentions and their political structures. Sixth, subsequent Song history devolved into a struggle between those who embraced the original intentions of the founders and those who promoted the New Policies and their continuing permutations. As we shall explore in Chapter 7, these six premises constitute a fully developed "grand allegory" of Song history that the Yuan historians used to organize the official *Song History* of 1345 and that still continues to influence modern scholarship on Song.

As we have seen at the beginning of this chapter, Lü Zhong's *Lectures* feature prominently in the pseudocommentary to the received version of Li Xinchuan's *Chronological Record*. Recent research indicates that late Song and early Yuan publishers took advantage of the popularity of Lü Zhong's *Lectures* to market publications on Song history to a public increasingly receptive of the *daoxue* academic curriculum. The pseudocommentary to the *Record* and the *Sagacious Administration from the Two Restoration Courts of the August Song* were not the only works to insert material from the *Lectures*. Commercial publishers, probably reacting to the return of the civil service examinations in 1315, also printed other chronological histories of Song "augumented with the collected opinions of many Confucians" (增入諸儒集議).[53] Surviving Yuan imprints of works that carry this designation attest that Lü Zhong was by far the most often quoted of these scholars. Liu Shiju's *Continuation of the Song Chronological Comprehensive Mirror for Administration* (*Xu Song biannian zizhi tongjian* 續宋編年資治通鑑), a short history of Southern Song, quotes Lü Zhong thirty-nine times within the work's fifteen *juan*. The much larger

[52] *Huangchao dashiji*, 1.35–38.
[53] For this expression see the printer's advertisement following the table of contents in Liu Shiju's *Xu Song biannian zizhi tongjian, mulu*, 4. For a similar phrase, *zengru mingru jiangyi* 增入名儒講議 in reference to the *Songshi quanwen*, see Balazs and Hervouet, *A Sung Bibliography*, 82.

Complete Texts of Song History (*Songshi quanwen* 宋史全文) quotes Lü Zhong a total of 210 times – 153 times in the Northern Song portion, ninety-seven in the Southern Song. These quotations are overwhelmingly from the third, "lecture" portion of Lü's work. The *Complete Texts*, however, introduces Lü Zhong's opinions using three different locutions: (1) as "Lü Zhong says" (呂中曰), (2) as the "*Record of Major Events*" (大事記), and (3) as the "*Lectures*" (講議). Wang Shengduo concludes from these variations that the scholars and editors whom the booksellers employed to insert "collected opinions" into their imprints relied upon multiple late Song editions of Lü Zhong's lectures.[54] This variety thus attests to the popularity of his works in late Song, and the insertion of these extracts into Yuan imprints confirms Lü Zhong's continuing influence in Yuan.

Daoxue Historiography

Before proceeding to examine how these late Song currents manifest themselves in the Yuan-period *Song History*, it may be useful to summarize the state of *daoxue* historiography at the end of Song. We may begin by distinguishing among the closely related concepts of *daoxue* historians, *daoxue* history, and *daoxue* historiography. *Daoxue* historians are historians who practice a distinctive *daoxue* historiography and whose works manifest a *daoxue* historical perspective. As outlined above, the major surviving authors are Zhu Xi, Chen Jun, and Lü Zhong. As used here, "*daoxue* perspective" does not correspond precisely to any modern definition of the "Learning of the Way" as a philosophical movement. As is well known, modern scholarship is not unanimous on the definition of Song *daoxue*, nor on its nature as a Song intellectual and political movement, nor on the relation of Song phenomena to developments in later Confucianism.[55]

Given this lack of consensus, it is difficult to align *daoxue* historiography precisely with any of the philosophical schools of Song Neo-Confucianism that modern historians have struggled to delineate. For example, Wang Shengduo notes that Lü Zhong's *Lectures* contain elements both from Cheng/Zhu

---

[54] Wang Shengduo and Chen Chaoyang, "*Songshi quanwen* chayin shilun wenxian yanjiu," 457–64. The pattern of Lü Zhong quotations in Liu Shiju's *Xu Song biannian zizhi tongjian* displays similar variety. The first *juan* cites the "*Zhongxing dashiji*" (中興大事記) sixteen times. There are no quotations in *juan* two through seven, then twenty-three quotations introduced by either "Lü Zhong says" or "Lü Zhong's *Lecture* says" (呂中議曰) occur in *juan* eight through fifteen. As related above, the *Yongle Encyclopedia* versions of the *Long Draft* and the *Chronological Record* also contain inserted quotations from Lü Zhong's *Lectures*. There are fifty-four such insertions into the commentary of the *Chronological Record*; all are cited as "Lü Zhong's *Record of Major Events*" (呂中大事記).

[55] For a survey of Song meanings of the term "*daoxue*" in relation to modern scholarship on Song "Neo-Confucianism" see De Weerdt, *Competition over Content*, 25–42.

Confucianism and from Eastern Zhe "statecraft" thinkers such as Chen Fuliang 陳傅良 (1137–1203) and Ye Shi; and he sees the *Complete Texts of Song History* as continuing to perpetrate such "contradictions."[56] However, viewed positively, one could likewise argue that the historical enterprise of *daoxue* both encompassed and transcended the movement's diverse philosophical currents. Although the three historians examined above all wrote in a similar *daoxue* mode, no consistent trajectory links or unifies their philosophical outlooks. As we have seen, Cheng/Zhu epistemology undergirds Zhu Xi's *Outline and Details of the Comprehensive Mirror*; but Chen Jun declined on a number of points to follow the master, and Lü Zhong drew upon the full range of the twelfth-century *daoxue* sources without regard to philosophical distinctions. Viewed from yet another perspective, the century between Zhu Xi and Lü Zhong witnessed a devolution in the practice of *daoxue* historiography, from major leaders of the movement (such as Zhu Xi himself), to scholars from lineages with national visibility (Chen Jun), to regional scholars of lesser renown (Lü Zhong), and finally to anonymous editors in the employ of commercial booksellers. Yet all of these authors practiced a distinct *daoxue* historiography that by the end of Song had produced a definitive *daoxue* history.

Reviewing the lives and works of these three historians, one can count at least six features that mark *daoxue* historiography. First, all agree that the purpose of history is to render moral judgments, principally on individual historical actors, so that readers may recognize and internalize the values that these judgments render. This propensity links them directly to the tradition of the *Spring and Autumn Annals*, a work in which Confucius supposedly imposed a moral order on otherwise random events. These authors freely apply the rhetorical dichotomy of *junzi* versus *xiaoren* to express their moral verdicts. Second, a contemporaneous context, and potential political application, underlie their historiography. Although the specific political targets differ in each period, in general the writers frame themselves and their audiences as political underdogs pitted against entrenched in-groups (principally, the four enemies of benevolent intent in Lü Zhong's schema) and literati proponents of the New Policies. Third, a combination of the first two concerns propels a highly teleological narrative that, seeking similarities between recent and past events, identifies and describes past actions in terms of present political struggles. The resulting discourse prioritizes the origins of institutions deemed positive and posits these back to the dynastic founders; in turn, pernicious deviations from the founders' purported intentions usually begin with Wang Anshi.

---

[56] Wang Shengduo and Chen Chaoyang, "*Songshi quanwen* chayin shilun wenxian yanjiu," 457, 464.

Fourth, in contrast to Sima Guang, Li Tao, and Li Xinchuan, who directed their works toward court historians and official policy makers (including the emperor), the *daoxue* historians wrote for a much wider audience of examination participants and interested literati. In this sense, their works are primarily pedagogical and were widely used at schools and academies, especially those that supported a *daoxue* curriculum. Fifth, the *daoxue* historians devised new formats that better accommodated the needs of their distinctive historiography. The new formats increasingly enabled *daoxue* historians to abridge the existing historical record in ways that foregrounded their moral and institutional concerns and belittled the status and power of their adversaries. Lastly, all of the major *daoxue* historians were from Fujian province. They benefited from the area's robust printing industry and often acted in consort with Fujian political leaders in Lin'an, for example Zhu Xi and Chen Junqing, Chen Jun and Zhen Dexiu, Lü Zhong and Xu Qingsou.

The second half of this volume delineates the motifs and narratives that comprise the *daoxue* historical vision and explores the origins of these rhetorical components in the vicissitudes of Song political history itself. We will focus on three clusters of motifs – the benevolent character of the Song dynastic enterprise; the deification of its founder, Taizu; and the moral conflict between *junzi* and *xiaoren* as a metaphor for Song political life. But, as we shall see, the *daoxue* historians did not invent these tropes. They merely repackaged and readjusted existing historical texts – often material from or on the margins of the official state historiographical operation itself. Thus, the textual material from which *daoxue* history was created pre-dates by many years the thirteenth-century finalization of that history.

However, a close correlation exists between the earlier works in which these rhetorical stances first arose and Li Xinchuan's tripartite periodization of the *daoxue* movement in the *Record of the Way*. In brief, during Li's first period, Sima Guang's *Su River Records* first defined the nature of the Song founding and then valorized the Qingli period of Emperor Renzong's reign as the ultimate expression of those values. During Li's second period, Fan Chong further refined this emphasis and positioned the Yuanyou period as an extension of Sima Guang's vision. Finally, in the third period, Zhao Ruyu's *The Ministers Memorials from the August Courts* and Zhu Xi's *Records of the Words and Deeds of Illustrious Ministers at Five Courts* codified in great detail the persons and policies that, in their view, had promoted this Taizu–Qingli–Yuanyou axis of political value. And, also in the third period, as we have seen above, Li Tao's *Long Draft* had already attempted (unsuccessfully) to codify and confirm this historical vision as accepted official history.

Writers such as Sima Guang, Fan Chong, and Zhao Ruyu embraced the first three of the six qualities that define *daoxue* historiography, but not the second three. In this sense, they may be regarded as proto-*daoxue* historians. They advocated literati governance, and their works shaped the rhetorical stances and framing narratives that contributed significantly to subsequent *daoxue* history. Zhu Xi, the intellectual force behind the creation of Song *daoxue*, is, as the first *daoxue* historian, the pivotal figure who bridged the transition between these earlier historians and Chen Jun and Lü Zhong a century later. Such a conception also helps to place the Sichuan historians in relation to the rise of *daoxue* historiography. Clearly, although neither Li Tao nor Li Xinchuan were *daoxue* historians, their works embraced similar political values and supporting historical narratives as those of the proto-*daoxue* writers, and their works were thus major sources of material for the proper *daoxue* historians of the thirteenth century. As Zhu Xi used Sima Guang, so Chen Jun and Lü Zhong used Li Tao and Li Xinchuan.

A comparison of coverage per Northern Song reign across four of the works under review will show how the *daoxue* historians utilized their sources to highlight this Taizu–Qingli–Yuanyou axis of political value. Decisions about allocation of coverage reflect authorial decisions about the relative importance of one period in Song history over another. Figure 4.5 compares the coverage devoted to each reign as a percentage of each work's total coverage for Northern Song, in the *State Compendium*, in Li Tao's *Long Draft*, in Chen Jun's *Outline and Details*, and in Lü Zhong's *Lectures*.[57]

The chart reveals a general trend from the *State Compendium* through the *Lectures* toward greater space allocation for those reigns that lay along the Taizu–Qingli–Yuanyou axis and decreased coverage for other periods. As argued above, the *State Compendium*, despite its own tortuous compilation and transmission history, offers our best view of the chronological range of

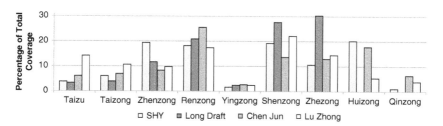

Figure 4.5 Relative coverage per Northern Song reign in the *Recovered Draft Compendium*, *Long Draft*, Chen Jun, and Lü Zhong

---

[57] *SHY* data measure, as explained above, unique datable entries per year, here aggregated by imperial reign. Data for the remaining works measure page counts in the Zhonghua shuju editions of the *Long Draft* and Chen Jun. The Lü Zhong data measure page counts in Zhang Qifan's 2014 edition. All data have been normalized to facilitate comparisons.

primary sources available to twelfth- and thirteenth-century historians. The *Long Draft* began the process of recasting relative chronological weight along the full spectrum of Northern Song history. Although Li Tao made no adjustments to coverage of the Taizu and Taizong reigns, he drastically decreased coverage for the Zhenzong reign while increasing Qingli, New Policies, and Yuanyou coverage. Subsequently, Chen Jun began increased coverage for the founding reigns of Taizu and Taizong, while continuing to de-emphasize the Zhenzong era, and to foreground Qingli. His relatively generous coverage of the Huizong and Qinzong eras focuses on negative appraisals of the New Policies in the context of their repeal in 1125 and 1126.

This chart also highlights the extreme steps taken by Lü Zhong during the last stage of this process to foreground the Taizu–Qingli–Yuanyou axis. Three trends are readily apparent. First, Lü Zhong has further increased coverage of the early reigns, especially that of Taizu. This change accords with the late *daoxue* elevation of Taizu to sage status and the historical narrative that posits him as the wellspring of benevolent governance. Second, Lü Zhong has reversed Chen Jun's coverage ratios of the Renzong–Yingzong versus Shenzong–Zhezong periods. The purpose of this reversal is harder to surmise. One reason may be that Lü Zhong posits so much of the positive Qingli ethos back to Taizu and Taizong that he can reduce Chen Jun's fuller coverage of Qingli. This shift, in turn, permits him to increase negative coverage of the anti-founder New Policies eras. Third, Lü Zhong has drastically reduced coverage of the Huizong–Qinzong reigns. This choice probably reflects the influence of the disastrous Song attempt to recover Kaifeng and the Mongol invasion of Sichuan in the mid-1230s, events that chronologically separate the works of Chen Jun and Lü Zhong.[58]

Finally, a comparison of the chronological coverage in the *State Compendium* versus the *Complete Texts of Song History* reveals the most extreme divergence between these two modes of historiography – in essence the alpha and the omega in the transition from official to *daoxue* history.[59] Two trends are noteworthy. First, Figure 4.6 reveals, for Northern Song, a full extension of the process begun by Li Tao of foregrounding the Taizu–Qingli–Yuanyou axis. However, the compilers of the *Complete Texts* have accordingly depressed coverage for the Zhenzong, Shenzong, and Huizong eras far beyond what their predecessors had attempted. Second, the drastic augmentation of

---

[58] Surviving woodblock exemplars of Chen Jun's history of Northern Song already show attempts to censor his vivid descriptions of the fall of Kaifeng in 1125–1127. Such passages were probably deemed too sensitive after the Duanping administration's failure to recover Kaifeng in 1234 cast doubt upon its ability to complete the Restoration. See Hartman, "Chen Jun's *Outline and Details*," 303–6.

[59] As above, *SHY* data measure entries per year. *Songshi quanwen* data measure page counts per year in the 2016 Zhonghua shuju edition.

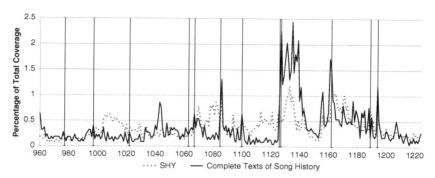

Figure 4.6 Coverage per year: *Complete Texts of Song History* versus *Recovered Draft Compendium*

coverage for the early Gaozong years stands out as the primary feature of Southern Song coverage. As we have seen above, an outsize emphasis on this period probably originated with Li Tao's first Restoration *huiyao* in 1170 and continued through the Southern Song portion of Lü Zhong's *Lectures*. This tendency reflects the growing trend over the course of Southern Song to posit Gaozong and his actions as restorative of the founder Taizu.

5   The *Song History*

Introduction: A Flawed History?

The *Song History* – at 496 *juan* and almost 5 million Chinese characters – is the longest of the twenty-four dynastic histories. Its nominal author, the Mongol chancellor Toghto (1314–1355), formed a committee of scholars in 1343 to compile the work, together with separate histories for the parallel Liao and Jin dynasties. The project proved controversial even before the committee completed its massive charge in 1345/10. Later, scholars in the Ming attempted unsuccessfully to undo the *Song History*'s official status and to redo its perspective on the history of the period. The great Qing historians of the eighteenth century criticized the *Song History* as the most problematic of all the official histories and dissected its many errors, omissions, and inconsistencies. Yet despite these problems, the work remains today the most systematic and comprehensive account of the dynasty's history. Many modern scholars, as they bemoan the work's infelicities and continue to ferret out its blemishes, still accept as authoritative its framing narratives and its presentation of the "grand allegory" of Song history.[1] This chapter, in addition to reviewing the work's compilation, its structure, and its meaning, will attempt to explain why otherwise competent historians compiled such a deeply problematic work.[2]

The Qing academicians who worked on the *Four Treasuries* project wrote a trenchant assessment of the *Song History*: "for the history of a single dynasty, the work is too massive to have been uniformly edited; furthermore, because its primary goal was to proclaim the Learning of the Way, other matters were given scant attention, so there are countless errors."[3] Qian Daxin 錢大昕 (1728–1804)

---

[1] For example, Chen Zhichao, "Song shi shiliao," 358–59.
[2] There is an extensive secondary scholarship on the *Song History*. Much of this research attempts to pinpoint, and sometimes resolve, contradictions between the *Song History* text and other sources. Modern examples in this genre include Gu Jichen, *Songshi bishi zhiyi* and *Songshi kaozheng*; Gao Jichun, *Songshi "benji" kaozheng*; Shu Renhui, *Dongdu shilüe yu Songshi bijiao yanjiu*; and Liu Yunjun, *Songshi zaifu liezhuan buzheng*. A useful collection of recent scholarship on the *Song History*, including major articles on its composition, is Luo Bingliang, *Songshi yanjiu*, which includes an extensive bibliography.
[3] Ji Yun et al., *Qinding Siku quanshu zongmu*, 46.635–36.

further specified that the Yuan historians used the *Song History* to promote the Zhu Xi school of *daoxue*.[4] The Qing scholars also observed that the Yuan historians merely copied verbatim large extracts from the Song dynasty's own state histories.[5] In short, they charged that the Yuan editors allowed their advocacy of *daoxue* to override their duty as historians. This judgment remains unchallenged to this day, even though its full implications have yet to be developed. Ge Zhaoguang, for example, accepts the Qing criticisms, but wonders why the same process and the same historians that produced the satisfactory histories of the Liao and Jin dynasties did not compile a different and better history of Song.[6]

The answer certainly rests in Toghto's decision to compile three separate histories and in the different nature of the Liao, Jin, and Song sources available to the Yuan historians.[7] In the case of Song, principal sources were the state histories and the veritable records. As we have seen in the Introduction and Chapter 1, these official sources provided fuller coverage for Northern Song, sparser coverage for early and mid-Southern Song, and little coverage at all after 1224. As early as the 1320s, Yuan Jue 袁桷 (1266–1327), in a thoughtful appraisal of the problem, informed the Yuan history office that the Song official histories were problematic and that extensive recourse to nonofficial works would be necessary to produce a reliable history.[8] Su Tianjue 蘇天爵 (1294–1352) repeated and reinforced this opinion again when work began in 1343.[9] Thus, Toghto and his committee knew that a more creditable historiographical process was not only possible but necessary. Their conscious choice to "cut and paste" from the existing Song histories expedited the project and met the immediate political needs of both Toghto and his compilers.

Nevertheless, despite their haste and the patchwork nature of their finished text, the Yuan historians devised a coherent, organized structure for the *Song History*. They did so with eyes that looked simultaneously backward to the Song *daoxue* tradition and forward to their own evolving position in Yuan politics. Accordingly, they arranged their Song sources onto an overarching framework in ways that showcased the lessons of Song history they had learned from their *daoxue* teachers. At the same time, they produced an official *Song History* that buttressed the legitimacy of Toghto and his allies in their political struggles against the forces of Mongol nativism. Modern scholarship on the *Song History* acknowledges the *daoxue* intellectual lineage of Toghto and his

[4] Qian Daxin, *Nian'er shi kaoyi*, 80.1106.
[5] Ji Yun et al., *Qinding Siku quanshu zongmu*, 46.636; Zhao Yi, *Nian'er shi zhaji jiaozheng*, 23.498–500.
[6] "Song guanxiu guoshi kao," 53–54.
[7] For details see Chan, "Chinese Official Historiography at the Yüan Court," 64–88, and *The Historiography of the Chin Dynasty*, 1–65.
[8] *Qingrong jushi ji*, 41.31a–41a; *QYW*, 23:712.140–46.
[9] *Ziqi wen gao*, 25.7a–15b; *QYW*, 40:1270.451–56.

compilers, but ignores Toghto's contemporaneous political agenda and how this political program shaped the message that his compilers foregrounded in the Song history they ultimately presented in 1345.

As we have seen in the Introduction, the three Song state histories that covered the Northern Song period had been completed in 1030 (for the years 960–1022), in 1082 (for 1023–1067), and in 1186 (for 1068–1127), well before a distinctive *daoxue* vision of that history arose later in the early thirteenth century. A state history for Southern Song was never completed, although portions were in draft by dynasty's end.[10] Therefore, the official Song state histories did not contain the dominant *daoxue* orientation of mid-thirteenth-century private histories such as those by Chen Jun and Lü Zhong. Although the official sources already contained major motifs of the grand allegory – such as the adulation of Taizu's "benevolence," denigration of the New Policies, and the Song monarchy's suppression of eunuchs and affinal political networks – Chen and Lü would paint such motifs with a much heavier *daoxue* brush. Thus, the Yuan compilers found Song official and private sources, both in substance and in ideology, better grist from which to fashion historical typologies for their Yuan political struggles than they did material from the Liao and Jin dynasties. First, the *Song History* would provide a plethora of precedents that Toghto could marshal against his political opposition; and second, the book could bolster the compilers' intellectual pedigree as heirs of Zhu Xi. The sparse coverage of Southern Song provided room for the compilers to exaggerate the historical importance of Zhu Xi's brand of *daoxue*, to cast his political and intellectual opponents in a lesser light, and to shift blame for *daoxue*'s contribution to dynastic decline.

In short, the Yuan compilers took the narratives of Song history they found in the *daoxue* historians of late Song as guidelines to "cut and paste" and thus to shape the official Song sources, which largely pre-dated the thirteenth century, into the official history of the dynasty. This historiographical process – and its resulting message – was not random, and there was no subterfuge. A total of 261 evaluations strategically placed throughout the work document the editors' efforts, clarify their purpose, and instruct the reader how to interpret the intervening text. Seventeen "eulogies" (*zan* 贊), one for each of the Song emperors; seventeen "prefaces" (*xu* 序) to the monographs and tables; and twenty-two prefaces to the classified groupings of biographies provide a macroscopic guide through the work and to the compilers' opinions on Song history. Finally, 205 "evaluations" (*lun* 論) interspersed throughout the nonclassified biographies provide further refinements and elaborations on major themes. Ouyang Xuan 歐陽玄 (1283–1357), effective editor in chief

---

[10] Ge Zhaoguang, "Song guanxiu guoshi kao," 47–53; Cai Chongbang, *Songdai xiushi zhidu yanjiu*, 117–48.

of the history, composed all these evaluations and provided ideological consistency for the project.[11]

The present text of the *Song History* thus represents the intersection and culmination of two processes that began in the dynasty itself. The text of the work descends largely from official histories of the Northern Song, yet its intellectual scaffolding descends from the *daoxue* ideologues of Southern Song. From the modern perspective, these two elements often appear to work at cross-purposes. Since the *Song History* indeed preserves only lightly edited extracts of the original Song sources, scholars usually attempt to embrace the text and jettison the scaffolding. Yet good evidence suggests that during the "cut-and-paste" process the scaffolding determined which passages were pasted into history and which were left on the cutting room floor.[12] This chapter contends, therefore, that this scaffolding, which shaped – so often in unseen ways – the contours of the *Song History*, continues to influence even the most meticulous of scholars who would use this work to understand the Song dynasty.

The Project and the Committee

Two factors account for the inability of the Yuan court to compile timely histories of its predecessors. As is well known, disagreements about "legitimate succession" (*zhengtong* 正統) impeded consensus about how best to frame the historical relationships among the three dynasties and about which dynasty the Yuan should declare its own immediate predecessor. Toghto resolved the issue by declaring the parallel legitimacy of Liao, Jin, and Song, and this equality between the ethnically Han and non-Han dynasties, more than any other factor, motivated Ming scholars to undo his decision. The issue is well studied and need not detain us here.[13] Less acknowledged is that after the death of the founder Khubilai (1215–1294) in 1294 the Yuan court divided sharply between

---

[11] Li Huarui, "*Songshi* lunzan pingxi." Li Shaoping, "Song, Liao, Jin san shi de shiji zhubian Ouyang Xuan," argues convincingly that Ouyang Xuan was the guiding intellectual force behind the *Song History*. Other scholars, for example Zhou Shengchun, emphasize the joint "team effort" of the editorial committee; see his "Guanyu Liao, Jin, Song san shi bianzhuan de jige wenti," 184.

[12] For the textual relationship between the Song state histories and the *Song History* see Hartman, "A Textual History of Cai Jing's Biography in the *Songshi*," 517–19. Liu Fengzhu and Li Xihou, "Yuan xiu Song, Liao, Jin san shi zai pingjie," also emphasize the value of the *Song History* as a repository of lightly edited Song primary texts. Gong Yanming, *Songshi zhiguanzhi buzheng*, Preface, 1–6, accepts this characterization but cautions that many passages in the *Song History*, especially the monographs, are so textually corrupt they cannot be considered actual primary sources and cannot be understood without extensive collation.

[13] For a succinct review see Chan, "Chinese Official Historiography at the Yüan Court," 68–74; for historical background see Chan, *Legitimation in Imperial China*; and Davis, "Historiography as Politics." For an extensive study of Ming efforts to revise the *Song History* see Wu Man, *Mingdai Songshixue yanjiu*.

two groups. On the one hand, Mongol nativists viewed the dynasty as part of the larger Mongol empire and were happy to divert Chinese resources to meet the demands of their engagement with the pan-Mongol polity. On the other hand, more sinicized Mongols and their native Chinese allies viewed the dynasty as a continuation of earlier states in China. They maintained that the Yuan dynasty should adopt and strengthen the Chinese imperial system and naturally objected to the diversion of resources which they feared would weaken its ability to govern in China. The first group was indifferent, if not hostile, to the history project; whereas the second embraced the proposed histories as another way to ground Mongol claims to legitimate rule in China and as a potentially useful rhetorical weapon against their nativist adversaries. The first group was naturally anti-Confucian; whereas the second group was pro-Confucian and, when in power, brought back the civil service examinations in 1315.[14]

The biography of Dong Wenbing 董文炳 (1216–1277), the Chinese general in Mongol service who secured the capital, Lin'an, in 1276, writes that Dong "recovered over 5,000 fascicles (*ce* 冊) of Song histories as well as all the records and notes" from the Song Imperial Library. He sent these archives north to the Yuan court history office, remarking that a state can be destroyed but not its history.[15] But just what did the Mongols retrieve? Yuan Jue's subsequent enumeration of twenty problematic issues in the Song sources then at hand focused exclusively on material in the state histories and veritable records.[16] Later, Su Tianjue reported that there were 3,000 *juan* of Song veritable records through 1224, 600 *juan* of state histories, and "over 1,000 *juan* of the chronological history," plus imperial genealogies, collected works, and "lesser opinions" (*xiaoshuo* 小說).[17] Absent the physical presence of the books themselves, precise biblio-graphic correlation between "fascicles" (*ce*) and "chapters" (*juan*) is always tenuous. However, Su's "chronological history" in 1,000 *juan* certainly refers to Li Tao's original *Long Draft*, in which one fascicle corresponded to one chapter.[18] Most probably this format was standard for clean copies of official historical works transcribed for the Imperial Library. A modern scholar has tabulated the three Northern Song state histories at 620 *juan*

[14] For the classic study see Dardess, *Conquerors and Confucians*; and his "Shun-ti and the End of Yüan Rule in China"; also Hsiao, "Mid-Yüan Politics."

[15] *YS*, 156.3672. See also Chan, "Chinese Official Historiography," 66; and C.F. Hung, "The Tung Brothers," 632. Hung understands the phrase "all the records and notes" (及諸注記) literally as "the *Diaries of Activity and Repose* [and] the *Records of Current Administration*" ([起居]注[時政]記). As explained below, I believe the phrase is best understood generally and refers to the veritable records.

[16] *Qingrong jushi ji*, 41.31a–41a; *QYW*, 23:712.140–46.

[17] *Ziqi wen gao*, 25.11b; *QYW*, 40:1270.453.

[18] Sudō Yoshiyuki, "Nan-Sō no Ri Tou," 488–89.

and the veritable records (through 1224) at 2,743 *juan*.[19] These figures correlate well with Su's estimates. Assuming an approximate one-to-one *ce* to *juan* equivalence would thus yield a total of 4,553 *ce* for the state histories, veritable records, and *Long Draft*. The remaining 447 *ce* from the roughly 5,000 *ce* that Dong Wenbing sent north were probably materials for the Southern Song state history and Lizong-era veritable records.

Dong thus took the two highest (and most redacted) levels of historical documentation – the state histories and veritable records – and left the lower (and more prolix) genres of court diaries and daily calendars. The state histories and the veritable records both ranked among the symbolic accouterments of dynastic legitimacy, their ritual status akin to imperial regalia such as seals, carriages, and sacrificial implements. The removal north to the Yuan capital of all these objects, including the most ritually significant material from the Imperial Library, symbolized the transfer of authority from Song to Yuan.[20] Thus, the decision to take only the state histories and veritable records arose from political and logistical, not historiographical, considerations. Furthermore, since the official historiographical function envisioned a clean progression through each of the four phases of redaction, in theory, the Song state histories alone should have been sufficient for the Yuan historians to compile the ultimate official history of the dynasty.

Taken together, the memoranda by Yuan Jue and by Su Tianjue provide an unvarnished assessment of the difficult choices the Yuan scholars confronted in their attempt to transform the archives retrieved from Lin'an into a finished, official history of the Song. These appraisals are also among the earliest and most perceptive analyses of fundamental and sometimes still unresolved issues in Song historiography. During the brief pro-Confucian administration from 1321 through 1323, the chancellor Baiji (d. 1323) tasked the Hanlin scholar Yuan Jue to survey prospects and progress on the three histories. Yuan had worked for twenty years in the Mongol history office and was descended from an illustrious Song literati clan from Ningbo. Three generation of his ancestors had served as Southern Song court historians, and his family still retained a substantial collection of their papers and copies of Song historical works.[21] Su Tianjue, on the contrary, was a northern scholar and a prominent Yuan literatus, whose career alternated between court academic appointments and significant provincial postings. He was first appointed to the Hanlin and History Academy (*Hanlin guoshi yuan* 翰林國史院) in 1324 and worked subsequently

---

[19] Cai Chongbang, *Songdai xiushi zhidu yanjiu*, 190.

[20] *YS*, 9.179. Jennifer W. Jay has suggested that Empress Xie negotiated the orderly transfer of imperial regalia to the Mongol army in exchange for lenient treatment of the Lin'an population; see Jay, *A Change in Dynasties*, 36–37.

[21] *QYW*, 23:712.140–41. Yuan mentions the historiographical service of his ancestors Yuan Xie (1144–1224), Yuan Shao (*jinshi* 1188), Yuan Fu (*jinshi* 1214), and Yuan Shang (*jinshi* 1223).

on the veritable records for the reigns of Emperors Khaisan (1308–1311) and Tugh Temür (1328–1332).[22] When Toghto ordered the three-histories project to begin in 1343, Su was not invited to join the compilation committee. He then sent "Some Questions about the Three Histories" (*San shi zhiyi* 三史質疑) directly to project director Ouyang Xuan. Sometime after the project was completed, Su wrote a funeral inscription for Yuan Jue, who had died about twenty years earlier in 1327. Su included a strong defense of Yuan's approach to Song history, a defense that also reads as an indictment of the history that Toghto and Ouyang had just completed.[23]

Yuan divided his observations into twenty items that addressed both specific and general problems of Song history and historiography. He argues that the official sources themselves – the state histories and veritable records – are not reliable because political pressures forced the Song historians to cover up sensitive events and to evade unpleasant realities. He maintains that only recourse to private works can amend these evasions in the official sources. Therefore, he appends to many of his twenty items lists of relevant private works, totaling about 140 titles, which he urges should be consulted. Since the Mongol history office lacked most of these works, Yuan proposed a systematic search in former Southern Song territory.[24] He argued that since the issues involved are no longer politically sensitive, the change in dynasties will facilitate this process of historical emendation and completion. Indirectly addressing the fact that his Song forebears were partially responsible for the pusillanimous sources he is criticizing, Yuan points out that famous historians of the past – Sima Qian, Ban Gu, Liu Zhiji – approached history writing as a multi-generational family enterprise: the later generation filled in what the earlier generation had been forced to omit. Yuan Jue thus maintains the soundness of his proposal, the stature of the work that will ensue, and the integrity of his family's reputation as historians.

Yuan's twenty items, plus the eight points in Su's memorandum that deal specifically with Song history, can be divided roughly into three categories of problems: (1) questions on general procedure; (2) perceived weaknesses in the existing Song histories that require rearrangement, deletions, or additions of new material; and (3) problems of omission and evasion that require further research and additions. Both Yuan and Su frame the project and its problems within the context of the established, official historiographical compilation protocol that they contend should not be abridged, despite the failure of the

---

[22] *YS*, 183.4224–27. For a detailed study see Sun Kekuan, *Yuandai Han wenhua zhi huodong*, 382–404; also Liu Yonghai, *Su Tianjue yanjiu*, 155–97.

[23] *QYW*, 40:1267.387–90.

[24] The history office clearly possessed copies of some works on Yuan's list, for example the *Long Draft*. But Yuan points out that the copies on hand are all fragmentary and incomplete. The office must obtain more reliable and complete versions.

Song historians to fulfill their responsibilities in this regard. Su begins by asking the basic question: "Do you plan a thorough revision [based on all the sources], or do you plan simply to copy the already completed state histories?" Su continues that even the latter procedure would be difficult, since the Song historians never completed the veritable records for Lizong's and later reigns. "Will you first compile veritable records for these reigns?"[25] Su insists the committee should follow his suggestion, since to omit the veritable-record stage of compilation would violate the established protocol.

Merging into the second category, both Yuan and Su underscored the uneven chronological coverage in the monographs and the biographical sections of the state histories. Yuan laments that the monographs on ritual, music, and fiscal administration do not reflect the pluralism of Song views on these subjects. Su further worries that no Yuan scholars are competent to revise the technical monographs on astronomy, the calendar, and geography. In the biographical sections of the state history, the selection and distribution of biographies do not properly reflect more recent historical judgments. Some biographies should be regrouped, others dropped entirely.[26] Others must be newly composed based on the drafts appended to the veritable records. Mirroring the scale of this concern, Yuan inserts his longest group of desired works (forty-eight titles) after his entry on biographies.[27]

Under the third category of evasions and omissions, Yuan and Su advocated that more light be shed on the darker corners of Song history, especially the actions and character of the three Song founders, Taizu, Taizong, and Zhao Pu. As the grand allegory had evolved in Song, Taizu assumed the status of deified founder, Taizu and Taizong became partners in fraternal comity, and Zhao Pu became an exemplar of the loyal councilor. In actuality, Taizu had usurped the throne from a child emperor whom he had sworn to protect; strong hints in some sources insinuated that Taizong had murdered Taizu to obtain the throne; and Zhao Pu had facilitated the deaths of Taizu's sons to curry favor with Taizong after he became emperor. Yuan and Su both advocate that the new history abandon their official Song personas and seek out private sources, reputed to exist, to present an unvarnished history of the Song founding. Su states directly that "the account of the solders' revolt at Chen Bridge in the Song state history has deceived later generations." He avers that the true story of Taizu's death can be intuited from the *Long Draft*. Yuan and Su both refer to

---

[25] *QYW*, 40:1270.453–54.

[26] *QYW*, 23:712.141. As an example of inappropriate grouping, Yuan cites the *Three Courts State History (Sanchao guoshi)* of 1030, where the biographies of Kou Zhun and Ding Wei occurred together in the same chapter. Subsequent historiography judged the former positively and the latter negatively. The received *Song History* has indeed separated their biographies, placing Kou Zhun in *juan* 281 and Ding Wei in *juan* 283 together with the other "negative" figures Wang Qinruo and Xia Song.

[27] *QYW*, 23:712.144.

Li Tao's private biography of Zhao Pu, which neither has seen, but which both suggest be sought out.[28]

Both scholars point out that because Emperor Gaozong was still alive when the *Four Courts State History*, which covered the last years of Northern Song, was composed between 1168 and 1186, its compilers were forced to omit references to Huizong's decision in 1120 to break Song's treaty with the Khitan and Tong Guan's mission in 1123 to occupy Yanjing, events that had precipitated the Jurchen invasion of Song in 1125. Likewise omitted were the subsequent siege of Kaifeng, the capture of Huizong and Qinzong, and their transport into northern captivity. Yuan suggests twenty private sources from which a history of these events could be reconstructed, the first being the *Compendium of Northern Treaties from Three Courts* (*Sanchao beimeng huibian*), which survives today and is indeed the major surviving source for these events. Yuan also notes that the copy of the *Long Draft* in the court history office is incomplete and lists thirteen works that can be sought out to supplement the lacunae.[29]

In short, Yuan and Su proposed to their colleagues in the Mongol history office a course of preparatory research that parallels the basic methodology of many modern scholars of Song history. These scholars accept the official sources (in this case, the finished *Song History*) as a baseline narrative, then sift an array of quasi-official and unofficial sources to validate that narrative and supplement any perceived deficiencies. Neither Yuan nor Su manifests an overt *daoxue* agenda. Although one may detect a note of resentment in Su's tone, an intellectual desire to produce a reliable history seems Yuan's primary motivation.

Yuan's tradition of family learning, plus his study of institutional history with his fellow Ningbo scholar, the polymath Wang Yinglin 王應麟 (1223–1296), followed by his study of poetry under Shu Yuexiang 舒嶽祥 (1236–1298), were the guiding forces in his early education. Both inclinations set him apart from adherents of Zhu Xi's *daoxue* lineage. Su's funeral inscription for Yuan notes his allegiance to his native Eastern Zhe scholarship, which focused on broad and deep knowledge of many subjects, all manifested through "real use, not empty words," a clear gibe at the *daoxue* scholars. Finally, Su avers that Yuan desired to produce a solidly researched and well-grounded history of Song, "not something thrown together and plagiarized in a wild rush to suit the trend of the times."[30] Since Su penned this phrase after the *Song History* had been completed, it may well constitute his assessment of the finished work. As we shall see, Toghto and his committee did search for relevant materials in the

---

[28] *QYW*, 40:1270.454.   [29] *QYW*, 23:712.142; *QYW*, 40:1270.455.

[30] *QYW*, 40:1267.388–90. Huang Zongxi, *Song Yuan xue'an*, 85.2876–81, places Yuan Jue among the students of Wang Yinglin, along with Hu Sanxing 胡三省 (1230–1287), the annotator of Sima Guang's *Comprehensive Mirror*.

south, and did adopt some of Yuan and Su's easier recommendations, such as regrouping the biographies. But, in the main, they ignored the more difficult recommendation that they reopen earlier stages of the official compilation process and integrate private sources.

Their decision arose largely from the politics of Toghto's rise to power and his complex relationship to contemporary *daoxue* scholarship. Since the installation of the thirteen-year-old Toghōn Temür as emperor in 1333, his first councilor Bayan the Merkid (1280–1340) dominated Yuan politics. He was a talented Mongol aristocrat with deep distrust of the growing Chinese and Confucian influence on Yuan political culture. In 1335, in an attempt to halt the increasing trend toward Sino-Mongol hybridization, he reactivated Khubilai's reign name (*Zhiyuan* 至元) and proclaimed a return to the "old norms" of the founder. He suspended the civil service examinations in favor of recruitment into office from the *kesigden*, the descendants of the hereditary guards of the Mongol founders, who numbered about 13,000, and were considered the "cradle of officialdom" and the "citadel of the Yuan ruling class."[31] The Bayan administration preferred these hereditary Mongol aristocrats with practical experience, supported by a large core of professional clerks, rather than Confucian scholars, as leaders of Yuan government. At the same time, Bayan accumulated vast personal assets and placed himself atop the complex web of interlocking court and palace offices that oversaw the patrimonial business interests of the Yuan royal house. His key ally in these interests was the Empress Dowager Budashiri (1307–1340) who had installed Toghōn Temür as emperor. Their alliance, in which Budashiri dominated the inner court and Bayan the civil and military administration, continued until 1340.[32]

Opposition to Bayan eventually arose both from aristocratic Mongol clans who were alienated by his autocratic domination of government and from younger Mongols and Chinese who had vested their careers in the examination system. Toghto, Bayan's twenty-six-year-old nephew, with the support of the emperor, staged a putsch in the spring of 1340 that displaced Bayan and Budashiri. Their removal from power marked a permanent end to Mongol nativist aspirations for a return to the supposed ethos of the earlier Khubilai era. Toghto brought back the civil service examinations, recalled Confucian scholars to the Hanlin academy, and reinstituted the imperial Classics Mat, the Imperial University, and the Chinese suburban sacrifices.[33] He proclaimed the new administration one of "renewal" (*genghua* 更化), a term used in Song

---

[31] Hsiao, *The Military Establishment of the Yüan Dynasty*, 39–41.
[32] Dardess, *Conquerors and Confucians*, 53–74; "Shun-ti and the End of Yüan Rule in China," 561–72.
[33] Quan Heng, *Gengshen waishi jianzheng*, 35–41; Schulte-Uffelage, *Das Keng-shen wai-shih*, 44–48.

politics to signal a return to the principles of literati governance after a period of authoritarian rule.[34]

When Toghto was young, his father had acquired for him a tutor from Jinhua in Zhejiang province, one Wu Zhifang 吳直方 (1275–1356), who taught him the Confucian classics and put him in touch with other Confucian scholars. The two formed a close relationship. Wu became a covert adviser to the young Mongol and his liaison to the Chinese Confucian community. According to his biographer, Song Lian 宋濂 (1310–1381), Wu was the impetus for the 1340 putsch against Bayan which he justified to Toghto with a phrase from the *Zuo Commentary*: "for the sake of a greater righteousness, one may destroy relatives."[35] In truth, as Dardess has concluded, Confucianism was the only ideology that could be used to justify the putsch and that could unify the multiethnic bureaucracy of the Yuan state.[36] "The triumph of Confucian politics" would soon make the language of Song *daoxue* the lingua franca of the Yuan political realm. And the *Song History* would be the first major work written in that language.

The composition of the committee to compile the three histories mirrored both the hybrid Sino-Mongol politics of the "renewal" and Toghto's links to the *daoxue* community. The 1343/3 edict that ordered work on the three histories to begin devised a four-tiered administrative structure for the *Song History*. Below Toghto as editor in chief, seven general editors (*zongcai guan* 總裁官) supervised twenty-five historians (*shiguan* 史官) and a support staff (*tidiao guan* 提調官) of twenty-three.[37] Most politically prominent among the general editors were the Qangli Turk Temür Tash (1302–1347) and the northern Chinese He Weiyi 賀惟一 (1301–1363), both key members of Toghto's "renewal" administration who acted as administrative co-ordinators for all three histories as well as concurrently supervising the emperor's Classics Mat.[38] The project's intellectual center, however, was the two general editors Zhang Qiyan 張起巖 (1285–1353) and Ouyang Xuan, a northern and southern Chinese respectively, who held precisely equal rank and office at the time of submission.

The enabling edict for the three histories authorized the general editors to correct drafts submitted by the historians, "to determine what was correct and

---

[34] Dardess, *Conquerors and Confucians*, 200 n. 2, cites two contemporary references to Toghto's advent as an era of *genghua*. For another see Huang Jin, *Wenxian ji*, 10B.54a. For Toghto's "renewal" agenda see *YS*, 138.3343; Dardess, *Conquerors and Confucians*, 73–81; Qiu Shusen, "Tuotuo he Liao, Jin, Song san shi," 98–103.

[35] Song Lian, *Wenxian ji*, 25.5b; Quan Heng, *Gengshen waishi jianzheng*, 24; Schulte-Uffelage, *Das Keng-shen wai-shih*, 35; Dardess, *Conquerors and Confucians*, 201 n. 13; Sun Kekuan, *Yuandai Jinhua xueshu*, 77–78.

[36] Dardess, *Conquerors and Confucians*, 74.

[37] These numbers are based on the name list that follows the *Song History* submission memorial; see *SS, fulu*, 14256–60. See also Zhou Shengchun, "Guanyu Liao, Jin, Song san shi bianzuan de jige wenti," 187–89, for some slight adjustments to these figures.

[38] Dardess, *Conquerors and Confucians*, 84–86.

what not," and thus to decide the final text.[39] Biographies of Zhang and Ouyang write that they both exercised this authority in accordance with their training and knowledge of *daoxue* principles.[40] The standard for historical correctness, in turn, was the "mental disposition" (*xinshu* 心術) of the historian, which, after a regimen of *daoxue* study and moral cultivation, would then become "straight/correct" (*zheng* 正), thus enabling proper historical judgments.[41] Zhang Qiyan was a native of Shandong descended from a family of late Jin officials who had submitted to the Mongols and entered Yuan service. The origin of his *daoxue* training is not recorded, but in 1315 he placed first on the Chinese roster in the first *jinshi* examination held under the Yuan, along with Ouyang Xuan and three of the other general editors of the *Song History*.[42] As is well known, the 1315 *jinshi* examinations were based on the *daoxue* learning of Zhu Xi. The preponderance of 1315 graduates on the editorial committee thus reflected the importance of this strain of Confucianism to Toghto's "renewal" and his commitment to imprinting *daoxue* historical views on the Song sources. After his *jinshi*, Zhang Qiyan served in the court academic agencies, including the history office where he worked on the veritable records of three Yuan emperors.

Ouyang Xuan had a similar career path. In his case, however, because his intellectual origins went back to Southern Song – and indeed straight to Zhu Xi – they are well recorded. Three generations of his direct ancestors were instructors at late Song academies where they taught a *daoxue* curriculum grounded in Zhu Xi's teachings. A family kinsman, Ouyang Shoudao 歐陽守道 (1209–?), was a leading *daoxue* scholar and headmaster at the famous Marchmount Hill Academy (*Yuelu shuyuan* 嶽麓書院) at Tanzhou 潭州, the modern Changsha in Hunan. In the early 1250s, about the time Ouyang Xuan's father, Ouyang Longsheng 歐陽龍生 (1251–1307), was born, Ouyang Shoudao invited Ouyang Xin 歐陽新, Ouyang Xuan's great-grandfather, to lecture at the academy. The family settled in Tanzhou, where Ouyang Xuan's grandfather continued as an instructor at the academy. Ouyang Longsheng grew up at Marchmount Hill, and went into reclusion at the fall of Song. He emerged again in 1293 to serve as headmaster of Cultured Tranquility Academy (*Wenjing shuyuan* 文靖書院), also in

---

[39] *Liaoshi, fulu*, 1554.

[40] For Zhang see *YS*, 182.4195; for Ouyang see *YS*, 182.4197–98, which is based on Wei Su's biographical sketch of Ouyang Xuan's life (*xingzhuang*), *QYW*, 48:1477.400–407.

[41] See Ouyang Xuan's "Inscription for the Reading Studio" of the Luling doctor Xiao Shangbin 蕭尚賓, *QYW*, 34:1098.553; and Jie Xisi's conversation with Toghto about the proper requirements for a historian, *YS*, 181.4186; also Fan Wenlan, *Zhengshi kaolüe*, 225; and Li Shaoping, "Song, Liao, Jin san shi de shiji zhubian Ouyang Xuan," 76.

[42] Of the seven general editors, five were 1315 *jinshi* graduates. In addition to Zhang and Ouyang were Li Haowen, Wang Yi, and Yang Zongrui; see Gui Qipeng, *Yuandai jinshi yanjiu*, 19–24.

Tanzhou, where young and old scholars flocked to hear his lectures on the *daoxue* curriculum.[43]

In addition to this tradition of Ouyang family learning, the *Song Yuan xue'an* also places Ouyang Xuan in the intellectual lineage of the so-called "Four Masters of Jinhua," Song dynasty Wuzhou 婺州, in central Zhejiang, the same locale that produced Toghto's mentor Wu Zhifang. The Jinhua 金華 lineage descended directly from Zhu Xi through his son-in-law and successor Huang Gan 黃幹 (1152–1221) to He Ji 何基 (1188–1268), who brought Zhu Xi's teachings back to his native Jinhua. The transmission then proceeded through Jin Lüxiang 金履祥 (1233–1303), to Xu Qian 許謙 (1270–1337), both from Jinhua, then to Ouyang Xuan and Jie Xisi 揭傒斯 (1274–1344).[44] Although the Jinhua masters were faithful interpreters of Zhu Xi's moral philosophy, they blended his teachings with the practical statecraft of thinkers from Eastern Zhejiang.[45] Jin Lüxiang, in particular, worked to refine Zhu Xi's application of *daoxue* moral philosophy to history and applied the insights of his refined paradigm to explicate the moral responsibility of government for maintaining proper moral and social order.[46] Ouyang Xuan's personal odyssey from the *daoxue* world of the late Song academies, through eremitism and the revival of the academies in the early Yuan, then, via the 1315 examinations, into a successful official career mirrored the intellectual path of many Yuan Confucians.[47]

Thus, politically, Toghto's committee to compile the *Song History* reflected the balanced and hybrid Sino-Mongol configuration that had brought about the "renewal." Intellectually, however, the committee reflected a much narrower focus that was descended from the dynasty's tentative embrace in 1315 of Zhu Xi Confucianism. Toghto chose seasoned historians and practical politicians, but they were also scholars who had benefited most from the dynasty's pro-Confucian turn and from Toghto's own embrace of that turn. The committee's direct links to the Song *daoxue* masters and their examination success gave

---

[43] For Ouyang Shoudao and Ouyang Xin see *SS*, 411.12364–65; Walton, *Academies and Society in Southern Sung China*, 151–52. See also Zhang Qiyan's spirit road inscription for Ouyang Longsheng, *QYW*, 36:1141.127–28; Wei Su's life of Ouyang Xuan, *QYW*, 48:1477.400–1; and Li Shaoping, "Song, Liao, Jin san shi de shiji zhubian Ouyang Xuan," 72.

[44] Huang Zongxi, *Song Yuan xue'an*, 82.2771–72. Ouyang Xuan's biographers do not mention his direct study with any of the "Four Masters of Jinhua," but the association is well accepted. See Sun Kekuan, *Yuandai Jinhua xueshu*, 44; Zhou Shengchun, "Yu Yunwen wannian shiji shulun," 122–24. Zhou also details the master–disciple *daoxue* lineages of four other Mongol and Chinese historians who worked on the *Song History*. The collected works of Wei Su, another *daoxue* historian who worked on the *Song History*, contain many details about his specific contributions to the project; see Kong Fanmin, "Wei Su yu *Songshi* de zuanxiu."

[45] There is a large body of scholarship on Song–Yuan period Jinhua; see Sun Kekuan, *Yuandai Jinhua xueshu*; Bol, "Neo-Confucianism and Local Society," and Langlois, "Political Thought in Chin-hua under Mongol Rule."

[46] Lee, "Different Mirrors of the Past," 253–315.

[47] Walton, "Family Fortunes in the Song–Yuan Transition."

them the moral and political authority to decide "what was correct and what not," and to this task they brought the historical viewpoints of their *daoxue* mentors.

Structure and Meaning

Despite its extended length and erratic editing, the *Song History* presents a coherent structure and a distinctive vision of the dynasty's history. At its most fundamental level, the book's division into annals, monographs/tables, and biographies adheres to the long-established tripartite structure of an official dynastic history. Although modern scholarship can rarely ascertain what proportion of text in any given *Song History* passage derives from Song sources as opposed to the Yuan editing of those sources, Ouyang Xuan – probably with the approval of Zhang Qiyan – certainly wrote the "eulogies" in the annals, the "prefaces" in the monographs, and the "prefaces" and "comments" in the biographies.[48] This editorial commentary provides an overarching structure of meaning for the work, despite the frequent inconsistencies that often lurk beneath.

The Imperial Eulogies

In the annals, the "eulogies" that cap the chronicles of each imperial reign permit the historian to comment on the character of each emperor and to summarize the nature of his rule. However, read together in sequence, the seventeen imperial eulogies also provide a macroscopic perspective on the dynasty's history. The Yuan editors used the eulogies to impose a periodization on Song history, and they used that periodization to introduce the major themes of their work. Following the annals, the more frequent "comments" in the more ample monographs and biographies reinforce these themes, provide amplifications, and supply supporting examples and details. Although the basic framework of this periodization is as old as Li Tao, the Yuan editors have reframed the story in *daoxue* terms and adjusted its focus to suit their own political needs. That said, within these self-imposed parameters, their eulogies often read as good-faith attempts to present balanced appraisals of the imperial personalities and historical trends of each reign, and these verdicts have influenced, and still influence, much scholarship on Song.

The most positive eulogies in the *Song History* are those for Emperors Taizu, Renzong, and Xiaozong. The choice of this trio projects a larger narrative in which Taizu's initial "benevolence" was perfected under Renzong, and then

---

[48] The claim that Ouyang Xuan composed these evaluations derives from his biography (*xing-zhuang*) by Wei Su, who was his subordinate on the project; see *QYW*, 48: 1477.404.

replicated, albeit to a lesser degree in Southern Song, under Xiaozong. As a contrast to these positives, the most negative eulogy is for Huizong, followed by those for Shenzong, Gaozong, and Ningzong. The Yuan historians apply judgments based on *daoxue* political ideals to create a waxing and waning barometer of the effectiveness of Song governance. The highly negative assessment throughout the *Song History* of Wang Anshi and the New Policies, an assessment that first appears in the eulogy for Shenzong, underlies this periodization and intensifies Li Tao's earlier judgment that Song history changed fundamentally in 1067. As will be explained in Chapter 8 below, the Taizu–Renzong axis of emphasis arose in early Southern Song. The addition of Xiaozong occurred in the mid-thirteenth century after the political triumph of *daoxue* had elevated Xiaozong's image as the emperor under whom the movement had grown to an earlier maturity. The Yuan editors inherited most of these positive evaluations from late Song *daoxue* historians such as Chen Jun and Lü Zhong.

Imperial "eulogies" were first drafted at the state-history stage of compilation. The Yuan historians would therefore have seen the earlier eulogies from the three state histories of Northern Song. Although these do not survive, the *Eastern Capital Miscellany* of 1186 preserves "historian comments" after each imperial reign that certainly reflect the spirit if not the actual language of the Northern Song state histories. These comments are all highly positive, since criticism of any Song emperor, especially in a highly visible and ritualistic genre like the state history, was not possible during Song. However, they contain a mid-twelfth-century, pre-*daoxue* vision of Song history and provide a useful point of comparison to evaluate what the Yuan historians took from their sources and what they devised on their own.

The *Miscellany*'s comments on the first four Song emperors present Song history before 1063 as a constantly escalating expansion of Taizu's "rectitude" and "benevolence." This posture originated in the *Three Courts State History* of 1030, when contemporary politics dictated adulation of the reigns of Taizong and Zhenzong, and then continued in this vein when Renzong was later added to the initial trio.[49] The *Song History* eulogies, however, depart sharply from these earlier and evenly positive evaluations. The Yuan writers not only elevated Taizu to a level far beyond his successors, they also interjected sharply discordant elements into the eulogies for Taizong and Zhenzong. The result is a trajectory of decline from Taizu's initial achievement, followed by subsequent renewal under Renzong.

The *Miscellany* comment for Taizu (translated in Chapter 9) limits itself to developing the trope that Taizu's "rectitude" equaled that of Yao and Shun

---

[49] See, for example, Shi Jie's preface to his *Sanchao shengzheng lu* in *Culai Shi xiansheng wenji*, 17.209–10.

because he obtained the throne through abdication and passed it on to his brother Taizong, not his own son. These historical parallels repose in turn on the Chen Bridge narrative of the founding and upon the Golden Box narrative of the Taizu–Taizong transition.[50] The *Song History* eulogy for Taizu retains and intensifies the Yao–Shun parallel by specifying that, in contrast to other emperors of the Five Dynasties, Heaven selected Taizu for his role: he restored tranquility to the people after the chaos these lesser monarchs had created. His Heaven-granted moral authority subdued other regional powers and enabled him to unify the country, "something that could not be easily accomplished by human might alone." The eulogy then lists his achievements after reunification: he disbanded the power of the military governors, rooted out clerical malfeasance and corruption, and personally supervised the appointment of local officials. He encouraged agriculture and learning, regulated punishments, and lowered taxation. The "canons and rules" of his seventeen-year reign laid the foundations for 300 years of Song rule and made the dynasty the equal of Han and Tang.[51]

In other words, according to the *Song History* eulogy, the centralized, civil-based, literati vision of imperial governance as advocated by the Song *daoxue* movement and its Yuan followers originated in Yao and Shun; then Heaven empowered Taizu to re-establish that governance again in 960. As we shall explore in the chapters to follow, elements of this paradigm emerged in the Northern Song, and thirteenth-century *daoxue* completed the process. The Yuan editors found this narrative a suitable model upon which to ground the *Song History* and to recommend to their own sovereign. In doing so, they rejected Yuan Jue's assertion that Taizu had usurped the Zhou throne and that the Golden Box narrative was Taizong's invention.

In addition to their deification of Taizu in the eulogy, the Yuan editors also inserted between the end of his annals and his eulogy a remarkable collection of fifteen vignettes about the Song founder, which we will examine in more detail in Chapter 6. This editorial procedure constitutes a feature of the *Song History* that is unique to the Taizu annals.[52] Each of the vignettes highlights an aspect of

---

[50] For the Chen Bridge narrative see Chapter 9 below. The Golden Box refers to the story of a supposed agreement between Taizu and his mother, Empress Du, that upon the emperor's death the succession would go to his brother Taizong rather than directly to Taizu's sons. She reportedly then summoned Councilor Zhao Pu to record and deposit Taizu's oath in a Golden Box for future reference. Historians have long suspected that Taizong and Zhao Pu forged the oath and contrived the story of the Golden Box to justify Taizong's questionable assumption of the throne. There is a sizable literature on the subject. See *Changbian*, 2.46–47; Sima Guang, *Sushui jiwen*, 1.9–10; Chaffee, *Branches of Heaven*, 25–30; Chang, "Inheritance Problems in the First Two Reigns of the Sung Dynasty," and the excellent master's thesis, Ten Harmsel, "Oath of the Golden Casket."

[51] *SS*, 3.50–51; *Dongdu shilüe*, 2.7b.

[52] *SS*, 3.49–50. The punctuation in the Zhonghua shuju edition obscures the independent textual origins of the fifteen vignettes.

Taizu's personality – his frugality, naturalness, openness, impartiality, foresight, abhorrence of violence, love of scholarship, and support for Taizong's ascension. Most of these undated stories were probably not part of the early historical record, but arose as quasi-fictional supplements to that record during the Northern Song. By the end of the eleventh century, they were routinely used singly and in various combinations to illustrate these purported qualities of the founder. Their insertion between the end of the Taizu annals and his eulogy prepares the way for the extravagant claims made on his behalf in the eulogy.

For example, the first story relates that soon after his ascension, Taizu rejected criticism that his frequent excursions in disguise outside the palace could endanger his life. He replied that Emperor Shi of the Zhou (r. 954–959) had killed any of his generals that bore an imperial physiognomy; but he himself came to no harm because Heaven had fated him to survive and become the Song emperor. This opening vignette, and many of the others, derive from Shi Jie's *Records of Sagacious Administration from the Three Courts*, compiled in 1038, and from Sima Guang's *Su River Records*. They were thus not part of the earliest, pre-1030 strata of official historiography, but arose during the reign of Renzong as part of literati efforts to mold an image of the founder that would be more in line with their aspirations for Renzong and his rule. Li Tao admits some of these vignettes into the *Long Draft*; but he signals his doubts about their reliability, noting their lack of dates and their earliest appearance in Shi Jie and Sima Guang.[53]

The *daoxue* movement continued to manipulate these vignettes to present Taizu as a model ruler whose cultivation of mind replicated the minds of Yao and Shun. In his famous 1188 audience with Emperor Xiaozong, Zhu Xi, quoting Taizu's words verbatim from Sima Guang's rendering of the story, reminded the emperor how Taizu had realigned (*zheng* 正) the gates of the palace so as to provide an unobstructed view into his inner quarters and thus into the rectitude of his mind. In the *daoxue* system, such "mental rectitude" (*zhengxin* 正心), especially on the part of the ruler, was the essential prerequisite for social and political order.[54] By the thirteenth century, the *daoxue* historians had turned this interpretation of the vignette into a standard motif of the Song founding.[55] It is difficult to determine when the particular combination of fifteen vignettes in the *Song History* came together – whether the Yuan historians inherited the collection intact or assembled it themselves. Hu Yigui 胡一桂 (1247–1315) commented on an unsourced passage that collected the first four of the vignettes in an order and diction that closely resembles the *Song History* insertion.[56] One may therefore document a direct line of *daoxue*

[53]   *Changbian*, 1.30–31; Sima Guang, *Sushui jiwen*, 1.4–5.
[54]   *Zhu Xi ji*, 11.467; Sima Guang, *Sushui jiwen*, 1.14.
[55]   Chen Jun, *Huangchao gangmu*, 2.28; Lü Zhong, *Huangchao dashiji*, 3.67–68.
[56]   See Xia Liangsheng, *Zhongyong yanyi*, 5.18b–19a.

transmission for the motif of the straightened gates from Zhu Xi, through Chen Jun and Lü Zhong, to Hu Yigui, and eventually to the Yuan historians.[57]

The *Song History* eulogies for Zhenzong and Renzong, compared to the historian's comments in the *Eastern Capital Miscellany*, present a study in marked contrasts. Since the Yuan historians endorsed the positive Song evaluation of Renzong, they needed only rephrase the earlier passage, which praises Renzong's magnanimity, compassion, forbearance, and frugality. They add, however, that although ills and problems existed, these did not impede the great achievements of his reign. In particular, his harmonious relations with his officials set the Song standard for "a government of loyalty and tolerance" (*zhonghou zhi zheng* 忠厚之政). Emphasizing that Renzong's reign marked a high point of Song history, they add that his successors' departure from his policies brought the dynasty to ruin.[58]

The *Miscellany* praises Zhenzong as a peacemaker for negotiating the treaty of Chanyuan, for the prosperity that ensued, and for the ritual perfection of the *feng* and *shan* sacrifices that he subsequently performed. Accordingly, the era of "Great Peace" (*taiping* 太平) over which he presided attained a perfection that had not been seen in a thousand years.[59] This official adulation of Zhenzong's reign was first articulated in the 1030s and persisted largely unchanged.[60] However, since the prosperity and institutional development of the Great Peace had occurred within a Daoist ritual context, Confucian scholars began privately to question the triumphalism of the official history. Sima Guang's *Su River Records* contains two entries that reflect negatively on Zhenzong. In the first, his early councilor Li Hang warns Wang Dan that the conclusion of the Chanyuan treaty may now free the emperor to indulge his natural penchant for extravagance (*chixin* 侈心), an incident that, as we have seen in Chapter 3, Li Xinchuan questioned. The second anecdote attributes the motive for Zhenzong's ritual excess to his councilor Wang Qinruo's suggestion that the Khitan, being highly superstitious, would be awed into submission by manifest and bounteous signs of Heaven's support for Song.[61] In 1099, Su Zhe penned a more elaborate version of this story, which Li Tao adopted into his main text narrative for the *Long Draft*.[62] The rise of *daoxue* increased pressure

[57] For earlier citations of this passage see Sima Guang, *Sushui jiwen*, 1.14; Luo Congyan, *Zun Yao lu*, 1.116–17. The story occurs in the Taizu basic annals at *Dongdu shilüe*, 2.31, under the date 963/4. Li Tao, *Changbian*, 9.199–200, places the event without comment in 968/1. As we have seen in the Introduction, in 1068 Qian Yi cited this story to Emperor Shenzong from the "state history," suggesting that this vignette may indeed have been part of the early historical record; see Zhao Ruyu, *Songchao zhuchen zouyi*, 2.11.
[58] *Dongdu shilüe*, 6.9a–b; *SS*, 12.251–51. [59] *Dongdu shilüe*, 4.8a–b.
[60] See, for example, Fu Bi's evaluation of Zhenzong's reign preserved in the anonymous *Taiping baoxun zhengshi jinian*, 84–85. Fu maintains that Zhenzong's "deep love for the people" brought about the economic prosperity of the era of Great Peace.
[61] *Sushui jiwen*, 6.120–21. [62] Su Zhe, *Longchuan bie zhi*, 1.72–73; *Changbian*, 67.1506–7.

on this positive image of Zhenzong. Zhu Xi, for example, privately questioned the enormous cost of the sacrifices.[63] In the main, however, overt criticism of Zhenzong remained muted even in the mid-thirteenth-century histories.[64]

The reign of Zhenzong thus presented a conundrum for the Yuan historians. Their ambivalent eulogy for him – the only one in the book – has given one modern scholar "the impression that they [were] reduced to shaking their heads."[65] Their eulogy develops Sima Guang's two anecdotes to portray Zhenzong as an intelligent but vain monarch who was easily misled by his ministers into ritual excess in order to impress the Khitan. In their attempt to camouflage their reliance upon Sima Guang, the Yuan historians explain that their research for the *Liao History* revealed to them the highly superstitious customs of the Khitans. They sanction the basic goal of Zhenzong's advisers to exploit this weakness of their powerful enemy, but conclude that the plan was flawed and its execution excessive. The one-issue eulogy then quickly transitions to more preferred and positive ground: "how wise was Renzong to bury the 'heavenly letters' with Zhenzong!"[66]

As may be expected, the *Miscellany* and *Song History* evaluations of Emperor Shenzong diverge radically. The former writes that Shenzong set out to reform imperfections that had gradually accumulated over the dynasty's first hundred years. He was an inspirational ruler who took antiquity as his model for governance. The *Miscellany* presents all his initiatives in positive terms, mixing the major New Policies with other actions such as reforms to imperial ritual and clan administration, the 1082 restructuring of government, and army reorganization. But he experienced "remorse" in his later years because his subordinates were unable to carry out his intentions.[67] For their part, the Yuan historians admit that Shenzong was a dedicated and inspirational leader whose goal was to complete the conquest of the northern lands. But his reliance upon Wang Anshi, who utilized the emperor's ambitions to implement the New Policies, cut short his early promise. Shenzong was never aware of the chaos that Wang brought to the country and confidently dismissed his critics, so that "in the end all the excellent policies and fine ideas of the ancestors were utterly destroyed; then steadily did the wicked advance, the will of the people was lost, and chaos ensued."[68] Thus, whereas the *Miscellany* never directly mentions Wang Anshi, the Yuan historians, still reluctant to criticize Shenzong

[63] *Zhuzi yulei*, 127.3044.
[64] Chen Jun, *Huangchao gangmu*, 7.146–48; Lü Zhong, *Huangchao dashiji*, 6.128–30.
[65] Cahill, "Taoism at the Sung Court," 37, where the full text of the eulogy is translated at 36.
[66] *SS*, 8.172. Sima Guang, Li Tao, and the *Song History* eulogy still dominate interpretive strategies for the Zhenzong reign; see Lau and Huang, "Founding and Consolitation of the Sung Dynasty," 270–73.
[67] *Dongdu shilüe*, 8.9a.   [68] *SS*, 16.314.

directly, place full blame upon Wang Anshi and the New Policies for the eventual fall of Northern Song.

Both histories are largely in accord on the reign of Zhezong. Both laud the regency of Empress Gao 高皇后 (1032–1093), when the Yuanyou administrators, whose governance "approached that of the Renzong era," were recalled. The *Song History*, however, explicitly states that the Yuanyou government rescinded the New Policies, then frames the political reversal after 1093 in moral terms: the "old nefarious" expelled "all the worthies." The *Miscellany* admits that Zhezong recalled the former reform officials, concluding simply that they did not serve him well. The Yuan historians do not comment on the personality of Zhezong, declining to repeat the earlier praise of him as "wise and resolute." In short, the *Miscellany* presents the reign of Zhezong as a simple reversal of political direction; the Yuan historians remove Zhezong himself from the equation and cast this reversal in the *daoxue* language of moral absolutes.[69]

The two historical works diverge most in their analysis of Huizong. Since Huizong's son, Emperor Gaozong, lived until 1187, the *Miscellany* comments reflect the enormous sensitivity in Southern Song to the historical problem of Huizong's responsibility for the demise of Northern Song. From the modern perspective, the *Miscellany* comments are a masterpiece of evasion. They focus solely on the beginning and the end of his reign. They relate that Huizong initially sought in 1100 to appoint the former Yuanyou administrator Fan Chunren 范純仁 (1027–1101) as councilor, but Fan was too ill to take office. There follows a generic statement that "loyal ministers" engender respect for the court; but chaos follows when "hordes of the dark are employed." A series of quotations from the *Book of Documents* then links Huizong to sage rulers of antiquity who realized their errors and so earned the support of the people. In 1125, "carefully attentive to the warnings of Heaven," he abdicated his crown, and in this way made possible the Restoration under Gaozong. Far from criticizing Huizong, the twelfth-century historian makes him the positive conduit through which the Yuanyou ethos was transmitted to the Restoration.[70]

Against these generalities, the Yuan historians devote considerable space (only their *zan* for Gaozong is longer) to citing specific incidents from Huizong's rule to dissect what they perceive as the baleful intersection of politics and personality in his reign. After a lengthy review of the diplomatic and military activity in the early 1120s, they conclude that if Huizong had not been emperor, the Jin, although powerful, could never have invaded Song. They describe Huizong as "a minor intelligence, egotistical and selfish in his motives" (私智小慧, 用心一偏). Cai Jing encouraged and exploited this

[69] *Dongdu shilüe*, 9.8a; *SS*, 18.354.
[70] *Dongdu shilüe*, 11.9b. For the *Shujing* quotations, see Legge, *The Shoo King*, 163–64, 180.

personality to encourage a cult of luxurious indulgence that infected and weakened the state. Disaster was assured when the eunuch Tong Guan was given command of the army's best troops. Huizong's imprisonment and loss of his state were not fated but resulted from his own cupidity. The Yuan historians also quote from the *Book of Documents* the admonition "do not what is unprofitable to the injury of what is profitable . . . [do] not value strange things to the contemning things that are useful."[71] The end of Northern Song arose from a combination of the continuation of the New Policies and Huizong's personal pursuit of strange, unprofitable things. Of those rulers who "destroyed all rules of conduct by indulging their own desires," he was the worst.[72]

The Yuan historians' appraisal of Huizong rests on the *daoxue* premise that the mind of the ruler determines the quality of political order during his reign. Thus, the fall of Northern Song followed as a natural result of the distorted proclivities of Huizong's mind (用心一偏). The *Song History* eulogies for the Restoration monarchs continue in this vein. The Yuan historians use the eulogies for Gaozong and Xiaozong to present their views on the nature and quality of the transmission from Northern to Southern Song; they evaluate the success of the Restoration, and they find it wanting. After a quick review of previous Restorations in Chinese history, of which they count five (in the Xia, Zhou, Han, Jin, and Tang dynasties), they find the Jin and Song attempts deficient because they did not recover all the dynasty's former territory.[73] They grant that Gaozong was respectful, frugal, benevolent, and generous. He used these qualities to continue the dynasty but was unable "to dispel disorder and return to orthodoxy" (*boluan fanzheng* 撥亂反正). This famous phrase derives from the *Gongyang Commentary* to the last entry in the *Spring and Autumn Annals*, where it describes Confucius' hope that his book may restore the fortunes of the Zhou dynasty. After 1127, the phrase became a rhetorical catchword to describe the task of Restoration; and after the peace of 1142 Qin Gui used the phrase to proclaim triumphantly that these goals had been attained.[74] The phrase implies not only a return to political and military stability but also moral realignment – the moral corollary of what Taizu did to the physical doors of the palace. By their specific use of this phrase, the Yuan historians, while admitting that Gaozong continued the dynasty, deny that he returned the dynasty to its Northern Song orthodoxy. Given the previous

---

[71] Legge, *The Shoo King*, 349.

[72] *SS*, 22.417–18. The last phrase also paraphrases the *Book of Documents*. Legge, *The Shoo King*, 207.

[73] This analogy culminates a discourse that began as early as 1127 when Chen Dong warned Gaozong that if he did not recover lost territory in the North, he would repeat the error the Eastern Jin had made in 317; see Hartman and Li, "The Rehabilitation of Chen Dong," 89–90.

[74] He Xiu, *Chunqiu Gongyang zhuan zhushu*, 28.21a. For an early Southern Song usage see the 1129 memorial of Hu Yin at *SS*, 435.12919. For a post-1142 usage see Li and Hartman, "A Newly Discovered Inscription," 415–17.

eulogies, "orthodoxy" must refer to the dynasty's pre-1067 Taizu and Renzong periods.

The eulogy concedes that the military and financial obstacles Gaozong confronted far exceeded those the other Restoration monarchs had faced. But they caution against allowing the magnitude of these difficulties to absolve him of responsibility for the Restoration's ultimate failure. As evidence they invoke the late Song *daoxue* opinion that – with Li Gang at court and Zong Ze in the field – Gaozong had in 1127 the wherewithal to recover the North. But, deceived by his early councilors, then manipulated by Qin Gui, he became indifferent and weak, and lost the opportunity to prevail over the Jurchen. Worse, he exiled Zhao Ding and Zhang Jun, and permitted the execution of Yue Fei, just as the general was on the point of victory.[75] The principled literati of his age detested him because he accepted humiliation in exchange for security. "He hid his resentment and abandoned his family; how tragic in the end he could not escape the scorn of later ages."[76]

The Yuan historians here extend to Gaozong's reign the *daoxue* concept of a "lineage of evil" councilors who originated in late Northern Song and that had oppressed a lineage of virtuous *daoxue*-inspired administrators – here Li Gang, Zhao Ding, and Zhang Jun. This historical construction began when Zhu Xi applied the Confucian dichotomy between *junzi* and *xiaoren* to Song history.[77] The motif will return in the *Song History* as a major organizing force in the biographies, where the lives of the *daoxue* masters stand in juxtaposition to those of the "nefarious ministers." When combined with the denial that he returned the dynasty to orthodoxy, the motif that Gaozong permitted this "lineage of evil" to extend into Southern Song implies that he merely prolonged the unorthodox deviations from "orthodoxy" that began under Shenzong. Therefore, his restoration was not only spatially but also morally incomplete: he was unable to recover the achievement of Taizu, the founder.

If the eulogy for Gaozong only implies this failure, the fully positive appraisal of Xiaozong begins unequivocally: Xiaozong excelled as emperor – the best in Southern Song – because he descended from Taizu. By stating this biological fact, the Yuan historians also assert a moral connection between Xiaozong and Northern Song orthodoxy as manifested under Taizu and Renzong, with whom Xiaozong is paired at the end of his eulogy. The historians specifically label Xiaozong a Confucian "worthy" (*xian* 賢). They praise his success in negotiating more favorable treaty terms from the Jin after the renewed outbreak of hostilities in the early 1160s. They claim that his support for military plans to recover the North earned the respect and fear of the Jin

---

[75] Indirect criticism of Gaozong along these lines first emerges after the 1234 Song invasion of the North; see Hartman and Li, "The Rehabilitation of Chen Dong," 139–40.
[76] *SS*, 32.612.   [77] See Hartman, "The Making of a Villain," 122–34.

court; and the ensuing peaceful détente between the two courts provided the population a welcome respite from war. In conclusion, they dwell at length on his filial piety. Considering he was not the biological son of Gaozong, they maintain that his filial devotion to his predecessor was unprecedented. As Renzong well deserves his temple name "the benevolent," so is Xiaozong well honored as "the filial."[78]

The Yuan eulogies for Gaozong and Xiaozong thus imply that the Restoration reached its apex under Xiaozong. The eulogies for the remaining Song emperors confirm this verdict. Although the Yuan historians laud both Guangzong and Ningzong for their early devotion to Confucian learning and their initial support for literati governance (Guangzong in 1190, Ningzong in 1194), they note that neither could sustain this initial commitment. Guangzong could not control the imperial affines of the inner court; Ningzong fell under the sway of autocratic councilors, first Han Tuozhou, then Shi Miyuan who diverted the rightful succession to Emperor Lizong. Ningzong's eulogy concludes with a direct parallel between Northern and Southern Song: after four emperors and 100 years, the Northern Song had come to Renzong; after four emperors and 100 years, the Southern Song had come to Ningzong. They then contrast the propriety of the transition from Renzong to Yingzong and the unseemliness of the transition from Ningzong to Lizong as a metaphor for the degree to which the Restoration had fallen short of its initial aspirations.[79]

The eulogy for Emperor Lizong compares the forty-year length of his reign to that of Renzong, but Lizong's continual reliance upon autocratic ministers (named are Shi Miyuan, Ding Daquan, and Jia Sidao) renders any further parallels superficial. The historians mock the duplicity of the Lizong court's dealings with the Mongols: having first allied with the Mongols to defeat the Jin in 1234, they then violated that alliance in a selfish attempt to grab Mongol territory in the North. The eulogy attacks Lizong personally, citing his sexual excess, his disinterest in government, his reliance upon autocratic councilors, and his pro forma attendance at Classics Mat sessions that were devoid of useful content. They close, however, by lauding his removal of Wang Anshi from the Confucian temple, his elevation of the *daoxue* masters to that status, and his promulgation of Zhu Xi's *Four Books*. His court was free of the persecutions that had marred the reigns of Huizong and Ningzong. Referring to the Mongol court's turn to Confucianism, the historians conclude that "our return to the good rule of the ancient kings through the study of principle ... began in truth under him." And they approve his temple name "the principled."[80]

A chronological reading of the imperial eulogies in the annals section of the *Song History* thus reveals an undulating trajectory of moral struggle, a struggle

---

[78] *SS*, 35.692.   [79] *SS*, 36.710, 40.781–82.   [80] *SS*, 45.888–89.

that takes place in the minds and the resulting political dispositions and policies of the Song emperors themselves. This perspective mirrors the Southern Song *daoxue* conviction, so forcefully expressed by Zhu Xi, that the mental disposition of the emperor determines the moral character and effectiveness of government. The prefaces and evaluations in the biographical sections of the history reinforce and add granularity to this cyclical pattern of moral tension. We will explore the Song origins of these conceptions in Chapter 11 on the rhythms of Song history.

The Prefaces and Evaluations

Like all dynastic histories, the biographies of the *Song History* comprise by far the largest portion of text and contain the most evaluative comments (*lun*). The division of these biographies into two groups, a single, large unclassified (general) collection and smaller collections of theme-related classified biographies is traditional in the genre. The *Eastern Capital Miscellany* contains a similar arrangement, and, once again, a comparison between this twelfth-century work and the *Song History* demonstrates how the Yuan historians modified their Song sources. Table 5.1 presents the organization of the biographical sections in both works. The *Miscellany*'s classified categories most probably derive from the *Two Courts State History* of 1082. Li Xinchuan writes that the *Miscellany* took its material from "the biographies in the [state] histories of the five courts [of Taizu, Taizong, Zhenzong, Renzong, and Yingzong] and the appended biographies in the veritable records of the four courts [of Shenzong, Zhezong, Huizong, and Qinzong], with some slight additions from private histories."[81] Li's formulation accurately describes the official Northern Song historical compilations such as they existed when the *Miscellany* was compiled in the mid-twelfth century: the two state histories of 1030 and 1082 and the individual veritable records for the last four reigns. The state history of 1030 was the first to have classified categories, and these were replicated in the subsequent history of 1082. The *Miscellany* categories therefore represent a quite old, mid-eleventh-century, and decidedly pre-*daoxue* sensibility. These largely moral divisions, although traditional, represent an increasing differentiation as compared to an earlier and simpler Song division that apparently contained no classified categories.[82]

This comparison demonstrates that the present configuration of biographies in the *Song History* represents an intentional structure devised by the Yuan historians. These intentions can be seen in the selection, designation, and order

---

[81] *Chaoye zaji, jia*, 4.113–14; also *Yuhai*, 46.51a.
[82] For the arrangement of biographies in the Northern Song state histories see Cai Chongbang, *Songdai xiushi zhidu yanjiu*, 119 (citing *Yuhai*, 46.46b) and 122.

Table 5.1 A comparison of the biographical sections in the *Eastern Capital Miscellany* and the *Song History*

Eastern Capital Miscellany				Song History			
Juan	Section		Preface	Juan	Section		Preface
13–14	世家	[Empresses]	13.1a	242–43	后妃	Empresses	242.8605–06
15–17	世家	[Princes]	15.1a-b	244–47	宗室	Imperial clan	244.8665–66
				248	公主	Princesses	None
18–109	列傳	[Unclassified biographies]	None	249–425	列傳	[Unclassified biographies]	None
110–11	忠義	Loyal and righteous	110.1a	426	循吏	Correct officials	426.12691
112	循史	Correct officials	112.1a	427–30	道學	Daoxue scholars	427.12709–10
113–14	儒學	Confucian scholarship	113.1a-b	431–38	儒林	Confucian scholars	None
115–16	文藝	Literary arts	115.1a-b	439–45	文苑	Literary writers	439.12997–98
117	卓行	Lofty conduct	117.1a	446–55	忠義	Loyal and righteous	446.13149–50
				456	孝義	Filial piety	456.13386
118	隱逸	Hermits	118.1a	457–59	隱逸	Hermits	457.13417
				460	列女	Virtuous women	460.13477–78
				461–62	方技	Physicians and diviners	461.13495–96
119	外戚	Imperial Affines	119.1	463–65	外戚	Imperial affines	463.13535
120–21	宦者	Eunuchs	120.1a-b	466–69	宦者	Eunuchs	466.13599–600
				470	佞幸	Favorites	470.13677
				471–74	姦臣	Nefarious ministers	471.13697
122	僭偽	Usurper	None	475–77	叛臣	Rebellious servitors	475.13789
				478–83	世家	[Conquered] houses	478.13853
				484	周三臣	The three Zhou servitors	484.13967
123–130	附錄	Liao, Jin, Xixia, Tibet, Vietnam	123.1a-b	485–92	外國	Foreign states	485.13981–82
				493–96	蠻夷	Southern Man tribes	493.14171

of the classified categories; in the assignment of individuals to specific groups; and in the group prefaces and individual comments. Table 5.1 shows how the historians have differentiated and rearranged the earlier Song categories. The overall order is similar, but the more complicated Yuan structure underscores an implicit divide between a "good" first half and a "bad" second half within the classified groups.[83] The first half begins with biographies of "correct officials" – selfless and dedicated, but not famous, civil servants. These idealized portraits of historically obscure but "correct" officials act as a prelude to the remaining "good" groups, which are organized on a descending scale of political importance, concluding with "virtuous women." "Physicians and diviners" marks the transition to the "bad" half, followed by "imperial affines," "eunuchs," and "favorites" – all potentially troublesome groups that the Yuan prefaces allege the Song successfully controlled. "Nefarious ministers" begins a series of increasingly destructive subsets of the "bad," whom the Song emperors managed less well to control. The subset concludes with "foreign" groups that are beyond the Song polity. The result is a hierarchical structure to the classified biographies in the *Song History* that pegs each group according to its relative positive or negative contribution to the health of an idealized *daoxue* vision of the Song body politic.

Careful readers will note that the Yuan editors have downgraded the "loyal and righteous," which led off the *Miscellany* classified categories, and upgraded "correct officials" to the initial category in the *Song History*. A comparative reading of the two prefaces explains the rationale for this move. "The loyal and righteous" refers to those who died in dynastic military actions, something akin to the "war heroes" of modern America. The *Miscellany* preface maintains that such heroes arise only during troubled times; therefore there have been few in Song. Only during the turbulent Jingkang period (1125–1126) did significant numbers appear. The *Miscellany* contains biographies of twenty-five heroes, half of whom died in various Tangut wars and half during the Jingkang period.[84] The *Miscellany* contains no biography of anyone who died in wars before the Qingli period. Probably, the grand-allegory narrative that the founders' "benevolence" had promoted a peaceful dynastic transition precluded mention of those who had died in the wars of consolidation under Taizu and Taizong. Taking a different tack, the *Song History* preface to its "loyal and righteous" category attributes to Taizu personally a return to the spirit of loyalism after its supposed decline in the Five Dynasties. The Yuan historians claim that Taizu's respect for those few who had chosen death out of loyalty to the former Zhou sovereign seeded a rebirth of loyalty that eventually inspired Song heroism during the Qingli wars.

[83] For a similar analysis see Li Huarui, "*Songshi* lunzan pingxi," 503–4.
[84] *Dongdu shilüe*, 110.1a.

Remarkably, they further attribute the full flowering of this loyalty to the Renzong period when memorials from literati such as Fan Zhongyan and Ouyang Xiu inspired the military to greater bravery and devotion to country. In their view, Taizu's original sentiment, thus reinforced, inspired the heroism of the Jingkang period and ultimately that of the Song subjects who had died resisting the Mongols. Once again, the Yuan historians posit a Taizu–Renzong ethos so strong that it shaped events until the end of the dynasty.[85]

The prefaces for the two transposed chapters on "correct officials" also demonstrate how the Yuan historians sharply adjusted a pre-*daoxue* Song focus. The classified category termed *xunli* 循吏, "law-abiding, reasonable, or correct officials," descended from the *Grand Scribe's Records*, where Sima Qian used the biographies of obscure but upright mid-Zhou officials to satirize the harsh governance of Emperor Wu.[86] This *Miscellany* chapter contains eleven biographies of minor, relatively unknown Northern Song officials. The accounts relate vivid incidents of how their actions as provincial administrators benefited the populace in reasonable, practical ways such as improving agriculture, providing famine relief, and fending off bandits. The *Miscellany* preface maintains that the accomplishments of these officials resulted from a consistent policy, extending from Taizu through Renzong, to encourage agriculture. Shenzong had the same intention, but officials intent on "merit and profit" (*gongli* 功利) derailed his policies; and the *Miscellany* features biographies of two officials who persevered in their efforts to help the people despite the complications of the New Policies.[87] In contrast, the *Song History* frames the "correct officials" as products of three Taizu policies to improve the quality of provincial administrators: (1) he personally selected them, (2) he closely supervised them, and (3) he severely punished infractions. There is no mention of agriculture or of other Song emperors. These Yuan adjustments, both in order and in content, signal a major redefinition of what it had meant to be a loyal servant of the Song state. The *Miscellany*, following the Northern Song *New History of Tang*, still gave pride of place to the "loyal and righteous," defining loyalty as an honorable death in the service of the dynasty. But the Yuan historians elevate "correct officials" into the primary position and

---

[85] *SS*, 446.13149–50. The historical portrayal of Song loyalists who resisted the Mongols presented a delicate problem for the Yuan historians. They append a long note to their preface to the "loyal and righteous" in which they relate that the general guidelines (*fanli*) for the three histories stipulated a frank presentation of their deeds. They differentiate, however, between four grades of heroism, depending on the deceased's motivation and the circumstances of his death. To some degree, the contention that the spirit of Taizu had continued to motivate the Song loyalists enabled the historians to finesse the problem of their intense resistance to the Mongols. The ten "loyal and righteous" chapters in the *Song History* contain the biographies of 277 individuals, seventy-seven, or 28 percent, of whom died at the end of the dynasty. See Jay, *A Change in Dynasties*, 68–71, 98–102, 265.

[86] Watson, *Records of the Grand Historian of China*, 2:413 n. 1.   [87] *Dongdu shilüe*, 112.1a.

downgrade the "loyal and righteous" three steps to a position below the Confucian scholars and litterateurs. In doing so, they signal a switch from a heroic military death to heroic civil service as the preferred standard for judging one's contribution to the body politic.

This focus also appears in the preface to the biographies of literary figures. Both the *Miscellany* and the *Song History* agree that the greatness of Song literature began with Ouyang Xiu, who swept away the overwrought decadence of the early Song Xikun 西崑 style of writing. The *Miscellany* frames this achievement in the context of long cycles of literary flourish and decline that extend back through the Tang into the Han. It compares Ouyang Xiu to Han Yu in the Tang but does not link him specifically to *guwen* 古文. After him, Wang Anshi, Zeng Gong 曾鞏 (1019–1083), and Su Shi broadened Song literary achievements that continue to this day. The *Song History*, however, directly attributes the Song literary renaissance to Taizu, whose replacement of military with civil officials laid the foundations for the emergence of "literati officials" (*wenshi* 文士). The preface directly links Ouyang Xiu to *guwen*, but laments that the "literary vitality" of Southern Song did not match that of Northern Song. The two prefaces to the biographies of literary figures thus replicate an established pattern: the *Miscellany* frames Song achievements as the result of sustained policies of the Song monarchy in general; the *Song History* attributes those same achievements to specific acts of Taizu personally and sees them as subsiding when subsequent monarchs did not follow his precedents.[88]

If the literatus as civil servant is the new hero in the *Song History*, the work's unprecedented treatment of "Confucians" signals in turn that the new standard will be based on the *daoxue* teachings of Zhu Xi. The Yuan historians divide Song Confucians into two groups: (1) "[masters] of the Learning of the Way" (*daoxue*), and (2) "the forest of Confucians" (*rulin* 儒林), a conventional term for Confucian scholarship as a whole. By foregrounding the *daoxue* biographies and by omitting a separate preface for the "forest of Confucians," the Yuan editors clearly signal that *daoxue* has now become the dominant flavor of Confucianism. Two factors govern the selection of figures for admission into the four-chapter *daoxue* group: Zhu Xi's opinion and the Yuan historians' opinion. The first two chapters contain biographies of the five Northern Song *daoxue* masters and their disciples as recorded by Zhu Xi in his *Record of the Origins of the [Teaching of the] Two Chengs* (*Yi Luo yuanyuan lu* 伊洛淵源錄). Both the texts of their biographies and the lengthy citations from their writings follow Zhu Xi. The second two chapters contain biographies of Zhu Xi and Zhang Shi 張栻 (1133–1180), followed by six disciples, headed by Huang Gan. The first two chapters thus reproduce Zhu Xi's reconstruction of his own origins; the second two chapters reproduce the Yuan historians' image of

---

[88] *Dongdu shilüe*, 115.1a–b; *SS*, 439.12997–98.

their own origins, the path by which Zhu Xi's teachings came to the Yuan state and to them.[89] As is well known, they consign other twelfth-century figures, such as Lü Zuqian and Lu Jiuyuan 陸九淵 (1139–1192), whom modern scholars often construe as forming a "fellowship of the *dao*," to the routine "forest of Confucians." The Yuan historians were adherents of Zhu Xi; however, they were not zealots, but scholars broadly conversant with many forms of Song Confucianism. Most likely, the *daoxue* chapters' exclusive focus on Zhu Xi more reflects official policy to support Zhu Xi's interpretation of the classics as the orthodox Yuan examination standard than it does the historians' private views or intellectual backgrounds.

The preface to the *daoxue* chapters is among the most vital orienting guides to the *Song History*. The historians first explain that, although the term *daoxue* was unknown in antiquity, in fact the teachings pervaded ancient society and government, and they benefited everyone in that society. They then summarize the standard account of the "lineage of the Way" (*daotong* 道統) – how these teachings passed to Confucius, died out with Mencius, and became adulterated in subsequent ages, but were then recovered in the Renzong era of the Song and perfected by Zhu Xi. In conclusion, they extend the "lineage of the Way" to their own time: "although *daoxue* flourished in Song, the Song did not perfect its application and even prohibited it. Contemporary monarchs and state rulers who aim to restore the governance of Heavenly virtue and the kingly Way would do well to find their standards here." The historians thus announce to their Mongol sovereign that the *Song History* presents the opportunity for him to learn from the mistakes of his Song predecessors and fully to restore the governance of antiquity.[90] This elevation of the Zhu Xi lineage affirms the Toghto network's support for the Song *daoxue* tradition of literati governance and for the hybrid Sino-Mongol alliance that had since 1313 embraced this political direction.

While the contents of most parallel prefaces in the *Miscellany* and the *Song History* differ substantially, those that introduce the biographies of imperial affines and eunuchs share similar language and themes. In other words, the Yuan historians saw no need to change the stance of the official Song histories on these groups. Both prefaces recite the standard line that the Song monarchs controlled imperial affines by granting them empty titles and high salaries but no authority. The affines were thus politically and militarily quiescent, unlike their Han dynasty forebears. The *Song History* adds that, among other benefits, the Song state enjoyed three tranquil regencies in the Northern Song under Empresses Liu, Cao, and Gao.[91] Both works take a similar tack on eunuchs.

---

[89] For a detailed study see Lu Zhongfeng, "Yuandai lixue yu *Songshi* 'daoxue liezhuan' de xueshushi tese."

[90] *SS*, 427.12709–10.   [91] *Dongdu shilüe*, 119.1a; *SS*, 463.13535.

They use the same examples to demonstrate that the first three Song emperors co-operated with their chief councilors to contain eunuch power. At this point, however, the two works diverge. The longer *Miscellany* preface details the breakdown of this control under Huizong. It admits that the latitude granted to Tong Guan and Liang Shicheng 梁師成 (d. 1126) undermined the proper exercise of literati governance and the political atmosphere approached the decadence of the final years of Han and Tang. Only the execution of the eunuchs brought the dynasty back from the brink of disaster. The *Song History* abbreviates these musings to one laconic sentence: "the disasters under Tong Guan and Liang Shicheng were not trivial."[92]

As the sequel to this volume will detail, the literati culture of Northern Song arose in opposition to the existing patrimonial structure of state governance, in which the affines and eunuchs played central roles. Literati distrust of these groups not only pre-dated Song but intensified in proportion to the growth of literati power over the course of the dynasty. This opprobrium is already ingrained in the *Miscellany* and continues unabated into the thirteenth-century *daoxue* historians and the *Song History*. The Yuan historians took at least two steps to reinforce the motif of monarchical and literati dominance over these groups. First, because the *Miscellany*'s frank admission about Tong Guan and Liang Shicheng undercuts the premise that the dynasty successfully contained eunuchs, the historians have curtailed its preface on eunuchs. Second, they place the biographies of the most powerful affines – Zhang Yue and Han Tuozhou – into the "favorites" and "nefarious ministers" categories. This move dilutes the fact that these affines indeed wielded great political authority in Southern Song, leaving only the "good" affines to confirm the motif of their subservience.

Both these *Song History* prefaces underscore the successful regencies in Northern Song, a contention that also dominates the preface on empresses. The motif of the dutiful empress arose after Empress Liu's death in 1033 to camouflage the extent of her independence and opposition to literati govern-ance, and grew in intensity and importance over the course of the dynasty. The *Miscellany* preface presents an elaborate comparison between the mothers of the founding empresses of the Xia and Zhou dynasties and Empress Du, queen mother for both Taizu and Taizong. Alluding to her supposed role in the Golden Box affair, the preface lauds her as the origin of the "family policies of the ancestors" (*zuzong jiafa* 祖宗家法), which have enabled successive Song emperors to "cultivate their persons, rectify their minds, and regulate their families." The Yuan historians accept the primacy of Empress Du as a model for Song affinal virtue, but omit the reference to the *Great Learning* catenation, since the allusion implies that rectification of the imperial mind might first

---

[92] *Dongdu shilüe*, 120.1a–b; *SS*, 466.13599–600.

require feminine-induced domestic tranquility. Instead, the *Song History* preface lists Empress Cao and Empress Gao (both of whom promoted the Yuanyou administrators), and, in Southern Song, Empress Meng and Empress Wu – all of whom, the editors claim, continued Empress Du's emulation of the queen mothers of antiquity. The Song thus experienced no interregnums such as the Han suffered under Wang Mang or the Tang under Empress Wu. The Yuan historians thus subtly realign the original Song motif of the virtuous empress to accord with their Taizu–Renzong–Yuanyou–Xiaozong axis of political value. This periodization bypasses the many empresses whose behavior fell short of the ancients – most prominently Empress Liu, Empress Li, and Empress Yang.[93] Once again, the negative examples are omitted to permit the positive examples to confirm the motif.

In addition to directly stated opinions, the Yuan editors also employ a number of structural features to convey their historical judgments in the biographies. First is overall length. Second is the placement of quotations within the biographies. Third are biographies that showcase a single event or quotation. Fourth is the placement of a subject's biography relative to other historical figures. The "average" biography of a major political figure occupies about ten pages in the Zhonghua edition. For example, Zhao Pu's biography is ten pages, Wang Dan's is ten, Han Qi's eleven, Fu Bi's nine. Anything above this length signals either a person to whom the Yuan editors attach special importance, or one whose biography they employ to emphasize some larger point beyond its subject's quotidian career. For example, the outsize biographies devoted to Li Gang (thirty-four pages), Yue Fei (twenty pages), and Zhang Jun (fifteen pages) develop a *daoxue* historiography of the Restoration, in which Emperor Gaozong's failure to follow their advice doomed the Restoration. These lengthy biographies and attached evaluations (*lun*) thus reinforce the Yuan historians' negative eulogy (*zan*) for Emperor Gaozong.[94] Other lengthy biographies are those for Sima Guang (thirteen pages), Su Shi (seventeen pages), Su Zhe (fifteen pages), and Zhu Xi (twenty pages). Several negative figures also command long biographies, the longest being that of Qin Gui at twenty-one pages.

The Yuan historians often quote extensively from the subject's writings to express their own judgments and opinions, and such quotations contribute significantly to the length of these biographies. The technique is old and especially strong in the "comprehensive mirror" tradition of Sima Guang, Li Tao, and Li Xinchuan. These historians, as we have seen above, often express their own opinions through carefully selected quotations from memorials. A comparison of surviving "appended biographies" from the Song veritable

---

[93] *Dongdu shilüe*, 13.1a; *SS*, 242.8605–6.
[94] *SS*, 359.11274, 361.11313–14, and 365.11396–97.

records and the corresponding biographies in the *Song History* confirms that extracts from the subject's writings were usually inserted into his biography at the state-history stage of compilation. Those in the veritable-records biographies rarely contained long quoted extracts.[95] The selection of these quotations, therefore, is a major vehicle by which the Yuan historians both indicate historical value and regulate the flow and intensity of their chosen motifs across the enormity of the *Song History*. In general, these memorials rehearse motifs of the grand allegory and profess the writer's support for the principles of literati governance.

For example, the seventeen-page biography of Su Shi contains five pages of anti-New Policies tracts. Almost half of Su Zhe's fifteen-page biography quotes a variety of memorials, including those against the New Policies and against political accommodation with their advocates.[96] Likewise, over half of Zhu Xi's biography quotes his memorials attacking Emperor Xiaozong's political practice and his reliance upon "favorites."[97] A telling example of this technique is the enormous two-*juan* biography of Li Gang that begins and dominates the Southern Song section of unclassified biographies. Li Gang played a prominent role in national politics for only two years, from 1125 through 1127, when Gaozong dismissed him as his first chief councilor. But he consistently opposed accommodation with the Jurchen, advocated military recovery of the North, and meticulously recorded and preserved these opinions for posterity in 180 *juan* of collected works. Zhu Xi recognized the historical value of Li Gang as a spokesman for the Restoration that might have been and as an antithesis to Qin Gui, who had shaped the Restoration as it actually was. Therefore, as Zhu Xi worked to vilify Qin Gui, he also worked to canonize Li Gang.[98] The Yuan historians use the biography of Li Gang, and especially its quotations, to express Zhu Xi's historical view of the Restoration. The first *juan* features a long summary of Li Gang's 1127 ten-point plan for political reform and a return to literati governance after the Huizong era. An enormous eight-page quotation, virtually the entire text of Li Gang's response to an 1135/3 edict soliciting opinion on logistical and diplomatic options for war versus peace, dominates the second *juan*.[99]

---

[95] Hartman, "A Textual History of Cai Jing's Biography in the *Songshi*," 531–36; Levine, "A House in Darkness," 204–308, 597–638.

[96] *SS*, 338.10801–8, 339.10822–23, 10829–30.   [97] *SS*, 429.12751–70.

[98] Hartman, "The Reluctant Historian," 138–39; Hartman and Li, "The Rehabilitation of Chen Dong," 117–18.

[99] *Yaolu*, 87.1674–88, contains summaries from ten respondents, including Qin Gui. For Li Gang's memorial, see *Li Gang quanji*, 78.793–805. The *Song History* also quotes shorter extracts from the other respondents, but only from those who advocated continued military operations; see *SS*, 375.11607–9, 11614–15, 379.11691–92. The biographies of Lü Yihao and Qin Gui do not cite their opinions on this issue.

Among the other respondents to the 1135 edict was Li Bing 李邴 (1085–1146), who had served as assisting chief councilor in 1129 but resigned over differences with Lü Yihao 呂頤浩 (1071–1139). Almost 70 percent of Li's biography consists of quotations from his response to the 1135 edict. Clearly, the historians have used his "biography" as a vehicle to insert his memorial into the *Song History*.[100] Li Bing's is one of a number of single-issue biographies whose focus resides not on the subject's life but on one text or event that advances the historians' larger agenda. It is often difficult to determine whether single-issue biographies derive from the Song state histories or were created by the Yuan historians. In the case of Li Bing, since the *Song History* quotation perfectly replicates Li Xinchuan's abridgment of the same memorial, one may surmise that the biography derives from the Southern Song state history, upon whose biographies Li Xinchuan worked after he completed the *Chronological Record*.[101]

The biography of Lin Xun 林勳 (*jinshi* 1115) presents a single-issue biography constructed by the Yuan historians, in this case Wei Su 危素 (1303–1372). Dispatched to the south on a search for source materials, Wei encountered Lin Xun's *Writings on the Root of Governance* (*Ben zheng shu* 本政書). Presented to the court in 1129, this work outlined how the ancient well-field system of agrarian land distribution could be adapted to modern times and could ease the burden of the existing "two-tax" system on the peasantry. Gaozong rejected the idea and opted instead for new cadastral surveys (*jingjie fa* 經界法). However, thinkers as diverse as Zhu Xi and Chen Liang 陳亮 (1143–1194) later endorsed Lin's ideas, and Chen Liang wrote a preface and printed the book. For *daoxue* historians, always sympathetic to tax reforms based on "well-field" precedents, the work became yet another example of the wrong choices Gaozong had made. Wei Su discovered a copy of Chen Liang's imprint in Songjiang and made a clean copy with the intention of printing the work himself. His own preface, dated 1346, explains that he inserted a synopsis of Lin's work into his *Song History* biography. Clearly, his superiors approved the draft; and the same synopsis also appears in the section on farmland in the monograph on fiscal administration.[102]

The biography of Lou Yinliang 婁寅亮 (*jinshi* 1112) provides yet another example of how the historians use the biographical format to foreground a single issue. Lou, an otherwise unremarkable official, suggested to Gaozong in 1130 that he designate an heir from the Taizu branch of the imperial clan. The emperor invited him to personally discuss the issue and accepted his suggestion. As will be discussed in Chapter 9, Lou's suggestion was part of an

---

[100] *SS*, 375.11606–9.   [101] *Yaolu*, 87.1683–88.
[102] *SS*, 422.12605–6. For detailed commentary on the monograph passage at *SS*, 170.4169–70, see Wada Sei and Nakajima Satoshi, *Sōshi shokkashi yakuchū*, 1:115–21; for Wei Su's preface see *QYW*, 48:1470.207.

elaborate effort to bolster the image of the Restoration during one of its darkest moments, and the rationale behind Lou's memorials became a cornerstone of Restoration rhetoric. Eighty-five percent of Lou's biography is given over to his memorials eulogizing Taizu and condemning the injustices done to his heirs. In this case, the showcased quotations are indeed historically significant, and Lou's "biography" provided a vehicle to insert these memorials into the *Song History*. Although the draft of the Southern Song state history probably included the present biography, its message is also central to the Yuan historians' adulation of Taizu. The remaining 15 percent of the biography also rehearses a favorite theme of the Yuan historians; for Qin Gui, jealous of Yin's potential influence over Gaozong, drummed up a legal inquisition against him and forced him from the capital.[103]

Virtually all of such featured quotations – long verbatim extracts – support the principles of literati governance or a historiographical perspective framed by the Southern Song *daoxue* masters. Such extracts thus occur in biographies of those figures whose historical personas the movement had cast in a positive light. Biographies of their antitheses – figures with negative personas that supposedly undermined literati governance – rely upon a different compositional technique. The most extreme negative personas are collected in the biographies of the "nefarious ministers" (*jianchen* 姦臣), whose origins, formation, and preface will be examined in Chapter 10. Since the actions of these figures were, by definition, inimical to literati governance, the historians do not cite their writings. Instead, they construct these biographies by fleshing out the "appended" veritable-records biographies not with extracts of the subject's own writings, but with quotations from the accusations and attacks of their political opponents and critics.[104]

Within the large section of unclassified biographies, the organization of biographies into *juan* and into larger groupings is complex and may appear at first sight somewhat quixotic. But the evaluations (*lun*), once again, provide a guide to the Yuan historians' intent. In general, the order is chronological, but not strictly so. Larger groupings resulting from combining the biographies of similar individuals often disrupt the chronology. For example, the two *juan* (*SS* 334–35) of military leaders who lived between 1082 and 1126 intervene between the biographies of political reformers and antireformers from the Shenzong era (1068–1085). The biographies of Wang Anshi and Sima Guang lead their respective political cohorts (Wang Anshi and followers at *juan* 327–29; Sima Guang's group at *juan* 336–41). In their evaluations, the historians make clear that they sanction the politics of one group over the other, and

[103] *SS*, 399.12132–33.

[104] Hartman, "A Textual History of Cai Jing's Biography in the *Songshi*," contains a detailed analysis of Cai Jing's biography. See also Hartman, "The Making of a Villain," 105–17, for a similar discussion of Qin Gui's biography.

they specify the precise relationship of each individual to the group. This structural pattern is replicated for all periods of Song history. *Juan* 282 contains positive biographies of the early chief councilors Li Hang and Wang Dan; the following *juan* 283 collects negative biographies of Wang Qinruo, Ding Wei 丁謂 (966–1037), and Xia Song 夏竦 (985–1051). *Juan* 358–361 extol Li Gang, Zong Ze, Zhao Ding, and Zhang Jun; while the evaluation for the following *juan* 362 chastises Zhu Shengfei 朱勝非 (1082–1144), Lü Yihao, Fan Zongyin 范宗尹 (1098–1136), Fan Zhixu 范致虛 (d. 1129), and Lü Haowen 呂好問 (1064–1131) for opposing the policies of the former group. Finally, the pattern replicates in Southern Song. *Juan* 392–393 begin with positive endorsements of Zhao Ruyu and members of his Qingyuan coalition of 1194; *juan* 394 follows with derision for their critics and opponents.

Cyclical Structure and Meaning in the Song History

The sum total of the evaluations and their supporting structures presents a picture of Song history as a series of alternating political and social cycles in which positive and negative forces compete to dominate one other. In traditional Confucian parlance, these forces are "gentlemen" versus "small men." Because neither group ever permanently vanquishes the other, the preface to the "nefarious ministers" biographies posits them as immutable categories locked in an unending struggle.[105] The four chapters of *daoxue* master biographies, however, parallel the four chapters of "nefarious minister" biographies both in length and in their respective positions in the positive and negative halves of the classified biography categories.[106] This tension between the lineage of *daoxue* as a political movement and a purported "lineage" of "nefarious ministers" is, as we have seen in Chapter 4, a central premise of the mid-thirteenth-century historians, and the Yuan editors have adopted this cyclical tension as an organizing principle for the *Song History*.

Two contentions undergird this cyclical tension. First, the advent of Wang Anshi and the New Policies marked a critical transition in Song history – a major change in the trajectory of cyclical movement. Second, the mental disposition of the sovereign determines the direction of this trajectory. Neither of these contentions is specifically *daoxue* in origin; but, after Zhu Xi juxtaposed the two ideas, the resulting synergy accelerated the momentum of *daoxue* historiography.[107] The *Song History* is replete with implications and

---

[105] *SS*, 471.13697.

[106] The "*daoxue* masters" are the second category in the "good" first half of the classified categories after the introductory "correct officials"; the "nefarious ministers" are far down the list in the "bad" second half.

[107] For a slightly different formulation of this idea see Li Huarui, "*Songshi* lunzan pingxi," 492–95.

direct statements of the importance of 1067 as a transition point in the dynasty's historical trajectory. For example, the important preface to the monograph on fiscal administration frames the advent of the New Policies as a downward turn in state finance that culminated in the ultimate collapse of political, financial, and social order.[108] The evaluation (*lun*) for Wang Anshi, perhaps the most important in the book, begins with a long quotation from Zhu Xi in which the master, late in life, summarizes his thoughts on Wang: he was a great writer with noble aspirations to restore the governance of antiquity. But his drive for financial and military reform forced him to employ unscrupulous agents whose oppression of the people "poisoned the four quarters" and brought on disaster. The Yuan editors lament that Emperor Shenzong ignored Han Qi's warning not to employ Wang Anshi as chief councilor. It was a tragedy for the dynasty and for Wang himself.[109]

Evaluations of individual officials reinforce the notion that the general quality and character of officialdom changed for the worse after 1067.[110] In addition, the Yuan historians also group together biographies that emphasize specific facets of this decline. For example, they gather together the biography of Ye Zuxia 葉祖洽 (*jinshi* 1070) and four other officials who placed first in *jinshi* examinations after 1070. The evaluation contends that New Policies changes to the examination system and its adoption of Wang Anshi's teachings as examination orthodoxy so deformed the pre-1067 system that "the habits of the literati were destroyed." Only those willing to parrot Wang orthodoxy passed, and those who parroted best passed first. Therefore, the historians explain, they have only included the biographies of seven of the eighteen first-place laureates between 1067 and 1125, including these five "despicable petty men." Referencing Mencius' desire to "rectify men's hearts, and put an end to those perverse doctrines," the historians conclude that such men mirror the "damage to the mentality of the people ... from which the state could not recover."[111]

At the peak of the political hierarchy, the mind of the sovereign both determined and indicated the mental outlook of the body politic. The evaluation to the biography of Zhang Jun begins with the central premise of *daoxue* political theory: the primary duty of the Confucian is to promote a "right and proper" (*zhengzhi* 正直) political atmosphere whose first objective is to "make

---

[108] *SS*, 173.4156.
[109] *SS*, 327.10553; for the original passage see Zhu Xi, *Chuci jizhu*, "Chuci houyu" 楚辭後語, 6.3a–b.
[110] For ten citations, five positive and five negative, see Li Huarui, "*Songshi* lunzan pingxi," 493–94.
[111] *SS*, 354.11172. For the Mencius quotation see Legge, *The Works of Mencius*, 284. The same quotation also occurs in the *Miscellany* evaluation of Wang Anshi: *Dongdu shilüe*, 79.7a. The five examinations in question occurred in 1070, 1079, 1103, 1105, and 1106; see Fu Xuancong, *Song dengkeji kao*, 299, 342, 474, 489, and 491.

right the mind of the sovereign" (*zheng junxin* 正君心).[112] Although the phrase and the concept are old, and had already been proposed as a program for the emperor in the early 1130s, Zhu Xi's emphasis on the cultivation of mental discipline as a prerequisite for political order in the *Great Learning* fore-grounded the concept as a criterion of *daoxue* historical value.[113] A number of evaluations insist that Wang Anshi's tenure as chief councilor robbed Emperor Shenzong of the tranquility of mind necessary to form impartial ("right and proper") decisions. Likewise, Cai Jing distorted Huizong's mind by encouraging his lust for the spoils of foreign conquest.[114] This rush of sovereigns and ministers alike toward the pursuit of riches started with Emperor Shenzong. Had he followed the model of Renzong, the tragedy of Wang Anshi could have been averted, for "the morals of the times and the manners of the literati are all tied to the aspirations of the ruler's thinking."[115]

It would be presumptuous to attempt to summarize the meaning of the *Song History*. However, one can easily summarize the Yuan historians' own state-ments about what they hoped its readers would understand. To wit, because Emperor Taizu, the Song founder, exercised a benevolent governance that promoted civil, literati values over military rule, Heaven conferred its mandate on him, and the excellence of his rule approached that of antiquity. His heirs, despite sporadic hurdles, built on this success, and a governance of "loyalty and toleration" culminated under Emperor Renzong (the benevolent ancestor). However, Emperor Shenzong and Wang Anshi changed course and departed from Taizu's policies; their New Policies led ultimately to the collapse of Northern Song. But Sima Guang's earlier reversion to the founders' policies during the Yuanyou period provided a sound model for the, alas, imperfect Restoration under Gaozong. His "pursuit of Yuanyou" culminated in turn under Xiaozong. Finally, Emperor Lizong transferred the monarchy's support from Wang Anshi to the *daoxue* masters, whose teachings now present the Yuan state with its best chance, once again, to revive the governance of antiquity.

Politics and Message

As we will explore in the chapters to follow, this synopsis presents a collage of themes and motifs that derive from Song imperial propaganda, *daoxue* histor-iography, and Yuan factional politics. We focus here, however, on the political and cultural context for which Toghto and his historians devised this synopsis and the message they hoped it would convey to their intended audience. We have seen that Toghto's Confucian allies characterized his overthrow of Bayan

---

[112] *SS*, 361.11313.
[113] *Zhuzi yulei*, 108.2678. For Hu Anguo's discourse to Emperor Gaozong that he should "set his mind straight" see Li and Hartman, "A Newly Discovered Inscription," 436–37.
[114] *SS*. 344.10949, 348.11046.   [115] *SS*, 355.11197.

in 1340 as a political "renewal" (*genghua*). The *Song History* evaluation for Sima Guang uses a similar phrase to describe his reversal of the New Policies in 1086. When read, once again, against the *Miscellany* comment on Sima Guang, the Yuan political context of the evaluation (*lun*) in his *Song History* biography becomes apparent. Whereas the *Miscellany* appraises Sima Guang's overall career and barely alludes to Wang Anshi, the Yuan editors focus exclusively on 1086. They craft an effusive paean to Sima Guang and literati governance as a contrast object to Wang Anshi and the New Policies. Few passages in the *Song History* juxtapose the two political orientations so directly and in such categorical terms. The oppressive "tax collectors" of the New Policies brought the populace twenty years of misery. The "nefarious and crooked" blocked dissent and monopolized government. But "worthies and gentlemen" united with the populace to plead for Sima's return. In one morning, he brought back the Renzong era, and the country greeted the return of literati governance "as rain that came at the height of the drought." Although Sima was old and ill, the Yuanyou interlude in the application of the New Policies mitigated their harmful effects, postponed the day of reckoning, and softened the severity of the crisis when it ultimately came.[116]

Much of this panegyric draws on *daoxue* hyperbole. But the drafters of the *Song History*, as well as their intended first audience, can hardly have failed to notice the parallels between 1086 and 1340. The stark contrast built into their evaluation of Sima Guang – a political tension that extends in many ways and on many levels throughout the book – invites, by typology, a comparison between Sima Guang and Toghto. Immediately, this type between the two "gentlemen" (*junzi*) then generates a corresponding and opposite type between the two "petty men" (*xiaoren*) – Wang Anshi and Bayan. These complementary types, plus the larger parallel between the "renewals" of 1086 and 1340, suggest a broader analogy between contrasting theories and practices of governance. The political struggle in Song between (1) literati governance as manifested in Yuanyou under Sima Guang and (2) the New Policies as manifested under Wang Anshi parallels the political struggle in Yuan between (1) the hybrid Sino-Mongol Confucianism as manifested under Toghto and (2) the Mongol-centered technocracy as manifested under Bayan. Finally, the combined force of these types and analogies generates a larger historical opposition between the two alternative models of government that I have characterized in the Introduction, and will revisit again in Chapter 11, as Confucian literati, or institutionalist, and technocratic: (1) a government staffed by examination-recruited officials rotating through established administrative units whose authority and relationship to other units is known and regulated by statute and precedent, versus (2) a government staffed by technocrats, recruited for

---

[116] *SS*, 336.10771–72; *Dongdu shilüe*, 87B.6b.

their specialized knowledge and employed in ad hoc administrative units with ill-defined and fluid relationships to each other. The Yuan historians, following their *daoxue* forebears in Song, clearly preferred the first alternative and framed its history in Song along the Taizu–Renzong–Xiaozong axis of "worthy administrators." They framed the second alternative as beginning with the New Policies and extending through an ensuing Cai Jing–Qin Gui–Han Tuozhou axis of "nefarious ministers."

This typological praxis enabled the editorial committee of the *Song History* to function simultaneously as state historians and as members of Toghto's political network. As Yuan politicians, they used Song history to give voice to their own aspirations and struggles to transform the Yuan polity into a Confucian-based, literati-dominated, institutionalist state. As historians, these political struggles provided a structure upon which to present and interpret the events of Song history. Granted, as we will explore in Chapter 6, much of this structure emerged preformed from the crucible of Song, and especially late Song, politics itself. But the emphasis added in Yuan was strong, and modern students should read the *Song History* with this Yuan praxis in mind. Thus guided by the eulogies, prefaces, and evaluations, every page of the *Song History* exhorts by analogy: "learn from what Song did well"; or warns: "take heed from what Song did badly."

At the end of their preface to the biographies of the *daoxue* masters, the Yuan historians had advised their sovereign that if he corrected the Song rulers' imperfect political application of the *daoxue* teachings, his own Yuan governance could attain the perfection of antiquity. They repeated this advice in the memorial that accompanied their submission of the completed work to the emperor in 1345/10. Composed by Ouyang Xuan in the allusive and elaborate parallel-prose style proper for important state pronouncements, the memorial nevertheless presents succinctly both the meaning and the message of the *Song History*. After framing their submission as the realization of Emperor Khubilai's initial order to preserve the history of Song, Ouyang Xuan, playing upon the rhetorical grandeur of the Song reign-period names, presents the grand allegory for Toghōn Temür's contemplation.

> For consider how
>> the great plans laid forth in "Eminence Established" and "Purity Transformed"
>> grew brilliant during "Spectacular Virtue" and "Total Tranquility."
>> So, in "Felicitous Chronometry" and "August Shelter"
>> did loyalty and tolerance bring beauty to their customs;
>> but in "Primal Abundance" and "Serene Peace"
>> those too clever and too bright disordered the established standards
>> and brought forth the turmoil of "Sagacity Continued"
>> and the chaos of "Exalted Peace."

Thus does

> our historical work make manifest
> the virtues and defects of governance;
> and what to have and to hold
> reposes in truth in Your Court.

> Then there were
> the plans to return
> during "Incandescence Established" and "Continued Ascendance"
> and secure stability
> during "Supernal Way" and "Pure Serenity."

Thus,

> if you employ the right and the proper,
> men there will be and governance will flourish.
> but when the crafty and crooked advance,
> the minister is demeaned, the ruler distressed . . .[117]

Ouyang Xuan's memorial then states the compositional principles that have generated this fusion of history and homily. He declares these to be the moral standards of the *daoxue* masters – here called "the teachings of the former Confucians on human nature and destiny." Expressing these principles (*li*) in Song history, "we laud the Way and its virtues; we condemn merit and profit" (*chong daode er chu gongli* 崇道德而黜功利). Modern scholars have rightly taken this key phrase as Ouyang Xuan's distillation of the message and meaning of the *Song History*.[118] In Song, the expression "merit and profit" – often expanded to "strategy and profit" (*quanmou gongli* 權謀功利) – referred historically to Legalist thinkers such as Guan Zhong and Shang Yang as opposed to Confucians such as Mencius. Therefore, his critics quickly labeled Wang Anshi and the New Policies as pursuit of "merit and profit," and Su Shi penned the classic link in his biography of Sima Guang.[119] Southern Song literati authors described technocratic continuations of the New Policies as "merit and profit" but also extended the term to castigate non-literati government in general. In 1180, for example, Zhu Xi accused Emperor Xiaozong's "close favorites" of deluding him with "base talk of merit and profit."[120] The juxtaposition of "virtue" (*daode*) and "profit" (*gongli*) arose in early Southern Song and gained traction with the rise of *daoxue*.[121] By 1211, Xu Fan 徐範

---

[117] *SS, fulu*, 14254; *QYW*, 34:1089.397.
[118] For the major study see Pei Rucheng, "Lüeping *Songshi* 'chong daode er chu kongli' de xiuzhuan yuanze"; also Lu Zhongfeng, "Yuandai lixue yu *Songshi* 'daoxue liezhuan' de xueshushi tese," 28.
[119] *Changbian*, 300.7305; *Su Shi wenji*, 16.489, often reproduced in Southern Song, for example, Lü Zuqian, *Song wen jian*, 137.1934.
[120] *SS*, 429.12754.
[121] For an early example see Chen Yuyi, *Jianzhai ji*, 2.2a. Later examples include Zhang Jun, *Mengzi zhuan*, 28.12a; Du Zheng, *Xingshan tang gao*, 9.9a; and Zhen Dexiu, *Daxue yanyi*, 14.11b.

(*jinshi* 1208) used the dichotomy to head a long litany of contrasting political and moral values whose contemporaneous reference is unmistakable.[122] In the language of Song politics, therefore, the phrases "the Way and its virtues" and "merit and profit" refer not only to ancient political theory but also to contemporaneous political orientations that align with the institutionalist and technocratic models of governance.

Yuan Confucian politicians were quick to apply this terminology to their opponents. For example, the *Yuan History* "nefarious minister" biography of Aḥmad, the Muslim financial mastermind of Khubilai's early court, describes him as "filled with the success of his pursuit of merit and profit."[123] Su Tianjue's "Preface to the *Record of the Origins of the Two Chengs*," dated 1343/10, posits a basic dichotomy between Confucian proponents of "virtue" and Legalist purveyors of "profit" that extended from Zhou times, through the Song *daoxue* masters, into the Yuan itself. Su maintains that, when the Yuan monarchy implemented civil service examinations based on *daoxue* texts in 1313, it endorsed "the Way and its virtues" as state policy. At the same time, it rejected "policies of strategy and profit," and he insists that Song *daoxue* writings now offer the best guide for state policy formulation.[124]

Good evidence also suggests that other Yuan literati would have understood the dichotomizing language of the submission memorial as relevant to Yuan politics. For example, the *Outside History of the Gengshen Period* (*Gengshen waishi* 庚申外史) by Quan Heng 權衡 uses the language of Song politics to refer to Chief Councilor El Temür as an "autocratic minister" (*quanchen* 權臣) who destroyed the "family policies of the ancestors" (i.e. Khubilai) (*zuzong jiafa* 祖宗家法).[125] The early Ming writer Ye Ziqi 葉子奇 states that, as councilor, Bayan "altered and disordered the old standards." Ye also quotes a popular ditty that circulated after Bayan's death. Its opening couplet contained the line "too clever and too bright, he wanted to disorder the former standards" (欲逞聰明亂舊章).[126] The line tracks the diction of the submission memorial's summary of Wang Anshi governance: "but in 'Primal Abundance' and 'Serene Peace' / those too clever and too bright disordered the established

[122] *SS*, 423.12628. Other opposites include "punishment" versus "mercy," "the various hegemons" versus "the pure sovereign," "heterodox ideas" versus "Confucian teaching," "cronies" versus "the straight," "indulgence" versus "frugality," "flattery" versus "honest advice," etc.
[123] *YS*, 205.4559. On Aḥmad see Morris Rossabi, "The Reign of Khubilai Khan," 473–74; and Herbert Franke's entry in Rachewiltz, *In the Service of the Khan*, 539–57. Dardess, *Conquerors and Confucians*, 32, terms the Mongol finance experts "crypto-Legalists."
[124] *QYW*, 40:1252.82–83.
[125] Quan Heng, *Gengshen waishi jianzheng*, 12; Schulte-Uffelage, *Das Keng-shen wai-shih*, 29–30. Of course, the designation of El Temür and Bayan as "autocratic ministers" may indeed accurately characterize their rule; see Hsiao, "Mid-Yüan Politics," 547–49, who argues that their usurpation of imperial authority marked a departure from the norms of earlier Mongol politics.
[126] *Caomuzi*, 3.13a, 4.7b.

standards" (元豐熙寧以聰明紊憲章). The precise relationship between the two texts is difficult to establish. However, their similarity suggests that when the Yuan historians linked Bayan and Wang Anshi they drew upon types and stereotypes widely recognized among the literate Confucian community. This similarity further suggests that that audience would have recognized political implications in other elements of the grand allegory of Song history that the historians present.

How the *Song History* treats at least three major themes related to the grand allegory reveals the influence of Yuan politics on its compilers. These themes are the elevation of Taizu, the praise for Song empresses, and the character of Song factionalism. For sure, earlier Song formulations of the allegory had contained all three themes; but the Yuan historians foregrounded and enhanced the focus on these themes in relation to other components of the allegory. As mentioned above, both Yuan Jue and Su Tianjue warned that the Song sources had so varnished the image of the Song founders that a credible history would need to recast the Song founding. Why did the Yuan historians ignore this advice and choose not to reopen the case on the moral character of Taizu and Taizong?

The political struggle between Bayan and Toghto also entailed a rhetorical struggle to define the historical character of the dynastic founder Khubilai. What exactly had been the "family policies" that Bayan supposedly sought to destroy? During Bayan's tenure as councilor in the mid-1330s, he discontinued civil service examinations, issued regulations to reserve top court and provincial offices to Mongols, and forbade Chinese to learn Mongol. As justification for these measures, he cited the precedent of Khubilai, under whom similar policies had been in effect. As evidence of his intent to restore the Khubilai era, in 1335 (and against Chinese precedent) he brought back the reign title "Ultimate Origin [or the Perfected Yuan]" (*Zhiyuan* 至元) that Khubilai had used from 1264 through 1294.[127] Bayan's claim on the historical legacy of Khubilai forced the Confucian party to develop another view of Khubilai the founder, one that cast him as the fountainhead of dynastic support for a Confucian governance based on institutionalism and *daoxue* ideology.

In the Confucian narrative, Yuan greatness arose from Khubilai's support for the Confucian scholar Xu Heng 許衡 (1209–1281). The renaissance under Ayurbawada (i.e. Renzong, r. 1312–1320), when civil service examinations were restored and institutions of Confucian governance were formed, flowed, in this version of Yuan history, from this initial support from the founder. Evidence for this narrative surfaces at the height of Bayan's administration in the late 1330s. For example, in 1338 Chen Lü 陳旅 (1287–1342) wrote a preface for the collected works of Wang Jie 王結 (1275–1336). According

---

[127] Dardess, *Conquerors and Confucians*, 60–61.

to Chen, Wang's success as a Confucian literatus resulted from Khubilai's support for Confucian scholarship and its renaissance under Ayurbawada. He noted the general decline of Confucian learning "in the past twenty years," and lamented that Wang's death had removed one of the few living connections to the earlier legacy.[128] Zhang Qiyan, one of the chief editors of the *Song History*, also employed a similar narrative in 1338. The magistrate of Jurong county had asked Zhang to compose an inscription to accompany copies of imperial edicts from 1330 that had enhanced the dynastic status of Confucius, his major disciples, and the Cheng brothers. The school planned to engrave a stone stele and print these edicts and Zhang's inscription. In essence, the magistrate asked Zhang to comment on the historical context of the 1330 edicts. His inscription drew a straight line from Khubilai's support for Xu Heng, through Ayurbawada's 1313 edict that ordered Xu Heng reburied in the imperial Confucian temple and honored together with nine Song *daoxue* masters, and the 1330 upgrade for Confucius. Disseminated at the height of Bayan's anti-Confucian campaign, Zhang's inscription counters Bayan's historical image of the founder and attempts to establish Khubilai as the fountainhead of Yuan Confucianism.[129]

Toghto's biography in the *Yuan History* records that he advanced a similar scenario to Toghōn Temür in 1343 as justification for his Confucian program and for the emperor's place in it. Critics had complained that the emperor spent too much time with Confucian scholars in his Classics Mat sessions reading the classics and histories. Toghto reminded him that Khubilai had ordered a Confucian education for his heir, Jingim 真金 (1243–1285), and that the heir's tutors had prepared for him a primer in Confucian political theory and practice. The emperor was greatly pleased and retrieved the work from the imperial library for perusal.[130]

In the context of this struggle over the historical definition of Khubilai's legacy, the Yuan historians doubtless found congenial the image, perfected by Song *daoxue*, of Taizu as a manifestation of the "the mind of Yao and Shun" and the ultimate source of Song greatness. Any diminution of this image would weaken the ability of the Yuan Confucians to create a type between Khubilai

[128] *QYW*, 37:1170.264–65; Wang Mingsun, *Yuandai de shiren yu zhengzhi*, 210–11, explores the development of this narrative, citing Chen Lü's preface and Su Tianjue's 1343 "Preface to the *Origins of the Two Chengs*." For Xu Heng, see Hok-lam Chan's extensive biographical entry in Rachewiltz, *In the Service of the Khan*, 416–47.

[129] *QYW*, 36:1140.82–83. For the 1330 edicts see *YS*, 34.763; Li Xinchuan, *Daoming lu*, 10.120–21, reproduces two memorials requesting enhancements for the Cheng brothers and the resulting edicts. The memorials cast the entire period between Mencius and the Cheng brothers as devoted to "merit and profit."

[130] *YS*, 138.3344. The work in question was probably the *Chenghua shilüe* 承華事略 by Wang Yun 王惲 (1227–1304), a version of which still survives; see Rachewiltz, *In the Service of the Khan*, 374, 382–83.

and Taizu and would thus undercut their efforts to posit Khubilai as the fountainhead of Yuan Confucianism. Once the type between Khubilai and Taizu was set, the ensuing parallels and analogies formed a compelling political and moral message to Toghōn Temür. Just as the initial seed of the founder flourished under a subsequent "Emperor of Benevolence" (Renzong, 1023–1063/Renzong, 1312–1320), so did an "autocratic minister" (Wang Anshi/Bayan) challenge the founder's legacy and undermine the success of the renaissance. The policy implications of this analogy were obvious: the Yuan monarchy now stood at the same juncture where the Song monarchy had stood in 1086: would it permit Toghto/Sima Guang to restore the rightful image of the founder and return the dynasty to its proper, Confucian roots, or would it continue its decline into technocratic autocracy?

The *Song History*'s inordinate focus on the virtue of the female monarchy in Song also grows from this tension between competing Yuan institutions and modalities of governance. As is well known, Mongol aristocratic women maintained in Yuan society the considerable power they exercised in their nomadic homeland. As a consequence, empresses, and especially empresses dowager – always a force in any imperial Chinese state – played an outsize role in Yuan history. As may be expected, they were, to a woman, allied with Mongol technocratic and patrimonial forces against the Sino-Mongol hybrid institutionalism of the literati. Empress Chabi (1225–1281) influenced Khubilai on important matters, although the founder's stature discouraged the extremes that would develop under his lesser successors. These began under Emperor Temür, whose Empress Bulukhan controlled the dynasty's finances and the imperial succession from 1300 through 1307. The dominance of the female monarchy crested – and assumed its classic form – in the person of Empress Dowager Targi (d. 1322), who formed a political alliance with the strongman and chief councilor Temüder (d. 1322). Her base in the Household Administration of the Empress Dowager (*Huizheng yuan* 徽政院) and in the Palace Provisions Commission (*Xuanhui yuan* 宣徽院) rivaled the power of the Court Secretariat and mirrored the divide between the competing conceptions of state power in Yuan. Formally branded a "nefarious minister" by his critics, Councilor Temüder and the empress battled the Confucian party during the reign of Ayurbarwada and beyond, until their deaths in 1322.[131]

The political relationship between Empress Dowager Budashiri and Bayan between 1332 and 1340 thus replicated the alliance twenty years earlier between Targi and Temüder, and continued the same conflicts with the Confucian party over political theory, practice, and power. Rumors even

---

[131] See, respectively, Rossabi, "The Reign of Khubilai Khan," 416–17, 426–27; and Hsiao, "Mid-Yüan Politics," 504–5 and 524–27.

persisted of a sexual relationship between the councilor and the dowager, who was under thirty at the time of Emperor Tugh Temür's death in 1332.[132] Given this background, the *Song History*'s insistence on the virtue of the female monarchy in Song reads easily as criticism of the lack of those virtues in Yuan and as an admonition to Toghōn Temür in 1345 to guard against the return of such relationships and the anti-institutionalist political structures they perpetrated. As we have seen above, the preface to the *Song History* biographies of empresses expanded the *Miscellany*'s focus on Empress Du – principal consort of Taizu – as the model for subsequent empresses. This focus also supports the primary emphasis on Taizu and occurs throughout the *Song History*. Qian Daxin, followed by Fan Wenlan, cites the three occurrences of Empress Du's burial and the conferral of her posthumous titles as an example of editorial oversight and careless duplication.[133] Might one speculate, however, that this duplication, although probably already present in the Song sources, was retained by the Yuan editors because it reinforced a positive type between Empress Du and Empress Chabi and a negative type between the subsequent virtuous empresses in Song and their antitypes in Yuan? A similar example of duplication – Emperor Guangzong's 1194 note to Chief Councilor Liu Zheng that indicated his desire to resign – occurs at five locations in the *Song History*.[134] The incident is historically crucial, not only because it justified the ascension of Emperor Ningzong, but also because it justified the ensuing purge of Guangzong's Empress Li and her faction, whose excesses had destabilized his reign. These repeated citations also underscore the "virtue" of Empress Dowager Wu, who supposedly co-operated with Zhao Ruyu to ensure an orderly imperial transition.[135]

Finally, the intense, violent nature of Yuan political factionalism probably prompted the Yuan historians to amplify their depiction of factional conflict in the *Song History*. As we have seen above, the structural contrast between the

---

[132] Quan Heng, *Gengshen waishi jianzheng*, 21; Schulte-Uffelage, *Das Keng-shen wai-shih*, 33. For Bayan and Budashiri see Dardess, *Conquerors and Confucians*, 58, 68, 75.

[133] Qian Daxin, *Nian'er shi kaoyi*, 70.987; Fan Wenlan, *Zhengshi kaolüe*, 229. See the annals (*SS*, 1.10), her biography (*SS*, 242.8607), and the monograph on ritual (SS, 123.2867).

[134] Qian Daxin, *Nian'er shi kaoyi*, 80.1118; Fan Wenlan, *Zhengshi kaolüe*, 229–30. These are the Ningzong annals (*SS*, 37.714) and the biographies of Ye Shi (*SS*, 434.12891), Liu Zheng (*SS*, 391.11975), Zhao Ruyu (*SS*, 392.11958), and Empress Wu (*SS*, 243.8648). Actually, the passage also occurs in the Guangzong annals (*SS*, 36.710) and in the biography of the eunuch Guan Li (*SS*, 469.13674).

[135] Fan Wenlan cites five examples of duplication. The other three also reinforce aspects of Yuan Confucian policies against the Mongol nativists: (1) a Su Shi essay on examinations quoted in his biography and in the monograph on examinations, (2) Han Qi's tract against the Green Sprouts policy quoted in his biography and in the monograph on fiscal administration, and (3) regulations concerning promotion into the "three preceptors and three dukes" (*san shi san gong* 三師三公) positions.

biographies of the *daoxue* masters and the biographies of the "nefarious ministers" presupposes unending conflict between morally positive and negative forces in the body politic. The ruler's duty is thus to recognize and restrain nefarious elements that "tyrannize the loyal and the straight, and reject the good and the true."[136] The Yuan Confucians employed language and motifs similar to those in the biographies of the nefarious ministers to indict the perceived oppressors in their own dynasty. For example, the collected works of Xu Youren 許有壬 (1287–1364) preserve a series of indictments that Xu, then investigating censor, directed in 1322 against Temüder and his sons as well as requests to rehabilitate those Temüder had oppressed. Xu describes Temüder as a "nefarious minister" who "stole imperial authority solely to carry out reprisals that destroyed the loyal and the good." These actions, which Xu links to those of the previous technocrats Aḥmad and Sangha, contravened "popular opinion." Finally, Xu compares Temüder to the Han dynasty strongman Liang Ji 梁冀, regent from 141 to 159, who, like Temüder, was the brother-in-law of the emperor and ruled in league with the empress dowager.[137]

Other evidence also indicates that political conflict in Yuan prompted the Confucians to sharpen the historical image of the struggle between the institutionalist and technocratic models of Song governance and to cast that struggle as one between adherents of *daoxue* and proponents of the New Policies. Ouyang Xuan wrote two inscriptions at the request of Zhao Yunweng 趙篔翁, a fellow *jinshi* recipient of 1315, and a sixth-generation descendent of the Song chief councilor Zhao Ding. His inscription for a shrine to Zhao Ding in Jiezhou 解州 in Shanxi, Zhao's native place, was composed in 1331; an inscription for a private academy in Chaozhou 潮州, where Zhao Ding had died a victim of Qin Gui's persecutions in 1147, was composed in 1342. The 1331 inscription, composed at the height of the El Temür and Bayan autocracy, places Zhao Ding in a narrative that frames Song history as a conflict between the teachings of the Cheng brothers and Wang Anshi: the Cheng adherents suffered repeated persecution at the hands of the Wang adherents but nonetheless always survived. In this context, Zhao Ding's political support for the Cheng teachings ensured their survival throughout the period of Qin Gui's autocracy. Thus, Zhao Ding's martyrdom served not only the Song, but also the Yuan state, which now adopted the Cheng teachings as orthodoxy.[138]

Again, as seen in Chapter 3, in 1333, Cheng Rongxiu, then supervisor of Confucian schools for Jiangzhe province and a direct descendent of Cheng Yi, enlarged Li Xinchuan's original *Record of the Way and Its Fate* in ways that enhanced the status of Cheng Yi and Zhu Xi and emphasized the book's history

---

[136] *SS*, 471.13697.
[137] *QYW*, 38:1183.48–56. For Liang Ji see Twitchett and Loewe, *Cambridge History of China, Volume 1*, 285–86.
[138] *QYW*, 34:1096.503–4, 520–21.

of Song *daoxue* as a series of persecutions at the hands of successive autocrats – Cai Jing, Qin Gui, and Han Tuozhou. In his preface, Cheng replied to those who might object to publicizing these venomous attacks against Cheng Yi and Zhu Xi. He answered that repressing this history of Song persecution would only enable it to recur in the future.

> Thus will petty men escape punishment for what they have done in the past and furthermore the historical evidence will be wiped out for the future ... Therefore I must publish this book so that the punishment for those petty men to come will be harsher, and future ages will be even more vigilant against them.[139]

Clearly, Cheng Rongxiu foresaw a contemporary and future context for Li Xinchuan's political history of Song *daoxue* and a utility in bringing that history up to date. The Mongol administrator of Jiangzhe province, the Confucian scholar Dorji (1304–1355), ordered Cheng's edition printed in 1333/2 during the interregnum between the death of Tugh Temür in 1332/8 and the ascension of Toghōn Temür in 1333/6, a time when the future direction of the Yuan polity under a new emperor remained unclear. The subsequent emergence of Bayan indeed fulfilled Cheng Rongxiu's prophecy against the return of the "petty men," and Bayan's anti-Confucian purges eventually reached Dorji in 1338.[140]

We may thus understand the overall political message of the *Song History* to be that Toghōn Temür – and by extension the entire Yuan state – should continue to promote the upholders of "virtue" against the purveyors of "profit," the Sino-Mongol institutionalists against the pan-Mongol technocrats, Toghto against Bayan – Sima Guang against Wang Anshi. However, the vagaries of Yuan politics scrambled this message even before the work was completed. Only the *Liao History*, submitted in 1344/3, bears Toghto's signature as official compiler and submitter. He resigned as chancellor of the right in 1344/5. Both the *Jin History*, submitted in 1344/11, and the *Song History*, submitted in 1345/10, bear the signature of his successor, Arughtu. A Mongol of the highest aristocratic lineage, Arughtu was, however, a temporary figurehead. He remarked to the emperor at the submission ceremony for the *Song History* that he did not read Chinese books and had no idea what the work was for.[141]

The next shaper of Yuan politics was Berke Buqa, a Mongol Confucian who had maneuvered for Toghto's removal, been named chancellor of the left in 1344/12, and eventually replaced Arughtu as chancellor of the right in 1347. Berke Buqa guided the Yuan state from 1344 through 1349, when Toghto returned for a second term as chancellor that lasted through 1354. The decade

---

[139] *QYW*, 31:1009.421.
[140] Hartman, "Bibliographic Notes on Sung Historical Works: The Original *Record of the Way and Its Destiny* by Li Hsin-ch'uan," 6–9. For Bayan's persecution against Dorji see Dardess, *Conquerors and Confucians*, 69–70.
[141] *YS*, 139.3361–62.

following the completion of the three histories was thus marked by political factionalism, not between Confucians and Mongol technocrats, but between two factions of Yuan Confucians. In truth, the sources of the conflict between Toghto and Berke Buqa rested upon intra-Mongol power struggles, not upon Confucian ideology. But, as Dardess has well explained, after Bayan's removal in 1340, the rhetoric of Song Confucian ideology became the dominant language of Yuan political struggle.[142] Adopting this rhetoric, Berke Buqa cast himself as a "conservative" Confucian in the mold of Sima Guang; by default, Toghto thus became a "reformist" in the mold of Wang Anshi, and one who pursued "merit and profit." In this case, their concrete policies and real actions supported this typing of Berke Buqa and Toghto. As had Sima Guang, Berke advocated local over centralized control; as had Wang Anshi, Toghto pursued top-down, activist interventions organized at the state level.[143]

Thus, the shifting ground of Yuan political conflict destroyed the immediate utility of the *Song History* as a source for concrete political precedents. Framed as a rhetorical source for Toghto to wield against Bayan, even before its completion the work had become a potential weapon for Berke Buqa to wield against Toghto. The original clarity of the Sima/Toghto versus Wang/Bayan typology was lost. However, the *Song History* was largely done; neither the work nor the committee was prepared to accommodate a new typology of Sima/Berke versus Wang/Toghto. The factional split among the Mongol Confucians – and the exceedingly negative way the *Song History* portrayed factionalism – removed almost immediately whatever rhetorical utility the book may have had for either side.

---

[142] "The events of 1340 had ensured that all future politics could henceforth be conducted only in Confucian terms. The . . . split between Toghto and Berke Buqa was one in which, for the first time in Yüan history, Confucian ideology predominated on both sides. By 1347, it can definitely be stated, Confucian political ideology had at last become a controlling force in Yüan government." Dardess, *Conquerors and Confucians*, 82.

[143] Dardess, *Conquerors and Confucians*, 2–3, 82–83, 93–94.

Part II

Narratives

History imposes syntax on time.
Nancy Partner

6   Political Precedents and the Origins of Historical Narrative

> If rhetoric is the politics of discourse, as discourse itself is the politics of language, then there is no such thing as politically innocent historiography.
>
> Hayden White[1]

The Power of Precedent

The creation of narrative from the uninterrupted and chaotic flow of events is the central task of the historian. As the epigram from Hayden White suggests, both politics and rhetoric pay significant roles in this historiographical process. Our examination of the major sources for Song history has revealed the extensive involvement of historians such as Sima Guang, Li Tao, and Zhao Ruyu in the politics of their time, as well as their extensive training in the (largely Confucian) rhetoric of political discourse. As we saw in Chapters 2 and 3, one often reads a Song historian defining his role as something akin to "searching out the beginnings and endings of an event"; in other words, creating a narrative.[2] For the Song official, however, a more immediate historiographical task was the identification of past events that might prove useful for current policy formulation. Such events were called simply "former events" or perhaps "precedent events" (*gushi* 故事).[3] The term implied an event selected from the routine stream of events submitted to the history office for its normative value as a precedent. To cite an event as a precedent highlighted or "foregrounded" that event in relation to others that had surrounded it in time or place; and the cited precedent thus became a justification for a proposed course of political action. A closely related term is "regulations and precedents"

---

[1] "Rhetoric and History," 24. The epigram on the preceding page is quoted from Nancy Partner, "Making Up Lost Time: Writing on the Writing of History," 97.

[2] See Zhao Ruyu's 1186 memorial seeking permission to submit *The Ministers Memorials*; *Songchao zhuchen zouyi*, appendix, 1724.

[3] *Gu* in the compound *gushi* is usually understand as "old, former," thus "former events." But *gu* as a single character, meaning something like "precedent," occurs as early as the *Zuozhuan*, where the early scholiast glossed the character as "old regulations" (*jiudian* 舊典); Du Yu, *Chunqiu Zuozhuan zhushu*, 56.4b.

(*diangu* 典故). The proffering of precedents was among the most common rhetorical techniques in the discourse of Song policy makers.

For example, in 1190 Prince Jia, only son of the recently installed Emperor Guangzong, lived in his own, separate establishment outside the Inner Palace. The prince had been ill, and Chief Councilor Liu Zheng proposed that he be immediately installed as heir apparent and moved into the heir's formal quarters inside the Inner Palace. After receiving no reply for two months, Liu repeated his request, but this time added a series of historical precedents supporting his argument that the establishment of an heir early in the reign of a new emperor fostered political stability. In addition to a Han-era precedent, he cited the Song example of Emperor Zhenzong's early identification of the future Renzong as heir. He appended additional material from two Northern Song memorials, one written by Lü Hui 呂誨 (1014–1071) in 1063 and another by Zhang Fangping in 1076. Lü had urged the recently installed but ailing Emperor Yingzong to appoint an immediate heir to assist in administration and to prevent the diffusion of power that an unsettled imperial succession might engender. Zhang had made similar arguments to Emperor Shenzong, who at that point was nine years into his reign and yet to designate an heir. Neither emperor had heeded the advice, and both had delayed formal designation of their successors until only days before their own deaths. These delays had prevented the gradual seasoning of the heirs for their future role as emperor and had created political instability.[4]

Liu Zheng's juxtaposition of the positive precedent of Renzong and the cautionary, negative example of Shenzong reposes upon and advocates a view of Northern Song history that privileges the reign of the former and questions that of the latter. Although only fragments of Liu Zheng's text survive, this combination of precedents and citations adroitly crafted a series of parallels between Emperor Guangzong's own circumstances and Northern Song history. Like Yingzong, Emperor Guangzong suffered from ill health; and, like Yingzong, his prolonged absence from court might require turning day-to-day administration over to the female monarchy. These historical parallels presented Guangzong with an implied choice: name an heir now and lay the groundwork for a repeat of the long and stable reign of Renzong; or, as Yingzong and Shenzong had done, delay and risk fragmentation of the monarchy and the political discord of those eras. Emperor Guangzong, of course, did not follow Liu Zheng's advice, and suffered consequences much as Liu Zheng's historical parallels implied he would.

The historical narrative that undergirds Liu Zheng's precedent privileged a Taizu–Qingli–Yuanyou axis of positive political value that evolved slowly

[4] *SS*, 391.11974. For the two memorials see Zhao Ruyu, *Songchao zhuchen zouyi*, 31.309–10.

over the course of the twelfth century. A major milestone, as explained above, was Li Tao's *Long Draft*, submitted in 1183. The next major expression of this paradigm for Northern Song history was *The Ministers Memorials from the August Courts* (*Huangchao zhuchen zouyi*), completed by Zhao Ruyu in 1186. We will examine this work and its political agenda in detail below. Liu Zheng was a close political ally of Zhao Ruyu, certainly knew the work, and most probably used it as a resource to construct his 1190 memorial. The section on imperial heirs in *The Ministers Memorials* contains thirty-two memorials, beginning with a suggestion in 997 by Tian Xi 田錫 (940–1003) to Emperor Zhenzong that he appoint an heir soon; it concludes with the two memorials by Lü Hui and Zhang Fangping that Liu Zheng cited in his precedent.[5]

Precedents could also be submitted as a separate, distinct genre of advice to the emperor. Examples found in the collected works of their authors are often labeled "presented precedents" (*jin gushi* 進故事), preceded by the date of submission. The genre consisted of two parts: a direct quotation of the precedent text, then a commentary that applied the precedent to a contemporary issue.[6] The practice of presenting precedents at the emperor's Classics Mat session began with a precedent presented by Fan Zuyu in 1087, and such early examples confine themselves largely to precedents from the Han and Tang dynasties.[7] The practice resumed in early Southern Song, and, over the course of the twelfth century, precedents were drawn increasingly from Northern Song sources, especially the *Precious Instructions from Three Courts* (*Sanchao baoxun*). By the end of Southern Song, authors drew their precedents largely from Song sources.

A good example of the genre is the "Presented Precedents from 1172/5" by Han Yuanji 韓元吉 (1118–1187). Han submitted his precedents following the torrent of protests from literati officials over Emperor Xiaozong's refusal to rescind the controversial appointment in 1171/3 of the imperial in-law Zhang Yue 張說 (d. 1180) as notary of the Bureau of Military Affairs. As his precedents, Han submitted two passages from biographies in the state history that preserved statements from the founding emperors Taizu and Taizong. In the first passage, Taizu expressed admiration for the Tang Emperor Taizong because the great Tang emperor had admitted his mistakes. But Taizu added that the wiser course was his own: because he accepted advice first, he made few mistakes. In the second precedent, Taizong tells his minister Lü Mengzheng 呂蒙正 (946–1011) that he prefers the "ancient" method of

---

[5] Zhao, *Songchao zhuchen zouyi*, 31.287–32.310.
[6] Deng Xiaonan, *Zuzong zhi fa*, 396–97; Hartwell, "Historical Analogism, Public Policy, and Social Science in Eleventh- and Twelfth-Century China," 698–99.
[7] *Yuhai*, 26.11a–12a; Fan Zuyu, *Fan Taishi ji*, 27.1a–20b, for example, has only one Song precedent, from 1062.

administration where the mutual and open exchange of opinion between sovereign and ministers fosters improved policy decisions.[8]

In his commentary on these two passages, Han Yuanji extols Taizu's ability to surpass Tang Taizong's legendary capacity for remonstrance – even to the point where remonstrance was seldom necessary, since he has made so few errors. As evidence of this administrative ability, Han cites from the state history "annals" (*benji* 本紀) another memoir of Taizu. One day after court a eunuch noticed that the emperor appeared dejected and asked him why. He replied, "You think it's easy to be emperor? I'm happy enough when I wake up, but if I make even a single mistake, then the historians will record it, so I am unhappy." Han Yuanji proceeded to parse out for Emperor Xiaozong the obvious lesson of these two "instructions" from his ancestors: if he would solicit opinion more widely before acting he could improve relations with his officials. In the context of the Zhang Yue affair, Han's "precedents" were one small piece of the literati campaign to thwart the influence of "close favorites" by persuading Xiaozong to accept literati opinion and rescind Zhang's appointment.[9]

Han Yuanji's story about Taizu's dejection belongs to a special category of generalized "event" that differs from the routine bureaucratic details that comprise the vast bulk of Song historical narrative. As we have seen above in Chapter 5, a short but unique section in the received *Song History* between the end of the Taizu annals and his "evaluation" gathers together fifteen such anecdotes.[10] Although several of these tales, including the dejection anecdote, were probably, as Han states, included in the state history of 1030, many seem to have made their first appearance in subsequent "precious instructions" and "sagacious administration" collections from the early Renzong period. Most also appear in private works on Northern Song history such as Sima Guang's *Su River Records* and Luo Congyan's *Record of Revering Yao* (*Zun Yao lu* 遵堯 錄), both of which we will examine in detail in Chapter 8. The frequent citation of these stories in official and unofficial histories acted not only to foreground those stories that had indeed appeared in the early state history and but also to introduce new "events" that made it possible for politicians and historians to adjust the image of Taizu to meet the needs of ongoing eleventh-century developments.

Li Tao took a reverent but cautious attitude toward this material. He grouped the account of Taizu's dejection together with three similar tales and placed them at the end of 960/12. But he admitted that the chronology of these events was uncertain and his placement arbitrary. He noted that all four stories occur in

---

[8] For versions of these passages in the received *Song History* see *SS*, 264.9111 and 265.9146. For a fuller version of the second passage see *Changbian*, 24.558–59.
[9] Han Yuanji, *Nanjian jiayi kao*, 11.1a–3a; *QSW*, 216:4794.128–30.   [10] *SS*, 3.49–50.

Shi Jie's *Records of Sagacious Administration from the Three Courts* and in Sima Guang's *Su River Records*. He was especially skeptical of the dejection story as he found it in the early state histories. The old veritable records, along with eleventh-century versions of the story in Shi Jie and Sima Guang, had named Wang Ji'en 王繼恩 (d. 999) as the eunuch in question.[11] But Li Tao noted that Wang was not a high-ranking eunuch until a decade later. He thus rewrote the passage to remove Wang Ji'en's name and simply wrote "a retainer." Also, without comment, he removed the reference to the court historian, probably because this detail duplicated another story in the group.[12]

Thus, each of the anecdotes that come together at *Songshi* 3.49–50 travelled its own way through the official Northern Song "precious instructions" (*baoxun*) collections, through Shi Jie, Sima Guang, and Luo Congyan, and into the hands of the Southern Song historians Li Tao, Chen Jun, Lü Zhong, the *Complete Texts of Song History* (*Songshi quanwen*), and eventually into the *Song History*. And throughout the dynasty – increasingly so in Southern Song – literati like Han Yuanji continued to cite such stories as "precedents," often adjusting the details to suit their own immediate political needs.

A comparison of the works listed in the section on "precedents" in the *Song History* monograph on bibliography versus the similar section in the private bibliography of Chen Zhensun provides some insight into the Song concept of the precedent.[13] The two bibliographies differ greatly in their scope and nature. The former is an official list, probably based on recorded holdings of the Song Imperial Library; the latter is a record of works actually held in one of the largest private libraries of the mid-thirteenth century. Both bibliographies agree that works in the genres of *baoxun* and "sagacious administration" (*shengzheng*) are collections of "precedents." Both bibliographies also include several titles in the genre of "audit records" for individual reign periods (*kuiji lu* 會計錄) as well as local financial records. Both mention Luo Congyan's *Record of Revering Yao* and the historical work known today as the *Administrative Records from the Period of Great Tranquility, Fully Classified* by Peng Baichuan. Unlike the *Song History*, however, Chen Zhensun included works in the *huiyao* genre, and he provided individual entries for the five major *huiyao* compilations in Song. He directly refuted the Imperial Library bibliography classification of *huiyao* as "encyclopedias" (*leishu* 類書), arguing that "the *huiyao* are exclusively devoted to relating regulations and precedents (*diangu*); they are not encyclopedias."[14]

---

[11] Shi Jie's text is quoted in Zeng Zao, *Leishuo*, 19.17a; for Sima Guang see *Sushui jiwen*, 1.5–6. Li Tao also notes that the "annals" (*benji*) version in the early state history, probably the same text copied by Han Yuanji, did not name the eunuch.
[12] *Changbian*, 1.30–31.   [13] *SS*, 203.5101–8; Chen Zhensun, *Zhizhai shulu jieti*, 5.158–70.
[14] Chen, *Zhizhai shulu jieti*, 5.161.

Both bibliographies include many works that modern historians view as undigested collections of primary sources but which Song readers understood to be in some sense pre-selected and thus foregrounded subsets of larger bodies of material. For example, as we have seen in Chapter 4, the work known today as the *Sagacious Administration from the Two Restoration Courts of the August Song* (*Huang Song zhongxing liangchao shengzheng*) remains for modern historians the most detailed chronology of the Xiaozong period, but both bibliographies classify the book – a *shengzheng* – as a collection of "precedents."[15]

The longer bibliography in the *Song History* encompasses a much greater range of works within the category of "precedent." Prominent are collections of precedents for specific government agencies, such as the Hanlin Academy, the Imperial Library, and the Censorate. There are also collections of memorials from single individuals as well as larger compilations such as the extant *Collection of Major Song Edicts* (*Song da zhaoling ji*). Also included are diaries, political memoirs, and personal accounts of specific events, such as Fu Bi's report of his diplomatic negotiations with the Khitan in 1043. Finally, the *Song History* counts both Sima Guang's *Su River Records* and Li Xinchuan's *Diverse Notes* as precedents (*gushi*), while Chen Zhensun classifies them as "miscellaneous histories" (*zashi* 雜史). Clearly, *gushi* was a fluid bibliographic category in Song.[16] I will demonstrate below that this uncertainty probably relates to twelfth-century disputes over the character of precedents and their proper use.

The inclusion of financial records and diplomatic reports suggests that works included in the *gushi* category were not only collections of existing precedents but were also perhaps viewed as possible source materials for locating and arguing "new" precedents in the future. Another conversation between Emperor Guangzong and Liu Zheng reveals this tension between the notion of precedents as a set body of unchanging statute and as justification for institutional change. Immediately after Guangzong came to the throne in 1189, some literati, as had Li Tao twenty years earlier, advocated for placing censors in each of the Six Ministries with authority to directly memorialize the emperor. Liu Zheng cited Northern Song precedents to support this change to existing practice. The emperor objected that all the precedents of the ancestors were known and understood; there was no reason to change anything. To which Liu Zheng replied, "The statutes governing these six censors are complete in every detail. If we can set up the posts, then all matters can be memorialized

---

[15] *SS*, 203.5103; Chen, *Zhizhai shulu jieti*, 5.168.

[16] Deng Xiaonan, *Zuzong zhi fa*, 371. The late twelfth-century *Suichutang shumu* of You Mao, for example, groups *baoxun*, *shengzheng*, and the standard histories together in a "state history" (*guoshi*) section. Its section on "dynastic precedents" (*benchao gushi*) concentrates on financial and diplomatic accounts; see You Mao, *Suichutang shumu*, 25b–27a.

upon. As Your Majesty has indeed instructed us, there is no need to change any of the old institutions."[17] This exchange manifests tension not over the existence or meaning of the precedents but rather about whether a given set of past precedents should be turned into present political reality.

Either as a rhetorical component of standard memorials or submitted as a distinct genre, precedents were a vital vehicle for literati participation in governance. As such, they straddle the line between policy formation and history. Clearly, although their precise definition and use varied over the course of the dynasty, they came to constitute an important subgenre of historical writing. Precedents were gathered into larger collections that were intended for general reference, or they might confine themselves to specific agencies or issues. They were compiled both by private individuals and as a routine function of official dynastic historiography.

The Policies of the Ancestors

The concept of the "policies of the ancestors" (*zuzong zhi fa*) first arose in the early Renzong period. Its continued development and intersection with the bureaucratic practice of submitting precedents created a powerful historiographical device that politicians could use to shape useful visions of the dynasty's past. This process continued until the very end of the dynasty, profoundly influencing the composition of the state histories and culminating in the present text of the *Song History*. As articulated in that work, the dynastic founders Taizu and Taizong had set forth a body of foundational principles upon which the subsequent stability of the dynasty had been based. When subsequent emperors adhered to these principles, political stability and prosperity ensued, but deviation had produced turmoil and the disaster of 1127.

Fa 法 is a broad but fundamental Chinese term that denotes "methods, laws, rites or a system of varying scope, depth and focus."[18] "Policies of the ancestors" can thus comprise specific statutes first promulgated in the early Song as well as the broad general principles of governance perceived to exist in those actions (for example, "centralize military power," "control eunuchs," etc.). The sum total of these *fa* were perceived to have formed a distinct political "system" that explained the historical uniqueness of Song.

Until the beginning of the present century, most historians accepted the position of the *Song History* that the "policies of the ancestors" were literally true; that is, that the founders had indeed set forth such policies and that subsequent dynastic history could be understood as the story of how well their descendants had maintained these policies. A simple adherence to this

---

[17] *SHY, yizhi*, 7.32b–33a; *SHY, zhiguan*, 55.26a–b.
[18] Lowell Skar in Kohn, *Daoism Handbook*, 456.

view drove many research agendas, and scholars combed the sparse historical record of early Song for the origins of the policies. This research focus, for example, led ultimately to the question whether Taizu or Taizong had been the principal intellectual force behind the "policies."

In 2004 Li Li questioned the assumption of many scholars that the "policies" could serve as an explanatory model for understanding the development of Song political institutions. He argued that *zuzong zhi fa* in the surviving historical record were a hopeless muddle of conflicting pronouncements and not a coherent body of policy. Accordingly, he concluded, any history of Song based upon this muddle was bound to be itself equally muddled. He pointed out that many scholars mistook Southern Song invocations of a given "policy of the founder" as evidence that such a policy had actually existed in Northern Song. He cited as an example the 1194/12 memorial of Peng Guinian against Han Tuozhou, in which Peng claimed that the founders controlled imperial in-laws by not appointing them to top civil or military positions and by banning them from access to the Inner Palace. And Li Li noted that many scholars often cite this passage as evidence of such a "policy."[19] Yet Peng's own memorial goes on to admit that these supposed early sanctions on access have long been abandoned.[20] As for Peng's assertion that the "policies" barred imperial in-laws from top government positions and thus, following this precedent, Han Tuozhou should be similarly barred, Li Li calculates that almost half of the imperial in-laws with biographies in the *Song History* actually held such posts.[21]

Deng Xiaonan's 2006 volume abandoned the traditional teleological model for understanding the "policies." Employing a rigorous historiographical analysis, she demonstrated the fluid and adaptable nature of the *zuzong zhi fa*. While not rejecting completely the notion that some actions of the founders might underpin these "policies," she emphasized the essential role that the literati had played in defining, explicating, and applying their content. Rather than being immutable policies from the founders, the "policies" grew and changed as generations of literati used the concept to articulate and justify their own political agendas. Not only did the specific content of the "policies" change over time, but disputes over the content of the policies often reflect contemporary political differences between opposing groups and even within the same group.[22] The *zuzong zhi fa*, and debates over their content, thus became a key vehicle and resource for the continuous formulation and adjustment of state policy.[23]

Deng provides examples of the relationship between these debates and our understanding of Song history. For example, she points out that officials who

---

[19] In addition to the scholars that Li cites see also Zhuge Yibing, "Lun Songdai houfei yu chaozheng"; and Miao Shumei, "Songdai zongshi, waiqi yu huanguan renyong zhidu shulun."
[20] *QSW*, 278:6299.186–88.
[21] Li Li, "Songdai zhengzhi zhidushi yanjiu fangfa zhi fansi," 27–33.
[22] Deng Xiaonan, *Zuzong zhi fa*, 495, 514–18.   [23] Deng Xiaonan, *Zuzong zhi fa*, 389–98.

served under Emperor Renzong, such as Fan Zhongyan, Fu Bi, Shi Jie, Wen Yanbo, and Sima Guang, did not view their monarch as an upholder of the policies of his ancestors. The image of Renzong as an advocate of a style of "benevolent rule," in accord with the example of the founders, dates from 1092. In that year, Fan Zuyu promoted this image of Renzong's administration as a vehicle to frame his opposition to the young Emperor Zhezong's plans to resume the New Policies of Wang Anshi. Fan reinforced his historical image of Renzong's rule with *Emperor Ren's Instructions and Statutes* (*Renhuang xundian* 仁皇訓典), which he prepared and submitted as reading material for the young emperor's Classics Mat lessons.[24] In other words, contention over the New Policies generated an image of Renzong as an inheritor and promoter of the "benevolent" policies of the dynastic founders as well as a corresponding image of the New Policies as a perversion of those policies.

As we shall see in Chapter 8, this image of the Renzong period as a culmination of the benevolent policies of the ancestors grew into one of the formative themes of Song history. The concept of *zuzong zhi fa* first arose in the early Renzong period not as an affirmation of contemporary policy but as a corrective to the perceived ills of that age.[25] A 1033 memorial in which Pang Ji 龐籍 (988–1063) frames political reform as a return to the policies of the ancestors opens the section entitled "Taking the Ancestors as Policy Models" (*fa zuzong* 法祖宗) in Zhao Ruyu's *The Ministers Memorials*. Pang argues for more stringent guidelines for appointments to top positions, for elimination of over-quota officials, for curtailment of unearned compensation, and for reductions in suburban sacrifice payments. He posits all of these ills as deteriorations of the practices of the founders and entitles his memorial "A Request to Return to the Old Statues of the Ancestors." Of course, all of these issues would later become planks in the Qingli reform agenda; and, as the political momentum toward reform grew during the late 1030s and early 1040s, so did the practice of casting reform as a return to supposedly original policies of the ancestors.[26]

The first concrete juncture of *zuzong zhi fa* and the practice of "precedents" occurs in a seminal work of the Qingli reformers entitled *Precedents from [and for] the Era of Great Peace* (*Taiping gushi* 太平故事), also known simply as the *Precedents of the Ancestors* (*Zuzong gushi*). As we have seen above in

[24] Deng Xiaonan, *Zuzong zhi fa*, 495–98; Chen Zhenxun, *Zhizhai shulu jieti*, 5.164. For Fan's two memorials see Zhao Ruyu, *Songchao zhuchen zouyi*, 12.108–9.

[25] Cao Jiaqi, "Zhao Song dangchao shengshi shuo zhi zaojiu ji qi yangxiang," provides many examples to show that ancestor policies were usually invoked in negative contexts against an action or a proposed action, arguing that the ancestors had warned against similar policies in the past.

[26] Zhao Ruyu, *Songchao zhuchen zouyi*, 12.104–5. Pang Ji was an early advocate of reform, an early supporter of Sima Guang, and a major source of early Song "precedents" that appear in Sima Guang's *Su River Records*.

Chapter 1, this work was closely connected to production of the first *State Compendium*. Less than three weeks after submission of the famous "ten-point memorial" – the blueprint for the Qingli reformers – Fu Bi received permission to compile a collection of explicated precedents from the first three Song reigns. His request posited appropriate standards and regulations (*fazhi* 法制) as the basis for a successful institutional system (*jigang* 紀綱). The actions of the first three Song sovereigns, in a steady and cumulative manner, had achieved, he argued, just such an age of "Great Peace." But that structure and its defining standards had now deteriorated, he continued. Because the Secretariat and the Bureau of Military Affairs now lack a definitive body of accepted precedent, they issue makeshift rulings that, despite their inadequacy, are nevertheless enacted, thus resulting in contradictory policy. As a result, corrupt officials proliferate, the people are exhausted, and the country is bankrupt. Fu Bi maintains, in short, that the state is on the verge of disintegration. He requests that "precedents" (*diangu*) from the three courts be selected and combined with effective actions and policies from the age of Great Peace into a classified compendium that shall be placed as models for administrative actions in the offices of the Secretariat and Bureau of Military Affairs. The emperor so ordered, and Wang Zhu headed the compilation team which submitted the work under Fu Bi's name one year later in 1044/9.[27]

Fu Bi's *Precedents* do not survive as an intact work, but numerous quotations remain scattered in Southern Song encyclopedias and in the interlinear commentaries of thirteenth-century histories.[28] The book's original twenty chapters contained ninety-six sections with extensive coverage of personnel management in the civil bureaucracy and in the military, fiscal control, and the importance of remonstrance. Within each section, the precedents were arranged chronologically and provided with an explicative commentary. Both Luo Congyan and Li Tao agree that the goal of the selected precedents and their explications was to link the Qingli reform agenda to the prestige of the founders. Luo even attributes the success and prosperity of Renzong's reign to those policies the *Precedents* had identified.[29] But, more to the point for the modern historian, the choices and explications of the *Precedents* became the historiographical baseline that defined the accomplishments of the ancestors. Luo took many of its entries into his own work in 1126. In 1138, Lü Yuan 呂源

---

[27] *Changbian*, 143.3455–56; Zhao Ruyu, *Sungchao zhuchen zouyi*, 12.105; Cheng Ju, *Lintai gushi*, 304–5; and *Yuhai*, 49.6b–7a. For modern studies see Chen Lesu, *Songshi yiwenzhi kaozheng*, 85–86; Kong Xue, "Songdai 'baoxun' zuanxiu kao," 57–58, and Deng Xiaonan, *Zuzong zhi fa*, 377–79.

[28] See Wang Shengduo and Chen Chaoyang, "*Songshi quanwen* chayin shilun wenxian yanjiu," 479–91. An anonymous Qing manuscript entitled *Taiping baoxun zhengshi jinian* 太平寶訓政事紀年 also relates in a manner yet undetermined to the Song work.

[29] Luo, *Zun Yao lu*, 4.48.

(d. 1143?) found an old printed copy of the work and submitted an updated version to the court.[30]

Lü Yuan's submission was timely. During the 1130s, the dynasty struggled to rebuild its institutions amid the debates and political struggle that surrounded the issue of continued war or negotiated peace with the Jurchen. In 1135/4, a string of military successes convinced the administration of Zhao Ding to favor an aggressive stance. Zhao's subordinate Fan Chong suggested that Emperor Gaozong copy out a chapter from the *Book of Documents* and mount the text on the walls of his Classics Mat chamber. The chapter, entitled "Against Luxurious Ease," urged the sovereign to be frugal and industrious, from which, the classic assured, two results will follow: the happiness of the people and the sovereign's ability to detect and evade nefarious ministers. Fan Chong recalled to the emperor that his father, Fan Zuyu, had urged a similar action in 1086 upon Emperor Zhezong, and had cited a Renzong-era precedent for the practice. Gaozong readily copied the chapter, and the assisting councilor Shen Yuqiu 沈與求 (1086–1137) remarked that if the emperor would make its content his "fundamental precedent," then recovery of the North would be assured. One notes in this event that the Zhao Ding administration advocated Renzong-era precedents, that Emperor Renzong had now become an "ancestor" (*zuzong*), and that the allusion in the *Documents* to nefarious ministers that referred unambiguously in 1086 to Wang Anshi now in 1135 alluded to Wang Anshi and Cai Jing as well as to Zhao Ding's political rivals, Lü Yihao, Zhu Shengfei, and perhaps Qin Gui.[31]

Precedents in Southern Song

By the end of the decade, however, circumstances had changed, and Gaozong appointed Qin Gui as chief councilor to negotiate a peace. And so one needed different precedents. In 1139/2, Gaozong remarked that the present situation would require precedents from the period after the peace treaty with the Khitan in 1005. He also added that he was confident his present focus on "tranquility and balance" would produce major benefits for the state. Qin Gui encouraged the emperor to pursue "dispassionate tranquility" and "in your every action, take the ancestors as your model." The reference to the peace treaty of 1005 and the Daoist flavor of this exchange suggest that Gaozong and Qin Gui had shifted to the Zhenzong period in their search for precedents to support peaceful coexistence with the Jurchen.[32] Crucial, however, is the fact that both sides

---

[30] Chen Zhensun, *Zhizhai shulu jieti*, 5.163–64.   [31] *SHY, chongru*, 6.15a–b; *Yaolu*, 88.1697.

[32] *Huangchao zhongxing jishi benmo*, 47.3b–4a; *Zhongxing xiaoli*, 26.307. Li Xinchuan's *Yaolu* does not record this exchange. The surviving accounts link this conversation to submission of the "veritable records of the ancestors" (*zuzong shilu* 祖宗實錄) on 1139/2/1. Wang Yinglin (*Yuhai*, 48.16a) understands *zuzong shilu* as a reference to the fifth version of the *Shenzong shilu*.

in the war–peace debates of the 1130s looked to the policies of the ancestors as a source of justification for their actions. As the two sides contended, each brought to the debate a different determination of what the appropriate policies of the ancestors had been and a correspondingly different interpretation of which periods in Northern Song history should be valued and which ignored as a source of precedents for the present.

As we have seen in Chapter 4, the rise of *daoxue* as an intellectual and political force during the reign of Emperor Xiaozong brought to the fore an appraisal of Northern Song history that heavily weighted the reign of Emperor Taizu and the Qingli and Yuanyou periods. The controversy over Lü Zuqian's anthology *Literary Mirror of the August Courts* (*Huangchao wenjian* 皇朝文鑑) reflects the growth of this vision and the opposition to it. The book originated in 1177 when Zhou Bida, then a Hanlin scholar, noted to Xiaozong that a Lin'an bookseller was about to print a mediocre anthology of Song dynasty literature entitled *Ocean of Literature* (*Wenhai* 文海). Zhou felt that the court could do better, and Lü Zuqian, having just completed work on the *Huizong Veritable Records*, was deputed to the task. When the manuscript was completed a year later, the emperor remarked that the memorials section could prove useful for governance and ordered Zhou Bida to compose a preface. But, as the work was going to print in 1179, a "close servitor," most probably Zeng Di or one of his associates, objected that the poetry selections insinuated veiled criticisms of the court and that the memorials "defamed the administration of the ancestors." His critics also charged that Lü Zuqian had taken a simple mandate to improve the bookshop edition and compiled a totally different, highly partisan work that privileged Qingli and Yuanyou authors, especially the Cheng brothers. Alarmed, the emperor ordered Cui Dunshi 崔敦詩 (1139–1182) to review and revise the work. Cui reported back that he had tried to even out the coverage and openly admitted that he had edited out "difficult language" from individual texts.[33]

If he is correct, then Gaozong is specifically rejecting the Shenzong period as a source of appropriate precedents. If, however, *zuzong shilu* is a generic reference to the early Song veritable records, then Gaozong seems to be requesting that the early Song veritable records be combed, presumably with a focus on the Zhenzong period, for suitable precedents. For another conversation between Gaozong and Qin Gui in 1141/10, in which the emperor links his personal practice of Daoist meditation, his general philosophy of administration, and the state policy of demilitarization, see *Yaolu*, 142.2679.

[33] *Chaoye zaji, yi*, 5.595–97, contains a careful narrative of the work's origins, including a quotation from the *Xiaozong Veritable Records* that contains the specific accusations against Lü Zuqian. Li Xinchuan points out that the *Xiaozong shilu* was composed under the Han Tuozhou administration when *daoxue* was proscribed, thus the author "defamed" Lü in this way. The passage nevertheless preserves a rare record of contemporary anti-*daoxue* sentiment. For Cui Dunshi's submission memorial, sometimes attributed to his brother Cui Dunli 崔敦禮 (d. 1181), see *QSW*, 269:6068.31.

The work was controversial even within *daoxue* circles. Zhang Shi wrote to Zhu Xi that the entire effort had no political value and was a waste of time. But Zhu Xi defended Lü Zuqian, writing that the selection of memorials offered a succinct historical survey of how subsequent ages had deformed the political models of the ancestors. He urged Zhao Ruyu to adopt Lü's basic outline for his own *The Ministers Memorials*. Then in the final year of his life, Lü Zuqian confessed that the criticisms of the anthology had unnerved him and he refused to speak about the matter. He complained that even Zhou Bida's preface had failed to understand and acknowledge the rationale for his selections.[34] In his later years Ye Shi took careful notes on the work. He held that Lü had chosen his selections based on content, not style, and that the work's basic goal was to distill the essence of the Northern Song political "Way."[35] A century later, Wang Yinglin understood the work as a pointed critique of Xiaozong's use of his close servitors to monitor and thwart the proper exercise of literati governance.[36]

The controversy over the *Literary Mirror* reflects tension within literati circles over the assignment of political value in Northern Song history, the sensitivity of the "close favorites" to a historical interpretation that questioned their past and present role in governance, and disagreement among *daoxue* scholars over the political and moral value of literary history. We have seen in Chapter 1 that Zhao Ruyu in 1180 initiated a politically motivated condensation of the *huiyao* corpus that eventually formed the basis of the present *Recovered Draft of the Song State Compendium*. He also undertook on his own initiative to enlarge greatly upon the 156 memorials that Lü Zuqian had included in the *Literary Mirror*. The resulting work, whose original title was *Memorials by Illustrious Ministers of the August Court* (*Huangchao mingchen zouyi* 皇朝名臣奏議) was completed in about 1186 and survives in a Song imprint of 1250. Zhao's preface and his memorial requesting permission to submit the work afford ample insights into his motivation and the political context of his compilation.

In his memorial, Zhao explained that he has condensed over 1,000 *juan* of Northern Song memorials into several hundred *juan*. He had categorized them by subject into over 100 topics and arranged them chronologically within each section. He claimed that reading chronologically within each section would

---

[34] *Zhu Xi ji*, 27.1147–48. Lü Zuqian's comments were recorded by his nephew Lü Qiaonian, who penned a defensive retrospective on the *Huangchao wenjian* early in the thirteenth century; see *QSW*, 304: 6940.94–96.

[35] *Xixue jiyan*, 47.1b, 50.15a. Chen Guangsheng, "Lü Zuqian yu *Song wenjian*," believes that, given Ye Shi's perception of the political goals for the work, the criticism of the "close servitor" was probably justified. A thirteenth-century source relates that the eunuch Gan Bian restricted access to the single copy of the *Literary Mirror* that Lü Zuqian submitted to Xiaozong; see Zhang Duanyi, *Gui'er ji*, 1.8.

[36] *Kunxue jiwen*, 15.1699–1701.

enable one to understand the successes and failures of government policy and to supplement the lacunae of the state histories. He insisted strongly that there was no need to look to distant antiquity or to earlier dynasties for precedents. The Northern Song memorials in his collection already articulated every idea needed to formulate contemporary policy. He requested permission to select "those pieces most essential for good government" and to submit them in installments of ten *juan* for his majesty's personal reading.[37]

Many scholars have noted that Zhao Ruyu's selections present a formal and detailed political agenda that heavily favors the policies of the Qingli and Yuanyou eras.[38] In this respect, his view of Northern Song history accords largely with that of Li Tao and Lü Zuqian. Zhao specifically mentions his indebtedness to the latter, and modern scholars have demonstrated that the precise chronological dating of texts in *The Ministers Memorials* derives from Li Tao's *Long Draft*.[39] The organization of the work is clearly based on the topical structure of the *huiyao* and the *baoxun* genres. Although its primary audience was the emperor, by structuring his book as a policy compendium based on a distinct historical view of Song history, Zhao also envisioned a larger literati audience, and he printed the work in Sichuan before his departure from the province in 1189.

Zhao's insistence that each dynasty govern through its own precedents targets the New Policies of Wang Anshi and those who would seek to bypass the policies of the dynastic ancestors through appeals to a higher antiquity. The selection of authors, subjects, and texts in *The Ministers Memorials* overwhelmingly foregrounds the "policies of the ancestors" as these were developed in the Qingli period and subsequently invoked against the New Policies. Zhao Ruyu, with a clear eye on the political battles of the late Xiaozong era, selected his memorials to create the impression of a direct link between those who had supported the Qingli reforms and those who had opposed the New Policies.

For example, Fan Zhongyan and Han Qi have nineteen and thirty-two memorials respectively. Fan's two sons, Fan Chunren and Fan Chuncui, opponents of the New Policies, have together forty-three memorials; but Han Qi's son, Han Zhongyan, tainted by his collaboration with Zeng Bu, has only one. Alternatively, Lü Yijian 呂夷簡 (979–1044), opponent of the Qingli reformers, has no memorials; but his son Lü Gongzhu 呂公著 (1018–1089), a senior Yuanyou official, has thirty-six. Memorials from the Fans of Huayang in Sichuan (Fan Zhen, Fan Zulu, and Fan Bailu) – a literati lineage that could boast both support for the Qingli reforms and opposition to the New Policies –

---

[37] For the text of this memorial see Zhao Ruyu, *Songchao zhuchen zouyi*, appendix, 1724; also *SHY, chongru*, 5.40a–b.

[38] Ji Yun et al., *Qinding Siku quanshu zongmu*, 55.776–77; and Chaffee, "Chao Ju-yü, Spurious Leaning, and Southern Sung Political Culture," 42–45.

[39] See the preface by Chen Zhichao to the 1999 edition, *Songchao zhuchen zouyi*, 8–20.

total eighty-one. Others with large selections include Ouyang Xiu (fifty-three), Wang Yansou (forty-five), Fu Bi (forty), Zhang Fangping (thirty-two), and Lü Hui (forty-five). There is token acknowledgment for proto-*daoxue* figures: Cheng Hao (eight), Cheng Yi (seven), Yang Shi (eleven). By far the most quoted minister, however, is Sima Guang, whose 146 memorials are triple the number for any other figure. Wang Anshi has six; Wang Gui three; Ding Wei, Kou Zhun, Xia Song, and Qin Gui one each.

In 1186, the same year that Zhao Ruyu completed *The Ministers Memorials*, Li Daxing 李大性 (1144?–1220?) submitted to the court a book entitled *Corrected Doubts about Precedents* (*Diangu bianyi* 典故辯疑). In the surviving preface, Li confronts the general concern over disreputable private or "wild" histories; he fears that their unreliable accounts may taint the official state sources. However, these concerns, he continues, have caused the state to ignore unofficial histories as a source of useful precedents. He has therefore combed such works for the edifying actions of noteworthy officials and confirmed the details of these private accounts against information in the official sources. His book contained two hundred such accounts along with their verifying documentation.[40]

Li's grandfather, Li Jizhong 李積中 (*jinshi* 1079), had been listed on the Yuanyou proscription stele in 1106, and Li himself was linked politically to Yang Wanli 楊萬里 (1127–1206), Chen Fuliang, and Peng Guinian. As had Li Tao before him, Li Daxing had also petitioned to install investigating censors in the Six Ministries with authority to memorialize the emperor directly.[41] Although Li is careful not to call his submitted accounts "precedents" (*gushi*), the title of his book, together with its preface, suggests that Li sought to provide documentation to expand the scope of ancestor precedents. If sanctioned, his "edifying" anecdotes could be used to justify policy proposals that his political allies and their *daoxue* colleagues favored. Within a year, such material indeed appeared in examination papers, and the Wang Huai administration took action to curb the trend, which it linked to the rise of *daoxue*.

In 1183, the censor Chen Jia, supported by Chief Councilor Wang Huai, had initiated the first political attack on *daoxue*.[42] In 1187, Chen, along with Hong Mai and Ge Bi 葛邲 (1135–1200), supervised the *jinshi* examinations and issued a report on general deficiencies in the papers they had read. Topping their list of concerns were improper references to the founders. They maintained that the state histories and institutional statutes constituted the sole source of "factual events concerning the founders." Many examination papers had drawn upon private, anecdotal works as sources to create strained and

---

[40] *Wenxian tongkao*, 200.5755–56; *QSW*, 259:5828.170–71.   [41] *SS*, 395.12048.
[42] Li Xinchuan, *Daoming lu*, 5.43–45; *Yongle dadian*, 8164.18b–20b; De Weerdt, *Competition over Content*, 194–96.

erroneous references. Using such sources and techniques, some papers had
ventured into areas "about which it is not proper to speak."[43]

Some quarters apparently interpreted this report as an attempt to ban all
citation of ancestor precedents from the examination system. He Dan 何澹
(1146–?), then rector of the Imperial University, objected to this interpretation
as an overreaction. He insisted that ancestor precedents were fundamental to
understanding the dynasty's history and that the examination system had
always sanctioned their citation. He agreed, however, that those who cited
wrongly or misinterpreted the precedents should not pass. The examiners
agreed to this compromise and affirmed that it had never been their intention
to ban the citation of ancestor precedent; they objected only to citations from
"unofficial and miscellaneous sources" and to strained explications.[44]

This compromise reflects the tension that had begun with Lü Zuqian's
Literary Mirror in 1177 and continued through Zhao Ruyu's *The Ministers'
Memorials* in 1186. These works, and the lost *Corrected Doubts about
Precedents*, sought to redefine dynastic precedents, as well as the corresponding interpretations of Northern Song history upon which they were based, and
bring the new amalgam into accord with *daoxue* political agendas. One will
recall that the final draft of Li Tao's *Long Draft* was submitted in 1183,
precisely during this period. Li Tao, who had, after all, also used "miscellaneous sources" to emend a politically outdated historical record, had appealed
to Emperor Xiaozong without success to convene a deliberative conference to
validate the *Long Draft*'s historical judgments. The examiners' report in 1187
confirmed that the state alone possessed the authority to determine the content
and interpretation of ancestor precedents.

This authority was demonstrated again in 1199 when Han Tuozhou, having
finally consolidated his hold on power following the death of Empress Wu in
1197, used the "explication" (*faming* 發明) of ancestor precedents to undertake
a formal and sweeping policy review. Two advisers devised a "strategic administrative agenda" divided into fifty topics similar to *baoxun* categories. Top
court officials and Classics Mat instructors convened every fortnight to discuss
one of the fifty topics. Each official was to submit in advance a "precedent" on
the topic that (1) reviewed the history of the issue, (2) cited a relevant ancestor
precedent, (3) discussed its connection to contemporary circumstances, and (4)
concluded with his own opinion. The process was to continue and result in
a reformulation and restatement of "major court policy."[45] On the one hand, the
process used ancestor precedents to update current policy; on the other hand, it
also confirmed which precedents and their interpretations had been formally

[43] *SHY, xuanju*, 5.10a–11a; De Weerdt, *Competition over Content*, 196–99.
[44] *SHY, xuanju*, 5.11b–12a; *QSW*, 282:6397.171.
[45] *Chaoye zaji, jia*, 6.144; *Xubian*, 5.94; Deng Xiaonan, *Zuzong zhi fa*, 391–92; Teraji Jun, "Kan Takuchū senken no seiritsu," 40.

deemed relevant to contemporary policy. This formal process thus ran counter to the *daoxue* recourse to "miscellaneous-source" precedents that had arisen during Xiaozong's reign.

For the remainder of Southern Song, the acceptance of precedents from "miscellaneous sources" rose and fell along with the political fortunes of the *daoxue* movement. Proscribed during the early years of the Han Tuozhou administration, *daoxue* gained gradual political acceptance after his murder in 1207. The new administration under Shi Miyuan inaugurated an era of mass historical revisionism that created the opportunity both to reinforce and rein- terpret old precedents and to create new ones. In short, as *daoxue* moved into the political mainstream, its "miscellaneous sources" also moved into the historiographical mainstream.

Precedents submitted by Hong Zikui 洪咨夔 (1176–1235), a major figure in the short-lived, *daoxue*-oriented, "minor Yuanyou" Duanping administration of 1234–1235, furnish examples of old precedents refurbished and new ones created. The military invasion launched in 1234/6 to recover northern territory exposed serious problems in army discipline. To persuade Emperor Lizong to address this issue, Hong submitted as "precedent" a conversation between Emperor Taizu and Li Chengjin 李承進, an old eunuch who had formerly served Emperor Zhuang of the Latter Tang dynasty (r. 923–925). Taizu asked the eunuch why Emperor Zhuang's reign had lasted only two years. The eunuch replied that his former master had been overly indulgent toward his troops. If his personal guard complained it was too cold for maneuvers, he would allow them to return to barracks. His management was inconsistent, and as a result his orders were not obeyed. Taizu replied that such emperorship was mere "child's play." Military leadership required strict discipline. In thirty years of managing his troops, "I have always been generous with rewards, but if they violate my rules, they get only my sword!" Hong Zikui drew for Lizong the evident connections between strict military discipline and an emperor's ability to exercise authority and ensure state security.[46]

In this case, Hong Zikui exercised a venerable Northern Song precedent.[47] As the Southern Song progressed into the thirteenth century, however, policy makers began to draw upon the actions of both Gaozong and Xiaozong as precedents. Hong also attempted to dissuade Emperor Lizong from accepting any of the plunder that Song military administrators had extracted during their

---

[46] Hong Zikui, *Pingzhai ji*, 8.1b–3a; *QSW*, 307:7007.152–53.

[47] In the surviving sources, a short version of the exchange between Taizu and Li Chengjin first appears in Zeng Gong, *Longping ji*, 2.11b–12a; for Luo Congyan's expanded version see *Zun Yao lu*, 1.112. In Southern Song, Li Tao's *Changbian*, 12.274, largely follows Luo Congyan. About 1182, Liu Guangzu included the precedent under the opening section on military management in his *Liangchao shengfan* (*QSW*, 279:6316.16). Finally, in the mid-thirteenth century, the story appears in both Chen Jun, *Huangchao gangmu*, 2.36–37; and Lü Zhong, *Huangchao dashiji*, 3.73–74.

campaign to recover Shandong and that they had sent to the emperor as private gifts. He argued that such behavior would hardly endear the Shandong populace to the Song cause. He urged Lizong to publically destroy the gifts as a signal both to the populace that the court was interested in their loyalty, not their property, and to the generals that imperial favor could not be purchased. The generals had also been rounding up and sending south large quantities of copper coin, and Hong cited a Shandong loyalist's remark, "once you have recovered a territory, why remove its money?"[48]

In this case, Hong used a story from the early months of Gaozong's reign as a precedent. In 1127/10, eunuchs from the former capital at Kaifeng had presented the young emperor with two bags of pearls from the imperial treasury. The young emperor immediately dumped the contents into the Bian Canal, remarking that he hoped thereby to emulate an ancient sovereign who, according to the *Zhuangzi*, had reduced thievery by publicly destroying his own valuables.[49] This story was part of the earliest historiographical layer of "Gaozong precedents" that the court history office began to compile into a *shengzheng* collection as soon as Gaozong abdicated in 1162; and the story of Gaozong and the pearls remains among the twenty entries that Lu You drafted for the *shengzheng* project in 1163. Lu You writes that Emperor Huizong's love of luxury brought on the Jurchen invasions, while Gaozong's embrace of frugality derived from his sincere desire to realize the Restoration.[50] By looking to Gaozong for precedents, Hong Zikui insinuates that Gaozong's actions are now on par with those of the Northern Song founders as sources of dynastic models.

In this latter case, Hong relied upon the official *shengzheng* compilation, completed in 1166, for his precedent. Other cases show him ranging much farther afield. For example, he urged Lizong to maintain his own notebook in order to keep track of the many details of imperial governance. As precedent, he offered the example of Emperor Xiaozong, who had taken notes during his audiences on small pieces of paper that he collected into a dossier and retained for future reference.[51] In this case, Hong's "precedent" came from a colophon that Zhou Bida had inscribed on such a note slip that Xiaozong had presented to him in 1184 as a reminder of actions they had taken a year earlier.[52]

[48] Hong Zikui, *Pingzhai ji*, 7.1a; *QSW*, 307:7006.140–41.
[49] Watson, *Complete Works of Chuang Tzu*, 110.
[50] For Lu You's original text see *Yongle dadian*, 12929.1b. The incident became a fixture of Southern Song history; see *Yaolu*, 10.266; *Zhongxing shengzheng*, 2.17b; *Zhongxing xiaoli*, 2.22; Wang Mingqing, *Huizhu lu*, *qianlu*, 1.6; and *Songshi quanwen*, 16A.1069–70. Li Xinchuan seems to understand Gaozong's destruction of the pearls as part of Li Gang's policy to free Gaozong from the influence of his predecessor's eunuchs; see *Yaolu*, 6.190.
[51] Hong Zikui, *Pingzhai ji*, 8.7a–b; *QSW*, 307:7007.157.
[52] Zhou Bida, *Wenzhong ji*, 14.13a–b; *QSW*, 230:5122.217–18; cf. *Yuhai*, 34.31b.

As economic and political conditions deteriorated over the course of the thirteenth century, writers increasingly looked to the Gaozong and Xiaozong eras as sources of precedents. As the Song drew to a close, these earlier periods, and especially the reign of Xiaozong in which *daoxue* had emerged as a political force, were increasingly seen as the golden period of Southern Song – a perspective that endures to this day in many quarters. Liu Kezhuang 劉克莊 (1187–1269), for example, submitted fifteen precedents between 1246 and 1262. They cited a total of sixteen sources (one drew upon two sources): six drew upon pre-Song history, six were from Northern Song, and four from Southern Song.[53] Although Liu's Song sources are all official, his Southern Song sources were compiled after the rise of *daoxue*, and they cast their sovereigns as paragon practitioners of the "policies of the ancestors." As vivid illustration of this trend, one may compare the "imperial precedents" submitted by Qi Chongli 綦崇禮 (1083–1142) in the early 1130s against a similar series submitted by Wu Yong 吳泳 (1181–1252+) a century later. Among Qi's seventeen precedents, fourteen draw from pre-Song sources; only three cite Northern Song monarchs. On the contrary, Wu Yong's entire series draws exclusively upon events undertaken by Gaozong and Xiaoxong.[54]

---

[53] *QSW*, 330:7594.147–7495.173.
[54] Qi Chongli, *Beihai ji*, 20.1a–13b, 21.1a–12a, 22.1a–12b; *QSW*, 167:3655.434–38; *QSW*,168:3656.1–20; Wu Yong, *Helin ji*, 15.1a–30b; *QSW*, 316:7253.314–33.

7   Song History as Grand Allegory

An Introduction

We noted in Chapter 4 a propensity for the moral categories of Song history writing to become increasingly well defined and rigid as the dynasty progressed, and we linked this propensity to the growth of *daoxue*.[1] As the reformulation of moral absolutes that began with the eleventh-century rise of the literati intensified into the twelfth-century *daoxue* movement, a drive also intensified for cleaner, thus more increasingly allegorized, interpretations of history. Although modern scholars recognize a sharp methodological divergence between Sima Guang and later *daoxue* historians, in truth Sima Guang had already planted seeds of this later transformation. Not without justification did many Southern Song scholars count Sima Guang as among the progenitors of *daoxue*.[2] The *Comprehensive Mirror* implants a thin chronology of "fact" within a "sublimated moral universe" that originated in the classical canon, especially the *Book of Documents* and the *Spring and Autumn Annals*.[3] Sima Guang expected his readers to apply values and structures from this moral universe to craft their own allegorical mediation between the world as it had been and the world as it could have been and might still be. The bulk of the *Comprehensive Mirror* – its lengthy quotations from memorials and earlier histories – forms a vast sourcebook of discourse on this moral universe to assist the reader in this interpretive task. Once the transition to the *daoxue* "outline-and-details" format was complete, the historian no longer asked the reader to craft his allegories for himself. Rather, they came prepackaged along with requisite "facts," and the transition to "pedagogical" history was complete.[4]

The following chapters argue that this "*daoxue* history" can be viewed as a metanarrative or grand allegory that came into being as the end product of *daoxue* historiography. To the degree that the *Song History* ratified this vision – and considering that scholars did not have practical access to the textual corpus

---

[1] The following five paragraphs are adapted from my article, "*Song History* Narratives as Grand Allegory," 38–39, 48–49.

[2] Hartman, "Li Hsin-ch'uan and the Historical Image," 338–39; Cai Hanmo, *Lishi de yanzhuang*, 399–400.

[3] Robert André LaFleur, "A Rhetoric of Remonstrance," 91–94.

[4] Hartman, "Chen Jun's *Outline and Details*," 275–81.

necessary to deconstruct that vision until the twentieth century – this *daoxue* history was for many centuries the grand allegory that explained the entirety of Song history. One may compare the notion of such a *daoxue* history with Herbert Butterfield's well-known critique of Whig history.[5] Butterfield charged that the needs of Whig politicians for historical justification had generated a history that led inexorably to their own political preferences for constitutional monarchy and British liberalism.

Seeking likenesses rather than unlikenesses between present and past, they created a narrative in which progress toward these political goals had flowed from the Reformation through Protestantism, the Glorious Revolution of 1688, the Whigs, and Parliament. In turn, they denigrated as retrograde and antiprogressive those countervailing forces that had run through Catholicism, the Tories, the king, and the absolute monarchy. Historical actors deemed to have fostered Whig goals received positive evaluations and became heroes; those who had opposed or thwarted them became villains. Whig historians employed radical abridgment of the complex and ambiguous primary historical record to foreground events that contributed to their preferred narrative and to omit those that did not. The result was a "giant optical illusion" so powerful that the research of most historians merely buttressed the illusion rather than challenged the basic story.[6]

There are many similarities between Butterfield's conception of how Whig politicians created a British history that rendered inevitable their political ascendency over the Tories and how the *daoxue* politicians created a Song history that led inexorably to their own political triumph in 1241. Both are blatantly presentist: historical events are chosen because they contain positive or negative value as guidelines for present or proposed future action. Both rely extensively upon abridgment to foreground these examples and prune away the profusion of unrelated detail. Both generate clear heroes and villains, whose earlier struggles presage the political conflicts of the present. And finally, both create a teleological trajectory of moral rectitude that ensures the ultimate intellectual and political triumph of the writer's own beliefs.

I use the term "grand allegory" because the Western notion of allegory indeed seems appropriate for how these late Song and Yuan historians accessed their own *daoxue* convictions to impose structure and meaning on the disparate data of Song history. In addition, Western allegories are often didactic, moral quests undertaken to explore grand existential struggles (think Dante, Spenser, Bunyan) similar to the absolute moral divide between the gentlemen (*junzi*) and

---

[5] I am grateful to Ho Koon-wan for suggesting to me a general affinity between *daoxue* and Whig history.

[6] Herbert Butterfield, *The Whig Interpretation of History*, 9–33.

the petty men (*xiaoren*) of the *Song History*, if not, of course, of Song history itself.

Similar to the practice of the Whig historians, the Yuan editors of the *Song History* constructed their work both to assert fidelity to their own intellectual masters in the Song *daoxue* movement and to serve the needs of their political masters at the Yuan court. The result is a distinctive grand allegory or master narrative of Song history. This chapter outlines the basic contours of this allegorical narrative and identifies three major thematic clusters. Chapters 8, 9, and 10 will then treat each cluster in detail and trace these themes to specific political issues within the history of the Song polity.

Each of these three themes arose at a different point in Song history. Briefly, they can be enumerated as follows. First, the weighting of the reign of Emperor Renzong, specifically the Qingli (1041–1048) and Jiayou (1056–1063) periods, as a golden age of Song governance arose first at the end of the eleventh century as a reaction against the New Policies of Wang Anshi. But, since these policies continued throughout the Huizong reign (1100–1125), the adulation of Renzong's rule as a pre-Wang Anshi utopia gained momentum only after 1125 and, as explained in Chapter 2, is a cornerstone of Li Tao's *Long Draft*. The resulting conception of 1067 as a fundamental dividing point in the political and moral history of Song became the guiding principle of the grand allegory.

Second, although important elements in the elevation of Emperor Taizu to iconic status as the pre-eminent Song founder can be traced to the *Precedents from the Era of Great Peace* and other works of the 1030s and 1040s, the glorification of Taizu is also a Southern Song political phenomenon, and closely tied to Emperor Gaozong's decision about 1130 to return the Song imperial line to Taizu's descendants. Li Tao also supported this development and labored mightily in the *Long Draft* against the paucity of his sources to frame Taizu as the ultimate source of Song greatness. Finally, toward the end of the twelfth century, the *daoxue* movement completed the deification of Taizu. He became a sage on par with the ancient paragons, an incarnation of the *daoxue* image of the perfect ruler.

Third, political opposition to the domination of government by Shi Miyuan and his nephew Shi Songzhi in the years after 1208 generated an image of Song history after Wang Anshi as a series of "nefarious ministers" (*jianchen*) whose policies were linked to the negative stereotype of the Confucian "petty man" (*xiaoren*). The *daoxue* movement, now at the height of its influence, framed Song history as a struggle between such "petty" yet powerful men with their numerous minions and their antithesis, the principled "gentlemen" (*junzi*), whom they had oppressed and driven from power. As the introduction to the biographies of nefarious ministers in the *Song History* explains, this opposition, like the interaction between *yin* and *yang* in the hexagrams, is inherent and constant.[7] This moral dichotomy between "gentlemen" and "petty men" was a fixture of Confucian moral rhetoric as old as the *Analects*. But after Ouyang Xiu introduced these terms into Song political discourse in the 1040s, their political use became standard in the factional struggles over the New Policies.[8] Yet, although inherently present in the motif of the golden age of Renzong, the systematic application of this dichotomy to a wide spectrum of Song historical actors did not mature until the theme of the nefarious minister had emerged and fused with the earlier two themes during the first half of the thirteenth century. The result of this maturity was the emergence of a widely accepted master narrative of dynastic history we seek to describe and whose evolution the following chapters will explore.

The evolution was slow and accumulative. Although each of these three themes originated under its own set of unique political circumstances, they all – but especially the first and third – grew from the politics of opposition. The process began in opposition to the New Policies and concluded in opposition to Shi Songzhi and the other late Song autocratic councilors. As they developed over time, these originally separate themes interacted with each other to create a coherent narrative of Song history. Major portions of this narrative had developed before the rise of *daoxue* in the 1170s; but this movement, at the height of its influence in the 1230s, dominated the final stage of the process and forged these elements into the grand allegory of struggle between two opposing political and ultimately moral forces.

Thus, before the thirteenth century, the grand allegory has no definitive formulation, no touchstone passage that contains all its elements. It was rather an assembly of themes, motifs, "types," and smaller allegories that late Song historians combined to express the values and structures that each perceived in their history. As I have demonstrated in Chapter 4, a major moment in this process occurred around 1229 when Chen Jun completed his *Outline and Details*, his two-part comprehensive history of Song. Taken together, his two works constituted the first attempt to compile a history of the Song from its inception in 960 to the author's own time, in this case the abdication of Emperor Xiaozong in 1189. Chen Jun, the grandnephew of the Xiaozong-era chief councilor Chen Junqing, was a declared disciple of Zhu Xi and closely allied to the political opposition to Shi Miyuan.

In 1229 the leading *daoxue* advocate Zhen Dexiu wrote a preface for Chen Jun's history in which he summarized the work's major themes and contents. He attributed the prosperity and stability of pre-1067 "grand governance" to four policies that Taizu had inaugurated and that his successors through

---

[7] *SS*, 471.13697.
[8] See Levine, *Divided by a Common Language*, 42–71; also my review of Levine in *Journal of Song-Yuan Studies* 40 (2010): 141–49.

Renzong had continued. But, Zhen insisted, changes to these policies after 1067 had "brought about chaos." First, the Song was founded upon the principle of "benevolence"; this changed after 1067 to one of expediency and advantage. Second, the founders adopted Confucianism as a moral base, but other doctrines later tainted this foundation. Third, Zhen maintained, there had been a gradualist quality, a deliberate and unhurried pace to pre-1067 administration, but after 1067 a precipitous rush to accomplish everything "in one reign" replaced this earlier consistency. Fourth, pre-1067 officials had been selected for their "genuine and natural" qualities; afterward they became sly and agile but morally "small."

Accordingly, Zhen continued, the pre-1067 consensus between sovereign and officials around these four principles had engendered respect for the fragility of the state and for effective administration. Wang Anshi and the New Policies, by interjecting Legalist and Buddhist elements, destroyed this unity and inflicted irreversible damage on the body politic. No longer able to generate officials with "genuine" pre-1067 qualities, state administration suffered at the hands of a continuation of nefarious officials such as Zhang Dun, Lü Huiqing, Cai Jing, and Cai Bian. This deterioration culminated in the military debacles on the northern borders precipitated by Wang Fu and Tong Guan in the early 1120s. Zhen concluded that Chen Jun's history provided, "at a glance, 167 years of events that you can savor and admire, but some that will also horrify you; truly this is a mirror of precedents for the future of our Song."[9]

This preface contains all three themes of the grand allegory. Because the first and second themes had experienced by this point in time a 100-year gestation, these are well developed in Zhen's preface. The third is present but incipient: the chain of negative political stereotypes that extends in the preface from Zhang Dun through Tong Guan is but the first installment of the more complete series that will culminate in the "nefarious ministers" chapters of the *Song History*. Several factors explain the still-incipient character of the third motif. First, when Zhen Dexiu wrote his preface in 1229, he had not yet seen Chen Jun's second work on Southern Song history, so he confined the scope of his preface to Northern Song. Also, in 1229 Shi Miyuan was still in power. The hostility between the Chen lineage of Putian in Fujian and the Shi lineage of Mingzhou 明州 originated in the political conflict between Shi Hao and Chen Junqing in the 1160s.[10] But Chen Jun was careful to hedge his bets: he also solicited a preface from Zheng Xingzhi, a major ally of Shi Miyuan.

---

[9] Zhen Dexiu, *Xishan wenji*, 27.1a–4a; *QSW*, 313:7169.140–42. By "167 years" Zhen refers to Northern Song, 960–1127. For a discussion of the full preface see Hartman, "Chen Jun's *Outline and Details*," 285–87.

[10] For Chen Jun's antipathy toward Shi Hao see Hartman, "Chen Jun's *Outline and Details*," 309–10.

Furthermore, Zhen Dexiu had moved only slowly toward *daoxue* and had a complex history with Shi Miyuan.

The following chapters attempt to trace in some detail the origins and development of these three themes. All arose from the rhetoric of political discourse. Although each experienced a long gestation, acute political crises elevated these three over many other possible elements within this larger political discourse. The identification of benevolence as a hallmark of Song rule and the location of the source of that benevolence in the character of Emperor Taizu both arose to prominence as a consequence of the political crisis that followed the Jurchen invasion of North China in 1125, the loss of Kaifeng, and the political Restoration under Emperor Gaozong after 1127. The final theme, the lineage of evil, rose to prominence following the crises of 1206–1208, the disastrous invasion of the North, the assassination of Han Tuozhou, and the transition to Shi Miyuan. This larger, threefold scenario underscores the idea that violent and drastic political change elevated to rhetorical dominance each major theme that would eventually form the grand allegory of Song history.

Yuanyou Origins

Li Tao, Zhao Ruyu, and Zhen Dexiu all viewed the reign of Emperor Renzong, especially the Qingli (1041–1047) and Jiayou (1056–1063) periods, as a time of political and cultural florescence founded on the principle of "benevolence." This notion of a Renzong florescence first emerged in 1092 when Fan Zuyu proposed to the young Emperor Zhezong that he should embrace Renzong-era political values rather than return to the New Policies that Sima Guang and the Yuanyou administration had halted in 1086. This antithetical link between the Renzong era and the Wang Anshi era – between the political value of "benevolence" and of "profit" – developed into a more nuanced and politically compelling motif as the late Northern Song debates and factional politics over the New Policies intensified.

When Zhezong died unexpectedly in 1100, the new Emperor Huizong and his regent urged the two opposing factions to form a coalition government. But the politics of this realignment required the removal of the entrenched pro-New Policies chief councilor Zhang Dun and his allies, and the process dragged on for nine months. Midway through this purge, Chen Shixi 陳師錫 (1053–1121) justified the move by casting parallels back to the history of Renzong's reign. He explained that Renzong's administrative style had combined an open and unbiased receptivity to remonstrance together with active style of personnel management. Renzong, Chen claimed, had used the information he received from remonstrance reports to evaluate quickly the performance of his senior officials and to make sweeping and effective changes in leadership. Renzong's impartial acceptance of remonstrance enabled him to separate the "worthy" from the "nefarious," and thus to advance the former and withdraw the latter.

Chen gave two examples where Renzong in a single action had replaced his entire senior administration. He then "promoted Du Yan, Fan Zhongyan, Fu Bi, and Han Qi and brought about the most florescent age of our dynasty, the Qingli and Jiayou governments, whose achievements surpassed those of Han and Tang and approached those of antiquity." To reinforce the parallel to Huizong, Chen carefully emphasized that Renzong had exercised this style of governance immediately upon beginning his personal rule in 1033. The message to Huizong was simple: the completed purge of Zhang Dun and his allies would set the stage for another period of "florescence" comparable to that under Renzong.[1]

The continuation of the New Policies throughout the Huizong era curtailed references to the motif of the Renzong florescence during this period. However, the Jurchen invasions in the winter of 1125 forced drastic political changes that once again freed the reference for use in active political discourse. Emperor Huizong abdicated in favor of Emperor Qinzong in 1125/12, and the Jurchen besieged Kaifeng on 1126/1/7. The resulting political turmoil unleashed a torrent of fault finding. Blame fell primarily on Cai Jing, who had been removed as chief councilor in 1125/4, but his former subordinates and allies still filled senior government ranks. Simultaneously, as Cai Jing's long-repressed political adversaries seized the opportunity to strike against him, his own coalition members struggled to disentangle themselves from his emerging legacy.

Thus, the Jurchen invasion forced a political turnabout that required a sudden revision of Song history, one that focused blame on Cai Jing but absolved those currently in power. Some evidence suggests that the Jurchen may have pressed the Song court to make this political transition as part of the negotiations in 1126/2 to lift their initial siege of Kaifeng. The Jurchen were doubtless eager to see a Song leadership less inclined to adopt an aggressive military posture against them. Historically, the Yuanyou administrators had advocated against expansive military adventures and favored a more defensive foreign posture. When the Jurchen returned in late 1126, they sent 100 troops to protect Sima Guang's tomb, sought out copies of Sima's works, including the *Comprehensive Mirror*, and burned the works of Wang Anshi in the Imperial Library.[2] According to one contemporaneous source, they also offered to make Sima Pu 司馬朴 (1091–1141?), Sima Guang's grandnephew, emperor of the puppet state they created to replace Song. When Sima Pu declined, the offer went to Zhang Bangchang 張邦昌 (1081–1127). The Jurchen took Sima Pu into northern captivity, but treated him well and continued to offer him positions in the Jin state.[3]

[1] Zhao Ruyu, *Songchao zhuchen zouyi*, 17.159–60; *QSW*, 93:2031.253–54. Zhao Ruyu dates this memorial to 1100/5. However, the present text contains the phrase "more than 150 years after the founding," or 1110, which Cao Jiaqi, "Zhao Song dangchao shengshi shuo," 79, accepts as the memorial's date.
[2] *Yaolu*, 1.28; Ding Teqi, *Jingkang jiwen*, 17–18. Zhu Xi also related information he obtained from Fan Zhongbiao, who was married to Sima Guang's granddaughter, about how the Jurchen troops had acted to protect Sima Guang's house in Luoyang and its surviving manuscripts, which then passed into the Fan family's possession; see *Zhu Xi ji*, 81.4176–78.
[3] Anonymous, *Jingkang xiaolu*, quoted at *Huibian*, 96.4a; also *Dongdu shilüe*, 108.6b–7a. For a detailed and still useful study of the Jurchen perspective on Song politics at the time of the invasion see Toyama Gunji, "Seikō no hen ni okeru shinkyū ryōhōtō no seiryoku kankei."

As the weakened government negotiated an end to the siege, on 1126/2/6 Emperor Qinzong rehabilitated Fan Zhongyan and Sima Guang and suspended prohibitions on the Yuanyou partisans.[4] His edict referenced a prior order to the major administrative agencies "fully to honor and to restore the policies of the ancestors." Similar language in other edicts from the second month of 1126 suggests that the policies of the ancestors were now set in stark historical opposition to the New Policies.[5] A corresponding historical narrative that foregrounded the motif of the Renzong florescence would soon follow. Bone fide Yuanyou partisans supported the new history because it privileged their own origins. At the same time, Cai Jing's partisans also found the new narrative more congenial than other options because it focused sole responsibility on Cai Jing and through him back to Zhang Dun and Wang Anshi, thus deflecting attention from their own origins in Cai Jing's political machine.

On 1126/2/12, two days after the Jurchen lifted the siege, Qinzong once again reaffirmed his intention to pursue a government based upon "the old institutions of the ancestors." He pledged to restore a fully functional ministerial system; to reduce the number of eunuchs, favorites, and patronage appointments; and to eliminate unwarranted compensation. In general, he ordered "an end to all manner of activities that prey upon the state and harm the people," a phrase that had negatively characterized the New Policies and now came to define Cai Jing.[6] Among the other actions taken immediately after the siege, Yang Shi was appointed rector of the Imperial University with a mandate to quiet a month-long series of strident protests against Cai Jing and the politics of his protégés currently in power. A disciple of Cheng Yi and fervent Yuanyou partisan, Yang had already urged Huizong to revise the existing Xuanhe-period (1119–1125) law codes to bring them into compliance with the ancient sage-kings' principle of "equilibrium" (*zhong* 中). He maintained that this principle had been latent in the original policies of the Song founders and manifested in the Yuanyou-period statutes, but since Wang Anshi had disfigured the former and Wang's followers had burned the latter in the 1090s, a reworking of the law code was necessary.[7] Since nothing had come of this earlier request, Yang took his appointment to the University as a mandate to dismantle a generation of New Policies educational practice and remove Wang Anshi from the Confucian temple at the University. Wang Anshi's commentaries to selected classics formed the basis of Song official education; therefore, to remove that foundation would undermine the careers of those who had already mastered Wang learning, a consequence that Yang Shi certainly understood.

---

[4] *Jingkang yaolu*, 2.251; *SHY, yizhi*, 12.18b.   [5] See, for example, *Jingkang yaolu*, 2.322.
[6] *Jingkang yaolu*, 2.302; *QSW*, 191:4215.243–44; *SS*, 23.425. For a similar, more specific action from 1126/2/29 see *Jingkang yaolu*, 3.418–19.
[7] *SS*, 428.12739; *QSW*, 124:2677.121.

Yang's radical policies heightened tension between the pro-Wang and pro-Yuanyou factions, and he was forced to resign in early 1126/5.[8] The remonstrator Feng Xie 馮澥 (d. 1140) suggested a compromise whereby both Wang Anshi- and Yuanyou-based learning would be accepted at the University. Feng's compromise confined political culpability to Cai Jing, questioned the viability of many ancestor precedents, and, by posing the Shenzong reign as a period of peace and prosperity, did not require an alternative to the existing historical narrative.[9] The opposition responded immediately with a series of memorials by the remonstrator Cui Yan 崔鷗 (1057–1126) and the censor Li Guang 李光 (1078–1159). Cui invoked the motif of the Renzong florescence to argue against the proposed compromise. Cui posited a direct historical link between the straightforward, honest personnel of the Renzong and Yingzong eras and the Yuanyou administrators under Sima Guang and Empress Gao. Cui thus placed his political and intellectual forebears in stark contrast to the minions of Wang Anshi, Zhang Dun, and Cai Jing.[10] His tract, in essence, created a historical narrative that supported his allies in the political battles against the entrenched New Policies advocates at the University and elsewhere in government. Cui Yan's memorial thus elaborated the historical link implied in the combined rehabilitation of Fan Zhongyan as representative of the consummate Qingli official and Sima Guang as the corresponding Yuanyou figure.[11]

The period between the Jurchen departure and their return the following winter witnessed concrete attempts to re-examine the policies of the ancestors for suitable replacements for the New Policies. To this end, the leadership had proposed on 1126/4/12 to establish an advisory committee to evaluate "the former policies of the ancestors." The remonstrator Chen Gongfu 陳公輔 (1077–1142), although lauding the goal, strongly objected to the mechanism. He condemned the proposal as a thinly veiled attempt to reinstitute an ad hoc agency that Cai Jing had proposed as early as 1094, and had actually convened outside the standard institutional structure to discuss and implement policy changes in 1104–1106. Chen pointed out that a similar committee reconvened in 1124 had produced only bloat and nepotism.

[8] Chu, *The Politics of Higher Education*, 197–99.
[9] See *Jingkang yaolu*, 6.754–56, 7.782–84, for Feng's memorials of 1126/5/10 and 5/13; also Hong Mai, *Rongzhai suibi, xubi*, 2.229.
[10] *QSW*, 128:2779.321–24. Southern Song sources widely cite Cui Yan's two memorials against Feng Xie; see *Changbian shibu*, 54.1718–23.
[11] For Li Guang's similar historical argument against official acceptance of the learning of both Wang Anshi and Sima Guang see his memorial at *QSW*, 154:3306.60–61; and *SS*, 363.11336. *Jingkang yaolu*, 7.803–10, contains additional sources for this debate, with excellent commentary. As usual, Zhao Ruyu, *Songchao zhuchen zouyi*, 83.899–901 cites the representative memorials by Yang Shi, Cui Yan, and Li Guang.

While Chen strongly endorsed a reconsideration of the policies of the ancestors, he maintained that these discussions should originate in the Six Ministries, then proceed to the State Council for deliberation and transmittal to the monarch. He maintained further that since the pre-1067 statutes still existed and had in fact been reactivated during the Yuanyou, they could be easily defined and re-implemented now. Those policies had fostered peaceful coexistence with neighbors, enabled the populace to thrive, and maintained a balanced prosperity between state and private interests. Chen concluded that a return to these policies could be realized simply by abolishing the New Policies still in force and, after a brief review, reinstituting the pre-1067 institutions.[12]

Several emerging middle-echelon officials, who would go on to play leading political roles in the early Southern Song, supported Yang Shi's call to revise both the legal code and educational policy to accord with the policies of the ancestors. Li Guang weighed in on the issue, affirming the centrality of ancestor precedents as base guidelines for institutional reform. He called for top administrators to select a committee of seasoned scholars to accomplish the task.[13] On 1126/6/7 Emperor Qinzong issued an edict noting that no progress had been made on these initiatives. The edict again placed blame for both problems on Cai Jing and used the expression "restoration" (*zhongxing*) to describe the political process that accomplishment of both efforts would promote.[14] A month later, Li Gang, then supervising troops in the north, added his support for these efforts to bring about the "restoration."[15]

Luo Congyan's *Record of Revering Yao*

Whatever progress the government may have made on this review stopped when the Jurchen returned to Kaifeng in the winter of 1126. But Luo Congyan 羅從彥 (1072–1135), a disciple of Yang Shi, took up the task in his capacity as a private scholar in his native Nanjian 南劍, Fujian, and compiled *Our Sagacious Song's Record of Revering Yao* (*Sheng Song Zun Yao lu* 聖宋遵堯錄). With a preface dated 1126/10, this surviving work documents the efforts among Yuanyou adherents in the final days of Northern Song to construct a detailed historical narrative that demonized the New Policies and justified replacing them with the policies of the ancestors. Luo's work both summarizes and develops the Renzong florescence motif and looks forward to further historiographical expansion and refinements to come in Southern Song.

Wang Yinglin described the *Record of Revering Yao* as "a collection of ancestor precedents that could be transmitted as policy to later ages, with

[12] *SHY, zhiguan*, 5.19a–20a.   [13] *QSW*, 154:3311.139.
[14] *Jingkang yaolu*, 8.833; *QSW*, 191:4219.302; *SS*, 23.429.   [15] *QSW*, 169:3692.193.

explanations and interpretations."[16] Luo's debt to his teacher Yang Shi and the Cheng brothers is clear. His preface anchored his historical argument in the concepts of "mind" and the "Way." He attributed the purity and perfection of pre-1067 Song institutions to the spiritual and mental qualities of the first four sovereigns, whom he equated with the sage-kings of antiquity. The preface posits Taizong and Renzong as faithful continuers of Taizu's legacy. Wang Anshi's mutilation of this legacy brought on the Jurchen invasion. Now, despite the new emperor's intention to revere his ancestors' precedents, Wang's adherents still dominate government. Therefore, Luo has composed this work, taking Wu Jing's 吳兢 (670–749) *Record of Zhenguan Government* (*Zhenguan zhengyao* 貞觀政要) and Shi Jie's *Records of Sagacious Administration* as models. In the rhetoric of Luo's preface, parallel quotations from the *Latter Han History* evaluation of Emperor Han Guangwu (r. 25–57) and from *Mencius* reinforce Luo's conception of his work as a handbook for ruler and minister to restore the benevolent government of the founders and "take us back to the Way."[17]

The surviving work presents 268 historical events; Luo does not indicate his source texts.[18] The eight-*juan* work contains one *juan* devoted to each of the first four Song emperors (Taizu, events #1–49; Taizong, #50–90; Zhenzong, #91–132; Renzong, #133–77); *juan* five treats Li Hang (#178–85), Kou Zhun (#186–91), Wang Dan (#192–203), and Wang Zeng (#204–11); *juan* six, Du Yan (#213–18), Han Qi (#219–30), Fan Zhongyan (#231–36), and Fu Bi (#237–43); and *juan* seven, Sima Guang (#244–51) and Cheng Hao (#252–68). An appended final *juan* prints Sima Guang memorials attacking Wang Anshi and Chen Guan memorials attacking Cai Jing. An absence of commentary, Luo explains in his preface, indicates his opinion that the relevance of the precedent for present times is obvious. Thirty-two "explanations," usually positive, accompany precedents whose import Luo fears may not be immediately obvious. Twenty-four events with appended "interpretations of subtleties" conclude each of the four *juan* on emperors and contain corrective comments on actions that Luo considers "not fully consistent with today's needs." This present format matches Chen Zhensun's description of the book in his 1250 bibliography.[19]

---

[16] *Yuhai*, 58.39a.   [17] Luo Congyan, *Zun Yao lu*, 105–6; *QSW*, 142:3060.157–58.
[18] Liang Tianxi, "*Zun Yao lu* shishi shuzheng, " numbers each event, lists textual variants, collects parallel sources, and provides helpful commentary. The numbering system used here is his.
[19] *Zhizhai shulu jieti*, 5.167. However, Chen saw an edition printed in 1214 by Liu Yunji 劉允濟 (*jinshi* 1178), who was then magistrate of Nanjian. Liu submitted his edition to the court with a petition to research Luo's career and confer upon him a posthumous name. The magistrate's actions were clearly part of local efforts to obtain a place for the native son in the then-forming pantheon of Northern Song *daoxue* paragons. For another such effort at this time see Hartman and Li, "The Rehabilitation of Chen Dong," 106–12. The petition was renewed in 1246 and finally granted in 1247. See Luo Congyan, *Yuzhang wenji*, 15.1a–9a; *Yuhai*, 58.39a. Liu Yunji's 1214 petition stated that Luo's manuscript had never circulated; and indeed, Li Tao, the most

Luo writes that he composed the book between 1126/2 and 1126/10, precisely during the hiatus between the two Jurchen sieges of Kaifeng, but was unable to submit his manuscript to court. The surviving book does not adhere strictly to the format of its models, Wu Jing and Shi Jie, but does conform well to the desiderata set forth by Yang Shi and his political allies for a review and restoration of ancestor precedents. Intended for the new administration of Emperor Qinzong, the *Record of Revering Yao* is a handbook for political behavior based on Confucian principles as articulated by the Cheng brothers and expressed through a selection and commentary on Northern Song historical events. The process generated both a group of foregrounded "precedents" and also a series of positive and negative political actors. Luo's aggressive Confucian theoretical base marginalized the Daoist origins of Song rule and thus purified the founders for linkage to the sage-kings of antiquity. At the same time, Luo's historical revisionism sought to undermine Wang Anshi's appeal to the antique "three ages" as a legitimate source of authority for the New Policies.

Because Luo's chosen "events" are now well known and his theoretical principles now sound like conventional Confucian platitudes, most modern scholars have ignored his work.[20] However, its importance resides neither in its uniqueness as a historical source nor in the brilliance of its theory, but rather in the particular constellation of historical choices that the work foregrounded to illustrate these principles. These choices – and the resulting narrative of what would soon be "Northern Song" history – were, in 1126, new. Liang Tianxi reads a major portion of the entries as illustrating four necessities for "benevolent government": (1) imperial self-cultivation, (2) insuring the welfare of the people, (3) appointing the proper individuals to office, and (4) accepting remonstrance.[21]

For example, Luo selected from Shi Jie the story of how Taizu ordered the palace remodeled so its doors and gates would be perfectly aligned and thus provide a straight, unobstructed view into his inner chamber – "and thus so shall be my heart, that all may see even the slightest deviation." Unlike Shi Jie, however, Luo's commentary links this vignette to the theory from the *Doctrine*

---

informed historian of the twelfth century, does not cite the work in his notes to the *Long Draft*. Furthermore, although Luo Congyan now occupies a secure place in the *daoxue* pantheon as a transmitter of the Way from Cheng Yi to Zhu Xi (Cheng Yi, Yang Shi, Luo Congyan, Li Tong, Zhu Xi), this status seems largely a creation of the thirteenth century. Luo's biography in the *daoxue* section of the *Song History* contains little beyond snippets from the *Zun Yao lu* (*SS*, 428.12743–45). Zhu Xi was aware of Luo as an associate of Yang Shi and of his own father, but did not include him in the *Yi Luo yuanyuan lu* (see *Zhu Xi ji*, 37.1616, 97.4972, 4984–85, 4988; *Zhuzi yulei*, 102.2596–97). The possibility remains, therefore, that Liu Yunji may have enhanced the manuscript to fit the historiographical tenor of the early thirteenth century.

[20] Useful summaries of the content, however, are Liang Tianxi, "Cong *Zun Yao lu* kan Songchu sichao zhi junshi yu zhengzhi"; and Chang Jianhua, "Cong *Zun Yao lu* kan Luo Congyan de zhengzhi sixiang."

[21] Liang Tianxi, "Cong *Zun Yao lu* kan Songchu," 203–6.

of the Mean that the mind of the sovereign, properly cultivated and aligned, is the ultimate origin of political order.[22] The first commentary in the book explicates an entry dated 960 about how Taizu approved a recommendation from Shen Lun 沈倫 (909–987), over the objections of others, that excess army stores be distributed to starving populations in Yangzhou 揚州 and Sizhou 泗州. Luo invokes the *Book of Documents* and *Mencius* to explain the relationship between a prosperous population and national stability: because grain comes from the labor of the people, and the army must consume grain to function as a source of order, the excess stored grain should be used to ensure the viability of the population in these areas.[23]

Luo also weighs in heavily on the side of "virtue" (*xian*) and "moral authority" (*de* 德) over "talent" (*cai* 才) as a fundamental requisite and a basic criterion for appointment to high office. It is the prime responsibility of the sovereign to distinguish the former from the latter when making appointments.[24] The final responsibility of the sovereign is to accept honest remonstrance and to keep the Censorate and remonstrance organs of government open, properly staffed, and robust.[25] All four of these categories derive from the Yuanyou discourse of opposition to the New Policies. And all four topics would soon become important conceptual frameworks for analyzing the political and economic problems of Southern Song.

New History for a New Regime

As Luo labored away in distant Fujian on his handbook for dynastic restoration, the fall of Kaifeng and the ascension of Emperor Gaozong on 1127/5/1 changed the personalities and the very definition of that restoration. But the fault lines from the 1126 debates lived on and intensified now that the Restoration had become hard political reality rather than abstract intellectual exercise. The historical vision of Renzong florescence that had emerged amid the internecine feuding during the last days of Kaifeng assumed new importance as the young emperor struggled to find political support and a historical narrative that would legitimate his ascension to his older brother's still-occupied throne.

On the second day of the new reign, Gaozong commanded that the existing veritable records composed during the 1090s be corrected to remove the slanderous accusation that Empress Gao had plotted to thwart the ascension

---

[22] *Zun Yao lu*, 1.116–17; Liang Tianxi, "*Zun Yao lu* shishi shuzheng," 70 (#39). See also *Zun Yao lu*, Liang Tianxi, "*Zun Yao lu* shishi shuzheng," 102 (#154), where Emperor Renzong begins the custom of distributing copies of the *Zhongyong* to *jinshi* recipients.

[23] *Zun Yao lu*, 1.109–10; Liang Tianxi, "*Zun Yao lu* shishi shuzheng," 60 (#9).

[24] *Zun Yao lu*, 5.168, 6.189–90; Liang Tianxi, "*Zun Yao lu* shishi shuzheng," 113–14, 133 (#189, 243).

[25] For examples, see Liang Tianxi, "Cong *Zun Yao lu* kan Songchu," 205–6; Chang Jianhua, "Cong *Zun Yao lu* kan Luo Congyan de zhengzhi sixiang," 35–36.

of the future Emperor Zhezong in favor of her own son.[26] There were at least two related issues behind his order. First, one of the few remaining Song "royals" not in Jurchen captivity was Empress Meng 孟皇后 (1077–1135), who, like Empress Gao, had opposed the New Policies, and had been removed as empress in 1096, reinstated in 1100 with the title "the Yuanyou Empress," and then demoted to the status of a Daoist nun in 1102. In 1126/4, the Jurchen quisling Zhang Bangchang rehabilitated her again and installed her as empress dowager in order to legitimate his own regime. However, she immediately endorsed the prospect that Gaozong should become emperor.[27] Her support provided a vital buttress to his own legitimacy and a historical link to the imperial past, a link that conveniently detoured around the New Policies and the embarrassing debacle (and present plight) of his own father and brother. Thus, the political relationship between Empress Meng and the future Emperor Gaozong required a history that validated the Yuanyou legacy. Second, the existing veritable records for the Shenzong and Zhezong reigns had been compiled by Cai Bian and other advocates of the New Policies; they not only "slandered" Empress Gao but criminalized the Yuanyou administrators. The return of these men's descendants to government service in sufficient numbers to legitimate Gaozong's restoration required a historical narrative that would reverse the existing historical verdicts and turn their fathers from criminals into heroes.

Deteriorating military conditions, however, soon overtook such considerations. After the flight south to Hangzhou and the suppression of the Miao–Liu mutiny in 1129/4, Gaozong issued another amnesty. Restating the theoretical underpinnings of the Restoration, the text linked the Renzong florescence, the Yuanyou administration, and the need to replace the existing Huizong-era law code. Among its provisions, the amnesty authorized the offspring of "Yuanyou ministers" to apply for reinstatement of their father's positions. Also, noting the longevity of Renzong's reign, the amnesty called for reinstatement of the Jiayou-period code.[28] As work commenced on the project, however, the difficulty of bringing back the age of florescence as legal reality rather than as historical inspiration soon emerged.

The amnesty provided some general guidelines for revision. For example, where the Jiayou code and the present code, the Zhenghe code of 1111, differed on the severity of a punishment, the lighter punishment was to be adopted. But

---

[26] *Yaolu*, 5.133–32; Zhou Hui, *Qingbo zazhi jiaozhu* 2.39–41.   [27] *Yaolu*, 4.120–21.

[28] The text of this amnesty survives only in fragments, a consequence perhaps of Qin Gui-era manipulation of the historical record. *QSW*, 201:4450.273–74, reprints the longest extract from *Huibian*, 128.8a–b, and appends other shorter fragments. Directly relevant to the discussion here is the passage quoted by Lu You in his 1164 *Zhongxing shengzheng cao*, which is preserved at *Yongle dadian*, 12929.5a. The *QSW* editors, however, have overlooked an important extract at *SHY, xingfa*, 1.33b–34a, that provides guidelines for updating the law code.

the Jiayou code pre-dated the New Policies, and many of the New Policies remained in effect; the earlier code also pre-dated the government reorganization of 1082, and thus, for example, lacked statutes governing the Six Ministries. As a result, in 1130 the Ministry of Justice was authorized to incorporate into the revision all statutes from the existing code that were absent from the Jiayou code.[29] According to Wang Yang 王洋 (1087–1153), a member of the compilation committee, Gaozong's amnesty had mandated an updating of the Jiayou code in the spirit of the policies of the ancestors.[30] But once permission was granted to reference the Zhenghe code, the details were relegated to clerks who were versant in that code, and they copied its statutes verbatim into the revision. Wang concluded that instead of reviving the spirit of the Renzong-era precedents, the new code merely perpetuated the late New Policies world of Cai Jing.[31] The completed work was presented on 1131/8/4 as an amalgam of the Jiayou and Zhenghe statutes and labeled the "Continuing Restoration" (*Shaoxing* 紹興) code to accord with the new reign period that had just begun.[32]

The inability of the revised code to restore the supposed legal foundations of the Renzong florescence could serve as a metaphor for the political predicament of early Southern Song. Between 1125 and 1129, the narrative that blamed the fall of Kaifeng on Wang Anshi's desecration of the founders' policies had become firmly established.[33] Despite the rhetorical appeal of a historical "return," with its adulation of the Renzong era and the Yuanyou administrators, the political establishment that survived the debacle of 1127 – its institutions, its laws, and its personalities – were products of the Huizong era. As military and financial pressures mounted on the new administration, its political divisions continued to widen along the fault lines that Huizong's abdication had opened in 1125/12.

Four days after his ascension Emperor Gaozong chose Li Gang as his first chief councilor. Li had advanced a robust military and negotiating posture against the Jurchen in 1126 and continued to advocate such policies, including moving the court to Xiangyang 襄陽 in order better to co-ordinate among the viable Song military forces that remained in the North. But before Li could arrive at Gaozong's court, Huang Qianshan 黃潛善 (d. 1129), whose good fortune had placed him at Gaozong's side when he ascended the throne, had already convinced the emperor to undertake a defensive move southeast toward

---

[29] *SHY, xingfa*, 1.33b–34a; *Yaolu*, 22.549.
[30] Wang's characterization matches Li Xinchuan's description of the mandate as "to revise and restore the Renzong precedents, to revere and adopt the Jiayou statutes"; see *Chaoye zaji, yi*, 5.592.
[31] *QSW*, 177:3871.105–6; *SHY, xingfa*, 1.34b–35a; *Yaolu*, 36.809.
[32] *SHY, xingfa*, 1.35a; *Yaolu*, 46.975.
[33] See, for example, the heartrending account of the fall of Kaifeng as a culmination of the failed New Policies in the anonymous *Jingkang xiaolu* from 1129 cited at *Huibian*, 96.1a–5a.

the modern city of Nanjing. Political tension between Li and his network and the emerging Huang network marked the early months of the new administration and culminated in the dismissal of Li Gang in 1127/8. Two months later the court moved southeast to Yangzhou.[34]

Hu Anguo's "Plans for the Restoration" and the Return of Qin Gui

During the tumultuous years of 1129–1130, the administration of Huang Qianshan, later joined by Wang Boyan 汪伯彦 (1069–1141), gave way to more competent hands such as Zhu Shengfei, Lü Yihao, and Fan Zongyin. These were seasoned Huizong-era bureaucrats who had survived the 1127 transition with their political networks largely intact. When Qin Gui returned from the North in 1130/10, he found a new emperor surrounded by entrenched political alliances that excluded him. But his uncompromising stance against the Jurchen in 1126 earned him the respect of Li Gang's supporters. Within a year, Qin Gui had formed an ad hoc political network of family members, younger officials, and descendants of Yuanyou administrators whose ban from politics prior to 1126 now rendered them political free agents. The head of the group, and Qin Gui's eventual secretary when he became chief councilor in 1131/8, was Hu Anguo 胡安國 (1074–1133), a scholar of the *Spring and Autumn Annals* and proponent of the learning of Cheng Yi.[35]

In 1129, Hu Anguo authored a series of fourteen essays called simply "Plans for the Restoration" (*Zhongxing ce* 中興策). The series grew into a developed statement of Hu's political and intellectual principles for the Restoration. He seems to have submitted individual essays in response to specific political issues as soon as he arrived at court in late 1131. In 1132/7, he proposed that the completed set of twenty-one "Essays on Contemporary Policy" (*Shizheng lun* 時政論), divided into twelve sectional rubrics, serve as the basis for formal discussion and subsequent adoption as "state policy" (*guoshi* 國是).[36] The series began with a review of the military and economic obstacles facing Restoration, discussed strategic considerations for locating the temporary capital at Jiankang as a base from which to recover the North, and detailed local corruption and governance abuses. Hu then moved to problems of central government organization and process, and concluded with five sections that directly addressed Gaozong's mental attitude and personal resolve. Sections

---

[34] For details see Hartman and Li, "The Rehabilitation of Chen Dong," 84–90.

[35] For a detailed discussion see Li and Hartman, "A Newly Discovered Inscription," 433–41; also Gao Jichun, "Qin Gui yu Luoxue."

[36] *QSW*, 146:3146.107–30; *Yuhai*, 62.19b–20a; *Yaolu*, 56.1138–39. Chen Jun inserts long passages from Hu Anguo's tracts in the commentarial portions of his Southern Song history; see *Zhongxing gangmu*, 1.25–26, 2.63, 63–65, 73–74, 3.111, and 4.159–62.

Six and Seven, "The Establishment of Government" (*Lizheng* 立政) and "The Verification of Truth" (*Heshi* 覈實) contain the kernel of Hu's thoughts on government structure and the political process. We focus here on his use of history in these sections and its relation to the politics of 1131–1132. These two sections simultaneously call for a return to Renzong-era government and issue a partisan attack on Qin Gui's political rivals – Lü Yihao, Zhu Shengfei, and Fan Zongyin.

Section Six takes its title from a chapter in the *Book of Documents* where the Duke of Zhou opines that the sovereign's choice of his three top ministers will determine the success of his rule. These carefully chosen ministers in turn select their subordinate officers to whom they delegate authority, and thus "establish government."[37] Hu Anguo argued that Gaozong's chief councilors, unlike their classical prototypes and despite the administrative reorganization of 1129 that merged the three departments, had failed to impartially staff and delegate authority to the Six Ministries. They neglected their primary duty of personal management and wasted time micromanaging lawsuits and taxation issues. Hu asked that Gaozong approve a request, first made by Sima Guang in 1086, to depute authorization to decide routine matters to the Six Ministries and thus simplify, and elevate, the duties of the councilors.[38] Hu then moved to a political denunciation of those responsible for these failures. He linked Huang Qianshan and his allies to the quisling government of Zhang Bangchang, to those who failed to defend Kaifeng, and to those who supported the Miao–Liu mutiny. He compared Zhang to Huafu Du 華父督 (d. 682 BCE), a minister of the ancient state of Song who murdered his fellow minister and his ruler, then bribed neighboring states, which shortly fell into political chaos, to accept his actions.[39] Hu thus implied that Gaozong's failure to punish Zhang Bangchang's collaborators likewise undermined imperial authority and imperiled the Restoration.

The next essay, "Verification of Truth," linked the image of Renzong florescence with Li Gang's role in recent history and, by implication, with Qin Gui's struggle against his political opponents. The essay draws parallels between the vitality of the remonstrance function under Renzong and its present weakness. Referencing the 1129/4 amnesty, Hu emphasized that the excellence of Renzong's governance resided in its balance of power between chief councilors and remonstrance officials. This balance insured that administrative decisions, especially personnel actions, were based on "truth" rather than "slander." The process was open and fair, therefore the public accepted punishment for bad actors like Ding Wei; and unjust slander against Kou Zhun, Fan Zhongyan, and

[37] *QSW*, 146:3146.120–22; Legge, *The Shoo King*, 508–22.
[38] For Sima Guang's memorial see Zhao Ruyu, *Songchao zhuchen zouyi*, 58.641–42.
[39] Legge, *The Ch'un Ts'ew*, 37–40.

Ouyang Xiu was successfully refuted. In contrast, Hu reviewed the political fates of the first three councilors under the new Restoration – Li Gang, Huang Qianshan, and Wang Boyan. Li Gang, slandered by Zheng Ku 鄭轂 (*jinshi* 1118), was dismissed and suffered distant exile, while Zheng was rewarded with promotion. Ma Shen 馬伸 (d. 1129), who had publicly criticized Huang Qianshan and Wang Boyan, was summarily executed by his critics. Huang and Wang then "closed down the speakers' road" and dismissed critics like Xu Han 許翰 (d. 1133), Yang Shi, Wu Ji 吳給, and Xu Jingheng 許景衡 (1072–1128). Hu Anguo concluded that such violations of "public opinion" must be redressed through a vigorous finding of truth, a purge of the slanderers, and rehabilitation for the victims and their offspring. Only in this way "can we restore the governance of Renzong."[40]

Thirteenth-century historians linked "Verification of Truth" to the transition of the councilorship from Fan Zongyin to Qin Gui in 1131/8. Five days after Qin Gui began his term, the court restored the academic titles of Li Gang, Xu Han, and another ally; and Li Gang's career enjoyed a brief resurgence.[41] In short, Hu Anguo's denunciation of Fan Zongyin's administration and its antecedents, his attempt to link Fan to the traitor Zhang Bangchang, and his insistence that Gaozong must purge these elements in order to preserve the Restoration were all intended to create political space for the new administration of Qin Gui, in which Hu believed there would be a role for Li Gang and his network.[42]

By emphasizing the vitality of its "public opinion," Hu's tract deepens the motif of the Renzong florescence, and the period's historical actors begin to assume the morally "good" and "bad" tags they will carry throughout subsequent history. More significantly, the essays demonstrate how the political dichotomies of early Southern Song generated a historical view that linked supporters of Li Gang such as Yang Shi, Ma Shen, Wu Ji, and Xu Jingheng back to their supposed *daoxue* origins in the Yuanyou period and thus to the Renzong florescence.[43] On the other hand, Li Gang's opponents, Huang Qianshan, Lü Yihao, Zhu Shengfei, and Fan Zongyin, would be framed as heirs of Cai Jing and precursors of the autocracy to come under Qin Gui. Qin Gui's first term as councilor ended in failure, and he would soon change tactics. But the alignment of contemporary policy, intellectual orientation, and historical vision that Hu Anguo created for Qin Gui's political use would endure and would soon pass to other hands.

---

[40] *QSW*, 146:3146.122–24.   [41] *Yaolu*, 46.980–81.

[42] Several weeks before the end of Qin Gui's tenure as councilor on 1132/8/27, Hu recommended Li Gang for major office; see *Yaolu*, 57.1149–50. For Hu's parting shot at Lü Yihao and Zhu Shengfei see *Yaolu*, 57.1153.

[43] For documentation of this process see Li Xinchuan, *Daoming lu*, 3.22–23, 27–30; *Yongle dadian*, 8,164.8b–9b, 11b–14b.

Zhao Ding, Fan Chong, and the Yuanyou Legacy

Several months after the amnesty of 1129/4, Zhao Ding, a refugee official from the North, submitted a series of memorials that negatively contrasted the pre-1067 Renzong florescence with the present. His review of Northern Song history stressed the importance of Empress Gao as a link back to the ancestors (and around Wang Anshi) because she "used Renzong's policies and used Renzong's people." Unfortunately, Zhao continued, Cai Jing had convinced Huizong to "be filial" and to resume the New Policies. Zhao argued further that surviving remnants from the Cai Jing and Wang Fu networks had successfully managed to "slow-walk" Qinzong's 1126 mandate to reverse the New Policies. He insisted that "public opinion" demanded more extensive measures to degrade these networks, and he advocated increased sanctions on Cai Jing's family and removal of Wang Anshi's status as acolyte in Shenzong's shrine. He also suggested that while the amnesty's focus on the "benevolence of the benevolent emperor" was appropriate, Renzong's achievements had built upon and continued the "martial qualities of Emperor Taizu." The Restoration demanded a balanced focus upon both, and Zhao recommended that Gaozong look to the first emperor for martial precedents.[44] We will see in the next chapter how soon and how literally Gaozong took this advice.

Zhao Ding was among the few officials who personally accompanied Gaozong on his flight to the open sea in 1129–1130, an experience that forged a strong bond between the two men. After their return to land, Zhao settled in Quzhou 衢州, where his affinal relative Fan Chong had just finished a tour as prefect. Fan Chong's son, Fan Zhongxiong 范仲熊, was married to Zhao Ding's daughter. This marriage connected Zhao to the heart of the Yuanyou administration, for Fan Chong was the son of Fan Zuyu, who had been principal author of the first *Shenzong Veritable Records* in 1091, and Sima Guang's collaborator on the *Comprehensive Mirror*. Another son of Fan Chong, Fan Zhongbiao 范仲彪, had married Sima Guang's granddaughter. Because both her father and her brother had died early, she was Sima Guang's only direct heir. Fan Chong thus came into the possession of Sima Guang's papers, and took responsibility for his remaining immediate family.

In his previous position, Fan Chong had begun to print the *Comprehensive Mirror*, but his successor halted the work in 1129/3 on the ground that Sima Guang had been a "nefarious person" and the book constituted "heterodox theory."[45] The court removed the official, and the printing was complete by 1133; but the incident reveals the nature and strength of the political forces against which Zhao Ding complained. Nonetheless, the court's public nod toward "benevolence," with its attendant historiographical needs, placed Fan

---

[44] *Yaolu*, 24.575; *QSW*, 174:3806.230–35.   [45] *Yaolu*, 26.606.

Chong in an enviable position as recipient of the manuscript legacy of both Sima Guang and Fan Zuyu. In 1130/7, Xie Kejia 謝克家 (d. 1134) requested that Fan Chong submit a copy of his father's *Emperor Ren's Instructions and Statutes*, the work that had begun the motif of Renzong florescence in 1093.[46] In the surviving preface, Fan Zuyu posits Renzong's benevolence back to Taizu the founder. He first taps into well-established Daoist rhetoric that made Taizu "divinely martial."[47] To this, however, he joins two other motifs: (1) because Taizu's "benevolence equaled Heaven," he was able to acquire the empire without killing; (2) because he bypassed his own sons and delivered the empire to his brother, the future Taizong, his actions parallel those of the sage-king Yao, who similarly passed authority not to his son but to his fellow sage, Shun. As a consequence, "magnificent were the founders of our dynasty, one sage succeeding another sage, their rule all honoring benevolence, but Renzong was the purest of these."[48]

War broke out between Song and the Jin buffer state of Qi at the end of 1133. The invasion from the north enhanced the political position of Zhao Ding, who supported a more aggressive Song military than did Zhu Shengfei. As a result, in mid-1134, Gaozong began to advance Zhao Ding into leadership posts; and, as Song generals successfully repulsed the invasion, Zhao eventually replaced Zhu Shengfei as chief councilor in 1134/9. For the first time, the dynasty now had an administration that espoused the historical notion of a Renzong florescence and its supposed continuation during the Yuanyou. Zhao Ding now wielded sufficient political and historiographical resources to imprint this view upon the official record. He also attempted to exploit Fan Chong's unique access to original Yuanyou texts to build an intellectual base upon which to strengthen his own political network. In contrast to the existing networks of Lü Yihao and Zhu Shengfei that were based on Wang Anshi's learning, Zhao sought to employ "Yuanyou learning" as defined by Fan Chong. We will examine below three aspects of Fan Chong's role as Zhao's cultural and political commissar between 1134 and 1136: (1) his revisions to the official Shenzong and Zhezong veritable records, (2) his 1136 edition of Sima Guang's *Su River Records*, and (3) his political use of the writings of the Cheng brothers.

Despite repeated entreaties from Empress Meng, Gaozong had not yet acted on his initial promise to remove the slanders against Empress Gao from the

---

[46] *SHY, chongru*, 5.30a. Xie Kejia was the son of Xie Liangzuo 謝良佐, considered in the 1130s as one of the three principal disciples of the Cheng brothers; see Li and Hartman, "A Newly Discovered Inscription," 440.

[47] The phrase *shenwu* derives from the *Yijing* (see Wilhelm, *The I Ching*, 317), is early associated with Taizu, and became part of Taizu's official title; see *Changbian*, 1.28, 9.207, 16.344.

[48] *Fan Taishi ji*, 36.10a–12a; *QSW*, 98:2145.258–59. The preface was commonly cited in Southern Song: see Lü Zuqian, *Song wenjian*, 91.1286–87; also Chen Jun, *Huangchao gangmu*, 23.574, where the passage translated above is featured.

veritable records.[49] The political ascendency of Zhao Ding, however, changed the politics of the issue, and in 1134/5 he appointed Fan Chong to the history office. Zhu Shengfei, still councilor, protested on two grounds. He questioned whether Fan Chong could be objective. The Cai brothers had criminalized Fan's father for his initial version of the *Shenzong Veritable Records*, then rewritten that version to suit their own needs. He doubted that Fan Chong could produce a third version that would satisfy Cai's political heirs. Second, Fan Chong's marriage connection to Zhao Ding disqualified him on technical grounds for the position. The emperor overruled his councilor on both counts and granted Fan a dispensation to accept the post, appointing Chang Tong 常同 (d. 1149) to assist in the work. In his previous post as censor, Chang Tong, whose father had suffered twenty years in exile for opposing Zhang Dun and Cai Jing, had attacked prominent members of Lü Yihao's network for their previous associations with Cai Jing and Wang Fu.[50] The emperor's insistence that Fan Chong and Chang Tong revise the veritable records shows his determination to produce a historical narrative with a pro-Yuanyou perspective.[51]

In actuality, the emperor and Fan Chong each had their own motivation for revising the historical record. Soon after appointing Fan, the emperor asked him how he planned to proceed. Fan began by positing the immutable nature of the "policies of the ancestors." By the Renzong period, however, the system had developed a few foibles. Lü Yijian preferred minor adjustments, but Fan Zhongyan wanted drastic change. Although the two differed on policy, Lü recognized Fan's integrity, and Fan eventually realized the impractical nature of his former aspirations.[52] Wang Anshi, however, deceived Emperor Shenzong, defamed and attacked his predecessors, and totally changed the policies. Fan emphasized that "the origin of the subsequent chaos was Wang Anshi; none of this was Shenzong's idea." The Yuanyou administrators had attempted to "return to the antiquity" of the ancestors. To which Gaozong replied, "Precisely. I treasure Yuanyou the most."[53]

---

[49] *Yaolu*, 40.881; *SS*, 243.8637, 382.11772–73. For a collection of relevant sources see Xu Peizao, "Song Gaozong yu *Shen Zhe shilu*."

[50] *Yaolu*, 73.1395–96; *SS*, 376.11625–26.

[51] *Yaolu*, 76.1440, 77.1460–61, 79.1497–98; Cai Chongbang, *Songdai xiushi zhidu yanjiu*, 88–92. As Li Xinchuan pointed out in his account of these revisions, the loss of Kaifeng deprived the early Southern court of access to the official copies of all the state histories. Furthermore, the court's shifting location in the early years hampered efforts to locate copies of the works in the south; see *Chaoye zaji, jia*, 7.109. Serious efforts to rebuild the court's historical archives seem to have begun only in 1133; see *SHY, chongru*, 4.22b–23b.

[52] This characterization of the Qingli reform and the relationship between Lü Yijian and Fan Zhongyan differs substantially from later twelfth-century views, which demonize Lü and sanctify Fan. This later view projected the moral and political dichotomies of the late Northern Song back to the Renzong period. Fan Chong's analysis, however, preserves the notion of Renzong florescence and the continuity of the policies of the ancestors from Taizu through Renzong.

[53] *Yaolu*, 79.1487–88; *Songshi quanwen*, 19A.1355–56. Interestingly, the *Songshi quanwen* text omits the phrase "I treasure Yuanyou the most."

Fan Chong emphasized that his father had intended, by his detailed account of New Policies failures in the first *Shenzong Veritable Records*, to place sole blame for those failures on Wang and thus to highlight the genuine achievements of Shenzong's rule. Fan likewise absolved Zhezong by explaining that the "continuation" was not Zhezong's continuing the policies of Shenzong, but Cai Jing continuing the policies of Wang Anshi. Fan admitted he had never seen the *Zhezong Veritable Records*, but they agreed the text was "nothing but the private opinion of nefarious ministers."[54] He agreed to remove the slander of Empress Gao, whom Gaozong proclaimed "the best of our empresses." Fan even attempted to absolve Huizong of responsibility for the persecution of the Yuanyou officials by citing a poetic couplet of the emperor that implied that Cai Jing should treat them lightly "so they need not fear coming home." In a slight rebuke to his father, Gaozong remarked that if, instead of writing poetry, Huizong had issued an edict and appointed several of the Yuanyou administrators to office, "this matter could have then been set right."

Agreed that the revisions will absolve the imperial house of Zhao, emperor and historian moved next to contemporary political considerations. Gaozong wondered why so many officials still trusted Wang Anshi and were actively promoting the New Policies. In reply, Fan Chong quoted an opinion he had heard from Cheng Yi: the New Policies were not the most harmful of Wang's legacies, since the emperor could easily reverse them. Rather the pernicious character of Wang's machinations, bent on personal profit, had infected the entire country and had now become the normal mentality of the dynasty. As evidence, Fan quoted a couplet from Wang's famous poem on Wang Zhaojun 王昭君, in which Wang portrayed with sympathy the affection that the heroine had developed for her barbarian family. Fan's Wang Zhaojun analogy connects the profit-oriented motive of Wang Anshi thought to the disloyalty of those Song officials who had defected to Liu Yu's rival Qi dynasty. And Cheng Yi thus became an oracle of Gaozong's most immediate problem.

Between Fan's initial appointment and 1134/8, when this conversation took place, Yue Fei had retaken Xiangyang; but the Song court was still ramping up a propaganda and military offensive against Liu Yu, the outcome of which would remain uncertain until late 1134.[55] These guidelines for revisions to the veritable records thus represent a bargain made at a historically specific moment between Gaozong and the emerging Zhao Ding network. First, by absolving the imperial ancestors of complicity in the New Policies, the new history will buttress Emperor Gaozong as heir to an unblemished imperial

---

[54] The history office did not acquire a copy of the *Zhezong shilu* until 1135/5. *Shilu* text for the final months of 1092 and the entire year of 1093, when Empress Gao was alleged to have plotted to thwart the ascension of Zhezong, was still missing as late as 1136/5 when Fan Chong issued a special call for this material; see *SHY, chongru*, 4.24b.

[55] For details see Li and Hartman, "Primary Sources for Song History," 323–33.

legacy and thus enhance his legitimacy against the rival state of Qi. Thus divorced from its erstwhile imperial sponsors, the revised, and now negative, political legacy of Wang Anshi and Cai Jing can be freely attached to Gaozong's political opponents – at the moment, Liu Yu and his supporters.[56] Second, by reversing the legal verdicts on the Yuanyou officials, enhancing the teachings of the Cheng brothers, and downgrading the politics of New Policies "continuers" such as Zhang Dun and Cai Jing, the new history will enhance the political capital of the emerging administration of Zhao Ding, who will soon replace Zhu Shengfei as chief councilor. In essence, the revised history will historically and politically legitimize the subordinates in Zhao Ding's network, and downgrade those in the rival networks of Lü Yihao and Zhu Shengfei. If Gaozong would truly "treasure Yuanyou," he will need more officials conversant with the insights of Cheng Yi. As we shall see below, Zhao Ding and Fan Chong intended to provide such officials through the mechanism of the triennial *jinshi* examinations the following year.

As implied in Fan Chong's opening analysis of the Renzong period, the new history's re-evaluation of the Yuanyou legacy implied a continuity between the two eras and thus enshrined in official history the notion of a Renzong florescence. Even though the existing histories of the Renzong period were not revised, the new history of the subsequent periods shaped the interpretation of the earlier period and created a Qingli–Yuanyou axis that would come to ground the grand allegory. The revised *Shenzong Veritable Records* were completed in 1136/1, and plans were soon drafted for revisions to the *Zhezong Veritable Records* as well, which were in turn completed in 1138/6.[57] Although subsequent political gyrations in 1137 and 1138 spawned yet another attempt to revise these histories, the project was abandoned. When Qin Gui re-emerged as chief councilor in 1138, neither his politics nor his policies required historical revisionism. Fan Chong's versions became "flash-frozen" in time as the definitive account of the Shenzong and Zhezong reigns, from 1067 through 1100, and, as we have seen in Chapter 2, this account then passed to Li Tao and into the standard history of Song.

As Zhao Ding's commissar of history and culture, Fan Chong also restated the case for Sima Guang's historical and political importance. He then crafted from Sima's remaining manuscripts an edition of the *Su River Records* that supported this assessment. As we have seen in Chapter 2, Li Tao relied extensively on this collection of Sima's notes to color his narrative in the *Long Draft*. Naturally, as the historical take on Wang Anshi turned increasingly negative after 1126, the take on Sima Guang grew in proportion increasingly

---

[56] For a Hu Yin memorial of 1135/5 that makes much the same argument, equating appeasement of the Qi and Jin with the legacy of Wang Anshi and Cai Jing, see *Yaolu*, 89.1720–22.

[57] *Yaolu*, 97.1854, 105.1973, 120.2234; Cai Chongbang, *Songdai xiushi zhidu yanjiu*, 98–101.

positive. Fan Chong's immediate printing of the *Comprehensive Mirror* in the south, his revisions to the veritable records for the reigns in which Sima Guang had opposed the New Policies, and his edition of the *Su River Records* profoundly influenced Sima Guang's historical image and insured that Sima Guang's political views would dominate the emerging narrative of Northern Song history. In short, while Fan Chong positioned his grandfather-in-law historically as the seminal literatus official on whom the continuity of the dynasty had depended, he also positioned his father-in-law Zhao Ding politically as the contemporary leader best able to effect that continuity.

The book known today as the *Su River Records* began as a collection of notes that Sima Guang kept on contemporary affairs – a daybook of personal experiences, political happenings, and gossip. Li Tao once saw several pages from Sima Guang's holograph *Diary* (*Riji* 日記), and wrote in his colophon on the manuscript that Sima Guang and Liu Shu 劉恕 (1032–1078) had intended to use such material in an unrealized "long-draft" sequel that would extend the historical narrative of the *Comprehensive Mirror* into the Song. He noted that in addition to the diary, there were also the *Su River Records* and another work called *Monthly Notes* (*Shuoji* 朔記), but that the versions of these works then in circulation were all fragmentary. Although Sima's heirs had carefully preserved the holographs in his ancestral temple during the inquisition, after 1126 they had become dispersed. He related that the diary pages he saw contained three categories of notes: (1) events that Sima had personally witnessed, (2) events about which he had heard from a participant, and (3) events about which he had heard through a third party. Some of the events differed from accounts in the official histories, and Li Tao believed that Sima Guang had preserved this material for eventual comparison against the official sources using "Sima's long-draft method to detect what was true."[58]

The story of the transmission of this material from Sima's holographs to the modern editions is complex and contested.[59] The revisionist historian Cai Shangxiang 蔡上翔 (1717–1810) maintained in 1804 that the work was not by Sima Guang but by later writers intent on slandering Wang Anshi.[60] No early printed editions survive; modern editions derive from Ming and Qing manuscript copies that represent at least three different "systems" of *juan* division, each probably descended from a different Southern Song edition. Despite this absence of surviving Song imprints, the work was nevertheless accessible and popular in Southern Song. Three twelfth-century works alone

---

[58] *Wenxian tongkao*, 197.5683; *QSW*, 210:4665.238–39.

[59] Deng Guangming and Zhang Xiqing's modern edition appeared at Zhonghua shuju in 1989, with a preface by Deng that attempted to refute twelfth-century reservations about the text and defend Sima Guang as its author. For a careful review of these reservations see Yu Jiaxi, *Siku tiyao bianzheng*, 892–95.

[60] Cai Shangxiang, *Wang Jinggong nianpu kaolüe*, preface, 2.

cite over two-thirds of the 496 entries in Deng Guangming's edition.[61] However, many Southern Song scholars doubted that all of this material had originated from Sima Guang's holograph. Specifically, Lü Benzhong 呂本中 (1084–1145) charged that Fan Chong had forged many entries, including several sections that cast his ancestor Lü Yijian in a bad light.[62] In the twelfth century, the opinion that many entries did not originate with Sima Guang was widespread.[63] For example, in his list of problematic "wild histories," Li Daxing wrote that "although the *Su River Records* go back to Sima Guang, there are many later additions."[64]

Because of Sima Guang's emerging centrality to the new revisionist history of Northern Song, when Emperor Gaozong learned of the work, he ordered Zhao Ding to tell Fan Chong to edit the material. In 1136/8 Fan Chong explained to Gaozong the history of Sima's holograph in terms that echo Li Tao's colophon: little remained of Sima's papers; the holograph notes were inchoate and incomplete, so Sima's heirs never showed them to anyone, but some material nonetheless had leaked into circulation. Therefore, Fan warned, producing a definitive edition would be difficult. He would edit the remaining holograph as lightly as possible, because, "in essence, although this book is not totally trustworthy, there is much here that can benefit good governance." Fan Chong arranged the material into ten fascicules and submitted them to court. And Li Xinchuan remarks that "his book now circulates widely."[65]

Also (and still) at issue is the relationship between Sima Guang's posthumous papers and the first edition, the so-called "black" edition of the *Shenzong Veritable Records*, completed by Fan Zuyu in 1091. Wang Mingqing related that the editors of the "black edition" had incorporated many of the *Su River Records* in order to color their negative evaluation of the New Policies. As a result, Cai Jing and Cai Bian excised these passages and inserted material from Wang Anshi's diary in the subsequent "red" edition. Deng Guangming has attempted to refute Wang Mingqing's contention, but he ignores the fact that Sima Guang's son, Sima Kang 司馬康 (1050–1090), served on the initial compilation committee together with Fan Zuyu and that Sima Kang deferred to Fan on most matters.[66] In 1100, Xu Ji 徐勣 (1046–1124) stated directly that

[61] Deng, *Sushui jiwen*, preface, 11–12 tabulates as follows: 196 entries in Jiang Shaoyu's *Shishi leiyuan* of 1145; 212 entries in Li Tao's *Long Draft* of 1183, and 128 entries in Zhu Xi's *Mingchen yanxing lu* series.

[62] Zhu Xi, *Wuchao mingchen yanxing lu*, 9.282–83; Wang Deyi, "Lü Yijian yu Fan Zhongyan," 182 n. 31.

[63] See, for example, Wu Zeng, *Nenggaizhai manlu*, 4.86–87; and Chen Zhensun, *Zhizhai shulu jieti*, 5.150.

[64] *Wenxian tongkao*, 200.5755; *QSW*, 259:5828.170–71.

[65] *Yaolu*, 104.1954–55. Deng, *Sushui jiwen*, preface, 3, omits Li Xinchuan's remark from his citation of this passage.

[66] Deng, *Sushui jiwen*, preface, 14–17; Cai Chongbang, *Songdai xiushi zhidu yanjiu*, 82–4.

because the "black" edition had relied heavily upon "notes stored in Sima Guang's house" and that because the Cai brothers had used Wang's diary, therefore the private notes of other leading officials from that time should be incorporated into yet another revision.[67]

If, as seems likely, Fan Zuyu and Sima Kang did introduce material from Sima Guang's posthumous papers into the first *Shenzong Veritable Records*, and if some of that material circulated subsequently as the *Su River Records*, then we can understand why Gaozong, Zhao Ding, and Fan Chong would be eager to insure that the *Su River Records* did not conflict with the just-revised official history. After all the evidence is considered, the present *Su River Records*, as reconstructed by Deng Guangming, reads best as precisely what the majority of twelfth-century scholars held it to be: draft notes by Sima Guang considerably enhanced in the mid-1130s by Fan Chong to meet the political needs of Emperor Gaozong and the Zhao Ding network.[68] A week after submitting his edition of the *Su River Records*, Fan Chong recommended Gou Tao 句濤 (d. 1141) for office. At audience, the emperor and Gou agreed that current policy should be based on "the policies of Jiayou and the administration of Yuanyou," precisely the two periods during which Sima Guang had been most active in government and which are thus treated in detail in Fan Chong's edition.[69]

Although it is impossible to determine how much of any single entry in the received *Su River Records* is Sima Guang and how much is Fan Chong, the assemblage and organization of the entire work accord with the major themes of post-1126 historical revisionism. The work's strong anti-Wang Anshi character grounds the work's perspective of a Taizu–Jiayou–Yuanyou axis of excellence in administrative practice. Many entries provide either positive or negative examples of institutionalist principles of governance, such as the proper relationship between ruler and minister or the centrality of a robust remonstrance function. Based on such principles, the work's constellation of positive (Kou Zhun, Fan Zhongyan, Han Qi, Sima Guang) versus negative (Wang Qinruo, Ding Wei, Wang Anshi) ministerial exemplars aligns well with later evaluations.

Fan Chong's recommendation of Gou Tao may illustrate yet a third dimension of his role in Zhao Ding's network – the historian as arbiter of political

---

[67] *Dongdu shilüe*, 105.1a; *Changbian shibu*, 16.603–4; *SS*, 348.11025. Deng Guangming (preface, 16–17) dismisses the relevance of this passage because it does not specifically name the *Su River Records* as among the "notes stored in Sima Guang's house."

[68] This view coincides largely with that of Yu Jiaxi; see note 59 above. Deng's edition suffers from a certain degree of circularity. Given the lack of Song imprints, he has reconstructed the text of many passages from quotations in later twelfth-century works. But these are the very passages whose attribution to Sima Guang twelfth-century observers questioned. For one example of this problem see Ji, *Politics and Conservatism in Northern Song China*, 208–9 n. 34.

[69] *Yaolu*, 104.1958.

pedigree. Fan Chong's historical revisionism went hand in hand with his role in the hardball politics of network creation, maintenance, and conflict. The 1126 tilt toward Yuanyou initiated a gradual removal of sanctions on the original Yuanyou administrators and their offspring, and a corresponding imposition of similar restrictions on their historical opponents and their offspring. The first such personnel action under Gaozong took place in 1127/7 when Li Jizhong, who had been sanctioned as recently as 1125/4 for his activity as a "Yuanfu submitter" (an official included on an 1102 list of those who had submitted policy criticism during the Yuanfu period, 1098–1100) was appointed prefect of Xiangyang.[70] Efforts accelerated throughout 1130 and 1131 to expedite this process.[71] For example, as soon as Qin Gui became councilor in 1131/8, he restored the academic titles of Su Shi and dismissed the three grandsons of Zhang Dun from capital office.[72] The inquisitions of the early Huizong years had generated lists of Yuanyou sympathizers, including those on the list of "Yuanfu submitters" and the 309 names on the "Yuanyou faction stele" of 1104. But because this documentation no longer survived, the court requested in 1131/10 that Yuanyou descendants submit their own claims to receive appointment to office.[73] However, with no access to proper documentation, the Ministry of Personnel had difficulty verifying these claims. Furthermore, it was acknowledged that Cai Jing had included on the lists many of his personal and political enemies who had no connection to Yuanyou policy and whose descendants thus should have no valid claim to current office.[74]

When Zhao Ding became councilor in 1134/9, he took steps to strengthen his own network and to degrade those of his opponents. In 1135/6, for example, Liu Dazhong 劉大中 (jinshi 1109), who had worked with Fan Chong on the *Shenzong Veritable Records*, denied the request of Deng Xiang 鄧襄 for a posthumous promotion for his father Deng Xunren 鄧洵仁 (d. 1135). Liu objected that the entire Deng family had been fervent and corrupt supporters of Wang Anshi and Cai Jing; therefore, a promotion for Deng Xunren conflicted with the current policy to advance Yuanyou men and their values. Zhao Ding then convinced the emperor to prohibit such requests on behalf of any official who had served in senior positions between 1102 and 1125 and to review the careers of all such officials who had served since 1067.[75] Zhang Jun, Zhao Ding's uneasy partner as co-councilor, warned that a policy of promotion based on ancestry or on the supposed political purity of one period over another was not sound administration.[76]

---

[70] *Yaolu*, 7.197; *SS*, 23.429; *SHY, zhiguan*, 69.17a–b; Gao Jichun, "Song Gaozong chao chunian de Wang Anshi pipan yu Luoxue zhi xing," 142.
[71] *Yaolu*, 35.799–800, 41.889.   [72] *Yaolu*, 46.966, 978.   [73] *Yaolu*, 48.1004.
[74] *Yaolu*, 67.1315; 73.1400.   [75] *Yaolu*, 90.1743–44; *Chaoye zaji, jia*, 5.120–21.
[76] *QSW*, 187:4124.355–58.

Nevertheless, throughout 1135 the political prospects of Yuanyou descendants and the number of claims to Yuanyou status rose dramatically. Absent a definitive list of those eligible for the Yuanyou preferment, Gaozong in 1136/4 eventually appointed Fan Chong and Ren Shenxian 任申先 (d. 1138), both sons of well-known Yuanyou officials, to screen claims to Yuanyou status.[77] Obviously, the emperor thought that Fan Chong's command of the historical sources, both his current work on the official veritable records and his access to private Yuanyou manuscript collections, would enable him to differentiate between legitimate and spurious claims to appointment via the Yuanyou preferment. Throughout this period, Fan submitted numerous recommendations for officials based on their Yuanyou status, including those for descendants of Lü Gongzhu and Sima Guang.[78]

According to the diary of his political adversary Zhu Shengfei, in addition to such appointments Fan Chong also attempted to turn the *jinshi* examinations of 1135 into a recruitment vehicle for the Zhao Ding network. Zhu explained how Fan Chong, claiming to have inherited manuscripts from Cheng Yi, printed and distributed these tracts as "Yichuan learning" to potential political allies. Zhu believed, however, that Fan Chong and his associates had themselves written these "shallow and vulgar pamphlets." When final placement of the candidates was determined at the palace examination, top places were given to those whose papers displayed mastery of "Yichuan learning."[79] Wang Yingchen, whose surviving paper indeed displays "Yichuan learning," was placed first.[80] Wang would subsequently play a leading role in the literati politics of the 1160s and, as we have seen in Chapter 2, was a major supporter of Li Tao.

By late 1136, however, both international and domestic politics began to erode Zhao Ding's position as councilor. As the rift between Zhao Ding and Zhang Jun widened, Zhao left the councilorship in 1136/12. Several weeks later, Chen Gongfu, with support from the now sole chief councilor Zhang Jun, protested against Zhao Ding's biased promotion of "Yichuan learning." His charge expands the implication in Zhu Shengfei's diary that Zhao Ding and Fan Chong had promoted Cheng Yi's teachings as a mechanism to build their own factional network. Significantly, Chen Gongfu framed this charge within the historical context of the Renzong florescence motif that Fan Chong himself had championed. He argued that the pre-1067 court embraced an impartial administrative style that fostered open debate, contained factionalism, and promoted harmony among officials. In contrast, once the court embraced Wang Anshi's "partial ideas" (*si yi* 私意), network factionalism destroyed administrative efficiency. Espousing a nondoctrinaire approach to the classic texts, free from

---

[77] *Yaolu*, 97.1848, 100.1898; *Chaoye zaji, jia*, 5.120.   [78] *Yaolu*, 103.1942, 104.1954–55.

[79] Li Xinchuan cites this passage from Zhu Shengfei's diary in the commentary at *Yaolu*, 88.-1708–9; see also Li and Hartman, "A Newly Discovered Inscription," 439.

[80] For the examinations of 1135 see Fu Xuancong, *Song dengkeji kao*, 702–21.

the partial explication of any single perspective, Chen cast Zhao Ding's support for Cheng Yi's teachings as a resurgence of the factional politics of the Cai Jing era. If not curtailed, this tendency would destroy Emperor Gaozong's drive to "restore the age of the ancestors."[81] Chen's memorial thus laid the intellectual groundwork for removing Zhao Ding's network members from power.

Although Zhao Ding returned briefly as councilor between 1137/9 and 1138/10, shortly after Qin Gui's return to the office in 1138/3, the last remnants of Zhao Ding's network, including Fan Chong, had left the capital.[82] The Jin dynasty in 1137/11 had dissolved the buffer state of Qi in preparation for entering into peace negotiations with the Song. Qin Gui was made councilor to negotiate the peace, and he remained in office until his death in 1155. Qin Gui had long ago abandoned his earlier embrace of Cheng learning; his own politics now eschewed any doctrinal "partiality," and he ruthlessly used Zhao Ding's and Zhang Jun's doctrinal inclinations against them. Although his personal training and preference favored Wang Anshi, Qin Gui publicly embraced an "impartial" stance toward educational policy that, by denying primacy to either Wang Anshi or Cheng Yi learning, promoted the authority of the monarchy.[83] As Chen Gongfu's memorial had made clear, such impartiality could be easily portrayed historically as a continuation of the Renzong florescence. Although Qin Gui persecuted Zhao Ding, literally to death in 1147, neither he nor Gaozong saw the need to abandon the new history that the abandoned politics of the mid-1130s had generated. After the peace treaty was concluded, Qin Gui and Gaozong agreed they should end the decades of doctrinal disputes about governance by returning to the "old policies of the ancestors" and "restoring the Qingli and Jiayou models."[84]

As a disciple of Wang Anshi, Qin Gui had little use for history. Although he expressed reservations about Fan Chong's work on the *Zhezong Veritable Records*, both he and Gaozong were content to let the revisions stand.[85] At the same time, as we have seen in the Introduction and Chapters 1 and 3, Qin Gui severely curtailed the operations of the court history office and enforced a ban on private histories. This ban attempted both to prevent the Zhao Ding

---

[81] *Yaolu*, 107.2019–20; *Daoming lu*, 3.24–25; *Yongle dadian*, 8164.9a–10b. Chen Gongfu had supported Li Gang in 1126, had been recommended by Fan Chong in 1136/6, and had attacked Wang Anshi learning in 1136/7. Thus his attack on Cheng Yi, and especially Zhang Jun's support for his memorial, became a serious historiographical problem once Zhu Xi established Cheng Yi as the fountainhead of *daoxue*. Li Xinchuan's commentary to the *Daoming lu* portrays Chen's memorial as an attempt to secure his own political position in the context of the rift between Zhao Ding and Zhang Jun and Gaozong's diminished enthusiasm for Cheng learning. Zhu Xi's biography of Zhang Jun omits his support for Chen's memorial (*Zhu Xi ji*, 95A.4845). Chen Jun, *Zhongxing gangmu*, 7.253, ruthlessly truncates the memorial, leaving only Chen's reprise of Cheng Yi's teaching and its popularity, and omits all mention of Zhang Jun.

[82] *Yaolu*, 119.2216, 124.2333.
[83] Li and Hartman, "A Newly Discovered Inscription," 410–19.   [84] *Yaolu*, 152.2872, 2873.
[85] *Yaolu*, 162.3065.

network from continuing to practice, even informally, its revisionism of Northern Song history and also to prevent the circulation of historical viewpoints that could be used to oppose the peace policy.[86] For Gaozong also, the peace treaty confirmed his own legitimacy as a Restoration monarch; the slanders against Empress Gao had been corrected; the time for historical revisions was over.[87] The court history office would remain largely dormant until the ascension of Emperor Xiaozong and the arrival of Li Tao in the 1160s.

Thus the concept of the Renzong florescence emerged between 1126 and 1136, almost exclusively as a by-product of the fall of Northern Song, the fixing of responsibility for the disaster, and the politics of the early Restoration. During this period, the theme is largely hortatory – an encouragement to re-establish the Song polity along the lines of an imagined pre-1067 golden age of governance. For, if the fall of Northern Song presented an epic debacle of governance, the ascension of Gaozong presented an opportunity to begin again. What had begun as criticism of the New Policies morphed into a call to remake the Song state in its original purity. But Gaozong and Qin Gui's professed enthusiasm for Renzong-era governance was political theater. As Gaozong noted, many officials openly advocated a return to the New Policies.[88] And the political structures during the Qin Gui years resembled those of the Cai Jing era in which both Gaozong and Qin Gui had come of age.

As imperial propaganda, the rhetoric of the Renzong florescence continued under Emperor Xiaozong. The edict announcing the decree examinations for 1174 lauded the Renzong era for producing an unprecedented fifteen successful examinees – as against the very few (actually two) during the twelve years of Xiaozong's own reign – and noted the difficulty of replicating the florescence under Renzong.[89] Already, however, as the edict implies, the theme of the Renzong florescence had once again assumed a critical, even ironic, tone as a rhetorical vehicle to attack perceived governance ills. For example, in 1165 Chen Junqing invoked the governance model of the Renzong period to attack the administration of the acting councilor Qian Duanli 錢端禮 (1109–1177). Chen charged that Qian's reliance upon imperial affines to staff his administration violated the system of morality-based personnel management that Renzong had perfected but that had deteriorated under Cai Jing and Qin Gui.[90] For the remainder of the dynasty, and especially after the political rise of *daoxue* in the 1160s and 1170s, political dissidents and critics would invoke the image of the Renzong florescence as an ironic parallel to the realities of the present.[91]

---

[86] Hartman, "The Making of a Villain," 86–105.   [87] *Yaolu*, 112.2098.   [88] *Yaolu*, 152.2872.
[89] *SHY, xuanju*, 11.32a–b.   [90] *Zhu Xi ji*, 96.4916–17; cf. Yang Wanli, *Chengzhai ji*, 123.7b–8a.
[91] For examples, see Li Huarui, "Lüelun Nan Song zhengzhi shang de 'fa zuzong' qingxiang," 213–20.

When Emperor Ningzong ascended the throne in 1194, his new councilor Zhao Ruyu came into office with long-standing hopes and plans to implement institutionalist reforms. A new reign title would, in two characters, reflect these priorities: the formulation "felicitous prime" (*Qingyuan* 慶元) combined the first elements in the reign titles Qingli and Yuanyou. Chen Fuliang composed the issuing edict that spoke to two dimensions of this choice: the Restoration had been founded on the policies of the Qingli and Yuanyou periods and these policies had now produced universal tranquility. Yet Chen's summary of the content of these policies – draw close the virtuous; reduce taxes – echoed the priorities of the past thirty years of government critics.[92] In two months, Zhao Ruyu would be dismissed as councilor, and he would be dead within the year. But the new administration under Han Tuozhou kept the reign title for the next six years. By the end of the twelfth century, the theme of the Renzong florescence and the ensuing Qingli–Yuanyou axis of political value had become so engrained throughout the body politic that even those against whom it had been directed came to accept its rhetorical stance as historical reality.

---

[92] *SHY, li*, 54.18a; Chen Fuliang, *Zhizhai ji*, 10.1a–b; *Chaoye zaji, jia*, 3.92.

9   From Soldier to Sage
Deifying the Prime Ancestor

Zhao Kuangyin 趙匡胤 (927–976) founded the Song dynasty on 960/1/3. Both the definition of this achievement and his image as the "prime ancestor" (Taizu 太祖) evolved over the subsequent course of the dynasty. These changes closely track the Song polity's evolving view of its own nature, of the challenges it faced, and of the proposed solutions to those challenges. In short, the character of Taizu mirrors the dynasty's perception of itself. Zhao Kuangyin was a general and military leader, one of the victors in the relentless warfare and political violence of the tenth century. Two hundred years later he had become a sage. His mind became an ontological first principle that had engendered the essence of the policies of the ancestors, the foundations and standards of all excellence in subsequent Song governance. To chart fully the course of this transition would require another book. The following discussion limits itself to outlining the history of this process, its relation to the Renzong florescence, and its centrality to the grand allegory.

As we have seen in Chapter 2, before his death in 1184, Li Tao wrote to Emperor Xiaozong, "Take Taizu as your master when planning for the future; take Renzong as your model when managing officials."[1] Li Tao, however, did not invent this link between the two sovereigns. A special identification of Taizu and Renzong with the principle of "benevolence" grew from the same early Southern Song politics that had developed the theme of the Renzong florescence. This process transformed "benevolence" from a personal characteristic of Renzong into a founding principle for the entire dynasty. Wei Jing's 衛涇 (1160–1226) first-place examination essay for 1184 epitomizes this link. Wei painted a wildly utopian vision of the Song founding. Enabled by Taizu's benevolence, "his armies were martial by their non-killing, his punishments awesome by their non-use, his finances rich by their frugality, and his officials virtuous by their non-guile. These were the basic ideas upon which he founded our state; successive emperors maintained them, and they became the policies of your house." Wei continued to explain that minor modifications in Qingli laid the basis for Jiayou governance, "a pinnacle never achieved even in

---

[1] Zhou Bida, *Wenzhong ji*, 66.21a; *QSW*, 232:5183.404; *SS*, 388.11919.

antiquity." These principles must therefore serve, Wei concluded, as the basis for improvements to current governance.[2]

To a large degree, the historiographical vacuum in which the dynasty began enabled generations of policy makers to create and manipulate successive images of the Song founder. Although the Latter Zhou dynasty's court history office continued to operate under Taizu, its archival duties were neglected in order to complete the histories of previous dynasties and thereby to bolster the Song claim to legitimacy. Accordingly, the office's historiographical mechanisms to document and preserve records of contemporary administration were not fully functional until the 990s, late into the reign of the second emperor, Taizong. Hu Meng 扈蒙 (915–986), whose services as a court historian began in the 950s under the Latter Zhou dynasty and continued into the 980s, lamented in 974/10 that the function of the history office as a repository for contemporary documents had lapsed with the coming of the Song in 960. The Song history office neither compiled a daily calendar nor received "records of current administration." Instead, only a perfunctory "inner Court calendar," maintained by the Bureau of Military Affairs, was submitted quarterly. This calendar was simply a copy of the imperial audience schedule and recorded neither the emperor's words nor his actions.[3] Again, in 987/9, more than ten years after Taizu's death, the historian Hu Dan 胡旦 (955–1034) delivered a stinging indictment of the deficient quality of the daily calendar and veritable records for the period 960 through 987. He maintained it would be impossible to compile a state history from such a poor archival base. The calendar, he wrote, consisted of little more than back copies of the *Court Gazette* (*baozhuang* 報狀), the "newspaper" for officials. He proposed an ambitious plan to recover the necessary documentation and drew up plans for the dynasty's first "state history," but the project was soon abandoned.[4]

The resulting dearth of contemporary documentation on Taizu's reign created in fact a *tabula rasa* on which much could be written. Furthermore, Taizu and Taizong were brothers, and Taizong's assumption of the throne after Taizu's sudden death in 976 bypassed two of Taizu's sons, both of whom came to questionable ends under Emperor Taizong. Many historians now believe that Taizong in fact usurped the throne; and some suggest even that Taizong murdered his brother to acquire the emperorship.[5] More certain is that

---

[2] Wei Jing, *Houle ji*, 9.15a–b; *QSW*, 291:6625.231–32.

[3] *Changbian*, 15.326; *SHY, zhiguan*, 6.30a.

[4] See Cheng Ju, *Lintai gushi*, 313–15; and the much abridged text at *Yuhai*, 168.13a. Neither the *Changbian* nor the *Song huiyao* contain Hu Dan's memorial. For a thorough review see Kurz, "The Consolidation of Official Historiography during the Early Northern Song Dynasty."

[5] There is an enormous secondary literature on these issues, which have become a de facto subdiscipline within the study of Song history. For a recent comprehensive study see Gu Hongyi, *Songchu zhengzhi yanjiu – yi huangwei shoushou wei zhongxin*. Gu (at 9–59) delineates the historiographical context. For a bibliography of the older Chinese scholarship see Fang

the base historical record of Taizu's reign, the *Taizu Veritable Records*, first completed in 980 and repeatedly revised over the next forty years under Taizong and his son, Zhenzong, concealed discord between the two brothers, accentuated the role of Taizong in the Song founding, and legitimated the Taizu–Taizong transition. A "new" *Taizu Veritable Records* was produced in 999, and the old version was formally recalled in 1007. The state history for the first two Song reigns was completed in 1016, but this draft was later incorporated into the *Three Courts State History* in 1030. The "old records" of 980 quickly became quite rare, while the revised "new records" of 999 and the 1030 state history became the official version of the Song founding.[6]

This manipulation of the early historical record, a major problem for Li Tao and for all subsequent historians of the dynasty, underpins the central problem of early Song history – who indeed was the real founder? Taizu or Taizong? Advocates for the former perceive Taizu as the innovator of key policies that led to early consolidation and centralization of Song power; they argue that the existing historical record, written under Taizong and Zhenzong, minimizes these accomplishments. Advocates for the latter perceive Taizu as a lackluster figurehead; they argue that Taizong and Chief Councilor Zhao Pu, regardless of the circumstances of the 976 transition, where nonetheless the principal "founders" whose policies, although perhaps formulated under Taizu, were brought to fruition under Taizong. An intermediate and now widespread position argues that the establishment of a distinctive Song polity was a protracted process that had deep origins in the Five Dynasties and was not completed until well into the reign of Zhenzong, with significant contributions by both Taizu and Taizong.[7]

During the Song, the official *Three Courts State History* of 1030 became the definitive history of the early dynasty. This work covered the reigns of Taizu, Taizong, and Zhenzong in full state-history format (annals, monographs, biographies). Although the history does not survive, it surely positioned the first three sovereigns as successive contributors to a cumulative process that had created a distinctive Song governance. In his 1038 preface to the *Records of Sagacious Administration from the Three Courts*, Shi Jie projected this composite view of the Song founders' successive contributions to governance and compared the Song "Great Peace" to the age of Yao and Shun. This view would

---

Jianxin, *Ershi shiji Song shi yanjiu lunzhu mulu*, 18–19. Xu Zhenxing, *Songji shouzhong kao yanjiu*, 45–91, contains useful summaries of the major secondary literature. In English, see Chang, "Inheritance Problems in the First Two Reigns of the Sung Dynasty"; and Ten Harmsel, "Oath of the Golden Casket." Lorge, *The Reunification of China*, reviews tensions between the two founders in the context of military and political reunification. For Sima Guang's take on the historiography of early Song see Lorge, "Sima Guang on Song Taizong."

[6] Cai Chongbang, *Songdai xiushi zhidu yanjiu*, 64–76.
[7] Worthy, "The Founding of Sung China"; Deng, *Zuzong zhi fa*, 184–280; Lau and Huang, "Founding and Consolidation of the Sung Dynasty," 206–78, esp. pp. 242–47.

remain the normal paradigm for the next hundred years.[8] The *Precedents from the Era of Great Peace* of 1044, as shown in Chapter 6, posited the age of Great Peace as a political achievement that, although resting upon Taizu's foundations, had been maintained and enlarged by his successors.[9] Fan Zuyu's *Emperor Ren's Instructions and Statutes* of 1093 did not challenge this model, but simply added Renzong to the sequence and changed the paramount standard of excellence from Great Peace to "benevolence."

"Benevolent" was a common element in the formal titles (*zunhao* 尊號) of both Taizu and Taizong. Taizu became the "benevolent sage" in 963, which was changed to "benevolent and filial" in 968. Taizong's title initially had no "benevolent" element, but in 984 he became "benevolent and moral" (*rende* 仁德). A shortening of his title in 989 eliminated "benevolence," but it returned in 992 as "benevolent and filial."[10] However, in 1008, when Emperor Zhenzong revised the titles of both emperors, the "benevolent" element was removed from Taizu's title, and Taizong's new title began with "supremely benevolent."[11] These changes show that "benevolence" was considered a formal element for both monarchs during their lifetimes, but that the titles were later adjusted to accord with Zhenzong's rewriting of the historical record. Only with the advent of the Qingli reformers and the *baoxun* genre of history writing in the late 1030s did Taizu and his supposed administrative style come to be associated with "benevolence" as a concept of Confucian governance. The term "benevolent government" (*renzheng* 仁政) from Mencius occurs for the first time in the *Long Draft* in 1029, but is then common after 1042.[12] Fu Bi's surviving appraisal of Taizu from the *Precedents from the Era of Great Peace* of 1044 – no doubt with the pending reforms and Emperor Renzong in mind – summarized Taizu's strengths: his love for the people made him benevolent, he readily corrected his mistakes, he was vigilant in administration, and he kept strict military discipline. For example, Fu Bi described Taizu's sympathy for innocents slain in the wars of consolidation as a manifestation of the "benevolent mind with which he approached the world."[13]

---

[8] Shi Jie, *Culai Shi xiansheng wenji*, 18.209–10. Cao Jiaqi, "Zhao Song dangchao shengshi shuo zhi zaojiu ji qi yingxiang," 70–76, cites other examples. Lü Yijian compared the aggregate "virtue" of the first three Song sovereigns in managing Inner Court personnel as "equal to Yao and Shun," cited at *Songshi quanwen*, 2.87.

[9] *Changbian*, 143.3455–56.   [10] Wang Mingqing, *Huizhu lu, houlu*, 1.47–48.

[11] *Changbian*, 69.1553.

[12] *Changbian* 107.2506. In an entry dated 962/1 Shen Lun advised Taizu to release military stores to feed the starving populace in the southeast and "practice benevolent government and thus elicit a harmonious spirit that will bring forth a good harvest." But Li Tao has inserted this entry into the *Long Draft* from the *Sanchao baoxun* and the *Taiping gushi*, both Qingli-period texts. See *Changbian* 3.60; and anonymous, *Taiping baoxun zhengshi jinian*, 9–10. A later version of these events in Luo Congyan's *Zun Yao lu* discussed above does not mention benevolence. See Chapter 8, note 23.

[13] Anonymous, *Taiping baoxun zhengzhi jinian*, 29–30; *Songshi quanwen*, 2.89.

However, developments in late Northern Song, especially the advent of the New Policies, weakened the official paradigm in which the early emperors shared equal credit for the foundations of Song governance. Wang Anshi had initially framed the New Policies as his own program to correct administrative deficiencies. But after Wang's dismissal in 1076 Shenzong assumed personal control over the reforms and sought to redefine both the New Policies and his own government reorganization of 1082 as affirmations of the "policies of the ancestors."[14] As a reflection of this redefinition, he ordered in 1080 and completed in 1082/11 a rebuilding of the Temple of Spectacular Numina (*Jingling gong* 景靈宮), previously a shrine to the dynasty's Daoist progenitor, as a religious venue that would "celebrate the Song dynasty and its history."[15]

Shenzong's own death in 1085, however, raised the question of where his own shrine would be placed within the now completed temple and how the New Policies would be placed in dynastic history. As soon as became emperor in 1100 Huizong ordered construction of a Western Temple of Spectacular Numina that would resolve these issues, and, at the same time, bolster his own legitimacy. A dedicatory inscription for the Western Temple, composed by Zeng Shu 曾紆 (1073–1135), son of sitting chief councilor Zeng Bu, makes no mention of Wang Anshi and frames the New Policies as manifestations of Shenzong's own inner perfection and as fulfillments of the "policies of the ancestors." Zeng's text created a complex series of historical parallels whereby an immediate successor brought to administrative perfection the principles of the dynastic founder – thus, King Cheng of Zhou perfected the work of his father, the Zhou founder King Wu; in Song, Taizong perfected the work of Taizu; and, by implication, the new Emperor Huizong will perfect the New Policies of his father, Shenzong.[16] These associations would not survive the fall of Northern Song, but the enhancement of Taizu over other Song rulers would soon form a staple of Southern Song imperial rhetoric and justification for the Restoration under Gaozong.

Other developments in late Northern Song, for example the advent of Cheng Yi's virulent Confucianism and Emperor Huizong's strong support for Daoism, also weakened the earlier image of the cumulative, corporate nature of the Song founding. The result is already apparent in Luo Congyan's *Record of Revering Yao* of 1126. His criticism of Zhenzong's Daoism (no doubt also intended as implied criticism of the state's extensive support for Daoism under Huizong)

---

[14] Deng Xiaonan, *Zuzong zhi fa*, 437–38; Fang Chengfeng, "Lun Beisong Xifeng Yuanyou nianjian de zhongshu tizhi," 113–16.

[15] Ebrey, "Portrait Sculptures in Imperial Ancestral Rites," 66.

[16] For Zeng Yu's inscription see Li You, *Songchao shishi*, 6. 17b–22a; *QSW*, 143:3084.212–15. For the attribution to Zeng Yu see Chen Zhensun, *Zhizhai shulu jieti*, 18.525. I am grateful to Zhao Yue of Sichuan University for calling Zeng Shu's inscription to my attention and for sharing with me his interpretation of the text.

continued a process that would undercut Zhenzong as a "founder" on par with his two predecessors.[17] Thus, the rise of the motif of the Renzong florescence, the reduced stature of Zhenzong, and the increased stature of Taizu all interacted to destabilize the old paradigm that had attributed historical value in roughly equal proportion to the first four sovereigns.

Very practical considerations under the new Emperor Gaozong, however, quickly elevated Taizu's status far beyond anything Luo Congyan could have imagined. Like all emperors from Zhenzong, Gaozong was descended from the Taizong branch of the imperial clan. Descendants of Taizu remained as clan members, but became increasingly marginalized in clan affairs under the eleventh-century Taizong line of emperors. Furthermore, clan policies under Cai Jing seem to have favored the Taizong branch by permitting its members to remain in Kaifeng while confining the Taizu line to compounds outside the capital.[18] Therefore, when Gaozong's only son died in 1129, and he faced the possibility of no further issue, he embarked on an extended plan to return the imperial succession to the Taizu line by selecting a number of seventh-generation descendants of Taizu and raising these boys within the palace, eventually to select one as his successor.[19]

Gaozong carefully adjusted the plan to encompass the necessary blend of practicality, propaganda, and historical revisionism. A memorial in 1131/6 by a provincial official, Lou Yinliang, blamed Cai Jing for impoverishing the Taizu branch. Lou cast the Song loss of the North as Heaven's retribution for this ill-treatment of Taizu's martial spirit, whose diminished vitality had caused the dynasty's reduced military might. Lou compared Taizu's own transmission of the throne to his brother Taizong, rather than to his own son, as parallel to the legendary Emperor Yao's transmission of imperial rule to his virtuous son-in-law Shun rather than to his own unworthy son. Tian Kuang 田況 (1005–1063) had already made this comparison in the mid-eleventh century, and Lou drew upon the long-standing general parallel between the Song founders and the ancient paragons Yao and Shun.[20] But the political context of the Restoration electrified the old parallel: Lou's memorial proposed to repeat the analogy – and history – this time by paralleling Gaozong as Yao and his future Taizu-branch successor as Shun. No wonder the historical record states that upon reading the memorial, "Gaozong had a great awakening!"[21]

---

[17] *Zun Yao lu*, 3.147–48. Already in 1085, Sima Guang, calling for a return to the policies of the ancestors, stipulated that those ancestors were Taizu and Taizong only; *Sima Guang ji*, 47.1007.
[18] Chaffee, *Branches of Heaven*, 95–103. [19] Chaffee, *Branches of Heaven*, 179–81.
[20] Tian Kuang, *Rulin gongyi*, 1.1a–b.
[21] *Yaolu*, 45.956–57; *Chaoye zaji, yi*, 1.496; Zhou Hui, *Qingbo zazhi*, 1.11–14. The Qing historian Wang Fuzhi 王夫之 (1619–1692) surmised, probably correctly, that Gaozong had already decided to engineer a transfer to the Taizu line and, through the sitting chief councilor Fan Zongyin, arranged to have Lou Yinliang submit this memorial (*Songlun*, 10.186). Otherwise, it

The ensuing court discussion reinforced these parallels and aligned the plan with the current policy to emulate Renzong-era administration. Assisting Councilor Zhang Shou 張守 (1084–1145) observed that because Taizu's sons had been indeed worthy of the throne, whereas Yao's son had been deficient, Taizu's selfless transmission to his worthier brother actually surpassed what Yao had done. Military Affairs Commissioner Li Hui 李回 (d. 1133) added that Taizu's decision had emerged from the founder's "utmost sincerity," making the subtle point that Gaozong's replication of Taizu's act would in fact serve to reconfirm Heaven's initial conferral of the mandate to rule on the Zhao house. Gaozong observed that he would "follow the precedent of Renzong," who, himself without a natural heir, had taken several young clan members, including his future successor, Yingzong, into the palace for imperial training.[22] Empress Meng, whose support was crucial to Gaozong's legitimacy, also approved the plan. In addition, Gaozong's embrace of Taizu, through his heirs, camouflaged his own origins in the New Policies world of his father Huizong and tapped directly into the purported source of original Song greatness. Finally, by bolstering his own legitimacy in this way, Gaozong countered challenges to his authority both from Liu Yu's Qi dynasty in the North and from at least three Taizu branch members who at this time seem to have made their own claims on the Song throne.[23]

But the political move to adopt a Taizu branch heir and thus enhance Gaozong's legitimacy also required an intellectually and historically enhanced Taizu. The official histories, for reasons explained above, could provide little help. Gaozong's political and cultural advisers, first under Qin Gui, then under Zhao Ding, looked, therefore, to the scholars of Yuanyou learning, freed since 1126 to criticize the New Policies and to formulate the necessary adjustments to political theory and to history. As mentioned above, already in 1130/7, the son of a major Cheng Yi disciple had asked Fan Chong to submit his father's *Emperor Ren's Instructions and Statutes*, which projected Renzong's "benevolence" back to Taizu and linked together the Yao–Shun and Taizu–Taizong transitions.[24]

---

is difficult to imagine how Lou, a person of otherwise little consequence, could have memorialized on such a sensitive subject. As we have seen in Chapter 5, his biography at *SS*, 399.12132–33 is merely a vehicle to include his memorial in the state history. Gaozong's embrace of Lou Yinliang's memorial was widely known in Southern Song; see *Zhuzi yulei*, 127.3053.

[22] *Yaolu*, 45.959–60.

[23] Chaffee, *Branches of Heaven*, 127–29; Gu Hongyi, *Songchu zhengzhi yanjiu*, 353–57; Lau, "The Absolutist Reign," 8–10.

[24] The present *Old History of the Five Dynasties* contains a document purporting to be the formal abdication of the Zhou dynasty child emperor Gongdi in favor of "our present emperor [Taizu]" (Chen Shangjun, *Jiu wudai shi xinji huizheng*, 10:3751–52). This document contains the passage: "Singers and litigants drew near to his perfect benevolence. Responding to Heaven, he followed the people and took as his model Yao's abdication to Shun" 謳謠獄訟, 附于至仁.

A year later, as the court was debating the Taizu branch option, Cheng Yi's titles were restored, and his teaching was described as the essence of the *Great Learning* – "rectified in mind, sincere in intention" (*zhengxin chengyi* 正心誠意). Simultaneously, this proto-*daoxue* learning was urged upon Gaozong as the key to restoring imperial governance.[25] As mentioned in Chapter 8, the fullest articulation came in the ninth of Hu Anguo's "Essays on Contemporary Policy," entitled "The Rectified Mind" (*zhengxin* 正心). Hu explained that an imperial mind trained to "utmost sincerity" (*zhicheng* 至誠) was the wellspring of good governance and urged Gaozong to apply this principle to the Restoration.[26] Li Hui had indeed identified this same mental sincerity as the source of Taizu's decision to emulate Yao. Gaozong's cultural commissars adopted the Cheng Yi school's vocabulary and focus on the *Great Learning* catenation, which linked personal cultivation and successful governance, to frame and buttress their political move to adopt a Taizu heir. In essence, the focus on "utmost sincerity" as a critical imperial value linked – and ultimately equated – Gaozong, Taizu, and Yao.

Already in 1126, Luo Congyan's commentary on the anecdote about Taizu's "rectification" of his palace alignment cited the *Great Learning*, thus linking the mind of Taizu to the governance of Yao and Shun.[27] Also related to this analogy was the emergence in late Northern Song of the concept of the "transmission of the Way" (*daotong* 道統) and its application to the Song monarchs. Precisely at the same time as Luo compiled the *Record of Revering Yao*, in 1126 the academician Li Ruoshui 李若水 (1093–1127) urged Council of State member He Li 何㮚 (1089–1126) to continue to suppress advocates of the New Policies. The historical revisionism of Li's letter – his adulation of Renzong and his anti-Wang Anshi rhetoric – is typical of other documents that date from the interval between the two Jurchen sieges of Kaifeng in 1126. However, Li also frames Taizu as the inheritor of a "succession of the Way," a method of perfected governance descended from Yao and largely lost since the mid-Zhou. This concept, subsequently refined by the same Cheng Yi-school emphasis on "rectification and sincerity" that forged the Yao–Taizu–Gaozong identity, would later appear in Qin Gui's 1155 inscription, where the term *daotong*

應天順民, 法堯禪舜. Both *Dongdu shilüe*, 1.4a, and *Songshi quanwen*, 1.5, reproduce this edict. Zhou Bida, however, questioned its integrity, noting that the supposedly original version in Zheng Xiang's *Wudai kaihuang ji* 五代開皇紀 of 1021 was totally different from the document in the *Taizu shilu* (*Wenzhong ji*, 180.1a–b); and Li Tao did not include either of these abdication edicts in the *Long Draft*. This edict and its links between Taizu, benevolence, and Yao–Shun is probably an eleventh-century fabrication.

[25] *Yaolu*, 44.939, 46.980–81, and 48.1008.
[26] *QSW*, 146:3146.126; Li and Hartman, "A Newly Discovered Inscription," 437.
[27] *Zun Yao lu*, 1.116–17; and see Chapter 8 above.

links Gaozong to Yao as the source of the Way and legitimizes him as ruler and teacher.[28]

Although Gaozong and Qin Gui soon abandoned their fleeting embrace of Cheng learning, the vocabulary, the political parallels, and especially the *Great Learning* emphasis on the Way remained central to the monarchy's political rhetoric. When Gaozong abdicated in favor of the future Emperor Xiaozong in 1162, a deliberative assembly was convened to determine a suitable title for the retired sovereign. The final formulation contained the two characters *guang Yao* 光堯, implying that Gaozong had "brightened Yao," that in fact his attainments surpassed those of the sage emperor, an implication already present in Qin Gui's inscription. Wang Yingchen objected that no one could "brighten Yao," but the phrase was nonetheless accepted.[29] In 1171, the title was expanded to include *ti dao* 體道, "who embodies the Way," further reinforcing the identity of Yao, Taizu, Gaozong, and the Way.[30]

Gaozong's elevated status as "retired emperor" sanctioned the use of this rhetorical nexus in both history and policy. The process began immediately. After recording Gaozong's assumption of the throne on 1127/5/1, Lu You's first draft comment for the *Sagacious Administration of the Restoration* reads,

We may understand why Yao and Shun alone surpassed all other sovereigns by looking at how they attained the world and how they passed it on. [Already] Tang [the founder of the Shang dynasty] was ashamed of his virtue, and Wu [the founder of the Zhou dynasty] was not perfectly good. And later ages? Gaozu of the Han and Taizong of Tang have been called virtuous rulers, but they attained the world through conquest, and there was near chaos when they passed it on. But awesome – our Emperor Taizu's receipt of the mandate and its Restoration by our Supreme Emperor [Gaozong]! Singers [of their praise] and litigants [seeking their judgment] flocked to them and would not disperse, so they could not choose but to accept the emperorship. And later, when they had found the best person for the world, having established our foundations, they passed these on to him, neither planning with advisers nor consulting oracles. They simply looked to where Heaven's will had rested. In the several thousand years since Yao and Shun, there have

---

[28] *QSW*, 185:4066.183–85; Li and Hartman, "A Newly Discovered Inscription," 432–41. In his preface to the "separate" *Zun Yao lu*, an appendix to the main work that contains Sima Guang's denunciations of Wang Anshi and Chen Guan's attack on Cai Jing, Luo Congyan terms this tradition of learning transmitted from Yao to Mencius "learning of the Way" (*daoxue*), one of the earliest Song uses of the phrase. In Luo's view, this learning was eclipsed by the teachings of Mozi and Yangzi in the Zhou, by Buddhism and Daoism in the Six Dynasties and Tang, and by Wang Anshi and Cai Jing in Song. Confucius wrote the *Spring and Autumn Annals* to harbor this learning from barbarian threats to the "central states" (*Zun Yao lu bielu*, 204; *QSW*, 142:3060. 158–59). All of these motifs recur in Qin Gui's inscription.

[29] For a lengthy synopsis of the deliberations see *Chaoye zaji, jia*, 2.71–72; also *SS*, 387.11879; Lau, "The Absolutist Reign," 36–37. The text of Gaozong's formal abdication ceremony pronounced that he had "trodden the lofty tracks of Yao and Shun" (*SS*, 110.2642).

[30] *Songshi quanwen*, 25B.2108.

never been times as extraordinary and flourishing as those of Taizu and our Supreme Emperor![31]

Lu You submitted this text in 1164. The passage was taken verbatim into the finished *Sagacious Administration of the Supreme Emperor* (*Taishang huang shengzheng* 太上皇聖政) of 1166 and became part of the formal rhetoric of the restoration.[32] The principal classical citation is to *Mencius* 5.A.5, where Mencius explains that it was not in fact Yao, but rather Heaven, that selected Shun to receive the mandate. Heaven indicated its choice through the actions of "ballad singers" who praised Shun and "litigants" who brought to him their lawsuits for settlement rather than to Yao's natural son. This citation supports the passage's central contention that Taizu and Gaozong attained their thrones not through violence but through the will of the people. As *Mencius* concludes with a quotation from the *Book of Documents*, "Heaven sees with the eyes of its people."[33] Lu You links the characterization of the Song founding as a spontaneous outpouring of support for Taizu from his soldiers to assume the emperorship at Chen Bridge in 960 and the Restoration as a gathering of displaced Song officials who rallied around Gaozong at Yingtian 應天 in 1127. The passage also flatters Xiaozong, positing him also as chosen by Heaven, acting through Gaozong alone, "neither planning with advisers nor consulting oracles."

The historian's comment (*zan*) that concludes the Taizu portion of the imperial annals in the *Eastern Capital Miscellany* probably dates from the mid-1180s and emphasizes Taizu's "rectitude":

The historian [Wang] Cheng remarks, [the rulers] before the three dynasties [of Xia, Shang, and Zhou] all obtained the world through rectitude. Yao and Shun passed it on to sages, but Yu [of Xia] passed it on to his own son. Although Tang and Wu replaced cruelty with benevolence, Tang was ashamed of his virtue; and Confucius said that Wu was not perfectly good. Therefore these two were only inadvertently "sages." Taizu's intelligence and insight were grave and sage; he obtained the world through abdication, as had Yao and Shun. When it came time to pass on his position, he did not pass it on to his son, but to his brother. Therefore, his saintliness surpasses Yu by far, not to speak of Tang and Wu. To obtain the world through benevolence and discard it like an old shoe –

---

[31] *Yongle dadian*, 12929.1a; Kong Xue, "Lu You ji *Gaozong shengzheng cao*," 34. For a detailed study of this work see Cai Hanmo [Charles Hartman], "Lu You *Zhongxing shengzheng cao* kao."

[32] *Zhongxing shengzheng*, 1.3b–4a; see also the quotation in the pseudocommentary at *Yaolu*, 5.131. For a description of the presentation ceremony for the *Taishang huang shengzheng* see Chen Kui, *Nan Song guan'ge lu*, 4.35–37. Emperor Xiaozong's own preface to this work and Chief Councilor Jiang Fu's submission record directly echo the rhetoric of Lu You's text: Gaozong is Yao; Xiaozong is Shun; the *Taishang huang shengzheng* is the *Shujing* (*Book of Documents*); see Qian Yueyou, *Xianchun Lin'an zhi*, 7.2a–4b; *QSW*, 210:4670.334, 236:5279.291. An anonymous Southern Song handbook of political rhetoric also cites Lu You's text; see *Hanyuan xinshu, houji, shang*, 2.2b.

[33] Lau, *Mencius*, 143–44.

in all the ages, of those who have continued the rectitude of Yao and Shun, there is only Taizu.[34]

The intertextuality between the Lu You and the Wang Cheng comments – especially the negative portrayals of Tang and Wu – suggests that the composite account of Taizu and Gaozong in the 1166 *shengzheng* influenced Wang's solo evaluation of Taizu. His evaluation seems crafted with Gaozong and his abdication to Xiaozong in mind. The emphasis on rectitude, here meaning the "rectified mind" of the *Great Learning*, reflects a continuation of the rhetoric of Southern Song emperorship that had been evolving since the 1130s.

As political propaganda, this rhetorical paradigm lauds the nonviolent, and thus "benevolent," nature of the Song monarchy, which it shares with the rule of Yao and Shun. Both the comments of Lu You and Wang Cheng are laudatory history, but the same rhetoric could easily be transformed into hortatory advocacy or direct criticism. In the mid-1170s Shi Hao submitted a series of precedents that urged Xiaozong to foster benevolence over profit, to delegate details to his chief councilor, and to concentrate on imperial essentials. As had Hu Anguo earlier, he defined the latter as "be rectified in mind, sincere in intention" from the *Great Learning*. Unlike Hu, however, Shi Hao placed this learning squarely in the context of the transmission of the Way that had begun with Yao, paused at Mencius, and then resumed in Song. In the imperial propaganda of the Qin Gui inscription, the Song emperors had resumed the Way; in the emerging Cheng–Zhu tradition of *daoxue*, the private scholar Cheng Hao had resumed the Way. Shi Hao's precedent, adopting the imperial rhetorical model, stated that Emperor Taizu had received the cumulative virtues of the Way's practitioners from Yao through Mencius. Thus, Taizu's founding of the Song dynasty resumed the political perfection of the Way that began with Yao. Gaozong had now restored this Way and had passed it on to Xiaozong. In conclusion, Shi Hao argued that Xiaozong can improve this tradition; for, as Confucius had proclaimed in the *Analects*, the benevolent man "gives extensively to the common people and brings help to the multitude . . . And even Yao and Shun would have found it difficult to accomplish as much."[35]

Zhu Xi, in his great memorial of 1188, invoked the openness of Taizu's newly aligned palace as a metaphor for the rectitude, the "straightness," of his mind. He emphasized to Xiaozong that Taizu had not attained this quality through ordinary study but through a direct transmission from Yao and Shun, "as when the two halves of a tally come together." Once again, Zhu emphasizes the *Great Learning* link between the mind of the ruler and governance: "when

[34] *Dongdu shilüe*, 2.7b. Wang Cheng submitted this work in 1186, but most of the contents were copied from the state histories; see Hartman, "The Reluctant Historian," 109–11. This comment, however, which carries his name, was probably composed close to the date of submission.
[35] Shi Hao, *Maofeng zhenyin manlu*,11.7b–10a; *QSW*, 200:4415.47–48; Lau, *Analects*, 85.

your mind is thus fully rectified, then no one near nor far will dare not to unite in your rectitude." In this case, Zhu Xi was not talking philosophy: his double negatives underscore his message that only the emperor, through the political exercise of his own personal rectitude, can curtail the activities of his personal retainers, the "close favorites," and thus eliminate "private interests" in his administration. The clear implication was that Xiaozong had failed to live up to the openness of the founder's design – for his mind, for his palace, or for his state.[36]

By the end of Song, the rise of *daoxue* completed the portrait of Taizu as a *daoxue* sovereign, a Song realization of the mind of Yao and Shun. Lü Zhong commented on Taizu's completion of his palace reconstruction that, although the ruler may dwell physically hidden within the palace, the quality of his mind will be apparent in the quality of governance manifest throughout the realm. He alluded to Zhu Xi's "Preface to the *Doctrine of the Mean*" that identified the famous "sixteen-character message" from the *Book of Documents* as the "the mind of the Way" that Yao and Shun had transmitted through the "succession of the Way" to later ages. Lü concluded, again citing Zhu Xi, that the accomplishment of the Song founding surpassed that of even the great Han dynasty because Taizu's "rectified mind matched like a tally" to the minds of the ancient sage-rulers.[37] By the thirteenth century, the *daoxue* phrase "principle first" (*daoli zui da* 道理最大) came to be understood as shorthand for the message of the sixteen characters and was used to describe Taizu's mind. By the end of the dynasty, "principle first" had become the essence of imperial governance, passed from Yao through the *daotong* to Taizu, and from him to each successive Song emperor.[38]

In summary, key elements and motifs in the process of deifying the founder occurred in Northern Song. Already by the 1030s, historians had associated the Zhao lineage collectively with the lineage of the primal sage-rulers. The Qingli reformers of the 1040s identified the character of Zhao rule as "benevolent." By 1068, Qian Yi had associated the anecdote about Taizu's realigned palace with the "rectified mind" of the *Great Learning*.[39] By 1093, Fan Zuyu had brought a number of these motifs together, strengthening Taizu's character and actions as "benevolent." Yet all these remained disparate and unconnected threads, and did not coalesce into revisions of history, despite Huizong's attempt in 1100 to

[36] *Zhu Xi ji*, 11.467.
[37] Lü Zhong, *Huangchao dashiji*, 3.67–68; *Songshi quanwen*, 2.60. For Zhu Xi's preface and the sixteen characters see *Sishu zhangju jizhu*, 14–16; Legge, *The Shoo King*, 61–62; and de Bary and Bloom, *Sources of Chinese Tradition*, 731–34, for an English translation and discussion.
[38] See Huang Yinglong's "Memorial on Study and the Way," in Huang Huai and Yang Shiqi, *Lidai mingchen zouyi*, 9.37a–39b; *QSW*, 347:8025.240–43; Deng Xiaonan, *Zuzong zhi fa*, 498–518.
[39] Qian Yi's 1068/10 "Memorial Addressing Ten Important Issues" opposed the New Policies. Each of the ten sections concluded with a founders' anecdote from the *baoxun* collections; see Zhao, *Songchao zhuchen zouyi*, 2.11–13; *QSW*, 48:1053.351–55.

equate Taizu and Shenzong. As long as Taizong's heirs controlled the monarchy, there was no political momentum to enhance Taizu's status above that of Taizong. In 1081 Emperor Shenzong himself had ordered Zeng Gong to combine the two existing state histories into a unified history of the dynasty. But when Zeng took the opportunity to enhance the status of Taizu over his successors, Shenzong rebuffed the idea and cancelled the project.[40] In addition, because Wang Anshi had sought to change policies that his opponents cast historically as continuations of those of the ancestors, he framed the New Policies intellectually as appeals to a fictive "antiquity," not to the actions of the Song founders. As long as the New Policies remained in effect, there was no rationale either to elevate Taizu over the other founders, or to devise a philosophical mechanism to connect Taizu, as the Song founder, more specifically to Yao, as founder of the political tradition of the Way.

As was the case with the theme of the Renzong florescence, the arrival of the Jurchen, the decline of the New Policies, and the liberation of Yuanyou learning enabled the creation of a new Taizu. Although Gaozong's physical impotence may have been the immediate impetus for his transfer of emperorship to the Taizu line, a historically refashioned Taizu would probably have emerged nonetheless. Its catalyst was the convergence in the early 1130s of two independent developments. First, the Cheng brothers interpreted the *Great Learning* against the *Doctrine of the Mean* as a juxtaposition of mind and Way that had originated with Yao. Second, the young Emperor Gaozong needed political legitimacy and a new propaganda line to promote the Restoration. Surviving documentation shows that Gaozong's advisers invoked the Yao–Shun parallel in order to justify transfer to the Taizu branch. Quite probably, however, they also engineered the switch as the foundation for a propaganda line that would link Gaozong and the Restoration with the moral legitimacy of Yao. This not only required a Taizu with a "rectified mind," but also mandated certain revisions to early Song history that would highlight how that mind had in turn rectified the state.

The monarchy, its official historians, private historians, and literati officials – each with their own agendas – all participated in this process of revision. The new times needed a new history. The early Southern Song penchant for advocating policy by recourse to Northern Song precedents – the earlier the better – reshaped the dynasty's history and bequeathed to posterity major elements of the grand allegory. As we have seen from the Introduction through Chapter 2, in the 1130s, the history of the post-1067 period was still in play; but the veritable records and state histories for the pre-1067 periods were long established, official, and could not be changed. There were two ways around

---

[40] *Changbian*, 317.7669–70, 318.7696, 325.7830; *Zeng Gong ji*, 10.170–75; Cai Chongbang, *Songdai xiushi zhidu yanjiu*, 123–27.

this problem. First, by selecting events from the existing official record and rearranging these selections, a historian could readjust the focus of an existing narrative, or create a new narrative. Second, the historian could foreground or "upgrade" an anecdote – an account usually not in the existing official history – and use it to create a new context against which existing official accounts could then be reread. The following sections examine two important events that shaped Taizu's role in the grand allegory: the dynastic founding at Chen Bridge and the so-called "taking back military power over a cup of wine" incident. The story of Chen Bridge illustrates the first method; "taking back military power" illustrates the second and shows how historians used anecdotes to shape history to the needs of contemporary policy.

Fighting over Chen Bridge

If a historian had been present at the founding of the Song dynasty on 960/1/4, his record of the events would not likely have survived.[41] Yet all histories of the Song begin with a telling of the events at Chen Bridge. All stress that the Song founding marked a new era in Chinese history because the dynastic transition from the Latter Zhou to Song was nonviolent in two ways. First, because Heaven chose Taizu, the people, and especially his soldiers, supported him: there was nearly universal consensus that he should be emperor. Second, Taizu himself was personally inclined toward nonviolence: his first command as emperor was to prohibit his troops from pillaging the capital, as had been routine in previous Five Dynasties transitions. The two oldest accounts of the founding, however, differ on who should get credit for this order.

The narrative in Sima Guang's *Su River Records* gives all the credit to Taizu himself. He is the sole actor in the drama at Chen Bridge. The narrative in Li Tao's *Long Draft*, however, posits the Song founding as a corporate affair that involved Taizu, his brother the future Taizong, and Zhao Pu. Modern scholars who posit Taizu as the real Song founder accept Sima Guang's account and argue that Li Tao relied too heavily upon the official histories that Taizong had doctored to enhance his own role in the founding. Rather than seek to resolve this issue, this section will orient the competing versions against the politics of the two periods from which they derive. The material for the Chen Bridge narrative in the *Su River Records* may well have originated with Sima Guang himself. However, as explained in Chapter 8, the present text derives from the

---

[41] The Qing academicians judged the surviving *Record of the Dragon Flying* (*Longfei ji* 龍飛記), attributed to one of the participants, Zhao Pu, to be a later fabrication; see Ji Yun et al., *Qinding Siku quanshu congmu*, 52.723. Indeed, Li Tao, who knew the title, does not cite any documents from the present text; see *Changbian*, 1.4; *SHY, li*, 54.1a; *SHY, chongru*, 7.69a. Gu Hongyi, *Songchu zhengzhi yanjiu*, 40–43, attempts to rehabilitate the *Longfei ji* as the earliest account of Chen Bridge; he considers the text a 981 revision of an earlier draft from 960.

edition that Fan Chong prepared for Emperor Gaozong in 1136. Therefore, the all-important Chen Bridge narrative that opens the book can be profitably read and interpreted against Restoration propaganda and the politics of the transition of emperorship to the Taizu line in the 1130s. As for the *Long Draft*, the section on Taizu was first submitted in 1163, but revised and resubmitted with the subsequent pre-1067 material in 1168, and the present text derives from this revision.

The *Eastern Capital Miscellany*, although technically a private work, presents a mid-twelfth-century, quasi-official view of Northern Song history. Its narrative of Chen Bridge has much in common with that in the *Su River Records* and is the best place to begin a comparative analysis of the different versions.

On 960/1/1, Zhen and Ding prefectures reported by express courier that Liu Chengjun in Taiyuan had joined with the Khitan and invaded across the border. And so Taizu was ordered to lead a large force on a northern expedition against them. The next day, the Palace Attendant Zhan Jurun held a farewell banquet for the departing army on the outskirts of the city. At the time there were many rumors in the capital of a plan to make the inspector general [i.e. Taizu] the Son of Heaven. When the soldiers reached Chen Bridge post-station, they deliberated together and decided to support Taizu. The next day, as they assembled at the post-station gate, suddenly all the officers came together and said, "We brave death in battle a thousand times to defeat the enemies of the state. But the Son of Heaven is a now a small child. Let's first make the inspector general the Son of Heaven, and then proceed on the northern expedition." Because he had consumed much food and drink at the farewell banquet, Taizu was sleeping drunk in his chamber and so was unaware of their plans. The next morning, the soldiers, with swords drawn, pounded on the bedroom door, and together they dragged him out into the main hall where they clothed him in a yellow robe. The officers saluted him and said, "We soldiers have no ruler. We wish to make you the Son of Heaven." Then they shouted out rounds of "Long Life" to the Emperor, and the sound could be heard for miles around. Taizu cursed them, but they would not relent. They crowded around Taizu, put him on a horse, and headed back to the capital. But Taizu drew up his reins and said to the officers, "I have accepted an order to proceed north, but you have decided to support me. If I issue an order, will you obey?" And they all said, "We await your order." Then Taizu said, "I have served the Empress and His Highness loyally. The court officials are my colleagues. Do not violate the palace or disturb the officials. These days, when rulers raise troops against a city, they allow the troops to loot and pillage. Do not sack this city nor loot its treasury. If you follow my orders, I will richly reward you. If you disobey, I will execute all of you." The officers saluted and received his order, and in strict formations they entered through the Gate of Benevolence and Harmony.[42]

This tight, carefully crafted narrative presents Taizu as a single actor who personally transformed the "pillaging" Five Dynasties into the "strictly formed" Song. The *Miscellany*'s unique mention of the farewell banquet – no

---

[42] *Dongdu shilüe*, 1.3a–4a.

other account contains this detail – both explains his inebriation and underlines his ignorance of the soldiers' plot against the infant Zhou emperor. Also unique among the other sources, the *Miscellany* does not mention either Taizong or Zhao Pu. It focuses exclusively on Taizu, on his personal confrontation and subsequent compact with the troops. During the conversation between the mounted Taizu and his officers, the inebriated and unwitting tool of mutiny quickly morphs into their unquestioned leader and majestic sovereign. His personal compact with the troops not to loot the capital turns a potential bloodbath into an orderly march back through the Gate of Benevolence and Harmony into the city, where, as the narrative continues, a nonviolent "abdication" of power from the Zhou to the new Song dynasty ensues.

The account in the *Su River Records* tallies closely with that of the *Miscellany*. There is, however, no banquet and therefore no inebriation. The soldiers do not force their way into Taizu's sleeping quarters, but rather Taizong makes his only appearance in the narrative as an emissary who transmits the troops' intentions to the still-sleeping Taizu. These differences lend an added aura of decorum to the Sima Guang/Fan Chong narrative. After the entry into the capital, their text adds, "the entire city was quiet, there was no alarm or disorder, and by nightfall the founding of the new house was complete." After this main narrative, Sima Guang appends a comment that his father made to him in 1033: the reason for the country's unification and continued prosperity was that Taizu had attained the mandate to rule "through his benevolence and rightness."[43]

Both the *Miscellany* and the *Su River Records* stress Taizu as a sole actor who obtained the mandate through nonviolence and benevolence. Although this focus could have originated in Sima Guang's desire to enhance Taizu as a legitimizing source for the "policies of the ancestors" against the New Policies, this sole-actor narrative fits equally well into the Taizu–Gaozong–Yao propaganda from the 1130s as outlined in Chapter 8. The Chen Bridge narrative was perhaps on Gaozong's mind when he made the decision to transfer to the Taizu line. When he passed through Hangzhou in 1132/1, he was delighted to learn that one of its counties was named Renhe 仁和 (benevolence and harmony). This coincidence between the name of the gate in Kaifeng and the name of the county in Hangzhou gave rise to his idea that Hangzhou might become his capital.[44] Furthermore, Fan Chong was personally involved in the education of the young candidates for the Taizu-line emperorship. At the urging of Chief Councilor Zhao Ding, in 1135/5 the court re-established the School for the Heir Apparent (*Zishan tang* 資善堂) in order to

---

[43] *Sushui jiwen*, 1.1–2.
[44] Liu Yiqing, *Qiantang yishi*, 1.4a. For the dating, see Tao, "The Move to the South and the Reign of Kao-tsung," 660–61.

educate the young heirs. Fan Chong was appointed one of the tutors. The future Emperor Xiaozong, then aged seven, was his student. Gaozong personally wrote out Fan Chong's appointment edict. He observed that Fan's grandfather had served as a policy critic in the Jiayou period and that his father had suffered for his Yuanyou affiliation. This background, plus Fan Chong's erudition and his work as a historian, made him especially qualified to serve as tutor to the Taizu-line candidates. The edict's implied parallel between the persecution of the Yuanyou administrators and the suppression of the Taizu branch rests on a revised vision of Song history in which imperial legitimacy passed from Taizu, through Renzong, to Gaozong, while scholarly legitimacy passed from Taizu, through the Jiayou and Yuanyou administrators, to the Zhao Ding network.[45] A year later, Fan Chong, at the height of his influence at court, carried out Gaozong's order to edit the *Su River Records*.

Li Tao's narrative of Chen Bridge is the most detailed among the surviving accounts. But these details add up to a very different vision of the founding. In the *Long Draft*, solar omens and rumors in the capital prefigure the impending regime change. And Taizong and Zhao Pu assume active roles in the events. The army officers, upon reaching the post-station, tell Taizong they intend to enthrone his older brother. Taizong immediately consults privately with Zhao Pu, but the officers barge into their deliberations. During the long confrontation that ensues, the pair maintain that, given Taizu's loyalty to the Zhou, he will never agree to be made emperor. The soldiers press their case and threaten to rebel. When Taizong and Zhao Pu realize the solders will not relent, they strike a bargain: if the officers will agree to maintain discipline and not loot the capital, the pair will condone their plan. To cement the bargain, they dispatch an emissary to alert key allies in the capital. The next morning Taizong and Zhao Pu enter Taizu's chamber to inform him of developments, but the officers pound on the door and demand, "We officers have no ruler. We wish to make you the Son of Heaven." Li Tao's narrative then continues much as the *Miscellany* does, but with one important exception. As the army is about to depart south, Taizong stands before Taizu's horse and requests an order that the city not be plundered. The conversation that ensues between Taizu and the troops thus comes at the suggestion of Taizong, who has indeed the day before already concluded the same agreement with the officers. Thus, Li Tao, while maintaining Taizu's innocence of the plot, credits the compact not to loot the city to Taizong and Zhao Pu and to their negotiations with the officers the previous day. Rather than the single-actor version of the *Su River Records* and the *Miscellany*, where all the credit goes to Taizu, Li Tao presents an image of the Song founding as a corporate event – a drama that involves Taizu, Taizong, and Zhao Pu.[46]

---

[45]   *Yaolu*, 89.1727–28; *SHY, fangyu*, 3.23b–25a; *Yuhai* 161.25a–26b. Fan Chong used Li Gonglin's hand-scroll illustrations for the *Classic of Filial Piety* to educate Xiaozong; see *Yaolu*, 90.1736.
[46]   *Changbian*, 1.1–3.

Li Tao's version thus presented a challenge to the single-actor versions that began with Sima Guang and that were current in the mid-twelfth century when he compiled the *Long Draft*. To understand why Li Tao rejected this account is to glimpse, at the very beginning of his work, his approach to his sources and his overall vision for the book. As we have seen in Chapter 2, Li Tao took a conservative stance toward his sources, adhering wherever possible to the text of the veritable records and state histories, which he believed should be amended only in cases of obvious error and always with documentation.[47] A careful reading of the *Long Draft* entries on early Song historiography shows that Li Tao discerned the questionable motives behind later revisions to the *Taizu Veritable Records* of 980. His notes to the Chen Bridge narrative in the *Long Draft* reveal his awareness of discrepancies in the official sources. Through the vehicle of these notes, Li Tao casts intentional doubt upon his own main narrative. His notes indicate (1) that the "old records" of 980 framed Taizu's compact with the soldiers not to loot the city as solely Taizu's initiative, (2) that the "new records" of 999 attributed this same idea to Taizong, and (3) that the *Three Courts State History* of 1030 contained details of Taizong's and Zhao Pu's knowledge about the soldiers' plan to support Taizu as emperor.

One may usefully think of any Chen Bridge narrative as a collection of textual snippets, each of which conveys a specific factoid about the event. After the first formulation in 980, new snippets were added to make the final official version of 1030. Subsequent writers rearranged these snippets, omitting some and sometimes adding new ones, in order to attain versions that suited their immediate needs. The Sima Guang–Fan Chong version itself is probably an accretion that may contain elements as early as Sima Guang's conversation with his father in 1033 and as late as Fan Chong's edition of 1136. Whenever and however this version came to be, it contradicted the official history of 1030 and must therefore have resulted from the purposeful omission of Taizong's role from that official version. The new focus in the 1130s on Taizu mandated a new history of his role in the dynastic founding.

Acting in the political interests of both the monarchy and Zhao Ding, Fan Chong had more authority and incentive than Sima Guang to undertake these changes. In essence, Gaozong sanctioned Fan Chong to use Sima Guang's anecdotes to bypass the monarchy's own official history. Relying upon Sima Guang's enhanced status as Yuanyou paragon, Fan used the draft *Su River* notes to propagate the single-actor version of Chen Bridge and thus to undercut the official accounts from 999 and 1030. The resulting and now current *Su River Records* accentuate the role of Taizu at the expense of Taizong, not only at Chen Bridge but throughout the book. The result is a drastic historical revision that

---

[47] Pei Rucheng and Xu Peizao, *Xu zizhi tongjian changbian kaolüe*, 39–72, esp. 56; cf. Hartman, "A Textual History of Cai Jing's Biography in the *Songshi*," 523–25.

posits a direct transmission of political value from Taizu, through Qingli and Yuanyou, to Gaozong and the Restoration.

Li Tao largely agreed with the political values of this trajectory, but he was a more conservative and much better historian than Fan Chong in terms of empiricism and quality control. As explained in Chapter 2, in general, Li Tao used the tension between his main narrative and his own commentary in the *Long Draft* to introduce doubt about those points in the narrative where his sources conflicted. The *Su River Records* were a major source for the *Long Draft*, whose notes cite the work almost three hundred times. So Li Tao knew the work well and used it often. But his Chen Bridge narrative totally ignores Sima Guang's version. Read together, his narrative and notes criticize the current single-actor scenario as a biased representation of the full range of the extant sources. Thus, although Li Tao knew that the corporate version derived from later revisions of the original 980 record, he was unwilling to abandon the "new records" of 999 and the *Three Courts State History* of 1030, as the single-actor versions had done. He sought to present, in contrast, a consistent version that incorporated as many elements as possible from the existing, official sources. In sum, Li Tao's account of Chen Bridge presents a reasoned, historical compromise on the major issues of the founding, as these were understood in the mid-twelfth century.

For example, there is anecdotal evidence that, despite the official, sanitized, and eulogizing versions of the founding, many Song literati did believe – as royal sensitivity on the issue suggests – that Chen Bridge had been a premeditated coup with Taizu's participation.[48] In concord with these popular suspicions, in Li Tao's version, the active roles assigned to Taizong and Zhao Pu, plus the emphasis on rumors and omens – elements derived from the revised sources of 999 and 1030 – all suggest premeditated action. But Li Tao insists on maintaining Taizu's loyalty to the Zhou and his ignorance of the impending regime change. Although the soldiers' insistence that Taizu become emperor is the driving force in all Chen Bridge narratives, the solar omen in Li Tao makes clear that Heaven has sanctioned this mandate. But, in Li Tao, that mandate comes to the Zhao house, as represented in the founding troika; in Sima Guang–Fan Chong, it comes to Taizu alone.

Gaozong's abdication in favor of Xiaozong in 1162/6 completed transfer of political authority to the Taizu branch line. But since Gaozong remained politically active in retirement, the monarchy was now more than ever a corporate body. In the rhetoric of imperial propaganda, Yao (Gaozong) and Shun (Xiaozong) now ruled in tandem. The new political reality of this parallel

[48] See, for example, Zhang Shunmin, *Huaman lu*, 16b; and Yuan Wen, *Wengyu xianping*, 8.76. In these two versions of the same anecdote, Taizu, at a banquet before his departure for the north, refuses to accept public prostrations from Tao Gu that would acknowledge him as the future emperor.

brought fresh attention and validity to the older Yao–Shun pair – Taizu and Taizong. Throughout his entire tenure as an official historian, Li Tao labored within the intricate ambiguities of the dual monarchy, divided between the retired Gaozong and the reigning Xiaozong. As a politician, he was allied with Wang Yingchen, Chen Junqing, and others who positioned themselves in the 1160s as successors to the political values that Zhao Ding and the historical revisionists of the 1130s, sanctioned by Gaozong and led by Fan Chong, had associated with Taizu. But as a more sober historian, Li Tao knew the importance of Taizong's contributions to the "policies of the ancestors." And as a courtier, his relationship to Emperor Xiaozong, which was central to his historical mission, was too important to endanger with an impolitic insistence on the single-actor model. The comity of the Song founding, in Li Tao's version, thus reflects not only his best historical judgment but also the political realities of the times in which he worked.

These realities are nowhere better reflected than in a series of surviving paintings that depict six of the Song founders engaged in a convivial game of kickball. The image survives in all the major formats – the hand scroll, fan, and perhaps the hanging scroll – and in paintings that carry attributions to Southern Song academy painters that range in time from the mid-twelfth-century Su Hanchen 蘇漢臣 (d. 1163+) through to Qian Xuan 錢選 (1235?–1301+), who spanned the Song–Yuan transition. The collected works of Yuan authors contain no less than six colophons on various versions of these paintings they had seen, and this number attests to the popularity of the image. A hand scroll attribution to Qian Xuan in the Shanghai Museum (Figure 9.1) carries a colophon in which Qian explained that he had copied an original that was once in the collection of the Song Imperial Library, and he identified the six figures.[49] The figure in the right forefront kicking the ball is Taizu; Zhao Pu is in the forefront directly to his left. Taizong is probably the figure in the upper left; General Shi Shouxin 石守信 (928–984) is upper center; upper right, behind Taizu, is General Dang Jin 党進. To the far left, behind Zhao Pu, is Chu Zhaofu 楚昭輔 (911–979).[50]

The Yuan scholar Wu Cheng 吳澄 (1249–1331) thought that the scene depicts the group before the Song founding in 960.[51] Since kickball was practiced as a form of military training and preparation, the colophon writers read the image as a paean to the sense of common purpose, group spirit, and

[49] Wu Cheng, *Wu Wenzheng ji*, 92.17a–b; Shu Di, *Zhensuzhai ji*, 5.12a–b. For the painting see Duan Shu'an, *Zhongguo gudai shuhua tumu*, 2:70, image no. 1-0144.
[50] Other colophons, perhaps describing another image, describe the figures as Taizu, Taizong, and Zhao Pu, plus a Daoist priest and attendants; see Wu Cheng, *Wu Wenzheng ji*, 92.1a; Wang Yun, *Qiujian ji*, 32.11b. For a version of this image, painted on a round fan, now in the National Palace Museum in Taipei, see Cahill, *An Index of Early Chinese Painters and Paintings*, 175.
[51] *Wu Wenzheng ji*, 92.1a, 92.17a–b.

Figure 9.1   Attributed to Qian Xuan, *Kickball*. Hand scroll. Shanghai Museum.

dedication that supposedly enabled the Song founding under Taizu. Whoever composed the initial image also framed the founding as a combination of military prowess and civil administration. Two of the figures, Zhao Pu and Chu Zhaofu, wear civil headgear as opposed to the turbans of the four military men. In short, the image extols the corporate nature of the founding and, if the composition indeed originated in the imperial painting academy, represents probably the same sanctioned, late twelfth-century vision of the Song founding found in Li Tao's *Long Draft*.

The two versions of the Song founding coexisted in tension for the remainder of the dynasty. And they continue down to modern times to supply evidence both for those scholars who advance Taizu as the pre-eminent founder and for those who counter that Taizong was the ultimate mastermind of the founding. Chen Jun's account in his 1229 *Outline and Details* condensed Li Tao's text, but expanded Taizong's speech before the mounted Taizu and inserted material that is not in the *Long Draft* or elsewhere. The new passage reads,

Kuangyi [ie. Taizong] restrained [Taizu's] horse and requested, "Those who would bring relief to the world must cause the people to respect him as they would an emperor. The capital is the foundation of the empire. I request that you order the generals to prevent pillage." And His Highness replied, "very well."[52]

In this passage, the phrase "restrain his horse" (*kouma* 叩馬) quotes the "Biography of Po Yi" in the *Grand Scribe's Records*, where the sage-recluses

___

[52] *Huangchao gangmu*, 1.1–2.

Po Yi and Shu Qi "restrain the horse" of Emperor Wu and thus admonish him against violence as he fights to found the Zhou dynasty.[53] This insertion of a literary allusion into Taizong's mouth on the eve of the Song founding, almost two hundred years after the event, underscores the continuing fluidity of the Chen Bridge narrative.

Alternatively – and in a rare example where Chen Jun and Lü Zhong do not agree – the most fervent *daoxue* historian of late Song retained the single-actor version espoused by Sima Guang and Zhu Xi. Lü Zhong's comment repeats the link between Mencius' focus on nonviolence and the transformative character of Taizu's mandate: as the elders of Pei village once flocked to Han Gaozu and beseeched him to become emperor, so did Taizu's soldiers rally around him and make him emperor. This total allegiance enabled him to end the militarism of the Five Dynasties and relieve the suffering of the populace.[54]

Given the strong *daoxue* commitment of the *Song History* compilers in the Yuan dynasty, the single-actor version dominates both their account of Chen Bridge and their evaluation of Taizu. In this sense, their treatment of the Song founding follows the *daoxue* line that descended from Fan Chong, through Zhu Xi, to Lü Zhong. As we have seen in Chapter 5, the Yuan historians, perhaps wisely, rejected the advice that they reopen the case on the Song founding. Their narrative of Chen Bridge at the beginning of the Taizu annals is sparse and avoids most of the contentious details; in turn, their eulogy pairs his civil and military talents but links both to the ancient sovereigns (civil: Yao and Shun; military: Tang and Wu). His seventeen-year rule ended the military chaos of the Five Dynasties and set the model for Song governance in which "the spirit of the Way and benevolence" prevailed.[55]

A Banquet for the Generals

The Song Military Problem

The Song academy painting of the corporate founders playing kickball may also visualize yet another of the grand allegory's projections of Taizu – his status as founder of the dynasty's unique system for administering military power. How best to balance the distribution of military power between the center – the court, the capital – and wherever that power had to be exercised – the border, the provinces – remained throughout the Song a perennial, unsolved problem. The issue involved much more than the political relationship between court and province. Given that military expenses consumed 80 percent of Song

---

[53] Sima Qian, *Shiji*, 61.2123; Nienhauser, *The Grand Scribe's Records*, 7:3.
[54] *Huangchao dashiji*, 2.48–49. The passage uses a quotation from Su Zhe, as cited in Zhu Xi's commentary to Mencius; see *Sishu zhangju jizhu*, 207.
[55] *SS*, 1.34, 3.50–51.

state revenue, the problem of military balance affected fiscal, monetary, and taxation policy as well. The grand allegory of Song history posits Taizu as the initiator of two policies that defined the dynasty's initial – and, according to the allegory, supposedly permanent – solutions to these problems: (1) he promoted the centralization of military and economic resources in the capital, a policy often abbreviated as "to strengthen the root and weaken the branches" (*qianggan ruozhi* 強幹弱枝), and (2) he promoted the use of civil over military officials, often abbreviated as "to weight the civil and lighten the military" (*zhongwen qingwu* 重文輕武). Modern scholarship has long moved past these platitudes and now understands the emergence of a distinctive Song governance as the result of a century-long process of social and economic change, in which the first Song emperor played an important but ultimately supporting role.[56]

No image, however, better defines Taizu's pivotal role in the grand allegory than the dramatic story of the "banquet at which he took back military power over a cup of wine" (*beijiu shi bingquan* 杯酒釋兵權). This single episode – even more than the story of the Chen bridge founding itself – came to define the essence of early Song distinctiveness and linked that essence to the persona of Taizu himself, especially to his reputation for benevolence: Taizu had ended the militarism of the Five Dynasties and set the foundations for the benevolent reign of Song – and the banquet was where he did it. Li Tao, with some hesitance, concluded that the event took place in 961/7, and scholars still debate whether the famous feast actually took place or not.[57] But regardless of the historicity of the occasion, the development of the story of the banquet – its evolution as an anecdote in Song – can be reconstructed and its textual history can then be read as a barometer of shifting attitudes toward the political and financial issues that the story embodies. Before embarking on this task, however, a review of the Song military problem may be helpful.

Histories of the Song military routinely distinguish between the standing professional army (*jinbing* 禁兵 "imperial troops") and various militias – part-time nonprofessional soldiers recruited from local populations. Taizu and Taizong began their careers as officers in a professional army whose origins can be traced to the mercenary armies of late Tang. During the Five Dynasties, the leaders of these armies sometimes became emperors, as did Taizu in 960. Army salaries then came directly from court funds that the leader, in his capacity as sovereign, collected from the population as general tax revenue.

---

[56] Wang, *The Structure of Power in North China during the Five Dynasties*, 1–6; Worthy, "The Founding of Sung China," 1–11; Huang K'uan-ch'ung, "Liang Song zhengce yu shifeng de bianhua"; Lorge, *The Reunification of China*, 1–21; Lau and Huang, "Founding and Consolidation of the Sung Dynasty," 215–220; more recently, Lau Nap-yin, "Bei Song pingjia wuren biaojun zai renshi."

[57] For the extensive scholarship see Fang Jianxin, *Ershi shiji Song shi yanjiu lunzhu mulu*, 18.

In the mature Song system of the Zhenzong era, these imperial troops were divided into "three commands" (*sanya* 三衙), with half the troops stationed in Kaifeng to defend the capital, and half stationed along the northern border and in the provinces.

In order to prevent military coups, the court rotated both commanders and battalions, usually at three-year intervals, between Kaifeng and provincial postings. This professional army enabled the Song monarchy to maintain complete operational and political control over a military force of a million men and so remained the preferred model for the first hundred years of the dynasty. The system, however, consumed enormous resources, usually at the expense of military preparedness. The intentional disjunction between commanders and troops undermined operational effectiveness and made it difficult to maintain readiness. Lastly, the professional army was the most expensive of the several options available. By 1065, the army consumed 83 percent of the state's cash income, and the government recorded its first overall financial deficit.[58]

For these reasons, in the early 1070s, Emperor Shenzong, with the goal of reducing military costs and eventually replacing the professional army, decided to develop a "mutual security" system (*baojia* 保甲) as part of the New Policies. Envisioned as a "peoples' army" (*minbing* 民兵), the *baojia* soon became a complex network of local militia units whose organizational hierarchy reflected the social structure of their communities: poorer peasants became simple militiamen, local landowners and magnates became their officers. The responsibilities of the new organization were soon expanded from general policing and bandit control to include tax collection. Critics cautioned against the dangers of militarizing the population on such a vast scale. When Sima Guang became chief councilor in 1085, he ordered the *baojia* units dismantled within five days, an act that created immediate bureaucratic chaos in local jurisdictions.[59]

When the New Policies were revived after 1094, the *baojia* system returned and remained in force for the remainder of Northern Song. In the usual understanding of the period, its growth undermined the professional army, and, combined with corruption in the *baojia* administration, rendered both organizations ineffective against the Jurchen invasions of 1125.[60] After years of chaos and forced experimentation, Emperor Gaozong restored his own revamped version of the professional military in 1141. The *baojia* system under the New Policies was the only time in the dynasty when the court advocated

---

[58] Wang Zengyu, *Songchao junzhi chutan*, 1–79, for data on Renzong-era battalion placements see 43–67. On the deficit see Smith, "Shen-tsung's Reign," 349.

[59] Smith, "Shen-tsung's Reign," 407–14, 427–29, 445–46; Levine, "Che-tsung's Reign," 494–96; Wang Zengyu, *Songchao junzhi chutan*, 153–57.

[60] *SS*, 187.4582; Wang Zengyu, *Songchao junzhi chutan*, 157.

a nationwide militia. But the notion of peasant-soldiers was enshrined in Confucian theory, and, in Southern Song, often in Confucian practice. The successful implementation in the Tang dynasty of the *fubing* 府兵 militia had inspired Wang Anshi and remained an attractive but elusive model for literati who opposed the heavy tax extractions that the professional army compelled. Civil literati often experimented with plans for local militias in their native areas and in jurisdictions where they were appointed.[61] Many literati administrators, especially those associated with the *daoxue* movement, encouraged local militias, often at the direct expense of the regular army, whose leaders naturally opposed their development.[62]

In fact, many of the most successful Southern Song fighting forces were variations on local militias or regional armies. Many troops in the so-called "house armies" of the 1130s, which Gaozong and Qin Gui transformed into the professional army after 1141, had evolved from late Northern Song *baojia* units. Well-organized militias enjoyed the advantage of closer communication between officers and soldiers, were better suited for local policing duties, and were generally much cheaper than the professional option. In 1168, for example, Wang Yan 王炎 (1115–1178) estimated the cost of one Jingnan "righteous brave" at only 5 percent of the cost of one regular army soldier.[63] Despite such tantalizing cost savings, however, the monarchy suspected any militia activity that was outside the purview of the Bureau of Military Affairs. The danger that ambitious leaders could use local forces to form alternative centers of regional military and political power – a variety of Song warlordism that Taizu had supposedly consigned to history – remained ever-present, especially after 1127.

Taizu is reputed to have abolished the system of military governors (*jiedu shi* 解度史) and attendant warlordism that the Song inherited from the Tang and Five Dynasties. In fact, however, similar mechanisms of regional military control endured throughout the dynasty as yet a third alternative form of military organization. In addition to the *baojia* militias, Emperor Shenzong also instituted "sectoral command measures" (*jiangbing fa* 將兵法) within the professional army that ended the earlier system of unit rotation. In a move to strengthen the links between commanders and troops and to improve training, the country was divided into about 150 regional commands, with designated units permanently attached to each command (*xijiang jinbing* 係將禁兵).[64]

Conceptually, military governors can be seen as a combination of features from both the professional and the militia systems. The governors were

---

[61] Lo, *The Life and Thought of Yeh Shih*, 105–10.
[62] Huang K'uan-ch'ung, *Nan Song difang wuli*. For excellent entries on the major Song militias and their relations with the regular army and the court see *Chaoye zaji, jia*, 18.407–24; also Wang Zengyu, *Songchao junzhi chutan*, 237–40.
[63] *Zhongxing shengzheng*, 47.1a; Wang Zengyu, *Songchao junzhi chutan*, 93.
[64] Wang Zengyu, *Songchao junzhi chutan*, 114–29.

professional soldiers who commanded professional troops. Neither rotated, but remained in a fixed location, often for long periods of time. During that time, they collected local tax revenues, and these funds formed the major source of their salaries. The governors had authority to manage personnel not only in their own army units but often in the local civil bureaucracy as well. Although their administration over the local population could be harsh, because morale in such armies was high they usually proved effective in combat. From the monarchy's perspective, the cost was intermediate between the two other systems. To the monarchy, the loyalty of the governor was naturally a paramount concern, since the court forfeited direct oversight over the areas the governor controlled.

The Song court resorted to this third option only under extreme duress. The Jin invasions of 1125 and the failure of Song forces to respond adequately destroyed the last vestiges of the early dynasty's theory and practice of military balance between center and province, between commander and troops. What remained after 1127 were disparate sectoral commands and militia units, all fighting locally with no unified command structure. At the same time, the Northern Song experience had left a rich legacy of concepts and structures for military reorganization. The complex history of the Song military between 1127 and 1141 presents repeated attempts to rebuild from these fragments a new military structure that would achieve two goals: (1) assemble and enlarge the disparate fragments into an effective fighting force, and (2) simultaneously reassert over the military the full imperial control of the pre-Shenzong era.[65]

The Restoration Context

As soon as Gaozong ascended the throne in 1127/5, Hu Shunzhi 胡舜陟 (1083–1143) and Li Gang recommended that he appoint military governors in north China, a move that would create an immediate political relationship between the new emperor and the local magnates then in place and fighting the Jin. As a precedent, Hu cited Emperor Taizu's policy of appointing trusted generals such as Guo Jin 郭進 (922–979) and Li Hanchao 李漢超 (d. 977) to long-term defensive positions on the borders and permitting them to retain taxes and exercise local authority.[66] The proposition was sidetracked as the court retreated south, but revived again in 1130/5 after the court's return from the sea. The Jurchen withdrawal north after the 1129 invasion had left massive banditry and lawlessness in the Yangzi valley and along the northern Henan border. Chief Councilor Fan Zongyin proposed that the court appoint thirty-

---

[65] Tao, "The Move to the South and the Reign of Kao-tsung," 662–71 provides a concise summary of early Southern Song military issues.
[66] *Yaolu*, 5.136; *Yuhai*, 18.34b.

nine "defense commissioners" (*zhenfu shi* 鎮撫史) in these areas and afford them extensive local autonomy. They could retain all land taxes, but not salt and wine monopoly revenues, which were still to be transmitted directly to the court. They could appoint local officials but prefectural-level appointments would require court approval. They could manage their own forces and conduct military operations without prior authorization. In response to critics of the plan, Fan replied that since the court did not control these areas anyway, it had little to lose from offering a political relationship to those who already exercised de facto control. These were a mixture of local magnates, military officers, and bandits. Only five of the initial appointments went to officials actually dispatched to these areas by the court.[67]

As precedent for the move, however, Fan did not use the precedent that Hu Shunzhi had cited earlier. He proposed, rather, a different take on Taizu's military policy: because the emperor and his councilor Zhao Pu had taken back power from the military governors, the dynasty had enjoyed 150 years of peace. But Fan argued that Taizu's policy had also led to the present enfeeblement of the dynasty's military capability in the face of the Jin invasions and should now be modified. The proposed "defense commissioners" would act as a defensive buffer between the court and the Jin. Fan's reference was clearly to the "banquet that took back power," but his formulation now cast doubt on the legacy of that venerable policy in order to justify his own reversal of it. In short, these early Southern Song deliberations over military policy reveal two antithetical interpretations of Taizu's thinking about the balance between court and provincial power: (1) that he placed trusted generals in long-term appointments that continued many features of the late Tang military-governor system; (2) that he ended such military governorships.

A month after Fan Zongyin created the "defense commissioners" in areas the court did not control, he formed the "Divinely Martial Army" (*Shenwu jun* 神武軍) to assert the fiction of a unified command under the Bureau of Military Affairs over the so-called "house armies."[68] By the mid-1130s, five such armies under Wu Jie, Yue Fei, Han Shizhong, Liu Guangshi 劉光世 (1089–1142), and Zhang Junn 張俊 (1086–1154) had grown steadily by absorbing weaker units and had become the Song's major fighting forces.[69] As the biography of Yue Fei illustrates, these leaders emerged through the chaos of the late 1120s and early 1130s to assume command over large armies whose subordinate officers were personally loyal to their leaders. The contemporary term "house [or

---

[67] *Yaolu*, 33.755–56. For the definitive study see Huang K'uan-ch'ung, *Nan Song difang wuli*, 145–202; also Wang Zengyu, *Songchao junzhi chutan*, 162–63. Most of the "defense commissioners" were quickly gone – killed, defected to the Jin, promoted, or absorbed into other units – but some remained in place as late as 1135.

[68] *Yaolu*, 34.780; Wang Zengyu, *Songchao junzhi chutan*, 164–70.

[69] I romanize 張俊 as Zhang Junn to distinguish him from his contemporary Zhang Jun 張浚.

family] army" (*jiajun* 家軍) alludes to the popular conception of these armies as extensions of the "family" of the top commander. Such armies violated the fundamental early Song premise of disjunction between commanders and troops. Lacking effective court oversight during this period, these armies had generated their own autonomous administration and collected taxes in areas they controlled.

"Divinely martial," the phrase the court adopted for its military reorganization in 1130/6, derives from the *Book of Changes* where the ancient sages were "possessed of divinely martial power yet did not kill" (神武而不殺者).[70] The phrase was early associated with Taizu and soon became part of his official title.[71] Renaming Song forces as the "Divinely Martial Army" was yet another attempt to cloak the Restoration in the rhetoric of the founder. In the second half of 1130, Emperor Gaozong ordered a review of dynastic military policy, and Wang Zhi 王銍 (1083?–1140), then an archivist at the Bureau of Military Affairs, produced a document collection of 200 *juan*, whose surviving preface summarizes his findings.[72] Wang posited Taizu as the personal creator of a military organization that perfectly balanced center and province and was perfectly administered through an interlocking system of financial and operational controls – the idealized professional army of the dynastic beginning. But Wang dealt gingerly with the issue of militias. He did not condemn them outright, but provided three examples, including the *baojia*, where emperors ordered militias discontinued because they overburdened the population. His conclusion placed his research squarely in the context of the emerging Yao–Taizu–Gaozong rhetoric of the time. He countered the standard image of Yao as an austere and frugal monarch, pointing instead to a passage in the *Book of Documents* that attributed his success to sagacity, spirituality, martial power, and civil virtues. The Song founders, Wang concluded, also embodied these four qualities and combined them to form the foundations of their military power: the essence of this combination could not be found in the historical "traces" he submitted but in the "mind of the sage."

Wang Zhi's politically delicate conclusion placed the resolution of the military problem squarely upon the emperor. Many voices cautioned Gaozong against the dangers of both the defense commissioners and the house armies. Wang Zao 汪藻 (1079–1154) wrote in 1131/2 that reasserting

---

[70] Wilhelm, *The I Ching*, 317.   [71] *Changbian*, 1.28, 9.207, 16.344, 43.923, 46.995.
[72] *Yaolu*, 35.805–6; Wang Mingqing, *Huizhu lu, yuhua*, 1.281–86, presents this text as the work of his father, Wang Zhi. The text of this preface also occurs as *juan* eight in Chen Fuliang's *Lidai bingzhi* 歷代兵制, and scholars have not questioned Chen's authorship. However, the text reads much better as part of the Taizu/Restoration rhetoric of 1130 than as late twelfth-century discourse. A close comparison of both versions reveals that Chen has rewritten Wang's original conclusion for his own purposes. Many scholars also accept this text as a primary source for early Song military organization; it represents, however, an early Southern Song utopian re-creation of Taizu's military accomplishments.

imperial control over these forces and rebalancing military power according to the founder's guidelines was crucial to the court's and to Gaozong's personal survival. Wang proposed a strategy to degrade the power of the generals by enticing capable but disgruntled subordinates to accept imperial commands over smaller subunits of troops that could be gradually pared off from the larger forces. Over time, a new imperial army (*yuqian* 御前) could thus be formed. Ten years later, a variation of this plan would serve as the base for the transformation of the house armies of the generals into the "house" army of Emperor Gaozong.[73]

The emperor and his advisers looked to Taizu, if not perhaps as a source of practical precedents to solve their problem, then certainly as a source of rhetoric in which to enfold the eventual solution. In 1132/12 Gaozong and Chief Councilor Lü Yihao were discussing proposed changes to the format for the *jinshi* examinations. The councilor suggested that the caliber of the man might perhaps be more important that the format of the examination. He had recently been reading anecdotes about how Taizu and his councilor Zhao Pu had established order and set down standards for the dynasty, which, if followed, they hoped would ensure its longevity. Gaozong replied, alluding to the banquet anecdote, that Zhao Pu's assistance had indeed been instrumental in removing the early Song military governors: in this, he had been a model councilor.[74] The subtext of this conversation is clearly the need to assert imperial control over Song military forces that, both emperor and councilor agree, now resemble the military governors of early Song. Having thus established the parallel nature of their historical circumstances, the interlocutors position themselves as aspirational parallels to Taizu and Zhao Pu. One may thus understand this exchange as Gaozong's sanction for Lü Yihao to pursue a stratagem to duplicate the outcome of the famous banquet, the success of which would ensure him a place in Song history akin to that of Zhao Pu.

Indeed, although there were many ideas, every chief councilor of the 1130s agreed that reassertion of imperial control over the army was essential to the success of the Restoration. As early as 1130/5, Zhao Ding had advocated bringing back the early Song "three commands" as part of a general "return

---

[73] *Huibian*, 145.1a–8b. Wang Zao's memorial is widely cited and abridged in southern Song histories: perfunctorily in the earlier sources, *Zhongxing shengzheng*, 9.4a–5a; and *Zhongxing xiaoli*, 10.123; at greater length and with a focus on military corruption in the later sources, *Huangchao zhongxing jishi benmo*, 16.3b–6a; *Yaolu*, 42.908–9; and *Zhongxing gangmu*, 3.123–24. For the full text see *QSW*, 157:3378.120–25. The generals, led by Liu Guangshi, pushed back against Wang Zao's attack on their loyalty and competence. They arranged for a response that pinned blame for the Song collapse squarely on civil authorities. Cai Jing and Wang Fu had been civil officials; civil officials had presided over the loss of Kaifeng and abandoned their posts when the Jurchen invaded. Worst of all, the two rival dynastic pretenders, Zhang Bangchang and Liu Yu were both Song civil officials. See *Huibian*, 145.9a–b; *Yaolu*, 42.910; Deng Xiaonan, *Zuzong zhi fa*, 460–64.

[74] *Yaolu*, 61.1211; *Zhongxing shengzheng*, 12.24b.

to the policies of the ancestors." He insisted that Gaozong reform and restore the palace guard as a first step toward bringing back the "three commands," the military organization that Taizu and Zhao Pu had devised to provide a long-lasting structure for dynastic security.[75] In 1135/12, under the joint councilorship of Zhao Ding and Zhang Jun, major progress was achieved in reviving the "three-command" structure and staffing it with commanders personally loyal to Gaozong.[76]

Sima Guang Again

Many of these issues were likely on Fan Chong's mind in 1136 when he received Gaozong's order to edit, based on the holograph notes that were then in his possession, Sima Guang's *Su River Records*. This undertaking, which we have examined in Chapter 8, now becomes relevant once again. The entry on the "banquet that took back power" in the *Su River Records* later became the dominant narrative in one of the grand allegory's seminal scenes. Li Tao began his *Long Draft* commentary on the banquet by lamenting that neither the standard histories nor the veritable records mentioned the incident. He admitted that he had therefore been forced to reconstruct it "retrospectively" (*zhuishu* 追書), meaning that, lacking contemporaneous documentation, he reconstructed the event from recollections recorded after the event itself. In addition to Sima Guang's account, Li Tao had two other sources: anecdote collections from Wang Zeng 王曾 (978–1038) and Ding Wei, both of whom had served in the early eleventh century as chief councilors under Emperor Zhenzong. The *Su River Records* version, however, is much longer than either of the earlier anecdotes:

After Taizu had attained the empire and destroyed Li Yun and Li Chongjin, he summoned Zhao Pu and asked, "The leadership has changed many times in the decades since the end of the Tang, and endless warfare has ground the people to dust. How can I develop a long-term plan for the state that will quiet this warfare?" Zhao Pu replied, "That you even speak of this will bring prosperity to everyone everywhere. The reason for the endless warfare and instability since the end of the Tang is simply the excessive power of the military governors: the ruler is weak, the servitor is strong. There is no special trick to bringing them under control now – just gradually take away their authority, control their revenue, and recall their best troops. Then the empire will find its own peace." Before he had finished talking, His Majesty said, "Don't speak of this again. I understand."

Sometime later, because court had run late, His Majesty was drinking together with his friends Shi Shouxin, Wang Shenqi, and others. When the wine had taken effect, he dismissed the servants and said, "I would never have been able to arrive here without your efforts. My memories of your virtues are boundless. But being the Son of Heaven is

---

[75] *Yaolu*, 33.765; *Zhongxing xiaoli*, 8.101.   [76] *Yaolu*, 96.1831; *Chaoye zaji, jia*, 18.401–2.

very difficult. It certainly does not compare with the joys of being a military governor. I have not dared so far to attempt a single full night's sleep."

Shi Shouxin and the others all said, "But why?"

His Majesty said, "It's not hard to understand. Who would not wish to be the one that holds this seat?"

Shouxin and the others all bowed low and said, "Why do you speak in this way? The mandate of Heaven is now established. Who would dare to think differently?"

His Majesty said, "Not so. Even though you have no such intentions, what if your subordinates should desire to become rich? If one morning, they put the yellow robe on you, even though you had no such desire, you could not resist." And so they all bowed their heads and wept, saying,

"Thoughtless as we are, we never considered this point. Only your compassion can lead us on the path toward a good life." And His Majesty replied,

"Human life is like the passing of a white colt glimpsed through a crack in the wall. And so those who enjoy wealth and status simply amass money, enjoy themselves, and free their descendants from want. You should relinquish your military authority, select and purchase good lands and villas, and so provide a stable future for your descendants. Take many singing boys and dancing girls, enjoy yourselves in daily drinking, and so live out the rest of your days. When there are no suspicions between ruler and servitor, both superior and inferior feel at ease. Is this not something good?" They all bowed once again and thanked him, saying,

"That Your Majesty shows such concern for his servitors is as it was once said 'to give life to the dead and flesh to bare bones.'"

The next day they all reported ill and requested to be relieved of their army authority. His Highness granted their requests, and all were given sinecures and repaired to their mansions. And so he bestowed upon them extensive rewards and considerations and formed marriage ties with them. He then devised a different system and implemented rotating commanders for his personal guard.

Later, he deployed transport commissioners and controllers general to oversee the provincial finances. He selected the best troops in the empire for the Imperial Guard. And all of these meritorious retainers ended their lives well, their descendants prosperous and honored down to the present day.

Without the long-term planning of Zhao Pu and the decisiveness of Taizu, the world would never have come to good rule. That today even old people have never seen war is due to the farsightedness of this "sage and worthy" (i.e. Taizu and Zhao Pu). Zhao Pu was crafty and cruel, and many were maliciously harmed during his time. Yet his descendants retain their fortune to this day. Few of the great ministers of the founding period were his equal, and his plan for the stability of the empire was his greatest achievement.[77]

This dramatic narrative artfully joins a number of motifs that transcend the immediate issue of military organization. First, the passage frames the banquet

---

[77] Sima Guang, *Sushui jiwen*, 1.11–13. For the white-colt quotation see Watson, *The Complete Works of Chuang Tzu*, 240. In the *Zuozhuan*, "To give life to the dead and flesh to bare bones" describes the advice given to a newly appointed councilor that he should dismiss his personal retainers who may threaten the sovereign and thus undermine his position; see Legge, *The Ch'un Ts'ew*, 494–96.

within the context of Emperor Taizu and Zhao Pu as an exemplary model of the ruler–minister relationship. The opening dialogue showcases this relationship. Taizu identifies a problem and asks his adviser for a long-term solution. Zhao obliges with historical analysis and a strategy for immediate action. Taizu is compassionate yet decisive; Zhao Pu is analytical yet practical. Although superior and inferior, they work together in an atmosphere of mutual trust. Labelled "sage and worthy" by the end of the passage, both play their proper roles in the structured dynamic of literati governance. Despite the "worthy's" sometimes unsavoury character, their relationship stands in contrast to the new ruler's relationship to his former colleagues-in-arms. Although loyal in the past and still now, their potential to threaten Taizu in his new position might undermine their relationship to him. The opening reference to Li Yun 李筠 (d. 960) and Li Chongjin 李重進 (d. 960) alludes to this threat, since these were generals who refused to accept the new dynasty. Taizu's last words to his former comrades mark the dramatic high point of the narrative: "When there are no suspicions between ruler and servitor, both superior and inferior feel at ease." The sentence describes equally well his present relation to Zhao Pu and his future relation with his comrades, if they accept his proposal. The phrase, in fact, encapsulates Sima Guang's most basic principle of literati government.[78] Read at the highest level of abstraction, this narrative depicts emperor and his top civil administrator peacefully incorporating those who wield military power into the hierarchical structure of dynastic governance.

Second, Taizu and Zhao Pu here co-operate to devise a plan that will both end the warlordism of the military governors and lay down a plan for dynastic stability based on imperial control of the military. The concrete plan to regain and centralize power develops from Zhao Pu's initial analysis that "the ruler is weak, the servitor is strong." This inversion of the proper hierarchical relationship engenders militarism, political fragmentation, and misery for the populace. Zhao Pu's plan to "take away their authority, control their revenue, and recall their best troops" and ultimately to deploy court officials to oversee provincial finances will restore this unnatural inversion. Peace will be the natural result of a military under central control. This narrative emphasizes the material benefits that accrue to all who accept their place in the model of centralized and hierarchical governance that the passage advocates. It is indeed not difficult to see why this narrative, composed largely of vivid, direct dialogue among the participants themselves, assumed its status as an iconic touchstone of Confucian literati governance.

Despite the anecdote's dramatic and theoretical attractions, Li Tao pointed out the basic contradiction: Zhao Pu's analysis and his plan of action target the

---

[78] For Sima Guang's ideas on the ideal ruler–minister relationship see Ji, *Politics and Conservatism in Northern Song China*, 35–49.

military governors, but Shi Shouxin and Wang Shenqi 王審琦 (925–974) are not military governors but high officers in the "three commands." While the first paragraph fulminates against the military governors, the rest of the passage shows Taizu convincing his comrades to accept positions as the very same military governors. Li concluded that Sima Guang had conflated two separate banquets – one in 961 at which the generals surrendered their "three-command" positions and another in 969 at which several military governors were indeed relieved of their commands.[79] Many modern scholars, developing Li Tao's lead, separate and omit the first paragraph when discussing his entry on the banquet.[80] Li Tao indeed reworked Sima Guang's text but retained the first paragraph intact, thus setting up a typical *Long Draft* tension between main text and commentary. To understand Li Tao's choices, it is necessary to first examine the other sources at his disposal. The earliest of these is probably the following passage attributed to Ding Wei:

When Zhao Pu was chief councilor, one day he said to Taizu, "Neither Shi Shouxin nor Wang Shenqi should be allowed to command troops." His Majesty said, "How would these two ever be willing to transgress?" Zhao said, "That's true. They would never be willing to do so. But I have carefully observed their incompetence, and I am worried they may not be able to control their subordinates. If they cannot control their subordinates, and troublemakers suddenly appear among their troops, then for a time they may not be their own masters." Taizu replied, "But we have so heavily rewarded these two, how could they possibly let me down?" Zhao said, "Perhaps just the same way you let down [Emperor Zhou] Shizong?" Then Taizu understood and agreed with him.[81]

Ding Wei's characterization of the relationship between Taizu and Zhao Pu differs greatly from that of Sima Guang. Here, Zhao initiates the conversation and actively pushes the issue against a vacillating, even recalcitrant, Taizu. There is no banquet; the generals are "incompetent"; and the conclusion alludes directly to Taizu's own usurpation of the Zhou throne. The focus is on Zhao's personal loyalty to Taizu, and his ability to persuade the emperor to undertake difficult but necessary actions. In its original location in the *Conversations of Ding Wei* (*Ding Jingong tanlu* 丁晉公談錄), this passage occurs as the last of six anecdotes that highlight aspects of Zhao Pu's leadership, his suitability for high office, and his relationship with Taizu. These passages show him able to stand up to Taizu yet also able to adapt flexibly to the emperor's many moods. This larger set of passages emphasizes their interpersonal "chemistry," not their paired institutional capacity to generate policy. Nor does this passage show any

---

[79] *Changbian*, 2.50, 10.233–34.

[80] Nie Chongqi, "Lun Song Taizu shou bingquan"; Deng Xiaonan, *Zuzong zhi fa*, 200–2; Worthy, "The Founding of Sung China," 174–75; Lorge, "The Entrance and Exit of the Song Founders," 60–61.

[81] *Ding Jingong tanlu*, 262.

larger concern for military balance or mention military governors. Ding Wei's sole focus is on Zhao's concern to protect Taizu from a potential military coup.

Ding Wei was exiled to the south in 1022 and remained there until his death in 1037. Song bibliographers suggest that his nephew put the *Conversations of Ding Wei* together during his exile, since the book mentions the death of Wang Qinruo in 1025.[82] The *Siku* editors fulminated against the work as a biased and partisan defense of Ding Wei and his policies.[83] Given these circumstances, the book's positive portrait of the Taizu–Zhao Pu relationship can be read as a historical and typological defense of Ding Wei's former relationship to Emperor Zhenzong: in Ding Wei's view, he and Zhenzong continued the exemplary relationship between Taizu and Zhao Pu. Of course, this larger context need not affect the veracity of the individual details in the anecdote, but these details serve a purpose very different from the longer and later version by Sima Guang. In short, one cannot arrange Li Tao's three sources on the banquet in simple chronological order and then read them as a cumulative amplification of the same narrative.

Li Tao's third source, an anecdote attributed to Ding Wei's political rival, Chief Councilor Wang Zeng, presents another view of the banquet:

When Taizu had been on the throne for many years after his ascension, Shi Shouxin, Wang Shenqi, and others still maintained their divided command of the Imperial Army, as they had before. Chief Councilor Zhao Pu often criticized them, but His Majesty strongly protected and sheltered them. Zhao Pu also secretly requested that they receive other commands. So Taizu had no choice but to invite Shi and the others to a banquet where he spoke of how long they had been friends, and then he notified them, "We have stood together as one family since the beginning. How could it be otherwise? Yet your critics have brought forth continual accusations. Now there is nothing to do but for you all to select a good location where each shall receive an external governorship and there shall be no discussion of transfers or replacements. Use the tax proceeds to maintain yourselves in enjoyment until the end of your days. I have numerous daughters in my inner apartments and shall arrange marriages with you as a sign there is nothing between us. I hope that in the future there will be no complications for you gentlemen." Shouxin and the others bowed low and thanked him. Therefore, husbands for imperial princesses were all selected from among the Gao, Shi, Wang, and Wei clans. And each retired to his military command, where for over twenty years they lived in honor and glory, united from beginning to end as one. In former times, even Emperor Han Guangzu did not surpass Taizu in such support and protection for meritorious retainers.[84]

This anecdote also presents Zhao Pu as the initiator against a reluctant emperor but does not dwell on their relationship as ruler and minister. Describing the transfer of the generals out of their "three-commands"

---

[82] Chen Zhensun, *Zhizhai shulu jieti*, 7.206; Chao Gongwu, *Junzhai dushuzhi jiaozheng*, 6.254–55.

[83] Ji Yun et al., *Qinding Siku quanshu zong mu*, 143.1889.

[84] *Wang Wenzheng gong bilu*, 267–68.

positions, it focuses on Taizu's generosity and largess toward these loyal supporters. In this narrative, the banquet symbolizes the strong relationship between Taizu and his generals. Accordingly, because the nature of Zhao Pu's criticisms against them is unspecified, there is no direct reference to a military coup or to insubordination. Their appointments as military governors outside the capital are portrayed here as fitting rewards for long and loyal service. The conclusion compares Taizu's promise to link himself to the generals through marriage to the similar policy of Emperor Guangzu of Han, who rewarded his early supporters with marriage ties to the dynasty.[85] This rhetorical parallel reinforces the main focus of the passage, the connection between just rewards for loyal service and dynastic stability – "united from beginning to end as one."

Thus, Li Tao confronted three source texts, none contemporaneous with the event itself and each written with a different purpose and perspective. In forging his "reconstruction," he adopted the focus of Wang Zeng's narrative, but took most of his actual language from the *Su River Records*. Because he believed that concerns about a coup were probably well founded, he also incorporated that portion of Ding Wei's dialogue. However, although he did not slavishly follow the *Su River Records*, he nevertheless allowed the contradiction between the first paragraph and the remainder of Sima Guang's text to stand. Since it is unlikely that Sima himself would have made such a basic historical blunder, Li Tao, by noting this contradiction in his commentary but retaining Sima's first paragraph in his main text, creates tension between text and commentary, and this tension alerts the reader to think toward a possible resolution.

In contrast to Wang Zeng's focus on Taizu and his generals, the first paragraph of the *Su River Records* – and indeed the entire anecdote – highlights the institutional relationship between Taizu and Zhao Pu as ruler and minister. But it does not address the central military issue that Sima Guang encountered during his lifetime – the regular army versus the *baojia* militia. However, the spirit and message of the first paragraph resonates perfectly with the court's efforts throughout the 1130s to reassert imperial control over the house armies. Zhao Pu's recipe for taking back military power presages precisely the policies and strategies that Zhang Jun, Zhao Ding, and ultimately Qin Gui pursued against the house armies.

Given the compilation history of the *Su River Records*, there is no way to know for sure who put together the existing "Sima Guang" narrative of the banquet. Sima Guang may indeed have penned the entire passage himself. More likely, as Li Tao hinted, the first paragraph was added as a preface in order to frame the principal narrative, a splice that most likely occurred sometime in the mid-1130s. For example, Luo Congyan's *Record of Revering Yao* from

---

[85] Twitchett and Loewe, *Cambridge History of China, Volume 1*, 275–76.

1126 begins with Taizu's dispatch of his trusted generals to guard the border, the same precedent with which Hu Shunzhi began his memorial in 1127/5, but Luo's collection, despite almost fifty anecdotes from the Taizu period, does not contain a version of the developed banquet narrative.[86] The first appearance of the received Sima Guang narrative – outside the *Su River Records* – occurs in the *Records of Things Heard and Seen in the Shao Family* (*Shaoshi wenjian lu* 邵氏聞見錄).[87]

The author of this work, Shao Bowen 邵伯溫 (1057–1134), was a Luoyang native, son of Shao Yong 邵雍 (1011–1077), and associate of Sima Guang. More importantly, he was also an early teacher of Zhao Ding; and his son, Shao Bo 邵博 (d. 1158), was a member of Zhao Ding's political network.[88] Although Shao Bowen's preface is dated 1132/12, a slightly later preface by Shao Bo relates that he selected, classified, and arranged his father's draft collection into its present twenty-chapter configuration. The conclusion to this preface frames the work as a contribution to ongoing efforts to correct the historical record of the post 1067 years.[89] As reviewed in Chapter 8, Fan Chong began supervision of the court's historical revision project in 1134 and edited the *Su River Records* in 1136. In 1138/10, upon the recommendation of Chief Councilor Zhao Ding, Gaozong conferred the *jinshi* degree upon Shao Bo, who was then appointed to the Imperial Library and history office.[90]

The strident advocacy in the *Shao Family Records* of Luoyang personalities and Yuanyou politics, its attacks on Wang Anshi and Cai Jing as responsible for the fall of Kaifeng, and especially its adulation of Taizu's virtues far above those of other Song monarchs – all mesh with the cultural politics of the 1130s, especially as these were crafted by Fan Chong for Emperor Gaozong and Zhao Ding. The first five chapters, a chronological series of anecdotes about Northern Song politics, offer an early articulation of the Taizu–Qingli–Yuanyou axis of political value. There is not a single mention of Taizong, and only one anecdote, a negative one, about Zhenzong. For the Shao family, the history of political value in Northern Song skipped directly from Taizu to Renzong, then declined, despite the best efforts of the Yuanyou politicians to counter Wang Anshi.

The textual history, therefore, for the earliest surviving version of the "Sima Guang" banquet narrative leads back to the *Shao Family Records* and the *Su River Records*. But it is impossible to know which came first. All of the authors involved – Shao Bowen, Shao Bo, and Fan Chong – had direct access to Sima Guang manuscripts, although Fan Chong's access was probably much better.

[86] *Zun Yao lu*, 1.107. *Zun Yao lu*, 1.116, does contain a brief account of the 969 banquet; see Liang Tianxi, "*Zun Yao lu* shishi shuzheng," 15 (#38).
[87] *Shaoshi wenjian lu*, 1.2–3.   [88] *SS*, 433.12853.
[89] *Shaoshi wenjian lu*, 231–32; *QSW*, 184:4055.391–92.
[90] *Yaolu*, 122.2276; *Chaoye zaji, jia*, 9.180.

The two works thus originated in the same ideological milieu and articulate a common political history. They also share a common vision for Restoration policy as a fulfillment of positive lessons to be learned from the then emerging revisionist history of Northern Song. Li Tao used both works as sources, but with constant caution. Given the extensive personal association of the three compilers and the extensive intertextuality between the two works, it is impossible to know who first spliced the two Sima Guang texts together. However it came into being, Fan Chong would have found the present version a most useful tale in 1136. It provided both a vintage precedent for reining in the house armies and also a flattering portrait of Taizu and Zhao Pu as institution builders in the Sima Guang mode. As Lü Yihao had used the tale in 1132/12, Fan Chong could now position Zhao Ding and Emperor Gaozong as pursuing the same venerable policy as had Zhao Pu and Taizu – rebalancing the distribution of military power and incorporating all its elements into the structures of civil governance.

As is well known, something similar happened in 1141/4 when Gaozong and Qin Gui convinced the generals Han Shizhong, Zhang Junn, and Yue Fei to attend a banquet on West Lake to celebrate their victories and reward their meritorious service. The real purpose was to convince them to surrender authority over their house armies in exchange for positions as commissioners in the Bureau of Military Affairs. Han and Zhang eventually agreed. Yue Fei did not and was executed. Modern historians see similarities (and many differences) between Taizu's consolidation of military power and Gaozong's in 1141. But, explained in the rhetoric of their time, Emperor Gaozong and his councilor Qin Gui had implemented the "policies of the ancestors" in a formal and visual way that demonstrated their Restoration of what Taizu and Zhao Pu had achieved at the dynasty's beginning.[91]

Now established as a central image of the Restoration, Li Tao had little choice but to adjust the Sima Guang narrative for the *Long Draft*. But the politics of the Xiaozong era and the rise of *daoxue* forced gradual reappraisals of the historical roles of Qin Gui and Yue Fei.[92] At the same time, the advent of the regional general command offices (*zongling suo* 總領所) to co-ordinate military funding and supply rapidly transformed the imperial armies into a bloated cancer at the center of Song government and took away much of the lustre of the achievement of 1141. These trends forced a detachment of the banquet narrative from its original context in the politics of the 1130s, and the story eventually acquired a new, updated interpretation. As usual, Zhu Xi laid the foundation when he characterized Zhao Pu's assistance to Taizu at the banquet as "an achievement of the benevolent."[93] In the early 1180s, Liu Guangzu 劉光祖 (1142–1222) joined

---

[91] *Yaolu*, 140.2633–34; Huang K'uan-ch'ung, "Li Qiong bingbian yu nan Song chuqi de zhengju," 88; Deng Xiaonan, *Zuzong zhi fa*, 464–65.

[92] Hartman, "The Making of a Villain," 117–43.   [93] *Songshi quanwen*, 1.20.

the banquet narrative with two other Taizu anecdotes to demonstrate that the founder had prevented powerful retainers from exercising unilateral military authority, affines from involving themselves in politics, and eunuchs from making decisions – all central concerns at the end of the Xiaozong era.[94] The greater narrative of the benevolent mind of Taizu as the fountainhead of dynastic stability had now engulfed the anecdote about how Taizu took back military power.

Lü Zhong's mid-thirteenth-century comment on the banquet narrative mirrors this development: Taizu's ability so quickly to assert his control over the military was an outward projection of his great inner authority – his skill as a manager of self, home, and court. Lü Zhong provided an array of historical examples to demonstrate that no ruler can control and project military power if he is unable to marshal the inner discipline necessary to control those closest to him, his affinal relatives, courtesans, eunuchs, and non-literati personnel at court. In Lü's telling, the Tang scourge of the military governors began when the decadent court under the favoured consort Yang Guifei 楊貴妃 (719–756) brought on the An Lushan rebellion; the scourge crested when corrupt eunuch administrators brought about murderous retribution from Zhu Wen. As his final example, Lü cited the words of the Tang chief councilor Pei Du 裴度 (765–839). After Pei had subjugated for Emperor Xianzong the military governors of the early ninth century, the emperor in 818 appointed as chief councilors two financial officials who had colluded with eunuchs. Pei Du resigned over the issue and warned the emperor that such appointments threatened to undo the court's military consolidation: "Only when the management of your own personnel is proper can you make the military governors submit."[95]

This late Song framing of the banquet narrative brings together all three major themes of the grand allegory – the benevolent character of Song rule, its origins in Taizu as founder, and the lineage of evil, autocratic councilors who corrupted these dynastic fundamentals. For a central premise in this final component of the allegory was the injunction from the *Great Learning* that the ruler must first regulate his own household before he can hope to govern the empire beyond. Failure to do so will result in devolution of his imperial authority, either by consent or by default, to autocrats who will wield power in his stead. As the Southern Song polity experienced successive periods of autocratic rule, this idea, amplified by strident voices within the *daoxue* movement, brought into place the last piece of the master narrative, a story that would sweep up the discordant flotsam of past events – as well as facts and anecdotes – into the grand allegory of Song history.

---

[94] *QSW*, 279:6314.30–31.
[95] *Huangchao dashiji*, 2.50–51; *Songshi quanwen*, 1.20. For earlier Song sources on Pei Du's comment see Sima Guang, *Zizhi tongjian*, 240.7752–53; Fan Zuyu, *Tangjian*, 18.10a–11a; for background see Twitchett, *Cambridge History of China, Volume 3*, 632–33.

10 The Lineage of Evil
Benevolence Undermined

Our previous review of the *Song History* in Chapter 5 showed that Ouyang Xiu and Song Qi first devised and inserted a biographical grouping called "nefarious ministers" (*jianchen* 姦臣) into the *New Tang History* they completed in 1060. They did not, however, define their new category. This task fell to Ouyang Xuan, the Yuan dynasty editor of the *Song History*, who continued the precedent of grouping together the biographies of high officials upon whom history had rendered a negative verdict. However, he brought to his work a clear sense of how the intervening centuries had come to define "nefarious ministers" and of whom this group should include. His preface to the *Song History*'s four *juan* of biographies of malevolent officials may appear at first a routine Confucian homily. But, properly read, Ouyang Xuan's short tract both presents a general theory of governance and also encapsulates the political perspective of late Song *daoxue* as filtered through Ouyang's own *daoxue* allegiance and his contemporary Yuan agenda.

The *Book of Changes* states, "The *yang* trigrams are mostly *yin*; the *yin* trigrams are mostly *yang*." Thus, even though gentlemen predominate, when the small man exercises authority, the image is *yin*. Even though petty men predominate, when the gentleman exercises authority, the image is *yang*.

At the start of the Song, the five planets converged in the Kui asterism; and the diviners considered this an omen for a great multiplicity of human talent. But, for the most part, during the age of Song, although the sage and the wise were not lacking, the nefarious and the evil outnumbered them. During the flourishing periods of Song, gentlemen held the reigns of political power, the small men obeyed their orders, and there were few problems. But during periods of decline, small men saw their ambitions realized and engaged in their cunning plots. They obstructed the ears of the sovereign and altered state policy (*guoshi*). They tyrannized the loyal and the straight; they rejected the good and the true. The gentlemen were out of office, and there was no remedy for chaos and disaster. How can those who hold the state not be careful to discriminate between the upright and the perverse? So we have made the biographies of the nefarious ministers.[1]

---

[1] *SS*, 471.13697.

The full context of the opening citation from the *Changes* and its traditional commentaries explain Ouyang Xuan's quotation: although each *yang* trigram has only one unbroken *yang* line and two broken *yin* lines, because the sum of the numerical values of the three lines is an uneven number (uneven numbers are *yang*; even are *yin*), the trigram is thus *yang*. Since an unbroken *yang* line represents the ruler and the gentleman, a *yang* trigram thus "images" a single ruler/gentleman dominant over two servitors/small men (the two broken *yin* lines). The opposite is true for a *yin* trigram, whose two *yang* lines compete for dominance over the trigram's single *yin* line.[2]

Since *yang* and *yin* symbolize two sets of correlatives (ruler and servitor; gentleman and small man), the *Changes* quotation can be understood in two ways. First, as Ouyang explains, the *yang* trigrams represent Song historical periods in which gentlemen, though few (only one line among three) dominate the small men (two lines). *Yin* trigrams, however, represent historical periods in which, although gentlemen outnumber small men (two to one), the small man predominates. But, since change is immutable, this situation is unavoidable and results from the inability of the ruler to "discriminate between the upright and the perverse." The purpose of the biographies is thus to assist the ruler "who holds the state" to identify small men and bend the trend toward the *yang* configuration and resulting periods of dynastic florescence.[3]

The second, latent interpretation of the quotation is that the nefarious officials – whose biographies will follow – instead of maintaining their proper, inferior position as servitor (*yin*) relative to the ruler (*yang*), usurped his authority, such that the state (the trigram) contained two rulers competing for the allegiance of a single servitor. Although cloaked in the number symbology of the *Changes*, this political indictment represents an accurate summary of the biographies of the major protagonists in the *jianchen* chapters: Cai Jing, Qin Gui, Han Tuozhou, Jia Sidao – a lineage of evil, authoritarian councilors who usurped the legitimate authority of the sovereign.[4]

Ouyang Xuan's preface thus presents both a theory of Song history and a theory of governance. We focus here on the first of these and consider the historical circumstances that gave rise to this construction of a lineage of evil and those forces that shaped it into the third and final motif of the grand allegory of Song history. For, although the final articulation is Yuan, the concept itself grows from the struggles in the twelfth and thirteenth centuries to incorporate

---

[2] Wang Bi, *Zhouyi zhengyi*, 12.12b–13a; Wilhelm, *The I Ching*, 337–38.
[3] For discussions of the *Yijing* and factional politics in Northern Song see Hon, *The* Yijing *and Chinese Politics*; and Levine, *Divided by a Common Language*, 32–34.
[4] *Songshi* chapters 471–474 contain biographies of twenty-two individuals, as follows: Cai Que, Wu Chuhou, Xing Shu, Lü Huiqing, Zhang Dun, Zeng Bu, An Dun (*juan* 471); Cai Jing and family members Cai Bian, Cai You, Cai Xiao, Cai Chong; then Zhao Liangsi, Zhang Jiao, and Guo Yaoshi (*juan* 472); Huang Qianshan, Wang Boyan, Qin Gui (*juan* 473); Moqi Xie, Han Tuozhou, Ding Daquan, and Jia Sidao (*juan* 474).

daoxue into the dynasty's political orthodoxy. In short, if the first and second themes of the grand allegory – the benevolence of the Song state and its origins in Taizu the founder – grew from the political struggles against the New Policies in the period after 1125, then the fully formed third theme developed much later, specifically, in the efforts to reimplement literati governance after the assassination of Han Tuozhou in 1207. To be sure, given the inclination of Chinese historians to view the world as an interaction of dichotomized polarities, as does Ouyang Xuan, the completed allegory demanded a negative narrative – a *yin* – to balance the overwhelmingly *yang* narrative of its first two, and chronologically earlier, components.

Certainly, the Yuan historians are responsible for the *Song History*'s assignment of specific biographies to the "nefarious" chapters. For example, scholars have long recognized that because Jia Sidao resisted the Mongol conquest, the Yuan historians typecast him as a "bad last minister" and framed his biography as a fitting conclusion to the lineage.[5] As the preface implies, the implication was that Emperor Shenzong's choice of Wang Anshi had sown the seeds of the Song fall in 1127 and again in 1279. In fact, the politics of 1125 that reversed the verdict on Wang Anshi and restored the historical and political viability of the Yuanyou administrators also spawned a corresponding lineage of the "nefarious." As we have seen in Chapter 8, this reversal culminated in a historical revisionism that assigned blame to a succession of Wang's "followers" such as Lü Huiqing, Zhang Dun, and Cai Jing. This process began only three days after Emperor Qinzong's ascension on 1125/12/24 when Chen Dong 陳東 (1086–1127), then an Imperial University student, submitted the first of three memorials that not only called for the execution of Cai Jing and his associates as "six felons," but also contained a historical critique of their policies as responsible for the Jurchen invasions.[6] Although this revisionism entailed a sense of historical progression, its subsequent focus remained largely on compiling a list of the politically culpable and their descendants, as Cai Jing had done with his proscriptions of the Yuanfu submitters and the Yuanyou administrators early in Huizong's reign. After 1125, those who had been *yin* became *yang*, and those who had been *yang* became *yin*.

The true genesis of the lineage of evil lies in the concurrence of two historiographical projects, one official, one quite unofficial. As for the first, the court history office made little progress on compiling the official state history for the period 1067–1127 until all the veritable records were complete and Li Tao had assumed control of the office in 1168. *The Four Courts State History [of Shenzong, Zhezong, Huizong, and Qinzong]* was finally completed

---

[5] Franke, "Chia Ssu-tao." For a recent, detailed account of this process see Mao Qin, "Lun Jia Sidao jianchen xingxiang de suzao."

[6] For the texts see *Changbian shibu*, 51.1594–99, 52.1615, and 1633–34; for a detailed discussion see Hartman and Li, "The Rehabilitation of Chen Dong," 84–90.

in 1186.[7] Although this work does not survive, the veritable-records biographies for the four major Northern Song "nefarious ministers" – Cai Que, Lü Huiqing, Zhang Dun, and Zeng Bu – do survive and can be compared against their biographies in the *Eastern Capital Miscellany* of 1187, which can be shown to be closely related to those in the lost state history of 1186. The earlier veritable-record biographies are relatively neutral, but the *Eastern Capital Miscellany* versions already show major textual manipulation to enhance the "nefarious" character of these individuals, and several of these biographies are largely identical to those in the *Song History*. This demonstrates that the initial "coloring" of these biographies – as well as that of Cai Jing – occurred between 1168 and 1186 and most probably under the supervision of Li Tao.[8] Thus, although the initial rehabilitation of the Yuanyou administrators in 1125 began a process that eventually determined the negative political personas of these New Policies ministers, textually, the fixing of their negative historical personas – the first installment of what would become the lineage of evil – was coterminous with the rise of *daoxue* during the reign of Emperor Xiaozong.

During this same period, Zhu Xi began a highly unofficial, but ultimately successful, campaign to mold the historical legacy of Qin Gui. In 1165/6, only ten years after Qin Gui's death, Zhu wrote a preface to *The Forthright Opinions of 1138* (*Wuwu dangyi* 戊午讜議). In this work, Wei Yanzhi 魏掞之 (1116–1173), a close associate of Zhu, had assembled documents written by opponents of the peace treaties that Qin Gui had negotiated with the Jin in 1138 and 1141. Wei had been present in 1147 when Zhao Ding's family felt forced to destroy Zhao's personal papers rather than permit Qin Gui to acquire them and use them further to prosecute the Zhao network. Wei probably intended his collection as a response to the Jin invasion of 1161, which violated the treaty and presented a political opening to the treaty's past and present opponents. Amid sporadic and inconclusive fighting, the court negotiated a new treaty, whose terms were announced in the spring of 1165, only months before Zhu Xi's preface.

Zhu bemoaned the contrast between the outpouring of "forthright opinion" in 1138 and the tepid response of officials to the crisis of the early 1160s: during court deliberations in 1163, only two officials, Zhang Chan 張闡 (1091–1164) and Hu Quan 胡銓 (1102–1180), had advocated for continued resistance rather than accepting yet another negotiated peace. Zhu interpreted this acquiescence as a moral failure of the state and placed historical responsibility directly on Qin Gui, whose machinations to obtain the earlier treaty had deceived Emperor Gaozong and destroyed the moral resolve of Song officialdom to resist:

[7] Cai Chongbang, *Songdai xiushi zhidu yanjiu*, 126–38.
[8] Hartman, "A Textual History of Cai Jing's Biography in the *Songshi*," 533–36; Levine, "A House in Darkness," 204–308, 597–638.

Qin Gui's crimes permeate the heavens and could not be redeemed even if he died ten thousand deaths. First by promoting his evil policies to deceive the state, then by using the influence of the barbarians to coerce his sovereign, he obscured proper relations between men and perverted the human heart.

In support of this sweeping condemnation, Zhu Xi summoned a highly imaginative and hyperbolic history of the Restoration: before Qin Gui's return from the North in 1131, Gaozong led a unified officialdom committed to recover the North and a military that had scored repeated victories against the enemy. The Restoration at this point was "eight- to nine-tenths complete." But Qin Gui, acting as an agent for the Jin, destroyed this unity; and so the opportunity to recover the North was lost.[9]

Writing less than thirty years after these events, Zhu Xi probably did not expect many to accept such an implausible version of Restoration history. His preface was rather addressed to a small circle of like-minded readers whom he knew would be sympathetic to his view. Yet, as his career advanced, he sharpened and made public his position on the historical role of Qin Gui and its negative legacy for Southern Song society. In 1182/8 he publically destroyed a shrine to Qin Gui in the district school at Yongjia 永嘉 and defended his action in a report that repeated his earlier charges.[10] He wrote prefaces and funeral inscriptions for Qin Gui's victims that teem with vivid details of his persecutions. The Conversations contain many passages that reveal Zhu Xi embellishing his negative persona of Qin Gui and defending it against sharp questioning from his interlocutors. These exchanges in the Conversations suggest that Zhu Xi's take on Qin Gui was considerably darker than the contemporary consensus. He insinuated several times that Qin Gui intended to murder Gaozong and usurp the throne. The Conversations, for example, are the textual origin for the story that Gaozong kept a dagger hidden in his boot to defend against a possible assassination attempt from Qin Gui. Finally, the last Conversations entry on Qin Gui formally brands him a "petty man" (xiaoren).[11] In his famous 1188 audience with the emperor, a year after Gaozong's death and a year before Xiaozong's abdication, Zhu Xi denounced Qin Gui for staffing the government with compliant and corrupt "clerks" who acquiesced in his usurpation of imperial authority and denounced those who resisted him, a style of governing that Zhu insinuated continued to the present.[12]

Evidence in surviving sources suggests that Zhu Xi's efforts to mold the historical image of Qin Gui began to influence official historiography in the early 1190s. Scholars have held that two surviving early histories of the Gaozong era, the Minor Calendar of the Restoration (Zhongxing xiaoli) and the

[9] Zhu Xi ji, 75.3929–32.   [10] Zhu Xi ji, 99.5090–91.   [11] Zhuzi yulei, 131.3153–63.
[12] Zhu Xi ji, 11.472–73; Darrobers, Zhu Xi: Mémoire scellé, 33–34. For a detailed study of Zhu Xi's construction of Qin Gui see Hartman, "The Making of a Villain," 126–34.

recently discovered *Topical Details of the Restoration of Our August Court* (*Huangchao zhongxing jishi benmo* 皇朝中興紀事本末), are different recensions of the same work by Xiong Ke. Recent scholarship, however, demonstrates that the two works are different: the former was indeed compiled by Xiong Ke in the late 1180s, but court academicians compiled the latter for use at Classics Mat sessions under Emperor Guangzong, who ruled 1189 through 1194. The former work contains fuller details of Qin Gui's exchanges with Gaozong, which the latter routinely truncates. For example, in 1142/7 Gaozong commented in detail on various legal problems that provincial authorities had submitted. Qin Gui replied that Gaozong's attention to such details ensured the success of the Restoration.[13] Later historians excised such passages on the ground they were mere empty flattery that Qin Gui's son, Qin Xi, had inserted into the daily calendar. Yet their subsequent excision from the official record changed the historical image of Gaozong and Qin Gui as partners in the Restoration to one where all the credit for its successes went to Gaozong alone – thus freeing Qin Gui to accept all the blame for its failings.

As recent discoveries have made clear, the rhetoric of *daoxue* encroached upon, and ultimately abrogated, the existing imperial rhetoric of the Song monarchy.[14] Many of Li Xinchuan's excisions detach, and thus camouflage, Qin Gui's promotion of this rhetoric. For example, in a court session in 1139/7, Gaozong remarked that if the court could distinguish between gentlemen and petty men, then "the way of good governance cannot but be accomplished." Qin Gui and the others admired the emperor's plan, observing that the proper placement of personnel had been the highest priority of government under the ancient sage-kings Yao, Shun, Yu, Tang, Wen, and Wu. Xiong Ke's *Minor Calendar* records the full exchange; the *Topical Details* truncates everything after "the emperor's plan"; Li Xinchuan's *Chronological Record*, however, retains only Gaozong's remark, excising entirely Qin Gui's analogy between Gaozong's personnel policies and those of Yao and Shun.[15] Such examples provide stark evidence of how the growth of *daoxue* necessitated a reappraisal of Qin Gui's historical role. This transition occurred during the twenty-year period between the death of Gaozong in 1187 and the new administration under

---

[13] See *Zhongxing xiaoli*, 30.362–63; and *Huangchao zhongxing jishi benmo*, 60.2a, where the latter text omits Qin Gui's remark. See Zhou Lizhi, "*Huangchao zhongxing jishi benmo* yu *Zhongxing xiaoli* zhi guanxi," 110–11, for additional examples. *Yaolu*, 146.2747, adopts the truncated version. In addition to the evidence that Zhou cites to distinguish the two titles as separate works, one could add that Chen Jun accords each title a separate entry in the list of works he consulted while preparing his *Huangchao biannian gangmu beiyao* of 1229; see *Huangchao gangmu*, front matter, 15–16.

[14] Li and Hartman, "A Newly Discovered Inscription," 441–46.

[15] *Zhongxing xiaoli*, 27.316; *Huangchao zhongxing jishi benmo*, 49.2a; *Yaolu*, 130.2443. For many more examples and an excellent discussion see Yan Yongcheng, *Nan Song shixue yanjiu*, 240–47.

Shi Miyuan in 1208. Finally, we have seen above in Chapter 3 how, during the end of this period, Lin Xinchuan utilized nonofficial sources to enhance the negative character of Qin Gui in the *Chronological Record*.

What little can be gleaned about the evolution of Qin Gui's biography in the *Song History* also highlights this period as a turning point in the formation of his ultimate historical persona as a "nefarious minister." The first official biography of Qin Gui would have been included in the *Gaozong Daily Calendar*, completed in 1176. As we have also seen in Chapter 3, this biography was certainly positive on Qin Gui and probably remained little changed in the *Gaozong Veritable Records* of 1202. However, privately compiled works, such as the *Remnant History of the Restoration*, submitted to the court between 1195 and 1200, and the *Record of Restoration Personalities* (*Zhongxing xing-shi lu* 中興姓氏錄) contained negative biographies of Qin Gui. The later may even have included Qin in its grouping of "nefarious and vile" (*jianxie* 姦邪) individuals.[16] As is well known, the biographies for the *Four Restoration Courts State History* (*Zhongxing sichao guoshi*) were never completed and thus never formally submitted to court.[17] However, at least two surviving quotations from "Qin Gui's state history biography," one from 1241 and another from 1246, indicate that Li Xinchuan and other thirteenth-century court historians had already begun to feed negative material from these private histories into a draft of Qin Gui's official biography.[18]

Although Zhu Xi had done much to demonize Qin Gui, the critical events that precipitated the construction of the lineage of evil – the succession of malevolent councilors whose biographies comprise the "nefarious ministers" section of the *Song History* – was the political fallout over the imperial succession of 1194. As is well known, Chief Councilor Zhao Ruyu – a key advocate of literati governance, initiator in 1180 of the *Comprehensive State Compendium* and compiler of the *The Ministers Memorials* in 1186 – co-operated with the imperial affine Han Tuozhou to effect the ascension of Emperor Ningzong in 1194. Subsequent disagreements led to Zhao's dismissal in 1195/2, his death the following year, and the rise of Han Tuozhou who remained de facto sole councilor until his execution in 1207. Beginning in

[16] Chen Lesu, "*Sanchao beiming huibian kao*," 284.
[17] Cai Chongbang, *Songdai xiushi zhidu yanjiu*, 138–44.
[18] Xie Caibo, *Mizhai biji*, 1.8, quotes an 1139 letter from Fan Rugui to Qin Gui. The passage is now in Fan's *Song History* biography, not in Qin Gui's; see *SS*, 381.11730. A precedent submitted by Liu Kezhuang in 1246 also quotes from a Qin Gui state biography; see *Liu Kezhuang ji jianjiao*, 86.3703–4. A version of this passage does occur in Qin's *Song History* biography; see *SS*, 473.13751. The passage concerns Gaozong's reaction to Qin Gui's statement that "southerners should return south; northerners should return north" and the emperor's involvement in the drafting of Qin Gui's dismissal notice in 1132/8. A quotation of this passages occurs in Xu Ziming, *Song zaifu biannian lu*, 15.982–83, which cites the *Zhongxing yishi* as its source. Li Xinchuan also relies heavily on the *Zhongxing yishi* for his account of these events; see *Yaolu*, 57.1160–61.

1196/8, the Han administration imposed a proscription on political associates of Zhao Ruyu, known to history as the "Qingyuan proscription" (*Qingyuan dangjin* 慶元黨禁), that lasted through 1202/2.[19] During this period, a total of fifty-nine officials were barred from holding office.[20]

Although branded an action against "false learning" (*weixue* 偽學), the proscription targeted officials who had attacked Han Tuozhou and his political allies. Many of these, although by no means all, were indeed proponents of *daoxue* whom Zhao Ruyu had attempted to bring into the new government in 1194. The moniker for the new administration (Qingyuan) fused the initial characters of the Qingli and Yuanyou reign periods and so announced their intentions to restore the political values of these Northern Song eras. Thus, Han Tuozhou's persecution strengthened the tendency of the persecuted to trace their political roots to these Northern Song eras and to frame their own persecution under Han as a cyclical repeat of the early Huizong-era proscription of the Yuanyou administrators under Cai Jing.

Beginning in the early 1190s, local officials erected replicas of the infamous "Yuanyou party register" (*Yuanyou dangji* 元祐黨籍), Cai Jing's stele of 1104 that had proscribed 309 officials linked to the Yuanyou administration. Two of these Southern Song steles in Guangxi province survived into modern times, and Song sources mention at least two others that have not survived.[21] At Guilin, the controller general Rao Zuyao 饒祖堯 erected a replica of the 1104 stele in 1198, at the height of the Qingyuan persecution. He did so at the request of Liang Lü 梁律, a local official on his staff, to commemorate the latter's ancestor, Liang Tao 梁燾 (1034–1097), who had been an important Yuanyou administrator. Another inscription at modern Rongshui 融水 county was erected in 1211 by Shen Wei 沈暐, then prefect of Rongzhou 融州 and a great-grandson of Shen Qian 沈千, whose name was also on the Yuanyou list. Both inscriptions contain postscripts that exonerate Huizong and laud Gaozong for his recall of the Yuanyou administrators. Both extol the power of public opinion (*gongyi*) expressed through history to clarify whose actions had been morally correct. Shen Wei writes, "wherever the state history is, there is public opinion." Cai Jing may have slandered the Yuanyou administrators as petty men;

---

[19] For these events see Davis, "The Reigns of Kuang-tsung (1189–1194) and Ning-tsung (1194–1224)," 766–89.

[20] For the list see *Chaoye zaji, jia*, 6.139–40. Earlier scholarship, following the late Song sources, interpreted the proscription of false learning largely as an intellectual movement against Zhu Xi. Schirokauer's 1975 article "Neo-Confucians under Attack" began to analyze the political aspects of the proscription. More recently, Chang Wei-ling, *Cong Nan Song zhongqi fan jinxi zhengzheng*, 134–48, frames the conflict between Zhao Ruyu and Han Tuozhou, including the proscription on false learning, as the culmination of political conflicts inherent since the early 1160s in Song government between literati and non-literati actors.

[21] For the surviving examples see Chen Lesu, "Guilin shike *Yuanyou dangji*," 68–71; Wang Mingqing, *Huizhu lu*, 1.64, mentions a replica erected at Yangzhou; Zheng Yao, *Jingding Yanzhou xuzhi*, 6.10a, mentions another in the Chun'an 淳安 county school in Yanzhou 嚴州.

but this republication of the 309 names of those he slandered reverses these incorrect judgments, and may, Rao Zuyao hoped, promote the cause of good governance.[22]

It is difficult not to read the Guilin inscription from 1198 as a direct attack on Han Tuozhou and the Qingyuan proscription.[23] But the wider chronological and geographical disbursement of these replicas suggests they were part of a larger movement of individuals to align themselves and their ancestors with the new historical narrative that emerged during this period, especially after Han Tuozhou's death. We have seen in Chapters 1 and 3 how the sudden political transition in 1208 affected both Li Xinchuan's *Chronological Record* and the new *Comprehensive State Compendium*.[24] The new administration of Shi Miyuan took immediate steps to rewrite the official history of the 1194–1207 years to remove pro-Han Tuozhou content from the primary sources for official history. The revisions were meant not only to formally label Han's supporters a "nefarious faction" (*jiandang* 姦黨) but also, by removing positive accounts of their prior actions from the historical record, to render more difficult any future appeals from them for political rehabilitation.[25] Just as the replicas of the Yuanyou party registers celebrated the reversal of the historical verdict on the Yuanyou administrators from their original designation as "petty men" to "gentlemen," so the new political and historical verdict on Han's supporters reversed them from "gentlemen" to "petty men."

When those who had criticized Han's policies returned to court they saw parallels between their own experience of persecution under Han and that of those who had suffered at the hands of autocratic ministers under earlier regimes. These parallels increased the rhetorical tendency to equate Qin Gui and Han Tuozhou. For example, for his consistent opposition to the Kaixi war, Han Tuozhou removed Xu Bangxian 徐邦憲 (1154–1210) to a temple sinecure in 1206. Xu returned to court after Han's death and told Emperor Ningzong that parallels between present circumstances and Qin Gui's death in 1155 were in fact not precise. It had been possible, Xu maintained, to restore political order after 1155, but Han Tuozhou's autocracy had "totally destroyed" any similar possibility for the moment.[26]

22 *QSW*, 293:6663.353; 304:6945.198–99.
23 Chen Lesu in fact suggested that the remote location of Guilin makes feasible this interpretation of the inscription; see his "Guilin shike *Yuanyou dangji*," 69.
24 One may perhaps also include the *Long Draft*, if my estimate of 1210 as the approximate date for Yang Zhongliang's reworking of the original *Long Draft* into the *Topical Narratives from the Long Draft* is correct; see Hartman, "Bibliographic Notes on Sung Historical Works: *Topical Narratives from the Long Draft*," 197.
25 See the 1209 memorial of Zhen Dexiu at *QSW*, 312:7143.173–76. For an account of the historical revisionism of this period see Hartman and Li, "The Rehabilitation of Chen Dong," 118.
26 *SS*, 404.12231–32.

As the rhetoric of the Qin–Han parallel suggests, the political reversals of 1208 required not simply revisions to recent history but realignments to earlier history as well. In Confucian parlance, autocracy suppressed "public opinion" (*gongyi*), as Han had done during the Qingyuan proscription. The historical revisionism of the period thus linked previous administrations that, in the emerging *daoxue* version of Song history, had acted in a similar way. In 1210, Zhen Dexiu extended this classic theory to Han Tuozhou. His memorial began by citing the view of Liu Anshi 劉安世 (1048–1125), a noted Yuanyou administrator, that public opinion represents "Heaven's Way" as lodged within the "mind of men." Thus public opinion, like Heaven, is eternal. Both, however, may suffer temporary periods of repression and eclipse for which there is always a political cost. Zhen then used this theory to link Wang Anshi, Qin Gui, and Han Tuozhou. He explained that although public opinion against the New Policies never ceased, their forced imposition sapped the economic vitality of the people. Similarly, Qin Gui pursued peace with the Jin against public opinion, and this violation strengthened the enemy. Zhen concludes by using these parallels to justify the removal of Han Tuozhou and urged Emperor Ningzong to be vigilant against the return of his supporters.[27]

Zhen Dexiu thus envisioned public opinion as a persistent, unchanging historical force; and his conception shares much with the stance of the postscript writers on the replicas of the Yuanyou party register. In short, a function of history is to record public opinion and thus prevent its permanent suppression. Li Xinchuan took a similar stance in the *Record of the Way and Its Fate*, a work that fuses this theory of public opinion with *daoxue* history. Li Xinchuan explained the term *daoxue* as a union of the "Way" – the political manifestation of Heaven's Way on earth – and "learning" – individual human understanding of that Way. When in office, a *daoxue* official implements the Way; out of office, his knowledge of the Way sustains and strengthens him for an eventual return to power. As explained in Chapter 3, the *Record of the Way* divides *daoxue* history into three periods, each with a similar political dynamic. Parties that oppose public opinion persecute parties that reflect that opinion: Zhang Dun and Cai Jing against Sima Guang; Qin Gui against Zhao Ding; Han Tuozhou against Zhao Ruyu. But the Way is insuppressible, and this rhetorical stance maintains that its true advocate – the honest voice of public opinion – will always prevail, if not now politically, then ultimately forever in history.[28]

The dynamics of this early Jiading-era historical revisionism also explain one of the greatest conundrums in the received master narrative of Song history: namely, why did the grand allegory come to posit officials who favored

---

[27] *QSW*, 312:7144.178–79. Both Liu Kezhuang in his biography of Zhen Dexiu and Wei Liaoweng in his spirit road inscription quote this memorial; see *QSW*, 330:7609.384–85 and 311:7110.69.
[28] Note that Zhen Dexiu's argument from 1210 closely parallels Lou Yue's appraisal of the *Chronological Record* from 1212. See Chapter 3 above, note 48.

military action against the Jurchen in the 1130s as heroic "gentlemen" (*junzi*) yet frame those who supported military action against the Jurchen in 1206 as craven "petty men" (*xiaoren*)? The answer turns on the differing geopolitical circumstances of the two periods and on shifting alliances among various elements within the Song polity. In brief, Emperor Gaozong and Qin Gui successfully framed the peace of 1142 as a political triumph, but the disastrous invasion of 1206 was an instant military and political failure. In the late 1130s, proto-*daoxue* figures such as Li Gang, Zhao Ding, and Zhang Jun supported the leaders of the house armies in their war against the Jurchen. As a consequence, as we have seen in Chapter 9, Qin Gui, with the support of Emperor Gaozong, achieved the peace of 1142 by simultaneously negotiating with the Jurchen and reining in both the house armies and those literati officials who also supported continued warfare. The resulting peace was promoted as a Restoration success and, despite the unpleasantness of the early 1160s, continued as "state policy" for the remainder of the eleventh century.

Two factors, however, gradually challenged this status quo. First, the integration of the house armies after 1142 transferred military control from semi-independent generals such as Han Shizhong and Yue Fei back to the monarchy. This transfer resulted in a bloated and corrupt military bureaucracy increasingly dominated by affinal kin and "favored close" within the monarchy. Second, the rise of *daoxue* during the Xiaozong reign drew political strength from the movement's opposition to these very elements within the monarchy and to their stranglehold on state resources. The political struggle between Zhao Ruyu and Han Tuozhou in 1194 was not a temporary clash of personalities but the climax of thirty years of tension between these two elements within the Song polity – Zhao the consummate practitioner of *daoxue* governance and Han the ultimate affinal kin.[29]

In this context, Han Tuozhou's invasion of the North in 1206 was the apex of the professional military's (and Emperor Xiaozong's) long-term, if perhaps rhetorical and disingenuous, support for full Restoration. But the army of 1206 was not the army of the 1130s. Many historians believe Han relaxed the Qingyuan proscription in 1202 in order to generate support among literati officials for his planned invasion. Eventually, many literati officials such as Li Bi (son of Li Tao), Ye Shi, and Zhang Ying 章潁 (1140–1217) did support the invasion.[30] After Han Tuozhou's assassination, these allies sought immediate political cover to disassociate themselves from the debacle. Early Jiading historiography thus heaped full blame on Han and his immediate associates, both for the defeat in 1206 and for the Qingyuan proscription, and whitewashed

---

[29] Chang Wei-ling, "Cong Nan Song zhongqi fan jinxi zhengzheng," 149–52.
[30] Zhang Ying played a prominent role in rewriting the history of the Han administration; see Hartman and Li, "The Rehabilitation of Chen Dong," 117–18.

their own participation in his regime. The resulting new historiographical narrative sidestepped previous stances on war and peace to focus instead on persecution at the hands of a lineage of autocratic councilors who had suppressed dissent regardless of its pro- or anti-war content. And so the successful peace of 1142 became a political and moral defeat; Qin Gui the successful negotiator became a *xiaoren* and a traitor to the state; Han Tuozhou became his incarnation; and officials who had supported him now recast themselves as the historical posterity of the heroic gentlemen who had opposed Qin Gui.

As this conception took shape, framers of the new historiography devoted increasing attention to tangible traces of those Northern Song figures who were now emerging as moral and political heroes. At the same time, traces of their contrasting political villains were devalued, if not destroyed. The writing of colophons on manuscripts, rubbings, and artwork flourished during this period, especially at the hands of officials with links to the *daoxue* movement.[31] The effort was not merely antiquarian but took pains to search out and interpret objects in ways that supported the newly emerging historical narratives. The Yuanyou replicas are one example of this trend.

Another is the extraordinary series of thirty-eight colophons composed between 1222 and 1259 on the supposed holograph manuscript of a memorial written by the Imperial University student Chen Dong to Emperor Gaozong in 1127. As we have seen earlier in this chapter, the three memorials Chen Dong wrote in 1125 and early 1126 contained the earliest historical assessments that framed Cai Jing, his family, and his associates as nefarious ministers. In 1127, Chen Dong, again claiming to represent the voice of public opinion, attacked Huang Qianshan and Wang Boyan, Gaozong's first two chief councilors, whom Chen held responsible for the decision to withdraw from northern China in the wake of the Jin invasions. Chen was publicly executed on 1127/8/15 in violation of the oath that Emperor Taizu had supposedly imposed on his imperial heirs not to execute literati officials.

Although the state apologized to Chen's heirs in 1129 and again in 1134, throughout the twelfth century Chen Dong's sacrifice remained largely unknown and his historical status uncertain. However, in 1199, the prefectural school at Zhenjiang erected a shrine to Chen Dong, who came from nearby Danyang 丹陽. Liu Zai, an important local *daoxue* scholar, composed an inscription for the shrine in 1204 that cast Chen Dong as the hero of an allegorical struggle between political good and evil. In Liu's historical analogy, Chen Dong, outspoken yet utterly loyal, ultimately triumphed morally and historically over the disloyal and self-serving chief councilors. Liu's rhetorical construction implied an unstated analogy between Chen Dong and himself (and Liu's *daoxue* readership), and between Gaozong's nefarious councilors and

[31] Hartman and Li, "The Rehabilitation of Chen Dong," 82–83.

Han Tuozhou. In short, Chen Dong becomes a type for those officials whom Han had persecuted, and Huang and Wang become types for the persecuting autocrat Han Tuozhou. Liu's allegorical narrative insinuated that Han would suffer the same historical fate as had Chen Dong's oppressors.[32]

In 1222 Chen Dong's great-grandson mounted his copy of his ancestor's memorial on a hand scroll and solicited colophons. The first writer was Liu Zai. For the next thirty-seven years, local scholars and officials – some well known but most not – plus officials from outside the area who rotated through local offices in the Zhenjiang area viewed the scroll and inscribed their reactions and thoughts. The series provides a remarkable view into local opinion on national events during the critical final phase of Song history. More specifically, the colophons reveal how the penetration of *daoxue* historiography at the local level both influenced the interpretation of political developments in the capital and, at the same time, defined with increasing sharpness the historical character of the nefarious minister.

An early colophon from 1222 frames Chen Dong's memorial in the context of a forty-year period of repression against the Yuanyou administrators that lasted from 1094 through the advent of Zhao Ding as chief councilor in 1134. This somewhat forced historical construction (restrictions on the Yuanyou administrators were in fact lifted in 1125) links Chen Dong's execution both to Cai Jing and, by implication, to Qin Gui. The writer accused his contemporaries of being, unlike Chen Dong, too apathetic and cowardly to submit frank criticism, despite Emperor Lizong's professed embrace of remonstrance. This accusation, by implication, places the sitting chief councilor Shi Miyuan in a lineage that began with Zhang Dun, Cai Jing, and Qin Gui, since, if the emperor permits remonstrance yet none is forthcoming, the chief councilor must be at fault. After Shi's death in 1233, the failed invasion of the North in 1234, and the advent of Shi Songzhi in 1237, the colophon writers increasingly link Chen Dong's executioners and the administration of Shi Songzhi. A colophon of 1240 makes a direct analogy between Qin Gui, Shi Miyuan, and Shi Songzhi. By 1246, in contrast, Chen Dong has been elevated to the status of a *daoxue* sage. Through the 1240s and 1250s, Song governance settled into a sustained struggle between literati who envisioned themselves as persecuted practitioners of the Yuanyou political heritage and autocratic councilors such as Shi Songzhi, Ding Daquan, and Jia Sidao. As these political struggles ground on, the stark moral dichotomies of *daoxue* historiography gained increasing appeal. The final colophons of 1259 introduce no new motifs to the series. They merely intensify the perfidy of an ever-continuing lineage of evil and laud the ability of history to render justice for Chen Dong and ultimately for themselves.[33]

---

[32] Hartman and Li, "The Rehabilitation of Chen Dong," 110–12.
[33] Hartman and Li, "The Rehabilitation of Chen Dong," 121–45.

The Chen Dong colophons document the wide diffusion of *daoxue* history – especially motifs associated with the lineage of evil – into thirteenth-century local culture. Zhenjiang was a metropolitan military garrison, a place hardly noted for its *daoxue* scholarship. Aside from Liu Zai and several others, few of the colophon authors have known *daoxue* affiliations; and most can hardly have been conversant with the intricacies of *daoxue* philosophy. Yet these local writers easily manipulated the *daoxue* narrative on Chen Dong and early Southern Song history and applied its rhetoric and its moral lessons to their own political world. Other more standard sources document the same chronological pace of this rhetoric's escalating intensity and the clarity of its contemporaneous import. We have seen in Chapter 7 that Zhen Dexiu's 1229 preface to Chen Jun's *Outline and Details* contained an inchoate version of a lineage that extended from Zhang Dun through Tong Guan. By 1241, Xie Caibo 謝采伯 (*jinshi* 1202) envisioned the lineage as Wang Anshi, Cai Jing, and Qin Gui, and added historical parallels between Wang Anshi and Wang Mang in the Han, Cai Jing and the imperial affines of the Eastern Han, and Qin Gui and the Tang minister Li Linfu 李林甫 (683–752). In Xie's view, Wang, Cai, and Qin were three "petty men" who had harmed the state despite the benevolence and probity of the Song rulers.[34]

In 1246, Liu Kezhuang, then serving as Secretariat drafter, refused to process an academic appointment for Shi Songzhi, who was then in mourning. Liu feared that the appointment could become a platform for Shi's eventual return as chief councilor. He submitted a precedent that reminded Emperor Lizong of Gaozong's experience with Qin Gui. According to Liu, Gaozong understood Qin's character and had personally drafted his dismissal notice in 1132; as a result, no one imagined that Qin could ever be councilor again. But Liu reminded the emperor that the nature of the "nefarious minister" is ever to plot his own return to power. Gaozong made the mistake of granting Qin an opening, and Qin began to plot against his political opponents. Liu argued that Zhao Ding and Zhang Jun would have negotiated a much more advantageous treaty with the Jin than Qin eventually did. But, after their removal, Gaozong had no option except to delegate that authority to Qin Gui, and Qin concluded a treaty more advantageous to himself than to Gaozong or to Song. And as long as Qin was alive, Gaozong could never recover his authority, lived in fear for his own life, and carried a dagger hidden in his boot. Liu concludes that if Emperor Lizong permits Shi's return to court, he will incur a similar fate for himself.[35]

---

[34] *Mizhai biji*, 1.16b. Xie's father, Xie Shenfu 謝深甫 (*jinshi* 1166), supported Han Tuozhou and was an architect of the Qingyuan proscription. That his son could nevertheless still invoke the Wang–Cai–Qin lineage at a time when others included Han Tuozhou as an extension of that group suggests the ubiquity and force of the conception of a historical lineage of evil that extended from Northern into Southern Song.

[35] *Liu Kezhuang ji jianjiao*, 84.3703–5; *QSW*, 330:7594.148–49. Liu made similar arguments against Shi Songzhi again in 1251; see his memorial quoted in his biography by Lin Xiyi 林希逸

Liu's precedent is remarkable not merely for its formal comparison between Qin Gui and Shi Songzhi but also for how closely Liu's account of Qin Gui's relationship with Gaozong anticipates both the narrative in Qin's *Song History* biography and the standard modern interpretation of the period. By the 1250s, as the Chen Dong colophons suggest, the concept of the lineage and its membership had become established elements of historical and political rhetoric. In 1256, for example, Yao Mian 姚勉 (1216–1262), arguing against a clampdown on protests by University students, invoked Cai Jing, Qin Gui, Han Tuozhou, and Shi Miyuan as councilors who had all acted similarly to suppress criticism and restrict legitimate remonstrance.[36]

This fully developed trope of a lineage of evil ministers who suppressed public opinion and harmed the state is central to Lü Zhong's *Lectures on Song History*, examined in Chapter 4. The introductory Southern Song essays framed the lineage as a driving dynamic of Song history. For example, the conclusion to the first essay seeks to explain the failure of Han Tuozhou and Shi Miyuan to retake the North and complete the Restoration. Lü attributed their failure not to military miscalculations but to each councilor's focus on political self-interest rather than on the founders' policies of benevolence and rightness. Lü traced the pro-war "mind of Han Tuozhou" back to the expansionism of Zhang Dun, Cai Jing, and Wang Fu; he traced the pro-peace "mind of Shi Miyuan" back to the accommodation policies of Huang Qianshan, Wang Boyan, Qin Gui, and Tang Situi. Despite their opposite approaches to war and peace, Lü argued that all these councilors had placed their own political network building over the larger interests of the state. Military action or inaction arose from their own self-interest rather than in response to policy as reflected in public opinion.[37]

Lü's second essay explained how these councilors' drive for political advantage corroded the institutional structures of the founders from within. He traced this tendency back to Wang Anshi's moves to "privatize" imperial government through changes that channeled institutional powers into the de facto hands of the chief councilor: instead of presiding as chief administrative officer over a network of interlocking institutions, the chief councilor presided over a private political network. The consequences were an end to the separation between the Secretariat and the Bureau of Military Affairs, a reduction in the scope of the emperor's "attendant officers" (*shicong* 使從), the shackling of the Censorate, and the privatization and corruption of military appointments. After Wang Anshi, the councilors Qin

(1193–1270+), *QSW*, 336:7739.37–38, which cites the 1246 and 1251 texts. See also Cheng Zhangcan, *Liu Kezhuang nianpu*, 217–18, 254–55, for the fuller context of both incidents.
[36] *QSW*, 351:8126.296–302.   [37] Lü Zhong, *Zhongxing dashiji*, 1.435–36.

Gui, Han Tuozhou, and Shi Miyuan all relied upon this governance model.[38]

As is well known, the lineage of evil ministers in the *Song History* ends with Jia Sidao. Yet this construction, which is certainly the work of the Yuan historians, also built on late Song criticism of Jia. For example, writing in 1269, Li Xinchuan's disciple Gao Side compared Jia Sidao to Cai Jing, Qin Gui, and Shi Miyuan. He noted that earlier nefarious ministers such as Cai, Qin, and Shi had been content to maintain a low profile as they built their autocratic regimes, but Jia did so while trying to preserve a reputation for integrity.[39] By the Song–Yuan transition, popular conceptions of the lineage included Jia Sidao and other late Song ministers. An early Yuan collection of anecdotes from late Song Lin'an quotes a lost work by Lü Zhong as fixing the Southern Song lineage as Qin Gui, Han Tuozhou, and Shi Miyuan. The writer adds that Lü's list should be extended to include Shi Songzhi, Ding Daquan, and Jia Sidao.[40]

There is no doubt that the Yuan historians determined whose biographies would be included among the nefarious ministers of the *Song History*. They clearly drew upon the established, late Song roster, but made two important exceptions – Wang Anshi and Shi Miyuan. As we have seen, Zhen Dexiu, Xie Caibo, and Lü Zhong all framed Wang Anshi as the initiator of the lineage. This tradition dated back to the earliest criticism of Wang as destructive of the policies of the ancestors and found its codification in Li Tao's *Long Draft*. Yet despite this criticism, Wang retained his position in the Confucian temple until 1241, and his works continued to be studied and cited in the exam system. More importantly, major *daoxue* voices, including Zhu Xi, respected his Confucian commitment and his political abilities.[41]

The exclusion of Shi Miyuan, which ran counter to almost universal literati opinion in late Song, reflects the *daoxue* sensitivities of the Yuan compilers. Unlike many nefarious ministers, Shi had been a member of a prestigious multigenerational literati family, and his father had served honorably as chief councilor under Emperor Xiaozong. In 1208, the early Shi Miyuan administration had returned to office many officials whom Han Tuozhou had persecuted and who embraced *daoxue* values. Even as Shi grew increasingly

---

[38] Lü Zhong, *Zhongxing dashiji*, 1.440–43. Lü's comments on individual entries frequently invoke the lineage. For example, commenting on Qin Gui's dismissal of Hong Xingzu 洪興祖 (1090–1155) in 1154, he observes that there have been five autocratic chief councilors – Wang Anshi, Zhang Dun, Cai Jing, Wang Fu, and Qin Gui – with each repression worse than the last; and he concludes that Han Tuozhou and Shi Miyuan "imitated Qin Gui." See *Zhongxing dashiji*, 13.641–42.

[39] *Chitang cungao*, 5.2b.

[40] Li You, *Gu Hang zaji*, 47B.32b–33a. For this passage see also Huang Huixian, "Lü Zhong yu *Huangchao dashiji* xintan," 906.

[41] On this last point see Yu Yingshi, *Zhu Xi de lishi shijie*, 1:314–337; 2:164.

autocratic and distanced himself from *daoxue* statesmen such as Zhen Dexiu and Wei Liaoweng, he never instituted, as did Cai Jing, Qin Gui, or Han Tuozhou, a formal proscription against *daoxue*. Lastly, under Shi Songzhi in 1241, the state recognized the *daoxue* teachings as state orthodoxy and finally removed Wang Anshi from the Confucian temple. For the Yuan historians, themselves beneficiaries of the state's embrace of *daoxue*, this fact alone precluded linking any member of the Shi family with the lineage of "nefarious ministers."

As the dynasty neared its end, the added rhetorical force of the lineage of evil gave rise to an image of Song dynastic history as an undulating pattern of political florescence followed by periods of repression and decline. This concept of an endless, cosmic struggle between the forces of good and evil conformed to the Chinese tendency to perceive cyclical patterns in time and prefigured, for example, the Yuan historians' preface to the nefarious ministers' biographies in the *Song History*.[1] With all three clusters of the grand allegory in place, metaphors of cyclicality were invoked both to explain specific issues and, as the dynasty approached its end, to construct sweeping summations of its entire history. For example, a commercial *daoxue* encyclopedia from the 1230s contains an entry entitled "human talents in the Qingli era." The author detected historical fluctuations in imperial personnel policies that had resulted in the Qingli florescence and mapped these onto the sequence of line changes throughout the cycle of the sixty-four hexagrams. In the author's analogy, the hexagram "Receptive" (*Kun*), six *yin* lines that depict the nadir of the cycle, corresponded to the Five Dynasties period whose rulers did nothing to foster literati talent. However, expanded recruitment through the examination system in early Song constituted "The Turning Point" (*Fu*), the hexagram in which the bottom *yin* line has changed to *yang*, thus initiating the eventual cyclic return up to the "Creative" (*Qian*) hexagram, six *yang* lines that represent the apex of the cycle. The author thus equated the profusion of political talent in the Qingli era to this "creative" apex in the cycle. But, of course, no apex is permanent, and the passage goes on to frame opposition to the Qingli reforms as the beginning of a political and moral downturn that eventually led to the New Policies, followed by yet another cyclical reversal under Yuanyou.[2]

As the dynasty ended, such schemes of explanatory cyclicality became increasingly detailed and comprehensive. The leading Zhu Xi disciple,

---

[1] On cyclicality as a general feature of Chinese historiography and its specific expression in Song see Hartman and DeBlasi, "The Growth of Historical Method in Tang China," 19–20; and Hartman, "*Song History* Narratives as Grand Allegory," 43–47.

[2] Lin Jiong, *Gujin yuanliu zhilun, qianqi*, 3.12b–17a; for a detailed study of this work see De Weerdt, *Competition over Content*, 271–79.

Huang Zhen 黃震 (1213–1280), in his reading notes on Zhu Xi's *Records of the Words and Deeds of Illustrious Ministers*, crafted yet another late Song vision of dynastic history as an undulating cycle of positive and negative forces, a vision that combined elements from all three thematic clusters of the grand allegory. In Huang's diaries, his notes on Song history follow four chapters that contain his reading notes on the standard dynastic histories from Sima Qian through the Five Dynasties. This placement thus accorded Zhu Xi's book a status equal to that of official dynastic history. At the end of his comments on specific individuals Huang appended a grand summary of Northern Song history that he distilled from lessons he perceived Zhu Xi to have embedded into the biographies. Huang divided Northern Song history into nine periods, each of which marked for him a significant political turning point, as follows:

(1) Taizu took back power from the military governors and established the foundations of Song peace and prosperity.

(2) However, Taizong's attempts to conquer the sixteen provinces and the Tanguts instigated unstable northern borders.[3]

(3) Chief Councilor Li Hang, under the banner of "control through purity and tranquility" (鎮以清靜) brought peace to the people.[4]

(4) Chief Councilor Kou Zhun, by convincing Emperor Zhenzong to personally lead Song forces at Chanyuan, brought about long-lasting border security.[5]

(5) Chief Councilor Wang Dan acceded to ill-considered sacrifices in connection with the Heavenly Letters, and state power declined.[6]

(6) Chief Councilor Wang Zeng protected the young Emperor Renzong, Han Qi assisted Emperor Yingzong and Shenzong, and through turbulent times the state was "as stable as Tai Mountain."

(7) Chief Councilor Wang Anshi promulgated the New Policies and promoted border expansion; the empire was again in turmoil.

(8) Empress Gao and Sima Guang restored order.

(9) Chief Councilor Fan Chunren employed gentlemen and petty men together and thus opened the door for Zhang Dun and Cai Jing to bring back the New Policies; the state was set on the disastrous path toward 1127.[7]

Huang concludes that this summary "illustrates the major points of florescence and decline" and that Zhu Xi's biographies thus "secretly lodge the history of our dynasty." Despite the familiarity of these events and periodization to modern students of Song history, Huang's focus is on the cyclicality of historical events. Events 1, 3, 4, 6, and 8 are positive; 2, 5, 7, and 9 are

---

[3] See Lau and Huang, "Founding and Consolidation," 251–52.   [4] *Changbian*, 34.758, 36.797.

[5] Lau and Huang, "Founding and Consolidation," 262–70.

[6] Lau and Huang, "Founding and Consolidation," 270–73.

[7] Huang Zhen, *Huangshi richao*, 50.42a–b; see also Wang Deyi, "Zhu Xi *Wuchao* ji *Sanchao mingchen yanxing lu* de shiliao jiazhi," 66.

negative. These positive and negative values derive in turn from the historiographical principles of the grand allegory. Taizu demilitarizes and brings about
civilian control; the resulting benevolent governance crests under Renzong; the
lineage of evil begins with Wang Anshi and the New Policies. Huang, in fact,
posited the lineage of evil back far earlier in the dynasty, since he here portrays
the Zhenzong-era councilor Wang Dan in negative terms, in contrast to the
positive exemplars Li Hang, Kou Zhun, Wang Zeng, and Han Qi.[8] Notable also
is the theme that military expansionism always leads to a decline in state power.
This theme follows from the foundational idea that Taizu's dynastic principle
was the containment of military power. Taizong's efforts to recover the sixteen
provinces are thus framed as a negative force, as is the Shenzong-era expansionism on the northwestern border. Although anti-militarism was a significant
factor in the literati project as early as Sima Guang, and accelerated as the
daoxue movement increasingly defined itself against technocratic military
interests under Xiaozong, the failed northern invasions of 1206 and 1234
increased attention to this theme.

Such explanatory scenarios increased the tendency for Confucian literati to
posit their own history in the context of these undulating patterns. As did Huang
Zhen, they conceived their own periods of political success as high points in the
undulating cycle, only to be frustrated by the eventual return of their opponents.
We have seen in Chapter 3, for example, how Li Xinchuan's *Record of the Way
and Its Fate* conceived of the history of *daoxue* as three cycles of florescence
and repression; and his preface to the *Record* concluded that the repressed must
persevere through difficult periods in anticipation of the resurgence to follow.
This perception of Song history became common toward the dynasty's end. Liu
Kezhuang, for example, framed the long history of Confucian attempts at
political reform undulating with successive repressive measures against those
efforts. He identified four cycles: the repression of the Qingli reformers, the
persecution of the Yuanyou administrators after 1094, the Qin Gui era (1138–
1155), and the Han Tuozhou era (1194–1207) – the last three of which match Li
Xinchuan's periodization.[9]

We have also seen above that the periods of active historiographical fer-
ment – periods in which private historiography moved to shape and transform
the official record – occurred in cycles of rhythmic alternation with these
periods of repressive, autocratic governance – in short, at high points in the
cycles either before or after periods of repressive governance. These are the
Qingli period, the Yuanyou period, the early (pre-Qin Gui) Shaoxing period

---

[8] For a characterization of Wang Dan as the first "autocratic" councilor see Olsson, "The Structure
of Power," 206–8.
[9] *Liu Kezhuang ji jianjiao*, 101.4253–55; *QSW*, 329:7576.253–54. Liu articulated this framework
in a colophon written on Huang Tianjian's holograph of the biography of Fan Pang 范滂,
a literatus executed for his opposition to the eunuchs in the Eastern Han.

(1131–1138), and the Jiading (1208–1224) period in Southern Song. All of these eras experienced either defensive or offensive wars that sparked domestic political upheavals, and these political conflicts then generated historiographical revisionism. The result was the emergence of a narrative of positive political value that moved from Taizu through Qingli and Yuanyou. This narrative of supposed Northern Song values and structures took shape under the descendants of the Yuanyou administrators in the mid-1130s, was then held in check during the Qin Gui years from 1138 through 1155, but took definitive form in Li Tao's *Long Draft*, composed over a forty-year period between the 1140s and 1183. Chen Jun then sharpened and popularized this narrative in his 1229 *Outline and Details*. In essence, our received narrative of Northern Song history grew from the political struggles of the Restoration. Later Southern Song historians then wrote the Restoration's own history by plotting its events back onto the earlier model their predecessors had created for the Northern Song.[10] Using the language of the Confucian historians of Song, a distillation of the grand allegory might read as follows:

Motivated by concern for the welfare of the people and assisted by Heaven, Emperor Taizu, the Song founder, sought to restore the Benevolent governance of Antiquity. In order to dispel the pernicious effects of long Military rule upon the country, he and his successors fostered Civil governance. For this task, they recruited Gentlemen who supported their vision and propagated governance in the Public interest that considered the needs of all the realm's people. But Petty Men – unruly elements within the monarchy such as imperial affines and eunuchs, recalcitrant military, and apostates among the Gentlemen – motivated by Selfish interests thwarted and deformed the Founders' model. Henceforth, the Upright and the Perverse contended, their struggles undermined the once-strong dynasty, and half its territory was lost to the barbarians. Weakened by decades of suppression, the Gentlemen could only effect a partial Restoration. The Petty Men regrouped under a Nefarious Minister who once again betrayed the Founders' commitment to Benevolence. Although the Gentlemen managed to resist and regroup, dynastic governance devolved into an unending cyclical struggle between the Upright and the Perverse, between advocates and opponents of the founders' original conception of Benevolent rule.[11]

All modern historians of Song will recognize in this morality tale a traditional, if somewhat banal, synopsis of the dynasty's history. Yet, even though scholars long ago abandoned many of these motifs, if we translate this allegory into the language of the modern historian, we obtain a master narrative to which most scholars of Song history could ascribe:

Taizu desired to end the militarism of the Five Dynasties and unify the country with a centralized, civil administration. He and his successors recruited such officials in large numbers, and they pursued a Confucian-based benevolent governance during the

[10] Hartman, "*Song History* Narratives as Grand Allegory," 56.
[11] Hartman, "*Song History* Narratives as Grand Allegory," 49.

Renzong period. However, after 1067 Emperor Shenzong and Wang Anshi, in order to raise revenue to finance the final conquest of North China, adopted New Policies, which undermined the governance of the founders. The resulting discord led to permanent factional division. The political ascendency of Wang's successors, especially Cai Jing, spurred renewed military expansionism, further weakened the state, and precipitated the Jurchen invasions of 1125. The Restoration under Emperor Gaozong, while rhetorically abjuring the New Policies, continued to employ many of their provisions. Opposition from the heirs of those who had opposed Wang Anshi, plus constant military threats from the North, fostered continued political division. Periods of authoritarian rule under Qin Gui, Han Tuozhou, and Shi Miyuan alternated with more benevolently inclined administrations favorable to *daoxue*. After Shi's death in 1233, Emperor Lizong kept the two sides locked in perpetual stalemate.[12]

A final question arises: if this grand allegory, in both its original Confucian and its modern version, is a historiographical construct that grew from Song political struggle, what can its formation, its rhetoric, its contours, tell us about those struggles? In the Introduction to this book, and repeatedly throughout these chapters, I have referred to two conceptions of governance, one that I have labeled Confucian literati or institutionalist, and the other technocratic. I have shown that the grand allegory is a product of the former, and, I contend, arose from political discourse directed largely against the latter. A naive reading of this allegorical narrative has led to a perception of the Song as "an age of Confucian rule."[13] Its deconstruction, however, suggests that the Song was rather an age in which a wide array of non-Confucian and/or non-literati actors within the Song polity, often the monarchs themselves and often even elements within the literati class itself, refused to accept the theory and practice of Confucian institutionalism and worked actively to oppose its influence. The undulating historiographical cycles of the allegory reflect not the moral battles between Confucian good and evil but the truly historical struggles between these two conceptions of the Song state.

In short, the multitude of facts and documents in the sources studied in this volume, once freed from their allegorical framework, may be read once again to tell the story of yet another narrative, one of conflict between these two modalities of Song governance. A subsequent volume on the structure of Song governance will define these two modalities, explore their historical origins and theoretical foundations, and describe their personnel and their formal institutions. It will also propose a new model for understanding Song government as a working symbiosis, sometimes successful but often not, between these two poles.

---

[12] Hartman, "*Song History* Narratives as Grand Allegory," 50.
[13] As in Kuhn, *The Age of Confucian Rule*.

Bibliography

Abbreviations

Changbian – Li Tao 李燾 (1115–1184). *Xu zizhi tongjian changbian* 續資治通鑑長編 [The Long Draft Continuation of the Comprehensive Mirror That Aids Administration]. Second edition. 20 vols. Beijing: Zhonghua shuju, 2004.

Changbian shibu – Huang Yizhou 黃以周 (1828–1899) et al. *Xu zizhi tongjian changbian shibu* 續資治通鑑長編拾捕 [Supplements to the Long Draft Continuation of the Comprehensive Mirror That Aids Administration]. Edited by Gu Jichen 顧吉辰. 4 vols. Beijing: Zhonghua shuju, 2004.

Chaoye zaji – Li Xinchuan 李心傳 (1167–1244). *Jianyan yilai chaoye zaji* 建炎以來朝野雜記 [Diverse Notes on Court and Province since 1127]. Edited by Xu Gui 徐規. 2 vols. Beijing: Zhonghua shuju, 2000.

Dongdu shilüe – Wang Cheng 王稱. *Dongdu shilüe* 東都事略 [Eastern Capital Miscellany]. 1186 edition. Reprinted, 4 vols. Taipei: Wenhai chubanshe, 1979.

Huangchao dashiji – Lü Zhong 呂中 (fl. 1250). In Lü Zhong. *Leibian Huangchao dashiji jiangyi. Leibian Huangchao zhongxing dashiji jiangyi* 類編皇朝大事記講義. 類編皇朝中興大事記講義 [Classified Lectures on Major Events of the August Courts. Classified Lectures on Major Events of the August Courts of the Restoration]. Edited by Zhang Qifan 張其凡 and Bai Xiaoxia 白曉霞. Shanghai: Shanghai renmin chubanshe, 2014, pp. 1–393.

Huangchao gangmu – Chen Jun 陳均 (1174–1244). *Huangchao biannian gangmu beiyao* 皇朝編年綱目備要 [Chronologically Arranged Complete Essentials in Outline and Detail of the August Courts]. Edited by Xu Peizao 許沛藻 et al. 2 vols. Beijing: Zhonghua shuju, 2006.

Huangchao zhongxing jishi benmo – anonymous. *Huangchao zhongxing jishi benmo* 皇朝中興紀事本末 [Topical Narratives from the August Courts of the Restoration]. Song editon. Reprinted as Xiong Ke 熊克, *Huangchao zhongxing jishi benmo*. 2 vols. Beijing: Beijing tushuguan chubanshe, 2005.

Huibian – Xu Mengxin 徐夢莘. *Sanchao beimeng huibian* 三朝北夢會編 [A Compendium on Treaties with the North at Three Courts]. 4 vols. Taipei: Dahua shuju, 1979.

Jingkang yaolu – Wang Zao 王藻 (1079–1154). *Jingkang yaolu jianzhu* 靖康要錄箋注 [The Chronological Record of the Jingkang Period, with Annotations]. Annotated by Wang Zhiyong 王智勇. 3 vols. Chengdu: Sichuan daxue chubanshe, 2008.

QSW – *Quan Song wen* 全宋文 [Complete Prose of the Song Dynasty]. Edited by Zeng Zaozhuang 曾棗莊 and Liu Lin 劉琳. 360 vols. Shanghai and Hefei: Shanghai cishu chubanshe and Anhui jiaoyu chubanshe, 2006.

QYW – *Quan Yuan wen* 全元文 [Complete Prose of the Yuan Dynasty]. Edited by Li Xiusheng 李修生. 60 vols. Nanjing: Jiangsu guji chubanshe, 2004.

SHY – Xu Song 徐松 (1781–1848) compiler. *Song huiyao jigao* 宋會要輯稿 [The Recovered Draft of the Collected Essential Documents of Song]. Edited by Liu Lin et al. 16 vols. Shanghai: Shanghai guji chubanshe, 2014. Originally published Beijing: Guoli Beiping tushuguan, 1936.

SS – Toghto 脫脫. *Songshi* 宋史 [History of the Song Dynasty]. 40 vols. Beijing: Zhonghua shuju, 1977.

Songshi quanwen – anonymous. *Songshi quanwen* 宋史全文 [Complete Texts of Song History]. Edited by Wang Shengduo 汪聖鐸. 9 vols. Beijing: Zhonghua shuju, 2016.

Wenxian tongkao – Ma Duanlin 馬端臨 (1254–1325). *Wenxian tongkao* 文獻通考 [Comprehensive Studies of Historical Documents]. 14 vols. Beijing: Zhonghua shuju, 2011.

Xubian – anonymous. *Xubian liangchao gangmu beiyao* 續編兩朝綱目備要 [Complete Essentials in Outline and Detail of the Two Courts, Continued]. Edited by Ru Qihe 汝企和. Beijing: Zhonghua shuju, 1995.

Yaolu – Li Xinchuan 李心傳 (1167–1244). *Jianyan yilai xinian yaolu* 建炎以來繫年要錄 [Chronological Record of Important Events since 1127]. Edited by Hu Kun 胡坤. 8 vols. Beijing: Zhonghua shuju, 2013.

Yongle dadian – Xie Jin 解縉 (1369–1415) and Yao Guangxiao 姚廣孝 (1335–1419). *Yongle dadian* 永樂大典 [Yongle Encyclopedia]. 10 vols. Beijing: Zhonghua shuju, 1986.

YS – Song Lian 宋濂 (1310–1381). *Yuanshi* 元史 [History of the Yuan Dynasty]. 15 vols. Beijing: Zhonghua shuju, 1976.

Yuhai – Wang Yinglin 王應麟 (1223–1296). *Yuhai* 玉海 [The Ocean of Jade]. 1883 edition. 8 vols. Shanghai: Jiangsu guji chubanshe, Shanghai shudian, 1988.

Zhongxing dashiji – Lü Zhong 呂中 (fl. 1250). In Lü Zhong. *Leibian Huangchao dashiji jiangyi. Leibian Huangchao zhongxing dashiji jiangyi* 類編皇朝大事記講義. 類編皇朝中興大事記講義 [Classified Lectures on Major Events of our August Dynasty. Classified Lectures on Major Events of the Restoration of Our August Dynasty]. Edited by Zhang Qifan and Bai Xiaoxia. Shanghai: Shanghai renmin chubanshe, 2014, pp. 395–858.

Zhongxing gangmu – Chen Jun 陳均 (1174–1244). *Zhongxing liangchao biannian gangmu* 中興兩朝編年綱目 [Chronologically Arranged Outline and Details of the Two Restoration Courts]. Edited by Yan Yongcheng 燕永成. Nanjing: Fenghuang chubanshe, 2018.

Zhongxing shengzheng – anonymous. *Huangchao zhongxing liangchao shengzheng* 皇朝中興兩朝聖政 [Sagacious Administration from the Two Restoration Courts of the August Song]. *Wanwei biezang* 宛委別藏 edition. Reprinted, 4 vols. Taipei: Wenhai chubanshe, 1967.

Zhongxing xiaoli – Xiong Ke 熊克 (1157 *jinshi*). *Zhongxing xiaoli* 中興小曆 [Minor Calendar of the Restoration]. Reprinted as Xiong Ke, *Zhongxing xiaoji* 中興小紀. Edited by Gu Jichen 顧吉辰 and Guo Qunyi 郭群一. Fuzhou: Fujian renmin chubanshe, 1984.

Abbreviations for collectanea

CSJC – Congshu jicheng 叢書集成 [Complete Collection of Assembled Books]. 3,467
vols. Shanghai: Shanghai yinshuguan, 1936–1940. Reprinted *Congshu jicheng
xinbian* 叢書集成新編. 120 vols. Taipei: Xinwenfeng chuban gongsi, 1985.
Quan Song biji – Shanghai shifan daxue. Guji zhengli yanjiusuo, ed. *Quan Song biji* 全
宋筆記 [Complete Song *biji*]. Zhengzhou: Daxiang chubanshe, 2003–
SBCK – *Sibu congkan* 四部叢刊 [Assembled Printings from the Four Divisions].
Reprinted, 100 vols. Taipei: Taiwan shangwu yinshuguan, 1979.
SKQS – *Yingyin Wenyuange Siku quanshu* 影印文淵閣四庫全書 [Photofacsimile
Reprint of the Wenyuan Pavilion Copy of the *Complete Books in the Four
Treasuries*]. 1,500 vols. Taipei: Taiwan shangwu yinshuguan, 1983–1986.

Primary Sources

Anonymous. *Hanyuan xinshu* 翰苑新書 [New writings from the Hanlin garden] (*SKQS*
edition).
Anonymous, *Nan Song guan'ge xulu*, in Chen Kui 陳騤. *Nan Song guan'ge lu, xulu* 南
宋館閣錄, 續錄 [An account of Southern Song Academic Institutions, and
a Supplemental Account]. Edited by Zhang Fuxiang 張富祥. Beijing: Zhonghua
shuju, 1998.
Anonymous. *Song da zhaoling ji* 宋大詔令集 [Collection of Major Song Edicts].
Beijing: Zhonghua shuju, 1962.
Anonymous. *Songji sanchao zhengyao jianzheng* 宋季三朝政要箋證 [Administrative
Essentials from the Last Three Courts of the Song, Annotated]. Edited by
Wang Ruilai 王瑞來. Beijing: Zhonghua shuju, 2010.
Anonymous. *Taiping baoxun zhengshi jinian* 太平寶訓政事紀年 [Administrative
Policies Year by Year from the *Precious Instructions from the Era of Great
Peace*]. Taipei: Wenhai chubanshe, 1980.
Cai Tao 蔡絛. *Tiewei shan congtan* 鐵圍山叢談 [Collected Conversations from the Iron
Encircling Mountain]. Beijing: Zhonghua shuju, 1983.
Chao Gongwu 晁公武. *Junzhai dushuzhi jiaozheng* 郡齋讀書志校證 [A Collated
Edition of *Notes on Reading Books in a Provincial Studio*]. Edited by Sun Meng
孫猛. Shanghai: Shanghai guji chubanshe, 1990.
Chen Fuliang 陳傅良. *Zhizhai ji* 止齋集 [Collected works of Chen Fuliang] (*SKQS*
edition).
Chen Kui 陳騤. *Nan Song guan'ge lu, xulu* 南宋館閣錄, 續錄 [An Account of Southern
Song Academic Institutions, and a Supplemental Account]. Edited by
Zhang Fuxiang 張富祥. Beijing: Zhonghua shuju, 1998.
Chen Shanjun 陳尚君. *Jiu wudai shi xinji huizheng* 舊五代史新輯彙證 [*The Old
History of the Five Dynasties*, Newly Compiled with Collected Annotation]. 12
vols. Shanghai: Fudan daxue chubanshe, 2005.
Chen Yuyi 陳與義. *Jianzhai ji* 簡齋集 [Collected Works of Chen Yuyi] (*SKQS* edition).
Chen Zhensun 陳振孫. *Zhizhai shulu jieti* 直齋書錄解題 [Notes and Comments on the
Books in My Library]. Shanghai: Shanghai guji chubanshe, 1987.
Cheng Ju 程俱. *Beishan ji* 北山集 [Collected Works of Cheng Ju] (*SKQS* edition).

Lintai gushi jiaozheng 臨臺故事校證 [A Collated Edition of *Precedents from the Imperial Library*]. Collated by Zhang Fuxiang 張富祥. Beijing: Zhonghua shuju, 2000.

Ding Teqi 丁特起. *Jingkang jiwen* 靖康紀聞 [Records of the Jingkang Period] (*CSJC* edition).

Ding Wei 丁謂. *Ding Jingong tanlu* 丁晉公談錄 [Conversations of Ding Wei] (*Quan Song biji* edition).

Du Yu 杜預. *Chunqiu Zuozhuan zhushu* 春秋左傳注疏 [Annotations on the *Spring and Autumn Annals* and the *Zuo Tradition*] (*SKQS* edition).

Du Zheng 度正. *Xingshan tang gao* 性善堂稿 [Collected Works of Du Zheng] (*SKQS* edition).

Fan Zuyu 范祖禹. *Fan Taishi ji* 范太史集 [Collected Works of Fan Zuyu] (*SKQS* edition).

Tangjian 唐鑒 [A Mirror of Tang Dynasty History] (*SKQS* edition).

Fu Zengxiang 傅增湘. *Songdai Shuwen jicun* 宋代蜀文輯存 [Surviving Writings from Song-Period Sichuan]. 1943 edition. Reprinted, 7 vols. Beijing: Beijing tushuguan chubanshe, 2005.

Songdai Shuwen jicun jiaobu 宋代蜀文輯存校補 [Surviving Writings from Song-Period Sichuan, Edited with Supplements]. Edited by Wu Hongze 吳洪澤. 6 vols. Chongqing: Chongqing daxue chubanshe, 2014.

Gao Side 高斯得. *Chitang cungao* 恥堂存藁 [Collected Works of Gao Side] (*SKQS* edition).

Han Biao 韓淲. *Jianquan riji* 澗泉日記 [Diaries of Han Biao] (*SKQS* edition).

Han Yuanji 韓元吉. *Nanjian jiayi gao* 南澗甲乙稿 [First and Second Drafts from South Gully] (*SKQS* edition).

He Xiu 何休. *Chunqiu Gongyang zhuan zhushu* 春秋公羊傳注疏 [Annotations on the Gongyang Commentary to the *Spring and Autumn Annals*] (*SKQS* edition).

Hong Mai 洪邁. *Rongzhai suibi* 容齋隨筆 [Random Notes of Hong Mai]. 2 vols. Shanghai: Shanghai guji chubanshe, 1978.

Huang Huai 黃淮 and Yang Shiqi 楊士奇, compilers. *Lidai mingchen zouyi* 歷代名臣奏議 [Memorials of Illustrious Ministers through the Ages]. 6 vols. Taipei: Taiwan xuesheng shuju, 1964.

Huang Jin 黃潛. *Wenxian ji* 文獻集 [Collected Works of Huang Jin] (*SKQS* edition).

Huang Yizhou 黃以周 et. al. *Xu zizhi tongjian changbian shibu* 續資治通鑑長編拾補 [Collected Supplements to the *Long Draft Continuation of the Comprehensive Mirror that Aids Administration*]. Edited by Gu Jichen 顧吉辰. 4 vols. Beijing: Zhonghua shuju, 2004.

Huang Zhen 黃震. *Huangshi richao* 黃氏日鈔 [The Diaries of Master Huang] (*SKQS* edition).

Huang Zongxi 黃宗羲. *Song Yuan xue'an* 宋元學案 [Scholars of the Song and Yuan]. Edited by Chen Jinsheng 陳金生 and Liang Yunhua 梁運華. 6 vols. Taipei: Huashi chubanshe, 1987.

Ji Yun 紀昀 et al. *Qinding Siku quanshu zongmu* 欽定四庫全書總目 [A General Catalogue of the Complete Books in the Four Categories]. 2 vols. Beijing: Zhonghua shuju, 1997.

Li Gang 李綱. *Li Gang quanji* 李綱全集 [Collected Works of Li Gang]. Edited by Wang Ruiming 王瑞明. 3 vols. Changsha: Yuelu chubanshe, 2004.

Li Jingde 黎靖德. *Zhuzi yulei* 朱子語類. [Conversations of Zhu Xi]. 8 vols. Beijing: Zhonghua shuju, 1994.

Li Xiaolong 李肖龍. *Cui Qingxian gong yanxing lu* 崔清獻公言行錄 [Record of the Words and Deeds of Cui Yuzhi] (*CSJC* edition).

Li Xinchuan 李心傳. *Daoming lu* 道命錄 [A Record of the Way and Its Fate] (*CSJC* edition).

Jianyan yilai xinian yaolu 建炎以來繫年要錄 [A Chronological Record of Important Events since 1127] (*SKQS* edition).

Jiuwen zhengwu 舊聞證誤 [Corrections of Errors in Old Accounts]. In Zhang Shinan 張世南 [and] Li Xinchuan. *Youhuan jiwen* 游宦紀聞 [and] *Jiuwen zhengwu*. Beijing: Zhonghua shuju, 1981.

Li You 李攸. *Songchao shishi* 宋朝事實 [True Events of the Song Court]. Taipei: Wenhai chubanshe, 1967.

Li You 李有. *Gu Hang zaji* 古杭雜記 [Diverse Accounts of Old Hangzhou]. In Tao Zongyi, comp., *Shuofu* (*SKQS* edition).

Li Yumin 李裕民, editor. *Sima Guang Riji jiaozhu* 司馬光日記校注 [Sima Guang's Diary, Collated with Commentary]. Beijing: Zhongguo shehui kexue chubanshe, 1994.

Songren shengzu xingnian kao 宋人生卒行年考 [Researches on the Birth and Death Dates of Song Persons]. Beijing: Zhonghua shuju, 2010.

Lin Jiong 林駉. *Gujin yuanliu zhilun* 古今源流至論 [Ultimate Essays as Origins and Developments from the Past to the Present] (*SKQS* edition).

Liu Kezhuang 劉克莊. *Liu Kezhuang ji jianjiao* 劉克莊集箋校 [The Collected Works of Liu Kezhuang with Commentary]. Edited with commentary by Xin Gengru 辛更儒. 16 vols. Beijing: Zhonghua shuju, 2011.

Liu Shiju 劉時舉. *Xu Song biannian zizhi tongjian* 續宋編年資治通鑑 [Continuation of the Song Chronological Comprehensive Mirror for Administration] (*CSJC* edition).

Liu Yiqing 劉一清. *Qiantang yishi* 錢塘遺事 [Surving Stories from Hangzhou] (*SKQS* edition).

Liu Zai 劉宰. *Mantang ji* 漫塘集 [Collected Works of Liu Zai] (*SKQS* edition).

Lou Yue 樓籥. *Gongkui ji* 攻媿集 [Collected Works of Lou Yue] (*SKQS* edition).

Lü Wu 呂午. *Zuoshi jiancao* 左史諫草 [Draft Remonstrance from the Historian of the Left] (*SKQS* edition).

Lü Zuqian 呂祖謙. *Donglai ji* 東萊集 [Collected Works of Lü Zuqian] (*SKQS* edition).

Song wenjian 宋文鑑 [The Song Literary Mirror]. Edited by Ji Zhiping 濟治平. 3 vols. Beijing: Zhonghua shuju, 1992.

Luo Congyan 羅從彥. *Yuzhang wenji* 豫章文集 [Collected Works of Luo Congyan] (*SKQS* edition).

Zun Yao lu 遵堯錄 [Record of Revering Emperor Yao] (*Quan Song biji* edition).

Mei Yaochen 梅堯臣. *Biyun xia* 碧雲騢 [The Blue Cloud Stallion] (*CSJC* edition).

Ouyang Xiu 歐陽修. *Ouyang wenzhong gong wenji* 歐陽文忠公文集 [Collected Works of Ouyang Xiu] (*SBCK* edition).

Ouyang Xiu quanji 歐陽修全集 [Collected Works of Ouyang Xiu]. Edited by Li Yi'an 李逸安. 6 vols. Beijing: Zhonghua shuju, 2001.

Xin Tang shu 新唐書 [New Tang History]. 20 vols. Beijing: Zhonghua shuju, 1975.

Peng Baichuan 彭百川. *Taiping zhiji tonglei* 太平治蹟統類 [Comprehensively Classified Governance of Great Peace]. 3 vols. Taipei: Chengwen chubanshe, 1966.

Qi Chongli 綦崇禮. *Beihai ji* 北海集 [Collected Works of Qi Chongli] (*SKQS* edition).

Qian Ruoshui 錢若水. *Song Taizong shilu* 宋太宗實錄 [The Veritable Records of the Song Emperor Taizong]. Edited by Yan Yongcheng. Lanzhou: Gansu renmin chubanshe, 2005.

Qian Yueyou 潛說友. *Xianchun Lin'an zhi* 咸淳臨安志 [Xianchun Period Gazetteer of Lin'an]. 1830 edition, reprinted in *Song Yuan difangzhi congshu*, Volume 7, pp. 3855–4826. Taipei: Dahua shuju, 1990.

Quan Heng 權衡. *Gengshen waishi jianzheng* 庚申外史箋证 [Notes on the *External History of the Gengshen Period*]. Annotated by Ren Chongyue 任崇岳. Zhengzhou: Zhongzhou guji chubanshe, 1991.

Shao Bowen 邵伯溫. *Shaoshi wenjian lu* 邵氏聞見錄 [A Record of Things Heard and Seen by the Shao Family]. Beijing: Zhonghua shuju, 1983.

Shi Hao 史浩. *Maofeng zhenyin manlu* 鄮峯真隱滿錄 [Collected Works of Shi Hao] (*SKQS* edition).

Shi Jie 石介. *Culai Shi xiansheng wenji* 徂徠石先生文集 [Collected Works of Shi Jie]. Edited by Chen Zhi'e 陳植鍔. Beijing: Zhonghua shuju, 1984.

Shu Di 舒頔. *Zhensuzhai ji* 真素齋集 [Collected Works of Shu Di] (*SKQS* edition).

Sima Guang 司馬光. *Jigu lu dianjiao ben* 稽古錄點校本 [A Collated Edition of the *Record of Investigating Antiquity*]. Edited by Wang Yiling 王亦令. Beijing: Zhongguo youyi chuban gongsi, 1987.

Shuyi 書儀 [Protocols for Writing] (*SKQS* edition).

Sima Guang ji 司馬光集 [The Collected Writings of Sima Guang]. Edited by Li Wenze 李文澤 and Xia Shaohui 霞紹暉. 3 vols. Chengdu: Sichuan daxue chubanshe, 2010.

Sushui jiwen 涑水記聞 [A Record of Things Heard by Su River]. Edited by Deng Guangming 鄧廣銘 and Zhang Xiqing 張希清. Beijing: Zhonghua shuju, 1989.

Zizhi tongjian 資治通鑒 [The Comprehensive Mirror for Aid in Governance]. Beijing: Guji chubanshe, 1956.

Sima Qian 司馬遷. *Shiji* 史記 [The Grand Scribe's Records]. Beijing: Zhonghua shuju, 1959.

Song Lian 宋濂. *Wenxian ji* 文憲集 [Collected Works of Song Lian] (*SKQS* edition).

Su Shi 蘇軾. *Su Shi wenji* 蘇軾文集 [Collected Prose of Su Shi]. Edited by Kong Fanli 孔凡禮. 6 vols. Beijing: Zhonghua shuju, 1986.

Su Tianjue 蘇天爵. *Ziqi wen gao* 滋溪文稿 [Collected Works of Su Tianjue] (*SKQS* edition).

Su Zhe 蘇轍. *Longchuan lüe zhi. Longchuan bie zhi* 龍川略志. 龍川別志 [A Brief Record from Longchuan. Another Record from Longchuan]. Beijing: Zhonghua shuju, 1982.

Sun Yirang 孫詒讓. *Zhouli zhengyi* 周禮正義 [Correct Meanings in the *Rituals of Zhou*]. Edited by Xu Jialu 許嘉璐. 10 vols. Beijing: Zhonghua shuju, 2015.

Sun Yuanxiang 孫原湘. *Tianzhenge ji* 天真閣集. Reprinted in Qingdai shiwen ji huibian bianzuan weiyuanhui. *Qingdai shiwen ji huibian* 清代詩文集彙編, Volume 464. Shanghai: Shanghai guji chubanshe, 2010.

Tian Kuang 田況. *Rulin gongyi* 儒林公議 [Public Discourse from the Confucian Forest] (*SKQS* edition).

Toghto. *Liaoshi* 遼史 [History of the Liao Dynasty]. 5 vols. Beijing: Zhonghua shuju, 1974.

Wang Bi 王弼. *Zhouyi zhushu* 周易注疏. [The Chou Dynasty Changes with Commentary and Subcommentary] (*SKQS* edition).

Wang Fuzhi 王夫之. *Song lun* 宋論 [A Discourse on the Song Dynasty]. Beijing: Zhonghua, 1964.

Wang Gui 王珪. *Huayang ji* 華陽集 [Collected Works of Wang Gui] (*SKQS* edition).

Wang Mingqing 王明清. *Huizhu lu* 揮麈錄 [Records While Waving the Duster]. Beijing: Zhonghua shuju, 1961.

   Touxia lu, Yuzhao xinzhi 投轄錄, 玉照新志 [Notebooks by Wang Mingqing]. Edited by Wang Xinsen 汪新森 and Zhu Juru 朱菊如. Shanghai: Shanghai guji chubanshe, 1991.

Wang Pizhi 王闢之. *Shengshui yantan lu* 澠水燕談錄 [A Record of Leisurely Conversations by the Sheng River]. Edited by Lü Youren 呂友仁. In Wang Pizhi, *Shengshui yantan lu* [and] Ouyang Xiu, *Guitian lu*. Beijing: Zhonghua shuju, 1981.

Wang Yingchen 汪應辰. *Wending ji* 文定集 [Collected Works of Wang Yingchen] (*SKQS* edition).

Wang Yinglin 王應麟. *Kunxue jiwen* 困學紀聞 [Notes on Things Learned from Arduous Study]. Edited by Luan Baoqun 欒保羣 et al. 3 vols. Shanghai: Shanghai guji chubanshe, 2008.

Wang Zeng 王曾. *Wang Wenzheng gong bilu* 王文正公筆錄 [Notes and Records of Wang Zeng] (*Quan Song biji* edition).

Wang Yun 王惲. *Qiujian ji* 秋澗集 [Collected Works of Wang Yun] (*SKQS* edition).

Wei Liaoweng 魏了翁. *Heshan xiansheng daquan wenji* 鶴山先生大全文集 [Collected Works of Wei Liaoweng] (*SKQS* edition).

Wenyuange Siku quanshu, dianziban 文淵閣四庫全書電子版 [*Wenyuange Siku quanshu*, electronic edition]. Hong Kong: Dizhi wenhua chuban youxian gongzi, 1999.

Wu Cheng 吳澄. *Wu Wenzheng ji* 吳文正集 [Collected Works of Wu Cheng] (*SKQS* edition).

Wu Yong 吳泳. *Helin ji* 鶴林集. [Collected Works of Wu Yong] (*SKQS* edition).

Wu Zeng 吳曾. *Nenggaizhai manlu* 能改齋漫錄 [Records from the Nenggai Studio]. 2 vols. Shanghai: Shanghai guji chubanshe, 1960.

Xia Liangsheng 夏良勝. *Zhongyong yanyi* 中庸衍義 [Extended Ideas about the *Doctrine of the Mean*] (*SKQS* edition).

Xie Caibo 謝采伯. *Mizhai biji* 密齋筆記 [Notes from the Secret Studio] (*CSJC* edition).

Xie Shenfu 謝深甫. *Qingyuan tiaofa shilei* 慶元條法事類 [Classified Regulations of the Qingyuan Period]. Taipei: Xinwenfeng chuban gongsi, 1976.

Xu Ziming 徐子明. *Song zaifu biannian lu jiaobu* 宋宰輔編年錄校補 [Chronological Records of Song Chief and Assisting Councilors, Edited and Supplemented]. Edited by Wang Ruilai 王瑞來. 4 vols. Beijing: Zhonghua shuju, 1986.

Yang Shiqi 楊士奇. *Wenyuange shumu* 文淵閣書目 [Catalogue of the Imperial Library] (*SKQS* edition).

Yang Wanli 楊萬里. *Chengzhai ji* 誠齋集 [Collected Works of Yang Wanli] (*SKQS* edition).

Ye Mengde 葉夢得. *Shilin yanyu* 石林燕語 [Shilin's Table Talk]. Edited by Yuwen Shaoyi 宇文紹奕 and Hou Zhongyi 候忠義. Beijing: Zhonghua shuju, 1984.

Ye Shaoweng 葉紹翁. *Sichao wenjian lu* 四朝聞見錄 [A Record of Things Seen and Heard at Four Courts]. Edited by Shen Xilin 沈錫麟 and Feng Huimin 馮惠民. Beijing: Zhonghua shuju, 1989.

Ye Shi 葉適. *Xixue jiyan* 習學記言 [Notes and Ideas from Repeated Study] (*SKQS* edition).

　Ye Shi ji 葉適集 [Collected Works of Ye Shi]. 3 vols. Beijing: Zhonghua shuju, 1961.

Ye Ziqi 葉子奇. *Caomuzi* 草木子 [[Notes from] The Master of Plants and Trees] (*SKQS* edition).

You Mao 尤袤. *Suichutang shumu* 遂初堂書目 [Bibliography of the Suichu Hall] (*SKQS* edition).

Yuan Jue 袁桷. *Qingrong jushi ji* 清容居士集 [Collected Works of Yuan Jue] (*SBCK* edition).

Yuan Wen 袁文. *Wengyu xianping* 甕牖閒評 [Leisurely Comments by the Small Window] (*CSJC* edition).

Zeng Gong 曾鞏. *Longping ji* 隆平集 [The Longping Collection] (*SKQS* edition).

　Zeng Gong ji 曾鞏集 [Collected Works of Zeng Gong]. Edited by Chen Xingzhen 陳杏珍 and Chao Jizhou 晁繼周. 2 vols. Beijing: Zhonghua shuju, 1984.

Zeng Zao 曾慥. *Leishuo* 類說 [Classified Discourses] (*SKQS* edition).

Zhang Duanyi 張端義. *Gui'er ji* 貴耳集. Beijing: Zhonghua shuju, 1958.

Zhang Gang 張綱. *Huayang ji* 華陽集 [Collected Works of Zhang Gang] (*SKQS* edition).

Zhang Jun 張浚. *Mengzi zhuan* 孟子傳 (*SKQS* edition).

Zhang Ruyu 張如愚. *Qunshu kaosuo* 羣書考索 [A Critical Compilation of All My Books] (*SKQS* edition).

Zhang Shunmin 張舜民. *Huaman lu* 畫墁錄 [Record of Worthless Scribbles] (*SKQS* edition).

Zhao Ruyu 趙汝愚. *Songchao zhuchen zouyi* 宋朝諸臣奏議 [The Ministers Memorials of the Song Court]. 2 vols. Shanghai: Shanghai guji chubanshe, 1999.

Zhen Dexiu 真德秀. *Daxue yanyi* 大學衍義 [Extended Ideas about the *Great Learning*] (*SKQS* edition).

　Xishan wenji 西山文集 [Collected Works of Zhen Dexiu] (*SKQS* edition).

Zheng Yao 鄭瑤. *Jingding Yanzhou xuzhi* 景定延州續志 [The Jingding Period Continuation of the Yanzhou Gazetteer]. In *Song Yuan difangzhi congshu*, Volume 11, pp. 6991–7056. Taipei: Dahua shuju, 1990.

Zhou Bida 周必大. *Wenzhong ji* 文忠集 [Collected Writings of Zhou Bida] (*SKQS* edition).

　Yutang zaji 玉堂雜記 [Miscellaneous Notes from the Jade Hall] (*Shuofu* edition).

Zhou Hui 周煇. *Qingbo zazhi jiaozhu* 清波雜志校注 [Annotated Edition of the *Various Accounts from the Qingbo Gate*]. Edited by Liu Yongxiang 劉永翔. Beijing: Zhonghua shuju, 1994.

Zhou Mi 周密. *Guixin zashi* 癸辛雜識 [Random Notes from the Guixin Quarter]. Edited by Wu Qiming 吳企明. Beijing: Zhonghua shuju, 1988.

　Qidong yeyu jiaozhu 齊東野語校注 [An Annotated Edition of *Rustic Conversations from Eastern Qi*]. Edited by Zhu Juru 朱菊如 et al. Shanghai: Huadong shifan daxue chubanshe, 1987.

Zhu Xi 朱熹. *Chuci jizhu* 楚辭集註 [Collected Annotations on the *Songs of the South*] (*SKQS* edition).

Sishu zhangju jizhu 四書章句集注 [Collected Commentaries on the Chapters and Verses of the *Four Books*]. Beijing: Zhonghua shuju, 1983.

Wuchao mingchen yanxing lu 五朝名臣言行錄 [Records of the Words and Deeds of Illustrious Ministers at Five Courts] (*SBCK* edition).

Zhu Xi ji 朱熹集 [The Collected Works of Zhu Xi]. Edited by Guo Qi 郭齊 and Yin Po 尹波. 10 vols. Chengdu: Sichuan jiaoyu chubanshe, 1996.

Zhuzi yulei 朱子語類 [Conversations of Zhu Xi]. Compiled by Li Jingde 黎靖德. 8 vols. Beijing: Zhonghua shuju, 1994.

Zhu Xi and Lü Zuqian 呂祖謙. *Jinsi lu* 近思錄 [Reflections on Things at Hand] (*SKQS* edition).

Zhuang Chuo 莊綽. *Jile bian* 雞肋編 [Chicken Rib Notes]. Beijing: Zhonghua shuju, 1983.

Zuo Tradition. Zuozhuan 左傳. *Commentary on the "Spring and Autumn Annals."* Translated and introduced by Stephen Durrant, Wai-yee Li, and David Schaberg. 3 vols. Seattle and London: University of Washington Press, 2016.

Secondary Sources

Aoyama Sadao 青山定雄. *Sōkaiyō kenkyū biyō: mokuroku* 宋会要研究備要: 目錄 [Research Essentials for the *Song Huiyao*: Index]. Tokyo: Tōyō bunko Sōdai kenkyū iinkai, 1970.

Balazs, Étienne. "L'histore comme guide de la pratique bureaucratique (les monographies, les encyclopédies, les recueils de statuts)." In *Historians of China and Japan*, edited by W.G. Beasley and E.G. Pulleyblank, pp. 78–94. London: School of Oriental and African Studies, 1961.

Balazs, Étienne and Hervouet, Yves. *A Sung Bibliography*. Hong Kong: The Chinese University Press, 1978.

Biot, Edouard, trans. *Le Tcheou-li, ou Rites des Tcheou*. 3 vols. Paris: Imprimerie nationale, 1851.

Bol, Peter K. "Neo-Confucianism and Local Society, Twelfth to Sixteenth Century: A Case Study." In *The Song–Yuan–Ming Transition in Chinese History*, edited by Paul Jakov Smith and Richard von Glahn, pp. 241–83. Cambridge, MA: Harvard University Asia Center, 2003.

   "This Culture of Ours": Intellectual Transitions in T'ang and Sung China. Stanford: Stanford University Press, 1992.

Butterfield, Herbert. *The Whig Interpretation of History*. London: G. Bell and Sons, 1931; reprinted 1959.

Cahill, James. *An Index of Early Chinese Painters and Paintings: T'ang, Sung, and Yüan*. Berkeley: University of California Press, 1980.

Cahill, Suzanne E. "Taoism at the Sung Court: The Heavenly Text Affair of 1008." *Bulletin of Sung–Yüan Studies* 16 (1980): 23–44.

Cai Chongbang 蔡崇榜. *Songdai xiushi zhidu yanjiu* 宋代修史制度研究 [Researches into the Song Period Institutions for the Compilation of History]. Taipei: Wenjin chubanshe, 1993.

Cai Shangxiang 蔡上翔. *Wang Jinggong nianpu kaolüe* 王荊公年谱考略 [A Chronological Biography of Wang Anshi]. Shanghai: Shanghai renmin chubanshe, 1959.

Cao Jiaqi 曹家齐. "Zhao Song dangchao shengshi shuo zhi zaojiu ji qi yingxiang – Songchao 'zuzong jiafa' yu 'Jiayou zhi zhi' xinlun" 赵宋当朝盛世说之造就及其影响 – 宋朝"祖宗家法"与"嘉祐之治"新论 [Emergence of the Idea of the 'Golden Age' in the Song Dynasty and Its Impact: A New Study on the 'Ancestors' Instructions' and the 'Age of Jiayou' in the Song Dynasty]. *Zhongguoshi yanjiu* (2007.4): 69–89.

Chaffee, John W. *Branches of Heaven: A History of the Imperial Clan of Sung China.* Cambridge, MA: Harvard University Asia Center, 1999.

"Chao Ju-yü, Spurious Leaning, and Southern Sung Political Culture." *Journal of Sung–Yuan Studies* 22 (1990–1992): 23–61.

"The Historian as Critic: Li Hsin-ch'uan and the Dilemmas of Statecraft in Southern Sung China." In *Ordering the World: Approaches to State and Society in Sung Dynasty China*, edited by Robert P. Hymes and Conrad Schirokauer, pp. 309–35. Berkeley: University of California Press, 1993.

"*Sung Biographies*, Supplementary Biography No. 2, Li Hsin-ch'üan (1167–1244)." *Journal of Sung–Yuan Studies* 24 (1994): 205–15.

Thorny Gates of Learning in Sung China. New edition. Albany: State University of New York Press, 1995.

Chaffee, John W. and Denis Twitchett, editors. *The Cambridge History of China. Volume 5. Part Two: Sung China, 960–1279.* Cambridge: Cambridge University Press, 2015.

Chan, Hok-lam. "Chinese Official Historiography at the Yüan Court: The Composition of the Liao, Chin, and Sung Histories." In *China under Mongol Rule*, edited by John D. Langlois Jr., pp. 56–106. Princeton: Princeton University Press, 1981.

The Historiography of the Chin Dynasty: Three Studies. Wiesbaden: Franz Steiner Verlag, 1970.

Legitimation in Imperial China: Discussions under the Jurchen Chin Dynasty. Seattle: University of Washington Press, 1984.

Chan, Wing-tsit, trans. *Reflections on Things at Hand: The Neo-Confucian Anthology Compiled by Chu Hsi and Lü Tsu-ch'ien.* New York: Columbia University Press, 1967.

Chang Bide 昌彼德, Wang Deyi 王德毅, et al. *Songren zhuanji ziliao suoyin* 宋人傳記資料索引 [Index to Bibliographical Materials of Song Figures]. 6 vols. Taipei: Dingwen shuju yinhang, 1976.

Chang, Curtis Chung. "Inheritance Problems in the First Two Reigns of the Sung Dynasty," *Chinese Culture* 9.4 (Dec. 1968): 10–44.

Chang Wei-ling 張維玲. *Cong Nan Song zhongqi fan jinxi zhengzheng kan daoxue xing shidafu dui "huifu" taidu de zhuanbian (1163–1207)* 從南宋中期反近習政爭看道學刑士大夫對"恢復"態度的轉變 (1163–1207) [The Changing Attitude toward "Recovery" among *Daoxue*-Style Officials Viewed from the Perspective of Their Political Struggles against the Close during the Middle Period of the Southern Song]. *Gudai lishi wenhua yanjiu jikan*. Third series, Volume 17. Taipei: Huamulan wenhua chubanshe, 2010.

Chavannes, Édouard. *Les mémoires historique de Si-ma Tsien.* 5 vols. Paris: Adrien-Maisonneuve, 1967.

Chen Guangsheng 陳廣勝. "Lü Zuqian yu *Song wenjian*" 呂祖謙與《宋文鑒》. *Shixueshi yanjiu* (1996.4): 54–59.

Chen Jian 陈坚 and Ma Wenda 马文大. *Song Yuan banke tushi* 宋元版刻图释 [Song and Yuan Woodbook Prints, Illustrated with Explanations]. 4 vols. Beijing: Xueyuan chubanshe, 2000.

Chen Lai 陈来. *Zhuzi shuxin biannian kaozheng* 朱子书信编年考证 [A Verified Chronology of Zhu Xi's Letters]. Revised edition. Beijing : Shenghuo, dushu, xinzhi sanlian shudian, 2011.

Chen Lesu 陳樂素. "Guilin shike *Yuanyou dangji*" 桂林石刻《元祐党籍》[The Yuanyou Party Registers Engraved on Stone at Guilin]. *Xueshu yanjiu* (1983.6): 63–71.

   "*Sanchao beimeng huibian* kao" 三朝北盟會編考 [A Study of the *Collected Documents Concerning Northern Treaties at Three Courts*]. *Lishi yuyan yanjiusuo jikan* 6.2 (1936): 193–341.

   Songshi yiwenzhi kaozheng 宋史藝文志考證 [A Textual Commentary on the Monograph on Bibliography in the *Song History*]. Guangzhou: Guangdong renmin chubanshe, 2002.

Chen Yinke 陳寅恪. *Chen Yinke xiansheng lunwenji* 陳寅恪先生論文集 [Collected Essays of Chen Yinke]. 2 vols. Taipei : Sanrenxing chubanshe yinhang, 1974.

Chen Zhichao 陈智超. *Jiekai* Song huiyao *zhi mi* 解开宋会要之谜 [Unlocking the Secrets of the *Song huiyao*]. Beijing: Shehui kexue wenxian chubanshe, 1995.

   "Song shi shiliao" 宋史史料 [Historical Sources for Song History]. In Chen Zhichao, *Song shi shi'er jiang* 宋史十二讲 [Twelve Lectures on Song History], pp. 335–79. Beijing: Qinghua daxue chubanshe, 2010.

   "Songdai renkou de zengzhang yu renkou fenbu de bianhua" 宋代人口的增长与人口分布的变化 [Increases in Song-Period Population and Changes in the Population Distribution]. In Chen Zhichao, *Song shi shi'er jiang*, pp. 205–34. Beijing: Qinghua daxue chubanshe, 2010.

Cheng Zhangcan 程章灿. *Liu Kezhuang nianpu* 刘克庄年谱 [A Chronological Biography of Liu Kezhuang]. Guiyang: Guizhou renmin chubanshe, 1993.

Chen Zhi'e 陈植锷. *Beisong wenhuashi shulun* 北宋文化史述论 [Studies on Northern Song cultural history]. Beijing: Zhongguo shehui kexue chubanshe, 1992.

Chia, Lucille. *Printing for Profit: The Commercial Publishers of Jianyang, Fujian (11th–17th Century)*. Cambridge, MA: Harvard University Asia Center, 2002.

Choi Sung-hei 蔡崇禧. "Li Tao (1115–1184) *Liuchao tongjian boyi* yanjiu" 李燾 (1115–1184)《六朝通鑑博議》研究 [A Study of Li Tao's *Extensive Discussions on the Six Dynasties Comprehensive Mirror*]. MA thesis, University of Hong Kong, 2004.

Chu Ming-kin. *The Politics of Higher Education: The Imperial University in Song China*. Hong Kong: Hong Kong University Press, 2020.

Dardess, John W. *Conquerors and Confucians: Aspects of Political Change in Late Yüan China*. New York: Columbia University Press, 1973.

   "Shun-ti and the End of Yüan Rule in China." In *Cambridge History of China. Volume 6. Alien Regimes and Border States, 907–1368*, edited by Herbert Franke and Denis Twitchett, pp. 561–86. Cambridge: Cambridge University Press, 1994.

Darrobers, Roger. *Zhu Xi: Mémoire scellé sur la situation de l'empire*. Paris: Les Belles Lettres, 2013.

Davis, Richard L. *Court and Family in Sung China, 960–1279: Bueaurcratic Success and Kinship Fortunes for the Shih of Ming-chou*. Durham, NC: Duke University Press, 1986.

"Historiography as Politics and Yang Wei-chen's 'Polemic on Legitimate Succession'," *T'oung Pao* 59 (1983): 33–72.

"The Reigns of Kuang-tsung (1189–1194) and Ning-tsung (1194–1224)." In *The Cambridge History of China. Volume 5. Part One: The Sung Dynasty and Its Precursors, 907–1279*, edited by Denis Twitchett and Paul Jakov Smith, pp. 756–838. Cambridge: Cambridge University Press, 2009.

de Bary, Wm. Theodore and Irene Bloom, eds. *Sources of Chinese Tradition. Volume 1.* Second edition. New York: Columbia University Press, 1999.

De Weerdt, Hilde. *Competition over Content: Negotiating Standards for the Civil Service Examinations in Imperial China (1127–1279)*. Cambridge, MA: Harvard University Asia Center, 2007.

Deng Guangming 鄧廣銘. "Dui youguan *Taiping zhiji tonglei* zhu wenti de xin kaosuo" 對有關《太平治跡統類》諸問題的新考索 [A New Study on All Questions Relating to the *Administrative Records from the Period of Great Peace, Fully Classified*]. In *Ji Xianlin jiaoshou bashi huadan jinian lunwenji*, edited by Li Zheng and Jiang Zhongxin, pp. 253–72. Nanchang: Jiangxi renmin chubanshe, 1991.

Deng Xiaonan 鄧小南. "Zouxiang 'huo' de zhidushi – yi Songdai guanliao zhengzhi zhidushi yanjiu wei li de diandi sikao" 走向"活"的制度史– 以宋代官僚政治制度史研究为例的点滴思考 [Toward a "Living" Institutional History: A Few Thoughts on the Study of Song Bureaucratic Government Institutions as an Example]. In *Songdai zhidushi yanjiu bainian (1900–2000)* 宋代制度史研究百年 (1900–2000), edited by Bao Weiming 包伟民, pp. 10–19. Beijing: Shangwu yinshuguan, 2004.

Zuzong zhi fa: bei Song qianqi zhengzhi shulüe 祖宗之法。北宋前期政治述略 (The Policies of the Ancestors and Early Northern Song Politics). Beijing: Shenghuo, dushu, xinzhi sanlian shudian, 2006.

Du Haijun 杜海军. *Lü Zuqian nianpu* 呂祖谦年谱 [Chronological Biography of Lü Zuqian]. Beijing: Zhonghua shuju, 2007.

Duan Shu'an 段書安. *Zhongguo gudai shuhua tumu* 中國古代書畫图目 [Index to Illustrated Catalogue of Selected Works of Ancient Chinese Painting and Calligraphy]. 24 vols. Beijing: Wenwu chubanshe, 1986–2001.

Ebrey, Patricia Buckley. *Emperor Huizong*. Cambridge, MA: Harvard University Press, 2014.

"Portrait Sculptures in Imperial Ancestral Rites in Song China." *T'oung Pao* 83 (1997): 42–92.

Fan Wenlan 范文瀾. *Zhengshi kaolüe* 正史考略 [Brief Studies on the Dynastic Histories]. 1931; reprint Shanghai: Shanghai shudian, 1989.

Fang Chengfeng 方誠峰. "Lun bei Song Xifeng Yuanyou nianjian de zhongshu tizhi" 論北宋熙豐、元祐年間的中樞體制變動 (1068–1093). [Changes in the Policy-Making System of the Northern Song between 1068 and 1093]. *Hanxue yanjiu* 28.4 (December 2010): 107–38.

Fang Jianxin 方建新. *Ershi shiji Song shi yanjiu lunzhu mulu* 二十世纪宋史研究论著目录 [An Index to Twentieth-Century Scholarship on Song History]. Beijing: Beijing tushuguan chubanshe, 2006.

Franke, Herbert. "Chia Ssu-tao (1213–1275): A 'Bad Last Minister'?" In *Confucian Personalities*, edited by Arthur F. Wright and Denis Twitchett, pp. 217–34. Stanford: Stanford University Press, 1962.

Sung Biographies. 3 vols. Wiesbaden: Franz Steiner Verlag, 1976.

Fu Xuancong 傅璇琮. *Song dengkeji kao* 宋登科記考 [A Study of Those Who Passed the *Jinshi* Examinations in the Song Dynasty]. 2 vols. Nanjing: Jiangsu jiaoyu chubanshe, 2009.

Gao Jichun 高纪春. "Qin Gui yu Luoxue" 秦桧与洛学 [Qin Gui and Cheng Learning]. *Zhongguoshi yanjiu* (2002.1): 97–108.

"Song Gaozong chao chunian de Wang Anshi pipan yu Luoxue zhi xing" 宋高宗朝初年的批判与洛学之兴 [Criticism of Wang Anshi during the Early Years of Song Gaozong's Reign and the Rise of Luo School Learning]. *Zhongzhou xuekan* (1996.1): 140–45.

Songshi "benji" kaozheng 《宋史本纪》考证 [Textual Criticism of the Annals Sections of the *Song History*]. Baoding: Hebei daxue chubanshe, 2000.

Ge Zhaoguang 葛兆光. "Cong *Tongjian* dao *Gangmu*" 从《通鉴》到《纲目》[From the *Comprehensive Mirror* to the *Outline and Details*]. *Yangzhou shiyuan xuebao* (1992.3): 154–58, 171.

"Song guanxiu guoshi kao" 宋官修国史考 [A Study of Official State Histories in Song]. *Shixueshi yanjiu* (1982.1): 47–54.

Gong Wei Ai [Jiang Weiai 江偉愛]. "The Reign of Hsiao-tsung (1162–1189)." In *Cambridge History of China. Volume 5. Part One: The Sung Dynasty and Its Precursors, 907–1279*, edited by Denis Twitchett and Paul Jakov Smith, pp. 710–55. Cambridge: Cambridge University Press, 2009.

Gong Yanming 龚延明. *Songdai guanzhi cidian* 宋代官制辞典 [Dictionary of the Song-Period Bureaucratic System]. Beijing: Zhonghua shuju, 1997.

Songshi zhiguanzhi buzheng 宋史职官志补正 (Corrections to the *Song History Monograph on Officials*). Revised edition. 2 vols. Beijing: Zhonghua shuju, 2009.

Gu Hongyi 顾宏义. *Songchu zhengzhi yanjiu – yi huangwei shoushou wei zhongxin* 宋初政治研究 – 以皇位授受为中心 [Studies in Early Song Government, with a focus on the Imperial Transition]. Shanghai: Huadong shifan daxue chubanshe, 2010.

Gu Jichen 顾吉辰. *Songshi bishi zhiyi* 《宋史》比事质疑 [Queries Concerning Parallel Passages in the *Song History*]. Beijing: Shumu wenxian chubanshe, 1987.

Songshi kaozheng 《宋史》考证 [Textual Criticism of the *Song History*]. Shanghai: Huadong ligong daxue chubanshe, 1994.

Gui Qipeng 桂栖鹏. *Yuandai jinshi yanjiu* 元代进士研究 [Researchs on Yuan-Period *Jinshi*]. Lanzhou: Lanzhou daxue chubanshe, 2001.

Guo Zhengzhong 郭正忠. "Nan Song zhongyang caizheng huobi suishou kaobian" 南宋中央财政货币岁收考辨 [An Examination of the Annual Currency Receipts of the Central Financial Administration in Southern Song]. In *Song Liao Jin shi luncong* 宋辽金史论从, edited by Zhongguo shehui kexueyuan lishi yanjiusuo Song Liao Jin Yuan shi yanjiushi, pp. 168–91. Beijing: Zhonghua shuju, 1985.

Hartman, Charles. "Bibliographic Notes on Sung Historical Works: The Original *Record of the Way and Its Destiny* (*Tao-ming lu*) by Li Hsin-ch'uan." *Journal of Sung–Yuan Studies* 30 (2000): 1–61.

"Bibliographic Notes on Sung Historical Works: *Topical Narratives from the Long Draft Continuation of the Comprehensive Mirror That Aids Administration* (*Hsü tzu-chih t'ung-chien ch'ang-pien chi-shih ben-mo* 續資治通鑑長編紀事本末) by Yang Chung-liang 楊仲良 and Related Texts." *Journal of Sung–Yuan Studies* 28 (1998): 177–200.

"Chen Jun's *Outline and Details*: Printing and Politics in Thirteenth-Century Pedagogical Histories." In *Knowledge and Text Production in an Age of Print: China, 900–1400*, edited by Lucille Chia and Hilde De Weerdt, pp. 273–315. Leiden: Brill, 2011.

"Chinese Historiography in the Age of Maturity, 960–1368." In *The Oxford History of Historical Writing. Volume 2: 400–1400*, edited by Sarah Foot and Chase F. Robinson, pp. 37–57. Oxford: Oxford University Press, 2012.

"Li Hsin-ch'uan and the Historical Image of Late Sung *Tao-hsüeh*." *Harvard Journal of Asiatic Studies* 61.2 (December 2001): 317–58.

[Cai Hanmo 蔡涵墨]. *Lishi de yanzhuang: jiedu daoxue yinying xia de nan Song shixue* 历史的严妆: 解读道学阴影下的南宋史学 [The Makeup of History: Understanding Southern Song Historiography in the Shadow of the "Learning of the Way" Movement]. Beijing: Zhonghua shuju, 2016.

[Cai Hanmo 蔡涵墨]. "Lu You *Zhongxing shengzheng cao* kao" 陆游《中兴圣政草》考 [A Study of the *Draft Entries for the Sagacious Policies of the Restoration* by Lu You]. *Lishi wenxian yanjiu* 36 (2016): 137–52.

"The Making of a Villain: Ch'in Kuei and *Tao-hsüeh*." *Harvard Journal of Asiatic Studies* 58.1 (June 1998): 59–146.

"The Reluctant Historian: Sun Ti, Chu Hsi, and the Fall of Northern Sung." *T'oung Pao* 89 (2003): 100–48.

"*Song History* Narratives as Grand Allegory." *Journal of Chinese History* 3.1 (2019): 35–57.

"Sung Government and Politics." In *The Cambridge History of China. Volume 5. Part Two: Sung China, 960–1279*, edited by John. W. Chaffee and Denis Twitchett, pp. 19–138. Cambridge: Cambridge University Press, 2015.

"The Tang Poet Du Fu and the Song Dynasty Literati." *Chinese Literature: Essays, Articles, Reviews* 30 (2008): 43–74.

"A Textual History of Cai Jing's Biography in the *Songshi*." In *Emperor Huizong and Late Northern Song China: The Politics of Culture and the Culture of Politics*, edited by Patricia Buckley Ebrey and Maggie Bickford, pp. 517–64. Cambridge, MA: Harvard University Asia Center, 2006.

Hartman, Charles and DeBlasi, Anthony. "The Growth of Historical Method in Tang China." In *The Oxford History of Historical Writing. Volume 2: 400–1400*, edited by Sarah Foot and Chase F. Robinson, pp. 17–36. Oxford: Oxford University Press, 2012.

Hartman, Charles and Cho-ying Li. "The Rehabilitation of Chen Dong." *Harvard Journal of Asiatic Studies* 75.1 (2015): 77–159.

Hartwell, Robert W. "Historical Analogism, Public Policy, and Social Science in Eleventh- and Twelfth-Century China." *American Historical Review* 76.3 (1971): 690–727.

He Yuhong 何玉红. "Nan Song chuanshan zhanqu junfei de xiaohao yu chouji" 南宋川陕战区军费的消耗与筹集 [The Raising and Consumption of Military Expenses for the Sichuan and Shaanxi War Zones during Southern Song]. *Zhongguo shehui jingjishi yanjiu* (2009.1): 31–39.

Hirata Shigeki 平田茂樹. "Sōdai no nikki shiryō kara mita seiji kōzō" 宋代の日記史料から見た政治構造 [The Political Structure of the Song Period as Perceived from Diaries]. In *Sōdai shakai no kūkan to komyunikēshon*, edited by Hirata Shigeki, Takatoshi Endō, and Motoshi Oka, pp. 29–67 (Tokyo: Kyūko Shoin), 2006.

Hoang, P. *Concordance des chronologies néoméniques chinoise et européenne.* Shanghai: Imprimerie de la Mission Catholique, 1910.

Hon, Tze-ki. *The* Yijing *and Chinese Politics: Classical Commentary and Literati Activism in the Northern Song Period, 960–1127.* Albany, NY: State University of New York Press, 2005.

Hsiao Ch'i-ch'ing. "Mid-Yüan Politics." In *Cambridge History of China. Volume 6: Alien Regimes and Border States, 907–1368*, edited by Herbert Franke and Denis Twitchett, pp. 490–560. Cambridge: Cambridge University Press, 1994.

The Military Establishment of the Yüan Dynasty. Cambridge, MA: Harvard University Press, 1978.

Huang Chün-chieh. "Chu Hsi as a Teacher of History." In *Zhongxi shixueshi yantaohui lunwenji (di'er jie)*, edited by Guoli Zhongxing daxue lishixi, pp. 307–66. Taipei: Jiuyang chubanshe, 1987.

Huang Huixian 黃彗嫻. "Lü Zhong yu *Huangchao dashiji* xintan" 呂中與皇朝大事記新探 [A New Study of Lü Zhong and the *Record of Major Events at the August Courts*]. In Lü Zhong, *Leibian Huangchao dashiji jiangyi: Leibian Huangchao zhongxing dashiji jiangyi*, pp. 898–924. Shanghai: Shanghai renmin chubanshe, 2014.

Huang K'uan-ch'ung 黃寬重. "Li Qiong bingbian yu nan Song chuqi de zhengju" 酈瓊兵變與南宋初期的政局 [The Rebellion of Li Qiong and the Politics of the Early Southern Song]. In Huang K'uan-ch'ung, *Nan Song junzheng yu wenxian tansuo*, pp. 51–89. Taipei: Xinwenfeng chuban gongsi, 1990.

"Liang Song zhengce yu shifeng de bianhua" 兩宋政策與士風的變化 [Song Government Policy and Changes in Literati Sentiment]. In *Jidiao yu bianzou: Qi zhi ershi shiji de Zhongguo*, edited by Huang K'uan-ch'ung, pp. 202–25. Taipei: Guoli Zhengzhi daxue lishi xuexi, 2008.

Nan Song difang wuli: difang jun yu minjian ziwei wuli de tantao 南宋地方武力 – 地方軍與民間自衛武力的探討 [Southern Song Regional Military Forces: Studies of Regional Armies and Self-Defense Forces]. Taipei: Dongda tushu gongsi, 2002.

Nan Song junzheng yu wenxian tansuo 南宋軍政與文獻探索 [Studies in Southern Song Military Affairs and in Primary Documentation]. Taipei: Xinwenfeng chuban gongsi, 1990.

Hung, C.F. "The Tung Brothers: Tung Wen-ping (1217–1278), Tung Wen-yung (1224–1297), Tung Wen-chung (1230–1281)." In *In the Service of the Khan: Eminent Personalities of the Early Mongol–Yüan Period (1200–1300)*, edited by Igor de Rachewiltz, pp. 620–45. Wiesbaden: Harrassowitz, 1993.

Jay, Jennifer W. *A Change in Dynasties: Loyalism in Thirteenth-Century China.* Bellingham, WA: Western Washington University, Center for East Asian Studies, 1991.

Ji Xiao-bin. *Politics and Conservatism in Northern Song China: The Career and Thought of Sima Guang (A.D. 1019–1086).* Hong Kong: The Chinese University Press, 2005.

Kaplan, Edward Harold. "Yueh Fei and the Founding of the Southern Sung (Volumes I and II)." PhD dissertation, University of Iowa, 1970.

Kohn, Livia, editor. *Daoism Handbook.* Leiden: Brill, 2000.

Kong Fanmin 孔繁敏. "Wei Su yu *Songshi* de zuanxiu" 危素與《宋史》的纂修 [Wei Su and the Composition of the *Song History*]. *Yanjing xuebao*, new series 2 (1996): 105–17 [Luo Bingliang, ed., *Songshi yanjiu*, pp. 160–75].

Kong Xue 孔學. "*Jianyan yilai xinian yaolu* qucai kao" 《建炎以來繫年要錄》取材考 [An Investigation of the Sources for the *Chronological Record*]. *Shixueshi yanjiu* (1995.2): 43–55.

"*Jianyan yilai xinian yaolu* zhushu shijian kao" 《建炎以來繫年要錄》著述時間考 [A Study of the Time of Composition of the *Chronological Record*]. *Henan daxue xuebao* 36.1 (January 1996): 53–56.

"*Jianyan yilai xinian yaolu* zhuwen bianxi" 《建炎以來繫年要錄》注文辨析 [Differentiating the Commentarial Notes to the *Chronological Record*]. *Shixueshi yanjiu* (1998.1): 46–55.

"Lu You ji *Gaozong shengzheng cao*" 陸游及《高宗聖政草》[Lu You and His *Draft Entries for the Gaozong Sagacious Administration*]. *Shixue yuekan* (1996.4): 32–38.

"Songdai 'baoxun' zuanxiu kao" 宋代《寶訓》纂修考 [A Study of the Composition of "Precious Instructions" in the Song]. *Shixueshi yanjiu* (1994.3): 56–64.

Kuhn, Dieter. *The Age of Confucian Rule: The Song Transformation of China.* Cambridge, MA: The Belknap Press of Harvard University Press, 2009.

Kurz, Johannes L. "The Consolidation of Official Historiography during the Early Northern Song Dynasty." *Journal of Asian History* 46.1 (2012): 13–45.

LaFleur, Robert André. "A Rhetoric of Remonstrance: History, Commentary, and Historical Imagination in Sima Guang's *Zizhi tongjian*." PhD dissertation, University of Chicago, 1996.

Lai Kehong 來可泓. *Li Xinchuan shiji zhuzuo biannian* 李心傳事跡著作編年 [A Chronological Study of Li Xinchuan's Life and Works]. Chengdu: Ba Shu shushe, 1990.

Lamouroux, Christian. *Fiscalité, comptes publics et politiques financières dans le Chine de Song: Le chapitre 179 du Songshi.* Paris: Collège de France, Institut des hautes études chinoises, 2003.

"Song Renzong's Court Landscape: Historical Writing and the Creation of a New Political Sphere (1022–1042)." *Journal of Song–Yuan Studies* 42 (2012): 45–93.

Lamouroux, Christian and Deng Xiaonan. "The 'Ancestors' Family Instructions': Authority and Sovereignty in Medieval China." *Journal of Song–Yuan Studies* 35 (2005): 69–97.

Langlois, John D., Jr. "Political Thought in Chin-hua under Mongol Rule." In *China under Mongol Rule*, edited by John D. Langlois, pp. 137–85. Princeton: Princeton University Press, 1981.

Lau, D.C. *The Analects.* Translated with an Introduction by D.C. Lau. Harmondsworth: Penguin Books, 1979.

Lau, D.C. *Mencius.* Translated with an Introduction by D.C. Lau. Harmondsworth: Penguin Books, 1970.

Lau Nap-yin [Liu Liyan 柳立言]. "The Absolutist Reign of Sung Hsiao-tsung (r. 1163–1189)." PhD dissertation, Princeton University, 1986.

"Bei Song pingjia wuren biaozhun zai renshi – chongwen jingwu zhi ling yimian" 北宋評價武人標準再認識–重文經武之另一面 [Revisiting the Criteria for Evaluating Military Officials in the Northern Song: Another Side to "Stressing the Civil over the Military"]. *Lishi yanjiu* (2018.2): 35–58.

Lau Nap-yin and Huang K'uan-chung. "Founding and Consolidation of the Sung Dynasty under T'ai-tsu (960–976), T'ai-tsung (976–997), and Chen-tsung

(997–1022)." In *The Cambridge History of China. Volume 5. Part One: The Sung Dynasty and Its Precursors, 907–1279*, edited by Denis Twitchett and Paul Jakov Smith, pp. 206–78. Cambridge: Cambridge University Press, 2009.

Lee Tsong-han. "Different Mirrors of the Past: Southern Song Historiography." PhD dissertation, Harvard University, 2008.

"Making Moral Decisions: Zhu Xi's *Outline and Details of the Comprehensive Mirror for Aid in Government*." *Journal of Song–Yuan Studies* 39 (2009): 43–84.

Legge, James, trans. *The Chinese Classics. Volume 1: Confucian Analects, The Great Learning, and the Doctrine of the Mean*. Reprinted Hong Kong: Hong Kong University Press, 1960.

The Chinese Classics. Volume 2: The Works of Mencius. Reprinted Hong Kong: Hong Kong University Press, 1960.

The Chinese Classics. Volume 3: The Shoo King. Reprinted Hong Kong: Hong Kong University Press, 1960.

The Chinese Classics. Volume 4: The She King. Reprinted Hong Kong: Hong Kong University Press, 1960.

The Chinese Classics. Volume 5: The Ch'un Ts'ew with the Tso Chuen. Reprinted Hong Kong: Hong Kong University Press, 1960.

Levine, Ari Daniel. "Che-tsung's Reign (1085–1100) and the Age of Faction." In *The Cambridge History of China. Volume 5. Part One: The Sung Dynasty and Its Precursors, 907–1279*, edited by Denis Twitchett and Paul Jakov Smith, pp. 484–555. Cambridge: Cambridge University Press, 2009.

Divided by a Common Language: Factional Conflict in Late Northern Song China. Honolulu: University of Hawaii Press, 2008.

"A House in Darkness: The Politics of History and the Language of Politics in the Late Northern Song, 1068–1104." PhD dissertation, Columbia University, 2002.

"A Performance of Transparency: Discourses and Practices of Veracity and Verification in Li Tao's *Long Draft*." In *Powerful Arguments: Standards of Validity in Late Imperial China*, edited by Martin Hofmann, Joachim Kurtz, and Ari Daniel Levine, pp. 90–134. Leiden: Brill, 2020.

Li Cho-ying and Charles Hartman, "A Newly Discovered Inscription by Qin Gui: Its Implications for the History of Song *Daoxue*." *Harvard Journal of Asiatic Studies* 70.2 (2010): 387–448.

"Primary Sources for Song History in the Collected Works of Wu Ne." *Journal of Song–Yuan Studies* 41 (2011): 295–341.

Li Fengzhu 李凤翥 and Li Xihou 李锡厚. "Yuan xiu Song, Liao, Jin san shi zai pingjie" 元修宋辽金三史的再评介 [A Reconsidered Evaluation of the Three Histories of Song, Liao, and Jin Composed in the Yuan Dynasty]. *Shehui kexue jikan* (1981.3): 94–98 [Luo Bingliang, ed. *Songshi yanjiu*, pp. 83–92].

Li Huarui 李华瑞. "Lüelun Nan Song zhengzhi shang de 'fa zuzong' qingxiang" 略论南宋政治上的"法祖宗"倾向 [A Brief Discussion of the Trend to "Take the Founders as a Model" in Southern Song Politics]. In *Song shi yanjiu luncong* 宋史研究论丛 [Collected Research Articles on Song History], edited by Jiang Xidong 姜锡东, pp. 199–226. Baoding: Hebei daxue chubanshe, 2005.

"*Songshi* lunzan pingxi" 宋史论赞评析 [An Analysis of the Evaluations in the *Song History*]. In *Song shi yanjiu lunwen ji (Dishiyi ji)* 宋史研究论文集 (第十一辑) [Collected Research Papers in Song History (Volume 11)]. Edited by Zhu Ruixi 朱

瑞熙, Wang Zengyu 王曾瑜, and Cai Dongzhou 蔡东洲. Chengdu: Bashu shushe, 2006.

Wang Anshi bianfa yanjiushi 王安石變法研究史 [A History of the Study of Wang Anshi's New Policies]. Beijing: Renmin chubanshi, 2004.

Li Li 李立. "Songdai zhengzhi zhidushi yanjiu fangfa zhi fansi" 宋代政治制度史研究方法之反思 [A Reconsideration of the Research Methodology for the History of Song Political Institutions]. In *Songdai zhidushi yanjiu bainian (1900–2000)* 宋代制度史研究百年 (1900–2000), edited by Bao Weiming 包伟民, pp. 20–39. Beijing: Shangwu yinshuguan, 2004.

Li Shaoping 李绍平. "Song, Liao, Jin san shi de shiji zhubian Ouyang Xuan" 宋辽金三史的实际主编欧阳玄 [Ouyang Xuan, the Real Editor of the Three Histories of Song, Liao, and Jin]. *Hunan shifan daxue shehui kexue xuebao* 20.1 (Jan. 1991): 72–76 [Luo Bingliang, ed., *Songshi yanjiu*, pp. 149–59].

Li Yumin 李裕民. *Songren shengzu xingnian kao* 宋人生卒行年考 [Studies of the Birth and Death Dates of Song Individuals]. Beijing: Zhonghua shuju, 2010.

Liang Taiji 梁太濟. "*Jianyan yilai xinian yaolu* qucai kao" 《建炎以來繫年要錄》取材考 [An Investigation of the Sources for the *Chronological Record*]. In Liang Taiji, *Tang Song lishi wenxian yanjiu conggao* 唐宋历史文献研究从稿 [Collected Research on Tang and Song Historical Documents], pp. 155–70. Shanghai: Shanghai guji chubanshe, 2004.

"*Shengzheng* jinben fei yuanben zhi jiu xiangbian" 《聖政》今本非原本之舊詳辨 [A Demonstration That the Present Edition of the *Sagacious Governance* Is Not the Original Version]. In Liang Taiji, *Tang Song lishi wenxian yanjiu conggao* 唐宋历史文献研究从稿 [Collected Research on Tang and Song Historical Documents], pp. 311–41. Shanghai: Shanghai guji chubanshe, 2004.

"*Xinian yaolu, Chaoye zaji* de qiyi jishu ji qi chengyin" 《繫年要錄》、《朝野雜記》的岐異記述及其成因 [Differences in the Accounts between the *Chronological Record* and the *Miscellaneous Notes* and Their Causes]. In Liang Taiji, *Tang Song lishi wenxian yanjiu conggao* 唐宋历史文献研究从稿 [Collected Research on Tang and Song Historical Documents], pp. 171–205. Shanghai: Shanghai guji chubanshe, 2004.

"*Yaolu* zizhu de neirong fanwei ji qi suo jieshi de xiuxuan tili" 《要錄》自注的内容范围及其所揭示的修纂体例 [The Content and Scope of the *Chronological Record*'s Self-Commentary and What It Reveals about the Work's Compilation System]. In Liang Taiji, *Tang Song lishi wenxian yanjiu conggao* 唐宋历史文献研究从稿 [Collected Research on Tang and Song Historical Documents], pp. 206–47. Shanghai: Shanghai guji chubanshe, 2004.

Liang Tianxi 梁天錫. "Cong *Zun Yao lu* kan Songchu sichao zhi junshi yu zhengzhi" 從遵堯錄看宋初四朝之軍事與政治 [Viewing the Military and Administrative Policies of the First Four Song Courts from the Vantage Point of the *Record of Revering Yao*]. *Dalu zazhi* 31.6 (September 30, 1965): 202–7.

Song Shumi yuan zhidu 宋樞密院制度 [The Bureau of Military Affairs Institution in Song]. 2 vols. Taipei: Liming wenhua shiye gongsi, 1981.

"*Zun Yao lu* shishi shuzheng" 遵堯錄史事疏證 [A Commentary on the Historical Events in the *Record of Revering Yao*]. *Xinya shuyuan xueshu niankan* 7 (1965): 55–144.

Lin Tianwei 林天蔚. *Songdai shishi zhiyi* 宋代史事質疑 [Doubts on Song-Period Historical Events]. Taibei: Taiwan shangwu yinshuguan, 1987.

Liu, James J.Y. [Liu Zijian 劉子健]. "The Sung Emperors and the Ming-t'ang or Hall of Enlightenment." In *Études Song, in memoriam Étienne Balazs*, edited by Françoise Aubin, pp. 45–58. Paris: Mouton & Co., 1973.

Liu Yonghai 刘永海. *Su Tianjue yanjiu* 苏天爵研究 [Research on Su Tianjue]. Beijing: Renmin chubanshe, 2015.

Liu Yunjun 刘云军. *Songshi zaifu liezhuan buzheng* 《宋史》宰辅列传补正 [Additions and Corrections to the Biographies of State Councilors in the *Song History*]. Baoding: Hebei daxue, 2016.

Lo, Winston W. *An Introduction to the Civil Service of Sung China, with Emphasis on Its Personnel Administration*. Honolulu: University of Hawaii Press, 1987.

The Life and Thought of Yeh Shih. Gainesville: University Presses of Florida, 1974.

Szechwan in Sung China: A Case Study in the Political Integration of the Chinese Empire. Taipei: University of Chinese Culture Press, 1982.

Loewe, Michael. *A Biographical Dictionary of the Qin, Former Han and Xin Periods (221 BC–AD 24)*. Leiden: Brill, 2000.

Lorge, Peter. "The Entrance and Exit of the Song Founders." *Journal of Sung–Yuan Studies* 29 (1999): 43–62.

The Reunification of China: Peace through War under the Song Dynasty. Cambridge: Cambridge University Press, 2015.

"Sima Guang on Song Taizong: Politics, History, and Historiography." *Journal of Song–Yuan Studies* 42 (2010): 5–43.

Lu Zhongfeng 卢钟锋. "Yuandai lixue yu *Songshi* 'daoxue liezhuan' de xueshushi tese" 元代理学与《宋史道学列传》的学术史特色 [Yuan-Period Neo-Confucianism and the Special Character of the History of Scholarship in the *Daoxue* Biographical Chapters of the *Song History*]. *Shixueshi yanjiu* (1990.3): 26–31, 52 [Luo Bingliang, ed. *Songshi yanjiu*, pp. 136–48].

Luo Bingliang 罗炳良, editor. *Songshi yanjiu* 《宋史》研究 [Researches on the *Song History*]. Beijing: Zhongguo dabaike quanshu chubanshe, 2009.

Mao Qin 毛钦. "Lun Jia Sidao jianchen xingxiang de suzao" 论贾似道奸臣形象的塑造 [On the Construction of the Image of Jia Sidao as a Nefarious Minister]. *Tianzhong xuekan* 30.6 (December 2015): 121–26.

Miao Shumei 苗书梅. "Songdai zongshi, waiqi yu huanguan renyong zhidu shulun" 宋代宗室外戚与宦官任用制度述论 [On the Employment System for Imperial Relatives, In-Laws, and Eunuchs in the Song Period]. *Shixue yuekan* (1995.2): 32–38.

Neskar, Ellen G. "The Cult of Worthies: A Study of Shrines Honoring Local Confucian Worthies in the Sung Dynasty (960–1279)." PhD dissertation, Columbia University, 1993.

Nie Chongqi 聶崇岐. "Lun Song Taizu shou bingquan" 論宋太祖收兵權 [On Emperor Song Taizu Taking Back Military Power]. In *Songshi congkao* 宋史叢考 [Collected Studies on Song History], pp. 263–82. Beijing: Zhonghua shuju, 1980.

"Songdai zhiju kaolüeh" 宋代制舉考略 [A Survey of the Song-Period Decree Examinations]. In *Songshi congkao*, pp. 171–203.

Songshi congkao 宋史叢考 [Collected Studies on Song History]. Beijing: Zhonghua shuju, 1980.

Nie Lehe 聂乐和. "*Jianyan yilai xinian yaolu* yanjiu" 《建炎以来系年要录》研究 [Studies in the Chronological Record of Important Events since 1127]. MA thesis, Beijing shifan daxue, 1987.

Nienhauser, William H, editor. *The Grand Scribe's Records*. 8 vols. to date. Bloomington, IN: Indiana University Press, 1994–.

Olsson, Karl Frederick. "The Structure of Power under the Third Emperor of Sung China: The Shifting Balance after the Peace of Shan-yuan." PhD dissertation, University of Chicago, 1974.

Partner, Nancy. "Making Up Lost Time: Writing on the Writing of History." *Speculum* 61.1 (1986): 90–117.

Pei Rucheng 裴汝诚, "Lüeping *Songshi* 'chong daode er chu kongli' de xiuzhuan yuanze" 略评《宋史》"崇道德而黜功利" 的修撰原则 [A Brief Critique of the Compositional Principle of "Lauding the Way and Its Virtue and Condemning Merit and Profit" in the *Song History*]. In Pei Rucheng, *Bansu ji* 半粟集, pp. 1–12. Baoding: Hebei daxue chubanshe, 2000.

"Songdai shiliao zhenshixing chuyi" 宋代史料真實性刍議 [Doubts on the Validity of Song Historical Sources]. In Deng Guangming and Qi Xia, eds., *Guoji Song shi yantaohui lunwen xuanji*, pp. 235–54. Baoding: Hebei daxue chubanshe, 1992.

Pei Rucheng 裴汝诚 and Xu Peizao 许沛藻. *Xu zizhi tongjian changbian kaolüe* 续资治通鉴长编考略 [A Study of the *Long Draft*]. Beijing: Zhonghua shuju, 1985.

Poon, Ming-sun. "Books and Printing in Sung China (960–1279)." 2 vols. PhD dissertation, University of Chicago, 1979.

Qian Daxin 錢大昕. *Nian'er shi kaoyi* 廿二史考異 [An Investigation of Differences in the Twenty-Two Dynastic Histories]. Edited by Fang Shiming 方詩銘 and Zhou Dianjie 周殿傑. 2 vols. Shanghai: Shanghai guji chubanshe, 2004.

Qian Mu 錢穆. *Zhuzi xin xue'an* 朱子新學案 [New Studies on Zhu Xi]. 5 vols. Taipei: Sanmin shuju, 1971.

Qian Zhongshu 錢鍾書. *Guanzhui bian* 管錐編 [Pipe Awl Chapters]. 4 vols. Beijing: Zhonghua shuju, 1979.

Qiu Shusen 邱树森. "Tuotuo he Liao, Jin, Song san shi" 脱脱和辽金宋三史 [Tuotuo and the Three Histories of Liao, Jin, and Song]. In *Songshi yanjiu* 《宋史》研究 [Researches on the *Song History*], edited by Luo Bingliang 罗炳良, pp. 93–115. Beijing: Zhongguo dabaike quanshu chubanshe, 2009.

Rachewiltz, Igor de, editor. *In the Service of the Khan: Eminent Personalities of the Early Mongol–Yüan Period (1200–1300)*. Wiesbaden: Harrassowitz, 1993.

Rossabi, Morris. "The Reign of Khubilai Khan." In *Cambridge History of China. Volume 6: Alien Regimes and Border States, 907–1368*, edited by Herbert Franke and Denis Twitchett, pp. 414–89. Cambridge: Cambridge University Press, 1994.

Schirokauer, Conrad M. "Neo-Confucians under Attack: The Condemnation of *Wei-hsüeh*." In *Crisis and Prosperity in Sung China*, edited by John Winthrop Haeger, pp. 163–98. Tucson: The University of Arizona Press, 1975.

Schulte-Uffelage, Helmut. *Das Keng-shen wai-shih. Eine Quelle zur späten Mongolenzeit*. Berlin: Akademie-Verlag, 1963.

Shu Renhui 舒仁辉. *Dongdu shilüe yu Songshi bijiao yanjiu* 《东都事略》与《宋史》比较研究 [A Comparative Study of the *Eastern Capital Miscellany* and the *Song History*]. Beijing: Shangwu yinshuguan, 2007.

Smith, Paul Jakov. "Shen-tsung's Reign and the Policies of Wang An-shih, 1067–1085." In *The Cambridge History of China. Volume 5. Part One: The Sung Dynasty and Its Precursors, 907–1279*, edited by Denis Twitchett and Paul Jakov Smith, pp. 347–483. Cambridge: Cambridge University Press, 2009.

Taxing Heaven's Storehouse: Horses, Bureaucrats, and the Destruction of the Sichuan Tea Industry, 1074–1224. Cambridge, MA: Council on East Asian Studies, Harvard University, 1991.

Song Limin 宋立民. *Songdai shiguan zhidu yanjiu* 宋代史官制度研究 [Studies in the Historiographical Institutions of the Song Period]. Changchun: Jilin renmin chubanshe, 1999.

Sudō Yoshiyuki 周藤吉之. "Nan-Sō no Ri Tou to *Zoku shiji tsugan chōhen* no seiritsu" 南宋の李燾と續資治通鑑長編の成立 [Li Tao and the Creation of the *Long Draft Continuation of the Comprehensive Mirror That Aids Administration*]. In Sudō Yoshiyuki, *Sōdai shi kenkyū* 宋代史研究, pp. 469–512. Tokyo: Tōyō bunko, 1969.

Sun Jianmin 孙建民. "Qushe zhi ji jian jingshen – lüelun *Jianyan yilai xinian yaolu* de qucai" 取舍之际见精神 – 略论《建炎以来系年要录》的取材 [Revealing the Essence through Textual Adoption and Rejection: A Brief Discussion of the Sources of the *Chronological Record of Important Events since 1127*]. *Shanghai shifan daxue* (1996.3): 82–88.

Sun Kekuan 孙可宽. *Yuandai Han wenhua zhi huodong* 元代漢文化之活動 [Chinese Cultural Activity during the Yuan Period]. Taipei: Taiwan Zhonghua shuju, 1968.

Yuandai Jinhua xueshu 元代金華學述 [Jinhua Scholarship in the Yuan Period]. Taizhong: Sili Donghai daxue, 1975.

Sung Chia-fu. "Between *Tortoise* and *Mirror*: Historians and Historiography in Eleventh-Century China." PhD dissertation, Harvard University, 2010.

Cong *Cefu yuangui* lun Beisong chuqi leishushi lishi shuxie caozuo de dianfan yiyi 從冊府元龜論北宋初期類書式歷史書寫操作的典範意義 [The Significance of the *Cefu Yuangui* as an Example of the Operation of Encyclopedia-Style Historical Writing in Early Song]. *Xinshixue* 25.4 (December 2014): 43–104.

"The Official Historiographical Operation of the Song Dynasty." *Journal of Song–Yuan Studies* 45 (2015): 175–206.

Tang Jianghao 汤江浩. "Li Tao zhuanjin *Xu zizhi tongjian changbian* zhi shi, ci, juan, ce xianyi"   李燾撰进《续资治通鉴长编》之时、次、卷、册献疑   [Doubts Concerning the Dates, Numbers of Chapters, and Numbers of Volumes in Li Tao's Submissions of the *Long Draft*]. *Lishi wenxian yanjiu* 24 (2005): 200–12.

"Li Tao zhuanjin *Xu zizhi tongjian changbian* zhi shi, ci, juan, ce xutan" 李燾撰进《续资治通鉴长编》之时、次、卷、册续探 [On the Dates, Numbers of Chapters, and Numbers of Volumes in Li Tao's Submissions of the *Long Draft*, Continued]. *Lishi wenxian yanjiu* 26 (2007): 157–70.

Tang Kaijian 汤开建 and Chen Wenyuan 陈文源. "*Shantang kaosuo* zhong baoliu de *Changbian* yiwen" 《山堂考索》中保留的《长编》佚文 [Fragments from the *Long Draft* Preserved in *Shantang's Investigations*]. *Songshi yanjiu tongxun* 15.2 (1989): 1–24.

Tao Jing-shen. "The Move to the South and the Reign of Kao-tsung (1127–1162)." In *Cambridge History of China. Volume 5. Part One: The Sung Dynasty and Its*

Precursors, 907–1279, edited by Denis Twitchett and Paul Jakov Smith, pp. 644–709. Cambridge: Cambridge University Press, 2009.

Ten Harmsel, Wayne Alan. "Oath of the Golden Casket: The Role of Chao P'u in the Imperial Succession of the Early Sung." MA thesis, University of Arizona, 1980.

Teraji Jun 寺地遵. "Kan Takuchū senken no seiritsu" 韓侂胄專權の成立 [The Establishment of Han Tuozhou's Autocratic Power]. *Shigaku kenkyū* 247 (2005): 20–47.

   Nan-Sō shoki seijishi kenkyū 南宋初期政治史研究 [Researches into Early Southern Song Political History]. Hiroshima: Keisuisha, 1988.

Tillman, Hoyt Cleveland. "The Rise of the *Tao-Hsüeh* Confucian Fellowship in Southern Sung." In *The Cambridge History of China. Volume 5. Part Two: Sung China, 960–1279*, edited by John W. Chaffee and Denis Twitchett, pp. 727–90. Cambridge: Cambridge University Press, 2015.

Toyama Gunji 外山軍治. "Seikō no hen ni okeru shinkyū ryōhōtō no seiryoku kankei" 靖康の變に於ける新舊兩法黨の勢力關係 [Antagonism between the Conservatives and the Progressives at the Time of the Downfall of Northern Sung in 1126]. In *Haneda Hakushi shōju kinen tōyō shi ronsō*, edited by Haneda Hakushi Kanreki Kinenkai 羽田博士還曆記念會, pp. 663–87. Kyoto: Tōyōshi Kenkyūkai, 1950.

Twitchett, Denis, editor. *The Cambridge History of China. Volume 3: Sui and T'ang China, 589–906, Part One*. Cambridge: Cambridge University Press, 1979.

   The Writing of Official History under the T'ang. Cambridge: Cambridge University Press, 1992.

Twitchett, Denis and Michael Loewe, editors. *The Cambridge History of China. Volume I. The Ch'in and Han Empires, 221 B.C.–A.D. 220*. Cambridge: Cambridge University Press, 1986.

Twitchett, Denis and Paul Jakov Smith, editors. *The Cambridge History of China. Volume 5. Part One: The Sung Dynasty and Its Precursors, 907–1279*. Cambridge: Cambridge University Press, 2009.

Veyne, Paul. *Writing History: Essay on Epistemology*. Middletown, CT: Wesleyan University Press, 1984.

Von Glahn, Richard. "The Origins of Paper Money in China." In *The Origins of Value: The Financial Innovations That Created Modern Capital Markets*, edited by William N. Goetzmann and K. Geert Rouwenhorst, pp. 65–85. Oxford and New York: Oxford University Press, 2005.

Wada Sei 和田清 and Nakajima Satoshi 中嶋敏. *Sōshi shokkashi yakuchū* 宋史食貨志譯註 [An Annotated Translation of the *Song History* Monograph on Fiscal Administration]. 6 vols. Tokyo: Tōyō Bunko, 1960–2006.

Walton, Linda. *Academies and Society in Southern Sung China*. Honolulu: University of Hawaii Press, 1999.

   "Family Fortunes in the Song–Yuan Transition: Academies and Chinese Elite Strategies for Success." *T'oung Pao* 97 (2011): 37–103.

Wang Chenglüe 王承略 and Yang Jinxian 楊錦先. *Li Tao xuexing shiwen jikao* 李燾學行詩文輯考 [A Collection of Li Tao's Writing and Documents Relating to His Life and Scholarship]. Shanghai: Shanghai guji chubanshe, 2004.

Wang Deyi 王德毅. "Bei Song jiuchao shilu zuanxiu kao" 北宋九朝實錄纂修考 [An Investigation of the Composition of Veritable Records for the Nine Northern Song

Emperors]. In Wang Deyi, *Song shi yanjiu lunji: Di er ji* 宋史研究論集: 第二輯 [Collected Research on Song History, Second Collection], pp. 71–117. Taipei: Dingwen shuju, 1972.

Li Tao fuzi nianpu 李燾父子年譜 [A Chronological Biography of Li Tao and His Sons]. Taibei: Zhongguo xueshu zhuzuo jiangzhu weiyuanhui, 1963.

"Li Xinchuan zhushu kao" 李心傳著述考 [A Study of Li Xinchuan's Writings]. Appended to Li Xinchuan, *Jianyan yilai xinian yaolu*, pp. 6771–88. Taipei: Wenhai chubanshe, 1980.

"Li Xiuyan xiansheng nianpu" 李秀巖先生年譜 [A Chronological Biography of Li Xinchuan]. Appended to Li Xinchuan, *Jianyan yilai xinian yaolu*, pp. 6695–769. Taipei: Wenhai chubanshe, 1980.

"Lü Yijian yu Fan Zhongyan" 呂夷簡與范仲淹 [Lü Yijian and Fan Zhongyan]. In Wang Deyi, *Song shi yanjiu lunji: Di er ji* 宋史研究論集: 第二輯 [Collected Research on Song History, Second Collection], pp. 119–84. Taipei: Dingwen shuju, 1972.

"Songdai de shengzheng he baoxun zhi yanjiu" 宋代的聖政和寶訓之研究 [Studies on the Song-Period "Sagacious Administration" and "Precious Instruction" Genres]. In *Song shi yanjiu ji*, no. 30, pp. 1–26. Taipei: Bianyi guan, 2000.

"Songdai Fujian de shixue" 宋代福建的史學 [The Study of History in Fujian during the Song Period]. *Wenshizhe xuebao* 52 (2000.6): 143–74.

"Zhu Xi *Wuchao* ji *Sanchao mingchen yanxing lu* de shiliao jiazhi" 朱熹五朝及三朝名臣言行錄的史料價值 [The Value of the Source Materials in Zhu Xi's *Records of the Words and Deeds of Illustrious Ministers in the Five Courts and Three Courts*]. In Wang Deyi, *Song shi yanjiu lunji: Di er ji* 宋史研究論集: 第二輯 [Collected Research on Song History, Second Collection], pp. 65–70. Taipei: Dingwen shuju, 1972.

Wang Deyi and Nie Chongqi 聶崇岐. *Songdai xianliang fangzheng ke ji cike kao* 宋代賢良方正科及詞科考 [Studies of Advanced Examinations in the Song Period]. Hong Kong: Chongwen shudian, 1971.

Wang Fengyang 王凤阳. *Gu ci bian* 古辞辨 [Old Expressions Explained]. Changchun: Jilin wenshi chubanshe, 1993.

Wang Gungwu. *The Structure of Power in North China during the Five Dynasties*. Kuala Lumpur: University of Malaya Press, 1963.

Wang Mingsun 王明蓀. *Yuandai de shiren yu zhengzhi* 元代的士人與政治 [Yuan-Period Literati and Government]. Taipei: Xuesheng shuju, 1992.

Wang Shengduo 汪圣铎. *Liang Song caizheng shi* 兩宋財政史 [A History of Financial Administration in the Song Dynasty]. 2 vols. Beijing: Zhonghua shuju, 1995.

"Songdai caizheng yu shangpin jingji fazhan" 宋代財政与商品经济发展 [Song-Period Financial Administration and the Development of the Commodity Economy]. In Wang Shengduo, *Songdai shehui shenghuo yanjiu* 宋代社会生活研究 [Studies in the Social Life of the Song Period], pp. 457–83. Beijing: Renmin chubanshe, 2007.

Wang Shengduo and Chen Chaoyang 陈朝阳. "*Songshi quanwen* chayin shilun wenxian yanjiu" 《宋史全文》插引史论文献研究 [Research on the Citations of Works of Historical Commentary in the *Songshi quanwen*]. In *Songshi yanjiu luncong* 15, pp. 452–97 (Baoding: Hebei daxue chubanshi, 2014); reprinted in *Songshi quanwen*, pp. 2959–3013 (Beijing: Zhonghua shuju, 2016).

Wang Sheng'en 王盛恩. *Songdai guanfang shixue yanjiu* 宋代官方史学研究 [Studies in the Official Historiography of the Song Period]. Beijing: Renmin chubanshe, 2008.

Wang Yunhai 王雲海. *Song huiyao jigao kaoxiao* 宋會要輯稿考校 [Investigations into the *Recovered Draft of the Song Compendium*]. Shanghai: Shanghai guji chubanshe, 1986.

Wang Yunhai wenji 王云海文集 [Collected Works of Wang Yunhai]. Kaifeng: Henan daxue chubanshe, 2006.

Wang Zengyu 王曾瑜. *Songchao junzhi chutan (zengding ben)* 宋朝军制初探 (增订本) [A Preliminary Inquiry into the Military System of the Song Dynasty. Revised edition]. Beijing: Zhonghua shuju, 2011.

Watson, Burton. *The Complete Works of Chuang Tzu*. New York: Columbia University Press, 1968.

Records of the Grand Historian of China: Translated from the Shih chi of Ssu-ma Ch'ien. 2 vols. New York: Columbia University Press, 1961.

White, Hayden. *The Content of the Form: Narrative Discourse and Historical Representation*. Baltimore and London: The Johns Hopkins University Press, 1987.

"Rhetoric and History." In *Theories of History: Papers Read at the Clark Library Seminar, March 6, 1976*, edited by Hayden White and Frank E. Manuel, pp. 1–25. Los Angeles: William Andrews Clark Memorial Library, 1978.

Tropics of Discourse: Essays in Cultural Criticism. Baltimore and London: The Johns Hopkins University Press, 1978.

Wilhelm, Richard. *The I Ching, or Book of Changes: The Richard Wilhelm Translation Rendered into English by Cary F. Baynes*. Third edition. Princeton: Princeton University Press, 1967.

Winkelman, John W. *The Imperial Library in Southern Sung China, 1127–1279: A Study of the Organization and Operation of the Scholarly Agencies of the Central Government*. Philadelphia: American Philosophical Society, 1974.

Worthy, Edmund Henry. "The Founding of Sung China, 950–1000: Integrative Changes in Military and Political Institutions." PhD dissertation, Princeton University, 1975.

Wu Man 吳漫. *Mingdai Songshixue yanjiu* 明代宋史学研究 [Research on the Study of Song History during the Ming Period]. Beijing: Renmin chubanshe, 2012.

Umehara Kaoru 梅原郁. *Sōkaiyō shūkō hennen sakuin* 宋會要輯稿編年索引 [Chronological Index to the *Songhui yao jigao*]. Kyoto: Kyōto daigaku jinbun kagaku kenkyūjo, 1995.

Xiong Bin 熊斌 and Huang Bo 黄博. "Yi shi lun zheng: Songdai Sichuan shijia de qianchaoshi yanjiu: yi Fan Zuyu, Li Tao wei zhuxian de kaocha" 以史论政：宋代四川史家的前朝史研究—以范祖禹、李焘为主线的考察 [Using History for Policy Discussion: Song-Period Sichuan Historians' Research on the History of Previous Dynasties, with a Focus on Fan Zuyu and Li Tao]. *Jilin shifan daxue xuebao* (2011.1): 60–63.

Xu Gui 徐規. "Li Tao nianbiao" 李焘年表 [A Chronological Biography of Li Tao]. In Li Tao, *Xu zizhi tongjian changbian* 續資治通鑑長編, Volume 1, pp. 35–102. Beijing: Zhonghua shuju, 1995.

"Nan Song Shaoxing shinian qianhou 'neiwai dajun' renshu kao" 南宋绍兴十年前后《内外大军》人数考 [A Study of Troop Numbers in Central Military Units about 1140]. In Xu Gui, *Yangsu ji* 仰素集, pp. 473–75. Hangzhou: Hangzhou daxue chubanshe, 1999.

Xu Peizao 许沛藻. "Song Gaozong yu *Shen Zhe shilu*" 宋高宗與神哲實錄 [Song Gaozong and the Veritable Records of Shenzong and Zhezong]. In *Qingzhu Deng Guangming jiaoshou jiushi huadan lunwenji*, pp. 625–32. Shijiazhuang: Hebei jiaoyu chubanshe, 1997.

Xu Zhenxing 許振興. "*Gujin yuanliu zhilun* zhong de Songdai *baoxun* yiwen" 《古今源流至沦》中的宋代《宝训》佚文 [Passages from Song-Period "Precious Instructions" in the *Gujin yuanliu zhilun*]. *Guji zhengli yanjiu xuekan* 86 (2000.4): 53–60.

  Songji shouzhong kao yanjiu 宋紀受終考研究 [Research on the *Songji shouzhong kao*]. Hong Kong: Ruirong qiye, 2005.

Yamauchi Masahiro 山内正博. "Ken'en irai keinen yōroku chūkoin hemmoku sakuin hika" 建炎以來繫年要錄注據引篇目索引控 [Notes for an Index to Citations in the Commentary to the *Chronological Record*]. *Miyazaki daigaku kyōiku gakubu kiyō* 22 (1967.10): 43–58.

  "*Sappu genki* to *Sō kaiyō*: sono kijutsu keishiki to keishō no igi" 册府元龜と宋會要: その記述刑式と繼承の意義 [The *Cefu yuangu* and the *Song huiyao*: Their Descriptive Form and the Significance of Their Succession]. *Shigaku kenkyū* 103.5 (May 1968): 20–39.

Yan Yongcheng 燕永成. *Nan Song shixue yanjiu* 南宋史学研究 [Research on Southern Song Historical Studies]. Lanzhou: Gansu renmin chubanshe, 2007.

  "Jin qichaoben *Xu zizhi tongjian changbian* tanyuan" 今七朝本《续资治通鉴长编》探源 [The Origin of the Modern Seven-Court Edition of the *Long Draft*]. *Guji zhengli yanjiu xuekan* 51 (1994.5): 8–12.

  "*Xu zizhi tongjian changbian* Shenzong chao qucai kao" 《续资治通鉴长编, 神宗朝》取材考 [An Investigation into the Sources of the Shenzong Section of the *Long Draft*]. *Shixueshi yanjiu* (1996.1): 61–67.

Yu Jiaxi 余嘉錫. *Siku tiyao bianzheng* 四庫提要辨證 [Corrections to the Evaluations in the Four Treasures]. 1937 edition. Reprinted, 2 vols., Kunming: Yunnan renmin chubanshe, 2004.

Yu Yingshi 余英時. *Zhu Xi de lishi shijie: Songdai shidafu zhengzhi wenhua de yanjiu* 朱熹的歷史世界: 宋代士大夫政治文化的研究 [Zhu Xi's Historical World: A Study of Literati Political Culture in the Song Period]. 2 vols. Taipei: Yunchen wenhua, 2003.

Zhang Jianhua 张建华. "Cong *Zun Yao lu* kan Luo Congyan de zhengzhi sixiang" 从《遵尧录》看罗从言的政治思想 [Luo Congyan's Political Thought as Viewed from the *Record of Revering Yao*]. *Tianjin shifan daxue xuebao* 196 (2008.1): 33–37.

Zhang Qifan 张其凡. "*Dashiji jiangyi* chutan" 《大事记讲义》初探 [A Preliminary Study of the *Lectures on Major Events*]. *Jinan xuebao* 21.2 (March 1999): 59–64.

Zhang Yuan 張元. "Tan Song shi jiaoxue zhong de shiliao fenxi" 談宋史教學中的史料分析 [A Discussion of the Analysis of Historical Sources in the Teaching of Song History]. In *Song shi jiaoxue yantaohui lunwenji* 宋史教學研討會論文, edited by Zhao Yashu 趙雅書, pp. 141–53. Taipei: Taiwan daxue lishixuexi, 1993.

Zhao Yi 趙翼. *Nian'er shi zhaji jiaozheng* 廿二史劄記校證 [Notes on the Twenty-Two Dynastic Histories]. Edited by Wang Shumin 王樹民. 2 vols. Beijing: Zhonghua shuju, 1984.

Zhou Lizhi 周立志. "*Huangchao zhongxing jishi benmo* yu *Zhongxing xiaoli* zhi guanxi" 皇朝中興紀事本末與中興小曆之關系 [On the Relationship between the *Topical Details of the Restoration of Our August Court* and the *Minor Calendar of the Restoration*]. *Wenxian jikan* (2010.3): 104–12.

Zhou Shengchun 周生春. "Guanyu Liao, Jin, Song san shi bianxuan de jige wenti" 关于辽金宋三史编撰的几个问题 [Regarding Several Questions Concerning the Compilation of the Three Histories of Liao, Jin, and Song]. *Lishi wenxian yanjiu*, new series 1 (1990): 179–89 [Luo Bingliang ed., *Songshi yanjiu*, pp. 124–35].

Zhuge Yibing 诸葛忆兵. "Lun Songdai houfei yu chaozheng" 论宋代后妃与朝政 [On Imperial Consorts and Court Governance in the Song Period]. In Zhuge Yibing, *Songdai wenshi kaolun*, pp. 231–42. Beijing: Zhonghua shuju, 2002.

Zou Zhiyong 邹志勇. "Zhengshi yu shuobu zhi huzheng: Li Xinchuan kaoju shixue bianxi" 正史與說部之互證：李心傳考據史學辨析 [Mutual Verification of Official and Nonofficial Sources: An Analysis of Li Xinchuan's Historiography of Textual Research]. *Shanxi shida xuebao* 30.4 (October 2003): 21–25.

Index

For EU product safety concerns, contact us at Calle de José Abascal, 56–1°, 28003 Madrid, Spain or eugpsr@cambridge.org.

www.ingramcontent.com/pod-product-compliance
Ingram Content Group UK Ltd.
Pitfield, Milton Keynes, MK11 3LW, UK
UKHW020402140625
459647UK00020B/2608